New Racism

Norma Romm

New Racism

Revisiting Researcher Accountabilities

 Springer

Norma Romm
Affiliate: University of South Africa
P.O. Box 1492
Manaba Beach
4276 South Africa
norma.romm@gmail.com

ISBN 978-90-481-8727-0   e-ISBN 978-90-481-8728-7
DOI 10.1007/978-90-481-8728-7
Springer Dordrecht Heidelberg London New York

Library of Congress Control Number: 2010924118

Printed on acid-free paper

Springer is part of Springer Science+Business Media (www.springer.com)

Preface

The idea for creating this book arose as I started reading various texts on racism – a topic that I had become increasingly interested in exploring over the last 6 years or so. While working with Carlis Douglas and Susan Weil on developing a book built around holding a (cross-racial) dialogue in which we probe together the multi-faceted dynamics of everyday institutional racism, and upon reading relevant texts, I identified a lacuna. I realized that while there is a myriad of writings aimed at investigating racism and what is called "new racism" across the globe, there is *no text specifically comparing the styles of inquiry* used to proceed in the explorations. With "new racism" seen as operating in more or less covert ways in social life, and not easily visible, the question arises as to how the investigation hereof can properly proceed. How can we go about organizing social inquiries around that which is admitted to be not easily detectable (as well as being a shifting terrain)?

I decided to embark on the specific project of examining in depth the variety of ways in which social researchers/inquirers have tried to study this terrain – looking closely at how they have justified their approach (insofar as they offer epistemological and methodological justifications). As I delved into the various approaches – and looked at these with a view to pinpointing the explicit and implicit justifications for the manner of proceeding – I located possibilities for how they might be redesigned and/or further developed. I concentrated on rethinking the methodologies in line with my previous work on the accountabilities of social researchers. For example, in my book *Accountability in Social Research* (2001), I offer suggestions for how social inquirers can display their accountabilities by being mindful of the potential impact of their inquiries on the continuing unfolding of the social worlds of which they are part. This implies paying particular attention to possible hidden consequences of taken-for-granted views of "knowing" and "knowledge making." This is not to say that none of those concerned with exploring (new) racism already do try to make provision for this. But it is to say that my attention in this book is directed toward considering more possibilities for creating such provision. I do this by drawing from some examples of research that I set out in the book, while expanding upon them, and also by offering some of my own examples.

The project of examining the range of literature in relation to inquiries around new racism and structuring all the arguments into a readable text, turned out to be a more complex process than I originally envisaged. I am hoping that the work that

I have put into detailing different approaches (exemplified with detailed reference to examples that I have chosen) and my proposals for extending them in specific ways will be helpful for inquirers – professional researchers and others – in their considerations for designing explorations around this area of concern.

As I explain in the book, I believe – with many others – that our ways of knowing are inextricably linked with our ways of living and being. Therefore, I believe that the suggestions that I advance for ways of exploring new racism are part of the process of our exploring options for revitalizing our humanity.

I would like to acknowledge that in writing this book I benefited immensely from input from the following people in particular, to whom I wish to express my heartfelt gratitude.

As regards my Chapter 1, which I found – as my starting chapter – almost the most difficult chapter to construct, many people helped me to define its development. Aleco Christakis, Sisinyane Makoena, Janet McIntyre-Mills, Tshimangodzo Mphilo, Phumla Nhlumayo, Abimbola Olateju, Elsa Onkenhout, Susan Schutte, and Susan Weil all read and offered commentary hereto. Susan Weil indicated to me (besides the additional commentary that she made suggesting points at which I should add clarifying material) that, in her words, "I so love how you ARE putting yourself more into your writing Norma ... I think we [Carlis and I] have had a big influence on you in this and in modeling different ways of doing this." She added that this is especially important in a context where "implicit pressures and norms ... support tendencies to disappear ourselves in academic writing and research." Tshimangodzo Mphilo pointed out to me the parts in the chapter that she found particularly meaningful and worth developing; and this also helped to give me direction.

As regards the rest of the book, in order not to ask too much of my friends, I asked different ones to offer feedback on different areas (although at times I gave the same sections of chapters to different ones hoping to receive a variety of perspectives). Aleco Christakis, Carlis Douglas, Veronica McKay, Phumla Nhlumayo, and Susan Weil all offered feedback that was invaluable both in helping me to see where the structure of chapters needed modification and where points that I had made needed development. Aleco's comments on Chapters 3, 7, and 8 helped me to concretize many of my statements; Carlis's comments in relation to Chapters 2, 7, and 9 helped me to see where I needed to extend the discussion; Veronica's comments on Chapter 2 likewise were useful in this way; Phumla's engagement with Chapters 5 and 6 opened up new insights for me; and Susan Weil's engagement with Chapters 2, 7, 8, and 9 helped to strengthen my "narrative" (as she calls it). Janet McIntyre-Mills kindly read almost the entire draft at its near-final stage – and I am grateful for her locating some places where I could clarify the text, but also for her summarizing for me how she was reading the book as a totality and how in her view I had proceeded to make a workable "flow" in the book. (I was also relieved to receive from all my commentators highly enthusiastic statements about the book, such as, for instance: that I had managed to weave together constructively threads from sociology, methodology, race, class, gender discussions, and so on – a job that "had to be done"; that the book was "very important toward the development of our understanding of new racism"; that my inquiry approach in the book made a very important contribution to the field and that it would surely be "well received.")

Meanwhile, discussions that I had with all these people (via face-to-face conversation, e-mail, and/or Skype) around the issues raised in the book also became useful material that became included in the text (and I have cited these conversations as "personal communications" therein). It is heartwarming to have received all the support offered to me – not only through people's material contributions, but also through their "being there" for me. I am also grateful to the anonymous reviewers chosen by Springer to review my initial proposal, which helped me in the structuring of the chapters.

In conclusion, the fact that I come from South Africa, where national and international icon Nelson Mandela spent 27 years in prison for his convictions on a humane and inclusive society meant that I could not but be inspired by the magnanimity of his spirit of wholeness. I hope that this spirit is reflected in this book.

July 2009

Contents

About the Author

Norma R.A. Romm is affiliated as Research Professor to the University of South Africa. She has worked for universities in South Africa, Swaziland, the United Kingdom, and Cyprus – holding the position of Dean in social science and humanity faculties in Swaziland and in Cyprus. She is the author of the books *The Methodologies of Positivism and Marxism* (1991) and *Accountability in Social Research* (2001). She is the co-author of *People's Education in Theoretical Perspective* (with Veronica McKay, 1992), *Diversity Management* (with Robert Flood, 1996), and *Assessment of the Impact of HIV and AIDS in the Informal Economy in Zambia* (with Veronica McKay, 2006). She is the co-editor of the books *Social Theory* (with Michael Sarakinsky, 1994) and *Critical Systems Thinking* (with Robert Flood, 1996). She has written over 85 articles in journals and in edited volumes on issues such as education (including adult education), social development, social theorizing in relation to development, the facilitation of co-learning in group processes, discursive accountability, systemic inquiry, and considerations of racism as a world problem.

Chapter 1
General Introduction

1.1 Introduction

The focus of this book is on providing a review of some of the ways in which inquiries around what is called "new racism" have been approached, with a view to reconsidering what is involved in such research endeavors. I look in particular into how our ways of "knowing" in this arena can be accounted for by rendering open to discursive accounting the pursuance of research aims.

Researchers highlighting new forms of racism consider these as different from what is called "old-fashioned racism" (as I explain in detail in Chapter 2). New racism is conceptualized as encompassing forms of racism that manifest in the patterning of social existence in less obvious ways than does old-fashioned racism. To understand this, it is argued that, calls for modes of inquiry equipped to delve into more covert coded expressions of racism (including instances where people may indeed not regard themselves as contributing to perpetuating racial hierarchies). In the book I examine and compare various ways of proceeding with such inquiry, and I offer proposals for how research options can be reworked and/or extended. To provide an indication of the terrain that I shall be covering in the book, I start off with some brief illustrations of how "new racism" has been conceptualized as differing from "old racism."

In the context of (contemporary) South Africa – for example – "old racism" is seen as manifested when White people blatantly make use of apartheid-styled racial labeling that denigrates others, marks them as inferior, and affronts their dignity, thus overtly still drawing on notions of White superiority.[1] Under the apartheid system, as Pampallis indicates, a mandate to "entrench the system of White supremacy" was given by the White electorate (in 1948). Social segregation in accordance with racial categories became enforced in that "Blacks living in close proximity to White residential and business areas were forcibly removed to segregated townships on

---

[1] Pampallis explains that in 1948 the National Party was elected to power (by the White electorate) under the slogan of "apartheid" (2008, p. 5). As regards derogatory racial labeling, which continues today, I have in mind in particularly the use of the word "Kaffir" (to refer to Black people), which is known to be insulting and offensive. (See also Footnote 140 in Chapter 5.)

N. Romm, *New Racism*, DOI 10.1007/978-90-481-8728-7_1,
© Springer Science+Business Media B.V. 2010

the outskirts of the cities," and the "political, social, and economic rights of all Blacks, and especially those of Africans, were severely restricted." In addition, "non-parliamentary opposition was ruthlessly restricted through a range of new legislation" (Pampallis, 2008, p. 5).

"New racism" in relation to this is seen as expressed more subtly, for instance, when people refuse to admit the continued need for social policies designed to redress past as well as continuing discrimination against those suffering the effects of apartheid following the move to a post-apartheid society (cf. Pillay & Collings, 2004).[2]

Considering options for addressing the manifestation of new forms of racism in South Africa (alongside "older" forms), the South African Human Rights Commission offers a report on an inquiry into the manner in which issues of race are portrayed in the media. The Commission notes that notwithstanding that post-1994 (in the transition to democracy) "political power in the new South Africa is in the hands of the Black majority," the power relations in the country are still skewed (in favor of Whites). The Commission points, for instance, to the ways in which individuals and communities can exercise power, and the ways in which corporations exercise power. The Commission points out that generally in a modern democratic state, state power is limited – thus rendering it important to understand power in "more nuanced ways" (2000, p. 54).

The Commission highlights the importance of sensitizing people toward under-standing "manifestations like structural forms of racism and the institutional character of racism" (2000, p. 54). They state that by racism they mean to include forms of racism that are linked not only to conscious intention to harm or discrimi-nate, but also to how "effects are felt" within society – whatever the intention (2000, p. 55). In the light hereof, they suggest that it is important to set up a dialogical pro-cess, where South Africans, through dialogue "will learn, understand, and have the facility to use race theory and analysis" (2000, p. 8). They see the purpose of their own inquiry into the media as having the potential to "engage all South Africans in seeking common solutions to racism and constructing a society free of racism" (2000, p. 8).

As another example of identification of less easily detectable forms of racism – this time in the context of the USA – Collins suggests that it is important to delve

---

[2]On the basis of his interviews with 400 Black workers spanning the years since South Africa's transition to a post-apartheid society (in 1994), Sitas indicates that 51% found the transition to be "extremely beneficial" (in that they became upwardly mobile), 25% remained "stuck" in their occupational milieu of the 1980s/early 1990s, and 22% experienced "rapid deterioration of life chances" (2004, p. 830). Of those in the last-named category, he notes that the majority attributes their position to their prior disadvantages: "no skills, no education, no nothing, now we are suf-fering" (2004, p. 840). Some of these expressed that the "Black elite" was being appeased by the (White) "Bosses" (those seen as having continued power) – and they expressed disappointment that the struggle movement (and comrades therein) had not been able to "look after them" in the post-apartheid era (2004, p. 840). (Sitas notes that the remaining 2% among those interviewed had got into serious "criminal trouble" by becoming involved in "violent crime and/or peddling drugs" – 2004, p. 833.)

into new racism in order to explore the ways in which, despite legislated deseg-regation in the USA, "actual segregation in everyday life" is still pervasive – but becomes masked by the media (2005, p. 6). She argues that part of the new racism in the USA consists in obscuring the manner in which "power relations that elevate some groups over others" continue to play themselves out in the "theater of race" (2005, p. 3). As she puts it, "in the post-civil rights era, the power relations that administer the theater of race in America are now far more hidden" (2005, p. 4). This means that:

> Recognizing that racism even exists remains a challenge for most White Americans and, increasingly, for many African Americans as well. They believe that the passage of civil rights legislation eliminated racially discriminatory practices and that any problems that Blacks may experience now are of their own doing. (2005, p. 5)

In order to provide an alternative to these views, she considers it crucial to find ways of exploring the "forms that new racism take in the post-civil rights era" – with the hope also of catalyzing an "effective anti-racist politics and contribut[ing] to a broader social justice agenda" (2005, p. 7).

And as yet another example, Kundnani refers to new forms of racism that he identifies as emerging in twenty-first century Britain (and elsewhere in Europe), characterized by intolerance toward that which is defined within the national story as "alien" – as perpetuated by the media, political stances on immigration, and so on. He notes how supposedly core British/national values can be used to set limits on multiculturalism, while allegiance to the defined (hegemonic) values becomes a factor in "assessing the merits of different categories of migration as well as a necessary condition for the settlement of immigrants" (2007, p. 122).

In Chapter 2, I present Table 2.1 that provides a summary indication of the kinds of social exclusions on which I am focusing in this book – which I shall be discussing (as do others) under the banner of "new racism." (See Chapter 2, Section 2.4.) The book is structured around my examining various ways of pro-ceeding to define and explore these forms of racism, and offering proposals for how such inquiries can be extended. My argument in the book is that all approaches to the study of racism (whether thought of within a continuum as more "old-fashioned" or "new") – as with research more generally – should be treated as being inextricably linked to developments in social life. That is, *the inquiries and the researchers should be understood as part of (and not apart from) the social fields being researched – of which researchers are indeed part* (cf. Weil, 1998, pp. 42–45; Ladson-Billings, 2003, pp. 398–402; Romm, 2006a, pp. 79–83). Through the book, I detail ways in which social inquirers can gear themselves to specifically take into account the potential (as considered by themselves and others) of their impactful involvements in the unfolding of the social fabric. I do this by drawing on, while also extending, what I see as the prospects offered via the examples of research that I discuss.

The suggestions for revisiting modes of inquiry around new racism that I for-ward in relation to my discussion of the relevance of my chosen examples follow from a specific constructivist stance that I argue for in the book following also from my work on researcher accountability (Romm, 2001, 2002a, 2002b, 2002c). With reference to the justification of research/inquiry endeavors, my suggestions relate to the understanding of both the process and the products of these endeavors. With regard to *research processes*, I discuss implications of recognizing that our use of methodological procedures[3] might itself evoke certain experiences at the point of exploring them through the research. And regarding the writing up of *research results (products)*, I underscore that we also need to be attuned to the possible social consequences of our style of presenting these. I make a case in the book for researchers practicing reflexivity in terms of an orientation as summarized by De Souza – as looking back at one's research practices in order to become more cognizant of, in her terms, "how social position, personal histories, and lived experiences matter" in the way in which research becomes constituted and the way in which it becomes presented (2004, p. 473). As De Souza notes, reflexivity implies an admission that these "matter" in our framing of the questions we ask as inquirers and the way in which answers are explored. As I hope to show in the book, different starting framings – as well as different understandings of what is involved in doing science/research – can make a difference to whether and how racism becomes detected and to the manner in which "recommendations" become posed for solution to any identified areas of concern. A stance of reflexivity, as understood by De Souza, enables researchers to portray an awareness hereof (to themselves and to others).

Not all researchers define reflexivity and its purpose in the same way. For example, Finlay points out that for some researchers, the process of reflexively monitoring and auditing the research process is argued to offer "truer" accounts of the research process in an effort to help "affirm the validity of the research" (defined in realist terms[4]) (2002, pp. 210–211). She indicates that realist-oriented accounts of reflexivity have been challenged by those pointing to and embracing the "socially constructed nature of the research experience" (2002, p. 211). She explains that "researchers of different theoretical persuasions . . . lay claim to competing accounts of the rationale and practices of reflexivity" (2002, p. 212). My own stance on reflexivity is linked to developing what I call *discursive accountability* as a way for would-be researchers to earn trust in their endeavors – as I explain in Section 1.6. My views on *reflexivity* are discussed in Section 1.5. But in essence, my suggestion is that reflexivity needs to be coupled with taking some responsibility for the ways in which our research practices can be considered socially consequential.

In line with my focus on reflexivity, which includes researchers' mindful admission of their own presence in the research process and its products, I would like

---

[3] I use the term "procedures" to point to the *processes of inquiry* that might become activated. Sometimes these are also called research *designs* or *strategies* – as, for example, in Romm and Adman (2000), Gray et al. (2007, p. 45), Bonilla-Silva and Baiocchi (2008, p. 140), and Vogt (2008, pp. 1–2).

[4] As we shall see in the chapters that follow, when validity is defined in realist terms, the focus is on trying to improve the likelihood that theoretical conceptualizations will correspond with (or match) the workings of reality. (See also Section 1.5.1 below.)

to offer a brief biographical narrative created here for the purposes of introducing myself to readers in some way. This might help readers to "place" some of my arguments developed in the book – by recognizing (with me) that they are a human production produced in terms of particular involvements of mine and particular social concerns (which form a starting point for the dialogues that I invite via this book).

1.2 A Brief Biographical Narrative

I was born in 1957 in South Africa into an English-speaking family of Jewish background. Being (defined as) White in apartheid South Africa, I became at some point conscious (I remember this consciousness as being most acute during my teenage years) that this afforded me immense opportunities and privileges. The reason that I can recall this consciousness arising at this point is that I remember joining the "Institute of Race Relations"[5] and organizing various charity events for the Institute, while participating in seminars aimed at considering ways of countering apartheid thinking and policy. I also taught (for 10 years) for Sached in South Africa – an organization that was set up to rectify the discrimination against Black students under apartheid.

I studied for my university degrees in Sociology – doing my DLitt et Phil while employed in the Sociology Department at the University of South Africa (UNISA), where I worked from 1982 to 1991. While working there (as Lecturer, Senior Lecturer, and Associate Professor), I became involved in the development of a "humanist" approach to examining the construction of social realities in official and everyday discourse. I was able (thanks to a humanist-oriented head of department – Prof. Cornie Alant) to write guides reaching thousands of (Black and White) students across the country – discussing racism as a social problem that dehumanizes social relationships.

I became head of the newly formed "humanist group" in the department, which focused on the implications of developing a symbolic view of "culture."[6] In this view, culture is not seen as encapsulating fixed ways of life that are supposedly shared among groups of people, but rather is considered as opening spaces for

---

[5]Because of the importance that this book gives to the way in which we use language – as part of the reproduction of our ways of seeing – I would suggest that it may be preferable to refer to the Institute of *Raced* Relations in order to show that the racialization of discourses and the *racing* of social relations (in terms of whatever definition of race" is used) is a historically variable mode of social existence (cf. Hercules, 2006, pp. 42–43; Kiguwa, 2006, pp. 127–130).

[6]For ease of teaching and organization, the department was organized along four lines: research methodology; conflict theory; systems approaches; and humanist sociology. I was appointed as head of the "humanist group," in which we explored implications of humanism for sociology – with a focus on humans as dialogical beings. This often involved us in heated conversation with those endorsing the specific value of (definitions of) "conflict theory" or "systems thinking" (with the latter understood at that time in terms of a view of social systems as organisms).

communication around ways of seeing and enacting social life (cf. Romm, 1990b, 1994; Alant & Romm, 1990; McKay & Romm, 1992). In the face of the prevalent reference to culture (now present in much of the international literature on ethnicity) as a "thing" that supposedly "belongs" to given (defined) groups, I feel that it is crucial to keep alive discussion around alternative definitions of the meaning of culture. My discussion in Chapter 2, Section 2.3.4, of new racism as involving what some authors have called "cultural racism" draws on and expands on the kinds of exchanges that we developed during our intensive debates with staff and students around these issues at UNISA.

When I left UNISA (at the point at which the head of department retired and I was not sure if the new head would appreciate the humanist argument and its implications), I worked in Swaziland on a 2-year contract (as Associate Professor and Dean of the Faculty of Social Sciences). There I met colleagues from a range of different countries and engaged in many conversations (with colleagues who became friends) around issues of "development" in Africa. I authored an article on the Tanzanian peasantry on insistence from a Tanzanian colleague (Prof. Sam Maghimbi), as he believed that my discussions with him on this (and my understanding of the issues) warranted it being "written up" in a book he was editing (1995a). I also co-authored with Prof. Apollo Rwomire (from Uganda), an article for a book that he was editing on African women and children (2001).

After the Swaziland contract, I decided to seek a research post, where I could concentrate on research and writing. I took up such a position at the University of Hull in the UK. The research position was in a newly formed Center for Systems Studies in the School of Management – a multi-disciplinary research center aimed at exploring research as systemic intervention. (I became its Deputy Director a few years later.) The University of Hull had a large student body of students from the Far East (especially its postgraduate degrees), and I developed strong relationships with many of my Masters and Ph.D. students from China, Taiwan, and Hong Kong with whom I had manifold discussions around different styles of working and interacting in social life. I also naturally learned a great deal from colleagues (again from various parts of the globe, including Africa, South America, the Netherlands, and of course the UK). After working at the university for just over 10 years, I took on a contract (for a year) in Cyprus as Professor of Sociology and Dean of Social Science and Humanities at Cyprus College. The College was in the process of becoming a University – the European University Cyprus – and my task was to help set up the required structures, including research ones. In Cyprus I was exposed to learning about the identifications of "Greek Cypriots" and "Turkish Cypriots" and the ways in which polarities around these identifications became historically reproduced.

I am currently affiliated (as Research Professor) to the University of South Africa, in the College of Human Sciences. For the past few years I have been co-organizing research around adult education in Southern African countries, with special reference to capacity building of educators (McKay & Romm, 2006a, 2006b), and also around HIV/AIDS in relation to the vulnerability of informal sector workers in Zambia (McKay & Romm, 2006c, 2008a, 2008b). I have also devoted much energy to investigating ways of organizing research – including my own primary research – to look into (new forms of) racism. (I hope that this book bears witness to this energy!) My interest in delving into research approaches in this field arose partly out of my involvement in a book that Carlis Douglas, myself, and Susan Weil are authoring in which we open a (cross-racial) dialogue around everyday institutional racism as we see it manifesting across the globe.

Turning to my other publications (which offer some sense of the range of issues over which I have written over the years) I have authored two books address-ing methodological issues in the social sciences. In the first book (Romm, 1991), I explored debates around the methodologies of positivism and of Marxism (in the process spelling out different interpretations of Marxist methodology). In the second book (2001), I examined issues of accountability in social research. I have co-authored three books: one on "people's education" (McKay & Romm, 1992); one on "diversity management" – which included proposals for managing the plurality of approaches to exploring social issues, with particular reference to organizational issues (Flood & Romm, 1996a); and one reporting on, and offering suggested routes toward dealing with, HIV and AIDS in the informal economy in Zambia (McKay & Romm, 2006c). And I have co-edited two books – one on social theory and the other on critical systems thinking (Romm & Sarakinsky, 1994; Flood & Romm, 1996b). I have also authored/co-authored over 85 articles in journals and edited volumes on diverse issues such as education, social development, social theorizing in relation to development, systemic practice, discursive accountability, dialogical intervention processes, and considerations of racism as a world problem.

All in all, my research work involves working across a variety of "disciplines" in the social sciences, with the aim of considering and at the same time helping others to consider fresh options for conceptualizing and acting in the social situations being researched/explored. This orientation is linked to my specific systemic approach to research practice, which highlights "knower(s)" and "knowing" as being part of the (unfolding) system being addressed (e.g., Romm, 1995b, 1996, 1997, 1998a, 1998b, 2001, 2002a, 2002b, 2006a, 2006b; Flood & Romm, 1996a; Adindu & Romm, 2001; Gregory & Romm, 2001, 2004; Romm & Hsu, 2002; Romm & Adman, 2004).

In deciding to embark on the preparation for this book, the question arose (in conversation with others and in relation to arguments in the literature) as to whether my being White in terms of the context of my upbringing in South Africa and in terms of my being seen as White in other countries too may serve as a disadvan-tage for me in relation to developing insight into the issues with which Black and other minority-status groupings of people have to contend. By virtue of privileges that could so easily be taken for granted and go "unnoticed" as I have interacted in daily life, could it be argued that I lack the necessary experience to offer an insightful account of ways of delving into (new) racism? In response to this ques-tion, I furnish readers with an outline of my interpretation of my experiences as follows:

I would suggest that already from my teenage years, I made some effort to be aware of the ordinarily unnoticed privileges accruing to me by virtue of being (taken as) White in the South African social system. I also tried in a range of ways to "make up" in some fashion for "everyday racism" (cf. Essed, 1991, 2001, 2002) such as, for instance, noticing Black people not being greeted in an elevator and being made to feel invisible. I specifically greeted and started conversation with Black people – despite what I saw as the unspoken taboo against creating such "cross-racial" exchanges. I also made efforts (since my teens) to undercut the use of derogatory language (including jokes) directed against Black people – and I found ways of reproving those using the language. In this sense I would argue that I displayed and also cultivated a sense of my own empathy, and tried to express what Bonilla-Silva calls a "loyalty to humanity" (2006, p. 230). I would argue that I could be classified as one of those "whites willing to tell the world when whites do or say things that disadvantage minority groups" (2006, p. 230).

As far as the development of what I would call my "progressiveness" is concerned, Bonilla-Silva proposes that "more research needs to be conducted to … specify what are the set of circumstances … and the conditions that lead actors to become racially progressive" (2006, p. 210). He noticed in his own research that working-class women (i.e., those he classified as working class in terms of some of their statements in interviews) tended to be a ("segment of the white population that is more progressive than others"). He suggests (tentatively) that working-class women experience two kinds of oppression in social life (by virtue of being both working class and women) – and thus possibly have the requisite experience to develop empathy with racial minorities. He points out that "in their narratives, many of these women used their own experiences to articulate their views on various hotly contested racial issues and, more specifically, to describe how discrimination occurs nowadays" (2006, p. 210).

Being a "woman" could well be argued to have impacted on my being able to empathize with targets of both old-fashioned and new racism. I have often heard old-fashioned ideas of women's (ascribed) inferiority expressed in various contexts in South Africa (and these expressions have not in my view disappeared). Furthermore, more subtle, covert ways of treating women as having less status (akin to the covertness associated with new forms of everyday racism) can also be seen as diffuse in South Africa as elsewhere. I can recall innumerable experiences encountering what I regard as unequal treatment in status due to my being (seen as) a woman, and when I speak with other women (Black and White) very soon stories of experiences of discrimination become recounted. But I admit that my being White has afforded me a different quality of experience (from those seen as Black) – and has been immensely helpful within social and work life as a route to "normal" (but oft-unnoticed) privileges.

As far as a consideration of my Jewish background is concerned, I believe that this has made me sensitive to how easily the misuse of ascriptive categories (based on people's ascribing characteristics to others in terms of an understanding of their background/heritage) can be employed in everyday life. Again I have many memories of this occurring in my presence – whether or not people were aware that I came from Jewish background. If I commented on how the use of derogatory labels based on ascriptive categories can have wider effects on social living and is not without consequence for the people concerned, and if I mentioned that I happened to be

Jewish, I would oft be told, as Bonilla-Silva puts it (in relation to the category of being Black), "you guys are hypersensitive" (2006, p. 211).

1.3 Creating Depth of Insight Through Developing Connectivity

Despite the above considerations around my experiences, it still could be argued that this does not adequately address the question as to whether my lack of social experience of being Black might disadvantage me unduly in my endeavor in this book to try to extend methodologies for exploring new racism. I now consider this question by taking as starting point some of the deliberations that Collins has provided in relation to her (brand of) standpoint thinking arising from experiences in the USA.

Collins points out in the *Preface* to the *first edition* of her book *Black Feminist Thought* (first appearing in 1990, but which she includes in the 2000 edition) that her writing on issues of racism arises from the standpoint of "placing Black women's experiences and ideas [in the USA] at the center of analysis" (2000, p. vii). She explains that the book expresses a concern with framing ideas in a way that resonates with Black women's experiences. She indicates that while admittedly writing from this standpoint and at the same time "privileging" African American women's ideas, she hopes also to "encourage White feminists, African American men, and all others to investigate the similarities and differences among their own standpoints and those of African American women" (2000, p. vii). Furthermore, she states that she does not wish to imply that "Black feminist thought" is a fully coherent set of ideas (and interests), and she hopes "to see other volumes emerge which will be more willing to present Black feminist thought as a shifting mosaic of competing ideas and interests" (2000, pp. viii–ix).

In her *Preface* to the *second edition*, Collins expands (and alters somewhat) her conception of the link between "Black feminist thought" and "alternative" positions. She remarks that:

> I have come to see how it is possible to be both centered in one's own experiences and engaged in coalitions with others. In this sense, Black feminist thought works on behalf of Black women, but does so in conjunction with other similar social justice projects. (2000, p. x)

Collins suggests that this shift in her thinking allowed her to

> emphasize particular dimensions that characterize Black feminist thought but are not unique to it. .... I tried to reject the binary thinking that frames so many Western definitions,[7] including my earlier ones of Black feminist thought and Black feminist epistemology [i.e.,

---

[7]Binary thinking is also sometimes referred to as thinking that relies on a type of logic where it is contradictory to state that, say, "p and not-p are both (socially) true." In her book on *Black Sexual Politics*, Collins clarifies the use of the term binary. She defines binary thinking as "a system of thought that divides concepts into two oppositional categories, for example, white/black, man/woman, heterosexual/homosexual, saint/sinner, reason/emotion, and normal/deviant" (2005, p. 349). She indicates that "both/and" thinking allows us to see the connections between the apparent oppositions.

conceptions of knowing processes in society]. Rather than drawing a firm line around Black feminist thought that aims to classify entities as *either* being Black feminist *or* not, I aimed for more fluidity . . . . (2000, p. xi)

Here Collins makes the point that the very decision to draw a boundary around the notion of Black feminist thought – seen as separated from "other" thinking (and experience) – was a decision that could be shifted. She now envisages a more fluid relationship with insights/experiences offered from arenas supposedly "outside" Black feminist thinking. Nevertheless, in the main text of the book she makes the point that, in her view, "It is more likely for Black women . . . to have insights into the condition of our oppression than it is for those who live outside those structures" (2000, p. 35). She argues that this does not imply for her that "others cannot participate" in the enterprise of trying to offer insight (2000, p. 35). But she avers that "the primary responsibility for defining one's own reality lies with the people who live that reality, who actually have those experiences" (2000, p. 35).

As we shall see throughout the various chapters of this book, the idea of giving credence to the experiences of people's lived realities is a theme that threads through my book. In this sense I concur with Collins that the power of defining experiences of oneself and of one's existence, and the power of constructing visions of social realities and of unfolding futures should not be ceded to others supposedly better equipped to "understand." In order to deflect "existing power hierarchies" (Collins, 2000, p. 36), it is *crucial that hierarchies in the production of "knowledge" too become revisited.* Collins cites Lorde as pointing out that "if we do not define ourselves for ourselves we will be defined by others" (Lorde, 1984, p. 45, as cited in Collins, 2000, p. 36).

Collins continues her argument by suggesting that

Black men, African women, White men, Latinas, White women, and members of other U.S. racial/ethnic groups, for example [as well as others outside of the U.S.] . . . can identify points of connection [in thought and suggested forms of action] that further social justice projects. (2000, p. 37)

Collins thus emphasizes the potential connectivity, rather than boundaries, between members of different (social) groups trying to further "social justice projects" – as I would suggest (and hope) I am trying to do via this book.

1.4 The "Reality" of Groupness

While Collins points to the potential connectivity between the social groups that she identifies, she also endeavors to deal with the issue of her apparently essentializing the different groups that she isolates as relevant. Before outlining her argument, it is worth noting that normally when one charges an author with being "essentialist" in orientation, this implies that the author making use of the concept of "group" is treating groups as if they are *entities with definite characteristics*, to which "members" necessarily belong. This is normally contrasted with a "non-essentialist" position that emphasizes *the processes by which social groupings are (re)created as social productions* within the course of social life. Anthias and Yuval-Davis elucidate that in their understanding, a *non-essentialist* position does not approach social reality as if there are groups to be *discovered* ("in reality"), but rather sees social realities (including social groupings) as "being created and recreated when practiced and discussed" (1996, p. 191). A non-essentialist position argues that "essentialist" categories of difference can all too easily be deployed to create a discourse of cultural difference that constrains unnecessarily people's conceptions of "who they are" (1996, p. 195).

Ways of treating the existence/development of groups in turn are often linked to ways of seeing the relationship between different possible forms of cultural expression supposedly connected with different "groups." Parekh, in criticizing an essentialist argument, calls upon people to revisit their way of relating to "culture," especially "in an age in which cultural boundaries are porous and permeable and in which culture both absorbs the influences and defines itself in relation to others" (1997, p. 61). Brubaker and Cooper also caution that we need to be wary – both as analysts and as practitioners – of working with a notion of "bounded groupness" (2000, p. 33). They point out that references to social groups can all too easily imply that members share "comprehensive identities and ways of life." Like Anthias and Yuval-Davis, they maintain that this way of seeing groups not only *posits* (as existing) the identified groups, but also *encourages* the reproduction of bounded groupness within the social process (2000, p. 33).

Also considering the matter of the boundedness of groups, Alleyne (2002) suggests that "we cannot live together in the global system if we hang on to our old essentializing identities." Instead of "hanging onto" an essentialized and reified conception of identity (as defined by an experience of a static "self"), we might try, as Alleyne cites certain "radicals" as trying, to "create new, more inclusive, transcultural, transracial . . . social identities" (2002, p. 179).

Collins's position in relation to her discussion of groups is that it is sometimes necessary for people sharing what can be regarded as common experiences to develop "safe spaces" where they can develop their ways of thinking about these experiences and about possible futures (2000, p. 110). She considers this in the light of her discussion of the (new) rhetoric of "color-blindness" – where inequality becomes legitimized by pretending that people are being treated equally (without regard to racial categorization), while they still continue to be categorized as racially "other" by those purporting color-blindness (Crenshaw, 1997, as cited in Collins, 2000, p. 110). As Collins explains:

> Despite protestations to the contrary, this new color-blind racism claimed not to see race yet managed to replicate racial hierarchy as effectively as the racial segregation of old. (2005, p. 3)

Collins suggests that in this social context, it becomes very difficult to maintain safe spaces for people experiencing continued (but now redefined) racism. As she puts it, "any group that organizes around its own self-interests runs the risk of being labeled 'separatist,' 'essentialist,' and anti-democratic" (2000, p. 110). She argues that racial boundaries continue to be preserved in the USA (as elsewhere), while the superiority of Whiteness is institutionalized – with attendant economic penalties being associated with Blackness.

Zuberi and Bonilla Silva support this account by likewise pointing to the ideology of color-blindness and arguing that it is important to develop ways of knowing and living that can counteract this ideology by being "openly race conscious" in orientation (2008, p. 333). They make the point that racialized structures "produce differences in life chances (i.e. inequality and exclusion) and in [social] identities"; and they indicate that their position is that "we advocate a move from race as soon as the conditions of racial stratification no longer exist" (2008, p. 333).

While Collins as well as Zuberi and Bonilla-Silva see the value of "identity politics" (where, say, Blackness as a political identity can offer a challenge to the perpetuation of normative Whiteness), they consider that identity politics could give way to alternative forms of effectively organizing. Collins proposes a model of "transversal politics [which] concerns coalitions of all sorts" and which can "accommodate the contradictions that seemingly distinguish identity politics and affinity politics" (where the latter involves people forming groups or communities[8] on the basis of some perceived affinity) (2000, p. 296). Likewise Zuberi and Bonilla-Silva point to the importance of producing knowledge and practices that will "ultimately help abolish race as a category of exclusion" (2008, p. 333).

The issue of how one should treat "groupness" in society can be seen as tied to the question of how "members" of the (posited) different groups are to be defined. In this book, I operate in terms of the understanding that the binary logic that separates supposed opposites such as White and Black, "us" and "them," and so on. (whether in terms of phenotypical or cultural markers), itself needs to be revisited.[9] Considering my own use of categories to "identify" myself in relation to what are

---

[8]Bouchard (2004) prefers to use the word "community" rather than the word "group." She argues that the word "group" already implies for her an "us/them" relationship between (groupings of) people. A similar suggestion is offered by Young (1990), who argues for the need to develop normative conceptions of communities where identifications with groups (or rather, communities) can emerge on the basis of understood affinities, while creating openings for people to "become acquainted with new and different people, [and] with different cultures and social experiences" (1990, p. 319).

[9]The term phenotype, as explained in wikipedia, is used to refer to "actual physical properties [of an organism], such as height, weight, hair color, and so on" (http://en.wikipedia.org/wiki/Genotype-phenotype_distinction). Considered in relation to phenotypical features associated with being Black or White, it is important to note that sometimes people are expressly called (and/or self-define themselves as) Black or White by virtue of their *social* behavior. For example, the use of the word *coconut* can be used to refer (normally derogatively) to someone with phenotypically "Black" features presumably trying to act "White" (see Chapter 5, Section 5.5). In contrast, sometimes calling someone with phenotypically "White" features as "Black" could refer favorably to their being able to empathize suitably with self-reported experiences of "Black" people (as I have heard through many anecdotes in South Africa as well as Britain). As another example, in the context of social relations in the USA, Aleco Christakis (of Greek heritage), indicated to me that he is a board member of the organization called "Americans for Indian Opportunity" and considers himself as Greek Native American (as one of his self-descriptors following on his feeling welcomed in the organization) – personal communication by e-mail with me, August 2008. (See also in this regard Chapter 7, Footnote 198; and see www.aio.org/programs.html as well as http://www.aio.org/21228%20Ambassador%20Newsletter.pdf)

seen to be "groups/groupings," it may be noted that when using the word White within my biographical narrative, I expressly capitalized it. The reason for my doing this is to emphasize that the racing of bodies with reference to supposedly observable features is not necessarily an "obvious" process – the importance of a feature such as Whiteness becomes obvious only when entrenched in a social order of raced relations.

In commenting on the practice by some authors of putting quotation marks around terms referring to social categories, Collins remarks that "putting brackets around the term 'Black woman' and pointing out its socially constructed nature does not erase the fact of living as a Black woman and all that it entails" (2000, p. 166). While Collins does not put quotation marks around racialized social categorizations, and prefers to use capital letters instead, she is of course aware of the way in which these constructions contribute to, and help to justify, the reproduction of unequal raced relations (see, for example, 2000, p. 138). In the remainder of this book I too – like Collins – will use capital letters to refer to these categories as well as to posit possibilities for reconstructing our conceptualizations of the status of the categories (and our attendant ways of living). (It should be noted that when citing other authors' arguments, if they themselves have not capitalized, I have chosen to leave their texts as is in the quotation.)

1.5 Notions of Reflexivity

As will become clearer as the book proceeds, the stance on reflexivity that I put forward in the book is one that calls for social inquirers to *take account of their involvements in social life* and to *acknowledge some responsibility for the possible social impacts* that their research arguably may be creating (see also Romm, 2002a, 2002b). When calling for an orientation of reflexivity in these terms, I at the same time try to address the various ways in which reflexivity can be conceptualized and practiced. In this section, I locate three accounts – linked to specific understandings of what is involved in the proper practice of inquiry – and I show why I wish to associate myself more with the third-named account.

1.5.1 A Realist-Oriented View

A realist-oriented understanding of the practice of (natural and social) science in society suggests that theories put forward in the process of inquiry can be tested for their closeness to the truth, where truth is defined as the accurate representation of facts, patterns, structures, and/or (in the case of social science) social meanings existing in reality.[10] (For more detail on these terms see, for example, Augoustinos,

---

[10]The term "realism" embraces a variety of positions that might be labeled under this banner. In my book *Accountability in Social Research* (Romm, 2001), I offer a discussion of four kinds of position that can be considered realist in orientation (albeit in different ways). These are *positivism* (a position focusing on the search through scientific inquiry to come to grips with natural and social regularities); *non-foundationalism* (a position that emphasizes the impossibility of obtaining

Walker, & Donaghue, 2006, p. 22; Gray, Williamson, Karp, & Dalphin, 2007, pp. 39–43.)

Within a realist position, the credibility of theoretical propositions is seen to rest on the degree to which they can be argued to have undergone appropriate tests in the face of competing claims about the operation of reality. All proposed claims put forward by researchers are regarded as needing to be adjudicated with respect to the relevant evidence. While there are various ways of trying to cater for this, Popper famously argued (1959, 1969) that scientists can try to determine via a process of *deduction* what empirical observations (if found) would constitute a *falsification* of their theoretical claims. The more scientists show that they have been prepared to seek such observations (instead of seeking only supporting evidence), the more credibility their propositions are awarded within the scientific community (1969, p. 256).[11]

According to Popper, the mechanisms of science cannot be used to generate *certainty* of knowledge about reality. As Delanty (referring to the Popperian argument) puts it: "Scientific knowledge is uncertain knowledge" (1997, p. 32). Nevertheless, as Delanty notes, Popper argues that it is the most certain kind of knowledge to which human beings can aspire. In similar vein, Gray et al. note that according to this account "theories are rarely completely proved or disproved. [But] ... findings influence theory by refining it, and making it a more precise tool of explanation" (2007, p. 6). They go on to state that scientists have been trained to use the scientific method (for testing theories) in a way that "decreases the probability of making errors in their observations and judgments" (2007, p. 8).

The central concern within this position, then, is to minimize errors that can be avoided in the process of coming to grips with reality. Researchers are considered as *biased* to the extent that they do not make sufficient effort to avoid preventable errors. Hammersley and Gomm (1997a) explain this position (to which they subscribe) by noting that researchers engaged in practicing science are required to "do their utmost to find and keep to the path which leads toward knowledge rather than error" (1997a, Paragraph 4.3).

In order not to be accused of being unduly biased, Hammersley states that it is crucial that researchers direct themselves toward the immediate goal of "the

---

indubitable proof); *scientific realism* (expressing a focus on excavating structures of reality); and *Weberian interpretivism* (expressing a focus on striving to understand meaning-making and its consequences in the *social* world).

[11] Many researchers in the "interpretivist" tradition have queried this argument of Popper as applied in the social sciences, and have argued for a more inductively based connection between empirical data and theoretical conceptualization (cf. Henwood and Pidgeon, 1993). However, Henwood and Pidgeon indicate that even within this tradition, it is understood that good theorizing needs to integrate "diverse levels of abstraction" as part of the process of developing a "conceptually rich understanding" that can be plausibly argued to "fit the data" (1993, pp. 21–22). Furthermore, they indicate that the "negative case analysis" often promoted within this tradition can be seen as paralleling "the Popperian strategy of ingeniously seeking wherever possible to falsify working hypotheses derived from the emergent model in that, as analysis of initial cases proceeds, further cases would be selected for their discomforting potential" (1993, pp. 25–26).

production of knowledge" (1995, p. 116). He qualifies this statement by stating that this does not mean that they need to abandon other goals, such as hoping that the research may "promote some political ideal or other to which he or she is committed" (1995, p. 116). But the primary purpose – and the one in terms of which all research is to be immediately directed – is that of producing knowledge.

In keeping with this argument, Hammersley suggests that we "draw a distinction between direct and indirect goals" and that we recognize that the *direct* goal to which researchers must properly be directed is "the production of valid and relevant knowledge" (1995, p. 116). He contends that in the research context, the aim is to "discover, through empirical investigation and rational discussion, which conclusions are sound and which are not, and why" (1995, p. 117).

Hammersley refers favorably to the Weberian view (accepted by many philosophers of science) concerning the fact/value distinction – that is, the distinction between the realm of "facts" and that of "values" (Weber, 1949). Hammersley argues that in outlining his view of social science (as indeed *science*[12]), Weber rightly recognizes the "need for detachment from [value-laden] political commitments," that is, the need to strive for "objectivity" (1995, p. 115). What Weber does not concentrate sufficiently on, according to Hammersley, is the "institutional requirements [in the scientific community] for this detachment" (1995, p. 115). Hammersley suggests that he "underestimates" somewhat the manner in which rational debate within the scientific community helps to generate less bias as a whole in the productions of science.

The realist conception of the goal of research to produce knowledge is tied to a specific notion of researcher reflexivity. Here reflexivity, defined as the "looking back at oneself" (aided by the scientific community), is seen as a process of trying *to locate potential biases in one's approach, with the aim of being able to minimize these biases* so as to better discover, in Hammersley's words, "which conclusions are sound and which are not, and why" (1995, p. 117). Davidson and Layder, writing from a somewhat different research approach from Hammersley in terms of their understanding of "empirical investigation," nevertheless concur with him on the import and aim of reflexivity in social research. Like him, they state a commitment to "research that is rigorous and reflexive" in the sense of trying to reflect back on the ways in which its biases can possibly be preempted (1994, p. 38). The aim is to produce knowledge that is "more objective than research which is sloppy and uncritical" (Davidson & Layder, 1994, p. 28).[13]

---

[12]Weber (1949) argues that social scientific inquiry is distinct from natural scientific inquiry, because social scientists can explore the realm of social *meaning making* that renders people's actions *understandable*. (See also Romm, 2001, pp. 55–66 for an exploration of ways of locating Weber's interpretivist argument in relation to other positions on social inquiry.)

[13]In terms of the labels proffered in Footnote 10, Hammersley subscribes to *non-foundationalism* (distinguishing his position from positivist *foundationalism or naïve empiricism*). Davidson and Layder invoke a *scientific realist* position – which relies on a different way of connecting "reason" with empirical "evidence" (sometimes called retroductive logic) so as to be able to excavate unobservable structures (Romm, 2001, p. 4). See Chapter 6, Section 6.1.2, as well as Chapter 8, for more detail on this.

In the chapters that follow, it will be seen that realist accounts of research and the attendant understandings of reflexivity can be argued to be decidedly influential within many of the examples of research around new racism that I have chosen to discuss. When discussing the examples, I show how realist positions can be revisited in the light of alternative conceptions of knowing processes and products.

Schmidt contends that researchers themselves can contribute to *altering societal expectations* in relation to the purpose of research endeavors. She notes that often researchers studying "minority–majority relations" in Western contexts and those studying "racism in the United States [USA]" operate in terms of an implicit realist epistemology and communicate this to the public (2008, p. 23). In this way they "reproduce a (popular) understanding of diverse research perspectives as something suspicious" – because it is taken for granted that "the purpose of research is not to think in varieties of possible understandings, but to produce a cohesive, monolithic description of 'reality'" (2008, p. 13). In the face hereof, Schmidt suggests that researchers should set out to highlight what she calls "epistemological variation" (i.e., alternative understandings of how "knowing" should be defined) as part of an effort to point to "the potential of alternative conceptualizations and framing" of what it means to engage in "research" (2008, p. 25). Below I point to some of these alternatives and I outline some implications hereof for the engagement in research around (new) racism.

1.5.2 A Constructivist-Oriented View

Certain authors who may be regarded as more constructivist oriented[14] have focused on the constructed nature of the worldviews developed within the scientific community. Kuhn – renowned for his book *The Structure of Scientific Revolutions* (1962), which was republished in 1970 in enlarged form – is sometimes cited as supporting a kind of constructivism with which those studying new forms of racism can sympathize (cf. Collins, 2000; Dunn & Geeraert, 2003; Cohen-Cole, 2005).

Kuhn's position, briefly put, is that scientific inquiry can be conceptualized as proceeding in terms of periods of what he calls "normal" and "revolutionary" science. During times of normal science – which he sees as characterizing most periods of scientific endeavor in the natural sciences – the scientific community works on solving problems or puzzles *set within a particular way of defining its field of study.* It develops "efficient instruments for solving the puzzles that its paradigms define" (1970, p. 166). Its approach to, and definition of, the defined objects of research (its worldview) are largely unquestioned – and it is indeed for this reason that scientists are able to explore in depth their defined puzzles.

---

[14] As with the term realism, the term "constructivism" embraces a variety of positions. For example, positions such as critical theory, anti-foundationalist feminism, and discursively oriented constructivism all query the realist focus on science as a process of generating increasingly improved access to independently existing (extra-linguistic) reality (Romm, 2001, pp. 5–7).

Kuhn avers that this exclusiveness of concentration on the part of scientists in the natural sciences implies a certain rigidity of perspective. But he states that there are times – "when the occasion demands" – that the "community can switch from paradigm to paradigm" (1970, p. 166). A revolutionary switch to a new way of addressing puzzles and problems then takes place within the scientific community. Nevertheless, this does not imply for Kuhn that through successive revolutions scientists can be said to make progress in getting, as he puts it, "closer and closer to the truth" (defined in realist terms) (1970, p. 170). He argues that this statement of his may "disturb many readers" – because "we are all deeply accustomed to seeing science as the one enterprise that draws constantly nearer to some goal set by nature [natural reality] in advance" (1970, p. 171). Yet he avers that there is no need to posit such a goal. As he explains:

> Does it really help to imagine that there is some one full, objective, true account of nature and that the proper measure of scientific achievement is the extent to which it brings us closer to that ultimate goal? (1970, p. 171)

His position is that it is *not necessary to make this assumption* – albeit that he admits that he cannot "specify in any detail the consequences of this alternative view" of science that he is forwarding (1970, p. 171).

Kuhn argues that in the case of the *social sciences*, they seem to be characterized by the simultaneous existence of a number of competing paradigms – among which social scientists have to make choices. Yet (given the paradigmatic character of all inquiry) these choices cannot be made with reference to an examination of the empirical evidence, because *"evidence" is already differently viewed depending on what paradigmatic language is being used to make observations.* Again Kuhn does not offer detail on how social scientists come to terms with what he calls "incommensurability" (or untranslatability) between different ways of approaching the research. He does suggest that one way of social scientists defending the approach adopted (and the choice of a research problem) – such as, say, exploring "the effects of racial discrimination or the causes of the business cycle" – is by considering "the social importance of achieving a solution" and how the research might contribute to this (1970, p. 164). However, he notes that any social science student is faced with having "constantly before him [or her] a number of competing and incommensurable solutions to these problems, solutions that he [or she] must ultimately evaluate for himself [or herself]" (1970, p. 165).

One can extrapolate that Kuhn's position would be that in which ever way social scientists do proceed, they should be aware that their choice of paradigm is indeed a choice, which leads them to frame questions for "solving" in a particular way.[15]

---

[15] Since Kuhn's work exploring the manner in which paradigms may frame our ways of perceiving, much debate has ensued around implications of this for processes of dialogue across paradigmatic positions (whether engaged in by professional researchers and/or others). While certain authors argue that people engaged in dialogue across paradigms necessarily in some ways *talk past each other* (as the languages are not fully translatable), others have pointed to the potential for *developing mutual engagement* – see, for instance, Tsing (1993), Flood and Romm (1996a), and Yuval-Davis (2004); and see my discussion in Chapter 4, Section 4.3.1.

This in turn would allow them (as well as others in society) to reflect upon the way in which research problems are becoming defined and answered – through a specific manner of perceiving and treating "the evidence." (See also Romm, 2001, pp. 100–101.) And it would allow readers/audiences of the studies to undercut the view of science as a process whereby scientists use reason/logic to assess theories in the light of the evidence supposedly supplied by reality.

Many authors who discuss the process of research in the context of their inquiries around (new) racism have commented on the continued dominance of the notion of science as ideally an arena of rational debate in relation to supposed factual evidence (e.g., Douglas, 1998; Collins, 2000; De Souza, 2002, 2004). The angle taken by such authors is that this view of science perpetuates binary oppositions embedded within (Western) discourse: oppositions such as, say, knower/known, subject/object, reason/emotion, fact/value, and so on. These oppositions serve to produce a worldview in which it is believed that scientists must try to access reality by separating the "knowing self" from the "known object" (Richards, 1980, p. 72, as cited in Collins, 2000, p. 70).

Collins remarks on how these binaries play themselves out in the course of practicing (Western-oriented) scientific processes. One of the binaries, for instance, is between feeling and thinking – which implies that "feelings cannot be incorporated in thought or even function in conjunction with it because in binary oppositional thinking, feelings retard thought and values obscure facts" (2000, p. 70). She argues that this kind of binary thinking denigrates knowing processes where their humanly created character (infused with people's feelings/concerns) is acknowledged and accounted for.[16]

In elucidating her epistemological position (regarding what is involved in human "knowing"), Collins indicates that she does not wish to "duplicate the positivist [realist] belief in one 'true' interpretation of reality" (2000, p. 297). Rather, she wishes to acknowledge that the statements made by her in relation to "the world" relate to a world that becomes presented by virtue of the values, concerns, and feelings that are brought to bear in its appearance. This is not to say that these all are to be seen as threats to the understanding of "reality." On the contrary, they are *part of the processes whereby constructed visions of humanly mediated reality are created* – in conjunction with others whose values, concerns, and feelings likewise need to be taken into account. (For an indication of how standpoint thinking can be disassociated from a realist epistemology – contrary to the claims of Hammersley & Gomm, 1997a, 1997b – see Romm, 1997, 1998c.)

Yuval-Davis explains that in terms of Collins's argument (1990, p. 236), operating from a "dialogical standpoint epistemology" implies recognizing that "from

---

[16]In similar vein, Ospina (2008, p. 441) notes that in order to cater for a stance where it can be admitted that thinking and feeling are inseparable, some people in Latin America refer to themselves as "feelthinkers" (via the concept of "*sentipensante*"). She refers to the way in which Fals-Borda (1985) drew on this concept in his writing about action research experiences in Latin America.

each positioning the world is seen differently, and thus any knowledge based on just one positioning is 'unfinished' [to differentiate from 'invalid']" (Collins, as cited in Yuval-Davis, 2004, p. 16). Yuval-Davis's inserted remark (in square brackets) on refraining from using the word "invalid" – and instead using the word "unfinished" – points to a distancing from a realist epistemology that is invoked when one defines a way of seeing as supposedly "invalid" in relation to some posited "true(r)" understanding of reality (2004, p. 16).

Reflexive thinking within a dialogically oriented epistemological approach is based on encouraging researching selves as whole beings to reflect back on their way of engaging with others – with the aim of instantiating dialogical forms of human relationship at the point of inquiry. The idea is also not to dehumanize the so-called researched object in the process of inquiries. Collins explains the importance of this kind of stance:

> ... because oppositional binaries rarely represent different but equal relationships, they are inherently unstable. Tension may be temporarily relieved by subordinating one half of the binary to the other. Thus Whites rule Blacks, men dominate women, reason is thought superior to emotion in ascertaining truth, facts supersede opinion in evaluating knowledge, and subjects rule objects. (2000, p. 71)

A reflexive approach thus would be aimed at reconsidering, and aiding others to reconsider, the kind of binary thinking that forms the "underpinning of this entire system of thought" – so as to avoid reproducing within the research process these concepts, which "imply relationships of superiority and inferiority" (2000, p. 71).

Collins provides a metaphor of "Black women's quilting" to express a quality of human relationships *not* built on upholding notions of superiority and inferiority. She sees the "theme of individual expression" in such quilting as pointing to an ethic of caring in that an effort is made to embrace "difference" arising from alternative forms of self-expression. As she explains: "Black women quilters place strong color and patterns next to one another and see the individual differences not as extracting from each piece but as enriching the whole quilt" (2000, p. 263). She argues that this metaphor provides an illustration of the importance of connectedness in the development of "the whole." And she sees the origins of this way of envisaging human being as "rooted in a tradition of African humanism" (2000, p. 263). Collins considers it crucial – as part of the (re)embracing of an ethic of caring – to provide a place for inquirers to reflect back on the quality of human relationships in social life in which they are complicit through the way in which they themselves conduct "research."

In the chapters that follow I shall show how these kinds of concerns that I have raised here can provide one entry point into revisiting some of the research examples that I outline and discuss. I also show how a third stance in relation to the question of reflexivity (see Section 1.5.3 below) – which I consider to be an extension of the second – can likewise provide an entry point into reconsidering the research examples.

1.5.3 A Trusting Constructivist View

Following on from the constructivist-oriented approach outlined above, a "trusting constructivist approach" (Romm, 2001) focuses on the importance of researchers assuming responsibility for their way of posing research questions, their way of generating "answers/insights," and their style of "write-up." My argument is that researchers need to earn people's trust (namely, that of colleagues, participants, and wider audiences) by showing that they are oriented to considering – with others – the potential consequences of their way of proceeding (see also Romm, 1990a, 1995, 1996, 1997, 2002a, 2002b, 2006a). (Deliberations around these consequences here can only be through discursive processes in which the humanly constructed character of the considerations is admitted.)

One of the ways in which this position can be practiced is by becoming attuned to consider the potential *self-fulfilling effects* that might be generated through the very act of supposedly knowing about the world. Jervis gives an example in relation to the "discovery" of social realities when he notes, for instance, that

> [journalistic] descriptions of the economic and social health of a neighborhood can be self-confirming because they depend in large measure on the characteristics, attitudes, and behavior of people who live there, which in turn are influenced by the descriptions people believe (and think others believe). Thus media spokespersons are incorrect to claim that they merely report what is happening . . . . (1997, pp. 148–149)

Just as journalistic reporters arguably contribute to *creating* the news on which they "report," so the same can be said of others involved in social inquiries.

In trying to address the question of to what extent both natural and social scientific inquiries should be regarded as implicated in the creation of realities, my suggestion is that this is a question that cannot be answered. We do not have the means of checking the extent to which, in any case in question, proffered constructions *are* generating specific impacts through the way in which they are being developed. (See, e.g., Hacking, 1995, 1999; Davis, 1997.) Nonetheless, I propose that, particularly in the realm of social inquiry, we need to work with the awareness that our way of organizing inquiries, and way of presenting "results," *might generate certain social effects* – as experienced and as argued for in processes of social discourse. (See Romm, 2002a, 2002b, 2007.)

Authors who support – and commit to – a realist-oriented approach as the basis for (natural and social) scientific inquiry assert that they too are concerned about the practical effects that research activities might have in society. But their argument is that they do not want this concern to detract from research efforts toward truth seeking. For them the prime task of researchers is to use the process of inquiry to strive to make advancements in moving closer to the truth. For example, Hammersley (1995) insists – following Popper (1969, 1994) – that just because absolute certainty is not available to scientists, it does not mean that they should relinquish the quest to get closer to the truth by following a path that is likely to lead to knowledge (rather than error). According to this position, science as traditionally understood (as directed toward knowledge production) enables people to act in terms of *more informed opinions* than they otherwise would have if science did not function as such as an institution in society in which scientists strive to generate increased knowledge of extra-linguistic reality.

However, this way of interpreting the purpose of scientific enterprises glides over the problem of *our affording undue credibility to the statements* that are presumed to flow from "scientific" activity (Romm, 1997, 1998b). As Jacobsen puts it, "the claim to speak on behalf of 'truth' and 'reality' is an effective way of authorizing knowledge claims" – where a "position of authority in wider society" becomes retrieved on this basis (2008, p. 32). But, as she notes, the issue of researcher power is not sufficiently problematized via this position. (She makes this point while arguing for an ethical responsibility of researchers exploring Muslim immigration in the Norwegian context, arguing that the way of framing the research issues can all too easily – through the power of the scientific language – serve to "naturalize boundaries between a national 'we' and foreign 'them'," with attendant social effects (2008, p. 34).[17])

The issue of researcher power and attendant responsibilities in the understanding of (new) racism is also raised as of primary consideration by, for example, Ladson-Billings when she asks: "who has the power to shape the public perception … ?" (2003, p. 417). Ladson-Billings states her concerns in her article by locating two divergent epistemological positions based on alternative central premises. She notes that the philosophy of René Descartes as an approach to knowing can be seen to articulate

> a central premise upon which European and (Euro-American) worldviews and epistemology rest – that the individual mind is the source of knowledge and existence. In contrast the African saying "Ubuntu", translated "I am because we are", asserts that the individual's existence (and knowledge) is contingent upon relationships with others. (2003, p. 398)[18]

She indicates that these divergent epistemological perspectives (which can be seen as similar to what have been labeled above as more realist- and constructivist-oriented approaches) are not merely matters of "preferences." She argues that the "preference" for the former kind of epistemology serves to reproduce a "dominant worldview and [attendant] knowledge production and acquisition processes"

---

[17]She notes, for instance, that when liberal notions such as "democracy, tolerance, and gender equality" are invoked with the aim of pointing (by contrast) to negative sides of Islam, the way in which these notions are defined can imply that they are themselves "beyond criticism" in their instantiation (2008, p. 41). Furthermore, the way in which the research is framed, reinforces negative stereotyping of Muslims, instead of "contextualizing, historicizing and displaying internal variation and differentiation among Muslims" (2008, p. 29). Regarding the question of whether their religion is to be conceived as a "stumbling block for integration," she notes that this question itself assumes a particular conception of what "integration" into the nation-state might imply – and can be seen to "uphold a notion of a unified national society or culture" (2008, p. 45). I return to this issue in my discussion of cultural racism in Chapter 2.

[18]Collins makes a similar point when discussing the "tradition of African humanism." She suggests that this tradition gains expression in "the polyrhythms of African American music, in which no one main beat subordinates the other" (2000, p. 263). Thus the *connectedness* becomes focused upon at the same time as individual uniqueness is acknowledged (2000, pp. 262–263).

in society (2003, p. 399). The realist epistemology, which implies that "knowers" can develop ways of accessing an independently existing world, indeed renders inferior a more participative approach (in which it is understood that the *claim to have the tools for better accessing apparently independently existing realities is already a problematic claim*). The dominant (realist) epistemology – based on the idea of "pure" and "elegant" scientific knowledge (2003, p. 401) – can already be said to be imbued with a view of human relationships, in which those with supposed access to the mechanisms for knowledge production (scientists) become equipped to authorize their visions/constructions in relation to others.

She argues that to call for an alternative epistemology to this dominant way of seeing "science," is *not* to suggest "that there are multiple and equally partial standpoints that are either [all] valid [the so-called relativist argument] or inexorably ranked hierarchically" (in terms of some criterion) (2003, p. 407). It is to pose a completely different way of seeing the way in which *social inquirers, as humans linked with others, render themselves accountable to others as part of the process of inquiry.*

She suggests (2003, p. 408) that what is called Critical Race Theory (CRT) (e.g., Delgado, 1995) as developed in the USA is significant for our considerations of an alternative epistemology (to mainstream orthodoxy) for addressing race issues. She explains that CRT offers a way of injecting the "cultural viewpoints of people of color" in efforts to "reconstruct a society crumbling under the burden of racial hegemony" (2003, p. 411). She points out that although there is no set of "doctrines or methodologies" to which all CRT scholars can be said to subscribe, they all consider that CRT as an analytic tool is equipped to inject into our discourses new worldviews as well as new ways of knowing itself (2003, p. 411). One way of doing this is by showing how storytelling, which enables, inter alia, the perspectives of the "dispossessed and marginalized" to be seen as "legitimate in the process of knowledge construction," can be capitalized upon in the inquiry process (2003, p. 411). This in turn implies revisiting the criteria for defining what counts as "knowing" within social life.

Ladson-Billings explains that already through trying to create a science that is directed toward offering an "apolitical authority" (as Collins, 1998, puts it), mainstream epistemology serves to de-authorize that which is deemed as less "objective" as a way of knowing (2003, p. 423). And she indicates that it is for *this* reason that an alternative epistemology, where people are called upon to reflect further on the political implications of all of our ways of knowing, is called for. She continues her plea for such an approach by noting that:

> Scholars must be challenged to ask not only *about whom* is the research, but also *for whom* is the research. The question of *for whom* is not merely about advocacy, but rather about who is capable to act and demonstrate agency. This agency is enacted through both epistemological and discursive forms. (2003, p. 415)

Here I understand Ladson-Billings as suggesting that when engaging in social inquiry it is crucial to create scope for people as research participants to become "agents" in the sense of participating both in the way the knowing process is developed and in the discourses that become constructed as part of the knowing process. Through the examples that I use in the book, I offer concrete suggestions for how I believe this can be organized within various research approaches.

Ladson-Billings also points out that as part of her own reflexive practice, she makes an effort, through her story about herself and her work, to "situate myself as a researcher – who I am, what I believe, what experiences I have had – because it affects what, how, and why I research" (2003, p. 416). As she further notes, "in CRT [Critical Race Theory] the researcher makes a deliberate appearance in his or her work" (2003, p. 424).

In terms of this understanding of reflexivity, it is not to be seen as a process of reflecting back on oneself in order to supposedly pre-empt biases springing from one's values. Rather, it is a process of recognizing, with others, how knowing is inevitably *shaped by situated selves*, who, together, can *reflect on their values, concerns, feelings, and so on, as part of the process of developing and expanding their perspectives on the humanly appropriated world.*

Ladson-Billings emphasizes that in affirming this alternative epistemological position, the aim is not to "dismiss the work of European and Euro-American scholars." Rather, it is about "defining the limits of such scholarship" by pointing to its potential effects in reinforcing, wittingly or unwittingly, hierarchical relationships in society (2003, p. 421). She suggests that it is on these terms that we need to understand why Collins (1990) "argues for concrete experiences as a criterion of meaning, the use of dialogue in the assessment of knowledge claims, an ethic of caring, and an ethic of personal accountability" (2003, p. 421).

As shown throughout the book, I take up and expand upon the argument of what I call trusting constructivism in order to exemplify how "personally accountable" research around new racism can become effected in practice in the design of research inquiries. My view of personal accountability (and trustworthiness) in the research process is linked with what I call discursive accountability. Inquirers can be considered as *discursively accountable* insofar as they can be seen (by those concerned) to embrace an orientation of being *sensitive to a range of considerations springing from engagement with alternative perspectives and values* (Romm, 2002b). Such an orientation in turn implies that one nurtures the capacity to take *seriously into account differences of viewpoint as the basis for developing one's sensitivities.* This is consistent with Collins's suggestion that the ethic of caring at the same time implies an openness to others' expressions of emotion and to recognizing "the appropriateness of emotions in dialogues" – rather than seeing "emotion" as separate from "intellect" (2000, p. 263).[19]

---

[19]This understanding of ethics (and ethical inquiry) has affinity with Aristotle's account of *virtue ethics* as outlined by Richardson and McMullen (2006). They suggest that the focus in such an ethics is not on the question of "what should I do?", but rather on "*what sort of person should I be?*" Translated into research ethics, it means that certain dispositions are encouraged in researchers (such as "honesty, sensitivity, respectfulness, reflexivity, etc.") – rather than trying to provide (via professional associations) "prescriptive or algorithmic rules or codes" (2007, p. 1128). Although Richardson and McMullen discuss virtue ethics in terms of Aristotle's account, others have argued

While I believe that a discursively accountable orientation is one that can be nurtured in "everyday" as well as in "professionally oriented" inquiry processes, I contend that one can still identify specific contours for the operation of what can be termed professional research. In the section below I elucidate my argument in this regard.

1.6 Contours of "Professional" Inquiry

1.6.1 Discursively Accounting for Research Strategies

It is sometimes said that a distinguishing mark of "scientific" or "professional" inquiry is that it makes its strategies of inquiry *recoverable* – so that these are visible for others wishing to appreciate or review the procedures used (cf. Shipman, 1982, p. xiii; Sharma, 1997, p. 792; Checkland & Holwell, 1998, p. 10; Douglas, 1998, Chapter 5; Burch, 2006, p. 9). In the context of the trusting constructivist stance outlined above, allowing for "recoverability" would mean that researchers seek to earn trust not only by making apparent the procedures used, but also by *elucidating the judgments* occurring in the process of choosing and working with those procedures. As I illustrate in the book, choosing and working in accordance with procedures also involves creative, innovative extensions thereof – in order to enhance the quality of engagement with colleagues, participants, and wider audiences. A discursive orientation on the part of researchers implies that they need to show how they are *engaging with concerns that might be raised by others* (or that might already have been raised when similar approaches have been employed in other research settings). In this process, they need to bear in mind a relationship not only with colleagues (taking into account different criteria that may be invoked to evaluate their work), but also with others (in the wider society).

Sharma's view is that other professionals as well as "lay principals" (research participants and wider audiences) can bring expectations – though not necessarily in the form of rules – to bear on inquirers to act responsibly. To build trust, I believe would-be professionals need to account for ways of conducting inquiries by considering debates in the professional as well as lay communities about acceptable inquiry processes. This is one way of embedding themselves, to use Sharma's terminology, in the social processes through which trust is awarded. But as part of the process of rendering themselves discursively accountable, they are also called upon to expand discursive repertoires operating in the scientific and wider communities – so that criteria used to judge research are not unnecessarily restrictive.

Alvesson and Sköldberg (2000) provide a good summary of what is involved in trying to reflexively reconsider modes of approach that may have become taken for granted as "frames of reference" (2000, p. 246). The idea is to cultivate the capacity

---

that it has roots in Chinese philosophy (cf. Hursthouse, 2007, pp. 1–2). And Collins considers the (related) ethic of caring as having roots in African humanism (2000, p. 263).

to reflect upon what is "*not* capable of saying" (or becoming manifest) within the particular frame, so as to extend one's repertoire. They propose that:

> Reflection means thinking about the conditions for what one is doing, investigating the way in which the theoretical, cultural and political context of individual and intellectual involvement affects interaction with whatever is being researched, often in ways difficult to become conscious of. (2000, p. 245)

They note that just because it is difficult to become conscious of the assumptions underlying inquiry processes, "the point of reflection is to break away from ... a narrow focus on a particular aspect [of what is being researched], ... to break up and change a particular language game" (2000, p. 246).

Through a variety of examples that I employ in the book, I show in what sense I believe that this notion of reflexivity has not been sufficiently embraced in certain processes of inquiry around new racism; I provide suggestions for shifting the "language games" guiding the research. In this respect it is worth noting Morawski's reference to Bond's attempts (1933, 1958) to lay bare the way in which the experimental methods of his time were "significantly infused with dominant cultural assumptions about human nature, specifically assumptions about human racial difference" (Morawski, 2005, p. 95). Morawski contends that still today "sciences *make* just as they discover human kinds" – through a "dynamic process of making and finding" (2005, p. 17, my italics). This contention relates to my argument above concerning the potential self-fulfilling effects of inquiry processes in the continued making/unfolding of social outcomes. I take up these arguments in depth in the text.

1.6.2 Creating Publicly Available Material

Scientific inquiry may be characterized also by an intention to present in some form to academic and other audiences the results created through an inquiry, no matter how tentatively they may be expressed. Part of the responsibilities of researchers is to make public to larger audiences than those involved in the particular localities where inquiries are conducted the results of the research, so that others – professional researchers, and lay practitioners – can assess their relevance in different contexts (cf. Flood & Romm, 1996a, p. 135; Hall, 1999, pp. 152–154; Pratto, 2002, pp. 196–197; Reay, 2004, pp. 1007–1008).

From a trusting constructivist viewpoint, it is stressed that when research material is "made public," this should not lead lay practitioners to passively accept authors' ways of defining the research outcomes and their (presumed) relevance in different social contexts. Research material as written up by authors should ideally make room for continued argumentation and contextualization by those wishing to consider its meaningfulness. The style of write-up is regarded as important within a constructivist position. It is suggested that the text should make provision for, rather than unnecessarily closing off, spaces for continued working *with as well as around* (rather than simply working *within*) frames provided (McIntyre-Mills, 2006a, p. 7).

This means in effect that the content of the results comes to matter less than the *discursive orientation* that authors and different audiences take toward it in argumentation (Romm, 2001, pp. 121–124). People judging the status of any inquiry should engage with arguments presented, as a way of exploring the potential of the inquiry to contribute to continuing productive discourse.

In order to highlight the impossibility of stepping outside of human discourse to check understandings against externally posited realities, some constructivists speak of theorizing as *narrative construction*. In terms of this conception of theorizing, it is suggested that narratives "worth listening to" can be fashioned, without authors or audiences regarding them as advancing knowledge defined as reflection of external realities (Barry & Elmes, 1997, p. 431). They can be seen as offering "interpretive lenses" (Barry & Elmes, 1997, p. 430) while at the same time inviting further understanding and meaning-making as people move around and past the stories proffered. The advantage of focusing on theorizing as a function of human discourse is that it allows people to engage with each other's accounts without trying to resolve these in some uniform view of "the facts." As Collins points out, this also caters for "sustaining dialogues across differences in power" – where different contributors are seen as "writing missing parts to the other writer's story" (2000, p. 38). As Gill elucidates, "individual perspectives are brought forward and retained in the overarching narrative, maintaining the multiple levels of meaning" (2001, p. 343). Furthermore, as Cobley remarks, in the contemporary understanding of narratives, "there is an enhanced sense of the capacity for participation [of audiences] in narrative" – due to an understanding of "the thoroughly constructed nature of narrative and the impossibility of producing true closure of time and space through the device of a conclusive ending" (2003, pp. 200–201).

On her reading of Section 1.6.2 of this chapter, Susan Weil's feedback commentary (May, 2009) was that despite my highlighting of "interpretive lenses" (which she liked), she was concerned that, as she puts it:

> This section could easily be read as what positivists do, in the sense that they anticipate arguments, [and] place their work in the context of previous academic literature [in this sense making it public]. If I am honest, it just misses the point in terms of the difference that makes the difference that you are exploring.

She suggested that this paragraph (above) does not give sufficient attention to "multiple ways of knowing without becoming entangled in a hierarchy." She also remarked that:

> I also am noticing how the notion of action research as being included in a continuum of meanings for scientific inquiry is marginalized, [and] made invisible here, so you are in a sense appealing to [reproducing] a dominant norm that indeed CRT and ... [others] have been attempting to dislodge in terms of determinants of validity.

She expressed concern that my paragraph could be read as "stay[ing] locked within an input–output notion of research" – rather than its

> including the possibility that some forms of critically reflexive action research, and so on. [as, for example, in Weil, 1997, 1998] make ongoing engagement with those whom the research is intended to benefit, and all the diverse stakeholders, integral to cycles of quality.

Moreover, ethics and power relations at play in research cannot be anticipated and controlled beforehand, as is expected now in most academic research.

She also pointed out that I had not [yet] opened up the "limits of the idea of the researcher even writing up the research alone." And she mentioned in this context that the "research assessment exercises" in the UK can operate to control what counts as "high quality dissemination, writing, etc., which favors, for example, individually-written work over collaborative work."

I have cited Weil's way of expressing her concerns because I believe that she has stated well the point that making research "public" needs to be seen in a way that indeed can dislodge positivist/realist-oriented visions of researchers' involvement in the social fabric.

In the chapters that follow I try to show that there are various ways in which research around new racism can be encouraged to generate disparate interpretations of how it can contribute to productive discourse in social life. And in Chapter 7 in particular, I refer to Weil's arguments around critically reflexive action research and I show how they link up with the kinds of constructivist/pragmatic approaches to defining research validity that I am forwarding in the book.

I now proceed to show how the rest of the book is structured.

1.7 Outline of Chapters 2–9

In *Chapter 2*, I provide an overview of some of the concepts developed by a variety of authors to differentiate "old-fashioned racism" from new manifestations of racism in contemporary social life. The chapter is aimed at detailing some of the central concepts that feature across the various examples used in the rest of the book. I also point out that when different theorists use apparently "same" concepts (such as, say, the concept of color-blind racism), they can be used with different theoretical meanings and implications. I offer an outline of different theoretical starting points that can be adopted in exploring (forms of) new racism and of different approaches to their study. In Chapter 2, I also devote a section to considering the geographical setting of research studies and I point to debates in relation to the transferability of concepts developed in particular geographical contexts to others.

Because Chapter 2 is organized around offering an account of a variety of theoretical conceptualizations of new racism and delving into the authors' arguments concerning the study hereof, it might be considered as a somewhat abstract (and also dense) discussion that is better "dipped into" by readers for a start – and later read in more detail. That is, it could be that only after reading the rest of the Chapters (3–9), which lend flesh to the discussions in Chapter 2, readers will find Chapter 2 more "readable." If Chapter 2 is not read in toto before moving on to the following chapters, I would suggest that readers still look at my summary table (Table 2.1) that I present toward the end of the chapter – before moving on to the following chapters. Nevertheless, some readers may decide indeed to plough through Chapter 2 from the start – to see how I am detailing the various theoretical conceptualizations that become drawn upon in later chapters.

In *Chapter 3*, I provide an exposition of experimental research as a procedure for exploring causal relationships between chosen variables (where variables are defined as any social phenomena that can vary and where variation can be measured), as a basis for creating recommendations to mitigate against the potential of racism. The experiments that I discuss are intended as enabling the researchers to look into race-oriented behaviors and their outcomes in society of which actors (especially White ones) may otherwise remain unaware. The argument of those instigating the experiments is that with new racism, people's feelings/attitudes in relation to race issues can manifest in ways unbeknownst to them. Scientifically organized experiments thus can become a way of generating increased knowledge of this. The focus on *White* people's responses is linked to the view that within new racism many White people profess that "race" does not matter in their thinking and behavior – and that experiments can be designed to investigate this contention. I discuss in the chapter how Black/minority people's deliberations have sometimes been, and should (I suggest) be further, incorporated within such designs. This also, I argue, can create openings for increased deliberation around the categories that become employed by people, including by the researchers.

To organize my discussion, I point to experiments conducted primarily in the USA (with some reference of authors to experimental work in Canada and in Europe). With reference to these examples, I try to show up limitations of this style of research, unless shifted/extended to express an increased engagement with those offering alternative epistemological, theoretical, and methodological proposals for researching what Harris-Lacewell calls "race politics" (2003, p. 222). I suggest that without this kind of engagement, particular ways of framing the research questions can well lead to the creation of policy recommendations implicitly (albeit unwittingly) buttressing these initial (and not sufficiently explored) ways of framing. This relates to my argument developed in *Accountability in Social Research* (2001), as expressed by McIntyre-Mills, that:

> Romm (2001) demonstrates cogently that accountability and responsibility go beyond merely research ethics and policy recommendations; they go to the very heart of a way a research project is designed or framed. (2003, p. 43)

With reference to the chosen examples in Chapter 3, I illustrate how experimenters can become more *oriented to accounting for the manner of framing and thereby indeed reach beyond their initial starting point of the research*. This, I suggest, can be done by introducing more space for "qualitative" discussion (with the concentration on words rather than numbers, including more space for cross-racial discussion).[20] Furthermore, I argue that more attention can be given (than

---

[20]My argument for considering experimental designs as not necessarily only *quantitative* in character is in line with Vogt's view that the quantitative/qualitative distinction is one affecting *data coding/measurement and analysis* (rather than the *research design* as such). He avers that designs – such as, say, experiments, surveys, and participant observation – do not carry with them a *necessary link* to the way in which data will be coded and analyzed (i.e., in more numerical or narrative form) (Vogt, 2008, p. 2). And my argument for including cross-racial discussion, is in line with Harris-Lacewell's observation that thus far Black people have been largely decentered through the way in

traditionally associated with experimentation) to exploring the status of the "results" as generated via the experiments. Through my discussion, I offer a proposal for how experimental research can be shifted/redirected to enable processes for *redefining* raced relations (that can be understood as having become raced through historically generated constructions).

In *Chapter 4*, I discuss survey research as a procedure, and the way it has been used in the study of new racism primarily with the intention of trying to *get to grips with attitudes and responses explicitly expressed by people around race issues*, again as a route to creating policy recommendations. The examples that I choose are of surveys exploring people's attitudes in the USA and attitudes explicitly expressed in Australia too. As with the experiments discussed in Chapter 3, surveys aimed at researching attitudes in regard to expressions of racism have tended to focus on *White* people's attitudes – and have been designed to uncover coded forms of racism among Whites. But I have also chosen to discuss in Chapter 4 examples of surveys where Whites were not the only respondents (e.g., in relation to views on affirmative action and multiculturalism).

As with Chapter 3, in all the examples that I discuss, I point to the potentially restrictive framing of research questions unless provision is specifically made to cater for this as a problem. I also point to possible problems created by not recognizing the self-fulfilling potential of "found" results, especially insofar as they are presented as *found* rather than *generated* (through the way the research is set up). I indicate what it might mean to employ survey research in a less "traditional" fashion, by taking further some of the examples that I outline. I show how these can be seen as providing the seeds of a novel way of practicing survey research so that through the research itself new forms of racism can be both explored and (at the same time) *undercut*. I suggest that this requires more space for posing questions to participants in terms of alternative frames (while also creating some additional openings for qualitative expression on their part), and also for researchers creating more reflexively oriented interpretations in which they reflect on the manner through which the research process might be generating the research material.

In *Chapter 5*, I open an exploration (introduced only briefly in Chapter 3 and 4) of the purpose of qualitatively oriented inquiry focused on excavating meanings through intensive (in-depth) interviewing, including focus group interviewing. I gear Chapter 5 toward showing how interviewing can enable processes of reviewing – with interviewees and wider audiences – the featuring of the race concept in historical and social contexts. It can thus become a suitable way of deconstructing the race concept as well as its social implications (see also James, 2008, p. 45). The examples that I choose in this chapter are interviews with Black women, enabling an in-depth exploration of their lives and their experiences/understandings of racism (in the Netherlands and the USA), and a focus group interview that I

---

which White scholars study "race politics" and that there appears to be a racial separation in the research community between those (largely Whites) studying "White racial attitudes" and those (largely Blacks) studying "Black politics" (2003, p. 241).

conducted in South Africa around cross-racial friendships (with Black and White school children). However, I suggest that particular attention needs to be given within interview research to the *role of interviewers in the way in which constructions of situations become generated*. This implies revisiting the (oft-underlying and more traditional) model of interviewing as a process of extracting "information." It also implies exploring the social relations between "interviewers" and "participants" as well as wider audiences of research reports (as pointed out by, e.g., Douglas, 1998; Parker & Lynn, 2002; Hoffman, 2007). I provide an indication in Chapter 5 of how I believe that interviewing can be (re)tuned to consider as of primary importance these concerns.

In *Chapter 6*, I explore ethnographic research (including autoethnography) as a mode of inquiry aimed at enabling an examination of the details of people's social interactions in specific social settings. Stewart indicates that the advantage of (qualitative) research focusing on people's interactions in social life is that it allows us to explore "the creation and maintenance of racial inequality through a series of social interactions" (2008, p. 124). He suggests that such research (more so than research that is "variable based") can be directed toward answering the question "how do social interactions create and maintain observed racial inequalities?" (2008, p. 124). In Chapter 6, I choose to discuss a study using a "Critical Race Theoretical" approach to examining Black children's narratives in the context of a school setting in the USA. Through this example, I discuss the normative intention of "critical theorizing" around racism, and I consider the question of how we should conceive the status of any analyses presented. I choose as another example in this chapter an autoethnography of my own involvement in a University setting in the UK (with Chinese students complaining of racial discrimination and with my trying to activate an institutional response to this). I use this example to again explore the way in which research reporting around experiences in social settings might be organized to enable audiences to recognize the author's presence in the development of conceptualizations.

In *Chapter 7*, I discuss in detail the epistemological arguments of those pleading for the creation of forums in society for participative co-inquiry around issues considered as problematic and as needing to be explored with a view to creating viable options for transformative action. I point to one example of a particular action-oriented approach in British organizational contexts (around the issue of institutional racism). I indicate what I consider to be the importance of this work in terms of exploring and practicing an "alternative epistemology" as a way of developing inquiries around new racism. I also point to an example of what I consider to be an innovative computer-aided form of structured dialogue to "harness collective wisdom" of co-inquirers – in this case in the social setting of Cyprus (where Greek Cypriots and Turkish Cypriots committed to unifying the island have been involved). I use both examples to highlight (and draw out) what I see as possibilities for activating collaborative ways of being and learning with others, while acknowledging personal accountability in the inquiry process.

In *Chapter 8*, I take up Marks's argument that studies of racism to date have not managed to build a "convincing theoretical foundation" (2008, p. 49) that will help

us to explain new racism. She argues that we still have not been able to produce
a convincing theory that can provide "meaningful explanations for simultaneous
progress [in trying to tackle racism] and stagnation" (in that racism still persists
across the globe albeit in altered form) (2008, p. 48). In view of Marks's location
of this lacuna, I devote Chapter 8 to offering an account of how structurally oriented theorizing around new racism might help to develop our theorizing – without
thereby claiming the "expert authority" that is of concern to authors such as Collins
(1990, 2000), Douglas (1998), and Ladson-Billings (2003). In the chapter I explore
in detail Bonilla-Silva's (2006) way of developing, and accounting for, his theoretical understanding of color-blind racism as the new racism (that he sees as having
penetrated not only the USA, but also the rest of the Americas and also Europe).
I concentrate on what criteria can be brought to bear in assessing the value of the
theorizing and what would be involved in invoking the requirement for discursive
accountability on the part of theorists/inquirers that I have proposed as important
throughout the book. (To this end, I compare some of Collins's arguments with those
of Bonilla-Silva.) In this chapter I also return to the debate that I raised in Chapter 2
regarding the transferability of ideas developed in one geographical setting to others.

In the final chapter (*Chapter 9*), I draw together various arguments as developed
in the book around what it might mean to develop inquiries that could be helpful
toward transforming the quality of our social existence:

- I reiterate my argument that our ways of knowing/inquiring cannot be separated
  from our ways of living and ways of being – and that transformation of social
  relationships implies revisiting our approaches to exploring (new) racism.
- I offer a discussion of methodological pluralism and make the point that the creative use of research approaches (whether used in mixed-research designs or on
  their own in any specific project) should be guided by trying to take into account,
  in deliberation with others, the potential social consequences of the manner of
  exploring (via the approaches) the issues seen to be at stake.
- I recap my conception of the status of any categories employed by people to
  delineate "differences" between (constructed) phenomena in social life.
- I point to some limitations of the book – in terms of issues not focused upon.
  Briefly, I would like to point out already here that the book has admittedly focused
  primarily on forms of racism that perpetuate hierarchical thinking and hierarchical patterns where "Whiteness" becomes privileged in the social fabric. Some
  commentators on sections of my draft book (from South Africa and Nigeria
  respectively, namely, Sisinyane Makoena and Abimbola Olateju) suggested to
  me (January 2009) that perhaps I should point out to readers that racism can
  relate to other social hierarchies. (They indicated to me that they were comfortable with my reporting on their expressed observations/experiences under their
  own names.) For instance, Sisinyane indicated that her husband's (Zulu) family tends to make her feel inferior by calling her a "Sotho girl," regarding her
  as lower in status (by virtue of being Sotho). She suggested that although her
  husband argues with his family that in post-apartheid South Africa she should
  not be treated like this, it is difficult for her to herself raise discussion around

this. Meanwhile, Abimbola recounted to me that she experiences countless incidents of Black people denigrating her on the basis of her being "kwerekwere" – a derogatory term used by some South African Black people to refer to (Black) "foreigners" in South Africa. In this book, I have not tried to explore in any detail these kinds of experiences (albeit with some brief reference to this in Chapter 2, when considering issues of cultural racism and its relation to xenophobia). The book is concentrated on the study of examples of forms of racism seen as perpetuating ideas of White superiority and perpetuating patterns of White advantage. To discuss other hierarchies in any detail would require another book. Nevertheless, I would suggest that my proposals for extending research approaches that I proffer in this book still might be found useful to be drawn upon in some way by those exploring such hierarchies.

Chapter 2
Conceptualizing New Racism in Relation to Old-Fashioned Racism: Concepts and Research Approaches

2.1 Introduction

In this chapter I offer an overview of some of the ways in which researchers have conceptualized what they call new forms of racism. I start off (Section 2.2.1) by discussing the label of new racism as used by authors who contrast what they see as "new racism" with more "old-fashioned" styles of racism in order to point to what they consider as mutations of racism primarily in the USA.[21] I then (Section 2.2.2) outline some accounts of the historical development of the concept of "race" in the European context. Again I show how older, more biologically based, forms of racism – and attendant views on race – are differentiated from developments toward more culturally based forms (which is not to say that "older" expressions of racism are seen as having disappeared from the landscape). I show how authors have tried to point to global implications of these developments.

Having provided this broad account of how new racism has been conceptually differentiated from more old-fashioned styles of racism, I turn to a detailed examination (Section 2.3) of definitions of forms of new racism by means of the concepts of, respectively, *symbolic racism*; *modern racism*; *aversive racism*; *cultural racism*; *institutional racism*; and *color-blind racism (as systemic)*. I exemplify the use of the concepts with reference to some examples from geographical settings such as the USA, Europe, and South Africa. At the same time I point to some debates around the manner in which theoretical concepts emerging in defined settings can become "transferable" across geographical contexts – an issue to which I return in Chapter 8.

I show during the course of my discussion of the various concepts in this chapter that not all authors considering new racism in relation to old-fashioned racism (and identifying particular kinds of new racism) need be understood as using these terms in the same way. Sometimes terms used – such as, say, the concept of "institutional discrimination" or "color-blind racism" – can be used with different

---

[21] Gaertner et al. use this analogy when they suggest that because racism has evolved into different forms (and has "mutated like a virus") it is now more difficult not only to "recognize but also to combat" (2005, p. 385).

N. Romm, *New Racism*, DOI 10.1007/978-90-481-8728-7_2,
© Springer Science+Business Media B.V. 2010

theoretical understandings being brought to bear. I provide some examples of theoretical debates around the usage of the different terms. I also make the point in my discussion that authors may differ in their views of the *process of scientific inquiry* itself, or what some would prefer to call *social inquiry* (to avoid the premises that they see as associated with defining research as "science"). Table 2.1 – which I provide at the end of Section 2.4 – summarizes my understanding of the different approaches.

This chapter, with my introduction of terms defining old and new racism as well as introduction of diverse theoretical understandings and research orientations, is meant to provide a basis for my in-depth examination in Chapter 3–8 of my chosen examples of research that I use as a basis for making proposals for shifting/extending the various modes of inquiry.

2.2 New Racism in Relation to Old-Fashioned Racism

2.2.1 Some Accounts of Old-Fashioned and New Racism in the USA

McConahay and Hough refer to the emergence in the 1970s in the USA of what they describe as "a new form of anti-black feelings, attitudes and behaviors among . . . [certain] segments of the American white population" (1976, pp. 23–24). They describe this new form of racism by contrasting it with *old-fashioned racism*. As they state: "It is not the racism of the red-neck bigots of old who spewed forth hatred, doctrines of racial inferiority, and support for de jure segregation" (1976, p. 24). They indicate that such expressions of racism can be called

> *old fashioned* because it is now out of style in sophisticated and opinion-making circles, and red-neck because it was (and is) most frequently expressed by the uneducated and by lower class Southern whites . . . . (1976, p. 24, my italics)

McConahay and Hough suggest that the new form of racism that they identify (modern or symbolic racism, discussed more fully in Sections 2.3.1 and 2.3.2) still expresses some of the negative feelings associated with "old-fashioned" or "red-neck" racism. However, the new form of racism is based on a different way of expressing attitudes and also on different behavioral manifestations from those associated with old-fashioned racism.

McConahay remarks that "those endorsing the ideology of modern racism [as he labels it] do not define their own beliefs and attitudes as racist" (1986, p. 93). This is because, for them, "racism" is seen as those attitudes and behaviors associated with old-fashioned racism, a form of racism that McConahay notes is "out of style in trendy circles" (1986, p. 93). He provides a historical account of these developments, stating that

The racial climate in America has changed dramatically since Hitler gave racism a bad name. In 1945, the legal codes of many states and localities [in the USA] – North and South – openly discriminated against blacks . . . . By 1954 these laws were being eliminated by the courts and by legislative bodies. By 1965, a new set of laws were in place making it illegal to discriminate. The legal situation had been reversed in only 20 years. White public opinion changed along with the laws. (1986, p. 91)

As I show in Sections 2.3.1 and 2.3.2, McConahay indicates that as old-fashioned racism became, in his terms, less trendy, some researchers began to concentrate on exploring different, newer forms of racism. He explains that the practical question for him, as well as various other researchers, became "How do we measure racial attitudes in the general public when the issues, the climate, and the structure of public opinion has changed?" (1986, p. 92).

Following in the same vein as McConahay, Sears (2005) comments that "old-fashioned racism" is associated with what is also called "Jim Crow racism,"[22] namely, "the racial ideology held by a majority of Whites in the US before the Second World War." He describes this kind of racism as having three main tenets:

(a) belief in the biological inferiority of African Americans; (b) support for formal discrimination against Blacks in many domains of life such as schools, public accommodations, and housing; and (c) racial segregation of Blacks in these domains, as well as in private domains such as marriages. (2005, p. 346)

Sears indicates that after the Second World War "support for that ideology began to wane in the North, and later, after the mid-1960s, gradually in the White South as well" (2005, p. 346). He avers, though, that this does not imply that racial prejudice has likewise disappeared. On the contrary, it can be regarded as appearing in new forms (as discussed in Section 2.3.1).

Bobo, Kluegel, and Smith (1996) concur with Sears' argument that despite evidence of the decline of old-fashioned racism in the USA, new forms of racism "live on" and are operative in all spheres of social and political life. They point out that although some scholars have argued that racism plays a diminishing role,

with equal plausibility, some scholars [such as Sears, 1988, Massey & Denton 1993, and Feagin & Sikes, 1994] argue that anti-black racism can be seen as powerfully influencing

---

[22] As the wikipedia indicates, the Jim Crow laws were state and local laws enacted in the Southern and border states of the USA and enforced between 1876 and 1965 – that mandated "separate but equal" status for black Americans. But "in reality, this led to treatment and accommodations that were almost always inferior to those provided to white Americans" (http://en.wikipedia.org/wiki/Jim_Crow_laws). The wikipedia continues:

After 1945, the Civil Rights movement gained momentum and used federal courts to attack Jim Crow. The Supreme Court declared . . . de jure public school segregation unconstitutional in 1954 [and] . . . the Civil Rights Act of 1964 . . . annulled Jim Crow laws that segregated restaurants, hotels and theaters.

Collins comments in this respect, though, that while racial integration is now the official policy of the United States, "large numbers of African Americans . . . remain confined to racially segregated, poor neighborhoods" (2005, p. 10).

politics, as well as a wide array of other social outcomes ... and day-to-day encounters between blacks and whites. (1996, p. 2)

Bobo, Kluegel, and Smith agree with authors such as Sears who discern a distancing from "Jim Crow" racism on the part of Whites after the Second World War. Like Sears, they comment on "the virtual disappearance of overt bigotry, of demands for strict segregation, of advocacy of government mandated discrimination, and of adherence to the belief that blacks are the categorical intellectual inferiors of whites" (1996, p. 2) – features which as noted above can be said to be associated with old-fashioned racism.[23] However, they claim that Sears' argument falls short in its way of theorizing "changes in whites' racial attitudes in the U.S." and is also not sufficiently equipped to explore the tenaciousness of institutionalized disadvantage (1996, p. 7).

Considering the question of to what extent "biological" arguments concerning Black inferiority have become transformed in popular acceptance, Bobo, Kluegel, and Smith agree with Sears that, in their terms, "most white Americans prefer a more volitional and cultural, as opposed to inherent and biological, interpretation of blacks' disadvantaged status" (1996, p. 3). They suggest that for the most part biological arguments are no longer relied upon (within racist discourse) and that more culturally based arguments are increasingly utilized as a way of explaining continued Black disadvantage.

Collins's understanding on this point is that White Americans routinely utilize "a dizzying array of biological and cultural arguments to explain African American's group conditions" (2005, p. 180). She explains that what is new for her in the new racism is "the ability of Whiteness to continue to obscure its own workings in the context of the greatly changed social conditions of the new racism" (2005, p. 180).

Also referring to what can be identified as differences between old-fashioned (Jim Crow) racism and the new racism (which relies on notions of "color-blindness"), Bonilla-Silva remarks that

Instead of relying on name calling (niggers, Spics, Chinks) color-blind racism otherizes softly ("these people are human too"); instead of proclaiming God placed minorities in the world in a servile position, it suggests that they are behind because they do not work hard enough; instead of viewing interracial marriage as wrong on a straight racial basis, it regards it as "problematic" because of concerns over the children, location, or the extra burden it places on couples. (2006, p. 3)

Bonilla-Silva explains the difference between old-fashioned and new racism as he sees it:

---

[23] Although Sears states that evidence of the virtual disappearance of old-fashioned racism is "rarely disputed" (2005, p. 346), one could of course argue that respondents of questionnaires supposedly measuring the extent of such racism could be "faking" their responses. Harris-Lacewell, for instance, points to "disturbing racial views" that sometimes can be drawn out through ethnographic "face-to-face discussion" – while surveys seem less equipped to draw out such views (2003, p. 243).

Much as Jim Crow racism served as the glue for defending a brutal and overt system of racial oppression in the pre-Civil Rights era, color-blind racism serves today as the ideological armor for a covert and institutionalized system in the post-Civil Rights era. And the beauty of this new ideology is that it aids in the maintenance of white privilege without fanfare, without naming those who it subjects and those who it rewards. (2006, pp. 3–4)

Bonilla-Silva comments that in contrast to old-fashioned racism, where "race" was clearly and overtly salient in social and political life, the new racism "denies the salience of race, scorns those who talk about race, and increasingly claims that 'We are all Americans'" (2006, p. 184). He argues that this kind of ideology is similar to the ideological discourses used in Latin America and indeed "rings Latin America all over." He avers that in Latin America, despite the operation of discrimination in practice, "any one trying to address racial divisions is likely to be chided" (2006, p. 184).

Interestingly, in commenting on a poll conducted in the USA by Associated Press and Yahoo News in September 2008 spurred by the Presidential candidacy of Barack Obama (and reporting that "40% of white Americans hold at least partly negative views toward blacks – including many Democrats and Independents"[24]), journalist Washington makes the point that Obama's candidacy seems to have begun to "spark a racial conversation that has clearly not [thus far] been had" (2008, p. 2). He cites Hawkins (an attorney specializing in counseling corporations on diversity) as stating that before Obama, "people had got a little bit frustrated and a little bit tired of the racial conversation in America. People were just as well to move onto the next issue" (Washington, 2008, p. 2).[25]

---

[24]This reporting was based on these Whites agreeing with some descriptors such as "'complaining', 'violent' or 'irresponsible'" to characterize Blacks (Washington, 2008, p. 2). The question on this in the questionnaire (as outlined by Sheppard, 2008) was constructed by asking Whites: "How well does each of these words describe most blacks?: 'Friendly, Determined to succeed, Law abiding, Hard-working, Intelligent at school, Smart at everyday things, Good neighbors, Dependable, Keep up their property, Violent, Boastful, Complaining, Lazy, Irresponsible'." Sheppard avers that the questionnaire itself was biased because, for instance, only Whites were asked to describe Blacks (in relation to this question in the questionnaire) – thus not making an opening for racist feelings of Blacks in relation to Whites to come to the fore. However, one could counter argue that at least the questionnaire could be used to *open up a public discussion on race*, such as pleaded for by authors/journalists such as Washington (2008). Furthermore, some authors – such as, say, Bonilla-Silva (2006) – would suggest that there is good reason why this poll had some response options only for *Whites* to fill in, in view of what Bonilla-Silva sees as structures of White domination and the unlikelihood that Blacks could "develop a racialized social system in the United States with Blacks as the dominant group" (2006, p. 173). I explore in detail in Chapter 4 the issue of how questionnaires are constructed and used in social life.

[25]This observation is supported by Gazel (2007). She indicates that from her own experience consulting in both the private and public sectors on "race relations and diversity" she learned that "excavating inequalities will not be welcome in the discourse." She indicates that comments to the effect that "I thought we were going to learn about different cultures" would be the kind of critique that she "would hear in seminar after seminar on 'challenging the racial status quo'" (2007, p. 534). When she later joined a University campus, she also found that "tolerance of diversity" (on the part of students) often went hand in hand with not wishing to "raise unpleasant issues such as structural inequality" (2007, p. 534).

Washington points out that although Obama's candidacy could be argued to have sparked some conversations about race, "not everyone is taking part in this conversation." As he notes,

> Some people claim race isn't a major factor in the election. [Meanwhile] ... U.S. Rep. Tony Scott [an Obama supporter] has argued that within the campaign "the best (race) dialogue would be no dialogue." (Washington, 2008, pp. 2–3)

Washington remarks that Obama himself, as he "courts the white voters crucial for victory, ... never emphasizes the social problems and issues that continue to affect minorities" (2008, p. 2). Clayton offers an alternative angle on this point when he indicates that "at the heart of his [Obama's] campaign is a message of hope that transcends race and attempts to bring a divided society together" (2007, p. 51). Space in this book (and its topic) does not permit a full discussion of the way in which Obama created a voice that earned him the trust of sufficient people in securing his position as President in the 4 November voting (2008).[26] But it is worth pointing to some of the ways in which he confronted issues of race during his campaign, as this offers a glimpse of his understanding of continued racial division in the USA.

In January 2008, Green, in writing about Obama's candidacy in "America.gov – telling America's story," entitled his report: "Barack Obama's U.S. Presidential Bid Bridges Racial Divisions." He refers to associate professor Cobb at Spelman College in Georgia, as stating that through his stirring oratory Obama is able to "connect to people of all different racial and ethnic backgrounds" and as stating that "Americans are attracted to Obama's message of bringing people together."

As part of his message of bringing people together, Obama did not shy from offering an explicit account of his view of racial division in America. For instance, on 18 March 2008, he presented what Huffington post calls a "race speech,"[27] largely in response to statements that his former pastor, Reverend Jeremiah Wright, had made – which he regarded as unduly racially divisive, and from which he wished to dissociate himself (Obama, 2008). He introduced his speech by referring to the principles of the American Constitution that, as he notes, "had at its very core the ideal of equal citizenship under the law; a Constitution that promised its people liberty, and justice, and a union that could be and should be perfected over time."

---

[26] In the November 24 2008 issue of *Time* magazine, reporter Capeheart suggests that in the light of Obama's style of winning trust we can speak about the "Obama effect," which she calls "that quality whereby the more you get to know a politician, the more you like or trust him or her." She suggests that "in future elections, politicians will have to factor in the Obama effect" (*Time*, 24 November 2008, p. 6).

[27] See http://www.huffingtonpost.com/2008/03/18/obama-race-speech-read-th_n_92077.html. Fox news also indicates that the speech has been billed as one on "race, politics and unifying America." See http://www.foxnews.com/politics/elections/2008/03/18/obama-condemns-wrights-rhetoric-but-defends-ongoing-relationship/.

But he points out that the

> words [of the Constitution] on a parchment would not be enough to deliver slaves from
> bondage, or provide men and women of every color and creed their full rights and obliga-
> tions as citizens of the United States. What would be needed were Americans in successive
> generations who were willing to do their part – through protests and struggle, on the streets
> and in the courts, through a civil war and civil disobedience and always at great risk – to
> narrow that gap between the promise of our ideals and the reality of their time.

He argues that one of the tasks that he considers as having been set forth at the
beginning of his campaign was to "continue the long march of those who came
before us, a march for a more just, more equal, more free, more caring and more
prosperous America." He goes on to indicate his perception that "American people
are hungry ... for this message of unity." But he also points to how race issues have
sometimes become problematic for him in the campaign. As he notes: "At various
stages in the campaign, some commentators have deemed me either 'too black' [to
appeal to Whites] or 'not black enough'" – that is, not sufficiently Black to represent
the experiences of African Americans.[28]

He also points to how the press (media) in America has tried to find evidence
among the electorate (via their scouring of exit polls) "of racial polarization, not
just in terms of white and black, but black and brown as well." And having set the
political context in this way, he notes that recently, "the discussion of race in this
campaign has taken a particularly divisive turn." He indicates that

> On one end of the spectrum, we've heard the implication that my candidacy is somehow
> an exercise in affirmative action; that it's based solely on the desire of wide-eyed liberals
> to purchase racial reconciliation on the cheap. On the other end, we've heard my former
> pastor, Reverend Jeremiah Wright, use incendiary language to express views that have the
> potential ... to widen the racial divide.

He remarks that he has already "condemned, in unequivocal terms, the statements
of Reverend Wright that have caused such controversy." One of the concerns that
he now raises with Wright's language is that Wright expresses a view of "racism as
endemic" – and thus seems not to offer hope for a future of unity. Obama comments
that this way of speaking, is itself

> divisive at a time when we need unity; racially charged at a time when we need to come
> together to solve a set of monumental problems – two wars, a terrorist threat, a falling
> economy, a chronic health care crisis and potentially devastating climate change; problems
> that are neither black or white or Latino or Asian, but rather problems that confront us all.

---

[28]Clayton explains that some African Americans argued that Obama should not be referred to as
"one of us" – because he did not "embody the experiences of most African Americans whose
ancestors had endured slavery, segregation, and the quest for civil rights" (2007, p. 56). Clayton
indicates that part of the promise of Obama's campaign is that he tries to move beyond dividing
America starkly into "White America" and "Black America." He remarks that Obama seems to be
arguing that we can become "something else together" (2007, p. 62). Walters for his part points
to the difficulties of choosing which cultural markers should be used to define a person as Black.
He suggests that to decide that someone is sufficiently Black "to share the experiences of [Black]
community" is ultimately a matter of trust. As he states, "cultural fit" turns out to be an issue of
political trust (2007, p. 13).

Obama makes reference to what he himself found valuable in the Trinity United Church of Christ (where the Reverend was his pastor), namely, that it was here that he heard stories of

> David and Goliath, Moses and Pharaoh, the Christians in the lion's den, Ezekiel's field of dry bones. Those stories – of survival, and freedom, and hope – became our story, my story; the blood that had spilled was our blood, the tears our tears; until this black church, on this bright day, seemed once more a vessel carrying the story of a people into future generations and into a larger world. Our trials and triumphs became at once unique and universal, black and more than black; in chronicling our journey, the stories and songs gave us a means to reclaim memories that we didn't need to feel shame about ... memories that all people might study and cherish – and with which we could start to rebuild.

He indicates that it is these memories that "help explain, perhaps, my relationship with Reverend Wright. As imperfect as he may be, he has been like family to me." It is for this reason that he notes that he

> can no more disown him than I can disown the black community. I can no more disown him than I can my white grandmother – a woman who helped raise me, a woman who sacrificed again and again for me, a woman who loves me as much as she loves anything in this world, but a woman who once confessed her fear of black men who passed by her on the street, and who on more than one occasion has uttered racial or ethnic stereotypes that made me cringe.

Here he points out the complexity of race issues in America, by noting how, just as he does not agree with Wright on certain scores, so too he has been "made to cringe" at some of the statements made by his White grandmother. Given this complexity, he suggests that "race is an issue that I believe this nation cannot afford to ignore right now." As he explains,

> comments that have been made [by Wright] and the issues that have surfaced over the last few weeks reflect the complexities of race in this country that we've never really worked through – a part of our union that we have yet to perfect. And if we walk away now, if we simply retreat into our respective corners, we will never be able to come together and solve challenges like health care, or education, or the need to find good jobs for every American.

Having said this, he indicates that considering the racial disparities that continue to exist,

> we do need to remind ourselves that so many of the disparities that exist in the African American community today can be directly traced to inequalities passed on from an earlier generation that suffered under the brutal legacy of slavery and Jim Crow.

He offers examples of the legacies that still remain:

> Segregated schools were, and are, inferior schools; we still haven't fixed them, fifty years after Brown v. Board of Education [see Footnote 43 below], and the inferior education they provided, then and now, helps explain the pervasive achievement gap between today's black and white students.

And he reminds people that

> Legalized discrimination – where blacks were prevented, often through violence, from owning property, or loans were not granted to African American business owners, or black homeowners could not access FHA mortgages, or blacks were excluded from unions, or

the police force, or fire departments – meant that black families could not amass any meaningful wealth to bequeath to future generations. That history helps explain the wealth and income gap between black and white, and the concentrated pockets of poverty that persists in so many of today's urban and rural communities.

He argues that as he sees it

What's remarkable is not how many failed in the face of discrimination, but rather how many men and women overcame the odds; how many were able to make a way out of no way for those like me who would come after them. But for all those who scratched and clawed their way to get a piece of the American Dream, there were many who didn't make it – those who were ultimately defeated, in one way or another, by discrimination. That legacy of defeat was passed on to future generations – those young men and increasingly young women who we see standing on street corners or languishing in our prisons, without hope or prospects for the future. Even for those blacks who did make it, questions of race, and racism, continue to define their worldview in fundamental ways.

Obama thus makes the point that questions of race, and continued racism, need to be brought fully to the fore in more public discussion, so that persistent racism can become more openly acknowledged and dealt with. However, he suggests that the Black anger such as that expressed by Wright is not always productive. And indeed it

prevents the African American community from forging the alliances it needs to bring about real change. But the anger is real; it is powerful; and to simply wish it away, to condemn it without understanding its roots, only serves to widen the chasm of misunderstanding that exists between the races.

Obama now refers to anger that he considers exists also "within segments of the white community." As he notes, "most working- and middle-class white Americans don't feel that they have been particularly privileged by their race." He explains how he sees their position:

They've worked hard all their lives, many times only to see their jobs shipped overseas or their pension dumped after a lifetime of labor. They are anxious about their futures, and feel their dreams slipping away; in an era of stagnant wages and global competition, opportunity comes to be seen as a zero sum game, in which your dreams come at my expense. So when they are told to bus their children to a school across town; when they hear that an African American is getting an advantage [as they perceive it] in landing a good job or a spot in a good college because of an injustice that they themselves never committed; when they're told that their fears about crime in urban neighborhoods are somehow prejudiced, resentment builds over time.

He comments how these feelings can affect White people's attitudes to certain social policies, noting that "anger over welfare and affirmative action helped forge the Reagan [conservative] Coalition." But he tries to place a new perspective on Black as well as White anger:

Just as black anger often proved counterproductive, so have these white resentments distracted attention from the real culprits of the middle class squeeze – a corporate culture rife with inside dealing, questionable accounting practices, and short-term greed; a Washington dominated by lobbyists and special interests; economic policies that favor the few over the many.

He summarizes that "this is where we are right now." And given his perception of this situation, he comments further on what he sees to be "the profound mistake of Reverend Wright's sermons." He argues that the mistake was not that he "spoke about racism in our society." It was that he

> spoke as if our society was static; as if no progress has been made; as if this country – a country that has made it possible for one of his own members to run for the highest office in the land and build a coalition of white and black, Latino and Asian, rich and poor, young and old – is still irrevocably bound to a tragic past.

He argues that Americans should rather be directed at having "hope – the audacity to hope – for what we can and must achieve tomorrow." He then states that what is required for a change to take place in the "white community," is for people to

> acknowledge that what ails the African American community does not just exist in the minds of black people; that the legacy of discrimination – and current incidents of discrimination, while less overt than in the past – are real and must be addressed.

And he indicates that this requires that people admit the need for

> investing in our schools and our communities; . . . enforcing our civil rights laws and ensuring fairness in our criminal justice system,[29] [and] . . . providing this generation with ladders of opportunity that were unavailable for previous generations.

He states that such a stance

> requires all Americans to realize that your dreams do not have to come at the expense of my dreams; that investing in the health, welfare, and education of black and brown and white children will ultimately help all of America prosper.

In this way, Obama calls for a change away from a "politics that breeds division, and conflict, and cynicism" toward a politics that speaks about issues that he believes are of concern to "all of America." He mentions, for instance, "the crumbling schools that are stealing the future of black children and white children and Asian children and Hispanic children and Native American children." He also points to a concern with how "the lines in the Emergency Room are filled with whites and blacks and Hispanics who do not have health care [and] who don't have the power on their own to overcome the special interests in Washington." And he points to a need to take on board that "the real problem is not that someone who doesn't look like you might take your job; it's that the corporation you work for will ship it overseas for nothing more than a profit." He also calls for unity by mentioning "the men and women of every color and creed" who "serve . . . ; fight, . . . and bleed together" in the name of the American flag.[30] He then proceeds to offer a story – as his closing statement of people working together to attend to social issues (in relation to care for the elderly) in unity.

---

[29]See Bobo and Thompson (2006) for an account of their research into unfairness in this system.

[30]He points out here, though, that it is unfortunate that America became involved in a war [the one in Iraq] that "never should've been authorized and never should've been waged."

Asante, in considering Obama's candidacy in relation to the "dilemma of power" (in an article written before the vote of 4 November 2008) offers an outline of what any US President would have to face once elected. His account for the most part tallies with the issues raised by Obama in the above speech (18 March 2008), namely, in Asante's terms:

(a) a budget that is out of control and a growing national deficit; (b) a military that cannot support the political commitments made by the government; (c) a broken immigration policy; (d) an increasingly criminalized society with prisons being built at an accelerated rate; (e) education standards that are falling behind ... ; (f) an inordinate relationship between the military and huge corporations; (g) health care and housing needs of millions of citizens; (h) a loss of American moral leadership in the world [due to its way of handling, *inter alia*, the Iraq invasion]; and (i) the persistence of income and wealth differentials between Whites and African Americans. (2007, p. 108)

Asante considers that what Obama brings to the electorate is "a call to a new agenda than the re-iteration of persistent partisan issues from the old agenda" (2007, p. 110). He believes that Obama's strength is that he appears to have "found the tone and the melody of the times." Asante also considers that Obama has the "intelligence and political savvy" to

go possibly where others because of their less committed stances would not even tread. If this is so, then Obama would be a trailblazing president with the potential of leaving a strong and positive legacy. (2007, p. 113)

Yet as Obama has pointed out, as detailed also in the above address, he does not see the problems that he identifies – including those relating to racial division – as capable of being dealt with in a single election. And it is not clear, as Washington (2008) remarks (as mentioned above), whether Obama's discourse has sparked or will continue to spark more open conversation in America involving "race-talk" (as Bonilla-Silva, 2006, too, advises).

What is important, as far as this book is concerned, is that Obama calls on people to recognize the continued legacy of racism and to acknowledge that, as he puts it, "the legacy of discrimination – and current incidents of discrimination, while less overt than in the past – ... must be addressed." It is in view of similar considerations that many authors writing about new racism urge people to keep alive discussions aimed at rendering more visible (and more open to exploration) these more covert manifestations of racism.

2.2.2 Some Accounts of the Development of (Old and New) Racism in Europe

In order to provide some background for discussions concerning our understanding of racism in the European context, I refer to Goldberg's argument regarding the original emergence of racialized discourses and their consolidation during "the Enlightenment."

Considering the history of the word "race," Goldberg (2002) argues that the concept of race appears to be absent in European social consciousness right until the fifteenth century. As he notes,

> Indeed, the first recorded reference to the sense of Europe as a collective "we" is in papal letters of the mid-fifteenth century, the first recorded usage of "race" shortly after that. It is only from this point on that social differentiation begins increasingly to take on a specifically racial sense. (2002, p. 284)

However, he comments that in the Middle Ages, certain people (e.g., Pygmies) were seen to represent a different stage of "development of man," a step "below humanity," and as not having the "discipline of rationally controlling instinct and imagination" (2002, p. 285). He remarks that this defining of humanity in relation to what was conceived as "rationality," served to introduce categories of inclusion and exclusion that "seem to mirror later racial categorizations" (2002, p. 285). Nevertheless, he argues that we still need to take care in labeling medieval thinking as *racism*. This is because "there was no explicit category of race or of racial differentiation" (2002, p. 286). Furthermore, there was "no catalog of racial groupings, no identification of individuals or groups ... in terms of racial membership" (2002, p. 286).

Goldberg argues that the sixteenth century marks the "divide in the rise of race consciousness" – concomitant with the Spanish and Portuguese exploration and conquering of West Africa and concomitant with the exploration and plundering of the New World. At this point "the concept of race becomes consciously and explicitly applied" (2002, p. 287). And with the rise of slavery, "racial difference came to define fitness for enslavement" (2002, p. 287). This kind of race consciousness, he suggests, was further consolidated with the emergence of "scientific domains of anthropology and biology" in the so-called "Enlightenment" period (beginning to emerge in the seventeenth century), where a "classificatory order of racial groupings" became established (pp. 289–290). He notes that while at first anthropology was concerned to catalog the otherness of *cultural* practices, it increasingly turned to "establishing the [supposed] *physical grounds* of racial difference" (2002, p. 290, my italics).

Like the authors cited in Section 2.2.1 above who identify alterations in racialized discourses following the Second World War, Goldberg too sees the aftermath of the War as marking a change. He refers to the associated shifts as linked to the use of the concept of "rights." As he states:

> It is pertinent ... that the contemporaneous critical attack on racial discourse and definition has been authorized in terms of rights: witness, most notably, the United Nations Declaration on Human Rights, the Civil Rights movement in the United States, and the various United Nations statements on race. (2002, p. 298)

But he cites favorably MacIntyre's condemning of the language of "rights" (seen as an abstraction that does not cater for concrete social practices of continuing exclusion). As Goldberg puts it, "moral fictions purport to furnish us with an objective and impersonal criterion of morality, but in practice do not" (2002, p. 300). He adds that "*formal* moral notions . . . are perniciously fictive in respect to racial and racial-izing discourse" (2002, p. 300). The formal language of rights as part of what might be called the discourse of new racism, serves to mask continued racialized social exclusion.

Bhavnani, Mirza, and Meetoo follow Goldberg in explaining shifts in European discourse. In line with Goldberg's historical understanding they indicate how, "with the growth of the slave trade in the seventeenth and eighteenth centuries, ideological constructions of superiority and inferiority between Africa and Europe began to emerge" (2005, p. 8). According to them:

> The separation of the world's peoples into designated "races" [at this point] thus involved economic gain through the ascription of certain differential traits which were reinforced through literature, science and philosophy of the time. (2005, p. 8)

Bhavnani, Mirza, and Meetoo comment that with the ascendancy of science, "phys-ical cause emerged as a predominant model in distinguishing 'races' in the 19th century" (2005, p. 8). As they elucidate:

> "Race" was seen as a way of distinguishing people into biological categories, and these were used to explain differences between people in differing cultures, particularly the superiority of the Europeans. (2005, p. 8)

They indicate that this "scientific" racism seeped into "populist racist pseu-doscience," and that despite being heavily challenged, these biologically and genetically based meanings of "race" have not completely vanished (2005, p. 9). But they agree with Goldberg and others who point to the Second World War as marking a shift:

> After the Second World War, the horrors of the genocide of Jewish people and Gypsies forced the academic community to challenge the so-called "scientific" basis of racial dif-ference. A variety of UNESCO statements between 1950 and 1960 appeared and papers on "race" and difference came into being . . . . These were to argue that the biological basis of "race" had no basis. (2005, pp. 9–10)

Despite this querying of old-fashioned racism in various forums, they suggest that the (misused) "power of early scientific thought . . ., coupled with the legacy of colonialism and slavery, has left large footprints in our current societies" (2005, p. 10).

They suggest that we can conceptualize the continuation of footprints of racism in terms of the way in which "the new racism in dominant discourse has moved from a scientific biological basis toward a concept of cultural racism" (2005, p. 11). They argue, citing authors such as Essed (1991) and Wimmar (1997), that the discourse of cultural differences can create a breeding ground for the culturalization of racism. They explain this argument with reference to a quotation from van Dijk (2000):

> They [those defined as "Other"] have a different culture, although in many respects there are deficiencies, such as single parent families, drug abuse, lacking achievement values, and dependence on welfare and affirmative action – "pathologies" that need to be corrected of course. (Van Dijk, 2000, p. 34, as cited in Bhavnani, Mirza, & Meetoo, 2005, p. 11)

Considering the prevalence of racism in Europe, Van Dijk explains that in the Netherlands (where he has conducted a large part of his research) and elsewhere in Europe, the notion that racism can be seen as endemic in the society is for the most part denied by the symbolic elites (politicians, writers, scholars, journalists, etc.). This, he suggests, is partly because "racism" is associated with what can be called the "old-fashioned form" (of overt bigotry) and hence efforts are seldom made to "look below the surface" and unpack the covert way in which "fundamental relations of group power are stacked against women and minorities" (2002, p. 481). Van Dijk avers that "in the upper divisions of the media, the universities and the corporate boardrooms [in the Netherlands] . . . people other than whites are still rare" (2002, p. 481). But he suggests that those who try to highlight this, face a kind of "institutional marginalization" because their claims regarding operative racism "produce so much cognitive and emotional dissonance" among those who believe otherwise (2002, p. 481).

Van Dijk reminds us that the problem in conducting research on racism is that "old-fashioned racism" is easier to detect and challenge than are new forms. (This echoes Collins's view that in the USA thus far none of the philosophies that has guided African American politics "has been successful in meeting the challenges of the new racism" (2005, p. 9).) Van Dijk proposes that in the face hereof (in Europe), "lots of radically critical research will be necessary on racism in the Netherlands and elsewhere in Europe" (Van Dijk, 2002, p. 485).

Wieviorka proposes to offer a framework for analyzing racism in European societies in terms of the way in which "immigrants" have been conceptualized. He suggests that following the Second World War in Europe, the economies of Europe were growing (1993, p. 56). At this point

> Given the demand for labor in many countries, immigration was thought to be useful for economic development. Immigrants were workers, mainly single men with plans to save money and then return to their homelands. Their cultural or religious traits were not a source of worry. (1993, p. 57)

Wieviorka states that in these circumstances, the racism directed against them mainly "took the form of 'inferiorization': immigrants were accepted into the host society but confined to the hardest, most tedious jobs. Their social visibility was practically naught" (1993, p. 57). Hence, "this racism did not arise out of a conflict between two traditions or cultures" (1993, p. 57). But Wieviorka claims that this kind of situation "started changing in the 1960s in the United Kingdom and somewhat later in other western European countries" (1993, p. 57). He sees a trend toward "narrow-minded, xenophobic nationalisms emerging, largely as a result of the new (economic) hard times aggravating unsettled social problems" (1993, p. 58). He suggests that this marks a shift in the way in which "immigration" came to be viewed. As he explains it:

> Immigrants used to be single "workers", who, exploited at work, had very low living standards. Nowadays they are being more perceived as Muslims, Arabs, Turks, Indians or Africans who have settled with their families in the host country. This change has been spectacular in France, the United Kingdom, Netherlands and Belgium. It is just starting in Italy. In Germany and Switzerland the situation is more complicated. Everywhere, social

and political debates refer ... more and more to the question of nationality and identity. (1993, p. 58)

Wieviorka argues that the kind of changes in racism that he has highlighted as trends in Europe can be compared with what some scholars in the USA have labeled as mutations from old-fashioned toward new racism.[31] He summarizes how the new (culturalized) form of racism can be seen as operating in Europe as well as in the USA:

> Immigrants in Europe are then accused of being the vectors of cultural forms – primarily Islam[32] – which are incompatible with the democratic principles of separating religion from politics or with the equality of women; blacks in the U.S. are accused of not subscribing to the American credo of working and bringing up a happy family with the aim of being upwardly socially mobile: in the eyes of "symbolic" racism they would prefer to live on welfare payments, do nothing and leave the family to disintegrate (Kinder & Sears, 1981). (Wieviorka, 2004, p. 285)

Wieviorka's account in relation to ways of seeing Muslim immigrants in Europe is supported by Kundnani, who takes issue with those who assert that democratic principles require the restriction of religion to a "private sphere" (separate from the public domain). He contends that there are alternative definitions of "secularism" that have thus far not been explored in Europe – to the detriment of Muslim communities. He points, for example, to "secularism as a form of pluralism based on the need to enable peaceful relationships between different value systems, including those embedded in different religious communities" (2007, p. 186). Such a pluralism recognizes that "for religious people, faith is a central part of their identity and values, and informs their reasoning." He argues that without this kind of pluralism in democratic societies, "secularism tends to involve discrimination against minorities." And he continues that "the danger of 'enlightenment' secularism is the exclusion from the public sphere of groups who define themselves by religion" (2007, p. 187). He argues that

> In the final analysis, the test of a secular society is whether it is capable of safeguarding freedom of belief and eliminating racisms based on religious difference. Today, driven by the attempt to legitimize a deeply unequal global order, racism has taken on new forms, at present directed specifically at Muslims and others perceived as 'alien'. Ultimately, the struggle against these forms of racism is not a fight for a particular religion or culture but

---

[31] For example, the notion of integration as used in Europe can invoke the idea, questioned by, for instance, Jacobsen, of a "unified national society or culture" into which "others" must supposedly integrate (Jacobsen, 2008, p. 45). Entzinger and Biezeveld also consider this in the context of discussion around multiculturalism and attempts to measure, for example, the extent of "multicultural optimism" (2003, p. 37).

[32] Byng indicates that after 9/11 the meaning of religious minority identity for Muslims in America became redefined – and it is now difficult to consider as "benign" the markers of difference that designate this boundary, along with other group boundaries, in the USA. She indicates that "even though *Muslim* is a religious label and not a racial one, since 9/11 Muslim American identity has been restructured to reflect the systemic inequality that is readily associated with racial minorities" (2008, p. 662). She bases her account on news stories from newspapers published in the northeast region of the USA and *The Washington Post* (between May 2002 and 2003).

a fight for universal human rights and against the vast economic and political inequalities of our world. … It is only through such a struggle that genuinely integrated and cohesive communities will emerge. (2007, pp. 187–188)

Kundnani's deliberations on this can be understood in the context of Entzinger and Biezeveld's remarks concerning "anti-immigrant attitudes among the population" of the various member states of the European Community, and their related comment that "politicians should sometimes take measures that are not very popular with certain parts of the electorate" (2003, p. 30). They make these remarks while considering changing orientations toward the acceptance of multiculturalism (or what Kundnani calls plurality) as a basis for "integrated" communities. They indicate that

for a certain period the multicultural model was endorsed by several … countries in the Northwest of Europe, in particular by the Netherlands and also, in varying degrees, by the Nordic countries, especially Sweden. More recently, however, it appears to have lost much of its appeal in those countries. (2003, p. 14)

In trying to revitalize the multicultural model as way of combating trends toward cultural racism, they remind us that "all European societies were culturally pluriform long before large-scale immigration began to gain momentum" (2003, p. 22).

Similar accounts of manifestations of new forms of racism have been offered by authors writing in relation to other geographical contexts too. For example, De Souza points to her own and others' research on experiences of migrant women in New Zealand. She reports that although (at the time of writing) "New Zealand migration policy had changed leading to a more culturally diverse population," she could identify various discourses drawn upon by health providers in relation to the needs of migrant mothers – discourses that could be seen as "unwittingly exclusionary, pathologizing, and homogenizing" (2004, pp. 465–466). She explores how these discourses invoke "assimilationist, sexist and ethnocentric assumptions" – with attendant "representation of migrant women as passive, invisible, backward, pathological and emotional" (2004, p. 2004). She shows how the "deficiency discourse" can be seen to be embedded in the "ideology of assimilation that views adaptation [of migrants to the host society] as a one way process" (2004, p. 467). As she comments: "Immigrants are expected to reject their own ways in order to fit into the host culture, whilst the dominant group's ways remain unchanged" (2004, p. 267). Meanwhile, she points to research suggesting that responses from western health workers in relation to migrant mothers' postpartum practices arguably range from "insensitive" (at best) to "derisory" (at worst) (2004, p. 267).

De Souza suggests that many health professionals in this context "would be shocked to be called racist" (2004, p. 469). Yet the notion of *institutionalized racism* can be helpful in understanding contexts where it seems that "health workers see western health practices as superior and come to expect minority women to assimilate to these practices" (as explored by, for instance, Marshall, 1992). In addition, she suggests that

Ng's concept of *commonsense racism* and sexism could also be useful for explaining the behavior of the midwives, as it refers to "those unintentional and unconscious acts that result in the silencing, exclusion, subordination and exploitation of minority group members." (Ng, 1995, p. 133, as cited in De Souza, 2004, p. 469, my italics)

As I indicated in Chapter 1, Section 1.1, De Souza does not hereby claim that social inquirers should present themselves as finding out about social realities unmediated by their own positionality and personhood. But she does suggest – in line with her views on reflexivity – that they need to reflect upon "how I might [as a researcher] be implicated in the maintenance of discourses that could be marginalizing to the participants" (2004, p. 472). She considers it important that researchers are attuned to finding strategies to "create new discursive spaces for representing difference and de-centering hegemonic [dominant] discourses" (2004, p. 476). I discuss these issues further in my accounts of cultural and institutional racism in Sections 2.3.4 and 2.3.5.

With this brief indication of how certain authors have pointed to what they see as the emergence of new racism in various contexts (which they differentiate conceptually from old-fashioned styles of racism), I now turn to more detailed definitions of the relevant concepts (by those forwarding them), namely, the concepts of

- symbolic racism;
- modern racism;
- aversive racism;
- cultural racism;
- institutional racism;
- color-blind racism as systemic.

My presentation is meant to provide a backdrop for my discussing in depth some examples of ways of employing these concepts in the following chapters (while also offering options for shifting/extending the different research approaches).

2.3 New Racism

2.3.1 Symbolic Racism

McConahay indicates that when a number of authors (including himself) began to conceptualize what was regarded as a new form of racism in America, the term chosen by them was "symbolic racism" (1986, p. 94). The reason that this term was chosen was first because, when conducting surveys to try to assess the operation of this new racism among Whites, the items designed by the researchers in the questionnaires contained many "code words and moral abstractions." The idea behind the survey designs was that when respondents were answering the questions, they would be reacting to "certain post-civil-rights-era policies, such as busing or affirmative action, that *symbolize to many whites* the unfair gains or demands of blacks"

(1986, p. 94, my italics). Second, the term symbolic racism also was chosen by these authors so as to highlight that the "new racism was rooted in abstract principles of justice and diffuse negative feelings acquired in early political and racial socialization and *not* in [respondents'] personal experience" (1986, p. 94).

McConahay states that he subsequently (around 1978) became dissatisfied with the term *symbolic racism* and preferred to use the term *modern racism* "to emphasize the contemporary, post-civil rights-movement nature of the tenets constituting the new ideology or belief system" (as held by Whites) (1986, p. 96). He points out that "Sears and his colleagues have kept the term *symbolic racism* because they think it is a better description of the phenomenon" (1986, p. 96). In the next section I turn to Sears' deliberations on the relevance of the concept of *symbolic racism* and on research efforts to identify/measure this form of racism. (In Section 2.3.2, I return to McConahay's argument.)

2.3.1.1 The Development of (Questionnaire) Items to Measure Symbolic Racism

Sears makes the point that "in the years since the concept of symbolic racism was developed, much research has been done refining and testing its claims, as well as responding to critiques." Over time, the concept has evolved as he and others working with it have taken into account the "accumulated evidence" (2005, p. 349). He indicates that in recent years the concept has been conceptualized and measured in terms of the following four themes:

(a) the denial of discrimination;
(b) criticism of Blacks' work ethic;
(c) resentment of Blacks' demands;
(d) resentment of unfair advantages given to Blacks by the broader society.

He states that the answers by Whites to questionnaires set in this (symbolic racist) language enable them to express their new racism – and allow researchers to discern it. Furthermore, he argues that in terms of these themes, the "political effects" of symbolic racism can be seen through the way in which respondents' answers to items on the symbolic racism scale correlate with their (lack of) support of, for example, federal assistance to blacks, and affirmative action and other policies (2005, p. 349).

One of the critiques of Sears' approach to which he responds is a critique leveled by Sniderman and Tetlock (1986), who argue that symbolic racist items in questionnaires can be regarded as tapping into *general political conservatism* rather than specifically *racial beliefs and motivations*. Sears counter-argues that the effects of (his measurements of) symbolic racism on "racially relevant variables" remain even after one has controlled, during the survey analysis, for political conservatism (2005, p. 349). Thus according to him, symbolic racism scales are *not* simply measuring

a (nonracial) politically conservative stance.[33] Tarman and Sears further indicate
that this point is important because otherwise it could be argued that the primary
reason why many (White) Americans oppose certain policies such as federal assistance, affirmative action, etc., has nothing to do with their racialization, but has to do
with the conservative belief that "interference" and "intervention" by governments
are generally to be restricted. In other words, it could be argued that the reluctance
to admit policies that could be viewed as "interference" in the market is about "the
optimal relative balance of governments and markets in modern societies" and is not
a reflection of "underlying racial animosity" (2005, p. 736). In the face of this argument, Tarman and Sears are at pains to show that measures of symbolic racism are
not the same as (or equivalent to) measures of (nonracial) political conservatism.[34]

    In considering this debate, Harris-Lacewell contends that one of the reasons
why Sniderman and Tetlock (1986) are able to make their claims about supposedly
nonracial political conservatism is that they ignore "the history of government-
supported racism and inequality in America" (2003, p. 236). For her, to claim that it
is possible to deracialize political responses is to "assume that political conservatism
is a race-neutral idea, when . . . American political history shows it to be linked with
racial ideology" (2003, p. 232). Thus she does not concur with Sniderman's account
of so-called principled politics (free of racial thinking). Nevertheless, she is critical more generally of the way in which what she calls scholars of "race politics"
whom she observes are primarily White (including Sears) seem to "marginalize
Black people in the study of race." She believes that the debate between authors
such as Sniderman and Sears would be better advanced if the opinions of Black
people, and the work of Black scholars, were appropriately included as part of the
discussion. She laments what appears to be a racial separation in the research community between those (largely Whites) studying "White racial attitudes" and those
(largely Blacks) studying "Black politics" (2003, p. 241). In Chapters 3 and 4, I
explore some options for how I see that Harris-Lacewell's critical observations can
be taken on board.

    Below I point to Tarman and Sears's elucidation of the questions constituting
what they call the "full symbolic racism scale" (2005, p. 738) and I show briefly how
one might locate problems in their research approach. In line with the four themes
into which they wish to tap via the scale, they explain their use of the questions
as follows (with the responses in brackets being coded as indicative of symbolic
racism)[35]:

---

[33]The argument of Sniderman and others is that there is a "tautological content overlap" between
the items measuring symbolic racism and items that measure conservative policy preferences
(Tarman & Sears, 2005, p. 734).

[34]The contention around whether *racism* or *conservatism* is being tapped into by these kinds of
questionnaires can also be seen in relation to the Associated Press–Yahoo News poll (September
2008) to which I referred in Section 2.2.1 (and in Footnote 24). See, for instance, Kuhn (2008) and
Sheppard (2008), who locate different ways of interpreting the data from the poll.

[35]Themes (a) and (b) as outlined by Sears (2005) as referred to above match the first two italicized
themes expressed by Tarman and Sears (2005), while (c) and (d) as outlined by Sears (2005)
become in turn the fourth and third italicized themes of Tarman and Sears (2005).

Items to tap into the (symbolic racist) theme of *Denial of Continuing Discrimination*:

Generations of Slavery: "Generations of slavery and discrimination have created conditions that make it difficult for blacks to work their way out of the lower class." (Disagree[36])

Discrimination: "How much discrimination against blacks do you feel there is in the United States today, limiting their chance to get ahead?[37] Would you say a lot, some, just a little, or none at all?" (A Little)

Real Change: "Has there been a lot of real change in the position of black people in the past few years?" (A Lot)

Items to tap into the (symbolic racist) theme of *Blacks Should Work Harder*:

Try Harder: "It's really a matter of some people not trying hard enough; if blacks would only try harder, they could be as well off as whites." (Agree)

Work Way Up: "Irish, Italian, Jewish and many other minorities overcame prejudice and worked their way up. Blacks should do the same without any special favors." (Agree)

Black Welfare: "Most blacks who receive money from welfare programs could get along without it if they tried." (Agree)

Items to tap into the (symbolic racist) theme of *Undeserved Advantage*:

Deserve Less: "Over the past few years, blacks have gotten less than they deserve." (Disagree)

Attention from Complaint: "Government officials usually pay less attention to a request or complaint from a black person than from a white person." (Disagree)

Deserve Attention: "Do blacks get much more attention from the government than they deserve: more attention, about the right amount, less attention, or much less attention from the government than they deserve?" (More Attention)

Items to tap into the (symbolic racist) theme of *Excessive Demands*:

Too Demanding: "Blacks are getting too demanding in their push for equal rights." (Agree)

Speed of Civil Rights: "Some say that the civil rights people have been trying to push too fast. Others feel that they haven't pushed fast enough. What about you: Do you think that civil rights leaders are pushing too fast, are going too slowly, or are they moving at about the right speed?"[38] (Too Fast)

Tarman and Sears argue (in keeping with Henry and Sears, 2002) that it is possible to subdivide the symbolic racism themes by contrasting the more "structural" items with the more "individual" items. They suggest that

external or *structural* attributions about race, primarily reflect denial of continuing racial discrimination and the belief that society provides blacks with too many undeserved special advantages. (2005, p. 743)

This can be contrasted with "internal or *individual* attributions about blacks, reflecting beliefs that blacks should try harder to get ahead and be less demanding in their calls for equality" (2005, p. 743).

---

[36]Respondents are given options here to: Strongly agree; Somewhat agree; Somewhat disagree; or Strongly Disagree (cf. http://condor.depaul.edu/~phenry1/SR2Kinstructions.htm).

[37]It is worth noting that the Associated Press–Yahoo Poll (September 2008) that I cited in Section 2.2.1 also contained the question: "How much discrimination against blacks do you feel there is in the United States today, limiting their chances to get ahead?"

[38]A similar question in the Associated Press–Yahoo Poll (September 2008) that I cited in Section 2.2.1 was phrased as: "Some people say that black leaders have been trying to push too fast. Others feel that they haven't pushed fast enough. What do you think?"

However, they note that the "structural" and "individual" items are highly correlated with each other (with high correlations existing between answers given by respondents on the structurally oriented items and answers given on the individually oriented ones). Their conclusion is thus that the variants of what can be called "structural" and "individual" symbolic racism are "closely related variants of the same underlying belief system" (2005, p. 744). Furthermore, they contend that both variants are indeed also strongly linked to "whites' opposition to racial policies." All measures of symbolic racism "have about the same effects" on the stance of Whites in relation to such policies (2002, p. 758).

Reflecting back on the theory of symbolic racism as a whole, Tarman and Sears argue that it "was initially more intuitively induced than rigorously deductive, and therefore somewhat imprecise." They state that "the process of critical scholarly scrutiny has unquestionably sharpened it" (2005, p. 758). Their view overall is that "on empirical examination, the theory proves to have generally been on the mark, and to remain current today" (2005, p. 759).

What Tarman and Sears do *not* reflect upon, though, is the possibility that their way of using their questionnaires already arguably *highlights and crystallizes* possible responses of Whites. For example, the items meant to tap into the belief that "Blacks should Work Harder" offers as an option the statement (with which Whites are asked to agree or disagree) that "Irish, Italian and Jewish and many other minorities overcame prejudice and worked their way up." This statement, it could be argued, already *makes this option for thinking specifically optionable for Whites (their respondents), without leaving room for a critical reflection (including a discussion between Blacks and Whites) on the historical differences between the opportunity structures that have been afforded.* Obama, for instance, points to the need for more discussion around these differences in his "race speech" of 18 March 2008 (cited in Section 2.2.1 above) when he raises for attention the continued aftermath of legalized discrimination against Blacks and when he notes that White people may find it difficult to connect with what ails the African American community. Harris-Lacewell for her part expresses her concern that surveyors studying "race politics" while ignoring/neglecting "Black agency" may easily serve to *perpetuate uninterrogated notions*, by the very way in which the research is set up. She tries to show, via her article, that in the study of race politics (by largely White researchers) to date "Black people are either invisible, wrongly excluded from the category 'American,'[39] or wrongly portrayed as monolithic assistance seekers" (2003, p. 234). And she insists that these exclusions need to be foregrounded and corrected for. In Chapter 3 and 4, I provide suggestions for how experimental and survey research in particular might be shifted accordingly to take into account Harris-Lacewell's concerns in this regard – in line with what I call a more discursively accountable approach.

---

[39]She cites here research examples of the pervasiveness of the term "citizen" or "American" when referring only to White citizens (2003, p. 230).

2.3.1.2 The Issue of Socially Desirable Responses Elicited Through Surveys

An issue that Tarman and Sears address is what they call "possible biases in survey research introduced by social desirability pressures" – which pressurize respondents not to directly express "racial antagonism" (2005, p. 758). They indicate that it is necessary to consider the matter of whether respondents' answers can be construed as being a response to what are believed to be "socially acceptable" answers, rather than these answers being *genuine attitudes* in relation to the questions being asked of them. They contend in this respect that "so far such biases do not seem to be of sufficient magnitude to jeopardize our main conclusions" (2005, p. 758). In other words, according to Tarman and Sears the main conclusions of their research regarding the extent of Whites' symbolic racist attitudes and the political effects hereof can be taken as sound.

Bonilla-Silva and Baiocchi, however – when considering survey research around racial attitudes more generally – make the point that because of the delegitimization in society of expressions of "racially-based feelings and viewpoints," surveys aimed at identifying racially based opinions and practices are to be regarded with caution (2008, p. 139). They consider that surveys on racial attitudes have "become like multiple choice exams where respondents work hard to choose the 'right' answers" (2008, p. 139). As we shall see in Chapter 4, I take up further the issue of how respondents' answers to survey questions designed to tap into their attitudes may be viewed within a variety of perspectives. This can be seen as relating to the issue of "reactivity" of respondents to research situations and how this issue is addressed within different perspectives – see also Section 2.3.2 on this. In Chapter 4, I make the point that the development of questionnaire items should not be treated in terms only of traditional understandings of the "reactivity problem." I propose that it is more important to make provision for the problem of questionnaires possibly *sedimenting* and *crystallizing* invoked social categories and attendant thinking (arguably leading to further polarization in social life) – rather than potentially undercutting this thinking.[40]

2.3.1.3 A Note on the Scope of Studies Exploring Symbolic Racism

Green, Staerklé, and Sears state that one limitation of studies (including their own) exploring symbolic racism and its effects in society is that "symbolic racism taps a belief system about a particular [target] group, Blacks, in a particular social context,

---

[40]Susan Weil, in providing me with feedback (by email) on an early draft of this chapter (August 2008), already considered that both McConahay's and Sears's manner of phrasing questions was itself polarizing – and she expressed concern that I had not sufficiently drawn this out in my original exposition of their approaches. She also pointed out – as what she calls my "critical friend" – that "there are issues of epistemology and power here that are not being stated." She considered that in my account of their stances I had not (yet) made manifest the tension that I may feel around the particular questionnaire constructions or the way in which "academic science" can use its power to develop items that then become "administered" for "agree/disagree" responses on the part of Whites.

the United States" (2006, p. 454). They note that constructs similar to the symbolic racism one (as defined through the questionnaire items that they employ to measure Whites' attitudes to Blacks in the USA) have been developed by other researchers to explore what can be considered as similar belief systems elsewhere. They cite, for example, studies exploring "the impact of 'subtle racism' on immigration attitudes in Europe" (2006, p. 450) – particularly in relation to immigrants from "non-European cultural backgrounds" (2006, p. 454). Thus they try to show the potential broadness of scope for studies examining forms of symbolic racism (expressed in coded language) in various parts of the globe.

They add the point that their construct of symbolic racism is considered as measuring "an explicit attitude to which people have conscious access" (2006, p. 449). It is not meant to cover "implicit and unconscious forms of racism" (2006, p. 449), for which alternative methodologies (other than surveys) are required. As we shall see in Section 2.3.3, this is one of the arguments of those concentrating on exploring what is called the "aversive" form of contemporary racism. But before turning to this, I discuss McConahay's understanding of "modern racism."

2.3.2 Modern Racism

As indicated above, McConahay argues that in about 1978 he became dissatisfied with the term symbolic racism and chose to "change the name of the concept in my thinking and writing" (1986, p. 96). The new term (for him) is "*modern racism* and the collection of items is called the Modern Racism Scale" (1986, p. 96). He indicates that in terms of his understanding, the items constituting the Modern Racism Scale can be regarded as subject to less "reactivity" than those used to measure old-fashioned racism (with the aim being to affect as little as possible what becomes answered by respondents through the way the items are phrased).[41]

In the light of the potential problem of reactivity, McConahay explains that because it is known by respondents that old-fashioned racism is indeed not "trendy," the "new items were developed to create valid, [relatively] nonreactive measures of anti-black prejudice" (1986, p. 97).[42] The reason that the items were regarded as being less reactive, is

---

[41] Speer and Hutchby do not agree with posing the question of reactivity in this way – a way that they indicate invokes certain (realist-oriented) assumptions. They criticize the assumption of a "supposedly pristine world to which researchers wish to gain unmediated access" – unaffected by interactional and contextual features (2003a, p. 334). They prefer an approach that makes more provision for the interactional relations (between researchers/research instruments and participants) taking place in all research contexts. Their approach is in line with the constructivist argument that I forward in the rest of the book and is also in line with Harris-Lacewell's suggestion regarding the importance of giving attention to the way in which the racial research context is experienced by people (2003, pp. 243–244).

[42] In his article considering the effects of race and racial attitudes in the context of simulated hiring decisions, he refers to the Modern Racism Scale as a "*relatively* nonreactive scale of racial attitudes" (1983, p. 551, my italics). In his 1986 article, he argues that "the Modern Racism Scale

in part because they tap into current issues about which there seems to be no clear consensus [in society] on the prejudiced and nonprejudiced position, and in part because for each item there is a plausible nonprejudiced explanation for endorsing the position scored as prejudiced on the scale. (1986, p. 97)

Hence McConahay avers that the scale can be considered as circumventing the problem that respondents may know, and respond in terms of, what are regarded as socially acceptable answers. According to McConahay, this is partly because there is no obvious understanding in contemporary society concerning "acceptable" answers to the items identified in the scale; and it is also because even when people respond in a way scored by researchers as prejudiced, the people could conceivably rationalize the responses as *not* implying racial prejudice. (This is especially insofar as they identify racism with traditional racist beliefs.) Dovidio and Gaertner explain McConahay's position:

> McConahay proposes that because modern racism involves the rejection of traditional racist beliefs and the displacement of anti-black feelings onto more abstract social and political issues, modern racists are also relatively unaware of their racist attitudes. (1986, p. 21)

McConahay (1986, p. 108) points to various stages of the development of the Modern Racism Scale, indicating that by 1984 the Modern Racism Scale could be contrasted with old-fashioned items as follows (with responses being scored on a 5-point scale):

Old-fashioned racism items
   I favor laws that permit black persons to rent or purchase housing even when the person offering the property for sale or rent does not wish to rent or sell to blacks. (Strongly Disagree = 5)
   Generally speaking, I favor full racial integration. (Strongly Disagree = 5)
   I am opposed to open or fair housing laws. (Strongly Agree = 5)
   It is a bad idea for blacks and whites to marry one another. (Strongly Agree = 5)
   Black people are generally not as smart as whites. (Strongly Agree = 5)
   If a black family with about the same income and education as I have moved next door, I would mind it a great deal. (Strongly Agree = 5)
   It was wrong for the United States Supreme Court to outlaw segregation in its 1954 decision. (Strongly Agree = 5)[43]

Modern racism items
   Over the past few years, the government and news media have shown more respect to blacks than they deserve. (Strongly Agree = 5)
   It is easy to understand the anger of black people in America. (Strongly Disagree = 5)
   Discrimination against blacks is no longer a problem in the United States. (Strongly Agree = 5)

---

was developed to be as nonreactive as possible" (1986, p. 110). In both cases he uses a definition of reactivity fitting a realist definition of validity, where validity is defined as the extent of correspondence between reality and its conceptualization by researchers. (See also Footnote 41.)

[43] In the 1954 *Brown v. Board of Education* ruling, the Supreme Court opened the door for school desegregation by declaring unconstitutional the "separate but equal" doctrine embraced by *Plessy v. Ferguson* (1896) (cf. Pfeifer & Bernstein, 2003).

Over the past few years blacks have gotten more economically than they deserve. (Strongly Agree = 5)
Blacks have more influence upon school desegregation plans than they ought to have. (Strongly Agree = 5)
Blacks are getting too demanding in their push for equal rights. (Strongly Agree = 5)
Blacks should not push themselves where they are not wanted. (Strongly Agree = 5)

In considering the modern racism scale, McConahay emphasizes that to speak of the ideology of modern racism is not to suggest that all Whites endorse the whole ideology. As he elucidates:

> Some whites endorse the whole ideology of modern racism, some buy none of it, and some whites believe in some tenets and not in others. That is why it is possible to develop a scale of individual differences along this dimension. (1986, p. 93)

Referring to the issue of the ambivalence of (some) White people, McConahay defines this as being "pulled in opposite directions at once" (1986, p. 99). He refers, inter alia, to Gaertner and Dovidio (1986a) on this score (see Section 2.3.3 below).[44] He suggests that the ambivalent person is marked by "sharp alterations of behavior" in different contexts, while the nonambivalent person is more consistent (1986, p. 99). He indicates (agreeing with Gaertner and Dovidio) that ambivalent people are likely to display "positive" (nonprejudicial) behavior under certain conditions (in order to appear, to themselves and others, as nonprejudicial). But in situations without clear norms or guides for behavior, Black actors can be targets of negative behavior, especially if (White) people can define the situation as "low in racial salience" – thus (re)defining their actions as not guided by racial considerations (1986, p. 100). He cites here an article by Gaertner and Dovidio (1981) as well as his own work (1983).

In terms of this account, McConahay notes that "we would expect the ambivalent person to score high on the Modern Racism Scale" – because the scale makes provision for people introducing justifications for their responses as being racially neutral (1986, p. 100).

---

[44]Sears for his part indicates that Myrdal first raised the question of Whites' ambivalence in his book *An American Dilemma* (1944). Sears argues that symbolic racism as a belief system (see Section 2.3.1 above) is consistent with support for equal treatment in the *abstract*; it incorporates the principle of equality of opportunity as holding in an abstract sense. But "Whites' responses to *concrete* public policies" are strongly influenced by symbolic racism. It is herein that the ambivalence lies (2005, p. 352). However, Harris-Lacewell is highly critical of Myrdal's manner of approaching American racial politics in a way that marginalizes Black people. Referring to Myrdal's calling the Negro "an American dilemma," she expresses her concerns as follows:

> This is also how Black people are treated in much of the work on race. But African Americans are not merely a problem or dilemma. Black people are political agents with attitudes and strategies that contribute to the politics of America, even when they are unobserved and unattended to by Whites. (2003, p. 228)

2.3.2.1 Symbolic/Modern Racism in Relation to Political Conservatism and Liberalism

McConahay points out that while earlier studies indicated links between the Modern Racism Scale scores (as well as symbolic racism ones) and the tendency to score highly on political conservatism scales, it is possible that these tendencies might have altered in the (USA) society. This is because, as he sees it, "more and more liberals appear to be joining with conservatives in adopting the tenets of modern racism" (1986, p. 121). Thus symbolic/modern racism is no longer clearly associated with the holding of a politically conservative stance. He argues that in any case, "white liberals" can be shown to display ambivalence as suggested via, for instance, the research of Gaertner and Dovidio. This is consistent with holding a modern racism position as he defines it (1986, p. 121).

2.3.2.2 Symbolic/Modern Racism and Self- and Group-Interests

McConahay addresses a question that has been asked in relation to symbolic/modern racism theorizing – namely, the question of whether modern racism could be seen to be linked to Whites' sense of preserving their self-interests. He notes that the research on modern (and symbolic) racism seems to indicate that people scoring highly "were no more likely than the low [scorers] to be [personally] objectively threatened by blacks or to perceive a personal threat" (1986, p. 122). But he suggests that this still does not answer the question of whether respondents' sense of self-interest may have been mediated by a sense of "group-interest" (depending on how they conceived the reference groups of relevance to them) (1986, p. 123).

McConahay claims that it is obvious that group conflict is a factor in producing modern racism. This, he argues, can be seen through the "resentment that whites high on the Modern Racism Scale feel toward the group demands and actions of blacks" (1986, p. 122). But what is not obvious, and what he believes still requires further research, is the "relative strengths of self-interest, group-interest, affect [emotions], and ambivalence in producing high or low Modern Racism Scale scores" (1986, p. 122).

As we shall see in the chapters that follow, what is also not obvious, though, as far as I see it, is *how such research is to be framed* and how *relations with participants and wider audiences are to be set up*. These questions, as noted by, for instance, Harris-Lacewell (2003, p. 245), need to be addressed in a way that "does not leave gaping holes" in our understandings. In her terms, they need to be addressed so as not to render invisible, or portray as monolithic, the agency of African Americans (via the way the questionnaires are framed and administered). My argument furthermore is that these issues, unattended to by McConahay, are important to address as part of the process of researchers acknowledging that research itself can *potentially contribute to a polarization (or alternatively de-polarization) of human relations.*

2.3.2.3 Some Applications of, and Developments in, Symbolic and Modern Racism Theorizing

The USA and Canada

In the USA, as indicated above, research around symbolic/modern racism is largely directed toward trying to determine, via surveys, Whites' racial attitudes and specifically considering these in relation to government policies. An example of such research is that of Green, Staerklé, and Sears (2006). Experimental research has also been undertaken in the USA and elsewhere in terms of the theory of symbolic/modern racism. As Pfeifer and Bernstein (2003) indicate, the theory suggests that if (White) people can *rationalize their behavior* in supposedly nonracist terms, then this provides them with an excuse to engage in discriminatory behavior (2003, p. 750). Experiments have accordingly been set up to try to see to what extent the behavior predicted to take place in terms of this theorizing, does indeed ensue. Pfeifer and Bernstein's work in the USA (2003) and Pfeifer and Ogloff's work in Canada (2003) provide examples hereof.

Sydell and Nelson have taken a somewhat different approach in their study of symbolic racism, by trying to explore differences in perception within a sample of Black and White students in regard to the current state of race relations in the USA (2000, p. 627). Through their survey, they explore the attitudes of both Blacks and Whites (with reference to the sample) in relation to the argument of the symbolic racist theorists that "Americans have moved from open hostility and aggressive racism to a more subdued, covert and even unconscious form of racism" (2000, p. 627). They state that their research showed up several differences in the way that the Black and White students perceived race relations. And they suggest that their exploration of these differences in perception is helpful in drawing out issues that currently appear to remain "below the surface of interracial dialogue" (2000, p. 628). They consider that their research could be helpful in "facilitating the efforts of educators, researchers, and counselors to establish some basis for clarification and identification of salient racial issues" (2000, p. 628). By drawing out issues that they consider have not been adequately probed thus far within symbolic/modern racist theorizing and research, they could be said to provide some corrective to the concern that Harris-Lacewell expresses (2003) with the concentration of such researchers on exploring *White* attitudes and on examining only *their* stance toward social policies. Sydell and Nelson's survey, as they themselves indicate, opens a way to set the stage for establishing possibilities for cross-racial dialogue. I explore some further options for this in Chapter 4.

Using Symbolic Racist Scales to Determine Anti-Arab Prejudice, with Special Reference to Europe

Drawing on the work of McConahay and Sears in the USA, Echebarria-Echabe and Guede have concentrated on exploring the operation of symbolic/modern racism in Europe in relation to Arabs – by developing a scale to examine Whites' attitudes in Europe vis-à-vis Arab immigrants. In explaining their creation of their "measure of anti-Arab prejudice," they indicate that the correlation between their new scale and an adapted version of McConahay's (1986) Modern Racism scale (adapted to reflect an Arab target group) was "very strong" (2007, p. 1077). This, they believe, helps to lend support to their notion that their new scale has "validity" in the sense of measuring, indeed, new forms of prejudice in Europe. Echebarria-Echabe and Guede indicate that their scale, like the symbolic and modern racism scales, has been set up to measure *explicit* attitudes that people express. As they note, there are also ways of measuring *implicit attitudes*, but this is not the subject of their research (2007, p. 1078). (They follow McConahay and Sears in suggesting that it is worthwhile to explore *explicitly expressed* attitudes, while also recognizing that other studies can be aimed at exploring implicit attitudes and attendant behavioral responses.[45])

In referring to their endeavors to create their scale of anti-Arab prejudice, Echebarria-Echabe and Guede indicate that the Modern Racism Scale has served to measure prejudice in

> Australia, Canada, The Netherlands, and Spain, with specific [target] groups in each case (Gomez & Huici, 1999; Gordijn, Koomen, & Stapel, 2001; Mellor, 2003; Navas, 1998; Pettigrew & Meertens, 1995; Pfeifer & Ogloff, 2003; Sonn, Bishop, & Humphries, 2000). (Echebarria-Echabe & Guede, 2007, p. 1078)

They point out that instead of simply using a version of the Modern Racism Scale adapted to an Arab target group, they considered it important to *reformulate the scale* (rather than merely adapt and translate it) for application outside of the USA because

> it is not the same to study prejudice against a native minority that shares most of the central elements of the majority culture ... (e.g. anti-black prejudice in the U.S.) as it is to study prejudice against immigrant communities with different cultural and religious worldviews (as in many European countries). (2007, p. 1078)

According to them, the selected items to be used in different contexts need to be attuned to the different "social realities" where the scales are to be applied – that is, to the "historical and contextual social environments" (2007, p. 1078). Thus, although Echebarria-Echabe and Guede acknowledge the importance of the research work underpinning the development of the Modern Racism scale, they consider it crucial to review this scale (including adapted versions thereof) in order to deal with new forms of anti-Arab prejudice emerging in Europe. They propose that their own scale serves this function. Below I provide a number of items included in this scale (which has 42 items) in order to give an idea of how the questions are phrased – with scores of course being assigned negatively or positively depending on the tenor of the item in terms of its understanding of Arab immigrants and Islam as a religion (2007, pp. 1080–1082):

---

[45]In Chapter 3, Sections 3.7, 3.8, and 3.9, I discuss the attempted measurement of what are regarded as implicit prejudicial attitudes that are posited to be operative at a *less-than-conscious level*; and I point to arguments concerning the tenuous relationship between measures of implicit and explicit attitudes.

- Islam is an archaic religion, unable to adapt to the present.
- Islam respects human rights.
- Islam is a threat for women.
- Europe should recognize Islam as an important religion.
- Arab immigrants are often involved in crime.
- Arab immigrants are ballast for our social services.
- Arabs have contributed to the European culture and science.
- The Western culture is superior to the Muslim culture.
- To be accepted, Arabic immigrants must promise to adapt to our customs and culture.
- It is unacceptable that women wear the Islamic veil in Europe.
- The immigrants of the second generation continue without integrating in our culture and maintain the tradition of their parents.
- Arabs are strangers for our cultural references (Rome and Greece).
- Islam is a great religion and culture and deserves our respect.
- Islam and Christianity share the same universal ethical principles.
- Islam preaches tolerance, respect for the human being, and peaceful coexistence among all countries.
- Arabs take advantage of European democracy to introduce their customs and culture.
- European police should pay special attention to Arab immigrants because they are a real threat for our countries.
- Arabs are suspicious of [or, for] supporting terrorism. They have to prove their pacifism.
- Arabs who do not accept our culture and traditions must return to their countries.
- The history of humanity is full of pages of civilization and tolerance written by Arabs.

As should be recognized when I discuss the concept of cultural racism below, the items on this scale are also relevant to the position of those positing *cultural racism* as a new form of (and justification for) social exclusion – in this case, of "Arab immigrants." However, as I pointed out when considering McConahay and Sears' constructions of their scales, which I suggested could be argued to potentially contribute to social polarization by virtue of the way the questionnaires have been constructed and administered in the USA (see Sections 2.3.1.2 and 2.3.2.2), the same could be said of Echebarria-Echabe and Guede's scale.

For instance, we can consider as an example their item stating that "To be accepted, Arabic immigrants must promise to adapt to our customs and culture." Already by posing/framing the question this way, and using the word "our" to refer to "our customs and culture," the question arguably *brings to the fore* in people's consciousness an *us/them mentality* while at the same time creating/reinforcing Whiteness as the norm for "our countries" in Europe (see also Section 2.3.4.1). The seemingly neutral questionnaire does not encourage respondents to reflect upon the issue of what is taken as normative – and thus can contribute to enabling what Ng

(1995) calls "commonsense racism." As I indicated in Section 2.3.1.1 with regard to Harris-Lacewell's (2003) concern that the scales as used in America can contribute to entrenching taken-for-granted assumptions, the same could be said of this scale. Using a similar argument, Jacobsen suggests that researchers exploring people's responses to Muslim immigrants need to pay attention to investigating how "theoretical and analytical frameworks enable (and disenable) particular descriptions of 'the other'" (2008, p. 40). As De Souza also cautions (citing Ng), researchers need to take some responsibility for trying to undercut discourses that pass as "commonsense." In Chapter 4, I make some suggestions for how I believe survey research can be shifted in order to make provision for this.

Measuring Continuing Old-Fashioned as Well as New Racism in South Africa

An example of research drawing on the work of McConahay and Sears in South Africa is that of Pillay and Collings, who proceed in terms of the attempt to measure, via the relevant scales, both old-fashioned and new styles of racism. They summarize the approach that guided their research:

> Although ostensibly less odious than its old-fashioned counterpart, it has been argued that modern or symbolic racism is "more insidious, entrenched and resilient because of its subtlety and apparent egalitarianism." (Augoustinos & Walker, 1995, p. 233, as cited in Pillay & Collings, 2004, pp. 607–608)

Pillay and Collings make the point that rather than seeing modern racism as having replaced or displaced old-fashioned racism in any society under consideration, we should recognize that "different forms of racism may in fact coexist, with different degrees of prominence, in any given society" (2004, p. 608). They thus highlight that research around modern/symbolic racism need not be seen as implying that old-fashioned forms of racism are no longer pervasive. In order to consider this issue in the context of South Africa, they administered a survey to a sample of university students on a campus in South Africa, where the items in their questionnaire were designed primarily to measure prejudice against Black people as the target group – with respondents in their sample being (classed as) Whites, Indians, Blacks, and Coloreds (2004, p. 609).[46] They remark that they utilized adapted versions of the

---

[46]Pillay and Collings point out that their use of these categories does not reflect their views regarding the meaningfulness of the classifications, "but rather the historical reality of an apartheid past which continues to have direct bearing on the notion of race in the contemporary South African context" (2004, p. 610). The Department of Education in South Africa also continues to employ these categories as a way of monitoring the involvement of different (groups of) students. For example, in a booklet produced by the Department entitled *A Guide for Schools: Into Higher Education,* it is stated that: South African higher education institutions have thrown open the doors of learning since 1994. In 1993 only 40% of students were African; today 60% – over 400,000 students – are African. White students make up 27% of enrolments, colored students 6% and Indian students 7%. (2008, p. 21)

Old-fashioned and Modern Racism Scales "to ensure that items were meaningful and relevant for South African audiences" (2004, p. 610). (They also combined this with certain open-ended questions to explore students' reactions to racial experiences – that is, with questions that gave leeway for the students to construct answers using their own words.)

On the closed-ended attitudinal questions, some of the items to measure old-fashioned racism were, for example (2004, p. 611):

- Black people are generally not as smart as white people.
- I favor laws that allow black people to rent or buy a property even if the owner of the property does not want to rent or sell to black people (reverse coded).
- It is a bad idea for people from different race groups to marry each other.

And also on the closed-ended attitudinal questions, some of the items to measure new racism were, for example:

- It is easy to understand the anger of black people (reverse coded).
- Over the past few years the government has shown more respect for black people than they deserve.
- I am opposed to affirmative action programs in the South African workplace.

In terms of the old-fashioned/modern racism distinction, the results of their survey indicated that "scores for modern racism were generally higher than scores for old-fashioned racism." But "a significant proportion of respondents endorsed statements reflecting both old-fashioned and modern forms of racism" (2004, p. 615).

The pattern of findings as far as *old-fashioned* racism was concerned was that such scores were "highest among white participants and lowest among black participants, with the other groups scoring between the extremes" (2004, p. 615). This is of course not surprising, given the nature of the items used (to measure prejudice mainly against Black people). Pillay and Collings do not try to explain why indeed Black students scored in the way that they did on both old-fashioned and modern racism scales and what their scores might imply. For instance, it is possible that middle class Black students on the campus were displaying some prejudice against those seen as lower class (or lower in status).[47] But Pillay and Collings's survey was not equipped to explore this possibility.

---

[47] This would tally with observations that were made by some participants in focus groups that I conducted in South Africa in 2007, where a number of Black participants stated that they were surprised/concerned at the way some of their middle-class Black friends/acquaintances treated Black people poorer than them. Examples were given of Black domestic workers being treated with little respect by the employers (the participants' friends) – but the participants felt that they could not intervene by expressing their concern over this matter. Perhaps the students on the campus studied by Pillay and Collings, if probed, would have indicated a similar stance against "poor Blacks" – possibly learned from their parents who afford Whites a higher status, no matter what their class position. Veronica McKay, in response to her reading of this (draft) chapter (September 2008), likewise indicated to me the lower status that she sees as sometimes being assigned (including by Black people) to the Black poor (relative to those perceived as the White poor).

As far as the patterns of findings for *modern racism* was concerned, Pillay and Collings note that these were "equivalent for whites and Indians, with blacks falling lowest, and coloreds falling between the extremes of the other groups" (2004, p. 615). In trying to provide an explanation for the equivalence of the Whites' and Indians' scoring for modern racism, Pillay and Collings suggest that "it is possible that the high scores for modern racism obtained by Indian respondents represent a covert attempt to retain the degree of relative advantage over blacks afforded by apartheid" (2004, p. 615). (Again, through the survey, it was not possible to make any conclusions regarding how the Indian students may have developed their understandings, and how this compares with those revealed by the White students in the survey.)

As far as the open-ended questions were concerned, Pillay and Collings noted that 242 out of their 433 respondents (55.9% of them) reported a total of 926 racially charged experiences (of felt discrimination) – with black students being "most likely to report [in the questionnaire] a racial incident and white students being less likely to report a racial experience" (2004, pp. 611–612). But none of the racial experiences had been reported to the University authorities. Reasons for non-reporting included

(a) the belief that reporting would not make any difference;
(b) a perceived absence of reporting structures on campus;
(c) fear of retaliation.

Pillay and Collings offer an interesting approach in their survey in that, first, they presented respondents with items deemed to measure *both old and new* expressions of racism – thus allowing older forms of racism along with new ones to come to the fore. Furthermore, they tried at least to consider the perceptions across a range of groups (and not only of White people) – albeit that the target group of their items (as in McConahay and Sears' formulations) was primarily Black people and albeit that this evokes the idea that attitudes *toward* Black people should be the focus of attention (as Harris-Lacewell complains – see Section 2.3.1.1 above). One could argue that at least through their open-ended questions Pillay and Collings afforded all respondents an opportunity to express in their own words what they took to be racially charged experiences – thus providing a channel for, inter alia, Black students to express some perspective on racial experiences.

But despite these qualifications/additions to the way in which they applied the modern/symbolic racism scale (in conjunction with the old-fashioned racism one), I would suggest that it is problematic that they do not seem to have made provision for *dereifying* the status of the race categories that they employed in posing their questions – even though in their write-up they mention that the categories do not reflect their views on the meaningfulness of the "classification of race or ethnicity" (2004, p. 610). In Chapter 4, I provide suggestions as to how survey research can better be tuned to make provision for de-essentializing any invoked categories.

It is worth noting here that Hercules, on the basis of his extensive interviews with a range of teachers and students in South Africa, makes the recommendation to the Department of Education to generate processes for undercutting the view (still springing from the apartheid era) that "races" exist. He makes this recommendation in the context of evaluating one of the programs set up by the Department, namely, the *Advanced Certificate in Education (ACE): Values and Human Rights in Education* (2003–2005), aimed at embedding a concern with values and human rights in teachers' as well as students' understandings. He remarks that

> The evaluator did find that the issue of "race", for example, was not grappled with in any serious manner by any of the implementing HEIs [Higher Education Institutions]. Students, lecturers and tutors alike, articulated an unproblematized notion of "race", namely that races exist, and that a fundamental message in support of a progressive human rights culture is to promote "peace between the races", "tolerance" and "racial harmony." (Hercules, 2006, p. 62)

He goes on to state that because the notion of race itself remains unproblematized – even in the human rights program – discussions about "race" (and "racial harmony") can still reproduce "the race concept," which he sees as "deeply entrenched and consolidated" within the society.

He argues that to de-solidify the "consolidation" of the race concept, an appropriate process would be to

> adopt a learning process, that problematizes the notion of "race", seeks to debunk and deconstruct the race myth, and attempts to deal with the serious question of building a nonracial classroom, school, community, and society in general.[48] A unity of people who uncritically believe that they are White, Colored, Indian or African in racial terms, is a rather precarious unity indeed! (2006, p. 62)

Hence, one could argue that insofar as Pillay and Collings's application of the symbolic/modern racism *fails to problematize the "race concept"* when they ask people to respond to the questionnaire items, the research itself can serve to further consolidate the categories (and ways of thinking in terms of the categories). In order for the research not be complicit in this process, this would require – I suggest – new usages of the survey approach as such and indeed new epistemological orientations, as argued for in Chapter 4.

In the next section I introduce the concept of *aversive racism* and I mention some strategies that have been advanced for ways of locating this as a form of racism by studying people's likely *behavioral responses*.

---

[48]While Hercules concentrates on making recommendations for learning processes *in educational institutions*, the Human Rights Commission report sees *the media* as an important locus for problematizing essentialist views on race and at the same time generating a dialogue around different forms of racism (as I noted in Chapter 1, Section 1.1).

2.3.3 Aversive Racism

The term aversive racism was originally developed by Kovel (1970) in order to distinguish "dominative" racism from "aversive" racism in the USA. Schutte (1995) explains Kovel's understanding hereof:

> Dominative racism ... was originally associated with slavery in a plantation economy. Blacks and whites were locked into one economic system run and dictated by whites. Their domination was complete in slavery. Aversive racism is more a feature of the North [of the USA] in the postemancipation era; it has [also] spread to other areas. (1995, p. 356)

Schutte indicates that according to Kovel, the aversive form of racism attained prevalence once the basis for dominative racism was destroyed – that is, with the demise of slavery. In dominative racism (in the form of slavery) Black and White people shared a lifeworld characterized by domination of Whites and submission of Blacks – which Schutte calls a "close though distorted relationship." In aversive racism, relations become characterized more by "rejection and symbolic distance" of Whites in relation to Blacks (1995, p. 357). Schutte indicates that according to Kovel, the "separate but [supposedly] equal" doctrine of the Jim Crow era can be regarded as one indicator marking a move toward this aversive form of racism. (See Footnote 22 in relation to the Jim Crow era.)

Kovel argues that in the post-civil rights era, new forms of racism in turn began to emerge, where the agents "are not racist in self-presentation" (Schutte, 1995, p. 357). But, as Schutte notes, "they [the agents] provide enough evidence that they think, or reason, along racial lines." They engage in a "group-way of-thinking ... but in a much more covert fashion" (1995, p. 357). Schutte explains that it is covert in the sense that "the way humans reason in the world of everyday life is taken for granted" (1995, p. 357).

While Kovel termed this new, covert form of racism "metaracism" (to highlight that these "racists" are not racist in their own eyes), Gaertner and Dovidio have chosen to continue to use the term aversive racism to refer to "the type of racial attitude that we believe characterizes many white Americans who possess strong egalitarian values" (1986a, p. 61).

Gaertner and Dovidio indicate that (those whom they call) aversive racists

> regard themselves as nonprejudiced and nondiscriminatory; but, almost unavoidably, possess negative feelings and beliefs about blacks. Because of the importance of the egalitarian value system to aversive racists' self-concept, these negative feelings and associated beliefs are typically excluded from self-awareness. (1986a, p. 62)

Gaertner and Dovidio point to what they see as a specific ambivalence in White American's orientations – namely, the ambivalence "between feelings and beliefs associated with a sincerely egalitarian value system and unacknowledged negative feelings and beliefs about blacks" (1986a, p. 62).

Considering the historical development of aversive racism, they suggest that it can be conceived as

> an adaptation resulting from an assimilation of an egalitarian value system with (1) feelings and beliefs derived from historical and contemporary culturally racist contexts, and (2)

impressions derived from human cognitive mechanisms that contribute to the development of stereotypes and prejudice. (1986a, p. 62)

Gaertner and Dovidio proceed to explain that when they refer to aversive racists' "negative feelings" toward blacks, such feelings are "not hostility or hate." Rather, the "negativity involves discomfort, uneasiness, disgust, and sometimes fear" (1986a, p. 63).

2.3.3.1 Aversive Racism and Liberalism

Dovidio and Gaertner indicate that their research work on aversive racism admittedly has been concentrated on a "relatively liberal segment of the population: college students attending northern universities" (1986, p. 22). Thus their term aversive racism is in some way linked to their understanding that "it reflects the ambivalence of political *liberals*" (1986, p. 22). They point out that one of the features that distinguishes their work from that of McConahay is that "McConahay's theory of modern racism developed from his work on symbolic racism. The focus of symbolic racism was on [White] *conservatives*" (1986, p. 22). They remark that in studies reported by McConahay and Hough, symbolic racism "was positively correlated with political conservatism and religious conventionalism" (1986, p. 22).[49] They here note that "at least as initially formulated, symbolic racism represented . . . subtle prejudice originating from the political right" (1986, p. 22).

As we saw when discussing the views of McConahay in Section 2.3.2.1, he believes that "more and more liberals appear to be joining with conservatives in adopting the tenets of modern racism" (1986, p. 121). Thus the idea that modern and aversive forms of racism are linked respectively to conservative versus liberal political orientations can be queried. Nevertheless, we should bear in mind Dovidio and Gaertner's caution that most of their research work has involved more liberally oriented samples – namely, college students of northern universities. In Chapter 3 – where I discuss experiments as a way of examining variables that are hypothesized as being relevant to race-related behavior – I offer an exposition of some of their examples of research in which they have been involved (using mainly students as experimental participants).

2.3.3.2 Ways of Locating Aversive Racism and Its Social Effects: Investigating (White) People's Behavioral Responses

Gaertner and Dovidio suggest that because of the "high salience of race and racially symbolic issues on questionnaires designed to measure racial prejudice," and because aversive racists are very sensitive to such issues, it would not be possible to develop "effective questionnaire measures of aversive racism" (1986a, p. 67).

---

[49] As mentioned in Footnote 33, Sniderman and Tetlock claim that this correlation is due to an overlap in the content of the scales measuring symbolic racism and political conservatism, a contention denied by Sears. See also Section 2.3.1.1.

They indicate, however, that this does not preclude them from exploring this form of racism – which operates below the level of explicit awareness of Whites. They point out that they have formulated the concept in such a way as to make possible certain predictions to be derived in relation to how aversive racists are likely to *behave* in different contexts (1986a, p. 66).

Their strategy for locating aversive racism relies on researchers being able to observe discriminatory behavior in "specially constructed situations of varying normative structure" (1986a, p. 67). One of the propositions of their theory is that when the normative structure within a social situation is "weak, ambiguous or conflicting ... the more negative components of aversive racists' attitudes may be more clearly observable." This is because in such instances "blacks can be treated unfavorably, ... yet whites can be spared the recognition that they behaved inappropriately" (1986a, p. 66). But when "norms prescribing appropriate behavior are clear and unambiguous, blacks would not be treated less favorably than would whites because wrongdoing would be obvious" (1986a, p. 66). They suggest that these predictions have been borne out by a range of experiments that they have undertaken. As they summarize, "the results of these experiments involving diverse experimental manipulations provide consistent support for [this] proposition of the aversive racism framework" (1986a, p. 73).

They point to another proposition of their theorizing in regard to aversive racism, namely, that "even when normative guidelines are relatively clear, aversive racists are sensitive to nonracial factors that can justify, rationalize, or legitimize behavior that more generally disadvantages blacks relative to whites." In other words, aversive racists seem able to "enhance the salience and potency of nonrace-related elements in a situation that would justify a negative response." That is, "they can attribute the reasons for their behavior to factors other than race" (1986a, p. 73). Gaertner and Dovidio give the example of busing:

> When busing became a tool to implement desegregation ... there was strong opposition. This protest was not about desegregation per se but about the nonracial element – busing. Thus people may discriminate against blacks while maintaining a nondiscriminating self-concept. (1986a, pp. 73–74)

By couching their opposition in terms other than racial ones, those opposed to busing could argue that they were not invoking racialized conceptualizations. I discuss in Section 2.3.6 the notion of color-blind racism as systemically embedded. But it is worth noting here that Dovidio draws on this concept when he suggests that "aversive racists ... frequently assert that they are color-blind. If they [purportedly] do not see race, then no one can accuse them of being racist" (1993, p. 53).

In order to lend detail to their propositions regarding the possible workings of aversive racism in the workplace, Dovidio and Gaertner (2000) refer to experimental research done (1989 and 1999) in which employment contexts were simulated by the researchers with a view to examining White respondents' (who were college students') hiring decisions. They indicate that results of these experiments on hiring decisions reveal that when both Black and White job candidates have obviously strong or obviously weak qualifications, there is no significant difference in the strength of recommendations for the candidates. But, as predicted by the theory, "ambiguously qualified black candidates were recommended significantly less strongly than were comparable white candidates" (2000, p. 317).

They comment that their results were as predicted by the "aversive-racism framework" and consistent with "other theories of modern racism (e.g. McConahay, 1986)" (2000, p. 318). They summarize their research over this period as implying that "aversive racism may account – at least in part – for the persistence of racial disparities in society despite significant decreases in expressed racial prejudice and stereotypes." But they point out that "this finding does not imply that old-fashioned racism is no longer a problem." They refer to continuing prejudice as openly expressed by certain respondents and note that

> In fact, the overall negative correlation between expressed prejudice and recommendations for black candidates suggests that traditional racism is a force that still exists and that can operate independently of contemporary forms of racism. (2000, p. 318)

They remark that in the case of the "aversive racists" in the studies, "the effect of race seemed to occur not in how the qualifications [of the candidates for hiring] were perceived, but in how they were considered and weighed." They go on to note that this tallies with their suggestions flowing from other research of theirs that

> the effects of aversive racism may be rooted substantially in intergroup biases based on social categorization processes. These biases reflect in-group favoritism as well as out-group derogation. (2000, p. 318)

In Chapter 3, I discuss in detail their argument in regard to social categorization, with special attention to the way in which they have conducted their research around this and to the way in which they present the results of the research (and their recommendations). I suggest that a critical exploration of what comes to be taken as normal and taken for granted in social life offers a potentially different starting point from that of Dovidio et al., who still see racism as rooted in "normal" psychological and social processes (cf. Dovidio, 1993, p. 52; Gaertner, Dovidio, Nier, Hodson, & Houlette, 2005, p. 385). I expand on this argument with reference to a range of literature and alternative arguments, including those springing from other ways of seeing "new racism" in contemporary society. I also suggest that while Dovidio et al. have offered a contribution in their experiments to examine not-easily-detectable forms of racism, one can expand upon their manner of conducting experiments in order to make openings for alternative ways of viewing what Harris-Lacewell calls "the politics of race" (2003, p. 244).

In the next section I turn to Dovidio and Gaertner's views on institutional discrimination – which lays some groundwork for my discussion of institutional racism in Section 2.3.5, where an alternative perspective on this is also offered.

2.3.3.3 Aversive Racism and Institutional Discrimination in the USA

As noted above, one of the concerns, *inter alia*, of Dovidio and Gaertner is the way in which the aversive form of racism can infuse workplace institutions (2000, p. 318). In more recent work, Gaertner et al. (2005) point out that

Labor statistics continue to demonstrate fundamental disparities in the economic status of Blacks relative to Whites – a gap that has not only persisted but also, in some important aspects (e.g. family income), has widened in recent years .... Aversive racism may be one factor that contributes to disparities in the workplace. Subtle biases can influence both the access of Blacks to the workplace and their performance in it. (2005, p. 383)

They indicate that continued experimentation by themselves and colleagues has led them to conclude that

The behavior of aversive racists is characterized by two types of inconsistency. First aversive racists exhibit an apparent contradiction between their expressed egalitarian attitudes and their biased (albeit subtle) behaviors. Second, sometimes (in clear situations) they act in an unbiased fashion, whereas at other times (in ambiguous situations) they are biased unintentionally against blacks. (2005, p. 384)

They state that they

have offered evidence [via research] across time, populations, and paradigms that illustrate how aversive racism – racism among people who are good and well-intentioned – can produce disparate outcomes between Blacks and Whites. (2005, p. 384)

Here Gaertner et al. emphasize that one does not need to posit that people are *intentionally* racist in order to be able to establish the operation of institutional discrimination.[50] This is also one of the arguments of Carmichael and Hamilton (1967), who coined the term *institutional racism*, but who pose the problem from what can be considered an alternative perspective from that proffered by Gaertner et al. – as I indicate in Section 2.3.5. (In this regard I would suggest that although Gaertner et al. state that they have worked "across ... paradigms" in their research, there is still far more ground for cross-paradigmatic discussion, as I detail in the rest of the book.)

Just as Gaertner et al. state that aversive racism as a concept helps to explain institutional outcomes in workplace settings, they argue that the concept can be used to explain other forms of institutional discrimination. For example, Henkel, Dovidio, and Gaertner use the concept to explain the impacts of Hurricane Katrina "which devastated New Orleans and had particular impact on its Black community" (2006, p. 100).[51] They argue that the inadequate response on the part of the government to the storm and the flooding does not appear to be a result of "obvious racism"; but nor do they agree with the Secretary of State's denial that "race had anything to do with Hurricane Katrina or the government's response to it" (2006, p. 100).

---

[50]Those using the terms symbolic or modern racism (see Sections 2.3.1 and 2.3.2) likewise argue that institutional discrimination can operate unintentionally by people rationalizing their (prejudicial) decision-making – through invoking nonracial explanations (cf. Pfeifer & Bernstein, 2003; Pfeifer & Ogloff, 2003).

[51]Walters indicates that a CNN poll taken in 2005 revealed that 60% of Black people believed that race was implicated in the slow response of government to the devastation, while 63% believed that poverty was also a factor. Walters notes that Senator Barack Obama at the time chose to characterize the slow response as due to the fact that "the administration's policies don't take into account the plight of poor communities" – rather than that "the administration doesn't care about Black people" (Obama, 2005, as cited in Walters, 2007, p. 18).

They argue that although one cannot explain the government's inadequate response as rooted in "overt antipathy or intention of decision makers," it is also important to "sensitize policy makers, officials, and future rescuers to how racial factors can play a role during such catastrophes" (2006, p. 100).

They remark in this regard that institutional racism refers to both "intentional and unintentional manipulation or toleration of institutional policies ... that unfairly restrict the opportunities of particular groups of people" (2006, p. 101). And they point out that in contemporary times, personal as well as institutional racism "often operate without Whites' intention to harm members of minority groups" (2006, p. 101). The same holds for cultural racism, which they define as "giving priority to the values of the majority group" (2006, p. 101). They note that cultural racism and institutional racism are "difficult-to-detect processes" and that "like institutional and cultural racism, individual prejudice is also commonly manifested subtly, often without conscious awareness or intention" – such as in aversive racism (2006, p. 102).

Again they draw on the argument re the "normality" of the psychological and social processes leading to the operation of racism, including new forms hereof. They state that

> because of a range of normal, cognitive, motivational and sociocultural processes that promote intergroup bias, most Whites also develop some negative feelings toward or beliefs about Blacks, of which they are unaware or from which they try to dissociate their nonprejudiced self-images. (2006, p. 103)

This argument of theirs relates to what Gaertner et al. call one of their "basic arguments" that they have made in their research on aversive racism, that is, as they put it,

> the negative feelings that develop toward other groups may be rooted, in part, in fundamental, normal psychological processes. One such process ... is the categorization of people into ingroups and outgroups – "we's" and "they's." People respond systematically more favorably to others whom they perceive to belong to their group than to different groups. (2005, p. 385)

Gaertner et al. make the point that "for aversive racists, part of the problem may be that there is no emotional connection to Blacks and other minorities and they [aversive racists] do not regard them as part of their circle of inclusion" (2005, p. 385). Gaertner et al. thus ask the question, which they pursue extensively in their research, "what if Whites perceived Blacks and other minorities, even temporarily, as members of their own group – as ingroup members?" (2005, p. 385). This question forms the basis for their research on social categorization and the discussion of appropriate interventions to address racism along these lines – and in Chapter 3, I return to their theoretical starting point for framing this research question. I set my discussion of this in the broader context of reconsidering their approach to "science" and to the way in which scientific results supposedly can inform recommendations for action.

2.3.3.4 Aversive Racism Outside of the USA

Although the research work on aversive racism was developed and has been applied mostly in the USA, the conceptual framework has been used in other geographical contexts too. For example, Hodson, Hooper, Dovidio, and Gaertner organized an experimental study aimed at investigating aversive racism in Britain by considering White participants' (college students') use of inadmissible evidence in legal decisions. They indicate that the social context of the study is one where "Blacks are overrepresented in prison by 800–900% based on general population levels . . . and are more likely to be stopped by police, questioned, and searched than are Whites" (2005, p. 438).

Their study was designed to test possible biases that may be infiltrating courtrooms – for example, when jurors are instructed to disregard information considered inadmissible. As Hodson et al. note, they sometimes do not; and indeed, they can make possible "substantial influence of this disallowed evidence" (2005, p. 438). In other words, jurors seem to make decisions that they believe are correct, rather than necessarily following the judge's instructions (2005, p. 438). Hodson et al. set out to test the hypothesis that Whites would choose to "examine information damning to a Black (vs White) defendant despite disregard instructions," while giving the benefit of the doubt to White defendants. They summarize the results of this research, as follows:

> . . . consistent with research on aversive racism, we found that after receiving orders from a judge stipulating that incriminating DNA evidence should not be utilized in making upcoming decisions, the Black defendant compared to the White defendant was considered to be more guilty, given longer sentence recommendations, seen as more likely to re-offend, and rated less likely to be rehabilitated. (2005, pp. 444–445)

In considering the importance of this experimental study, they remark that

> To our knowledge the present investigation is the first *experiment* to uncover aversive racism in Britain, a country with strong egalitarian values yet a substantially different racial history from the U.S. (2005, p. 445)

They argue that the research supports their suggestion that "aversive racists" seek to be able to justify their decisions to themselves and others by finding "a nonracial motive" to account for them. They indicate that in the experiment, the "inadmissible evidence condition" presents a situation to participants in which they can draw on a supposedly nonracial motive, namely "the desire to avoid letting a guilty person go unpunished" (2005, p. 445). But as borne out by the outcomes of the research, this "reasoning" still enables discrimination (unnoticed) to affect decisions made.

They also remark in this context that the Modern Racism Scale – designed to *directly measure* prejudice (by asking people to respond to questionnaire items) – is not equipped to uncover the covert, subtle forms of prejudice operative in participants' behavioral responses (2005, p. 445).[52] Hence they reiterate the importance of their kind of (experimental) research design.

Their conclusion is that

> The present experiment continues to show the subtlety of contemporary racism, its persistent effect in the courtroom even when procedures to help ensure comprehension and fairness are implanted, and its pervasiveness beyond North America. (2005, p. 446)

It is also worth noting that besides its application to potentially understanding new forms of *racism*, certain researchers have extended the argument about aversive forms of prejudice to *other areas of discrimination*. For example, Bromgard and Stephan apply the argument when considering discrimination against homosexuals (in Mexico), suggesting that there "may be a disjunction between overt messages stigmatized people receive from others and more covert behaviors" (2006, pp. 2436–2437); and Deal examines "aversive disablism" as "subtle prejudice toward disabled people" in Britain (2007, p. 93).

2.3.4 Cultural Racism

Dovidio and Gaertner refer to the concept of cultural racism as explored by Jones to emphasize the "total social and cultural context within which prejudiced attitudes develop, are supported and reinforced, and are transmitted" (1986, p. 15). They indicate that Jones (1983) has questioned the experimental procedure with its focus on the behavior of the individual – at the expense of "culture- and system-related variables" (1986, p. 15). They suggest that his work, along with others pointing to these (macro-social) factors, offers a crucial contribution to the study of racism. In their view, racism cannot be understood without a full consideration of "basic perceptual, cognitive, interpersonal, intergroup, social, historical, and cultural factors" (1986b, p. 329). They summarize Jones' position in relation to the USA: "Racial issues . . . are often actually cultural issues involving conflict between Euro-American and Afro-American perspectives" (1986, p. 28). For this reason, they claim, "in addition to individual-level influences in racism, the effects of culture and social power must be considered" (1986, p. 28).

The reason why I have started the section on cultural racism with Dovidio and Gaertner's account hereof (in summarizing Jones' argument) is to show that the term has and can be used within a variety of theoretical perspectives. Dovidio and Gaertner use the term as a way of highlighting the cultural and social context in which (individual) attitudes develop. It appears that they incorporate the "cultural racism" argument as a way of moving away from what they would agree to be narrowly individualist perspectives in the study of racism (in the USA as elsewhere). But as we shall see in following chapters, they still concentrate on the *cognitive processes* utilized by individuals (albeit in the context of trying to explore group

---

[52]For an elucidation of research questions concerning *direct* versus *indirect* measures of what are considered as *explicitly* and *implicitly* held attitudes, see Chapter 3, Section 3.9.1.

relations) in their research agenda. And it is this aspect of their argument that I review in the rest of the book.

Turning to Jones' argument itself, Jones indicates that for him, at the heart of the notion of cultural racism is the problem that

> whites are in positions of power, ... and have been in positions to structure black environments such that adaptation to them decreases the likelihood of developing those characteristics rewarded by the supposed meritocracy within the broader society. (1986, p. 293)

He suggests that part of the structuring of black environments (in terms of historical legacy and current functioning) means that basic opportunities become unavailable. Jones goes on to state also that the cultural framework of dominance is predicated on certain values, namely, "individuality, future-orientation, written and material approaches to accomplishments" (1986, p. 293). These values are not universal, but reflect specific cultural orientations. In this context, "if a group has evolved from a cultural legacy and tradition at variance with this framework, it too is at a collective disadvantage" (1986, p. 293).

Jones remarks that "black motivational and ability deficiencies" are invoked by "individual-blame proponents" as a way of putting the blame on blacks for observed racial disparities in the social system (1986, p. 294). This "reasoning" is "based in part on the notion that blacks have inherent (genetic or cultural) tendencies and/or capacities that put them at a disadvantage in an open, competitive meritocracy." In contrast to these explanations:

> The *cultural perspective* on black-white disparities suggests that negative adaptations to slavery and oppression have left blacks with behavioral, cognitive, and attitudinal characteristics that run counter to the norms of this society. (1986, p. 294, my italics)

The "individual-blame approach" can thus be contrasted with the cultural approach – where the latter focuses on providing an understanding of racism at "increasingly macro-systemic levels of society" (1986, p. 290). With a focus on these levels, one can create the concept of cultural racism to point to *cultural racists' denial of the continuing legacy of slavery and oppression coupled with their pressing for Blacks to conform to supposedly obvious social norms.*

In somewhat similar vein to Jones, who calls for a reviewing of what is regarded as "normative" in social life, Collins too calls for this, arguing that there still has not been sufficient questioning – including by "contemporary African Americans" – of norms associating "strength" with "male dominance of jobs, wealth, and political power" (2005, p. 201). She laments the seeming acceptance of the "narrow equation of strength with financial well-being, especially well-being gained through profiteering and inherited family wealth" (2005, p. 201). She makes this statement in the context of her concern that

> With the exception of a handful of wealthy African Americans, the majority of people of African descent, regardless of gender, have been harmed by the corporate irresponsibility of globalization. Most are disproportionately poor and powerless. (2005, p. 201)

Considering the "irresponsibility of globalization," Collins argues for the importance of a critical perspective, rooted in a "commitment to social justice, not exclusively for African American men and women, but for all human beings" (2005, p. 9).

Collins's understanding of cultural critique as a way of working toward the development of social justice is linked to her emphasis on exploring the "contemporary closing door of opportunity" in practice within "the emerging structures of the new racism" (2005, p. 84). Her account of the need for critique of forms of cultural racism is thus set in the context of her exploring the embeddedness of new racism in "emerging social structures" – as I explain further in Section 2.3.6.[53]

Strickland also calls for cultural critique in the USA when he avers that new visions are called for in order to address what he sees as "things falling apart." He makes the point that the (age-old) struggle of Black Americans to be treated "just like everybody else" is no longer sufficient when one considers that this fails to address the question of how the "Ship of State called America" is to be steered (2004, p. 7). He explains that the struggle cannot simply be about inclusion, and that people need to become aware that the "movement for real social change ... is not simply political but also profoundly cultural" (2004, p. 7).

Strickland explains that in the current cultural context, there are "multiple categories of victims." He argues that the issues at stake can be seen as providing potential raw material for a "Rainbow Coalition" as a critical mass of possible change makers (ideally transcending racial, class, and ethnic boundaries) – who can act against a system falling morally apart.[54]

Teasley and Tyson elucidate further this kind of suggestion when they quote South African freedom fighter Steve Biko, who in 1968 stated that "We reject the power-based society of the Westerner that seems to be ever concerned with perfecting their technological know-how while losing out on their spiritual dimension" (Biko, 2002, p. 47, as cited in Teasley & Tyson, 2007, p. 407). As part of their argument they suggest that while trying to "give the world a new human face," Black people are "challenged [at the same time] to engage in a multicultural dialogue with other versions of human" (2007, p. 407).

In the context of South Africa, the Human Rights Commission (2000) expresses a related argument when pointing to their concern that

---

[53] Here she suggests that any focus on culture should not be at the expense of a focus on structure. Entzinger and Biezeveld too suggest that a focus on issues of culture in the case of the European context (where their research is set) must include an exploration of *structural discrimination*, which they define as "imped[ing] the integration process of migrants in the labor force and keep[ing] them at a level of deprivation" (2003, p. 28).

[54] As indicated in Section 2.2.1 above, Asante states that if Obama is able to establish himself as an innovator in addressing the issues as outlined in his campaign, he may be able to leave a strong and positive (moral) legacy. But Asante indicates that he will have to navigate some "treacherous waters between his heritage and White racial domination and globalization strategies" (2007, p. 115).

In the nature of things, there is a veritable history of dominance by the European culture and world view in South Africa to the extent that such a uni-polar world view has come to be taken for granted. (2000, p. 57)

They suggest that the challenge in South Africa, faced with this dominance, is for people to

recognize the multiplicity of value systems, institutions and structures and to understand the ways in which these interact in the formation of contemporary South African society. Where this is not recognized, then the systems and institutions serve only a hegemonic function [perpetuating the dominant culture]. It appears that that is something the South African media are yet to embrace. (2000, p. 57)

The idea behind many of those who point to the problem of cultural racism, then, is that this form of racism is coupled (often unnoticed) with a denigration of Black (and other minority) cultural contributions/expressions – to the detriment of generating a discussion on guiding social norms.

2.3.4.1 Globalization and Cultural Racism in Europe

Bhavnani, Mirza, and Meetoo contend that new racism in its culturally racist form (including religious expression, as mentioned in Sections 2.2.2 and "Using Symbolic Racist Scales to Determine Anti-Arab Prejudice, with Special Reference to Europe" above) should be understood as linked to macro processes of globalization. Through processes of globalization, nations become increasingly interdependent and this is coupled with mass movements of those who seek work across the globe. Culturally racist discourses play on people's insecurities and fears by introducing (and regenerating) conceptions of "racialized aliens" (2005, p. 153). Bhavnani, Mirza, and Meetoo argue that it is crucial in such contexts to "highlight the fictions that pervade 'common-sense' fears of swamping and invasion by the alien 'other'" (2005, p. 153). They indicate how ideas about culturally "other" people have been fostered in debates led by politicians and the media (2005, p. 40). For example, they note how "Margaret Thatcher, former British Prime Minister, talked about the 'swamping' of Britain by 'different' cultures" (2005, p. 43).

In his foreword to Kundnani's book *The End of Tolerance* (2007), Sivanandan protests that the new discourse in Britain is moving in the direction of adopting Europe's assimilationist policies – with the underlying rationale being that "western civilization and values are superior to all others" and should be "visited on the rest of the world" (2007, p. vii). Meanwhile

Globalization, the process that underpins and advances that project, engenders a monolithic economic system which immiserates and displaces Third World populations and throws them up on the shores of Europe. (Sivanandan, 2007, p. vii)

Kundnani explains that "in a deeply divided global order," stigmatizing discourses in various guises have developed across the globe – but all "converge on the same fears and insecurities" (2007, p. 4). He points out that particularly after 9/11, it became increasingly feared that "Europe was threatened by an alien culture that brought division and unrest" (2007, p. 5).[55] In Britain and the Netherlands (with histories of officially accepting cultural diversity), this has, inter alia, led to multiculturalism coming under attack, as minorities became required to now "subsume themselves to a prescribed set of national values" (2007, p. 5).[56] And in France and Germany, "any signs of cultural difference" expressed, for example, by Muslim communities become "interpreted as signs of anti-Western aggression" (2007, p. 5).[57]

He provides an exposition of how cultural racism can be seen as having come to the fore specifically in Britain (the focus of his book). He explains that with the rise of the British Empire, "British nationality had been expanded to cover a multiracial empire," and it was "this legal notion of nationality that facilitated settlement in Britain from India, Pakistan and the Caribbean in the 1940s and 1950s." He adds that

> The 1948 Nationality Act confirmed that citizens of Commonwealth nations were to be British subjects – partly to allow for immigration of colonial workers to meet demand for labor in the UK and partly to sustain Britain's "links" with the empire after independence. (2007, p. 19)

But he notes how from 1950, a Conservative MP (Enoch Powell) was leading a campaign arguing that there existed a contradiction between "the legal version of nationality and the version of nationality felt by the people, in which being white was a pre-requisite to being British" (2007, p. 20). Kundnani indicates that Powell's vision was "of a white cultural identity engaged in defending itself against threats that landed on British soil itself" (2007, p. 20). And he indicates that the 1962 *Commonwealth Immigrants Act* reflected Powell's concerns. The immigration legislation was "marked by convoluted attempts to divide between 'Old Commonwealth' immigrants [from Canada, Australia, etc.] and 'New

---

[55] As noted in Footnote 32, Byng provides an analysis of the complex inequalities that became generated also in the USA in relation to the "religious minority identity of Muslim Americans following 9/11" (2008, p. 659).

[56] A similar analysis is offered by Fekete, who argues that "across Europe, the 'war on terror' is having a major impact on race relations policies. New legislation, policing and counter-terrorist measures are casting Muslims, whether settled or immigrant, as the 'enemy within'" (2004, p. 3). She states that: "Islam is seen as a threat to Europe, which is responding not only with draconian attacks on civil rights but also with moves to roll back multiculturalism and promote monocultural homogeneity through assimilation" (2004, p. 3).

[57] Entzinger and Biezeveld indicate that "in the European literature" the United Kingdom is usually seen as providing a prototype for the *multicultural* model, where immigrants are defined "as full members of their new society, although primarily in terms of their ethnic or national origin." In this approach (and insofar as the multicultural model is adopted), immigration is seen as having reinforced the multicultural character of society. They compare the multicultural model with, for instance, the "*assimilation model*, of which France is usually cited as a prototype." They note that in this model, "immigrants are expected to assimilate to their hosts" (2003, p. 14). With reference to Germany, they indicate that Germany is sometimes considered prototypical of a *guestworker model*, where immigration is "largely determined by the (conjunctural) needs of the labor market, and the immigrants' presence is seen as temporary. As a consequence, there is no need to reinforce their legal status, nor to reflect on the consequences of increased cultural diversity" (2003, p. 15).

Commonwealth' immigrants from India, Pakistan and the Caribbean, who had to be barred." The 1971 Immigration Act "achieved the same outcome" by granting access if you could "trace your ancestry back to Britain in the two preceding generations." As Kundnani notes "it was a polite way of allowing whites in and keeping 'coloreds' out" (2007, p. 21). Thus the "immigration laws ... implicitly defined Britain as white" (2007, p. 22).[58]

Kundnani argues that currently the "managed" migration policies are aimed at

carefully regulating the supply of migration into the country to produce ... a pool of disposable and easily exploitable migrant workers and, at the same time, to recruit skilled workers from abroad in those fields where shortages exist. (2007, p. 7)

Potential migrants are meanwhile ranked in terms of their "perceived assimilability to 'British values'" (2007, p. 7). He suggests that official government policy, political discourse and media coverage of the issues, seem to preclude creating "a true sense of cohesion in British society today" (2007, p. 9). Instead, racial(ized) tension is fostered through the creation of a "clear sense of 'them' and 'us'" (2007, p. 7).

Kundnani's account of the way in which a sense of "them" and "us" becomes created in cultural (and religious) racism, mirrors attempts by a range of researchers in various parts of the globe, who have all pointed to how these kinds of discourses have become increasingly acceptable as a way of generating exclusionary practices. (See, e.g., Taguieff, 1999; Henry & Tator, 2002; Jayasuriya, 2002, 2003; Anderson, 2003; Arber, 2000, 2003; Dunn & Geeraert, 2003; Amin, 2004; and Amirauz & Simon, 2006.)

Cultural Racism Within Far-Right Discourses

Rydgren makes the point that cultural racist orientations can readily be encouraged within the discourses of far-right political parties in Europe. He develops his argument in the context of comparing the kinds of discourses developing in France and Sweden. He contextualizes his account by suggesting that "it is not an exaggeration to claim that the extreme right for the first time since the Second World War constitutes a significant force in West European democracies" (2003, p. 46). His argument is directed toward showing that the emergence of "radical right populist" (RRP) parties themselves "may cause an increase in racism and xenophobia" (2003,

---

[58]Douglas likewise points to the implications of the 1971 Act, which "removed *all* controls on the immigration of Commonwealth citizens who have at least one British-born grandparent." She points out that:

When we examine this Act more closely and apply this new entry criterion to various groups of Commonwealth citizens, ... the underlying racist ideology becomes visible. It is now clear that the concern was not to restrict the flow of immigrants into Britain per se, but rather to keep out those considered as being undesirable i.e. Black people. (1998, Chapter 4, p. 18)

p. 46). This is because of the "legitimization effects" that they have in rendering more acceptable a culturally racist discourse in the political space of the society. He notes that

> This type of "new" or "cultural" racism[59] comes close to the conception of "xenophobia", that is, fear of individuals who are different or "strange". Like the new cultural racism, xenophobia also is characterized by a belief that it is "natural" for people to live amongst others of "their own kind", and a corresponding hostility toward the presence of people of a "different" kind. (2003, p. 48)

Rydgren introduces a distinction between "latent" and "manifest" xenophobia and argues that the RRP parties have managed to increase the importance (in people's ways of seeing issues) of the *socio-cultural cleavage* dimension at the expense of the *economic dimension*. In other words, people's thoughts/perceptions now become increasingly framed in terms of *these* potential cleavages that can be created/constructed in the society, rather than, for instance, choosing to give prime attention to potential conflicts between, say, "workers and capital" (2003, p. 55). As he explains:

> Hence, partly as a result of the emergence of the RRP [radical right populist] parties the salience of the economic cleavage dimension has decreased, which means that many who previously defined themselves ... in terms of their economic position, now instead define themselves and their adversaries in terms of ethnicity and nationality. (2003, p. 55)[60]

Rydgren explains that this has also been coupled with the RRP parties placing high on the political agenda the immigration issue, as they define immigrants as "problems" in a number of ways, all the time reiterating the distinction between "ourselves" ("us") and "them" (2003, p. 57).

Rydgren contends that, in comparing the French and Swedish cases, there are crucial differences in terms of the way cleavages have traditionally been defined and this also makes a difference to how people align their thinking. He claims that the emergence of the (radical right) Front National in France "resulted in a dramatic increase in manifest, politicized xenophobia" as the discourse spread to people who had previously refrained from this way of thinking/seeing (because of the stigma previously associated with it). In France, indeed, the established

---

[59]Rydgren argues that occasionally the cultural racist discourse can still invoke an implicit biological racism, as when RRP parties instruct people to take a look in the streets, in the schools, etc. to "verify" that there are too many immigrants (on the basis of physical features) (2003, p. 63). This tallies with Collins's argument suggesting that a "dizzying array" of biological and cultural arguments can become invoked in racist argumentation (2005, p. 180). See also Section 2.2.1.

[60]Considering patterns of voting in 20 Western countries, Achterberg puts forward the argument that "the old politics of class have come to share the stage with new issues" – including "environmental and cultural issues" (2006, p. 254). Yet he does not believe that class issues should be considered as thereby having disappeared. He suggests rather that new issues (over and above class-related ones) have "increased in salience in most countries" (2006, p. 254). Nevertheless, he found (in similar fashion to Rydgren) that "traditional class-party alignments are weaker in contexts where new issues are of greater importance, and that in these contexts cultural and environmental motives affect voting more strongly" (2006, p. 254).

right wing parties began to appropriate the Front National's xenophobic language, whereas Rydgren does not see this as having occurred to the same extent in Sweden (2003, p. 57).[61] Thus he sees the increases in manifest politicized xenophobia in different societies as being a variable that depends on a number of social conditions.

In any case, Rydgren (2003) points out how cultural racism can move toward "politicized xenophobia," as ways of speaking about "the other" as being socially problematic and threatening become increasingly socially available. By framing "others" (those defined as socio-culturally other) as creating problems for "us," the cultural racist discourse as appropriated by the far right, can increasingly enter the range of acceptable (rather than stigmatized) languaging and policymaking in society.

In similar vein, Sciolino reports (2007) that in Switzerland, the far-right Swiss party (the Swiss People's Party) has served to "divide the nation on the immigrant issue." She comments on how political posters for the party depict "three white sheep standing on the Swiss flag, as one of them kicks a single black sheep away." She remarks that "the poster is not the creation of a fringe movement, but of the most powerful party in Switzerland's federal Parliament and a member of the coalition government."[62] She notes that during the election campaign (2007), the poster was distributed "in a mass mailing to Swiss households, reproduced in newspapers and magazines and hung as huge billboards across the country" – and sparked a "nationwide debate over the place of immigrants ... and what it means to be Swiss." Rydgren's concern again would be that in this way far-right parties can inject, and make legitimate, culturally racist discourses – through the way immigrants are constructed in the first place as socially problematic.[63]

---

[61] Jacobsen, however, makes the point that since the 1990s multicultural politics have come under attack in Sweden (as in Norway). She indicates that the "ideological trend shifted from problematizing structural limitations [within the society] toward culturalizing social problems." She points to "growing arguments" in public administration "for limiting cultural pluralism and down-playing the importance of racism" (2008, p. 34).

[62] *Twentieth century History* reports on similar developments in Austria, via the far-right Freedom Party coming into power (through a coalition with the conservative People's Party) in 2000. As stated by *twentieth Century History*, the parties used explicit "anti-foreigner" and "anti-immigration" language in speaking about their policies.

[63] Leontidou suggests that it is important for researchers not to apply labels to "nations" in terms of "national averages" in regard to the measurement of native's racism or xenophobia. She argues that the Eurobarometer (EUMC) survey (2001) – through its purportedly measuring "national averages" – is not an appropriate way to "approach this sensitive matter." She proposes that it is more appropriate to try to explore "ambivalence and fluidity of perceptions of 'the immigrant'" (as, e.g., can be drawn out in interviews) in order to try to shift people's configurations. This is in line with the argument that I develop in the following chapters regarding the potential of research to *draw out/develop* differing understandings.

2.3.4.2 A Note on Cultural Racism and Xenophobic Attacks in South Africa

The 2008 xenophobic attacks in various parts of South Africa against "foreigners" (widely reported by media across the globe) can be said to draw on a similar discourse of foreigners constructed as creating social problems (albeit that in the face of the attacks the government posted advertisements trying to curb the negative sentiments). Interviews by reporters with Black South Africans either perpetrating the attacks or supporting their perpetration, pointed to ways in which foreigners were considered as drawing on South African social services and as taking jobs that otherwise may be available for South Africans (by agreeing to work for lower pay due to their lower negotiating power).

Gumede (reporting in *The Independent*) summarizes that

> The specific incidents in Alexandria, which started the violent attacks had much to do with the failure of government to deliver services to the poor. The trouble was sparked by a combination of grievances over lack of delivery of local services, such as housing, and the economy's failure to create jobs, as well as perceptions of local corruption. In these townships, there is a feeling that foreigners bribe local government officials to access housing and trading licenses, while locals have to wait for years.[64] Some South African-owned small businesses have also been attacked, for allegedly employing "foreigners" and not locals. (Gumede, 2008, p. 2)

Gumede continues his report by noting that "the newly democratic institutions are often indifferent to them [the poor] . . . [and] "having no outlet for their grievances, those on the bottom rung vent them on foreign Africans" (2008, p. 2).[65]

Geci, Hemson, and Carter's research on the "outbursts of xenophobia" in South Africa also points to the government's "failure to respond to poor people and to communicate with this section of the electorate." They argue that South Africa is yet to develop what can be said to be a "responsive political system" (2009). They suggest that

---

[64]In conversations I had with some people (September 2008) in which I probed this perception, they suggested that it is because foreigners have a practice of pooling all family resources in order to obtain the relevant finances for this. In any case, Gumede can be seen as raising for attention this feeling – as one of the bases for the xenophobia.

[65]As Veronica McKay (personal communication, August 2008) notes, "this becomes [or includes] a social class argument" – especially insofar as we recognize that it is in the poorer sections of South Africa where people are expected to bear the brunt of the strain on services, jobs, etc. Zegeye, in his discussion of Black youth culture (where he notes that there are "uneven levels of consciousness" about the identity of Blackness – 2004, p. 853), refers to the extremes of wealth and poverty in South Africa, rivaled only by Brazil (2004, p. 868). Zegeye sets his discussion in the context of considering how within global capitalism, the nation-state may lose its power, but not necessarily its influence to try to establish more social justice (2004, p. 869). Sitas also notes how, during his interviews with (Black) workers, they indicated that one cannot expect capitalists to solve their experienced problems (including when they are, or became, unemployed). But they could expect some solutions to be generated by government. Sitas thus reports on the "mounting pressure for job creation and state intervention" (2004, p. 845). All these comments are consistent with an attempt to review the issues so as to concentrate on worker vulnerabilities (including those of the unemployed) – while not forgetting the historical legacy of the racialization of poverty.

For the rich and middle classes this is not problematic as they are able to mobilize resources to protect their interests and demand good governance and therefore quality services. However, the poor who have much more to lose in a relative sense do not have the resources to confront a largely indifferent bureaucracy that is buffeted through non-responsive structures. (2009, in press)[66]

Gumede's (2008) and Geci, Hemson, and Carter's (2009) accounts hereof are consistent with conversations that I initiated with people around this (September 2008), in which they expressed that they do not hate foreigners but that their only way of getting government to pay some attention to their own experienced social conditions is to "attack the foreigners" – so that government will recognize that something needs to be done. People indicated that their trying to raise for government attention strains on social services, lack of employment opportunities, lack of sufficient skilling programs, etc., does not seem to create a response on the part of government – but that attacking foreigners does create one, as government then "has to act." They suggested, therefore, that it is not hatred (of foreigners) that is driving them, but the attempt to find a route to action.[67]

As part of his reporting on the issues, Gumede indicates that xenophobic responses have not been confined only to those living in "the townships." Furthermore, he notes that "the xenophobic sentiment cuts across race and levels of income." As examples he reports that

White farmers pay black immigrant workers pitiable wages. Black professionals think white companies use them as "scabs", rather than appointing more local blacks. Africans [those seen as "foreign"] are regularly accused by the police, media and local politicians of fuelling the country's high crime rate. Police routinely stop and search foreign Africans, sometimes even mistaking locals for foreigners, and [arrange to] deport them if they don't have their identity documents with them.[68]

Regarding these developments, Gumede expresses his view that "given its immediate history of overcoming colonialism and racialized segregation, South Africans were supposed to be more tolerant" (2008, p. 1).

Gumede's reporting on his detection of an exclusiveness of approach to "others" from outside of South Africa is supported also by an anecdotal story told to me by Abimbola Olateju, originally from Nigeria, whose experience I referred to in

---

[66]They suggest that the izimbizo's (public meetings) often seem to be carried out "to ensure certain performance criteria [of public officials] are met, rather than being used as a valuable opportunity to engage with the masses" (2009).

[67]My conversations were with a group of domestic workers and their friends, as well as with some taxi drivers and their friends. The conversations were organized along the lines of our considering what kinds of action might be undertaken and what alternative relations with those seen as foreigners could be created – for example, possibly asking these people to help them to learn skills (such as working with electricity and plumbing), and considering ways in which the government could practically contribute to the development of alternative relations.

[68]Gumede indicates that up till now, as far as government policy is concerned, the government does not appear to have decided whether to adopt "European-style fortress policies" in relation to immigrants or alternative ones (2008, p. 1).

Chapter 1 (which she was comfortable with reporting in this book).[69] She indicated to me that often when (Black) people hear her Nigerian accent they remark to each other that she is "kwerekwere" – a derogatory term for being a foreigner.[70] When I asked her how she responds, she indicated that this is mostly done behind her back, so she cannot respond. But when she does get an opportunity, she tells them that if they are from another Province in South Africa, they are also "outsiders." In this way, she told me, she tries to point out that it is not clear what an "outsider" is.

In considering the "re-theorization of identity" in South Africa after apartheid in relation to xenophobia, Kiguwa indicates that we need to give attention (as theorists, whose theorizations are themselves not without social import) to "the functioning of social constructions' in the society" (2006, p. 131). She argues that the project of "nation building" – entwined with "nationalist ideology and categorization" – has meant that "constructs of a South African identity" can contradict "constructs of an African identity" (2006, p. 131). She points to Harris's (2003) identification of "two discourses that continue to be prevalent following the country's transition to democracy":

> (1) a discourse of the "New South Africa" (through which we are able to speak of rebuilding the nation, of unity, and of national identity), and (2) a discourse of an "African Renaissance" (which constructs identities that are transnational) . . . . (Harris, 2003, as cited in Kiguwa, 2006, p. 131)

Similarly to the way in which I have argued the point in Chapter 1, Kiguwa mentions that what she sees as crucial in regard to the constructions is the "functioning of [and status afforded to] such constructions" (2006, p. 131). She points out that "traditional conceptualizations of identities" and groups tend to "reproduce essentialized constructs of identity and groups," but that

> Researchers [such as herself] utilizing social constructionist frameworks seek to emphasize the processes by which individuals and groups construct themselves and others in specific social and historical contexts . . . . Ethnicity, gender, and race, especially as seen in cases of xenophobic violence, [can be] . . . shown to be groupings and identities in the service of particular agendas. (2006, p. 133)

She suggests therefore that to address the (cultural) racism associated with xenophobia requires developing an alternative (more constructivist-oriented) account of

---

[69]This story was told in the course of our discussions that we had at Sandringham Gardens, where my mother used to reside and be cared for, and where the care workers and I (with my mother making comments too) often had intense conversations – including Abimbola here cited and Sisinyane Makoena as part of the process of our developing a friendship.

[70]The term "kwerekwere" is a term reserved for *Black* foreigners – as pointed out to me through a story told by another friend. She indicated to me that she sometimes refers jokingly to her German boyfriend as being "kwerekwere" when (as White South African herself) she introduces him to Black colleagues and friends. They find this reference amusing, because they know that it is only Black foreigners who become treated in this way (no matter what their social status may be). She suggested to me that this story highlights some of the discrepancies between people's treatment of those considered as White or Black "foreigners" in South Africa. She suggested that through the legacy of apartheid, racialized thinking is still here pervasive.

the constructs of "us" and "them" – which encourages people to take into account their historically constructed character (2006, p. 132).

2.3.5 Institutional Racism

Singh indicates that Carmichael and Hamilton (1967), Black Power activists and writers in the USA, coined the concept of "institutional racism" to help explain the "persistence of socio-economic inequalities in the midst of social and legal reforms" (2000, pp. 29–30). Their use of the term signaled a shift in the analysis of racism: "moving away from *individual acts* of prejudice, toward the role of *racist power structures* in the generation and reproduction of racialized division" (2000, p. 30, my italics). According to Carmichael and Hamilton, institutional racism could be identified irrespective of people's individual intentions and actions – it was identified as networks or patterns that, as Singh puts it, are "covert, hidden in the organization of the society" (Singh, 2000, p. 31). In referring to different levels of racism, and insisting that it can operate at an *institutional* level, they suggested that instead of focusing on tackling this form of racism by trying to work primarily at the level of individual (whether conscious or relatively unaware of) beliefs and behavior, new forms of action were required to act against *patterns/policies/practices that reproduce Black disadvantage*.

Singh notes that the term was "soon taken up and reproduced by both American and British academics from the early 1970s onwards" (2000, p. 30). An understanding of the term was seen as aiding people to account for racism in terms of the way in which policies and practices/processes in institutions "systematically reflect and produce social inequalities" (2000, p. 30). For example, he notes that in Britain, by the 1980s, "the concept of institutional racism began to be used extensively to identify how particular institutions, such as housing agencies, schools, the health services, and social services generated and reproduced racialized divisions" (2000, p. 30). And the Macpherson report (1999) pointing to institutional racism in the Metropolitan Police also referred to the work of Carmichael and Hamilton.[71] As Murji also notes:

> The Macpherson report's discussion of institutional racism draws extensively on evidence submitted by several sociologists to the inquiry – which it describes as "very helpful" – as well as the 1967 book, *Black Power* by Stokely Carmichael (later known as Kwame Ture) and Charles Hamilton, in which they first developed the main features of the term. (2007, p. 844)[72]

---

[71] Sir William Macpherson chaired the Stephen Lawrence Inquiry into the murder by white youths of Black teenager Stephen Lawrence. See my further discussion hereof in Section 2.3.6.

[72] Anthias argues, though, that Macpherson still did not adequately take into account the way in which Carmichael and Hamilton located racism in the wider social context of collective social power and domination (1999, Paragraph 2.5).

Singh points out that the concept can furthermore be seen as encapsulated/echoed in the 1976 Race Relations Legislation in Britain – via the notion of "indirect discrimination." The (previous) 1968 Race Relations Act made provision only for direct discrimination (where a person discriminates knowingly). Thus to "prove" discrimination it had been necessary to prove discriminatory intent. The notion of indirect discrimination allows for discrimination to be considered as at play even without intent to discriminate. He indicates that this was in tune with the approach that the US Court had taken to the meaning of discrimination in the 1964 Civil Rights Act – with the idea being to "go beyond an individualistic account of discrimination" (2002, p. 30). The Human Rights Commission report on an inquiry into racism in the media in South Africa (2000) makes the point, though, that in the USA some intention still appears to be a requirement of US jurisdiction, whereas this requirement is not a feature of South African law (2000, p. 77). The Commission concurs with the South African approach and states that "this approach, we submit, is also consistent with the definition of racial discrimination in the International Convention on the Elimination of Racial Discrimination" (2000, p. 77).

Using this definition of structural discrimination, the International Labor Organization, for example, has organized research in a number of member states in Europe and has come to the conclusion that "discrimination indeed does occur quite frequently in many places" (as cited in Entzinger & Biezeveld 2003, p. 29) – albeit that this is not easy to prove in a legal sense.

Considering the importance of offering sociological analyses of persistent racism at the level of the institutions of society, Bobo (2001) points out that in the USA this would involve giving attention, inter alia, to

> such tangible indicators as the persistent problem of racial segregation of neighborhoods and schools, discrimination in access to housing and employment, [and] innumerable everyday acts of racial bias. (2001, p. 266)

To understand the dynamics at play that generate racism at the level of *institutional outcomes* requires what Bobo, Kluegel, and Smith call the development of a *sociological theory*, rather than (merely) a socio-cultural theory. They argue that the explication of "symbolic racism" (as developed by, e.g., Kinder and Sears, 1981) is "explicitly premised on a sociocultural theory" and "places central importance on social learning and the psychological-affective nature of racial attitudes." They believe that a *group position theory* of prejudice, which examines "prejudice" in the context of economic and political needs of advantaged groups, is better equipped to appreciate "persistent black oppression in the United States, but now in a manner appropriate to a modern, nation-wide, post-industrial free labor economy and polity" (1996, p. 7).

Within the framework that they present, they suggest that the terms "symbolic racism" and "modern racism" *do not suitably direct us to the forces operating to sustain Black and other minority disadvantage.* They consider that a more suitable term for understanding the style of racism operative in what they call a "post-industrial free labor economy" is *"laissez-faire* racism" (1996, p. 7). (This tallies with Collins's suggestion that a "global marketplace ... seemingly controls every-thing, but no-one is responsible for the poverty, homelessness, poor health, and hunger that persists among a large proportion of the world's population" – 2005, p. 10.[73])

In discussing the research methods that have been used to support theorizing around symbolic/modern racism, Bobo (2001) notes that questionnaires designed by, for instance, Sears (1988) and Kinder and Sanders (1996), can be interpreted as possibly drawing attention to certain factors operating at a societal level. But he proposes that in order to fully appreciate institutional racism, one needs to find a way of examining the "institutionalized structural conditions" in which human courses of action are embedded.

While Bobo tries to move the theoretical analysis of racism to a more soci-etal level than he sees provided by those concentrating on individual attitudes, Bonilla-Silva argues that Bobo and his associates still focus on "prejudice and its psychological baggage rooted in interracial hostility" (2006, p. 7). Bonilla-Silva avers that in order to explore the dynamics of institutional racism, a yet more struc-turally oriented theoretical conception is necessary – upon which I elaborate in Section 2.3.6.

Omi and Winant's position in regard to the concept of institutional racism (as developed within various social movements[74]) is that it has been specifically helpful in moving the discussion of racism toward focusing on the "structural dimensions of racism" (1994, p. 70). And they indicate that it also offers a counterpoint to individual-oriented approaches that neglect the "continuing organization of social inequality and oppression along racial lines" (1994, p. 70). In the light of current contestation over the meaning of racism, they propose their own suggestion, namely, that we can define racism as "a racial project [that] *creates or reproduces structures of domination based on essentialist categories of race*" (1994, p. 71). They point in this regard to the importance of the distinction between *racial awareness* and *racial essentialism*.[75] (See also Chapter 1, Section 1.4.)

---

[73]Of course, the ways in which interventions can be created toward more social justice in what Collins calls the "global marketplace" is subject to much controversy – but Bobo's point (and that of Collins) is that some responsibility needs to be taken for the (racialized) patterns of advantage and disadvantage.

[74]Omi and Winant point to the "black power" movement of the 1960s (and later the "brown power," red power" and "yellow power" ones) and the associated conception of racism as a "product of centuries of systematic exclusion, exploitation, and disregard of racially defined minorities" (1994, p. 69).

[75]Omi and Winant clarify that they define essentialism by drawing on the book of Fuss enti-tled *Essentially Speaking* (1989). In this understanding, essentialism implies a "belief in real, true human essences, existing outside of or impervious to social and historical context" (Fuss, 1989, p. xi, as cited in Omi & Winant, 2002a, p. 140). They suggest that a consideration of the difference between racial awareness and racial essentialism is helpful as it allows us to understand that, for example, the former could involve an effort to "to attribute merits, allocate values or resources to, and/or represent individuals or groups on the basis of racial identity" – and should not as such be

In considering Omi and Winant's approach, Bonilla-Silva suggests that despite the importance of Omi and Winant's work in proposing a definition of racism as practices that create or reproduce structures of domination based on essentialist categories of race, their argument still does not give sufficient attention to racism as a "sociopolitical concept" that refers to a "racial ideology that glues a particular social order" (2006, p. 173). I return to Bonilla-Silva's argument in Section 2.3.6 and again in Chapter 8 (where I discuss it in relation to alternatives).

2.3.5.1   Connections Between the Terms Cultural and Institutional Racism

Many authors making use of the term "cultural racism" at the same time invoke the term "institutional racism" to point to the need to analyze the historical development and reproduction of racism via social institutions. (See, for instance, Bhavnani et al., 2005, p. 28, Amirauz & Simon, 2006, p. 206, and Kundnani, 2007, p. 123.)

For example, writing in the context of Britain, Kundnani indicates that the Brixton riots of 1981 were explained in the Scarman report in terms of the "ethnic characteristics" of minorities, rather than being seen as a consequence of the "racist institutions that British society had produced" (2007, p. 45).[76] Kundnani thus sees a link between cultural and institutional racism in the sense that the "alien" cultures of minority groups become focused upon to explain failure – rather than recognizing the institutional failure created within the society (2007, p. 45).

Also writing in the context of Britain, Bhavnani, Mirza, and Meetoo too point to the difficulty of unraveling the cultural and institutional dimensions of the (new) racism when trying to challenge it. They sum up the problem as they see it:

> [The] lack of clarity in unraveling racism, in all its facets, is closely connected to a lack of clear definition of "success" in relation to an intervention. What does "successful" mean when you are tackling a problem which has not only been around for several hundred years, but keeps changing form and appearing in different ways, in different societies, including being reproduced at all levels of society. (2005, p. 30)

And Entzinger and Biezeveld caution that if one focuses too much attention on the notion of cultural racism (in Europe), one can lose sight of the need to explore the *structural discrimination* that prohibits opportunities for particular immigrants to "participate in the major institutional arrangements of a society" (2003, p. 9).

Meanwhile, writing in relation to what they call "the South" – with special reference to South Africa and India – Sayed, Soudien, and Carrim point out the importance when considering institutional racism of paying attention to the historical context in which specific forms of exclusionary practices have developed. They argue that

---

regarded as "racist." As they state, such a project "may in fact be quite benign" (1994, p. 71) – as I explain in my related discussion in Chapter 1, Section 1.4.

[76] Murji (2007, p. 849) notes that Scarman (1981) specifically rejected the notion of invoking what he took to be "unseen factors" (as implied by the concept of institutional racism).

Unfortunately, the seeds of what is often a destructive divisiveness continue to be watered in institutions precisely because the histories and legacies of exclusion are so deep-rooted. (2003, p. 241)

Sayed, Soudien, and Carrim argue that in order to adequately address deeply rooted institutional forms of racism, it is insufficient to "operate around somewhat crude categorizations of various social groups in relation to power and access to goods and services." They emphasize that the taking for granted of "unproblematized identities within the broader society" (by using "unproblematized homogenous categories" – 2003, p. 241) also needs to be tackled in order to "find a way through the thickets of injustice" (2003, pp. 242–243). The focus on culture as a factor of "difference" and the placing of people in terms of these "identities" also does not tackle the problem of intersecting exclusions in terms of "race, gender, class, region, and language" – which generate a "complex context in which injustice occurs" (2003, p. 243). Sayed, Soudien, and Carrim's proposal in addressing forms of institutional racism is to recognize the specificities of particular social contexts – but in any case not to rely on using any essentialized categories as a basis for defining people's apparent "inclusion" or "exclusion" (2003, p. 236).

An example supporting Sayed, Soudien, and Carrim's remarks in the context of South Africa can be found in Sitas (2004), who reports on some interviews with Black middle managers who complained that in their interactions with their White managers as well as those of Indian descent, they were subjected to "endless evaluations" and that they had to "bow and scrape to their goodwill to tolerate us" (2004, p. 835). Thus their "inclusion" in the workplace – even as managers – did not mean that they did not have to face being, in their terms, demeaned and humiliated. Sitas states that these Black managers felt that the apartheid-created mental models (of racial superiority) were still in force. Sitas detects a nascent racial populism emerging in response – where "Indians" and "Whites" are seen as a problem in a zero sum game of either "us" or "them." This is reflected in the Black managers' positing the need for an end to what are seen as "Eurocentric/apartheid/racist" blockages and performance standards (2004, p. 836). It is also reflected in their derogatory statements that they make in relation to Whites and Indians.

Sitas believes that "despite the fact that such ideas are held by a small percentage of the broader mobile cohort [of people whom he interviewed], they are bound to have a major impact" in South Africa. He also refers to arguments made by others in this (mobile) cohort, who stated that nonracialism for them did not mean that "blacks will prove that they are capable of being equals – through education, competence building and training." Rather, they insisted that it is the "others [nonblacks] instead who have to prove their nonracism" – through acts of solidarity. They have to "prove that they are 'brothers and sisters'" (2004, p. 837). Sitas points out that it is within this "mobile cohort" (as he puts it), that issues of race featured most extensively. For the rest (those who experience themselves as "stuck" or those who have experienced a "deterioration" in life conditions), issues around defending and protecting jobs, or finding a way of gaining employment, featured most strongly (2004, p. 840).

In considering the question of how to examine institutional racism in South Africa, the Human Rights Commission suggests the importance of investigating the ways in which life chances continue to be skewed along racialized lines. As they note:

> Statistics reveal that the indices for poverty are that a disproportionate number of black South Africans live in extreme poverty, more blacks are unemployed, live in informal squatter camps, are homeless, and suffer from diseases like TB and HIV/AIDS. Representations of poverty in our society show a stark black/white face. Resort to the concept of power, therefore, must be done with the understanding that the meaning of power has become very complex and one cannot use simplistic notions of power when the concept has undergone transformation of meaning and content in the new South Africa. (2000, p. 55)

For the Human Rights Commission (2000), as for Sayed et al. (2003), the exploration of institutional racism is linked to a commitment to exploring "the complex context" (and historical specificity) of the "thickets of injustice."

I now turn to my final conceptualization of racism as identified by a range of authors – namely, the notion of color-blind racism (especially as conceptualized through a systemic approach).

2.3.6 Color-Blind Racism as Systemic

Schofield (1986) traces the notion of color-blind racism as a way of understanding racism in the USA to Rist (1974), who defined "*the color-blind perspective* as a point of view which sees racial and ethnic group membership as irrelevant to the ways individuals are treated" (1986, p. 232). She indicates that there is evidence that this perspective is "widespread in American schools, either as official policy or as an informal … social norm" (1986, p. 233). And a color-blind approach is also frequently espoused as a goal "in many other realms such as employment practices, judicial proceedings, and the like" (1986, p. 233).

Authors from a variety of theoretical perspectives have drawn on the notion of color-blind racism to critically examine the implications of people's purporting a color-blind orientation. Sears (in discussing his symbolic racism argument) notes that ironically one of the justifications for racially conservative political positions in the USA is an appeal to Martin Luther King, Jr., who argued for a world in which character rather than color would be the basis for social judgment (2005, p. 354). Dovidio for his part indicates that aversive racists "frequently assert that they are color-blind," as a way of denying that they can be viewed as racist (1993, p. 53). And Bonilla-Silva points to the "curious racial ideology" which he sees as operative in Europe that "combines ethnonationalism with a race-blind ideology similar to the color-blind racism of the United States today" (2006, p. 184).

The *European–American Collaborative Challenging Whiteness* Institute indicates in this context that in order to learn about race, "white people [need to] become able to make race, especially their own, a 'discussable'" (2005a, p. 56). White people cannot ignore the role of race in the reproduction of social inequalities. The *European–American Collaborative Challenging Whiteness* Institute (2005a, p. 57) offers the following suggestion based on their citing of Parker's advice: "The first thing you do is forget that I'm Black. Second, you must never forget that I'm Black" (Parker, 1990, p. 297). Race cognizance is seen here as a way of avoiding the pitfalls of supposed color-blindness, which purports to be color-blind while ignoring the manner in which race is factored into the social institutional fabric. They argue further that because of the pervasiveness of assumptions rooted in a color-blind perspective, it is important to encourage "transformative learning [as] a process of making visible perspectives and assumptions that have been made invisible" (2005b, p. 248).

To provide an indication of how certain authors have worked with the notion of color-blind racism to try to render more visible the invisible assumptions reinforcing institutional racism, I turn briefly to examples from the work of Bhavnani (2001), Bobo (2003), Bonilla-Silva (2006) and Collins (2005).

Bhavnani offers an example of how in relation to queries regarding institutional racism in the police force in Britain (during the Macpherson Inquiry – see Section 2.3.5 above), a resort to professional "impartiality" was often justified by the color-blindness ideology (2001, p. 60). She appraises interview material obtained from police officers' comments in relation to their investigation of the Stephen Lawrence murder – a murder by white youths of a black youth while calling him a "nigger." Considering some of the interview material, she notes how one mechanism for denial of racism by the police is by reference to professionalism, liberalism or objectivity, such as in comments by officers suggesting that (2001, p. 61)

> "Whether someone is black or white is totally irrelevant";
> or:
> "I would say it was treated as any other murder at the time of the house to house";
> or:
> "I did my job as a professional officer."

In this way, Bhavnani remarks, the racist nature of the incident could be ignored. *The apparent color-blindness masks the failure to treat the incident as a serious racist crime.*

Bhavnani tries to provoke more considered thinking in her own write-up of the material, hoping that audiences will recognize that "in an ideal world we would want to get beyond race, but this cannot begin to happen until racial stereotyping and racism are acknowledged" (2001, p. 70). She here displays her own values (her conception of an "ideal world") while inviting us, with her, to acknowledge the effects of color-blind ideological justifications in terms of rendering race issues undiscussable.

Similarly, writing in the context of the USA, Bobo indicates (2003) that he hopes to "stir the pot" in his discussion of affirmative action in relation to a particular Supreme Court set of cases. In considering the issues, he remarks that the US society "is in the process of becoming comfortably ensconced in a new form of systematic, institutionally and ideologically embedded racial inequality" – via a color-blind ideology that denies the continuing pervasiveness of discrimination. Here Bobo highlights the way in which, as he sees it, the laissez-faire system (see Section 2.3.5) is linked to the entrenchment of systematic racial and ethnic inequality. To explore this, he suggests, requires inquiry tools directed toward the institutional level of the system to render this more visible.

Bonilla-Silva also argues for what he calls a "structural interpretation" of racism (1997, p. 465). However, he believes that his approach goes yet further than those concentrating on what he calls the "institutionalist perspective" (1997, p. 466) – of which he sees Bobo as an exemplar. He argues that while Carmichael and Hamilton and others forwarding this perspective define racism by considering it as involving not only individual racism but also the racial outcomes resulting from the "normal" operation of social institutions, it is possible to surpass this definition of racism.[77] While their view of racism does contribute to our understanding by "stressing the social and systemic nature of racism," he believes that this perspective still does not provide a sufficiently "rigorous conceptual framework that allows analysts to study the operation of racially stratified societies" (1997, p. 466).

He contends that it is important to understand ideology (which would include the current pervasiveness of the color-blind perspective) by seeing this in the context of what he calls a "racialized social system" (1997, p. 467). He argues that this allows us to better explore the "contemporary materiality or structure" of the operation of the system – rather than seeing racism in terms only of vestiges of past legacies (1997, p. 468). He defines a racialized social system as follows:

> In all racialized social systems the placement of people in racial categories involves some form of hierarchy that produces definite social relations between the races. . . . . The totality of these racialized social relations and practices constitutes the racial structure of the society. (1997, pp. 469–470)

Bonilla-Silva's development of concepts to explore what he calls racialized social systems means that he conceptualizes "attitudes" in a specific way: Instead of trying to locate attitudes at the *individual level*, he prefers to see individuals themselves as "*embodiments of race relations*" (2006, p. 219, my italics). He admits that he is here paraphrasing Marx's words – and that, like Marx, his theorization is "structural and societal-wide" (2006, p. 219) – despite his not agreeing with Marx and neo-Marxism on other scores (1997, p. 468). (See Section 8.3.2 for more detail.)

He outlines what this means to him in terms of the potential for transformation of racialized social systems:

> Accordingly, individuals are not the ones who create larger social systems such as "capitalism," "patriarchy" or "racialized social systems", but they are the cogs that allow these systems to run. If the "cogs" were to *change their beliefs, and, more importantly, their behaviors, these systems would not be able to run.* (2006, p. 221, my italics)

---

[77]He refers also to the work of Chesler (1976) in forwarding this perspective – whom he argues "developed the most succinct definition of racism produced by any author in this tradition: the prejudice plus power definition" (2001, p. 26). He states that this perspective "helped to move the discussion about race in academic and nonacademic circles from the realm of people's attitudes to the realm of institutions and organizations" (2001, p. 26). But he argues that the problem with authors in this tradition is that they "do not identify the mechanisms whereby racism is produced and reproduced" (2001, p. 27).

Because he considers that ways of thinking do play a part in the reproduction of social systems, he regards it as important to mount a challenge on, *inter alia*, the (new) color-blind ideology (2006, p. 25).

As part of his argument, Bonilla-Silva also shows concern that certain "contemporary scholars" themselves can unwittingly "help reinforce the social order" by themselves "fail[ing] to highlight the social dynamics that produce ... racial differences" (2006, p. 8). He argues that it is important to indeed underline that

> When race emerged in human history, it formed a social structure (a racialized social system) that awarded systemic privileges to Europeans (the people who became "white") over non-Europeans (the people who became "nonwhite"). Racialized social systems ... became global and affected all societies where Europeans extended their reach. (2006, p. 9)

Here he summarizes his understanding that race (as with other social categories) *should be theorized in a manner that allows us to see it as a social construction rooted in specific social structures*, where ideologies emerge to support (buttress) these structures.[78] The new color-blind ideology, in his terms, operates to buttress new forms of racism across the globe.

Taking a somewhat similar approach to that taken by Bonilla-Silva, Collins provides her own structurally oriented angle on the new racism, which she too sees as supported by an ideology of color-blindness. Commenting on ways of perceiving the new racism, she suggests that we can compare past forms of racism with present ones by considering "emerging structures" as constituting a "reformulation of former racial formations" (2005, p. 84). As an example, she suggests that the (past) slavery of enslaved Africans in the American South can be compared today with the plight of, say, illegal immigrants across the globe who become "held in debt bondage to pay off the cost of their passage." She considers this a "reworked version of slavery" – if one defines slavery as "the total control of one person by another for the purpose of economic exploitation" (2005, p. 84). Meanwhile, she points to a variety of ways in which the "door of racial opportunity of the post civil-rights era" in the USA appears to be closing (2005, p. 84). As she states:

> The contemporary closing door of opportunity must be judged in the context of prior racial formations dedicated to maintaining the "parallel lines" of separate and unequal opportunities and outcomes. Legal changes are necessary, but they are far from sufficient in responding to a new seemingly color-blind racism, where the past is ever present. (2005, p. 85)

She continues her account by noting that in terms of this color-blind ideology:

> The joblessness, poor schools, racially segregated neighborhoods, and unequal public services that characterize American society vanish, and social class hierarchies in the United States, as well as patterns of social mobility within them, become explained solely by issues of individual values, motivation, and morals. (2005, p. 178)

---

[78]By pointing to the importance of defining "race" in this way, Bonilla-Silva remarks that his position bears similarity to that of Omi and Winant (1994) in terms of their conceptualizing race as "an organizing principle of social relationships that shapes the identity of individual actors at the micro level and shapes all spheres of life at the macro level" (1997, p. 466).

Collins offers her argument in the context of considering how different forms of oppression produced by classed, gendered, and raced relations all contribute to "different expressions of the disappearing hope that the closing door of opportunity presents" in practice (2005, p. 85). I discuss her views, and style of inquiry approach, in relation to those of Bonilla-Silva in more detail in Chapter 8.

2.4 The Use of Concepts Across Geographical Contexts

As has been shown in Sections 2.2 and 2.3, concepts used to explicate the development of new forms of racism have sometimes been created with a particular geographical context in mind and then been applied/transposed to other ones. In elucidating the various concepts, I have tried to locate them in the theorizing of the authors advancing their use and then shown how they or others have drawn on them to discuss other settings. But it could be argued that this manner of treating the concepts does not lend sufficient specificity to how the emergence of racism (and new forms thereof) needs to be understood in different historical settings.

Hanchard comments on this problem when he notes that he has been accused (by Bourdieu and Wacquant, 1999) of traveling to Brazil "utilizing a normative lens about race ground and framed in the United States" (2003, p. 5). He was accused of "evaluating Brazil and the Brazilian black movement according to the contours of race relations in the United States" and attempting to "convince movement activists that their movement should resemble the U.S. Civil Rights movement" (2003, p. 5). The critique was that the singular (unique) historical traditions that constituted the US situation became then the "bi-polar model" of race relations that he tried to import into his exploration of Brazil.

Hanchard responds to this critique by suggesting that Bourdieu and Wacquant did not seem to be aware that "the so-called U.S. Civil Rights movement was not limited to the United States and the 'black' struggle was not entirely black" (2003, p. 11). Nor was the movement a "monolithic entity." He argues that a further, broader response to Bourdieu and Wacquant is to note that their analytic methods "privilege the nation state and national culture as the sole object of comparative analysis" (2003, p. 6). He suggests that the problem with their approach is that

> both the black Brazilian movement and the U.S. Civil Rights movement are analyzed solely as national-territorial and entirely self-referential ... phenomena, with no linkages inbetween. (2003, p. 6)

He states that while Bourdieu and Wacquant accuse him of taking an "imperialist" approach in the sense that he tries to impose a US lens of understanding onto Brazil, his approach can rather be perceived as supporting a "transnational approach" (2003, p. 7). Thus instead of privileging in one's analysis the "politics of nation states," one can choose to work across national borders in one's analysis and one's attendant view of options for appropriate intervention.

He argues that in any case, there is no reason to consider that "options for political assembly and protest" are so specific as to be completely "immobile." There is no reason why certain ideas and options for action developed in one context cannot be offered as options for consideration in others.As he notes:

> Ghandi's tactics of civil disobedience, informed in part by the writings of ...Thoreau [an American] did not transform him into an "American", nor the national struggle in India into one beholden to the United States. Nor did Ghandi's anti-racist resistance to Boers in South Africa convert India into the Union of South Africa. (2003, p. 10)

Hanchard's suggestion is that ideas developed in one context can well be used to help cast light on issues in others; there is thus no reason to regard concepts as being "immobile" and "untransportable." He contends that as long as the transmission of ideas between the USA and the rest of the world is not one-way or unilinear, there is little cause for concern. The exchange of ideas across contexts can help to activate what he calls "political imagination" (2003, p. 12).

Bourdieu and Wacquant's concern, nonetheless, is that one may still need to be wary of the power of American research to the extent that the "themes of American social doxa" attain a "power of attraction" (1999, p. 46). They argue that we need to be careful of importing the "products of American research" – which seem to have acquired an "international stature" (1999, p. 46). In other words, we need to be wary of the

> tendency of the American world-view, scholarly or semi-scholarly, to impose itself as a universal point of view, especially when it comes to issues such as that of "race", where the particularity of the American situation is particularly flagrant and particularly far from exemplary. (1999, p. 46)

They indicate that their concern is that thus far the "intellectual current flows in one direction only" (1999, p. 46), even when so-called exchanges of ideas are supposedly encouraged via "exchanges of researchers and students" (1999, p. 46). As we saw from Hanchard's response (2003), he does not believe that the intellectual current needs to be interpreted as being one-way; and, therefore, he is less concerned about this problem than are Bourdieu and Wacquant.

Considering the debate between Hanchard (2003) and Bourdieu and Wacquant (1999), and relating this to Brazilian race(d) relations, Alvarez (2003) draws on the argument of French (2003) to make the point that

> both accusations of U.S. "cultural imperialist imposition" and simplistic charges of "mimicry" by Afro-Brazilian activists neglect "the dynamics ... through which 'foreign' ideas come to be incorporated into national intellectual fields." (French, 2003, p. 376, as cited in Alvarez, 2003)

Alvarez thus supports Hanchard's highlighting of overlapping interests and commonalities across the boundaries of "nations" and "national cultures," along with his highlighting of possibilities for "local appropriation of ideas" (Alvarez, 2003). I return to this issue in Section 8.6 of Chapter 8.

Before concluding this chapter, I present a table (Table 2.1) offering a rendition of the various conceptions of new racism as elucidated in the chapter.

Table 2.1 Comparing understandings of new racism

| | Ways of defining | | | Ways of researching | |
	Feelings	Belief system	Expected behavior	Mode(s) of inquiry	Scientific inquiry
Symbolic racism	Feelings include diffuse negative, anti-Black stances acquired by Whites in early political and racial socialization. Anti-Black feelings are displaced onto more abstract (symbolic) issues – expressed in coded language	Denial of discrimination; criticism of Blacks' work ethic; resentment of Blacks' demands; resentment of perceived unfair advantages to Blacks	When people can locate a (presumed) nonracial reason for their attitudes and behavior, bias is likely to be displayed. Symbolic racism is also highly correlated with political conservatism	Research strategies involve primarily survey research – with questionnaires developed by researchers to measure explicit attitudes to which people have conscious access (and on which they can self-report)	Empirical examination suggests that the theory "proves to have generally been on the mark" (e.g., Tarman and Sears)
Modern racism	As in symbolic racism, modern racism is definable in terms of anti-Black feelings becoming displaced onto more abstract social and political issues	Similar to symbolic racism themes, with more focus on group-level abstractions rooted in early racial socialization. (Group conflict is pinpointed as a factor in producing modern racism.)	Ambivalent Whites, whose behavior is pulled in different directions, score highly on the modern racism scale. More liberals are joining conservatives in adopting the tenets of modern racism (and associated behavior)	As in symbolic racism – with questionnaire items specifically designed to circumvent the problem that respondents may know, and respond in terms of, socially desirable answers. Experiments also can be designed to consider people's behavior in ambiguous situations	Research to date shows evidence of (degrees of) modern racism among both conservatives and liberals. More research is needed on how people's sense of self-interest may be mediated by a sense of group-interest (e.g., McConahay)

Table 2.1 (continued)

Aversive racism	Feelings	Belief system	Expected behavior	Mode(s) of inquiry	Scientific inquiry
	Whites' negative feelings toward Blacks and associated beliefs are typically excluded from self-awareness. Negativity is evidenced in discomfort, uneasiness, disgust, and sometimes fear	Ambivalence arises through Whites' upholding an egalitarian value system and negative feelings and beliefs about Blacks. Feelings and beliefs are derived from culturally racist contexts, and impressions derived from human cognitive mechanisms	Aversive racists are sensitive to nonracial factors that can justify, and rationalize, behavior that disadvantages Blacks relative to Whites. They enhance the salience of (perceived) nonrace-related elements	Because of the high salience of racially symbolic issues in questionnaire items measuring modern/symbolic racism and because aversive racists are sensitive to such issues, questionnaire measures of aversive racism are not possible. Experiments are needed. Other approaches, such as field observations, also can be of use	Results of experiments in particular involving diverse experimental manipulations provide support for the aversive racism theoretical framework (e.g., Dovidio and Gaertner)

Table 2.1 (continued)

Cultural racism	Focus on essentialized cultural differences	Exclusivist orientation	Social manifestation	Mode(s) of inquiry	Social inquiry
	In contrast to ideologies stressing the importance of physical specificities differentiating groups (from which to deduce inferiority), inferiority now is deduced from posited (irremedial) cultural difference	Those "culturally different" are regarded as fundamentally incapable of being socially integrated into mainstream society. "Others" are regarded as threatening and/or as creating social problems	Priority is given (in more or less unrecognized ways) to the values of the majority group. Cultural racism can also be linked to xenophobic nationalism – which can be rendered more or less acceptable in social and political discourses	An exploration is needed (via suitable modes of inquiry) of how discourses are created in different social contexts, with attention to possible social effects of these discourses in justifying exploitative practices. Researchers may admit that they bring values to bear in their approach	Inquirers can offer conceptual frameworks to express (and open to further exploration) their insights into emerging trends and potentialities across the globe. (Cultural racism is seen as global in its pervasiveness – e.g., Bhavnani, Mirza, & Meetoo; Kundnani; Teasley & Tyson; Wieviorka)

Table 2.1 (continued)

Institutional racism	Institutional operation	Social embeddedness	Social manifestation	Mode(s) of inquiry	Social inquiry
	Racism is constituted through the persistence of socio-economic inequalities in the midst of formal social and legal reforms supposedly meant to tackle racial discrimination	Racism is to be understood as embedded in networks and patterns across the social institutions of society. (It requires analysis beyond a focus on individual decision-making)	Policies and practices in institutions (e.g., the workplace, housing agencies, schools, the health services, social services, and the legal system) generate and reproduce racialized divisions	Explanations are sought for the tenaciousness of institutional-level disadvantage across the institutions of society. Any research strategy that serves this explanatory end, such as generating oral histories and exploring patterns in institutional documentation, can be used	Working with the concept of institutional racism implies sociological theorizing – rather than focusing on psychological and socio-cultural learning. Assumptions and ideals of researchers can be explored as part of the research (e.g., Bobo; Carmichael and Hamilton; Sayed, Soudien, and Carrim)

Table 2.1 (continued)

Color-blind racism as systemic	Systemic invisibility	Ideological buttressing	Social manifestation	Mode(s) of inquiry	Social inquiry
	Within contemporary racialized social systems, White privilege can be maintained without naming those whom it rewards and whom it disadvantages. Color-blind ideology can function as a mechanism to chide race-talk	Color-blind racism serves as a new ideological framework for covert and institutionalized racism (with new social patternings)	Racial inequality is reinforced through the frames provided by the color-blind ideology (with one of the frames being the cultural one associated with cultural racism[79])	Some attention should be given to evoking storytelling to help develop insights into how racial ideology is (re)produced in communicative interaction. Questionnaires can also be helpful – especially insofar as they are "mixed" with additional (and historically informed) inquiry options	Theorizing needs to include theorists' trying to render transparent the positionality of their research and their social concerns – for the benefit of readers and potential critics (e.g., Bonilla-Silva; Collins; European–American Collaborative Challenging Whiteness)

[79] In this way authors considering color-blind racism as *systemic* also are able to invoke the notion of cultural racism as part of their explanations. (Refer, e.g., to my discussions in Sections 2.3.4 and 2.3.5 where I show how Collins – similarly to Bonilla-Silva – draws on a view of cultural racism, and the need for cultural critique, as part of her understanding *of institutional/systemic* racism.)

Rows 1–3 in the table (symbolic, modern, and aversive racism) encapsulate the theoretical concentration on *prejudicial (biased) feelings and attitudes and on social learning processes* as the basis for the reproduction of new racism. I label these theorists' approach to their research as being *scientific inquiry* in order to point to my consideration of their reliance on the model of science that I outlined in Chapter 1, Section 1.5.1, as a way of validating their inquiries. Rows 4–6 (cultural racism, institutional racism, and color-blind racism as systemic) introduce analyses and explanations of new racism focusing more on *discursive, institutional, and systemic social processes and structures*. Here I label the approach to the research as *social inquiry* to point to the espoused link between inquiry and social action that I see as often being invoked to validate the inquiries – and that can be regarded as embracing some of the epistemological arguments that I outlined in Sections 1.5.2 and 1.5.3 of Chapter 1.

2.5 Conclusion

In this chapter I have pointed to ways in which the conceptualization of new racism has been approached by a variety of authors. My focus in the chapter was on showing how these authors differentiate old-fashioned from newer forms of racism and how they believe that new racism can be inquired into. This is not to say that the authors subscribe to the view that old-fashioned racism has for the most part given way to new forms of racism. Different authors may have different opinions concerning the extent of still operative old-fashioned forms of racism in the contexts under consideration.

For example, writing about the USA, Bobo, Kluegel, and Smith (1996) and Sears (2005) refer to "the virtual disappearance of overt bigotry" – while Dovidio and Gaertner (2000) indicate that their findings on aversive racism "do not imply that old-fashioned racism is no longer a problem." Indeed they suggest that their research indicates that "traditional racism is a force that still exists and that can operate independently of contemporary forms of racism" (2000, p. 318). Collins for her part proposes that new racism can be seen as "past-in-present forms of racial oppression" (2005, p. 201). While suggesting that in the USA certain old-fashioned beliefs have largely been "discredited," she also notes that such beliefs are still propagated in "White Supremacist literature" (2005, p. 6). But she concentrates her attention on exploring what is "new" in the global patterning of new racism. Bonilla-Silva also finds it important to concentrate on the contemporary "materiality" (as he puts it) of the new racism (2006). In the context of Europe and elsewhere, I have likewise directed my discussion around inquiries concerning emerging new forms of racism, rather than focusing on the research of those trying to explore the continuance of old-fashioned/traditional racism.

As Pillay and Collings point out, the concepts of old-fashioned and/or new racism when employed in any context can be employed on the understanding that, as they put it, "different forms of racism may ... coexist, with different degrees of prominence, in any given society" (2004, p. 608). (They make this remark in the context of their explorations of racism in South Africa.)

The categories of *old-fashioned* and *new racism* themselves, of course, need not be seen as clearly separable from each other (in terms of clear conceptual boundaries) or as being unalterable as tools for analysis/understanding. As with all categories, whose status I have tried to show should be treated as human constructions, the status of the categories for me here gain their meaning from the way in which they aid the further discussion of, and possibilities for addressing, certain issues isolated for attention. Insofar as the ways of conceptualizing "new racism" helps to bring to the fore what might have been more or less undiscussable (as many authors have argued) and hence creates possibilities for developing "better" styles of human relationship, the category can be seen as a worthwhile one to use. That is, it becomes then, indeed, a starting point for discussion of issues seen to be of concern.

The same goes for all the concepts that have been forwarded by the different theorists – for example, the concepts of symbolic, modern, aversive, cultural, institutional, and color-blind racism. Their value lies, for me, in their status/potential in opening up possibilities for people, together, to re-explore issues around their human relations and the patterning of social life (as experienced by people) that have been raised as problematic via the use of the concepts.

All the authors to whose explorations around new racism I have referred wish their research to be *useful* in some way to the furthering of "better" (less racist) forms of social existence. However, how they conceive their research as contributing to this project is argued for differently, depending on the epistemological orientation that they bring to bear. In Chapter 1, I showed that in terms of a realist-oriented epistemology, so-called political goals are argued to be separable from the goal of "knowledge production" in society. And it is argued that the practices of science – when practiced properly – are geared toward producing credible knowledge products. The utility of any knowledge/research results as put forward by researchers is seen as being a function *of its perceived likelihood of apprehending "real" (extra-linguistic) reality*. In Table 2.1 above, I have labeled research exploring *modern*, *symbolic*, and *aversive* racism as "scientific inquiry" to point to what I see as an underpinning realist epistemological orientation informing the research work and its practical utility.

I have labeled research around *cultural, institutional,* and *color-blind racism as systemic racism* as all being "social inquiry" to point to the often normatively oriented approach employed and the oft-espoused link to furthering social justice projects. I show in the book, however, that diverse epistemological arguments can be invoked to justify the approach to inquiry adopted. Different accounts of the link between knowing and acting are proffered by different authors – and can be considered as more or less realist- or constructivist-oriented *depending on how the link is argued for*. In the chapters that follow I explore in depth various positions that can be drawn out of the specific research examples (as discussed by the authors and by others) and I thereby extend the epistemological discussion.

Again, in this regard it could be claimed that it looks like I am treating the categories of "realism" and "constructivism" as referring to "real" positions that authors may adopt. My point here is rather that the constructions of realism and constructivism can be seen as *tools to open up a discussion around different arguments/orientations that authors seem to invoke* – and in this sense are useful as starting points for a discussion of issues seen to be at stake, namely, in this case, epistemological issues. As I proceed in the book, my understanding of how it is helpful to employ, say, the term *constructivism* as differentiated from *realism* for the purpose of epistemological discussion, will hopefully become clearer.

I now continue in the rest of the book to delve into these various issues connected with the exploration of new racism and how research around this can be practiced and justified, with reference to my in-depth discussion of examples.

Chapter 3
Experimental Research: Studying Variables to Examine Causal Effects in Terms of Mitigating Against the Potential of Racism

3.1 Introduction

In this Chapter I discuss in detail a number of experiments that I have chosen as examples of research examining causal connections between variables (phenomena that can vary) that the researchers present as contributing to our understanding of possibilities for mitigating against the exclusionary practices associated with (new) racism. They suggest that the experimental research designed to look into the hypothesized causal influence of certain variables that they isolate for attention offers a basis for increasing our understanding of what may be effective routes to circumvent/mitigate against social exclusion. That is, they conceive the research as providing a basis for making practical recommendations for interventive action in society in view of the scientific results as they define their social significance. As I discuss the research, I point to how the experiments that were conducted can be revisited, and at the same time I offer suggestions for how they, as with other experimental research, could be redesigned.

In the first research example that I discuss in detail (Nier et al., 2001) – with one study set up in laboratory conditions and another "in the field" – the variables of relevance were

- *(re)categorization of identity* (e.g., separate identity versus team identity);
- *perception of identity* (measured by questions regarding the situation set up in the laboratory);
- *race* (defined in this research as Black or White);
- *evaluative responses of White people toward others* (ranging from positive to negative evaluations);
- *affective responses* (over a range of emotions); and
- *helping behavior* (defined in terms of a specific indicator of helpfulness).

In the second example (Monteith, Voils, & Ashburn-Nardo, 2001), the researchers were interested in examining the connection between the variables of

- *magnitude of performance of Whites on a test: the Implicit Racial Association Test - IAT* (designed to measure implicit preferences);

N. Romm, *New Racism*, DOI 10.1007/978-90-481-8728-7_3,
© Springer Science+Business Media B.V. 2010

- *self-recognition of IAT bias*;
- *reaction to such (recognized) bias*;
- *awareness of discrepancies in how participants should and would respond in situations involving Blacks*; and
- *ability to self-regulate responses.*

In related research work with African American participants. Ashburn-Nardo et al. (2007) concentrated on the connection between the variables of

- *performance of Blacks on the Implicit Racial Association Test*;
- *Black cultural immersion*;
- *ingroup identity*;
- *perceived ingroup-directed prejudice*;
- *psychological well-being*; and
- *psychological distress.*

In all these examples, the experiments were conducted in the USA. However, in my discussion of the research, I point to how the work connects to other (related) experiments in relation to people's manner of identifying and categorizing in various geographical contexts.

In my discussion I follow up Harris-Lacewell's indication that experimentation, conceived as an opportunity to "manipulate racial contexts," can – if undertaken in a particular way – provide a route to filling certain "gaping holes" that she has located in our understanding of racial politics (2003, pp. 244–245).[80] Harris-Lacewell is concerned that thus far in survey and experimental research (largely organized by White researchers) in relation to *Whites'* racial attitudes and behavior, what she calls "Black agency" has become decentered, while monolithic notions of the social meaning of being Black at the same time remain uninterrogated. (See also Chapter 2, Sections 2.3.1.1 and 2.3.2.2.) I discuss with reference to the studies by Nier et al. (2001) and by Monteith et al. (2001) what it might entail, in terms of the design of the experiments, to create openings for making more central the kinds of issues to which Harris-Lacewell points. I suggest that this would require, inter alia, creating opportunities for the people involved to explore different racialized social construc-tions that might be harbored – including generating explorations hereof through cross-racial discussion across race(d) groups.

---

[80]Harris-Lacewell's use of the analogy of filling "gaping holes" can be compared with Collins's comments that any knowledge based on just one positioning is "unfinished". (See Chapter 1, Section 1.5.2) Harris-Lacewell suggests that a more complete understanding can be advanced if we set out to "fill holes" – such as the ones she identifies. This does not itself commit her to a realist account of what it means to attain a "truer" (in the sense of more comprehensive) under-standing – albeit that she invokes the language of truth seeking when she argues that "through careful attention to historical and contemporary Black agency race researchers can finally capture the true heart of the politics of race" (2003, p. 246).

I also indicate that while Ashburn-Nardo et al. (2007) could be seen as providing a corrective to the focus on *White* responses in the field of "race politics" (as Harris-Lacewell puts it), they still do not appear to have sufficiently considered *what may be left* out due to the way their starting hypotheses are framed and the issues explored in terms of the variables that they have isolated. I argue that due to the manner in which this experiment, as other experiments, is designed, opportunities are unnecessarily closed for furthering a (re)consideration – with others – of starting assumptions. I offer suggestions for extending experimental designs in accordance with these concerns.

3.1.1 Some Considerations Around Experimentation as a Research Design

When explaining experimentation as a research design, Gray et al. make the point that experimentation is actually a feature of everyday as well as scientific practice. It involves, in their terms, "systematically altering some feature of the environment" in order to examine possible effects thereof (2007, p. 264). They state that "the presumed purpose of our everyday experimentation is to assert the existence of a causal connection, or systematic relationship between two or more variables" (2007, p. 264). What distinguishes *scientific* from everyday experimentation is that "most of us typically do not go to the trouble of creating rigorous safeguards to ensure the correctness of the causal relationship suggested by our everyday experiments" (2007, p. 264). They continue:

> To make "safe" causal inferences, we must somehow ensure that factors wholly unrelated to what we presume to be the cause of some phenomenon can be excluded or discounted. (2007, p. 264)

Experimenters must thus design experiments ideally to manipulate (create variations in) only what is called the *independent variable* (or variables) hypothesized to have a causal influence on a dependent variable or variables. This, they explain, allows researchers to "control for" factors other than the experimental treatment (manipulation) that could account for any changes observed in dependent variables. They summarize that:

> Experimental research, therefore, may be defined as *an investigation in which the experimenter manipulates one or more variables under carefully controlled conditions*. The task of scientists is to assess the effects of their experimental manipulation by measuring changes in a specified variable [the dependent variable]. (2007, p. 265)

In the experiments discussed in this chapter, situations were indeed set up in accordance with the intention of investigating the effects of manipulating independent variables (on hypothesized dependent variables). As I refer to the detail of the examples, and provide a discussion around the handling of the research, I offer proposals for how practices of experimentation – thus conceived – might be shifted/extended. I suggest that the traditional notion of scientific experiments as a route to examining in a controlled fashion causal relationships between chosen variables and as a route to offering "informed" recommendations based on the results of studies can and should be reviewed. My suggestions relate not only to the quantified character of the variables under consideration but primarily to whether and how *definitions of concepts – such as in this case, say, definitions of "race" – can be problematized* during the experimental process. My suggestions also relate to the (related) question of what *status should be afforded to any research material* that becomes generated via the research process. As I review the experiments, I point to possibilities for how experimentation might open a space for more "straight talk" (to use Bonilla-Silva's 2006 terminology) around racialized relationships – with experimenters, participants, and wider audiences.

As I mentioned in Chapter 1, although experimentation is usually treated as a quantitative approach, this way of portraying experimental research designs can be misleading in that, as Vogt notes, the designs (like all research designs) can make provision for both quantitative *and* qualitative coding and analysis (2008, p. 2). My concentration in this chapter is on making provision for *qualitative input* in a specific way (as an invitation for *participant discussion with others around issues seen to be at stake*), as well as on making provision for *reconsidering the status of the results produced* via the experimental logic.

3.1.1.1 Traditional Conception of Scientific Experimentation as Guided by the Logic of Deduction

Gray et al. indicate that experimentation as a scientific mode of approach is considered to be guided by the logic of deduction (2007, p. 264). In discussing the logic of deduction, they state that it involves "begin[ning] with a theory and then . . . subject[ing] it to observation" (2007, p. 23). They further explain that "deductive theory does not emerge immediately from the data; it is conceived beforehand and applied to the data" (2007, p. 23). Popper, who propounds that deductive logic is indeed the logic of science (1959, 1969), suggests that this logic allows us to test hypotheses about posited causal relationships between variables with respect to observed empirical information.[81] According to Popper, deductive logic can be used to ascertain what observed outcomes (if observed), could reasonably be taken as falsifying a given hypothesis. If we are repeatedly unable to obtain falsifying observations, and are meanwhile able to confirm predictions in relation to expected observations (expected in terms of hypothesized causal linkages), we may take the hypothesis as being tentatively corroborated (1969, p. 256).

---

[81] Popper argues that *inductive logic* is not the logic by which science proceeds. He takes the strong position that, as he puts it, "*there is no induction:* we never argue from facts to theories, unless by way of refutation or falsification" (1978, p. 86). He suggests that although what is called induction – generalizing from observed facts to more general statements – may be useful as a way of generating hypotheses (by speculating about general statements), it has no other scientific importance. Once speculations (as hypotheses) have been developed, they must be tested via deductive logic.

Popper recognizes that deductive logic can never be used to arrive at certainty of knowledge claims, because there is always the possibility that subsequent observations may lead to the hypothesis being refuted at some point. But he argues that the more research work is done in which hypotheses are repeatedly shown to stand up to the test of observation, the more we can accept them as having the *status of being well tested.* (See Chapter 1, Section 1.5.1.) Popper emphasizes that none of the statements of science, including "basic statements" about particular observed occurrences, can ever be considered as indubitable. Hence empirical observation does not constitute a firm foundation on which science can be seen to rest.[82] As with more general statements (such as those referring to causal relationships between variables), decisions have to be made as to whether to accept statements about specific observations as "satisfactory" in the sense that we may, in Popper's terms, "desist from justifying them by further arguments (or by further tests)." But he points out that "should the need arise, these [basic] statements [as others] can . . . become tested further" (1959, p. 105).

Popper argues that despite the tentativeness of all statements, it is still true to say that "our knowledge is vast and impressive" (1994, p. 100). Yet he contends that it is also true to say that "our ignorance is boundless and overwhelming" (1994, p. 100). Popper suggests that "both of these theses are true, and their clash characterizes our knowledge-situation" (1994, p. 100). In other words, while he avers that no statement can ever be fully verified, he believes that this should not lead us to reject the idea that *science makes advancements in knowledge about reality* via the process of deduction (rigorous testing of hypotheses). In the course of my discussion in the chapter, I elucidate how this kind of realist epistemological stance can be seen as underpinning the way in which authors chosen as examples in the chapter explain the status of their findings.

3.1.2 Examples Discussed and Revisited

I begin with a discussion (Section 3.2) of Nier et al.'s account of two studies – one laboratory experiment and one conducted "in the field" – both aimed at examining the effects of a "common group identity" on "changing interracial evaluations and behavior" (2001, p. 298). (The article to which I refer is authored by Nier, Gaertner,

---

[82]Hammersley and Gomm adopt a similar argument and label their position as *non-foundationalism* in order to express the lack of a firm foundation for science. Like Popper, they indicate that we can never be sure of the cognitive status of any specific statement or set of statements made in the search for knowledge (1997a, paragraph 2.6). Nonetheless (following Popper) they assert that the admission of uncertainty should not commit communities of inquirers to relinquish the quest for knowledge (defined as accurate representation of reality). On the contrary, for them, it is still crucial for inquirers to develop a concern to "do their utmost to find and keep a path which leads toward knowledge" (1997a, paragraph 4.3). They believe that as humans, people cannot live by relinquishing this quest (1997b). However, my alternative proposal (1997, 1998c, 2001), faced with the admission that we cannot be provided with any assurance regarding the status of particular claims made, is to consider embracing an *alternative epistemology* to realism.

Dovidio, Banker, Ward, and Rust, and it encapsulates some of the arguments developed by Dovidio and Gaertner as explored in Chapter 2, Section 2.3.3.) Having outlined their exposition of their research, and their account of its connection to related research work, I turn to revisiting their arguments. I point to a theoretical lacuna in their not bringing sufficiently to the fore (for participants or for audiences) *processual and social relational accounts of the meaning of race(d) and other social groupings* (as highlighted by, e.g., Alleyne, 2002; Yuval-Davis, 2004; De la Rúa 2007). As I develop this argument, I question the relationship between experimenters and research participants that were set up via the research (as portrayed by the researchers). And I offer a discussion of how the research "results" in relation to the Common Ingroup Identity Model (cf. Dovidio & Gaertner, 1999) can be re-examined. I show how it might be possible to reopen to discussion the meaning of identity invoked by the experimenters, while revisiting ways of exploring (lay) people's categorization processes – both those of (defined) Whites and other groupings. In my discussion, I also refer to some other authors' work as cited by Nier et al. (2001) – such as Crisp and Hewstone (1999) – and I show how alternative interpretations of this work can be provided.

I then (Section 3.7) turn to Monteith et al.'s (2001) experiment aimed at exploring the implicit prejudices of White participants toward "outgroup" members. In discussing their mode of approach, I try to extend the scope of the research to disturb (rather than potentially reproduce) taken-for-granted categorization. I also show how Ashburn-Nardo et al.'s (2007) experimental work with African Americans (discussed in Section 3.8) too can be revisited – by reconsidering the relationship with participants set up in this experiment and by reviewing the way in which "results" became interpreted (by the researchers). With reference to both examples, I re-examine the status of the Implicit Association Tests (IATs) used as part of the experiments, and I offer suggestions for how such tests may be used in such a way as to enhance social discussion in relation to race(d) groups. I discuss the issue of the status of research results also with reference to some material offering another way of conceiving people's responses in IATs – such as provided in Dasgupta and Greenwald (2001), Govan and Williams (2004), De Houwer (2006), and Banaji and Greenwald (2008). And I indicate implications hereof for our understanding of research results as possibly being activated through the way in which research settings are devised.

3.2 Nier et al.'s Experiments in Relation to Common Group Identity (Delaware, USA)

3.2.1 Study 1: The Laboratory Experiment

3.2.1.1 The Design of the Experiment

In this first study as reported in Nier et al.'s article (2001), 53 White female students who were enrolled in a General Psychology course at the University of Delaware

(USA) became participants. Their participation in the study offered them points toward the fulfillment of their course requirements (2001, p. 302). Female students were used due to their availability. But Nier et al. explain that they do not regard the gender restriction as likely to have affected their research results, because "previous work on the Common Ingroup Identity Model (see Gaertner & Dovidio, 2000) has not revealed evidence of systematic sex differences in this area" (2001, p. 313, Note 1).

The participants were randomly assigned to participate in certain sessions set up during the experiment. The sessions were created such that each session consisted of three people: a White participant; a Black or White "experimental confederate" (given instructions by the experimenters as to how to contribute in terms of scripted information); and another White participant.[83] As part of the experimental design, Nier et al. introduced what they call a *categorization manipulation* by

> varying participants' perceptions that they were interacting with the Black or White confederate and another White participant either as a member of the *same work group* or as *separate individuals*. (2001, p. 302, my italics)

The three-personed sessions were thus varied in terms of whether participants were induced to see themselves as a *team* or as *separate individuals* as well as in terms of whether the experimental confederate was *Black* or *White*. As Nier et al. explain, "the study therefore involved a 2 (*Race of Confederate*: Black or White) × 2 (*Categorization*: Independent Participants or Team) design" (2001, p. 302, my italics).

Participants in all sessions were asked to solve what is called the Winter Survival Problem (Johnson & Johnson, 1975). This requires participants "to imagine that their plane has crash-landed in the woods ... and to rank-order 10 items salvaged from the plane ... in terms of their importance for the group's survival" (2001, p. 303). The participants had the task of doing this ranking.

In the (manipulated) *team condition*, Nier et al. indicate (2001, p. 303) that the group members "sat at the same table, wore identical University of Delaware t-shirts, and were assigned a group name (as in Dovidio et al., 1997; Gaertner, Mann, Murrell, and Dovidio, 1989; Gaertner, Mann, Dovidio, Murrell, and Pomare, 1990)." And upon reaching consensus in solving the Winter Survival Problem, "the group's solution was read aloud by the participant while the entire group was facing a video camera." These manipulations were all set up to "enhance the sense of common group membership" (2001, p. 303). By contrast, in the "*individual participants* condition," the people in the session

> sat at separate tables dispersed around the perimeter of the room, were not given University of Delaware logo t-shirts to wear, and they solved the Winter Survival Problem individually (see Gaertner et al., 1989). At the end of the work period each person verbally identified

---

[83] Nier et al. note that the additional White student who was present was actually a participant in a different, related study, and that in the experiment under discussion the researchers were interested specifically in the evaluations that were made of the *White and Black experimental confederates* (2001, p. 303).

herself and then read her solution to the problem aloud, ostensibly for the video camera that
was focused uniquely on her during this individual presentation. (2001, p. 303)

By asking people to read aloud their solution (ostensibly) to the camera, the
researchers ensured that participants in this condition would still hear the scripted
ideas that were provided by the experimental confederate.

Nier et al. were particularly interested in establishing how participants in the
manipulated *team condition* and the manipulated *separate individuals* condition
were conceptualizing the conditions in which they had been placed. Participants
were thus asked (via a number of items in a questionnaire) to report on what
Nier et al. call their "conceptions of the aggregate." Nier et al. explain that this
was in order to measure their "cognitive representations" of the situation (2001,
p. 303). The idea here was to ascertain to what extent the categorization manipulation induced participants to represent the aggregate as one group. The participants
were asked to report

the extent (1 = not at all; 7 = very much) to which they perceived the three people in the
laboratory as a group ("it felt as though we were all members of a group"), and as a team
("it felt as though we were all on the same team"). (2001, p. 303)

Participants were also asked to respond to a single item "regarding how much they
perceived the three people in the laboratory to be 'separate individuals'" (2001,
p. 303). Questions regarding conceptions of the aggregate were asked directly after
the categorization manipulation as well as in the post-experimental questionnaire.

Other questions asked in the post-experimental questionnaire were aimed at measuring participants' "evaluative and affective responses" to the Black and White
confederate who had been present, as well as to the other (White) participant in the
situation. Participants were asked

to rate the extent to which (1 = not at all; 7 = very much) 13 traits described each individual
(likable, responsible, reliable, foolish, wise, cooperative, hardworking, valuable, intelligent,
good, creative, bad, trustworthy). After reverse scoring "bad" and "foolish", these responses
constituted participants' positive evaluation of each person. (2001, p. 303)

Also as part of the questionnaire, participants were asked "to express their degree
of agreement (1–7) with eight items regarding how each of the other people 'made
them feel'" (2001, p. 303). This was in order to assess their "affective responses."
The items were

accepted, awkward, self-conscious, confident, happy, irritated, defensive and impatient.
After reverse scoring the responses to the negative feelings (e.g., awkward), these responses
constituted a measure of participants' positive affective reactions to each person. (2001,
pp. 303–304)

Nier et al. indicate that upon statistical analysis it was shown that the two sets of
items – measuring evaluations and affective responses respectively – were "highly
intercorrelated," and so they created "an average of all 21 items, reflecting the
overall evaluation done by each individual" (2001, p. 304).

3.2.1.2 Nier et al.'s Discussion of the Results of Study 1

Nier et al. indicate that their results (from their statistical analysis of variances) suggest that, as expected in terms of the Common Ingroup Identity Model, participants in the *team condition* rated the confederate more positively than those participants who had been in the *separate individuals* condition. Furthermore, again as expected, this effect was qualified by the "*Categorization × Race* interaction" (2001, p. 304, my italics). That is, "participants who shared a common team membership with the Black confederate rated her more positively ... than those in the Individual Participants condition" (2001, pp. 304–305). Nier et al. also wished to examine (statistically) whether the *perceptions of people that they shared a common group membership was a mediating factor* in the "positivity of evaluation" of the Black confederate (2001, p. 305). To this end, a series of regression equations were undertaken. They explain what is involved in defining a variable as a mediating one:

> Mediation is established by the co-occurrence of a series of effects. First, when the dependent variable (*Evaluation of Confederate*) is regressed on the independent variable (*Categorization manipulation*), it should be shown that the independent variable predicts the dependent variable. Second, the independent variable should predict the potential mediator (i.e. *perceptions of common group membership*). Third, when the dependent variable (*Evaluation of Confederate*) is regressed on the independent variable simultaneously with the potential mediator [*perceptions of common group membership*], the potential mediator should relate to the dependent variable. Also, in this last equation, the effect of the independent variable on the dependent variable should be weaker than in the first equation .... (2001, p. 305, my italics)

Nier et al. state that the results of the series of regressions that they conducted point to the partial mediating influence of perceived "salience of common group membership" as a factor in generating positivity of evaluation of the Black confederate (2001, p. 306). That is, people's sense (perception) of the salience of the "common group" made a positive difference to the evaluation results that were observed. As Nier et al. put it: "Overall, the results suggest that the relation between the *same team manipulation* and the *evaluation of the Black confederate* was partially mediated through *perceptions of group membership*" (2001, p. 306, my italics). Thus Nier et al. conclude that, as expected in terms of the Common Ingroup Identity Model, the way in which people (the White participants) *perceive the aggregate* can be taken as contributing toward creating the effects observed in the dependent variable (the perceived positivity of the Black confederate).

But they state that it is still necessary to explain why there was only a modest effect of the categorization manipulation on participants' evaluations of the *White* confederate. They offer some explanations for why it was found that the categorization manipulation (toward a team condition) had a *relatively modest effect for White partners* and a *far more robust one for Black ones* – admitting that their explanations are based on reasoning which is "speculative" (2001, p. 307). I refer to their attempted explanations below.

Modest Effect of the Categorization Manipulation for White Partners

As a way of explaining the modest effect of the categorization manipulation for White partners, Nier et al. comment that whether in the same team condition or separate individuals condition, White confederates would in any case probably have been seen as a "member of a common group, based on automatic racial categorization" (2001, p. 307). But in contrast,

> when the confederate was Black, the manipulation of common team membership changed the status of the confederate's membership from that of an *outgroup* member to that of a new *ingroup* member, . . . and differences in evaluations between conditions were thus obtained. (2001, p. 307, my italics)

They thus consider that "automatic racial categorization" of White confederates as already "ingroup" would mean that the manipulation of the "team condition" would make little difference to the evaluation of the confederate.

Robust Effect of the Categorization Manipulation for Black Partners

Nier et al. indicate that another way of explaining the results would be to try to account for the robustness of the effect of the categorization manipulation for Black partners. To this end, they refer to research by, for example, Crisp and Hewstone (1999) on crossed categorization (see Section 3.5). Following on from this work, Nier et al. remark that there is "substantial support for the social inclusion pattern," which suggests that "individuals who are ingroup members along just *one dimension* . . . are evaluated as positively as those who are ingroup members on *both dimensions*" (that can be evoked to categorize people) (2001, p. 307, my italics). Hence in this study, because Whites would have been seen as ingroup members on the dimension of race, they did not also need to be seen as team members (on the dimension of team identity) in order to be evaluated positively by the (White) participants. That is, they were evaluated positively whether or not they shared team membership. And when Black confederates were seen as sharing "team membership" (sharedness on the dimension of team identity), this too could be sufficient to generate an "inclusiveness" in the White participants' representations. As Nier et al. put it:

> In terms of the present study, White confederates who are racial ingroup members with our White participants were evaluated positively whether or not they also shared common team membership. In contrast, Black confederates in the team condition who shared common membership with these White participants [thus being ingroup on the dimension of team identity] were evaluated more positively than when they shared neither racial nor common team identity (i.e. in the separate individuals condition). (2001, p. 307)

Yet another explanation for the stronger impact of the team manipulation for Black than for White participants can be found in research suggesting that "newcomers" to a group are "often greeted with particularly favorable responses" (2001, p. 307). Nier et al. here cite Dovidio and Gaertner's (1993) work, as follows:

To the extent that Blacks are normally viewed, often automatically and unconsciously (Dovidio & Gaertner, 1993), as members of a different group by Whites, they may be seen more as "newcomers" in the team condition. (2001, pp. 307–308)

Nier et al. go on to suggest that:

The finding that the common group identity condition improved evaluations for Black, but not for White, confederates also reveals that within the context of a common super-ordinate identity our participants were not "color blind" and thus likely regarded the Black confederate with a "dual identity" involving both race and team membership. (2001, p. 308)

This statement of Nier et al. in relation to Whites' assigning a dual identity "involving both race and team membership" and operating according to this kind of categorizing will be explored further in Section 3.4.1.

Participant Responses in the Individual Participants Condition:
No Discrimination Observed

Considering participants' responses in the *individual participants* condition, Nier et al. point out that contrary to what they had initially expected, in this condition "Black confederates were not evaluated reliably less favorably ... than White confederates" (2001, p. 305). That is, no discrimination was observed: "Black and White confederates were responded to equally favorably" in this condition (2001, p. 308). Nier et al. remark that they find this difficult to explain – as it seems that they would have expected some "racial bias" in the individual participants condition (2001, p. 308). (I return to this issue in Section 3.2.2.3, where I show how they invoke the theory of aversive racism to account for why the particular social contexts in Study 1 as well as Study 2 may indeed not draw out biased responses on the part of Whites.)

Possible Influence of "Demand Characteristics"?

Remarking on the status of the results from Study 1, Nier et al. consider the question of whether, given the "relatively obvious nature of the manipulations" (to the participants), their responses may have been geared in terms of what are called "demand characteristics" (2001, p. 308). In terms of a "demand characteristics argument," participants become aware of what a socially desirable response on their part will be (in relation to how they believe experimenters will view their responses – see also Chapter 2, Section 2.3.1.2 on this). Thus, for instance, when answering items on the questionnaire supposedly measuring their evaluative and affective responses, they might well have answered in reaction to the research situation. For instance, when referring to Fazio, Jackson, Dunton, and Carol's (1995) work in this regard, Blinder contends that:

Survey questions about racial attitudes, even relatively subtle ones, offer the opportunity to mask any underlying negative stereotyping by applying egalitarian socially desirable racial norms. (2007, p. 313)

He points out that "this tendency is especially potent among younger respondents who have grown up with anti-racist norms" (which would apply to the students participating in Nier et al.'s study) (2007, p. 313). Blinder avers that more so than others, younger cohorts may have an "increased tendency ... to suppress seemingly biased responses" (2007, p. 314).

Nier et al. do not discount such possibilities (related to the normative pressure to create socially desirable responses) – although they propose that the pattern of the results in their study suggests that "the findings are not simply a result of demand characteristics" (2001, p. 308). They argue that what is not easily explicable in terms of social desirability pressures is why, say, "Blacks should be rated much more favorably than Whites in the Same Team condition but similarly to Whites in the Individual Participants condition" (2001, p. 308). Nevertheless, they argue that because of the laboratory nature of the study they cannot discount entirely the explanation regarding normative pressure that can affect responses.

Their second study – discussed below – was designed to focus on the "potential of a common ingroup membership to promote prosocial interracial behavior in a natural rather than laboratory setting" (2001, p. 308).

3.2.2 Study 2: The Field Experiment

This study set out to

> explore whether the beneficial effects of common identity from Study 1, obtained on self-report measures in a laboratory context, may generalize to interracial behaviors observed outside of the laboratory. (2001, p. 308)

In explaining the import of Study 2, Nier et al. indicate that there is evidence from various laboratory studies that "the development of a common ingroup identity can promote more positive intergroup behaviors, such as helping and self-disclosure, as well as evaluations – at least with laboratory groups (Dovidio et al., 1997)" (2001, p. 308).[84] That is, they indicate that due to the steps that have been taken toward establishing (internal) validity within these studies, the laboratory research conducted – with Study 1 being one example – can be considered as increasing our understanding of the causal influence of "common ingroup identity," at least as this manifests within the laboratory settings. But they point out that the generalizability of the research work (which is sometimes classed as an issue of "external validity" – see Romm, 2001, p. 138) may still be in question.

They indicate that the present study (Study 2) was thus set up to assess whether "this positive effect" of common ingroup identity (when groups become

---

[84]In my book on *Accountability in Social Research* (Romm, 2001), I devote a chapter to examining this experiment of Dovidio et al. (1997). I offer a detailed critical examination of the procedure as well as the interpretation of results – which I explore from seven different (epistemological) positions: positivism; non-foundationalism; scientific realism; interpretivism; critical theory; anti-foundational feminism; and trusting constructivism.

created in the laboratory) holds in situations of "interracial interactions – involving … powerful forms of categorization with a history of conflict, distrust and tension" (2001, p. 309). Furthermore, they wished to examine whether, without the explicit cooperative interdependence that characterized Study 1 (via working together on the Winter Survival Problem), a sense of common identity alone might be "sufficient to reduce bias" (2001, p. 308). They indicate that previous studies in relation to the development of common ingroup identity have suggested that this is indeed the case (e.g., Gaertner et al., 1990). But, despite these earlier studies:

> It remains an empirical question as to whether these findings will generalize to contexts involving racial and ethnic categorizations. As a result, the second purpose of the present study was to demonstrate that Whites will respond more favorably to a Black person with whom they share common group membership, even in the absence of cooperative interaction and interdependence. (2001, p. 309)

In order to examine this question, the field experiment was set up. The Study was set in the University of Delaware football stadium, just prior to a match with a football team from another university. The experimenters assumed that "the salience of the fans' university identities would be particularly high at that time" (2001, p. 309).

3.2.2.1 The Design of the Field Experiment

The field experiment was designed as follows:

> Fans [White spectators of the football match] were approached shortly before they were about to enter the stadium by either a Black or White research assistant who asked if they would agree to complete at this time a brief interview about their food preferences. The Black and White interviewers systematically varied whether they wore a University of Delaware or West Chester State University logo hat so as to vary their apparent University affiliation. (2001, p. 309)

Nier et al. indicate that the interviewers proceeded to approach the fans – 183 White spectators (73 men and 110 women) – for assistance by asking them if they were prepared to be interviewed. As they proceeded, they varied whether the fans were approached by a Black or White interviewer and whether the interviewer could be identified as having the same or different university affiliation than themselves. The procedure resulted in a 2 (*Race of Interviewer*: Black or White) × 2 (*Categorization*: Same University or Different University) design (2001, p. 310, my italics).

Twelve interviewers were utilized in the study, and race and gender were equally represented among the interviewers. Interviewers (who arrived at the stadium an hour and 15 min prior to the match) interviewed people at six locations spread around the stadium. They altered their university affiliation (by switching hats) and location around the stadium every 15 min. Interviewers approached people only of the same gender as themselves, asking them if they had a few minutes to complete a survey about food preferences.

Nier et al. indicate that they expected to find that:

Among the White fans, ... the beneficial effect of common university affiliation would be stronger for the Black than for the White interviewers. Similar to the rationale for Study 1, we expected that White fans would be more likely to categorize the White interviewers as ingroup members regardless of the university affiliation manipulation, whereas Black interviewers would be regarded as ingroup members only when they were affiliated with the same university as the participants. (2001, p. 309)

3.2.2.2 Nier et al.'s Discussion of the Results of Study 2

The results of the study (obtained via statistical analysis), revealed that, as expected, the White participants were more likely to "to extend prosocial behavior to Black interviewers with the same university affiliation as themselves compared to Black interviewers affiliated with the opposing university" (2001, p. 310). (Prosocial behavior on the part of participants was measured by their agreeing to be interviewed by the interviewers.) Nier et al. comment that this finding of the study "suggests that a common ingroup identity does indeed have positive effects on behavior directed toward members of a racial outgroup."

Nier et al. point out that, as in Study 1, "there were no significant effects of common team affiliation for participants with White interviewers." That is, White interviewers did not receive significantly more agreeable responses whether they were affiliated with the same team or not. Thus, Nier et al. comment that over the two studies, "a very similar pattern of results emerged – and probably for similar reasons" (as were discussed in "Modest Effect of the Categorization Manipulation for White Partners" and "Robust Effect of the Categorization Manipulation for Black Partners" as discussed under Section 3.2.1.2). They summarize that

the modest benefit of the common group identity for White partners becomes substantially more pronounced for Black partners – cultural "newcomers" to the common group membership created by our manipulation. (2001, p. 311)

They suggest that as Black people become "members" of the group through what could be called their cultural entry into it via the university affiliation, so they are regarded as "ingroup" and accorded the relevant "prosocial behavior" toward them. As they note:

Black interviewers were helped more frequently when they were affiliated with the same school [university] as the participants, relative to when they were associated with the opposing school. (2001, pp. 311–312)

They contend that:

These results indicate that the beneficial effects of recategorization may indeed generalize to interracial behavior. Further, the positive impact of recategorization occurred in the absence of explicit cooperative interdependence among the participants and the person requesting assistance [the interviewer]. (2001, p. 311)

In Nier et al.'s understanding, processes of recategorization here amounted to recategorizing the person (in this case, the interviewer) as "ingroup" on the basis of their being seen as part of the same group – in this case, the university.

Nier et al. add that in both Studies 1 and 2

the reactions of our participants to Blacks in the *different group* (i.e. different team or university) conditions were *roughly equivalent* to their reactions to Whites. That is, relative to
the other conditions, Blacks who were portrayed as sharing common identity with our participants were treated *particularly positively* relative to each of the other conditions. (2001,
p. 312, my italics)

In other words, just as no discrimination was found in Study 1, in Study 2 likewise no bias was displayed by the White participants toward the Black interviewers.
Meanwhile, a very positive treatment was given to "Blacks who share identity with
White respondents" – a finding consistent with the Common Ingroup Identity Model
(2001, p. 312). Nier et al. thus consider that the observed findings of both Study 1
and Study 2 are consistent with theorizing in terms of the Common Ingroup Identity
Model.

3.2.2.3 The Perspective of Aversive Racism to Explain Whites' Reactions (Apparently Non-discriminatory)

Nier et al. consider as a theoretical possibility that the form of racism called *aversive
racism* could account for the "especially positive reaction to racial outgroup members in the common group conditions" (2001, p. 312). They indicate that in terms of
the "aversive racism perspective, . . . bias by Whites against Blacks occurs primarily
when it can be rationalized on the basis of some factor other than race (Gaertner &
Dovidio, 1986a)." However, "in the Common University condition, in which the
interviewer is from the respondent's own institution, [a] nonracial rationalization
for refusing to participate is unavailable" (2001, p. 312). And additionally, because
nonrace-related justifications are "absent,"

respondents in the Common University condition may be especially likely to comply with
a Black interviewer's request, to avoid acting in a way that could be attributed to racial
prejudice. (2001, p. 312)

Nier et al. thus consider that the theory of aversive racism – where White people
take pains not to appear prejudiced – could serve to explain Whites' particularly
favorable responses to Blacks in the "Common University condition."

They comment, though, that their finding in both studies that White participants
simply did not respond more negatively to Black confederates (in either the "common" or "separate" conditions) than to White confederates may still seem at odds
with the literature – which posits that some subtle forms of racism are likely to
be operative (2001, pp. 312–313). Nonetheless, they remark that they believe the
results are largely consistent with the findings of earlier research, because contexts
in which people are able to rationalize their (discriminatory) behavior are the ones
in which one would expect bias to manifest itself – and these contexts were not the
ones created in the experimental situations. (See also Chapter 2, Section 2.3.3.2.)

3.2.3 Nier et al.'s Conclusions: Benefits of Recategorization

Considering the overall results from both Studies 1 and 2, Nier et al. conclude that recategorization processes such as the ones they induced via their experiments "are capable of overcoming powerful ethnic and racial differences between groups" (2001, p. 313). When "racial outgroup" members become recategorized on some basis as "ingroup," this can be shown to have a positive influence on evaluations and behaviors toward them. They point out that because the "common identity manipulation largely influenced reactions to Blacks but not to Whites" – in the sense that the "team" or "common university" condition had a robust effect on responses to *Black* people but not to *White* ones – this indicates that Whites do not forego their perceptions of "race" and are not "color-blind" in their responses. As they put it, "White participants were capable of maintaining a 'dual identity' representation for Blacks in which both *race* and *same team* identity were salient" (2001, p. 313, my italics).

Nier et al. argue that the positive responses and behaviors shown toward Blacks as a result of the (induced) common ingroup identity in these experiments could extend more generally in society to "the sharing of resources" as well as "the special assistance [such as via affirmative action, for instance] that may be important for combating historical racial disadvantage" (2001, p. 313). They believe that their contribution to the Common Ingroup Identity Model (which includes as one option people's recategorizing in terms of a superordinate category, while still retaining the racial "subcategories" in their cognition) is of both theoretical and practical value:

- Its theoretical value lies in its offering an understanding of causal connections between *cognitive representations* and *evaluations of, and behavior toward, recategorized ingroup members.*
- Its practical value lies in its suggestion that *altering people's representations* (via inducing a common ingroup identity) may be a route to enabling people to consider "sharing of resources" as well as favoring policies and practices aimed at rectifying "historical racial disadvantage."

3.3 Related Work on Recategorization

Nier et al.'s two studies form part of an extensive research agenda around the Common Ingroup Identity Model. When discussing their work on developing this model, Dovidio and Gaertner (co-authors of the Nier et al. article) explain the implications of this for new forms of racism:

> Changing the basis of categorization from race to an alternative dimension can alter who is a "we" and who is a "they," undermining a contributing force to contemporary forms of racism, such as aversive racism. (Dovidio & Gaertner, 1999, p. 103)

They provide a graphic account (see Fig. 3.1) of the major elements of the model – including the four types of cognitive representations (representational mediators) identified by it:

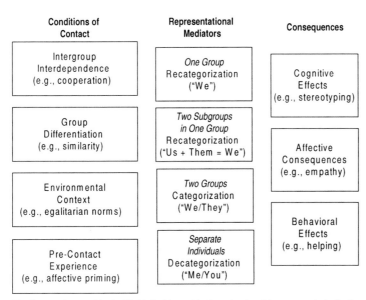

The Common Ingroup Identity Model: In this model, elements of an intergroup contact situation (e.g., intergroup interdependence) influence cognitive representations of the groups as one superordinate group (recategorization), as two subgroups in one group (recategorization involving a dual identity), as two groups (categorization), or as separate individuals (decategorization). Recategorization and decategorization, in turn, can both reduce cognitive, affective, and behavioral biases, but in different ways. Recategorization reduces bias by extending the benefits of in-group favoritism to former out-group members. Attitudes and behavior toward these former out-group members thus become more favorable, approaching attitudes and behaviors toward in-group members. Decategorization, in contrast, reduces favoritism toward original in-group members as they become perceived as separate individuals rather than members of one's own group.

Fig. 3.1 The Common Ingroup Identity Model. Source: Dovidio and Gaertner (1999, p. 104)

As can be seen through the way in which they explain the model (and the relations between elements therein), Dovidio and Gaertner use realist-oriented language to point to what they see as the operative causal links between the variables of *Conditions of Contact, Representational Mediators,* and people's *Cognitive, Affective, and Behavioral responses.* I would like to point out too that their label of "Two Subgroups in One Group Recategorization" (as one kind of representational mediator) is what they mean by retaining "dual identity" in cognitive representations. (See Section "Robust Effect of the Categorization Manipulation for Black

Partners" as discussed under Section 3.2.1.2, and Section 3.2.3.) That is, people may be seen as "possess[ing] dual identities," in which "original and superordinate group memberships are simultaneously salient" (1999, p. 103). They state that this option is "explicitly considered in the model" (1999, p. 103).

Dovidio, Gaertner, Niemann, and Snider argue that the provision in the model for "dual identity" representations is important also in terms of what they call the "attitudes, experiences, and intentions" of minority group members (2001, p. 171). While Nier et al. refer to the way in which *Whites* seem to invoke the notion of a dual identity in their representation of Blacks in the experimental conditions of the studies, in Dovidio et al. the researchers included an exploration of perceptions of *majority as well as minority groups* (2001, p. 179). These studies involved experimental as well as survey research, using as participants (in different studies) White, Black, Hispanic, and Asian full-time faculty members from various universities (in North America), as well as students. From these studies, Dovidio et al. came to the conclusion that:

> Establishing a common superordinate identity while simultaneously maintaining the salience of subgroup identities (i.e. developing a dual identity as two subgroups within one group) may be particularly effective because it permits the benefits of a common ingroup identity to operate without arousing countervailing motivations to achieve positive distinctiveness. (2001, p. 179)

In other words, if people wish to have a sense of the "distinctiveness" of a group to which they see themselves belonging, the dual identity kind of categorization achieves this purpose, because people can identify with this group as well as with the superordinate one. Dovidio et al. argue that "this type of categorization may be particularly effective when people have strong allegiances to their original groups" (2001, p. 179).

They contend that if for some reason – such as that the(ir) group is seen as having a "high status" or, alternatively, when there are "highly visible cues" as to which group people belong – it may not be possible for people, either as self-identifying with a group or as perceivers (of others), to relinquish the subgroup categorizations (2001, p. 179).

Dovidio et al. indicate that this is not to say that all people will have the same attitude toward the notion of a "dual identity." They argue that there is evidence to suggest that

> whereas minority group members often tend to want to retain their cultural identity, majority group members favor assimilation of minority groups into one single culture (a traditional "melting pot" orientation): the dominant culture .... (2001, p. 180)

They cite as evidence the work of, for example, Van Oudenhoven, Prins, and Buunk (1998) in the Netherlands, who found that the

> Dutch majority group members preferred an *assimilation* of minority groups ... whereas Turkish and Moroccan immigrants most strongly endorsed *integration* (in which they would retain their own cultural identity while also valuing the dominant Dutch culture). (2001, p. 180, my italics)

Dovidio et al. refer to further related research (with their North American participants) in which they specifically asked the participants questions pertaining to their orientation to group relations, in order to explore different people's preferences in terms of the four main representations considered by the Common Ingroup Identity Model, namely:

(1)   different groups on the same team (subgroup and superordinate group identities are high);
(2)   different groups (subgroup identity is high and superordinate identity is low);
(3)   one group (subgroup identity is low and superordinate identity is high); and
(4)   separate individuals (subgroup and superordinate identities are low).[85]

The results of their analysis of people's responses, as expected by them, was that Whites' positive perceptions of intergroup contact were mediated by "one-group representations," which Dovidio et al. see as reflecting an *assimilation* perspective, while the "racial and ethnic minorities" tended toward a *"pluralist integration* perspective that recognizes both one's racial or ethnic group identity and superordinate identity: a dual identity" (2001, p. 181, my italics). Dovidio et al. indicate that these findings are important in terms of developing strategies for "improving intergroup relations," as follows:

> Because White values and culture have been the traditionally dominant ones in the United States, Whites may see an assimilation model, in which members of other cultural groups are absorbed into the "mainstream" as the most comfortable and effective strategy .... For people of color, this model, which denies the value of their culture and traditions, and the

---

[85]Dovidio et al. indicate that this relates to Berry's (1984) typology, where he classified four types of orientations that may be exhibited by immigrants in plural societies, namely:

- integration, when cultural identities are retained and positive relations with the larger society are sought;
- separatism, when cultural identities are retained, but positive relations with the larger society are not sought;
- assimilation, when cultural identities are abandoned, and positive relations with the larger society are desired; and
- marginalization, when cultural identities are abandoned and are not replaced by positive identification with the larger society. (Berry, as cited in Dovidio et al., 2001, p. 180).

This typology was based on asking respondents two questions, namely:

- *Are cultural identity and customs of value to be retained?* and
- *Are positive relations with the larger society of value, and to be sought?*

My concerns in this regard are that this way of posing the questions already can limit people's conceptions of possible options for human relationship. I would suggest similarly that Brug and Verkuyten's research conducted among ethnic minority and majority youth in the Netherlands (2007), in which they also try to identify adolescents' approaches for dealing with cultural diversity, likewise operates by presenting descriptions of models to people, which itself can serve to limit the possible options. However, at least in their research conclusions they indicate that they regard it as important to "investigate the boundaries and limits of the different societal models" (2007, p. 129). They do not indicate, though, how such an investigation might proceed.

reality of their experience of stigma, may be perceived as not only less desirable but also as threatening to their personal and social identity. (2001, p. 183)

Besides this research work undertaken in the USA, Dovidio has participated in research (Esses, Dovidio, Jackson, and Armstrong, 2001) in both Canada and the USA aimed at exploring how White people might respond to "editorial messages" with different emphases. For example, they point to an experiment in Canada in which participants were presented with four different editorials in relation to immigrants, namely, one *neutral*; one emphasizing *common ethnic roots* (between participants and immigrants); one emphasizing *common national identity*; and one emphasizing *common ethnic roots as well as common national identity* (2001, pp. 405–406). (The editorial emphasizing *common ethnic identity* suggested that immigrants have a long history in the country and that the participants themselves could probably trace their own ethnic roots – albeit not the same ethnic roots for all people. The editorial emphasizing *common national identity* pointed to a common present and future for participants and immigrants.)

According to their findings, even for those people who strongly believed that "the world involves competition between groups for resources,"[86] the three editorials that were "designed to induce a common ingroup identity produced more positive attitudes [toward immigrants] than did the neutral editorial" (2001, p. 406). They interpret these results as allowing, in the participants' consciousness, for "a dual identity in which ethnic groups maintain their ethnic identity while joining in a common national identity" (2001, p. 407).

3.3.1 Dual Identity Representations, Decategorization, and Recategorization

In summarizing the data that they have attained over the years (with colleagues) in relation to the Common Ingroup Identity Model, Gaertner and Dovidio state that

we have found that although across different domains of group life a purely one-group representation is consistently associated with more harmonious intergroup relations, a dual identity is sometimes associated with positive and sometimes with negative intergroup relations (e.g., Gaertner, Rust, Dovidio, Bachman, & Anastasio, 1996). (Gaertner & Dovidio, 2005, p. 635)

They thus indicate that the results concerning a "dual identity" in terms of effects on "harmonious intergroup relations" are not consistent. They add that their research also indicates that

---

[86]Esses et al. note that this belief is associated with what Sidanius and Pratto (1999) call a Social Dominance Orientation – measured in terms of the strength of belief in group hierarchies and the associated belief that "the world involves competition between groups for resources." (See also Chapter 4, Sections 4.2.2 and 4.4.)

whereas majority group members prefer a one-group representation, a dual identity relates to better adjustment and more positive intergroup attitudes for minority
group members (Dovidio, Kawakami, & Gaertner, 2000). (Gaertner & Dovidio, 2005,
p. 635)

It is important to note that Dovidio et al. recognize that alongside possibilities for *recategorization* (in terms of, for instance, a one-group representation or
a dual identity representation), there are other ways in which biased responses
in intergroup relations can be reduced, as explored by other researchers. For
example, they refer (2001, p. 171) to Brewer and Miller's research in relation to *decategorization*, which involves cognizing people as discrete individuals
as one engages in social interaction (Brewer & Miller, 1984, 1996). Dovidio
et al. suggest that recategorization can work alongside decategorization. As they
explain:

> *Recategorization*, either in terms of a one-group or dual-identity representation, reduces bias
> by extending the benefits of ingroup favoritism to former outgroup members. Attitudes and
> behavior toward former outgroup members thus become more favorable, approaching those
> toward ingroup members. In contrast, *decategorization* reduces favoritism toward original
> ingroup members as they become perceived as separate individuals rather than [simply] as
> members of one's own group. (2001, p. 171, my italics)

As shown above, their research concentrates on processes of *recategorization* in
relation to a concept of common ingroup identity. They explain that the approach
that they adopted has been as follows:

> Our own work, leading to the development of the Common Ingroup Identity Model, capital-
> ized on the proposed *positive* consequences of ingroup membership. Rather than focusing
> on the benefits of decategorization in which members of two groups are induced to regard
> the aggregate as individuals, we began to explore the potential benefits of recategorization.
> (Gaertner & Dovidio, 2005, pp. 267–268)

In other words, their research agenda was guided by the hypothesis that via recategorization, prosocial behavior that proceeds from seeing people as "ingroup" would
take place across the "group lines." They suggest that this hypothesis (which they
believe has now been well tested) is compatible with research work on decategorization. As they put it, "it may be possible to engineer a *recategorization* or
decategorization of perceived group boundaries in ways that reduce the original
intergroup bias and conflict" (2005, p. 628).[87]

---

[87] Miller explains that experimental work on decategorization is consistent with, and complements,
the work of Gaertner and Dovidio in relation to the Common Ingroup Identity Model. He suggests that one way of achieving decategorization is "by applying or making salient a superordinate
identity" (2002, p. 395). His argument is outlined in Section 3.6.

3.3.2 Dovidio's Exposition of the "Normality" of Social Categorization

Before turning to a detailed assessment of the research discussed above, I would like to draw attention to Dovidio's claims regarding the development of racial categorization in society. Dovidio's argument is based on his views concerning the "normality" of social categorization processes in general. Dovidio explains in this regard that the "negative feelings and beliefs" associated with aversive racism "are rooted in three types of normal . . . psychological processes" (1993, p. 52):

- The first process referred to by Dovidio is, in his terms, "a cognitive . . . process called social categorization. In this normal process, we all categorize others into groups, typically in terms that delineate our own group from others" (1993, p. 52). He argues that immediately once the categorization process is set in motion, bias becomes *automatically* activated – "we begin to value those in our group more and often to devalue people in other groups". And he suggests that "because race is one of the aspects of another person that we notice first, racial categorization can form a foundation for prejudice" (1993, p. 52).
- The second "normal process" that Dovidio identifies is "the motivational process of satisfying basic needs for power and control for ourselves and our group." He avers that "in a world of limited resources, one way to maintain control or power is to keep competing groups down" (1993, p. 52).
- A third "normal process" relates to sociocultural influences. Dovidio remarks that we often adopt uncritically the "values of society." He suggests that it is unfortunate that "many of the values of American society reflect racist traditions" (1993, p. 52).

Dovidio argues that once we understand the normal process of categorizing people into "in-groups, 'we,' and out-groups, 'they'," we can gain a better appreciation of how racism develops and also how it can mutate into new forms (1993, p. 55). He admits that "this is not to say that the we/they distinction explains all racism or bias." But it is to remind us that "normal processes may contribute to subtle, unintentional forms of bias" (1993, p. 55).

He explains that what he calls subtle, unintentional bias can occur at the "cultural, individual, and institutional levels" of society and that strategies to combat bias need to be directed at all levels. At the structural level, for example, equal opportunity and affirmative action programs require that the "subject is visibly supported by senior management" (1993, p. 57). At the cultural level, educating people about subtle bias and training them to recognize it" can also help to "ensure fairness" (1993, p. 57). And at the individual level, it is crucial to set up "frequent and constructive interracial contact" – as research has shown that this contact can "decrease bias, enhance group cohesiveness and increase productivity" (through generating trust relationships) (1993, p. 57).

As shown via their extensive research work and recommendations springing therefrom (as mentioned in Chapter 2 and as exemplified in this chapter), Nier et al.

(2001) along with Dovidio (1993) offer suggestions as to how *recategorization* can draw on "normal" cognitive processes of social categorization – while offering a route to minimize/cut out racial bias.

3.4 Revisiting the Experiments and Their Theoretical Framing

In this section, I review the experiments as set up by Nier et al. and the related theoretical framing of the research agenda. I suggest that the research framing can be seen to be unduly restrictive in that it does not leave sufficient room for approaching the issues from alternative angles. I suggest that the realist-oriented language – referring to the study of relationships between variables "in reality" – already has the effect of drawing attention away from the researchers' specific constructions. The way in which the experimenters themselves (and their presentation of results) may be constructing, and reproducing, ways of seeing and acting (on their part as well as on the part of others – participants and other audiences) has not in my view being sufficiently opened to critical reflection.

3.4.1 The Experimental Reliance on Racial Group Categorization

The experimental designs of Nier et al. rely on the notion that people could be identified for purposes of the experiment in terms of their "race" as Black or White. For example, they explain that in Study 1, the design was set up as a "2 (*Race of Confederate: Black or White*) × 2 (*Categorization: Independent Participants* or *Team*) design" (2001, p. 302, my italics). And in Study 2, by virtue of utilizing Black and White interviewers, they suggest that the procedure resulted in a "2 (*Race of Interviewer: Black or White*) × 2 (*Categorization: Same University* or *Different University*)" design (2001, p. 310, my italics). Because participants were visibly Black or White, this defined their *Race* in terms of the experiments.

The idea that race is "visible" in social life is indicated in Dovidio's statement in his prior article (1993) that: "because race is one of the aspects of another person that we notice first, racial categorization can form a foundation for prejudice" (1993, p. 52). Here, Dovidio seems to draw on (and reproduce) the "common-sense" notion – also carried forward by Nier et al. (2001) – that because of the (presumed) visibility of "race," people become placed/categorized in social life in particular racial groups. Furthermore, Dovidio et al.'s (2001) conclusions – also carried forward by Nier et al. (2001) – about the way in which participants in social life construct each other in terms of group membership can be gleaned from their statement that:

> When group identities and the associated cultural values are central to members' functioning or when they are associated with high status or highly visible cues to group membership, it would be *undesirable* or *impossible* for people to relinquish these group identities, or, as perceivers, to be "color-blind". (Dovidio et al., 2001, p. 179, my italics)

Their claim that "when there are … highly visible cues to group membership" it would be undesirable or indeed impossible for "group identity" to be relinquished (either by those "belonging" to the group, or by "perceivers") is a statement that seems to refer to what really is "impossible." But by making this statement, the researchers *exclude from consideration the notion that "race" is a historically created category used to create binary distinctions* between supposedly different groups and to suggest that people "belong" as members in one or the other group along the dimension of race. (See my discussion of Collins's (2000) argument in this respect in Chapter 1, Section 1.1, as well as my discussion of Omi and Winant's (1994) position in Chapter 2, Section 2.3.5.) In terms of these considerations, it is *not impossible* that people could unlearn patterns of response where "highly visible cues" become used to place people in particular, racialized group memberships. Thus, for instance, Yuval-Davis speaks of the potential of a transversal politics to transcend binary divisions so as to open the way for people to participate in "mutually reconstruct[ing] themselves and others" as part of a social dialogue (2004, p. 27). Within such a political stance, the positioning of "the subject" under consideration cannot be fixated with reference to any set of social categories and groupings (2004, p. 22). Alleyne explains the implications hereof for the construal of "identity":

> How, why, by whom, and for what are identities constructed? Projects of identity are always unfinished, because both history and the individual life expressed as biography are in constant movement. (2002, p. 178)

Omi for his part suggests that it may be worthwhile at this historical juncture to revitalize discussions around multiraciality as a way of drawing attention to the "inherent fluidity and slipperiness of our concepts of race" (2001, p. 248). While the term "multiracial" may imply a conception of the prior existence of "pure" and "discrete" races, the term, like that of "racial hybridity," can also be used to point to "the fundamental instability of all racial categories." It can be used in addition to enable people "to discern particular dimensions of racialized power," while opening up for discussion a "host of political issues" (2001, p. 248). In whatever way the discussion around racialized categorization is opened up, Omi considers it crucial that researchers/analysts display "imagination" in their research work and do not slip into "treat[ing] the category of race in an unproblematic fashion" (2001, p. 260). He thus calls on social scientists to display a sensitivity toward "problematizing race in our work" (2001, p. 260).

Milner IV suggests that in terms of what is called Critical Race Theory (CRT) – such as developed by, for instance, Delgado (1995), Ladson-Billings and Tate (1995), and Ladson-Billings (2003, 2004) – researchers are urged to consider as one of their pertinent questions:

> What do my [the] participants believe about race and culture in society and education, and how do they and I attend to the tensions inherent in my and their convictions and beliefs about race and culture in the research process? (2007, p. 395)

If one leaves in abeyance these questions, and uses the category of "race" without giving participants and experimenters an opportunity to discuss their views of race, the questions are silenced. And as Harris-Lacewell comments, this means that certain notions remain uninterrogated through the way in which the research is formulated (2003, p. 234). For example, the research might be set up in such a way that (White) respondents become disposed to treat Blacks as a "monolithic group" (2003, p. 241).

In the light of concerns such as those raised by Omi, Milner IV, and Harris-Lacewell, we can now consider how Nier et al. could approach their study differently: I would suggest that in Nier et al.'s Study 1 – which consisted of participants chosen as White, as well as White and Black "experimental confederates" – questions regarding the meanings of "race" could well have been asked of the participants and of the (defined) Black and White confederates. The participants and confederates could have been involved individually and/or in focus group sessions, with the focus being on asking people to consider for instance, "what it means to be a white person or person of color in a race-conscious society" (as Tatum, 2003, p. xviii, puts it). Nier et al. could have chosen to generate discussion around this in the post-experimental situation – rather than simply administering a questionnaire asking the students who had participated their conceptions of "the aggregate" and asking them about their evaluations and affective responses toward the confederates.

This could all have been done as part of a so-called debriefing session, which often in any case is considered as apt when conducting experiments, where participants become informed about what the experiment has been about (cf. Dobbs & Crano, 2001, p. 359; Govan & Williams, 2004, p. 359; Gray et al., 2007, p. 90; Lowery, Knowles, & Unzueta, 2007, p. 1239). As it happens, Nier et al. do not report having undertaking any kind of debriefing process. But my suggestion is that when experimenters do organize "debriefings," they can consider this as an *opportunity to discuss the racial categorizations that they (as others) may have been using during the experimental process*. Without this discussion, the consequence is that some view of race – such as the one implicit in Dovidio's understanding hereof (1993) or as expressed by Dovidio et al. (2001) – takes priority in the write-up of the research results.

Thus, for instance, in setting out their findings of Study 1, Nier et al. indicate that the White participants most likely "regarded the Black confederate with a 'dual identity' involving both race and team membership" (2001, p. 308). At no point do they question what it might mean to speak of "race membership" as something that might be seen as a problematic notion when used by (social) analysts or by people in everyday life. Instead of making a conjecture as to the "most likely" perception by Whites of the Black confederate, Nier et al. *could have engaged participants in a discussion of what it means to attribute "race membership" to people*. Participants could have been encouraged to reconsider what it may mean to view someone as "belonging" to some defined racial group category and at the same time to consider how processes of *racialization* can generate what Tatum calls a historically produced "race conscious" society (2003, p. xviii).

Furthermore, Nier et al.'s participants could have been asked also to reconsider what it might mean to develop identifications in social life – instead of the researchers taking it that people are inclined to ascribe group "identity" (in terms of,

say, positing race membership, or race and team membership, or team membership).
De la Rúa suggests in this regard that:

> The notion of identity, because of its essentialist, unifying, and reifying connotations
> becomes analytically sterile. In its place, following the proposal of Brubaker and Cooper
> (2000), it is preferable to adopt the concept of "identification", which is free from the rigid
> semantic connotations of the word "identity". (2007, p. 683)[88]

In Study 1, Nier et al. asked people to express their conception of "the aggregate" by
responding to questions such as "it felt as though we were all members of a group',"
and "it felt as though we were all on the same team" (2001, p. 303). This was in
order to enable the researchers to measure the extent of people's "group identity".
But the researchers' conception of identity here already frames the information and
its interpretation by them in their analysis – as if people's conceptions of groups
and groupings require no further discussion. Again, this could have been explored
via Study 1 (e.g., in a post-experimental debriefing) as a way of enabling people
to (re)consider what may be involved in developing *identification – by researchers,
say, raising for discussion issues concerning identification as a social relational
process.*

And in Study 2, even though there was no bringing together of participants and
experimenters in a post-experimental stage, some of the football fans could have
been approached after the match, asking them to reflect on their understanding
of "team membership" and of "Black and White" (ostensible) interviewers at the
match. This may have provided all those participating in the discussion an entry
point to indeed reconsider the meaning of their "affiliations" and would also enable
audiences of the report by Nier et al. to reflect upon the way in which categories to
label people can become (de)constructed in social life.

I use the term deconstruction in the sense defined by Butler when she suggests
that "to deconstruct is ... to call into question and, perhaps most important, to
open up a term ... to reusage or redeployment that previously has not been authorized" (1994, p. 165). In future chapters I offer further detail on the question of

---

[88]It should be noted that De la Rúa's conception of identification here offers an alternative to
attempts to measure "it" in the way that is often used by those relying on so-called identification
scales. For example, Stathi and Crisp (2008), when examining "national identification" in the context of an experiment, indicate how they asked participants to complete an "identification scale"
(adapted from Branscombe et al., 1993) by rating the extent to which they agree to the following
statements (with ratings ranging from 1, not at all, to 7, very much): "*I identify strongly with other
people who share my nationality"; My nationality is an important part of who I am"; I feel strong
ties with other people who share my nationality; I feel a strong sense of solidarity with other people who share my nationality*" (2008, p. 948). This way of measuring identification, however, in
terms of De la Rúa's argument, clearly does not provide for participants to *reflect on processes* of
identifying with created groupings within *particular social contexts*; nor does it allow for them to
reconsider terms such as "my nationality" in terms *other than as a possession*. Harris-Lacewell
proposes that experimental research contexts could become a social context in which a "more tex-
tured" account of the ways in which (in this case) Black and White people affect one another in
their interactions could be developed (2003, p. 244). But this requires (re)examining potentially
uninterrogated notions.

how categorizations may be treated – but for the time being I wish to show how Nier et al.'s conceptualization of "dual identity" (e.g., in terms of race membership and some other categorical membership) seems to be infused with their particular understandings – that can be revisited as the central terms become redeployed or reconfigured.

It is noteworthy that when considering the results of both Studies 1 and 2, Nier et al. suggest that Black partners could be interpreted (in terms of the researchers' theoretical framework) as having been seen by Whites as cultural "newcomers" to the "common group membership" created by the experimental manipulation (2001, p. 311). Because of the lack of discussion between experimenters and participants, inevitably Nier et al.'s write-up of the research reproduces their own understandings of the categories of Black, White, Newcomer, based on the assumed reference to factual features of reality – thereby reinforcing their seeming "existence" in society. My concern is that the very way in which the experiments were set up, and the results presented, means that opportunities become lost to reframe the initial conceptualizations. And, as Harris-Lacewell has pointed out, insofar as assumptions remain uninterrogated, the "holes" that she locates are not appreciated (2003, p. 245).

3.4.2 Providing for Alternative Interpretive Frames in Processes of "Knowing"

Milner IV proposes that researchers should consider the "social, political, historical, and contextual nuances" that might have shaped participants' "racial and cultural ways or systems of knowing, both past and present" (2007, p. 395). Furthermore, they should consider to what extent their own ways of "coming to know" may themselves be influenced by their experiences of a specific history that shapes their understanding. In setting up a conversation in relation to the different voices and perspectives of those involved, he suggests that researchers can avoid their own "voice" from "overshadowing the voices of the researched and *vice versa*" (2007, p. 396). Milner IV remarks that "the [resulting] tensions in the interpretation and explanation are forms of data in themselves and can be beneficial and useful for consumers [audiences] of the research" (2007, p. 396).

Considering Nier et al.'s research and Dovidio et al.'s related research in the light of Milner IV's argument, their own voices can be seen to overshadow the way in which the central terms become understood. Let us consider, for instance, Nier et al.'s suggestion (2001, p. 313) that the concept of dual identity seemed to be invoked by White participants (when they represented in this case Blacks as a subgroup within a postulated more inclusive group), as well as Dovidio et al.'s suggestion that the notion of dual identity is often invoked by minority groups – as it can offer a counterpoint to the assimilation model (2001, p. 183). My contention is that what is left out of these analyses is that efforts on the part of "minority groups" to *counteract the assimilation perspective* need not be linked to a concept of groupness in the same way as, say, Nier et al. and Dovidio et al. conceptualize it. Koppelman points out in this regard (1996, p. 86) that in the context of the USA, when minorities have tried to re-assert their cultural and social status, there are a variety of ways of deploying "group thinking."[89] And he suggests indeed that "anti-discrimination law" itself – as part of a project of social reconstruction – needs to be coupled with attention to symbolic considerations so as to "disrupt the machineries of universe maintenance," which contributes to the stigmatizing in practice of those ascribed as "belonging" to assigned groups. The strength of this symbolic world, he propounds, "lies largely in its invisibility" (1996, p. 100). To deconstruct the apparent obviousness of the existence of groups "in" the social world, should thus be seen as part of the project of reversing discriminatory practice.

In trying to take into consideration the manner in which categorization can "play a role in the rationalization of the existing social order," Yzerbyt, Rocher, and Schadron point to research in various arenas, including gender and race stereotyping (1997, p. 22). They cite studies suggesting that "people in privileged positions . . . are more willing to endorse an essentialist view of existing social categories than members of the nonprivileged groups" (1997, p. 42). They point out that this makes sense in that essentialism posits that group members' *dispositions* (whether biologically or culturally derived) can be used to explain social outcomes (1997, p. 43). This means that those who "essentialize" are able to neglect/underestimate the impact of *situational factors* in affecting group members' life chances (1997, p. 45). In this (essentialist) reading of groups, then, *social discrimination* as a factor accounting for observed outcomes can be underestimated.

In more recent research by Morton, Hornsey, and Postmes (2009), they set out (through experiments that they conducted in Australia and in Britain) to consider what they call the variable deployment, by people from privileged groups, of essentialist categorization.[90] They explored whether White people's treatment of social

---

[89]Schutte illustrates, for instance, how the meaning of "race" became employed by African Americans as a political category after the civil rights era in the face of evidence of the "continued and intensifying racial disadvantage of African Americans and Hispanics as *groups*, not as individuals" (1995, p. 347, my italics). He suggests that it was in *this context* that in the USA:

> the disadvantaged have realized that the egalitarian rhetoric of the dominant discourse brought them nothing. Instead, group membership has become the basis for achieving a degree of power from a position of disempowerment. (1995, p. 349)

Schutte cites in this regard Outlaw's critical race theoretical approach, where it is understood that organizing around group differences is linked to the demand that social justice be "measured by results" (Outlaw, 1990, p. 60, as cited in Schutte, 1995, p. 349). This tallies with Harris-Lacewell's insistence that Black agency needs to be adequately accounted for in exploring the politics of race (2003).

[90]I became aware of this article through Stephanie Demoulin (in November 2008) after I asked her via e-mail (in relation to an article of hers and colleagues on essentialism and nationalism) "whether any of your research work can be seen as making an intervention in helping people to see social categories as social constructions." I mentioned in my e-mail that "my main interest is on accountability in social research" and that "I am specifically interested in how research can be used to help people to reconsider their ways of thinking/seeing – in this case in regard to social constructions." In her reply she mentioned that Morton and colleagues

categories might vary according to strategic purposes. Their experiments were based on setting up conditions where, in the "White exclusion condition," White people became treated as excluded – in this case, from a prize competition in the experimental situation. The results of their experiments suggest that when essentialism can be deployed as a way of excluding *others*, it tends to be more readily drawn upon; but when their *own* exclusion on the basis of group membership may be at stake, people can invoke, in Morton, Hornsey, and Postmes's terms, a social constructivist understanding of categories. For example, Morton, Hornsey, and Postmes remark, in relation to their Australian study, that "indeed, when race is being used to implicitly exclude their own [on the basis of a posited group membership], prejudiced participants might appear more like social constructivists than essentialists" (2009, p. 45). To explore further what might be driving participants' responses, Morton, Hornsey, and Postmes undertook their related study in Britain (2009, p. 46).

They comment in relation to the British study in particular that "prejudiced participants' de-essentialism of race in response to the exclusion of someone for 'being white'" was mediated by their purported endorsement of egalitarian values (2009, p. 53). That is, "prejudiced participants ... emphasized the value of equality and downplayed the meaningfulness of race" in response to their being excluded (2009, p. 53). In this way, Morton, Hornsey, and Postmes remark, "their responses are likely to be experienced as a principled objection to the use of race" (2009, p. 53).

The results generated by Morton, Hornsey, and Postmes via their studies lend support to those who have argued for the slipperiness of color-blindness as an ideology – such as Collins (2005), and Bonilla-Silva (2006) as discussed further in Chapter 8. Morton, Hornsey, and Postmes themselves state that they believe that it is important to connect experimental psychology to arguments "outside of psychology," where, as they put it, "discussions of essentialism emphasize the fluid, dynamic, and political nature of such beliefs" (2009, p. 36). In this way they aim to develop some bridges between "psychologically oriented research" and research created by those emphasizing the politicized manner of drawing on beliefs/ideology.

What I wish to foreground here is an issue raised by Morton, Hornsey, and Postmes in relation to the status of their findings. In considering their analysis that they undertook, they concede that "although our analysis suggests that essentialist beliefs are strategic constructions, alternative explanations exist" (2009, p. 55). They indicate that one explanation to account for findings that they observed could be that

the emphasis on egalitarian values and de-essentialism of race by prejudiced participants in the "white exclusion" condition was not strategic but genuine. That is, experiencing racial

---

look at how group essentialism is situationally determined. That is, they demonstrate that people use essentialism as a strategic tool in social interaction in order to serve their current goals. It does not answer your question directly but might be a nice article for you to think of ways to *indeed help people deconstruct arbitrary social categories*. (my italics)

I believe, with Demoulin, that this work is relevant in this respect – especially if the experimental approach becomes extended in the way I suggest below.

exclusion directed toward their ingroup might have opened prejudiced participants' eyes to the reality of discrimination. This experience may have caused them to actually become less prejudiced, and thus *truly* more egalitarian and less essentialist in their thinking. (2009, p. 55)

In other words, they suggest that it is possible that the experimental conditions themselves, in which White subjects were subjected to racial exclusion, might have generated an understanding on their part leading to less essentialist thinking (than the researchers observed in the other conditions) about "groupness."

For Morton, Hornsey, and Postmes, the research task is to try to determine the genuineness of these people's expressed beliefs. They indicate that to solve this research problem would require more longitudinal studies and in different social contexts too. As they indicate:

Without examining participants' beliefs across time and contexts, it is impossible to say whether the racial de-essentialism observed in these studies is of the context dependent and strategic kind that we suggest, or reflective of a genuine and enduring change in beliefs. (2009, p. 55)

They conclude by suggesting that it is unlikely that genuine changes of beliefs might have become generated via the experiment (2009, p. 56).

My response to this conclusion of theirs is that possibly the space *can be created* during experimentation to explore – with participants – their way of expressing beliefs following experiences of discrimination, and that this in itself might indeed become then a mechanism to *draw out and discuss issues relating to social categorization*. The question of the "reality" of beliefs that become "observed/generated" then becomes of less import than the question of how experimentation itself *can bring to the fore (and raise to attention) different ways of treating social categories*. I would suggest here, as with my earlier suggestions for using the "debriefing" process as an opportunity to engender critical discussion, that this too could be done in Morton, Horney, and Postmes's studies.

Likewise I would suggest that Dovidio et al.'s (2001) account of how they used different "editorials" to expose different people (defined as non-immigrants) to particular messages in regard to their connection (or not) with those defined as immigrants could have provided an opportunity in later debriefings to explore these possible connections. This again would require that "debriefing" – insofar as it is undertaken as part of the experiment – becomes a *forum for discussion* in which *researchers also take responsibility for the kinds of images which become rendered accessible to participants (via the research)*.

I would suggest that trying to open the space for increased discussion is especially important in the light of the exclusivist thinking associated with essentialism. Leyens et al. have indicated, for instance, that in the context of considerations around nationalism (in different geographical contexts), nationalists refuse to consider that "others" can share with them a "common identity" – because of the supposed (inherent) differences between the groups. They indicate that for these nationalists it is understood that "the differences between the groups may be so fundamental that the groups cannot be perceived as part of a superordinate [inclusive] category" (Leyens et al., 2003, p. 714). Leyens et al. point out that "nationalists will again claim that their refusal is not a racist one, but a radical respect of differences. The 'others' are so different that they should be viewed as belonging to a completely other category" (2003, p. 714). Leyens et al. propose that:

> The theoretical solution is to find conditions where differences between groups are not essentialized. The main weakness of our model and of our research is that we were not yet able to locate such conditions [in their experiments]. (2003, p. 714)

They state that "to solve this problem, we are currently scrutinizing other models or theories" (2003, p. 712). One of these models that they still see as of relevance is the Common Ingroup Identity Model (of which they cite Gaertner and Dovidio, 2000). However, my argument is that just because this model posits identity as something that group members *possess* as a result of their group "membership" (see Dovidio & Gaertner, 1999, p.103), little provision is made theoretically and practically for people to *review the group constructions in terms of their political implications.* The model makes provision for inclusive recategorization – but as Leyens et al. themselves admit, when essentialists consider that the differences between groups requires "others" to be placed in a different category, *they do not include them* as part of the "ingroup." Hence I suggest that researchers need to be specifically alert to the ways in which their research work can itself reinforce this kind of group thinking – through the language used to speak of groups (including so-called ingroups and outgroups). As Gallagher indicates, researchers need to take seriously any possibilities for instantiating an anti-essentialist epistemology or methodology, which would provide scope for, as he puts it, asking questions that "challenge our respondents to think about race as a political category" (2008, p. 176).

My contention, thus, is that Dovidio et al. (2001) do not make sufficient provision for exploring what Omi calls "different forms of power" that may come into effect in relation to social categorization – such as the "power to control resources, the power to push a political agenda, and the power to culturally represent themselves and other groups" (2001, p. 252).

Gaertner and Dovidio might counter-argue that they are clearly aware that often minority groups are expected to conform to the pressures of "white middle-class culture" (1986b, p. 326). They make the point that such pressure to conform is problematic because it precludes "the opportunity for the total aggregate to profit from diversity" (1986b, p. 326). As an example of how "successful" diversity might be generated in the corporate world, they point to Schoennauer's (1967) research suggesting that:

> Successful mergers [between corporations] were associated with an integration pattern in which in the first stage the two management teams joined together without either company being required to conform to the style of the other, followed by a second stage in which the merged company developed a culture that represented a blend of the two corporate cultures. (1986b, p. 326)

But in this example Gaertner and Dovidio do not provide sufficient detail for us to be able to appraise how the dialogue leading to the supposed blend/combination was effected and whether "success" was still possibly defined in terms of some dominant definition thereof.

hooks [sic[91]] takes up the question of how one might begin to address the dominant cultural climate when she suggests that a radical alteration of our culture is needed to revitalize what she calls a "love ethic" (which includes the ethic of caring that I introduced in Chapter 1, Section 1.5.2). In making her plea to revitalize this ethic, she affirms the importance of literature that "invites us to re-evaluate the values that undergird our lives and make choices that affirm our connectedness with others" (2001, p. 94). She elucidates that dimensions of love include "care, commitment, trust, responsibility, respect and knowledge" (2001, p. 94). She expresses disquiet that

> The small groups of people who produce most of the images we see in this [USA] culture have heretofore shown no interest in learning how to represent images of love in ways that will capture and stir our cultural imagination. (2001, p. 95)

She highlights that debates around ways of practicing love seem to be largely lacking in the social fabric (2001, p. 12). This lacuna in turn allows for practices of corporate and other forms of greed to indeed become normative – rather than (re)opened for public discussion (2001, p. 71). She laments that the "hopeful vision of justice and love" evoked by the civil rights and other struggles,[92] and the radical movements thereafter aiming to make the world a "democratic place where resources could be shared" have become all but eroded as "folks stopped talking about love" (2001, p. 107). She points to what she sees as a shift in the way the good life is now being portrayed (since the late 1970s):

> The good life was no longer to be found in community and connection; it was to be found in accumulation and the fulfillment of hedonistic, materialistic desire. In keeping with this shift from a people-oriented to a thing-oriented society, the rich and famous . . . began to be seen as the only relevant cultural icons. (2001, p. 108)

She argues that the worship of money became expressed by privileged people by, for example, ostentatiously "parad[ing] . . . material luxury," while "among the poor and the other underclasses," the worship of money became differently expressed. It became "most evident by the unprecedented increase in the street drug industry, one of the rare locations where capitalism worked well for a few individuals" (2001, p. 109). She summarizes that greed became the order of the day. As she puts it:

---

[91] hooks specifically chooses not to capitalize her name.

[92] She indicates her concern that the sixties' Black Power movement put the emphasis "more on power" than the civil rights movement, which, under the leadership of Martin Luther King, was "fundamentally rooted in a love ethic" (1994, p. 290). She indicates that following what she sees as a shift away from this love ethic in the Black Power movement, "it is not surprising that the sexism that had always undermined the black liberation struggle intensified," as "the equation of freedom with patriarchal manhood became a norm among black political leaders, almost all of whom were male" (1994, p. 291). She points to the positive side of the Black Power movement in its shifting the focus of struggle from reform to revolution in its critique of imperialism. But she feels that despite the apparent "success" of both the civil rights and Black Power movements, "black people collectively experienced intense pain and anguish about our future" (1994, p. 292).

"Mirroring the dominant capitalist culture, a few individuals in poor communities prospered while the vast majority suffered endless unsatisfied cravings" (2001, p. 110).

hooks sets her discussion in a social context in which she states that "one fifth of America's children live in poverty" and "half of our African American children live in poverty" (2001, p. 122), while "we are all witnessing the ever-widening gap between the rich and the poor" (2001, p. 123). By asking readers of her book to notice as problematic our witnessing of the widening gap between rich and poor, hooks appeals to us to question the (dominant) culture of consumption underpinned by an unrestrained and loveless capitalism.

I have offered this account of hooks's way of presenting what she sees as central deficiencies in the arena of public discussion – as a backdrop to showing how her statements/visions of cultural debate move beyond the style of recommendation provided by Nier et al., as also shown in the following section.

3.4.3   Implications of the Status of Nier et al.'s Conclusions for Practical Recommendations

One of the conclusions that Nier et al. suggest can be drawn from both the experiments upon which they report (supported by other research to which they refer) is that the presence of a *common identity*, along with *dual identity representations*, "increased the occurrence of positive attitudes and behaviors [of the White participants] toward Blacks" (2001, p. 313). They go on to suggest that "these positive behaviors" which resulted from the manipulation of the common ingroup identity show that helping behavior can be induced via the creation of a common ingroup identity. As indicated above, they remark that these results "may be critical for providing the sharing of resources . . . and the special assistance that may be important for combating historical disadvantage" (2001, p. 313).

Considering the practical implications of their work in terms of such possibilities, it is worth drawing attention to the tentative character of their conclusions (generalizations) regarding the potential for sharing and caring behavior in the USA (and possibly elsewhere?). That is, they indicate that their results "*may be* critical for providing the sharing of resources . . . and the special assistance" needed for (re)generating policies and practices to combat historical racial disadvantage (2001, p. 313, my italics). Nevertheless, they still seem to propose that the results *do* point in this direction.

In their article they do not offer reasoning as to why they believe that the results could be generalized to settings in which issues of affirmative action, welfare policies, policies on redistributing wealth in other ways, and so on are at stake. Thus it is difficult to engage dialogically with their argument or to widen the discussion so as to include the kinds of issues raised by, for example, hooks (2001) as discussed above. Furthermore, space is not so far generated in their presentation to focus on the broader economic parameters (linked to, say, an exploration of capitalist social relations) that might set limits on what Nier et al. call the "sharing of resources" or contribute to what hooks calls the problem of the widening gap between the rich and the poor, which she explains has racialized dimensions (2001, p. 123).

My suggestion is that it is crucial for Nier et al., as others, to display with caution their view that creation of a common ingroup identity is likely in general to lead to "positive behavior" such as sharing of resources and providing "special assistance." Alternative theoretical angles on this would, at least, need to be alluded to. Interestingly, it is worth noting that Nier et al. state that their results regarding the development of a common ingroup identity "may be *critical* [crucial] for providing the sharing of resources ... and the special assistance that may be important for combating historical disadvantage" (2001, p. 313, my italics). This seems to suggest that Nier et al. regard as paramount for addressing racism the psychological process of seeing people as "ingroup" – so that the necessary "prosocial behavior" can come into play.

As shown in Section 3.4.2, it is possible to take a different starting point so to focus more on the *failure of public discussion to revitalize a sharing and caring cultural orientation*, while at the same time highlighting concerns regarding the power dynamics at play in stultifying this kind of discussion. Such an alternative starting point offers what critical race theorists would call a counternarrative (cf. Parker & Lynn, 2002) that can be brought into the research frame so that differing interpretations and attendant views on recommendations for action can become presented – as a precurser to a wider social dialogue. This would enable us, for instance, to *reopen discussion* around cultural discourses that seems to endorse the notion that, as hooks puts it, "I can only care about you if *you're like me*," as well as the notion that "I can only show compassion toward you if *something in your experience relates to something I've experienced*" (2001, p. 278, my italics). In terms of these considerations, Nier et al.'s pointing to identification of "commonality" as the basis for so-called pro-social behavior become seen as an unduly restrictive perspective – framed by a particular way of setting up the research.

Nyamnjoh, writing from his experiences in Africa, offers a proposal in regard to further possibilities for inviting participant and wider audience discussion in processes of social research – linked to the advent of the internet. He proposes that:

> The scientific community must continue to explore more innovative ways of participation for individuals and communities who have traditionally been acted upon by, rather than interacting with, the researcher. (2007, p. 8)

He argues that the internet

> promises a more interactive research process, wherein informality and equality or electronic democracy can effectively replace the age-old unilinear, elitist model of scientific inquiry and its modes of celebrating achievements [such as its supposed advances in knowledge]. (2007, p. 8)

He sees the internet as providing the potential for the "scientific community" to reconsider issues of research ethics so as to include electronically facilitated innovative styles of interacting with, and relating to, participants and audiences. His suggestions tie in with the arguments of Collins (1990, 2000) and Ladson-Billings (2003) regarding the exemplification via the research endeavor, of (more) dialogical forms of human engagement around the issues seen to be at stake.

In the next section I continue to discuss, and offer alternative angles for envisioning, the research results as presented by Nier et al. I do this by referring to some of the literature on "crossed categorization," which Nier et al. note adds substantiation to their own research work (2001, p. 307).

3.5 Complementary Work on Crossed Categorization (In Various Geographical Contexts)

Nier et al. (2001, p. 307) refer to Crisp and Hewstone's (1999) research on what is called crossed categorization. In this section, I refer in some detail to arguments by Crisp and colleagues, who have undertaken research on crossed categorization in a number of geographical contexts, including Northern Ireland, Britain, and North America (Crisp, Hewstone, & Cairns, 2001; Crisp, Walsh, & Hewstone, 2006; Crisp et al., 2002). After offering an account of this research, in which I show how it relates to work on the Common Ingroup Identity Model, I provide an account of how it too can be revisited.

Crisp et al. state that research into crossed categorization is aimed at describing and explaining "the processes and outcomes that occur when two or more dimensions of group membership become simultaneously salient." They remark that such research is a logical extension of work on "categorization . . . as a pervasive psychological process" (2002, p. 35.) The notion of crossed categorization, they note, was developed to answer the question of whether "people really use multiple categories in person perception." Or, put another way, Crisp et al. ask, "does crossed categorization have any validity as a realistic reflection of intergroup relations?" (2002, p. 36). That is, they indicate that they are considering research around crossed categorization in terms of its helping to advance our understanding of the realities of people's interactions in specific contexts. (As with the research of Dovidio et al., much of Crisp et al.'s work has been conducted in laboratory settings; but, like Dovidio et al., they argue that results can be regarded as holding in settings outside of the laboratory.)

To elucidate the concept of crossed categorization, they give an example of a situation where "race and gender group memberships" become crossed (2002, p. 40). As they state:

> We can define the four composite groups created by, for instance, crossing race and gender group memberships as follows: For the Black female perceiver, other Black females are double in-group members (sharing categorizations on both dimensions of categorization), Black males and White females are mixed group members (sharing a categorization with the perceiver on only one of the two dimensions of categorization) whilst White males are double out-group members. (2002, pp. 40–41)

Crisp et al. refer to the link between their work on crossed categorization and that of Gaertner and Dovidio (and colleagues) on superordinate categorization when they speak about "category inclusiveness," as follows:

> Category inclusiveness can be defined as the extent to which categorization is at a more superordinate level, subsuming other social categorizations in the immediate intergroup context; e.g., "European" is a more inclusive social category than "British" or "French". (2002, p. 50)

They here draw on the account of superordinate categorization in terms of a more inclusive group, as explained in Section 3.3. They propose that just as superordinate categorization "helps to alleviate intergroup bias on a *single subordinate category dimension*" (as argued by, e.g., Gaertner & Dovidio, 2000), so

> making a superordinate categorization salient [such as described in work on common ingroup identity] in a *crossed categorization situation* will promote a reduction in bias, *via recategorization of mixed or double outgroup members into a common ingroup*. (2002, p. 50, my italics)

Much of their experimental work has been aimed at further testing this proposition, by "priming superordinate identity" (2002, p. 51) – inducing people in crossed categorization contexts to feel part of a superordinate group.

Crisp et al. indicate that, in keeping with the Common Ingroup Identity model, their model also addresses decategorization (See Section 3.6.). By providing access to individuating information, which enables participants to see the individuals as indeed individuals, this can lead to "decategorizing the crossed category context" (2002, p. 51). They point out that within the model, recategorization (via superordinate categorization) is "predicted to have the same process and outcome implications as the decategorization effect" (2002, p. 51). In both cases, reductions in bias (across the group lines) are expected.

They proceed to offer an indication of "empirical support for the model" (2002, p. 51). The model includes a consideration of *cognitive* priming (changing patterns of cognitive structure or cognitive representations) as well as *affective* priming (changing perceived mood). They offer an account of the complex links between "cognitive and affective mediators" which can influence people's patterns of responses in intergroup situations (2002, p. 60). They suggest that in considering both cognitive priming and affective priming, it may be best to postulate that there is no need to regard cognitive and affective mediators of people's responses as being mutually exclusive. As they state, it is possible that "the effect of affective moderation are themselves moderated by [cognitive] category salience." They believe that further research work in this direction is required (2002, pp. 64–65).

They explain the import of this kind of research agenda in view of the current world situation:

> In a world that is increasingly characterized by multiple, cross-cutting group affiliations the study of the psychological processes and implications of such intergroup relations is becoming increasingly pertinent. (2002, p. 68)

They propose that while experimental work into crossed categorization is

> still in relative infancy ... the future clarification and refinement of the extant phenomena associated with such complex intergroup affiliation will greatly aid our attempts to understand the nature of social classification, prejudice and intergroup conflict. (2002, p. 68)

3.5.1 Further Exploring the Common Ingroup Identity Model (In Relation to Crossed Category Groups)

In exploring the links between their own further work and the Common Ingroup Identity Model, Crisp et al. (2006) again present the research to date on this. (Their terminology that they use in their presentation is important – as I show in Section 3.5.2.1.)

They point to Gaertner and Dovidio's (2000) review of the model, which they summarize in their own words as follows:

> When perceivers in simple dichotomous categorization settings are encouraged to form a common ingroup identity (i.e. representing members of both groups as included within one overall category), the initial ingroup-favoring bias will disappear due to the enhanced evaluation of previous outgroup members. (2006, p. 1205)

They explain:

> Because both in- and out-group members are then in one overall group, all members of this common group will be perceived as more similar to the self and bias will be attenuated accordingly. (2006, p. 1205)

They indicate that the key mediating variable in such contexts, which is

> responsible for reducing bias in ingroup contexts has been identified as *reduced intercategory differentiation* (i.e. perceivers report that the context feels *less "like two groups"* and *more like "one overall group"*). (2006, p. 1205, my italics)

They go on to consider the results of their own further experiments examining the effects of "a common categorization in complex contexts defined by crossed category groups" (2006, p. 1206), in which they gave specific attention to the importance of the existing categorizations to perceivers. They point to an example where participants (in Britain) were presented with "a list of social categories that they ranked in terms of most and least important." The list of supplied categories was as follows:

- Age (young adult, old adult);
- Political beliefs (labor, conservative);
- Nationality (British citizen, non-British citizen);
- Subject studied (humanities student, science student);
- Childhood environment (urban, rural);
- University affiliation (Aston student, Birmingham student);

- Graduate status (undergraduate student, postgraduate student); and
- Membership of university sports team (team member, not a team member).

Participants were then presented with a sheet of paper with two affiliations from the list that they had ranked (in terms of importance) and asked to circle their own group memberships. Crisp, Walsh, and Hewstone indicate that this was in order to "increase the salience of participants' own group membership" (2006, p. 1209). As part of the experiment, these categories were manipulated in that half of the participants were given the two categories that they rated as most important and half the categories that they rated as least important. Participants were in addition asked a set of questions designed to measure the extent of identification – as a check on the assignment of importance – which Crisp, Walsh, and Hewstone note is a "commonly used measure to assess perceived importance of social identities" (2006, p. 1210). The items to which participants were asked to respond here were as follows (adapted from Hornsey and Hogg, 2000) – with their being instructed to assign scores ranging from 1 (not at all) to 9 (very much):

- "In terms of general attitudes, I feel similar to other ———— [actual groups inserted]."
- "I feel a sense of belonging with other ———— [actual groups inserted]."
- "In general, I like other ———— [actual groups inserted]."

The experiment was designed so that the researchers could examine the effects of an experimental "manipulation of a common ingroup context over and above the two cross-cutting target categorizations" (2006, p. 1209). (For the purposes of my discussion, the details of how they achieved this is less relevant than the way in which they measured what they considered to be the importance of categories to perceivers – as it is this on which I am concentrating in this section.)

They indicate that their findings that arose from their experiment can be linked up with "recent developments in the common ingroup identity literature," namely, findings suggesting that

> simply making a superordinate classification salient does not always reduce intergroup bias but that *recategorization can sometimes be resisted when subgroup identities are important to perceivers* ([e.g.] ... Gaertner & Dovidio, 2000; Hewstone, 1996). (2006, p. 1216, my italics)

They state that this was supported by their own experiment:

> A common identity did [in their research] improve the pattern of evaluations across the crossed category groups, but this was optimally effective when participants did not perceive their original category identities as highly important. (2006, p. 1216)

In conclusion they explain that their results have shown that:

> Adding a further layer of [superordinate] group membership onto the initially complex pattern of affiliation defined by crossed categorizations can lead to predictable variation in evaluations [done by members], and also ... this is further moderated by the perceived importance of these categorizations. (2006, p. 1217)

They elucidate what can be concluded from this research as follows:

These findings add to [the] growing literature by illustrating the complex, but definable, interplay of cognitive and contextual processes involved in multiple social categorizations. (2006, p. 1217)

3.5.2 Revisiting Work on Crossed Categorization in Relation to Group Categorization

In this section I revisit Crisp et al.'s mode of approach – in much the same way as I delved into Nier et al.'s experiments in Section 3.4.

3.5.2.1 Group Membership as a Seemingly "Obvious" Conceptualization

As noted above, Crisp et al. (2006) compare their research work on crossed categorization with work on common ingroup identity. They state that while research to date on the Common Ingroup Identity Model has concentrated on the effects of inducing/generating a common ingroup identity in *simple* contexts of intergroup relations, their crossed categorization model considers the effects of "a common categorization in *complex contexts* defined by crossed category groups." That is, they have extended the Common Ingroup Identity Model to concentrate on people's original representations of *multiple subgroups* and the effects of generating a common ingroup identity in *such* situations (2006, p. 1216).

In outlining findings generated by experimental work on the Common Ingroup Identity Model, they explain that when people recategorize a situation in terms of common ingroup identity, so that "members are then classed in one overall group," what occurs is that "all members of this common group will be perceived as more similar to the self and bias will be attenuated accordingly" (2006, p. 1205). They indicate that the mediating variable here is the extent to which people "*report that the context feels less "like two groups" and more like "one overall group"* (2006, p. 1205, my italics).

But in terms of the argument that I am developing, we should *not take for granted the psychological processes* that they see at play when a common ingroup identity is induced (e.g., via Dovidio et al.'s experiments). Although Crisp et al. may believe they have evidence for the processes which they report coming into play (in their 2006 article, they cite as evidence people's responses to questions concerning whether the situation *feels like one group*), this can be revisited. I would suggest here that there is nothing preventing experimental researchers from *engaging in conversation with participants around matters such as these*. Discussions could, for instance, be generated around what it might mean to speak of a "group" in contexts of social interaction; and what status should be given to social labels identifying (and marking) various groups.

While Crisp et al. might argue that they have made provision for participants to express whether they consider particular categories as important to them, I would suggest that the problem lies in the way this "importance" is studied. Supplying participants with a list of categories and asking them to rank them from least to most important still does not require participants to engage with the issue of the socially constructed character of the groupings. For example, participants may well still consider, say, nationality as referring to "something" that people essentially "have" – even though the possession may be less or more important for different people (see also Footnote 88 in regard to the measurement of national identification). Presenting people with a list and asking them to rank the different social categories *does not raise for consideration the issue of the status of the categories*. I would suggest that in discussion with participants (in some kind of debriefing), the different items on the list could have been used as an opening to ask people to reflect on whether, say, nationality (or for that matter, race as a social category[93]) should be treated similarly to, say, the decision to join a sports team. Moreover, the check that the experimenters undertook on the perceived importance of identity by asking people about whether they "feel similar" to others, whether they feel a sense of "belonging," and whether they "like" others (in that category) preframes people's thinking about categories. As I have argued in earlier sections, this itself becomes hyperaccessible as a way of conceiving categories – and researchers therefore need to take more seriously the issue of how they present "options for thinking" to participants.

Hence, while Crisp et al.'s work could conceivably open up avenues for us to explore further what they call the "contextual processes involved in multiple social categorizations" (2006, p. 1217), my concern is with the way in which experiments have been set up to make findings in terms of specific framings. As I see it, the way their experiments are set up (including the way measurements of "importance of categories" and of "social identifications" are undertaken) does not create sufficient space for participants and others to *reflect upon the standing of the constructions*. The point I wish to emphasize here – as in Section 3.4.1 – is that researchers need to be cognizant of the way in which their uses of categories could contribute to reinforcing *essentialist treatment* hereof in society, and that this itself is not without social consequence. (In responding to my argument developed in this book and offering her commentary – May 2009 – Janet McIntyre-Mills summarized well for me that "your [my] book explores the way in which research designs can construct or deconstruct racism"; and she points out that I am imploring people to be mindful hereof.)

Louis casts additional light on the problem of people tending to essentialize group categorizations when he points out that "within the racial paradigm, ostensibly benign descriptions of difference and sameness are never that, but [are] placed in hierarchical order through their relationship to each other" (2005, p. 360). The (group) thinking in terms of identities "possessed" by people, which marks their "differences" from one another, thus itself cannot be considered to be benign. He notes in this respect that interestingly, the effect of the "native-/foreign-born

---

[93]In the research cited by Crisp et al. (2006), they did not use race(d) categories – but used other ones in their effort to consider the effects of importance to perceivers of defined social categories.

dichotomy" in the USA to mark a distinction between African Americans born in the USA and African immigrants seems not to have punctured the salience of race in people's consciousness. Those Africans who are foreign born are seen as demonstrating "a culture of industry and discipline, while the native-born are taken to represent a 'culture of poverty' that is seen as innate to their character" (2005, p. 360). Thus the understanding of seemingly innate (essential) qualities continues to be racialized – but now in increasingly cultural terms. (See also my discussion of cultural racism in Chapter 2, Section 2.3.4.)

Louis argues that in our attempts to understand the "symbolic and material meanings of racialized identification [we] might usefully *pause for reflection* on the substantive, ethical, and political basis of that identity" (2005, p. 361, my italics). Taking on board Louis's caution to "pause for reflection," my concern is that Crisp and colleagues' work is not set up to provide the opportunity for us (as participants and audiences of the research) to pause to *reconsider the meaning(s) of "group membership."*

3.5.2.2 Reviewing the "Empirically Observed" Everyday Use of Categories Such as Race and Gender: Posing an Intersectional Alternative

In outlining their views on social categorization Crisp, Hewstone, and Cairns attempt to engage with the question of how the identification of groups along the dimensions of, for example, race and gender proceeds in everyday life. As part of their consideration hereof, they cite research referring to the socially used distinction between what they call "more general characteristics of an individual (e.g. gender or race)," and "more specific details (e.g. occupation)" (2001, p. 504). They suggest that there is empirical evidence demonstrating "the relative primacy" of the more "general" characteristics over more "specific attributes." For instance, they cite research by Stangor, Lynch, Duan, and Glass (1992) showing that

> participants used categories such as gender and race to categorize individuals who could potentially be categorized in any number of other ways. More specific bases for classification (e.g. style of dress) were used less . . . . (2001, pp. 504–505)

However, it is important to note that the manner in which this use of categories is "measured empirically" by the researchers is by referring to the way participants in everyday life appear to utilize group categorizations *when a number of "categories" are made available to them.* What is not considered is whether, if other options for treating the status of "categorizations" were presented, people *might be able to rethink their way of employing the social categorizations.* Also, to say that it has been empirically demonstrated that people do tend to use categories such as race and gender in preference to "more specific bases of classification," is to assume that the other bases *are obviously* "more specific." But what we now refer to as specific attributes (such as occupation, dress style, etc.) could conceivably be considered by people socialized differently as being of more general interest. For instance, a concern with the lifestyle choices adopted by people (of which dress style could be an indicator) could become a more central concern in certain contexts and for certain observers. Furthermore, the apparently obvious group categorizations based on the dimensions of race and gender *can be conceptualized (by professional researchers and others) as open to de- and re-construction in processes of social interaction.* This would mean that the "multiple categorizations" to which Crisp, Walsh, and Hewstone point (2006), and which their research invokes, *could be understood to be (and to become) more open to revision than their theorizing suggests.*

Focusing on the definition of "gender," Squires and Weldes (2007) indicate how theorizing around this is increasingly challenging the assumption that "sex is a stable category around which gendered identities are constructed" (2007, p. 186). They explain that "the category of 'sex' itself comes under scrutiny" as theorists – such as, for example, Haraway (1991) – "challenge the idea of 'being' male or female'" (2007, p. 186). They explain further that theorizing around the notion of *intersectionality* – as in the work of, for instance, Anthias and Yuval-Davis (1983), Collins (1999), and Yuval-Davis (2006) – amounts to defining gender in terms of its linkage to other systems of unequal power relationships (such as those based on race or class).[94] Gender is here defined as a "constellation of ideas and social practices that are historically situated within, and that mutually construct, multiple systems of oppression" (2007, p. 187). The term intersectionality thus opens a way for trying to situate historically, while re-examining the status of, constructed categories in terms of their embeddedness in systems of oppression that, in Squires and Weldes's terms, "reflects an intersection of multiple forms of discrimination."

It is significant in this regard that Omi and Winant argue that not only can "gender" and "race" be recognized to be fluid constructions,[95] but also even the concept of *class* need not be theorized in terms of a fixed notion of it. Hence they make the point that "a static and fixed notion of class provides little room for understanding how race (and gender) could shape class categories, consciousness and organization" (2002b, p. 456).[96] They point in this respect to research highlighting, inter alia, "our continuing capacity to reinterpret the meaning of relationships and identities in social interaction" (2002b, p. 457).

Essed and Goldberg further highlight that theorizing can involve not only *pointing to* potential fluidity, but making space for *encouraging* it. Hence, when discussing the work of Markus in their Introduction to their edited book *Race*

---

[94]Squires and Weldes state that the term intersectionality emerged in Britain at the end of the 1970s in relation to the triple oppression of Black working-class women, and was popularized by Crenshaw in the USA in the 1990s (2007, p. 187). But they aver that in Crenshaw's account (1991), the different axes of discrimination are still seen as distinct rather than as *mutually constructive* of each other. They suggest that in a transversal politics this mutuality is what becomes focused upon.

[95]Omi and Winant make the point that there is no reason to regard gender as being different from race on the supposed ground that gender has some biological basis (based on the biological division of humans into sexes). But they note that because of the biological division of humans into sexes (two at least, and possibly intermediate ones), people have been able to resort to arguments invoking so-called natural gender divisions. They indicate that no equivalent arguments can be invoked in relation to race categorizations (2002a, p. 139, Note 1).

[96]They indicate that to theorize in this way, implies a "rethinking of Marxism." See my discussion on structurally oriented theorizing, including Marxist theorizing, in Chapter 8.

Critical Theories (2002), they note that "Markus ... drawing from her own experiences of migration, encourages us not only to *shift*, but to *lift boundaries* of taken-for-granted identifications" (Essed & Goldberg, 2002, p. 10, my italics). I discuss Essed's methodological arguments, and her way of instantiating research around intersectionality, in Chapter 5. At present I wish to make the point that work on intersectionality can offer an alternative way than that provided by Crisp and colleagues for viewing processes of social categorization.

3.6 Decategorization in Relation to the Understanding of Group Categorization

Both Nier et al. and Crisp et al. cite the research work that Brewer and Miller (1984, 1996) have undertaken on decategorization. (See also Fig. 3.1.) In order to show how this work relates to work on the Common Ingroup Identity Model supported by Nier et al. (2001) and Crisp et al. (2002), I refer to Miller's (2002) exposition – in which he presents a summary account of the process of decategorization.

With respect to Brewer and Miller's (1984) conceptualization, Miller explains that decategorization can firstly take the form of *differentiation* (2002, p. 390). That is, it can involve what he calls "differentiated perceptions of ingroup and outgroup members." In this process, the perceiver notices "differences among [different] group members" in terms of an understanding of "group variability" (2002, p. 391).

Miller explains that in Brewer and Miller's (1984) account, decategorization can also take the form of *personalization*. Here, group membership is "relatively unimportant." Instead, persons are categorized primarily in terms of their "similarity or dissimilarity to self":

Miller elucidates the difference between these two kinds of (decategorized) responding as follows:

> In *differentiated* responding, information about a given category member is processed in terms of a prototype of the category. When processing information in this mode one assesses whether the individual *fits the prototype well or poorly*. (2002, p. 391, my italics)

In contrast, in more *personalized* interaction,

> the key comparison process involved in noting the important attributes of another person is *not made with respect to the groups to which that other and oneself respectively belong*. Instead, attributes of the other are noted primarily in terms of self-other comparisons. (2002, p. 391, my italics)

Interestingly, Miller still draws on the idea that individuals – even those involved in what he calls "personalized interaction" – still belong to groups; hence he speaks of the groups to which they "respectively belong." This relates to Miller and Brewer's (1986) definition of personalized interaction as a process in which the actor operates by "*reducing the role* that category membership plays" (1986, p. 216, my italics). As Miller explains it, reducing the role that category membership plays clearly does not mean that the categories themselves are *given a different status* in people's consciousness (as, for example, fluid and socially contingent social constructions, as I mentioned as possibilities in Section 3.4.1). Miller himself remarks that decategorization in social life does "not necessarily imply a perceptual elimination of the category boundaries that differentiate the ingroup from the outgroup" (2002, p. 395).

Johnston and Hewstone (1990) concur with this understanding of Miller when they point to the social advantages of the practice – even in processes involving decategorization – of actors "maintain[ing] group boundaries" in their cognitions. They suggest that the development of contacts between people then becomes a process in which the "positive effects" of interacting with individual members from "other" groups (i.e., of so-called outgroups) can then be "generalized to all outgroup members." In other words, personalized contact then becomes helpful in ensuring the "acceptance of the whole group and not just selected individuals" (1990, p. 193). They thus make the point that Brewer and Miller should not over-emphasize "the need for increased differentiation and personalization of groups, in order to enhance the development of interpersonal relationships" (1990, p. 193).

Miller for his part notes that experimental work that has been undertaken on decategorization is consistent with the work of Gaertner and Dovidio in relation to the Common Ingroup Identity Model. He describes the Common Ingroup Identity Model as postulating that

> bias toward outgroup members is reduced by changing a person's perception of an intergroup context from one that involves members of different groups to one that involves members of a single common or superordinate group. Former outgroup members are recategorized as ingroup members within a superordinate category that they respectively share with one another. (2002, p. 393)

Relating his understanding of social processes of decategorization to the Common Ingroup Identity Model, Miller suggests that, aside from differentiation and personalization,

> decategorization can also be achieved by applying, or making salient, a superordinate identity. Thus decategorization is a broader concept than individuation or differentiation among group members. (2002, p. 395)

Miller considers that what authors such as Gaertner and Dovidio call making salient a "superordinate category" (to enable people to regard each other anew in terms of an inclusive category) is similar to (and indeed can be called a kind of) decategorization. He argues that further research work is required to try to establish the effects of different strategies (such as differentiation, personalization, and recategorization) in terms of their "beneficial effects" for intergroup relations (2002, p. 407). But he believes that his discussion "may succeed in adding useful or constructive nuances to one small portion of the palette from which intergroup research and interventions are drawn" (2002, p. 407).

What I wish to highlight in relation to Brewer and Miller's (1984, 1986), and Miller's (2002) argument, is their continued acceptance – within their understanding of various options for "decategorizing – of people's conceptions of *being "members" of groups.* Thus, as in Nier et al.'s and Crisp et al.'s work, they do not explore possibilities for subjects (via the relevant experiments) to review the status assigned to social categorizations by the researchers and others – and *to reflect on their character as social constructions*. In subsequent chapters, I offer accounts of research approaches that are geared to focusing more on the social processes of producing social constructions – and I point to their potential to point to options for deconstruction. But as I indicated when discussing, for example, Morton, Hornsey, and Postmes's experimentation (2009), as well as possibilities for shifting Nier et al.'s research style, I believe that these options need not be precluded by experimental designs.

In the next section I discuss as an innovative style of experimentation an experiment by Monteith, Voils, and Ashburn-Nardo (2001) in which they expressly set out to create an intervention at the moment of doing the experiment (in relation to White people's implicit racial associations). Following my discussion hereof, I explore further research by Ashburn-Nardo et al. (2007) with African American participants. After revisiting both of these studies and offering an indication of how they could be constructively extended, I turn to other researchers' suggestions for exploring people's implicit associations (and considering possibilities for category redefinition).

3.7 Monteith, Voils, and Ashburn-Nardo's Experiment: Exploring White People's Reactions to Implicit Racial Bias (Kentucky, USA)

In this section I concentrate on discussing the experiment by Monteith, Voils, and Ashburn-Nardo (2001) in which they set out, while organizing the experiment, to create opportunities for White people self-regulating their (otherwise unreflected upon) responses to Blacks. I consider that their approach – appropriately extended – offers an interesting way of researching, while making people more conscious of, their racialized responses. Nevertheless, their research still takes as read that, as Monteith and Winters remark, there appears to be "ample evidence" to back up the science behind social identity theory (2002, p. 49) – which posits the "deep-seated drive" to categorize in terms of "us" and "them." Given this understanding of identity theory, they ask the question: "If categorization and bias come so easily, are people doomed to xenophobia and racism?" (2002, p. 49). They explain their own position in relation to this question:

> It's pretty clear that we are susceptible to prejudice and that there is an unconscious desire to divide the world into "us" and "them". Fortunately, however, new research [such as the research discussed below] also shows that prejudices are fluid and that when we become conscious of our biases we can take active – and successful – steps to combat them. (2002, p. 50)

I now examine in some detail Monteith, Voils, and Ashburn-Nardo's study (2001), in which they tried, inter alia, to render White participants more conscious of biases that they may hold at an implicit level. I show in the course of my discussion that Monteith and colleagues' understanding of identity theory and its supposed scientific backing too can become revisited.

3.7.1 The Social Context of the Experiment and Its Goals

Monteith, Voils, and Ashburn-Nardo (2001) elucidate the contemporary social context for their experiment in terms of their understanding that White people today are less inclined to express racial prejudice as such in *blatant* form. They cite favorably Dovidio's work (along with that of other authors) in this respect (2001, p. 395). But they contend that empirical research around racial biases that may be operative outside of conscious awareness has thus far not focused sufficiently on whether, given the chance to "look underground," people are "willing and able to attribute their responses to prejudiced tendencies" (2001, p. 396).

They note that they consider this to be an important question to address because "awareness of subtle biases and willingness to attribute them to internal forces are critical for learning to control them" (2001, p. 396). It is for this reason they consider it worthwhile to offer "lay persons the opportunity to take a look underground at their own implicit racial biases" (2001, p. 397). One way of "looking underground" is via *IATs* – as in Greenwald, McGhee, and Schwartz's research (1998). This refers to a process of testing that is designed to measure people's implicit preferences – operating outside their immediate conscious awareness. (The word "implicit" here suggests attitudes held at a level below people's conscious appreciation; that is, attitudes normally hidden from consciousness.[97]) Fazio and Olson provide a succinct account of the IAT procedure as developed by Greenwald, McGhee, and Schwartz:

> In the Greenwald et al. (1998) IAT concerning racial attitudes, participants were first asked to categorize names (e.g., "Latonya" or "Betsy") as typical of blacks versus whites. Here, race is the target concept and the keys are labeled "black" and "white." Participants then categorized a variety of clearly valenced words (e.g., "poison" or "gift") as pleasant or unpleasant, which constitutes the attribute dimension. In the critical phase of the experiment these two categorization tasks were combined. Participants performed this combined task twice – once with one response key signifying black/pleasant and the other labeled white/unpleasant, and once with one key meaning black/unpleasant and the other white/pleasant – in counterbalanced order. The question concerns *which response mapping participants find easier to use.* (Fazio & Olson, 2003, p. 299, my italics)

---

[97] De Houwer, Geldof, and De Bruycker (2005, p. 237) suggest that we can consider the IAT as "measuring similarity between fairly complex stimuli and concepts in an *indirect* manner (my italics)." They consider that it is advisable to use the word *indirect* to refer to the *manner in which we are measuring* (in this case, through *indirect means* - rather than through directly posing questions to respondents). This avoids confusion between the manner of measuring (e.g., *direct* or *indirect*) and what is supposedly being measured (e.g., *explicit* or more *implicit* attitudes). See also De Houwer (2001, 2003, 2006) in this regard.

Monteith, Voils, and Ashburn Nardo likewise elucidate that in terms of the IAT procedure, automatic racial bias on the part of Whites is revealed "if Whites have an easier time pairing White names with pleasant stimuli and Black names with unpleasant stimuli than the reverse (i.e., Black names with pleasant stimuli and White names with unpleasant stimuli)" (2001, p. 397).[98] In the research reported upon in their article (2001), Monteith, Voils, and Ashburn Nardo mention that several goals were operative:

1. Firstly, they wanted to examine the magnitude of relation between IAT performance – how (White) participants fared on the IAT – and reports of "feeling" the IAT effect (i.e., a sense on the part of participants that they had shown some hidden bias). The researchers were interested in knowing whether only those who have an especially strong IAT bias (as measured by the IAT test) were able to detect this, or whether such detection is more general (2001, p. 397).
2. Secondly, they were interested in "how people interpret and react to the detection of biased performance on the IAT" (2001, p. 397). They mention that it is of course possible that even if people "feel" the IAT effect, they may differ in their interpretations thereof.
3. Thirdly, they were interested in exploring the possible moderating effect of individual differences on IAT performance and reactions to such performance. They explored this in the light of previous findings regarding discrepancies between how Whites report that they *should* respond in a variety of situations that involve Blacks, based on their beliefs about what is appropriate, and their reports about how they *would* respond in such situations. The "difference between participants' *should* and *would* ratings is taken for each scenario to index the extent to which people would respond with greater prejudice than they believe is appropriate" – that is, the extent to which there is a discrepancy (in each case). Monteith Voils, and Ashburn-Nardo indicate that they were considering the role that "self-reported proneness to discrepancies would play in people's interpretations of and

---

[98] Brendl, Markman, and Messner qualify the significance of IAT tests (done to assess people's biases) by noting that "an IAT effect does not unambiguously indicate prejudice, because it can have multiple causes" (2001, p. 769). For instance, "the influence of familiarity [with names used in the test] compromises the IAT as an ambiguous marker" (2001, p. 770). Also, when two groups are measured [by respondents] relative to one another, it is possible for one group to be preferred to another without the second group being evaluated negatively (2001, p. 770). The IAT thus appears to measure only "relative preferences" and not necessarily *prejudice* against others. (Greenwald, 2008, agrees that we need not consider that *prejudice* is being measured, but rather, *implicit preferences*.) Other authors have argued that IAT tests may not necessarily be measuring individual people's evaluative responses to the categories (e.g., Black and White), but may be measuring the prevalence of *stereotypical images* in the society in general. (For instance, Nier, 2006 points to controversies around whether White Americans' performance on the IAT could be reflecting "their knowledge of these negative stereotypes" (existing in the society). Meanwhile, other authors ask questions concerning the stability of IAT effects. They suggest that effects as observed by researchers depend crucially on how the tests are administered. (See Section 3.10.)

reactions to their IAT performance" (2001, p, 399). They wondered whether people would "experience negative self-directed affect (e.g. guilt) when they realized they had engaged in prejudiced response" (2001, p. 399). They were also interested in the implications of raising awareness of discrepant responses for the subsequent self-regulation of prejudiced responses.

Monteith, Voils, and Ashburn-Nardo designed the research to examine these three areas of interest, using as participants students studying Psychology at the University of Kentucky. They indicate that "prejudice and discrepancy scores" were obtained through a mass survey that had been administered earlier, and participants (79 of them) were recruited telephonically from this larger pool. They received research credits toward their Introductory Psychology course in return for participating in the experiment (2001, p. 400). These participants began their involvement in the experiment by completing the IAT tests – after a White experimenter had explained the task to them (2001, p. 402).[99] After they completed the IAT, the experimenter provided them with a questionnaire. This was aimed at assessing their awareness of the extent to which they showed bias on the IAT, as well as their affective reactions to any biases they may have had (2001, p. 403). As part of the questionnaire, participants were asked whether they thought they were particularly slow or particularly fast on some parts of the IAT test. They were asked to consider their slowness and fastness in regard to the classification of various presented stimuli:

- White and Black names;
- Pleasant and unpleasant words;
- White names paired with pleasant words;
- Black names paired with unpleasant words;
- White names paired with unpleasant words; and
- Black names paired with pleasant words.

Participants were also asked in the questionnaire – via an open-ended question – to speculate as to why they may have been especially slow for certain conditions (trials). Their speculations were later examined (through content-analysis) to consider the way in which they explained any perceived difficulties with the IAT. The questionnaire also asked people how they felt "as a consequence of the experimental procedures": They were asked to indicate how they felt about the task by circling a number between 1 (=does not apply) and 7 (=applies very much) on 32 affect items (2001, p. 404). This was designed to ascertain the existence and extent of any negative feelings about their own biases (as measured by the IAT tests) that

---

[99]Although Monteith, Voils, and Ashburn-Nardo do not specify that the participants too were White, this becomes evident from the context of the rest of the article, aimed at exploring White people's prejudicial responses.

people might have experienced when their scores were revealed to them by the researchers.

3.7.2 Monteith, Voils, and Ashburn-Nardo's Discussion of Results Generated via the Research

Considering the results regarding the IAT scores, Monteith, Voils, and Ashburn-Nardo indicate that "only four participants had negative IAT scores, such that they responded faster on incongruent trials than on congruent trials" (2001, p. 405). (i.e., they responded faster to Black American names paired with pleasant words and White American names paired with unpleasant words than to Black American names paired with unpleasant words and White American names paired with pleasant words.) The rest showed a bias in favor of Whites – although there was a "good deal of variability in the extent of bias" shown by the different participants (2001, p. 405).

The researchers examined statistically the relationship between participants' actual IAT scores and their own detection (recognition) of an IAT bias. A moderate-sized correlation was found. Monteith, Voils, and Ashburn-Nardo point out that the fact that there was not a strong correlation here indicates that "it is not just participants who have an especially strong IAT bias who can feel the IAT effect" (2001, p. 406).

The next question Monteith, Voils, and Ashburn-Nardo explored was how people themselves react to and interpret a biased IAT performance (i.e., how they react to their bias as measured by the IAT test). This was examined by considering the "affect [feelings] they reported in relation to the IAT task" (2001, p. 406). An examination of the affect indexes showed that, interestingly, the (statistical) relationship between the actual extent of IAT bias and negself (negative feelings about one's reactions) was not significant. This suggests that it is the person's "detection of IAT bias [that] drives negself feelings rather than the magnitude of IAT bias" (2001, p. 407).

Monteith, Voils, and Ashburn-Nardo also content-analyzed participants' written explanations for why they thought they were particularly slow on certain trials. This was in order to determine how the participants interpreted their IAT performance. The responses were coded according to three categories: One coding category was used if people indicated that racial associations or stereotypes caused a slowing of response; another coding category was used if people indicated that color associations caused the slowing; and a third coding category was used when the response had nothing to do with race or color (e.g., if people mentioned the fact that "Black names are unfamiliar and harder, so they went better with the unpleasant words" or "I know this is a test on racial bias, but I felt that since the White names were paired with the pleasant things first, that set the pattern") (2001, p. 407). The results of the coding were that 37% of people did attribute their slowness to race or stereotypical reactions. And (as would be expected) "participants who interpreted their biased

IAT performance as related to racial associations tended to report greater feelings of guilt than participants who made other attributions of their performance" (2001, pp. 407–408).

Monteith, Voils, and Ashburn-Nardo were further interested in establishing whether participants who self-report a discrepancy between their standards and their actual behavior (as measured by *should/would* discrepancy scales) are "less prone to automatic associations revealed by the IAT than other participants" (2001, p. 408). In addition, they wished to establish whether discrepancy scores were related to participants' detection of their own IAT biases, as well as to their interpretations of and reactions to this detection. The findings indicate that

> participants who reported that they were not prone to discrepancies showed just as much evidence of implicit racial bias as their discrepancy-prone counterparts and were just as likely to detect the IAT effect. However, they were less likely to feel guilty in relation to their IAT bias and were less likely to interpret the bias as reflecting race-related factors. (2001, p. 411)

The researchers' overall understanding is that completing the IAT and having the opportunity to detect a biased IAT performance can serve to "highlight implicit racial biases for some individuals" – while other individuals explained the bias with reference to nonracial factors (2001, p. 411). They remark that:

> The finding that many individuals (particularly those who are discrepancy-prone) recognized their implicit biases, and felt guilty in relation to them, increased our confidence that many people are willing to detect prejudiced responses when they occur and self-regulate in relation to them. (2001, p. 412)

They conclude that tools such as the IAT may be useful devices to provide people with self-insight into racial bias and may indeed allow them to self-reflect on their way of interacting with others. For example, they indicate that

> perpetrators of discrimination may well recognize that their group discriminates against others but, because of the unsettling and image-threatening effects of recognizing personal discrimination within oneself ... people may be motivated to deny it at the personal level. (2001, pp. 413–414)

According to Monteith, Voils, and Ashburn-Nardo, when faced with a biased IAT performance and the possibility of detecting and interpreting their score, this may lead people to be more *self-conscious* about their own way of responding in future behavior. However, they comment that one disturbing finding from the research is that low-prejudice participants with small discrepancy scores "were resistant to interpreting their IAT performance as having anything to do with racial biases, and they did not feel guilty about their biased performance" (2001, p. 415). This implies (for the researchers) that it is possible that people sometimes do respond in prejudiced ways, but do not recognize their responses as prejudiced or self-regulate in relation to them" (2001, p. 415). They make the final point that

> people cannot possibly gain control over a process or its effects if they are not aware that the process is occurring .... This underscores the crucial need to encourage people to take a look underground at their implicit racial biases. (2001, p. 415)

3.8 Ashburn-Nardo et al.'s Related Work with African American Participants (Kentucky, USA)

While Monteith, Voils, and Ashburn-Nardo (2001) directed their experiment toward trying to assess and at the same time render White people more aware of possible racial biases, Ashburn-Nardo et al. (2007) organized an experiment with 316 African American students (with all but 7 attending the University of Kentucky). During this experiment – with White experimenters being employed in 65% of the sessions and non-White ones in 24.3% thereof[100] – the students completed, among other things, a "typical racial IAT." They also completed some self-report questionnaires in which the researchers were trying to measure the constructs of "Black cultural immersion, ingroup identity, perceived ingroup directed prejudice, psychological well-being and psychological distress" (2007, p. 477). Participants completed the study individually – that is, they individually completed the IAT and the packet of self-report questionnaires.

To measure the construct of *Black cultural immersion*, students were asked to report on the following percentages (with greater values indicating deeper immersion):

1. What percentage of your parents' friends was Black?
2. While you were growing up, what percentage of your friends was Black?
3. While you were growing up, what percentage of your close friends was Black?

To measure the construct of *ingroup identity*, students completed the "eight-item racial centrality subscale of the Multidimensional Inventory of Black identity," as developed by Sellers et al. (1998). The items included questions such as "In general, being Black is an important part of my self-identity" – and were aimed at "assessing the degree of overlap between self and racial ingroup" (2007, p. 477).

To measure *perceived ingroup directed prejudice*, the researchers drew on a number of scales, including items such as "I believe that most Whites think they are superior to Blacks" and "Blacks are not respected by the broader society." Ashburn-Nardo et al. explain that these items "assess the extent to which participants believe that Whites or society at large hold their ingroup in negative esteem" (2007, p. 477). Items were also included to "assess the degree to which participants have been or expect to be mistreated due to their race" (2007, p. 477).

To measure *psychological well-being*, questions from scales designed to assess self-esteem, satisfaction with life, and hope were used; and to measure *psychological distress*, a depression inventory was used (2007, p. 478).

---

[100]Data on this was missing for some sessions (10.7% of them) due to recording errors (2007, p. 476). And Ashburn-Nardo et al. indicate that there were "too few instances of Black experimenters to differentiate non-White experimenters" (2007, p. 478).

The researchers were trying to explore during this study different "theoretical perspectives" in relation to the link between ingroup identity, people's understandings of perceived prejudice toward their ingroup, and the possible role of Black cultural immersion in affecting implicit racial attitudes, ingroup identity, and psychological health. They were also trying to establish the direction of certain causal relationships, such, as, say, identity as an *antecedent* of perceived (ingroup directed) prejudice; identity as a *consequence* of perceived prejudice; and identity as a *moderator* of perceived prejudice (2007, p. 474).

In commenting on their use of the IAT within the study, Ashburn-Nardo et al. point out that "in the study of racial prejudice, most of the research employing implicit methodology has focused on Whites' implicit attitudes." But they note that there have been some recent studies assessing the attitudes of African Americans. On average, these studies have found that African American samples "have exhibited either a lack of implicit ingroup bias ... or an implicit preference for Whites" (2007, p. 473).

Because Ashburn-Nardo et al. are aware of the debate around whether IAT scores could be argued to be assessing *extra-personal* culturally acquired associations/stereotypes (in relation to White and Black people) rather than people's *personal* attitudes, they tried to deal with this by administering to a separate sample (of 60 students) a modified IAT (2007, p. 485). In this IAT, the category label *pleasant* (which could be argued to be associated with general ideas in society of what is regarded as pleasant) is replaced by *I like*; and *unpleasant* by *I don't like*. This they considered (following Olson and Fazio, 2004) would make people's *personal evaluations* more salient (instead of their responses being reflective of socially available and socially rehearsed responses to Black and White people). But they point out that despite organizing this IAT, their participants who completed this one did not fare differently (in terms of exhibiting different associations/evaluations) from the participants who filled in the original IAT. As they note:

> If the original IAT is susceptible to extrapersonal influences [from the larger society] ... then one would expect participants to exhibit less favorable ingroup associations [in this case, in relation to Black people] on the original versus the modified IAT. This was not the case. Rather, means and standard deviations were comparable across IAT versions. (2007, p. 485)

One of the findings of their study was that the implicit racial attitudes (as measured by the IAT) "predicted both well-being and distress, such that implicitly favoring their ingroup relative to Whites was associated with more positive psychological functioning and less depression" (2007, p. 482). They argue that to their knowledge "this is the first empirical demonstration of the personal significance of such associations for the global mental health of a stigmatized group" (2007, p. 482).

As far as the variable of "identity" is concerned, where the researchers were looking to see whether it seemed to function as an *antecedent*, *consequent*, or *moderator* of perceived prejudice, they found that "identity appeared to function as a 'resource' for stigmatized persons ... resulting from their experiences with, and perceptions of, prejudice" (2007, p. 483).

And as far as the variable of "Black cultural immersion" (developing Black cultural ties through contacts with Black people) was concerned, they found that "Black cultural immersion did not directly predict either psychological well-being or psychological distress." But they found that implicit racial attitudes (as measured by the IAT), ingroup identity, and perceived prejudice toward their ingroup, *did* predict well-being or distress (2007, p. 484). They furthermore point out that "racial attitudes appear to stem from an immersion in Black culture at an early age" (2007, p. 486).

They indicate that overall from the study "what is clear is that there is nothing straightforward about these variables and their implications for psychological health" (2007, p. 486). In the light of their own and previous findings they state that:

> It is perhaps safest to conclude that ingroup identity and perceived prejudice operate in a cyclical manner, with stronger identity increasing one's awareness of ingroup-directed prejudice, and increased perceptions of prejudice strengthening ingroup ties and ultimately protecting individuals from further psychological harm. (2007, p. 486)

They state their conclusion (and attendant recommendation) thus:

> In conclusion, our results suggest that providing good models of and encouraging close relationships with ingroup members from an early age are good pieces of advice for promoting positive ingroup identity, and, in turn, psychological welfare in stigmatized persons. Although this strategy may also increase attention to ingroup-directed prejudice, the negative effects appear to be outweighed by the benefits. (2007, p. 487)

Ashburn-Nardo et al. thus consider that strategies to increase a sense of ingroup identity among, in this case, African Americans are recommended in terms of the results of their research.

3.9 Revisiting Monteith, Voils, and Ashburn-Nardo's and Ashburn-Nardo et al.'s Experiments

3.9.1 Revisiting the Experiment with White Participants

Monteith, Voils, and Ashburn-Nardo suggest that in this experiment, the participants were offered a device – via the IAT – to rethink their way of relating to others. Helping people to "look underground," they hoped, could bring more to the surface people's favored responses, as a precurser to people self-regulating them. Their argument in this regard tallies to some extent with Douglas's suggestion that prejudice (or what can here be called "implicit preferences[101]") can be seen as operating as "sets of unconscious coded and programmed messages" that allow people to "act

---

[101] Greenwald indicates that he and Banaji use the term *preference* (rather than prejudice) in order to avoid using the unqualified word "prejudice" when considering what the IAT may be measuring. He suggests that this is because "prejudice" is "ordinarily understood as a state of mind that leads to *intentional* discriminatory behavior" (2008, p. 4, my italics).

quickly in a complex world" (1998, Chapter 10, p. 17). Douglas indicates that in terms of this understanding, the challenging of prejudice means that we have to first "raise it to the conscious mind and question a part of an individual's organizing frame for engaging with the world" (1998, Chapter 10, p. 17).[102]

I would suggest that Monteith, Voils, and Ashburn-Nardo have tried to develop an innovative way of using experiments as a possible mechanism for creating, in Douglas's terms, a reframing of, in this case, White people's "software/programming" for engaging with the world. Douglas indicates, nevertheless, that in her experience as a Black woman manager (and as action researcher in a variety of institutional contexts in Britain – see Chapter 5 and Chapter 7 below) trying to challenge one's cognitive software "produces high anxiety, defenses, and resistance." For this reason, she suggests that unlearning prejudice requires what she calls "higher order learning." Douglas's view is that processes for developing higher-order learning go beyond merely cognitive reprocessing, and require work to be done around people's "anxieties" (1998, Chapter 10, p. 17). This caution of Douglas needs to be borne in mind when considering the potential of interventive experiments such as Monteith, Voils, and Ashburn-Nardo's one to develop "regulation" of people's responses in practice.

However, what I would like to raise at this point when considering Monteith, Voils, and Ashburn-Nardo's research with the participants and its potential for intervention is the way in which they set up the experimental design so that the researchers themselves could adjudicate on the meaning of the IAT results and interpret participants' comments on their (measured) IAT scores. In terms of their relationship with the participants, my concern is that this research – especially because it is couched in terms of being a "finding out" exercise on the part of the researchers – can restrict *discursive exploration* of apparently "found" inconsistencies in White people's racialized thinking, which could potentially become better thought through in social discussion. I would suggest that without having to treat the status of IAT testing as pointing to "real" (albeit implicit) attitudes, the participants could be *invited to participate in a discussion around the meaning of the IAT results.* For example, a discussion concerning why some of the White participants stated that they were unfamiliar with the Black names presented to them could be opened up – which may lead the talk in the direction of how more familiarity can be enhanced (by, e.g., engaging in more cross-racial interaction across race(d) groupings).

Monteith, Voils, and Ashburn-Nardo contend that it is highly unlikely that when participants attributed (biased) IAT scores to nonracial factors that this was a correct attribution on their part. This is because research on the racial IAT shows that performance on the IAT is related to other priming measures for assessing racial bias;

---

[102]Douglas conceptualizes prejudicial responses as operating both unconsciously and consciously. What is important for her is to find a way of conceptualizing prejudice without reducing it solely to an understanding of *individual* responses. She points out that she rejects the either-or dichotomized mode of thinking that "lacks recognition of the complexity of the problem" and that leads to "unending debates about behavior or attitude change; [and] change of individuals or change of culture" (1998, Chapter 4, p. 15).

and also in their own research, participants' performance was linked to explicit self-reported attitudes, as long as "there is not a complete dissociation between implicit and explicit attitudes" (2001, p. 412). But Fazio and Olson point to the discordance that has often been found between indirect and direct (self-report) measures of attitudes. They indicate that discussion around this in the research literature "has raised a conceptual question. The question is: *"Is the 'real' attitude the one represented by the implicit measure or is it the one reflected in the explicit measure?"* (2003, p. 304, my italics). And they indicate that this also raises the question of *"what does 'real' mean"*? (2003, p. 304, my italics). They remark that this question cannot be resolved with reference to "a measure's predictive validity," because "both implicit and explicit measures can be predictive of judgments and behavior" (2003, p. 305).

In commenting on the debate around what the IAT may be considered as measuring, Greenwald makes the point that IAT scores have proved particularly useful in predicting some kinds of behavior. For instance, he indicates that:

> In one type of experiment that has been done a few times, researchers video-recorded the behavior of a White person who had previously taken the IAT, talking to a Black person in an ordinary conversation. The videotapes were then scored for indicators of discomfort, such as speech errors, maintaining distance, and turning away. (2008, p. 5)

The finding of these studies, he notes, is that "these indicators of discomfort are better predicted by the race IAT than by the same person's self-reported race attitudes" (2008, p. 5). This implies that IAT results need to be taken seriously as they can offer a window to develop better understanding of people than a reliance on self-report procedures (2008, p. 5). Banaji similarly notes that it seems that at least in certain domains "this test outpredicts the usual questions about human behavior that are directly posed to respondents in survey-type measure" (2008, p. 6). Banaji adds that:

> I think we have taken the position that this test is useful for two purposes: as a scientific tool, and for the education at the individual level and at the level of communities discussing its meaning and use. (2008, p. 6)

Here Banaji points out that for her it might be important to *open up a discussion*, at *individual and community level*, regarding the meaning and use of the IAT. That is, the meaning of it in terms of what it is supposedly "measuring" can be subjected to discussion. I would suggest in this regard that the video experiments reported by Greenwald (2008) could also become opportunities to open up such discussion. For example, after White participants have been shown the IAT results as scored by the test, and shown the judges' scoring of their discomfort in interacting with the Black conversation partner, both parties (including the experimenters) could be brought together again to discuss the possible value of the IAT – as well as to discuss various interpretations thereof. I contend again that this could be done without their having to adjudicate on the "real" reality of what the IAT is supposedly measuring. For example, it could be argued that one reason why White people in the experiments reported by Greenwald feel discomfort in ordinary conversation with Black conversation partners is that they are not used to interacting with Black people – and that this is an issue that needs addressal at a *societal level*. As with the familiarity issue, then, the issue of discomfort could serve to open up a wider discussion than concentrating on individual attitudes (and trying to decide what is being measured by the IAT).

Sommers and Norton point out that many psychologists consider "discomfort/unfamiliarity" as an indicator of (modern) racism, while they also point to the "ambiguous nature" of such racism (2006, p. 131). Sommers and Norton suggest that in lay terms, however, this kind of understanding of racism "has not entrenched itself in consensus lay conceptions" (2006, p. 132). This is all the more reason, I would argue, why these kinds of research settings could be used as opportunities to indeed open to further discussion the issues that the various participants see to be at stake. In other words, these experimental situations could become mechanisms for helping to generate more open talk in regard to racial matters (as, for instance, pleaded for by Bonilla-Silva, 2006, pp. 73–75, and as discussed in later chapters) – without the discussion revolving around the "reality" of attitudes apparently located.

Such a discussion with participants in the experiment (individually or in focus group sessions) could in turn set the stage for people to work together, in natural settings, to reconsider and revise ways of dealing with racialized situations in more deliberative ways. In Chapter 8, I show how Bonilla-Silva chooses not to set the terms of discussion around racism as an *attitudinal* approach – but wishes rather to explore the *functioning of ideological discourse* (2006, p. 198). He defines ideology as "collective representations" which, in this case, help Whites to "manufacture accounts on a variety of racial matters" (2006, p. 208). And he concentrates on *opening these accounts to public debate and reconsideration*, with the intention of enabling people to review the perpetuation of (racialized) social inequalities (2006, p. 220).

As far as Monteith, Voils, and Ashburn's experiment aimed at helping (White) people to "look underground" is concerned, then, I would suggest that they have developed an inventive way of creating some scope for enabling people to explore the potential fluidity in their responses (and thus to recreate/reform their manner of seeing and acting). Nonetheless, one of the problems with *the framework supplied by the researchers* – in this case, as directed toward locating *individual attitudes* and at capitalizing on people's potential *self-guilt* – is that it can preclude alternative ways of approaching and addressing the issues. These, I suggest, could potentially be drawn out through participant discussion. And also some cross-racial discussion designed into the experiment (by setting this up at the point of discussion with participants) may be helpful in drawing out frameworks other than the one that seems to be framing the research focus in this case.

3.9.2 Revisiting the Experiment with African American Participants

Turning to Ashburn-Nardo et al.'s research exploring the psychological well-being of African Americans, here the researchers did not try to introduce an interventionist component at the point of involvement with participants (during the research process) – but offered various recommendations for intervention springing from what they took to be the findings of the study. In regard to this experiment, I would like to make a few brief points, linked to my arguments that I have developed earlier in the chapter.

Firstly, Ashburn-Nardo et al. have ventured to explore ways in which African Americans can be protected, as they put it, from "further psychological harm" (2007, p. 486). Clearly, their focus is on the level of *individual psychological responses* on the part of African Americans to their continued stigmatized status as a group in the USA. One recommendation that the researchers make, is "encouraging close relationships with ingroup members from an early age" in order to in turn promote "positive ingroup identity" (2009, p. 487). However, the problem with this advice is that attention may become detracted from the alternative ways of African Americans choosing to address the racialized landscape in the USA. That is, alternative (political) options are not made manifest either to the participants or to wider audiences. Moreover, by encouraging in their recommendations for action "close relationships with ingroup members" the researchers could unwittingly serve to reinforce bounded group styles of living at a wider social level in the society; and by encouraging the promotion of "positive ingroup identity" possibilities for de-essentializing "identity" may become left out of the equation. The research focus here was on exploring African Americans "identity" – defined by items such as "Being Black is an important part of my self-image" (2007, p. 477). But the meaning of being Black is never discussed with the participants – and this itself may not be without social consequence (again, for both the participants involved and for readers of the article). Thus, although the research may provide some corrective to Harris-Lacewell expressed concern (2003) with research that is directed primarily toward displaying *White* responses in relation to race matters, I would suggest that the starting framework here operates as still unduly restrictive. That is, little provision is made in this research to question the starting hypotheses focusing on psychological "well-being" or "distress" of African Americans and little provision is made for exploring more politicized conceptions of "identity" and "group belonging." Hence, many notions remain "uninterrogated" (to use Harris-Lacewell's terminology, 2003, p. 223). Of course the researchers could argue that any research study necessarily has to create *some* cut off points when deciding what to study and what hypotheses to investigate. But as I have argued earlier, the problem is when what may hereby become "left out" is not seriously considered – and when few openings are made for their continued exploration (with participants and/or wider audiences).

As far as the researchers' conception of their way of developing "findings" in relation to what they observed, it is worth noting that Ashburn-Nardo et al. consider that the completion of the racial IAT, for instance, offers information about how Black participants "really" relate (in terms of their implicit preferences) to what is seen as their ingroup or outgroup. Ashburn-Nardo et al. state that:

> African American participants who respond faster when the categories *Black* and *pleasant* share one response key and *White* and *unpleasant* share the other response key than when the reverse pairings occur *exhibit more positive associations with Blacks than Whites (i.e. ingroup favoritism)*. (2007, p. 477, my italics)

Here Ashburn-Nardo et al. posit the existence of ingroups and outgroups and consider that "positive associations with Blacks" on the IAT can be taken to be an indication of "ingroup favoritism." Likewise, for those Black respondents who did *not* respond faster when the categories *Black* and *pleasant* share one response key and *White* and *unpleasant* share the other response key than their responses in the reverse pairings, this is taken as an indicator of *outgroup favoritism*. That is, this is considered by the researchers as favoring a "group" (Whites) other than the one to which they "belong" (Blacks). As noted above, there are other possible interpretations of the results of the IAT scoring – other than speaking in terms of ingroup and outgroup favoritism. I would suggest that as with the experiment with White participants, so with this experiment, opportunities for discussion around the IAT measures could have been provided for. And while in Monteith, Voils, and Ashburn-Nardo (2001) those conducting the experiment were White (as were the participants), in this experiment with African Americans 65% of the sessions had White experimenters. This means that potentially interesting cross-racial discussions individually and/or in focus groups could readily have been set up between race(d) groupings – in this case between some of the experimenters and the participants.[103]

My concern with this experiment again is that conceiving researchers as scientifically equipped to develop understanding in relation to those being "researched," can restrict possibilities for establishing an alternative, more dialogical, relationship with participants as well as audiences. As I pointed out in Chapter 1, Ladson-Billings (2003), for instance, poses a view of accountable "knowing" in social life, where researchers acknowledge that their own concerns have been brought to bear in their way of seeing, and use this awareness as an opportunity to expand their perspectives – together with others – on the (humanly constructed) world (2003, p. 497). By operating in this way, different kinds of human relationship can become exemplified through the research process.

My argument concerning ways of exemplifying and practicing new forms of human relationship – as part of the movement toward undercutting different forms of social domination (including racism) – is elaborated further throughout the book.

---

[103] In an e-mail to Margo Monteith (November 2008) I asked her whether in any of her and colleagues' research work with Black participants, they "at the same time have White participants in the same experiment? And is it possible that after the experiment you are able to organize a discussion between the participants asking them to reflect together on the issues that the experiment is raising and exploring?" Her reply on this point was that "Your ideas about organizing discussions between Black and White participants *would be very interesting to pursue*, but these are not issues that I have addressed in published work that I can send along" (my italics). Although she indicates that thus far such work has not been published, she clearly does not preclude this as a viable possibility. My suggestion is that especially as there were many White experimenters involved with the (in this case, Black) participants, the opportunity could have been created already here for some kind of cross-racial discussion.

3.10 Some Other Experimental Work on the IAT: The Influence of the Stimulus Items

Monteith et al. (2001) as well as Ashburn-Nardo et al. (2007) used versions of what Govan and Williams (2004) call the "standard IAT" in terms of the way in which stimulus items were chosen for the participants to respond to. In the standard IAT, also called the "typical IAT" by Govan and Williams (2004, p. 360), "the stimulus items for Black were a set of typical Black names, and the stimulus items for White were a set of typical White names." But Govan and Williams point out that further research has been aimed at exploring whether, if these stimulus items are replaced with others, different IAT effects become manifested. They point to research in this direction by, for instance, Dasgupta and Greenwald (2001), where

> the pro-White IAT effect was substantially reduced (but not eliminated) by exposing participants to *disliked White* and *admired Black* exemplars prior to the completion of the IAT. (2004, p. 360, my italics)[104]

In order to examine further the effect on IAT results of the *specific stimulus items* to which individuals are exposed, Govan and Williams set up an experiment in a University in Australia to examine "the difference between a standard Black/White IAT and a disliked White/liked Black IAT" (2004, p. 360). In this study, participants (Introductory Psychology students – White[105]) participated in either a typical (standard) IAT or an atypical one (see Fig. 3.2) – in order that the experimenters could compare the IAT effects. They note that:

> For the typical IAT, the stimulus items for Black were Theo, Leroy, Tyrone, Lakisha, and Ebony, and the stimulus items for White were Chip, Josh, Todd, Amber, and Betsy. For the atypical IAT, the stimulus items for Black were Michael Jordan, Bill Cosby, Eddie Murphy, Cathy Freeman, and Ernie Dingo, and the stimulus items for White were Charles Manson, Adolph Hitler, Hannibal Lechter, Pauline Hanson, and Martin Bryant. (2004, p. 360)

In commenting on their choice of stimulus items, they remark that in Australia, Pauline Hanson is regarded as a "disliked politician, Martin Bryant as a mass murderer, Cathy Freeman as a popular athlete, and Ernie Dingo as a popular actor" (2004, p. 360).

The results of this experiment were that pro-White responses were shown on the typical IAT but not on the atypical IAT one (2004, p. 360). The graph below expresses these results.

Govan and Williams try to account for why the results did not show pro-Black preferences when the *atypical IAT* was used, given that the White exemplars used here were undesirable. They suggest that it is possible that own-race preference

---

[104]To organize this process, Dasgupta and Greenwald asked participants to complete an ostensible "general knowledge test" (Govan & Williams, 2004, p. 360).

[105]Govan and Williams do not specify that White participant responses were being assessed – but this becomes clearer in their discussion of the results: When explaining the scores for an atypical task (see Fig. 3.2), they note that it is possible that "own-race preference" creates an element of a "stronger association between *White* and *pleasant*" (2004, p. 361).

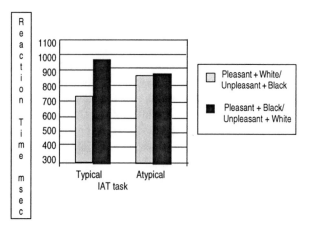

Fig. 3.2 Results for Typical & Atypical IAT Tasks. Source: Govan and Williams (2004, p. 360) IAT Results for [This] Study: Reaction times as a function of IAT task (typical or atypical) and categorization pairing (pleasant+white/unpleasant+black, or pleasant+black/unpleasant+white).

"is a ... practiced and culturally instilled attitude" – thus creating some element of a "strong association between White and pleasant" (2004, p. 361). This could explain the "finding of an elimination, *but not reversal*, of the pro-White effect in the atypical IAT" (2004, p. 361, my italics).

But they suggest that the difference between the *typical* IAT and the *atypical* IAT effects, which shows that "the stimulus items can influence the IAT effect" can be seen as supporting the notion that participants can and do temporarily redefine the categories (White and Black) by virtue of the stimulus items to which they are exposed. Otherwise put, they suggest that this experiment can be seen as pointing to the possibility that participants *can engage in category redefinition* and therefore respond on the basis of their redefinitions.

To support their inference regarding category redefinition, they set up another study, in which participants completed what they call a "*Category IAT* " (2004, p. 361). This study consisted of various stages. In Stage 1, the researchers used animals and plants, and located positively and negatively valenced exemplars of each category. Then:

> Half the participants completed an IAT for which the stimulus items were comprised of negatively valenced (i.e., *nasty*) animals and positively valenced (i.e., *nice*) plants, and half the participants completed an IAT in which the stimulus lists were comprised of *nice* animals and *nasty* plants. (2004, p. 361)

In Stage 2, participants completed a filler task. Participants were presented with a letter string in the center of the computer screen, and their task was to decide whether the string was a word or non-word. Words consisting of positively and negatively valenced plants and animals were used here (with different items used from the ones used in Stage 1).

In Stage 3 of the study (the Category IAT), the researchers used as category labels pleasant/unpleasant and animal/plant. And the stimulus items for the categories *animal* and *plant* were simply "animal" and "plant." Their idea was that, if category redefinition were operative, then participants would be

> redefining the category *animal* to *nice animal* (in Stage 1) and then they should be faster at the Category IAT when *pleasant* and *animal* shared a response key than when *pleasant* and *plant* shared a response key. Similarly, if participants were redefining the category *plant* to *nice plant* (in Stage 1), then they should be faster at the Category IAT when pleasant and plant shared a response key than when *pleasant* and *animal* shared a response key. (2004, p. 361)

The results of the experiment showed that, indeed, as hypothesized,

> participants who completed the nice animal/nasty plant IAT in Stage 1 responded faster in the Category IAT when *pleasant* and *animal* shared a response key ... than when *pleasant* and *plant* shared a response key .... Participants who completed the nasty animal/nice plant IAT in Stage 1 responded faster in the Category IAT when *pleasant* and *plant* shared a response key ... than when *pleasant* and *animal* shared a response key. (2004, p. 362)

These results, they argue, give support to the "redefinition of categories hypothesis" (2004, p. 362). That is, they see both their studies as providing support for the hypothesis that "IAT effects are not solely a function of category labels" and that indeed these labels can be (temporarily) redefined. But they see the results as having a more fundamental significance, namely, that:

> Perhaps these results speak to individuals' abilities to disregard category labels and stereotypes if they are sufficiently infused with members of a category that are incongruent with their stereotypes. (2004, p. 363)

They remind us that their results from their Black/White atypical IAT "showed an elimination of the pro-White effect, suggesting that participants were able to override the stereotypical response automatically" (2004, p. 363).

They regard it as crucial to recognize that the stimulus items chosen (by researchers) to represent the category labels are important, and may be seen as "driving participants to re-define the categories." They urge researchers not to regard this as being "merely a methodological footnote for IAT research" (2004, p. 363).

Govan and Williams also raise for reconsideration the interpretation of "what we are measuring with the IAT" (2004, p. 363). They consider the question as to whether the IAT should be conceived as "a measure of the *true* attitude" of people. They suggest that the conception of the IAT in this way "might need to be altered" (2004, p. 363). At the very least, they suggest, we need to recognize that the IAT can be treated as a "useful way of ... measuring an attitude toward a concept [category], *where that concept is defined by the representing set of stimulus items*" (2004, p. 363, my italics). That is, instead of seeing IAT effects as revealing fixed orientations toward category labels as used by people, we need to recognize that the "found" results *might have become activated by the researchers via specific presented stimuli.*

In this way, Govan and Williams cast a different perspective on Monteith et al.'s (2001) and Ashburn-Nardo et al.'s (2007) conception of hidden (true) attitudes that supposedly become "found" via the IAT – by pointing to the influence of researchers' *specific manner of conducting the studies* on the way the

IAT effects become generated. The idea of research choices as themselves being influential in shaping results, as I have argued in Sections 3.4.2, 3.5.2.2, and 3.9, has import for researchers' style of engagement with participants and with larger audiences.

De Houwer casts yet another perspective on the way in which IAT effects can be seen as being generated in the research process, when he suggests that participants can influence the outcome of an IAT by "paying attention to certain features or by intentionally retrieving certain information" (2006, p. 179). He proposes that Dasgupta and Greenwald's (2001) study – which showed less favoring of Whites as measured by the IAT "when participants saw names of admired Black Americans and disliked White Americans before completing the race IAT" (2006, p. 179) – suggests that IAT effects can indeed be influenced by "non-automatic processes." He believes that "conscious propositional knowledge" used by participants could account for some of the IAT effects observed by the researchers. In any case, he questions the assumption that IAT measures necessarily provide a reflection of "automatically formed associations" (2006, p. 178). De Houwer supports his contention that perhaps IAT measures could be picking up (and generating) "*non-automatic processes*" by referring to a study where researchers' instructions to participants were "sufficient to induce a change in valence as measured by the IAT" (2006, p. 180). (The study was set in Ghent University – Belgium – with first year psychology or sports science students as participants.)

What I find important in these considerations around the IAT as advanced by Govan and Williams and by De Houwer is that the influence of the research context (and researchers' choices) become increasingly highlighted as relevant to the so-called observed IAT effects. What is observed now becomes seen to be dependent at least in part on how the studies are set up. Of course, faced with these considerations, researchers may try to develop research tools that enable better access to what "really is the case" independently of researchers' influences. However, an alternative approach to considering the influence of researchers' manner of designing and framing studies is to suggest that *people's attitudes/responses/ways of using categories, and so on should be understood as context-dependent.* The research context can then be seen as a *social context that, like others, affects what becomes activated by people in social life.*

3.11 Conclusion

In this chapter, I offered a detailed examination of a number of experiments and suggested that the manner of proceeding by the experimenters did not reflect sufficient acknowledgment of the possible social consequences of approaching the research questions in the ways that were chosen. I suggested that insufficient space was provided for people – including experimenters/participants/audiences – to review the initial frameworks/paradigms for puzzle setting (to use Kuhn's, 1962 terminology) that I located via my discussion of the experiments.

In considering the oft-cited distinction between the realm of *facts* supposedly being explored through the research process and the realm of *values* supposedly meant (in terms of a realist epistemological stance) not to intrude on this process (see Chapter 1, Section 1.5.1), Habermas makes the point that any statements of "fact" (and any theoretical statements apparently resting on them) "is derived within a normative framework which is capable of *critical* but not of deductive-empirical justification" (1974a, p. 213). According to him, it is only through *critical discussion* that we can decide (or try to decide) on the *standards in terms of which we will be both seeing and defending our vision of "the facts"*[106] This implies that researchers need to attempt to make visible the preferences/orientation in terms of which they are framing their studies/inquiries so as to open this (value-laden) frame to critical assessment. Through this process of critical discussion, which includes a discussion around values, alternative ways of seeing "facts" and alternative ways of thinking about the values in terms of which human relationships can come to be guided can be generated. Taking into account Habermas's arguments, along with those offered by critical race theorists, I pointed to ways in which the various studies could be regarded as incorporating a number of uninterrogated notions, which I suggested require further consideration. I indicated how experimental research could be designed to provide more space for social discussion around the frameworks provided – including discussion around how "results" become generated through the process of research.

Bonilla-Silva argues that in any case, when trying to find ways of addressing racism, an appeal to facts (as if these are devoid of values) is not likely to be productive, because "racial facts are highly contested." He elucidates the context of contestation (in the USA) as follows:

> In the eyes of most whites ... evidence of racial disparity in income, wealth, education, and other relevant matters becomes evidence that there is something wrong with minorities themselves; evidence of minorities' overrepresentation in the criminal justice system or on death row is interpreted as evidence of overrepresentation in criminal activity; evidence of black and Latino underperformance in standardized tests is a confirmation that there is something ... wrong with them. (2006, p. 208)

In view of Bonilla-Silva's understanding of contestation around "the evidence," it seems unlikely that the solutions to issues of racism as offered by the experimenters considered in this chapter are sufficiently forward looking. Habermas for his part suggests that the appeal to some form of deductive logic (such as the Popperian-espoused one) to supposedly explore the realm of "facts" distinct from values can result in what he calls the reproduction of quasi-causal relationships – where *quasi-causal links become reproduced insofar as people continue to act them out.* For instance, it could be argued that focusing on ingroup identification and the supposed link between this and developing positive responses to those considered "ingroup" *encourages* the continuing patterning of the social world into defined "groups" (as

---

[106]In Chapter 6, Sections 6.3.2 and 6.3.2.1, I discuss in more detail considerations of the status of Habermas's own theorizing. And I extend further this discussion in Chapter 8.

I tried to show in Section 3.4.1). I suggested therefore that research be designed to better equip people to *participate in social discussion around viable ways of social living*.

As far as the critical assessment of research results within the social fabric is concerned, as noted in Section 3.4.3, Nyamnjoh points to opportunities hitherto unthought of as having been opened up through the "advent of the internet" (2007, p. 2). With the advent hereof, the "game of approval and disapproval" of research results need not be limited to (professional) researchers and their peers (2007, p. 2). Rather, facilitated through, for instance, the internet, it can become an "ongoing process of exchange with those studied" (and with others concerned) (2007, p. 2). Nyamnjoh calls upon people to question the idea of findings created by experts and assessed by peers – to make room for "findings" to be treated *as open to involvement* from the general public – in processes of ongoing exchange (2007, p. 2).

Bearing in mind these arguments, I now offer some proposals for revisiting researcher accountability in experimental research and for how I believe this style of research can be reworked as a way of exploring, inter alia, (new) racism.

3.11.1 Revisiting Researcher Accountability in Experimental Research

Considering the various authors' write-ups of their experiments as discussed in this chapter, their concentration in their presentation is on showing how they are developing reasonable inferences/interpretations about the connections between the variables under consideration. The uneasiness that I have expressed in this chapter relates to my argument that the researchers have not engaged seriously with the kinds of concerns that have been raised by others who have *questioned the goal set in traditional experimentation* – namely, the goal of developing knowledge of causal connections apparently free of values and political frameworks brought to bear on the research.

It appears that even when general concerns have been raised by certain scholars about the assumption that scientific procedures are equipped to generate findings that become closer and closer to "the truth," *these voices also seem not to have been heeded with sufficient seriousness* (to the point that they are engaged with in any way in the write-up of the research). Cohen-Cole offers an account of a number of contesting voices of those who have questioned the idea of science as a process of discovering "islands of truth." She cites, for instance, the work of Bruner, Goodnow, and Austin (1956) entitled *A Study of Thinking*. She indicates that they considered their understanding of science as opposing the view of science as a "voyage of discovery" en route to "discover the islands of truth" (2005, p. 129). These authors argued that "science and commonsense inquiry alike do not discover the ways in which events are grouped in the world; they *invent* ways of grouping" (Cohen-Cole, 2005, p. 129).

She remarks that Bruner, Goodnow, and Austin in turn were drawing on authors (such as Mayr, 1952), who, with reference to the biological sciences were arguing that "species are not 'discovered' but 'invented'" (Bruner et al., 1956, p. 19, as cited in Cohen-Cole, 2005, p. 120). She refers to Bruner's argument that processes of perception do not involve reacting to "stimuli," but rather to (valued) "stimulus information." As Bruner puts it:

> what we wish to denote here is not the energy characteristics of stimulation, but the cue characteristics provided by stimulation – its signaling value .... The data of the scientist are not the raw cues of stimulation, but the perceptions of the scientist which occur when those cues confirm perceptual hypotheses which he [sic] has acquired. In this important sense, then, the scientist's *data are not found, but created*. (Bruner, 1951, as cited in Cohen-Cole, 2005, p. 121, my italics)

Cohen-Cole indicates that these suggestions of Bruner were based on

> a series of experiments he conducted on how expectation determines what people see. For historians of science the most notable of these experiments is one that examines how individuals experience Gestalt switches in their perception when viewing mis-colored playing cards such as black hearts (Bruner & Postman, 1949). This paper was one of Thomas Kuhn's central examples of Gestalt switching in The Structure of Scientific Revolutions. (Cohen-Cole, p. 130, Note 33)

As I indicated in Chapter 1, Kuhn's constructivist-oriented arguments have been seen as relevant by authors such as Collins (1990, 2000) who sees them as supporting an understanding of research accountability not resting on a view of science as "discovery" but on a view of social research as dialogical inquiry. I have suggested (via my detailed examination of the particular experiments) that such conceptions of accountability need, at least, to be seriously engaged with.

3.11.2 Extending Research Options

The experimental work discussed in this chapter has been designed to investigate particular variables and their connections – on the understanding that if we can find out more about the causal factors influencing social exclusionary responses/behaviors on the part of people, we can create interventions to mitigate against these patterns of exclusion. As noted in Chapter 2, one of the reasons why certain researchers studying new forms of racism have concentrated on experimental designs is because it is argued that such designs may be best equipped to uncover what people in everyday life may be reluctant to notice. The hope is also that the scientific experiments can contribute to finding ways of addressing racism that would not otherwise appear to people in their everyday life and that in any case would not have been subjected to the rigorous testing that is required of scientific propositions.

While I can appreciate that these researchers are considering their scientific work as aimed toward providing information and interpretations that can contribute to addressing new (subtle and often not admitted) forms of racism, I have tried to show that there are other ways of relating with various participants and with audiences (as well as with colleagues expressing alternative visions) – other than the ones displayed by these inquirers.

Through the detail of my discussion around the experimental work, I suggested that insofar as some kind of experimental procedure is chosen to be used, it should become reworked from its more traditional usage. In order to manifest a more discursively oriented accountability (which I have tried to explicate as a viable way of conceiving researcher accountability), I suggest that the experimenters would need to

- express some recognition that their framing of hypotheses may already be reflecting pre-formed images of "what the world must be" (Miller, 1963, pp. 149–150, as cited in Cohen-Cole, 2005, p. 126). This in turn involves acknowledging a preparedness to engage with alternative values/visions that can be – and/or have been – invoked by others. In this way provision can be made for viewing "truth" as what Nyamnjoh calls a "negotiated truth derived from competing perspectives" (2007, p. 8), while also tying truth-seeking (or processes of inquiry) consciously to a critical discussion of values, as, for instance, suggested by certain critical race theorists (CRT) (cf. Parker & Lynn, 2002, p. 11);
- make provision for participant involvement (together with the experimenters) in post-experimental discussion (individually and/or in focus groups). Hereby, the way becomes opened for possible tensions between researchers' starting convictions (in terms of beliefs about race and culture) and starting views of different participants *to become brought to the fore for discussion* (as explained by Milner IV, 2007, p. 395). To this end it may be important within experimental studies to make provision for interpretations of people who have had different historical experiences, in order to bring to bear variegated understandings of racism. Hence I would suggest that experimenters seek some opportunities to engender cross-racial discussion (across race(d) groupings) – as part of the research agenda. This also caters for Harris-Lacewell's concern (2003) that otherwise monolithic conceptions of "the other" can become reinforced through the research process; and
- make more provision for expressing in their presentation of their write-up a variety of theoretical lenses that can be used to cast radically different light on ways of setting research questions – and at the same time suggest ways in which debate around these can be used to extend repertoires of visioning and of acting. To do this requires that inquirers cultivate their reflexive capacities to reflect on what is *not* capable of being said within their initial way of setting their research questions/puzzles (cf. Alvesson & Sköldberg, 2000, p. 246) so as to open the space for further audience participation in engaging with any apparently "found" (or rather, *generated*) results.

In relation to the last bullet point, I propose that the CRT suggestion that particular narratives – including those created by professional researchers – can wittingly or unwittingly serve to preclude alternative ways of seeing needs to be taken on board, so as to develop an orientation toward inviting "counter-story" telling (cf. Delgado, 1989; Parker & Lynn, 2002). This is one way of preventing an inclination to, as Ladson-Billings puts it, "seize intellectual space" – such as she considers as associated with Euro-American cultural logic (2003, p. 417). To invite counter-story telling as part of the process of knowing, as I see it, means that all stories are admitted to be capable of being reframed. Parker and Lynn cite Hayman (1995) in regard to the status to be given to proffered conceptualizations. Hayman suggests that CRT can be seen as having postmodern threads[107] in that, as Parker and Lynn state, both postmodernism and CRT "reject the assertion that established doctrine and texts have objective truth and universal meanings" (2002, p. 11). But Parker and Lynn remark that CRT more explicitly encapsulates the idea of extending repertoires of (socially constructed) visioning to the practical interest in social justice. Therefore research validity is defined as inextricably linked to *social justice validity* in this conception – even though it is recognized that there may not be an overarching theory of justice to which we can appeal (2002, p. 11). In this conception, our ways of knowing are seen as inseparable from our ways of exploring options for humane modes of living. (See again Chapter 1, Section 1.5.3.)

While in this chapter I have tried to show how a discursive orientation to knowing and living can be pursued via an extended style of experimental research exploring, inter alia, factors identified as relevant to discussions around racism, in the following chapters I offer examinations of other procedures that have been used – starting with survey research in Chapter 4.

Figure Credits

Figure 3.1 printed with permission of the publisher; from Dovidio, J. F., & Gaertner, S. L. Reducing prejudice: Combating intergroup biases. *Current Directions in Psychological Science, 8*(4), 101–105 @ 1999 Wiley-Blackwell.

Figure 3.2 printed with permission of the publisher; from Govan, C. L., & Williams, K. D. Changing the affective valence of the stimulus items influences the IAT by redefining the category labels. *Journal of Experimental Social Psychology, 40*(3), 357–365 @ 2004, Elsevier Inc.

---

[107]As Fraser and Nicholson note, not all authors whom others characterize as postmodern in orientation label themselves this way. But they indicate that Lyotard in his *The Postmodern Condition* (1984) "is one of the few social thinkers widely considered postmodern who actually uses the term; indeed it was he who introduced it into critical discussions of philosophy, politics, society and social theory" (1994, p. 244). According to this argument, as Fraser and Nicholson explain, there are no special tribunals (such as, say, scientific courts of appeal) set apart from the sites where inquiry is practiced. Hence practitioners have to "assume responsibility for legitimizing their own practice" (1994, p. 246). Fraser and Nicholson also note that examples of "local stories" which form the basis for social criticism can be found in those told by Foucault (1979) – who is often also considered as postmodernist (1994, p. 247). See also Lemert's account of Foucault's relation to postmodern politics (1994, p. 268).

Chapter 4
Survey Research: Examining Expressed Feelings and Views on Racial(ized) Issues as Variables Along with Other Variables

4.1 Introduction

In this chapter I turn to a discussion of some examples of survey research that have been organized to examine people's feelings and attitudes/views in relation to specific racial(ized) issues and to consider connections between variables isolated. I show how the researchers see their work as helping to formulate workable social interventions for engaging with (detected) forms of racism. But first – in line with my concentration on examining methodologies – I place my discussion in the context of a number of authors' accounts of survey research as a research design.

Acquah offers an indication of what is involved in the design of survey research when he outlines its advantages and disadvantages in relation to other approaches, which he considers while exploring challenges and responsibilities for social research in Africa. He points out that:

> The advantage of the sample survey lies in its potential for quantification [of the variables under consideration], replication [in that the survey questions can be re-administered at other points in time], and the fact that results obtained can be generalized over a broader or larger population [insofar as the sample is considered as representative hereof[108]]. (2007, p. 129)

However, he indicates that he considers it ethically problematic when researchers use surveys simply to "mine" data for a research paper or dissertation – in such a way that "the community is 'used' to achieve this purpose" (2007, p. 127). He looks at survey research specifically in relation to more participatory styles of research (such as the ones I explicate in Chapter 7), which he sees as having the advantage of being more equipped to involve communities in "discussing items that concern them and identifying problems and their causes" (2007, p. 129). As he notes, in

---

[108]The confidence with which we can assume that the sample indeed represents the population (based on inferences of probability) is sometimes called "population validity." This is similar in experimentation to external validity – namely, the extent to which any observed connections between the variables that have been isolated for attention in the experimental situation can be taken as holding more generally (outside of this situation). (See Romm & Adman, 2000; Romm, 2001, p. 138.)

N. Romm, *New Racism*, DOI 10.1007/978-90-481-8728-7_4,

"participatory research" people in the community "are expected to participate more actively in the discussions [about problems and their causes] compared to those outside the community" (2007, p. 130). But he also points out that survey research itself can be used in a more responsible manner than as a tool to "mine" data for research purposes. As shown in the course of the chapter, I take up a similar position to Acquah in regard to the accountable use of survey research, where the terms of research as well as its "results" are rendered discursively accountable.

Some researchers explain what is involved in survey research as a research design by considering it in relation to the attempt to establish causality as striven for in experiments. For instance, Bryman compares survey research with a logic of experimentation based on creating (or manipulating) variation in an independent variable or variables in order to examine causal effects hereof on other variables. He points out that considered in relation to experimental designs, survey researchers need to *rely more on theoretical interpretations* to make inferences regarding the direction of causality of any observed correlations between the variables under consideration. As he remarks:

> The old maxim – correlation cannot imply cause – ostensibly implies that the social scientist's ability to establish causality from social survey research is severely limited. However, survey researchers have by no means been deterred and have developed a variety of procedures for the elucidation of causality by means of . . . reconstruction of the "logic of causal order" . . .. (1992, p. 31)

Put differently, Bryman suggests that in considering variations in the data collected from the survey in terms of some theoretical understanding, researchers can make decisions, if appropriate, on which variables can be regarded as the one(s) influencing the others.

As far as the *collection of data* is concerned, De Vaus indicates that in survey research, as in experiments, a range of data-collection techniques may be employed, including questionnaires (which consist largely of closed questions, but which can include some open-ended ones[109]), structured interviewing (with pre-set questions), in-depth interviewing (semi-structured or unstructured), (direct) observation, and content analysis (De Vaus, 1996, p. 6). As he explains,

> the technique by which we generate the data need not be highly structured so long as we obtain each case's attribute on each variable [in which we are interested]. Because questionnaires are the easiest way of ensuring the structured data matrix they are the most common technique used in survey research. But there is no *necessary* connection. (1996, p. 5)

Following De Vaus, Seale and Filmer also comment that social surveys do not "always involve rigidly fixed questioning devices" (1998, p. 128). They note that "qualitative data" as gathered through, for example, interviewing processes, can

---

[109]In a closed response format, respondents are given set options from which to choose their answers to the questions, while an open-ended response format means it is left open for them to construct answers in their own words.

later be quantified by putting them into a form that allows us to measure differences – if it is felt that this fits in with the aim of the project being undertaken
(1998, p. 128).

As Vogt likewise indicates,

> we know that coding and analysis are not matters of design [to which different designs are
> necessarily linked] from the simple fact that all research designs can be, and have been,
> used to generate either quantitative or qualitative data. (2008, p. 2)

Vogt argues that because surveys "quite often contain open-ended questions,"
respondents are able to "express their beliefs and attitudes in their own words, sometimes at length." He points out that "these expressions of opinion are qualitative data
and are usually analyzed using qualitative techniques" (2008, p. 2). But he adds that
"surveys are also quantitative" in that:

> Many of the questions included in a typical survey are written to generate answers that are
> best analyzed using quantitative techniques. In sum, although the analysis of survey data
> is frequently quantitative, it is not exclusively so. Surveys, like all research designs, can be
> used to collect either qualitative or quantitative evidence – or both. (2008, p. 2)

Interestingly, Vogt makes the point that although survey research is "usually
categorized as a quantitative method," it can be considered as indeed including a
"qualitative" component at the point at which the questions (to be answered by
respondents) are composed (2008, p. 2). He notes that deciding on questions is "a
delicate and nuanced art that requires a great deal of thought about what words mean
to people" (2008, p. 2). He gives an example of the importance of word choices
chosen by researchers, by noting that

> studies have shown that respondents often answer survey questions about a proposed law
> differently depending on which two seemingly equivalent phrases is used to describe it:
> Should X "be forbidden" or should X "not be allowed"? (2008, p. 2)

Vogt does not explore further this point in terms of a consideration of how
research results might therefore be regarded as a product of the way questions are set
– as his main focus is on exploring the manner in which researchers choose research
designs. However, the issues on which I concentrate in this chapter revolve around
the way in which the *evocation of data through surveys may be conceptualized*, and
the way in which any derived *correlations between the variables studied might be
treated*. I consider in depth the question of the status to be given to "found" correlations between variables. I take up the position – also advised by Acquah – that some
engagement with respondents/participants participating in the survey as well as with
members of the wider community needs to be set up – so as to provide opportunities
for dialogue around what participants and others in the community may expect and
what the "results" of the survey show (2007, p. 130). As Acquah notes:

> Sometimes the results of a survey may turn out to be different from what the community
> expected. A workshop is an opportunity for discrepancies in the results to be discussed and
> compromise solutions arrived at. (2007, p. 131)

Acquah states his view that researchers should not present "results" as having the status of being undiscussable: through discussion it is possible that compromise solutions as to how to consider the results may be generated. Via the examples that I use in the chapter, I explore further various options for rendering results more discussable (other than the workshop option presented by Acquah as appropriate in the context of research within African communities).

4.1.1 Examples Discussed and Revisited

In this chapter I have selected for discussion three surveys exploring feelings and attitudes in relation to racial(ized) issues – set in the USA and Australia. The first survey (as reported in Rabinowitz, Wittig, von Braun, Franke, and Zander-Music, 2005) is with White and Asian high school students in Los Angeles as respondents. The second (Haley and Sidanius, 2006) is with White, Black, and Latino residents of Los Angeles. And the third (Dunn and Geeraert, 2003) is with respondents (from different educational and cultural backgrounds) from various geographical areas in Australia.

In considering the study of Rabinowitz et al., I make the point that survey research can all too easily reinforce specific schemas of interpretation (on the part of the research subjects as well as other audiences) insofar as provision is not made for questioning these schemas. I show that Rabinowitz et al.'s own understanding of the variables under consideration, which formed the basis for setting up questions for members from "high status groups" to answer, could easily influence the respondents', as well as others', continued framing of the issues. As I indicated in Chapter 2, Harris-Lacewell expresses concern with those scientific studies of race directed primarily to explore the views of "high status groups" – arguing that in this way certain assumptions (of researchers and respondents) often remain uninterrogated (2003, p. 223). By offering a detailed discussion of this survey, I try to illustrate the importance of designing surveys differently (and writing them up differently) so as to open the space for the questioning of starting frameworks.

I then discuss briefly the survey of Haley and Sidanius (2006) to point to its potential in acknowledging how survey questions can influence respondents' conceptions of issues, such as in this case, issues relating to *affirmative action*. But I make the point that although their research highlights how the framing of issues in relation to affirmative action might influence respondents' attitudes toward them, they do not concentrate on explicating how they themselves – through their research – may be gearing research responses. I suggest therefore that their research does not sufficiently carry forward the implications of acknowledging the *potential consequences of research framing* on participant responses and the potential consequences of interpretations of "results" on wider audiences.[110]

---

[110]Harris-Lacewell likewise identifies limitations in Sidanius and Pratto's (1999) attempt to explore both "the attitudes of White Americans and ... the agency of African Americans" (2003,

I use the survey of Dunn and Geeraert (2003) to illustrate that although they espouse a constructivist argument, their way of posing questions in their survey still may reinforce people's perceptions of particular groups as existing "in reality." I indicate what I see as possibilities in their approach for asking questions in a different way – based on the kinds of questions that they pose as "Student Activities" at the end of their article. I suggest that some of these questions could be incorporated within the survey processes itself. In this way respondents could be offered opportunities to generate less univocal responses – which in turn may make a difference to audiences' understandings. I also suggest that raising additional questions for audiences to consider, via the style of write-up, offers a potential novel way of engaging with them. I propose that catering for this kind of relationship with respondents/participants and wider audiences would then tally with Acquah's suggestions regarding the (ethical) importance of gaining community participation in relation to the treatment of any "information" created via survey research (2007, p. 131).

4.2 Rabinowitz et al.'s Survey Exploring the Relationship Between Egalitarianism and Affective Bias (Los Angeles, USA)

4.2.1 The Social Context of the Research

In explaining the social context of their research (which involved utilizing and analyzing data from a sample of 112 high school students from a number of schools in Los Angeles), Rabinowitz et al. elucidate that:

> One of the challenges for social scientists has been to discover ways to promote group equality and inclusiveness in society. Although answering this challenge has always been difficult – perhaps especially so now that affirmative action programs in the United States are under fire – this endeavor is also one of the oldest in social psychology. For the better part of a century, a number of applied and basic research programs in social psychology have concentrated on issues of prejudice and discrimination and how to reduce them both. (2005, p. 526)

They indicate that the study was set up to explore how "equality beliefs" (beliefs that the adolescents had about the value of equality) may be related to prejudice (against those perceived to be members of low status groups) via two other variables identified by the researchers, namely, "strength of ethnic identity" and "outgroup orientation." (Their definitions of these terms are given in Table 4.1 in Section 4.2.3 below.) The questionnaire utilized in the study was administered to respondents from different schools. Data were actually collected at two time points in the

---

p. 239). Her main concern is that the inclusion of Black agency within their Social Dominance Theory is too ahistorical (2003, p. 240) and does not serve to "enrich our understanding of the complex and multifaceted relationship of Blacks to American race politics" (2003, p. 241).

schools, partly to help in an evaluation of the effectiveness of anti-bias peer train-ing that was being undertaken in the schools. However, the data that the researchers used (and upon which they report in their article) were from the time period *before* any "anti-bias intervention" took place – that is from "time 1 only" (2005, p. 535). The idea was to examine theoretically (via an analysis of this data) the relationships between the variables isolated.

Rabinowitz et al. remark that in organizing their study, they concentrated on the views of adolescents from "high status groups" – that is, the views of White and Asian students as their population under study. They indicate that:

> It is necessary to note that there is a high degree of consensus within the American social system as to which groups are dominant and which subordinate. Sidanius and Pratto (1999) showed that, among four racially diverse samples of university students, there was a very high level of consensus in the status ratings of five ethnic groups. The average perceived social status ratings were ordered from highest status to lowest: (1) Whites, (2) Asians (3) Arabs, (4) Blacks, and (5) Latinos. (2005, p. 533)

Rabinowitz et al. also cite empirical evidence that "young Asian Americans have mean levels of prejudice as high as – if not higher than – their European American peers (Jackson, 2002; Lowery, Hardin, & Sinclair, 2001)" (2005, p. 533). On the basis of this empirical information, Rabinowitz et al. suggest that "it makes empir-ical sense as well as theoretical sense to combine Asian American and White respondents" (2005, p. 533).

4.2.2 The (Societal-Level) Focus on Egalitarian Beliefs

Rabinowitz et al. note that in their study, they wished to focus on social equality beliefs of people, because this, for them, represents

> a broader societal-level focus than measures of the conditions of intergroup contact, which generally focus on the immediate environment (usually at the school or even classroom level). (2005, p. 533)

They believe that through the choice of constructs as used in the study, they can provide a broader (societal-level) focus than other psychological studies of prejudice and possibilities for its attenuation. They point out that this applies specifically to the construct of "egalitarianism," which they note is

> prescriptive rather than perceptual; that is, equality beliefs represent individuals' beliefs about the way social arrangements *should* be, rather than simply their perceptions of what *is*. Thus, we shift the focus from perceptions of conditions of contact as predictors of prejudice toward individuals' prescriptive beliefs about social equality. (2005, pp. 533–534)

They indicate that the choice of the construct of egalitarianism as a possibly impor-tant variable influencing intergroup prejudice is based on their acknowledgment that beliefs about equality have "historically shown strong effects" (2005, p. 529).

They also point out that within what is called Social Dominance Theory (STD), egalitarian beliefs feature as an important variable, via the concept of Social Dominance Orientation (SDO). Within this theorizing, an SDO, they note, is defined in terms of the value that individuals place on "nonegalitarian and hierarchically structured relationships among social groups (Pratto, Sidanius, Stallwort, & Malle, 1994; Rabinowitz, 1999)" (Rabinowitz et al., 2005, p. 530).

The study that they set up was based on what they call a strategy for combining the variable of *egalitarianism* and the variables of *strength of ethnic identity* and *outgroup orientation* in a model that tests the impact these variables have on *prejudice* (2005, p. 529). They consider that the potency of the STD on which they draw is that it does not

> restrict its explanation of discrimination or prejudice to the intrapsychic conflicts and mechanics of individual actors, but rather examines how individuals influence and are influenced by inequitable social structures. SDT . . . posits that the origins of prejudice derive, in part, from unequal distribution of resources and status within society and the need to maintain and justify these unequal distributions by those groups that take advantage of them. (2005, p. 530)

Rabinowitz et al. elucidate another concept that is important in terms of STD – the concept of "legitimizing myths" (2005, p. 531). They suggest that the content of these myths, when accepted by people, mediates between

> a desire for group-based inegalitarianism (e.g., SDO) and support for hierarchy-enhancing social policies and behaviors that lead to an inequitable, group-based hierarchy in a given society. (2005, p. 531)

That is, to the extent that people embrace the content of "legitimizing myths" that may be prevalent in a society, group-based hierarchical relationships become endorsed and practiced by people. Indeed, Rabinowitz et al. remark that the definition of a legitimizing myth is that it performs this legitimizing function. As they put it, "the mediating role of such variables defines them as legitimizing myths" (2005, p. 531). Rabinowitz et al. indicate that one kind of legitimizing myth is political conservatism, which can be used to justify opposition to policies such as affirmative action. (See also Chapter 2, Section 2.3.1.1.) They see another legitimizing myth as provided by symbolic racism. (See again Chapter 2, Section 2.3.1.1.) As they state:

> Research on social dominance theory has shown that symbolic racism mediates the relationship between inegalitarianism and individuals' stances on social policies, such as affirmative action. (2005, p. 531)

Here they refer to research that suggests that people's scores on symbolic racism scales have been shown to be (negatively) correlated with responses to particular policies such as affirmative action.

Rabinowitz et al. indicate that *hierarchy-enhancing* legitimizing myths (such as those involved in symbolic racism) stand in opposition to *hierarchy-attenuating* legitimizing myths. They provide examples of hierarchy-attenuating beliefs in society as including "Christian brotherhood, socialism and feminism" (2005, p. 531).

4.2.3 Possible (Hypothesized) Mediators of Prejudice: Strength of Ingroup Ethnic Identity and Outgroup Orientation

In terms of their understanding of the import of STD, Rabinowitz et al. posit two possible mediators of the operation of prejudice, namely, ethnic identity and outgroup orientation. They consider *strength of ingroup ethnic identity* as "a hierarchy-enhancing ideology (at least for high status groups)" (2005, p. 532) because "it refers to individuals' closeness to the ingroup without regard to the other groups" (2005, p. 533). They suggest that *outgroup orientation* can be "characterized as a hierarchy-attenuating ideology" (2005, p. 531) because it refers to people's orientation to "know, understand, and interact with outgroups" (2005, p. 533).

They elucidate their definition of these terms by drawing on the work of Berry, Trimble, and Olmedo (1986) as follows:

- Ethnic identity is most frequently defined as the part of social identity that we associate with the ethnic group(s) to which we belong. Further, ethnic identification describes the degree of concern with maintaining the cultural identity and characteristics of one's ingroup (2005, p. 528).
- Outgroup orientation reflects one's degree of concern for developing and maintaining relationships with other groups (2005, p. 528).

In relation to these variables, they offer the hypotheses that:

First, we hypothesize that egalitarianism will negatively predict level of prejudice. Second, egalitarianism will predict outgroup orientation positively and strength of ethnic identity negatively. Third, we expect that both ... outgroup orientation and strength of ethnic identity will predict level of prejudice. (2005, p. 534)

They explain that in testing these hypotheses the following measures of the relevant variables (with some questions in the questionnaire being reverse coded) were utilized – as expressed in Table 4.1 below:

Table 4.1 Rabinowitz et al.'s (2005, p. 536) constructs (with item wordings)

Egalitarianism
1. Providing equal opportunities for different groups is important if America is to stay strong
2. Our society cannot afford to guarantee each person an equal opportunity to succeed in life (reversed)
3. We should not be concerned about maintaining a "level playing field" for everyone to succeed (reversed)
4. All groups should be given an equal chance in life
5. It's not very important if some individuals are given more of a chance to succeed in life (reversed)
6. Every person in this society should be given exactly the same opportunities to succeed

Strength of ethnic identity
1. I am happy that I am a member of the ethnic group I belong to
2. I have a strong sense of belonging to my own ethnic group

Table 4.1   (continued)

3. I have a lot of pride in my ethnic group and its accomplishments
4. I feel a strong attachment toward my own ethnic group

Outgroup orientation
1. I like meeting and getting to know people from ethnic groups other than my own
2. I often spend time with people from ethnic groups other than my own
3. I am involved in activities with people from other ethnic groups
4. I enjoy being around people from ethnic groups other than my own

Affective bias
1. I feel like I could develop an intimate relationship with someone from a different race
   (reversed)
2. When I have children of my own, I would feel O.K. about my son or daughter dating someone
   from a different race (reversed)
3. It would be fine with me if people of a different race than me moved in next door to my home
   (reversed)
4. I think it is better if people marry within their own race

Rabinowitz et al. point out that both the constructs of *outgroup orientation and strength of ethnic identity* were assessed using 7-point scale items, ranging from 1 (*Strongly disagree*) to 7 (*Strongly agree*). (Higher scores on these scales express, respectively, higher levels of outgroup orientation, and stronger ethnic ingroup identity.) *Egalitarianism* was also measured with a 7-point scale. *Affective bias* was measured with a subscale of the Quick Discrimination Index (QDI).

4.2.4 Rabinowitz et al.'s Discussion of Results

In discussing the findings of the research, Rabinowitz et al. indicate that the results "are consistent with our hypothesis that equality beliefs are a predictor of intergroup affective bias" (prejudice) (2005, p. 539). They find it interesting that in terms of the statistical equations set up to observe mediations, "ethnic identity does not serve a mediating function [between egalitarianism and affective bias], but outgroup orientation may" (2005, p. 539). According to the test of mediation that they used, it was revealed that "outgroup orientation was a statistically significant mediator ... but that strength of identity was not" (2005, p. 539).

They suggest that their (hypothesized) attempt to "implicate" the variables of strength of ethnic identity as well as outgroup orientation as mediators of the relationship between egalitarianism and affective bias can thus be regarded as "partly successful" (2005, p. 539). As they explain:

> Willingness to interact with members of outgroups and positive feelings about such interactions [items connected with the variable of outgroup orientation] were shown to explain a significant portion of the relationship between egalitarianism and prejudice. (2005, p. 539)

They also point out that research is ongoing regarding people's "outgroup orientation" and regarding the possible "need to feel secure in one's identity as a mechanism for tolerance of others" (2005, p. 539).

As far as the role of ethnic identity is concerned, they remind us that:

> We expected to find that ethnic identification would serve as a hierarchy-enhancing legit-
> imizing myth, in that greater closeness to one's own group would drive, to some degree,
> greater affective bias against outgroups. Although the path coefficients were in the hypoth-
> esized directions, the results provide little evidence to suggest that ethnic identification
> is a mediator of the egalitarianism-to-prejudice relationship in any manner – either in a
> hierarchy-enhancing or a hierarchy-attenuating way. (2005, p. 540)

In trying to explain this unexpected finding, they suggest that it is possible that
students are aware that

> in a multicultural society, there is nothing inherently wrong with or counterproductive about
> taking pride in one's own ethnic group. It is possible, according to this cultural pluralism
> argument, for individuals to desire and work for a truly egalitarian society while still feeling
> close to their own ethnic heritages. As such, beliefs about equality would be independent
> of feelings toward the ingroup. This would explain the lack of a relationship in our data
> between egalitarianism and ethnic identity. (2005, p. 540)

They point out in this regard that it is noteworthy that they found no correlations
between "outgroup orientation" and "ethnic identity." This they interpret as meaning that "how close students feel to their own ethnic group tells us nothing about
how willing they are to interact with different ethnic groups" (2005, p. 540). They
indicate that this lack of a relationship as revealed by their findings can be considered as "consistent with the lessons of cultural pluralism" in the sense that a cultural
pluralist approach to group relations "stresses respect for other groups as well as
one's own groups" (2005, p. 540).

They indicate that their findings are compatible with recent research conducted
by Whitehead, Wittig, and Ainsworth (2005), which shows that "the relationship between strength of ethnic identity and positive feelings toward outgroups
is mediated by positive feelings toward one's ingroup" (Rabinowitz et al., 2005,
p. 541). They remark that this has important implications for ways of approaching
multicultural education. As they put it:

> If this result is robust, the challenge to multicultural education is clear: Focus on promoting
> ethnic identity based on pride in one's membership in an ethnic group with a positive history,
> customs, and traditions that are unique in their forms, but which share with other ethnic
> groups many common features. An ethnic identity based on such insights is compatible
> with the egalitarian principles necessary for a multicultural society. (2005, p. 541)

According to them, then, their research, coupled with some of the results found by
others, shows that one can foster an egalitarian society by encouraging members of
different "ethnic groups" to take pride in their membership thereof, while simultaneously encouraging principles of egalitarianism. They spell out their conception
of implications of this research for "diversity in education" as well for "affirmative
action in education" in the two concluding sections of their article.

4.2.4.1 Implications for Diversity in Education

In setting out the implications of the findings of their research for diversity in
education, they state that "the present article has demonstrated a relationship

between students' egalitarian beliefs and their levels of affective bias toward other racial/ethnic groups" (2005, p. 541). They indicate that because they have shown that egalitarian beliefs are negatively correlated with affective bias (prejudice), their research "justifies efforts to design interventions to foster such beliefs" (2005, p. 541). They also point out that their research results suggest that "students' levels of prejudice can be reduced in a couple of ways" (2005, p. 541):

> First, interventions that increase levels of egalitarianism are likely to reduce prejudice. Second, to the degree that interventions can enhance outgroup orientation, they are likely to improve attitudes toward outgroups. (2005, p. 541)

They conclude from this that interventions designed to effect attitude changes toward more egalitarianism and toward enhanced outgroup orientations "among high-status group members at the high school level hold promise for paving the way for smoother intergroup relations in colleges and workplaces" (2005, p. 541).

They suggest that, in the light of previous research showing that the absence of bias (on the part of high status groups) is linked to better academic performance of all students in the setting, the strategy that they have suggested should be seen as part of an overall strategy to "elicit the best academic performance from students of all races" (2005, p. 542). They suggest that in the long term, this could reduce the need for "programs such as affirmative action" (2005, p. 542). They believe that it is important to convince "future leaders and decision makers" that "maintaining social diversity should be the default for a multicultural society – even in the absence of a set policy" (2005, p. 542). They thus stress the importance of maintaining such diversity.

4.2.4.2 Implications for Affirmative Action in Education

Rabinowitz et al. begin their deliberations on this by pointing to the importance of schools in bringing, in their words, "children and youth of all races" together – at a time when, as Patterson (1997) suggests, "their life-long attitudes are being formed" (Rabinowitz et al., 2005, p. 542, citing Patterson, 1997, p. 191). In considering the formation of "life-long attitudes," they indicate that in their view (based on their research), "chief among these attitudes are those that support equal opportunity and 'leveling the playing field' for all groups" (2005, p. 542).

In referring to their own write-up of the research, they point out that:

> The present report focusing on adolescents from high-status ethnic groups is consistent with a growing body of research suggesting that such egalitarian beliefs are associated with lower prejudice. (2005, p. 542)

They now indicate that as far as affirmative action is concerned, if we consider

> the history of U.S. Supreme Court decisions over the last 30 years, it seems likely that affirmative action in education will undergo a gradual shift toward a class- or income-based policy. (2005, p. 542)

Faced with this possible scenario, they suggest that it is crucial that we recognize that

a continuing commitment to egalitarianism on the part of the majority of U.S. citizens will
be an essential component of the feasibility and success of all such social policies that are
designed to equalize opportunities to acquire skills that are essential to competence – skills
that are mainly available through education. (2005, p. 542)

They thus conclude that whether or not affirmative action policies endure in their
present form, it will be essential that citizens continue to commit to egalitarian principles so that, at least, opportunities to acquire skills (in schools and universities)
will not be thwarted.

4.3 Revisiting Rabinowitz et al.'s Research

My review of Rabinowitz et al.'s research in this section revolves around my suggestion that the way of posing questions to their "high status group" respondents and the
very focus on *groups*, on *group identity* and on *group thinking* already frames the
research endeavor and generates "results" accordingly. Furthermore, it reinforces
the idea, as Harris-Lacewell complains about many studies of race politics (2003),
that "others" – such as "other ethnic groups" or those from a "different race" are
indeed "others" to be seen as such.

One of the assumptions that informs their research is that the categories of
race/ethnic groups to which they refer are obviously "given" in social life, namely,
the five ethnic groups that they isolated: (1) Whites, (2) Asians (3) Arabs, (4) Blacks,
and (5) Latinos (2005, p. 533). The research which they cite showing that there is
high degree of consensus in America "as to which groups are dominant and which
subordinate" (2005, p. 533) seems to be based on the idea that these groups exist as
entities "in" the social system.

Omi comments in this regard that researchers, as others, can all too easily reify
what Hollinger (1995) calls the American ethno-racial pentagon (2001, p. 252). In
terms of a reified account of the "pentagon,"

Blacks, Hispanics, American Indians/Alaska Natives, Asians/Pacific Islanders, and Whites
are now seen as the five basic demographic blocs we treat as the subjects of multiculturalism. The problem is that these groups do not represent distinct and mutually exclusive
"cultures" [as is implied by isolating them as "ethnic groups"]. (2001, p. 252)

Omi considers it crucial that we

rethink what we mean by the terms "race" and "culture," and ... critically interrogate
the manner in which we articulate the connection between the two in research and policy
studies. (2001, p. 252)

Following on from this proposal of Omi's, I would suggest that Rabinowitz
et al.'s research, as with previous research that they cite in relation to the positioning of "ethnic groups," does not provide sufficient opportunities for people to
interrogate the way in which the "groups" might be conceived in the first place. To
illustrate this point, we can (re)consider the way of setting the questions meant to tap
into people's strength of ethnic identity in Rabinowitz et al.'s study. The questions
that were posed are

1. I am happy that I am a member of the ethnic group I belong to.
2. I have a strong sense of belonging to my own ethnic group.
3. I have a lot of pride in my ethnic group and its accomplishments.
4. I feel a strong attachment toward my own ethnic group.

By posing these questions, it seems to me that no space is left for people to revisit the apparently obvious ethnicization of social life (obvious to the researchers). It is assumed that people really "belong" to some ethnic group and that they can be more or less happy that they are a member hereof (Question 1). And the remaining matters then become how strong their sense of "belonging" is (Question 2); how much pride they take in "their" ethnic group (as if it is a possession – Question 3); and how attached they feel to their "own" ethnic group (Question 4).

Consider also the way of setting the questions meant to tap into people's outgroup orientation. The questions that were posed are as follows:

1. I like meeting and getting to know people from ethnic groups other than my own.
2. I often spend time with people from ethnic groups other than my own.
3. I am involved in activities with people from other ethnic groups.
4. I enjoy being around people from ethnic groups other than my own.

Again here I would suggest that no space is left for people to revisit the apparently obvious division of the social world into bounded ethnic groups; and meanwhile the "othering" of others (in this case, those who are not White or Asian) can become encouraged via this mode of questioning. The questions are already focused on directing people to seeing themselves as belonging to some group – and *in these terms* orienting to "others." It is assumed that people are obviously socially situated in some "group," and that when they make choices to interact with others they will be considering them in terms of their "belonging" to some "other" group. So the questions are posed to ask people to consider how much time they spend with people who are "from" other ethnic groups and how much they enjoy interacting with people defined as "from" another group.

As I argued in Chapter 2, and again in Chapter 3, this way of framing is not the only possible option for analysts or practitioners in conceiving our way of developing social relationships. Furthermore, by strengthening the salience of "ethnic groups" as a schema of interpretation (which the researchers may unwittingly be doing by treating as obvious the fact that there "are" ethnic groups *in* social reality), the researchers may be contributing to creating the conditions for people to conceivably focus on competition between "the groups." As Brubaker, Loveman, and Stamatov argue, if the ethnic competition schema is easily activated, people may be more prone to see and experience competition in ethnic rather than in other terms. One key aspect of ethnicization is that ethnic schemas become hyper-accessible and in effect crowd out other interpretive schemas. (2004, p. 44)

So, considering the framing of the questions in Rabinowitz et al.'s study, I suggest that by (re)activating a sense of ethnic groups as given entities, and by using the research to "find out" how people experience "their" group's achievements, the research already makes ethnic schemas "hyper-accessible" in social life. Trying to then "undo" relations of stereotyping and affective bias in the society, by hoping to teach "equality" is not necessarily helpful. Although Rabinowitz et al. have shown that there is (in terms of their measures of constructs) a correlation between egalitarian beliefs and low levels of affective bias (prejudice toward outgroups), they do not show how one could *set about nurturing the egalitarian beliefs* that they consider crucial to prejudice reduction in (USA) society. Another way, not posed by them, would be to help people to *deconstruct the apparent obviousness of ethnicized schemas*, so that people are not thought of in terms of their naturally being "members" of some supposedly identifiable group. (See also Chapter 8, Section 8.3.4.2, for a discussion of the use and critique of the "naturalization" frame as identified by Bonilla-Silva, 2006.)

4.3.1 Rabinowitz et al.'s Conception of Multicultural Education

Rabinowitz et al. consider that one of the implications of their findings for multicultural education is that such education could/should focus on

promoting ethnic identity based on pride in one's membership in an ethnic group with a positive history, customs, and traditions that are unique in their forms, but which share with other ethnic groups many common features. (2005, p. 541)

They argue that arising from their research, it would appear that "an ethnic identity based on such insights is compatible with the egalitarian principles necessary for a multicultural society" (2005, p. 541).

The disquiet that I have with this framing of the issues is that Rabinowitz et al. do not consider that this way of approaching multiculturalism *already presupposes* the existence of groups as if these are entities *in* the social world. Other strategies (not provided for by the language that they seem to be unreflexively employing) for developing different social relationships between people thereby become excluded, but without recognition of this exclusion.

Meanwhile, Bhavnani et al. suggest, in contrast to what Rabinowitz et al. are proposing as a recommendation, that when those trying to foster "diversity" in schools focus on the "groups" to which people are considered as "belonging," this itself can be counterproductive. With reference to Bigler's work in the USA on school interventions designed to counter stereotyping, Bhavnani et al. state that *drawing attention to a group* and its characteristics can be argued to "facilitate inter-group bias" (Bigler, 1999, cited in Bhavnani et al., 2005, p. 138). Omi similarly remarks that "multiculturalism" has sometimes been criticized for "unwittingly increas[ing] racial tensions" – especially insofar as "race" and "culture" tend to be conflated in apparently "multicultural" projects (2001, p. 252).

Bhavnani et al. indicate that in the context of Britain, "some [multicultural] interventions . . . could be construed as entrenching segregation and artificially separating 'racialized' groups" (2005, p. 117). They indicate that their primary concern with "multicultural intervention" is when "diversity" projects are set up in terms of a specific (narrow) conception of the diversity of cultural forms and of "'cultural' difference." They remark in this regard that "by examining 'difference' between and among communities against a narrow definition of culture, 'culture' can become 'fixed' and interpreted as unable to change" (2005, p. 117).

Kundnani deliberations on the social effects of different understandings of multiculturalism in Twenty-first Century Britain are of relevance too in making a case for reconsidering its meaning. He argues that the "policies that were implemented in the 1980s [in Britain] in the name of multiculturalism" became a mode of control. They were focused around managing the identity of ethnic communities so that these do not become "disruptive" of what were seen as English traditions such as "respect for authority and decency" (2007, p. 44). He explains:

> Multiculturalism in this sense referred to a set of policies directed toward taking African-Caribbean and Asian cultures off the streets – where they had been politicized and turned into rebellions against the state – and putting them on the council chamber, in the classroom and on the television, where they could be institutionalized, managed and commodified. Black culture was turned from a living movement into an object of passive contemplation, something to be "celebrated" rather than acted on. (2007, p. 44)

He avers that it was in this political context that "multicultural policies confused anti-racism with a superficial sort of cultural recognition" (2007, p. 46). He proposes that it is an easy (and dangerous) step from this understanding of multiculturalism to argue that "culture" has an "anthropological meaning: a distinctive way of life in which a people is rooted, organically, holistically, and traditionally" (2007, p. 49). This in turn implies that "genuine interaction between cultures" is not possible (2007, p. 50). He argues that for ethnic minority communities, the "new politics of ethnic difference" had disastrous consequences. They were now officially defined "not by color, or nationality, or immigration, status, but by culture – which was proving to be the most ambiguous of concepts" (2007, pp. 51–52).

Kundnani thus argues that we need to be careful of ways in which multiculturalism becomes understood, and we need, at the very least, to make provision for more dynamic forms of multiculturalism,[111] where participation in discussion around social values is provided for, and where culture is not essentialized as a "thing." (See also Chapter 2, Section 2.3.4 and Chapter 3, Section 3.4.2.) The idea

---

[111] This would tie in with Alibhai-Brown's proposal that we need to move away from what she calls "laissez-faire multiculturalism" and move more toward teaching children in schools the "skills for critical interrogation" (2000, p. 70).

here, as Janet McIntyre-Mills further points out – in offering feedback to me, May 2009 – is to point to the "sharing of essential values of being human as a basis of social dialogue."

Considering these deliberations around ways of interpreting multiculturalism in different contexts, I would suggest that when Rabinowitz et al. provide for their respondents the wording: "I have a lot of pride in my ethnic group and its accomplishments," no option is provided for people to consider cultural heritages or forms of expression as *processes in-the-making – made in relation to involvement with others*. Parekh suggests that such a processual view is important in an age in which, as he puts it, "cultural boundaries are ... permeable and in which culture both absorbs the influences and defines itself in relation to others" (1997, p. 61). By Rabinowitz et al. focusing the students' attention on "my" ethnic group, they already provide a frame for participants that encourages seeing "their" culture in a specific way – and the space for acknowledging learning between cultural expressions hereby already becomes shrunk.

Laitin offers an interesting conceptualization of culture that allows us (analysts as well as practitioners in society) to envisage (and practice) culture as an ongoing process – rather than treating "it" as consisting of set values, ways of life, or, in Rabinowitz et al.'s terms, "accomplishments." He suggests that we can envisage culture as "points of concern to be debated" (Laitin, 1988, p. 589). We can then locate "cultural arenas" by looking out for the kinds of issues that are raised as *points of debate* in some (cultural) setting – that is, as issues that people in that setting regard as *important to address*. But it is understood in this conception of culture that there is no univocal solution offered to address problems of concern to people participating in a cultural arena. In terms of this definition of culture, then, culture is conceptualized as *offering symbolic vehicles for debating* what are considered to be "issues of concern" – offering options for living which are never finalized.

The advantage of this way of viewing culture is that we can then imagine fostering processes of transcultural communication – where people are encouraged to become geared to considering a variety of ways of contributing to debates being explored in different settings. At the same time, it means that people do not have to link their so-called pride to being able to defend the various components of *their* cultural "possessions." Rather, they can take pride in developing their capacities to move beyond seemingly fixed repertoires of seeing and acting, and in being open to mutually interrogate – with others – elements of (any) culture.

Berbrier expresses a similar stance when he suggests that it can become problematic when the "pluralist master frame" becomes (ab)used to emphasize "the immeasurable value of diversity and cultural survival" at the expense of creating opportunities for dialogue across differing perspectives (2004, p. 55). Rabinowitz et al. have remarked that the high school students in their survey may have been aware of the *cultural pluralism stance*, where it is understood that people can "work for a truly egalitarian society while still feeling close to their own ethnic heritages" and where "respect for other groups as well as one's own groups" is stressed (2005, p. 540). But I would contend that Rabinowitz et al. also *foster* this kind of orientation (rather than an orientation of, say, mutual criticism and learning[112]) when they pose questions around the issue of "pride" in "my" ethnic group.

In considering some of the debates around ways of developing more dialogical human relationships across different cultural expressions, Simpson addresses the question of what might be involved in such a dialogue (and whether it is possible to talk across the languages provided by different cultural expressions). He suggests that understanding of "the other" implies participating in a dialogue that is "linguistically enabled" (2000, p. 436). For Simpson, language is a vehicle that can be used to "reconfigure boundaries and transform difference, and therefore also the borders separating and defining Self and Other" (2000, p. 437). He points out that through language (discourse), people's frameworks can become enlarged; and in this way, as he puts it, "my resources for self-description get enlarged and my self accordingly gets reconfigured, my boundaries redrawn" (2000, p. 437).

Simpson also points out that "in order to understand the new, we are sometimes required to expand intelligibly a given paradigm [in terms of which we may be thinking] or decisively reconfigure it" (2000, p. 438). And by doing so, we change ourselves and our relationship to what was previously seen as "other." This implies a reconceptualization of the way in which "diversity" of cultural resources is appreciated. This is consistent with Brubaker, Loveman, and Stamatov's suggestion that we need not see the social world as divided into "cultural blocs" with "bounded groups as basic constituents of social life" (2004, p. 45). We can rather envisage "collective cultural representations" as "widely shared ways of seeing, thinking, parsing social experience, and interpreting the social world" (2004, p. 45), which at the same time, can also form the basis of dialogue across "ways of seeing" and ways of life (through transcultural communication).

Bauman puts forward the suggestion that the capacity to move across borders that we may have drawn in our imagination is part of our humanity. But he also notes that, unfortunately, our capacities to "transcend our reciprocal otherness" keeps being "used up, diverted, channeled away, squandered by . . . commercialized pseudo-multiculturalism . . . in lieu of genuine conversation" (2003, p. 215).

Reay et al. take up Bauman's arguments when they criticize forms of multiculturalism that they see as "caught within" what they call "multicultural capitalism." They argue (on the basis of their interview research with families in London) that middle-class White children "exposed" to "ethnic and classed others," can all too easily make use of "a conveniently accessible . . . ethnic other in order to gain valued global multicultural capital" (2007, p. 1053). Reay et al. indicate that being

---

[112] To illustrate the option of encouraging mutual criticism, it is worth noting Hampden-Turner and Trompenaars' suggestions for doing this by locating pathologies attendant on "taking too far" any specific codes. For example, considering the cultural codes associated with "individualism," they suggest that one pathology of individualism is the "runaway greed it celebrates" (2000, pp. 78–79). And a pathology that they locate in communitarian-oriented cultural contexts is that people can feel "savagely censured" if they try to "escape their shared fate" (whatever this may be) (2000, p. 82). Through people's involvement in locating pathologies/disadvantages in different "cultural codes," the way arguably becomes opened for dialogue across alternative styles of living.

"exposed" to different cultures can be seen strategically as offering White children skills to (later) work and live in ethnically mixed settings. Thus a "use value" is put on exposure to "other" cultures – where "white middle classes further enrich themselves through the consumption of ethnic diversity" (2007, p. 1051). They indicate that in terms of Bauman's outlook, a different way of approaching a commitment to multiculturalism would be to be genuinely concerned with the welfare of "the other." They suggest that thus far the tension (identified by Bauman) between "the acquisitive individualized self and commitment to civic responsibility and the common good" has not been given sufficient attention in public conceptualizations of multiculturalism (2007, p. 1051).

Reconsidering Rabinowitz et al.'s study in the light hereof, it could be argued that their research process, as well as the recommendations that apparently spring therefrom, could well limit these students' (their participants') and wider audiences' possible appreciation of forms of *processual multiculturalism*, where *transcultural communication toward building new forms of relationship is encouraged.*

4.3.2 Possibilities for Developing Reframing

Having illustrated by way of my discussion of Rabinowitz et al.'s study that survey research might serve to reinforce certain uninterrogated notions with respect to race/ethnicity/culture, and so on, I now ask whether survey research could potentially be operated differently – that is, in a way that sets the stage for reframing. But before exploring this matter, I would like to reiterate that I am querying the assumption that survey research can be considered as a process that serves (more or less accurately) to *uncover* already existing attitudes/views/affective responses which merely become (self-)reported via the questions asked by researchers. As I have tried to show with reference to the items/questions used by Rabinowitz et al. to supposedly tap into people's "real" orientations, it can be argued that the researchers are *rendering certain ways of thinking and ways of feeling hyper-accessible* at the point at which the questions are asked (to use Brubaker, Loveman, and Stamatov's terminology, 2004, p. 44). By posing questions in another way, *other frames may become relevant and could then "come to the fore" in the answers provided by the respondents.*

So, for instance, if Rabinowitz et al. made provision for posing questions in a way that concentrated on possibilities for learning across cultural expressions (where such expressions are not seen as a "possession" of some "ethnic group"), these ways of conceptualizing their human relationships may become more accessible to people – as the questions may enable people to bring to the fore in consciousness some examples of this occurring in their experience.

The idea that research can be treated as itself *forming* the attitudes that it may be attempting to "uncover" has been mooted by many researchers – especially those operating within a more "qualitative" tradition of research (cf. Mann, 2006). But Mann notes that despite this being what she calls "methodological staple" in relation to various topics of research, it seems that there has been little attempt to consider this as an issue in "nationalism scholarship and in relation to its specific dimensions" (2006, Paragraph 1.5). She cites Brubaker's (2004) argument that, as Mann paraphrases it, "greater attention needs to be paid to how ethnic, national and racial categories are used by analysts themselves" (2006, Paragraph 1.5). Based on Brubaker's caution, she notes that interviewers' own talk in processes of interviewing "could well betray 'assumptions' and 'common sense habits'." Her argument is that the manner in which researchers draw out/generate the interviewees' expressed ways of seeing is specifically of importance when talking to people around issues of nationalism/ethnicity/race – where initial assumptions about their "facticity" can easily be reinforced unless specifically probed (or as Mann puts it "unhinged") during the interview encounter.

Mann asks readers of her article to consider to what extent the use of, say, national or ethnic categories by an interviewer in formulating questions can be seen to "reproduce and reinforce" a respondent's use of the categories (2006, Paragraph 4.6). Her own deliberations around this question are as follows:

> This question identifies the central problematic that this article seeks to address .... It is perhaps not surprising that respondents should reproduce the "having" of a national identity in a self-evident unproblematic fashion if they are prompted to do so. At the same time such framing by the [interview] question[s] also provides an enclosure to work against .... (2006, paragraph 4.6)

Mann's suggestion is that it is important for interviewers/inquirers to indeed admit the way in which their questioning can reinforce a sense of "self-evidence" in the use of categories. By being conscious hereof, they can in turn see their frames as something for both interviewer and interviewees to work against in their apparent obviousness. Mann goes on to provide for readers a number of examples of ways in which "talking against" national and ethnic categories emerged in some of the interviews on which she reports (2006, Paragraph 5.2).

Mann sets up her argument in the context of considering the role of interviewers in more or less unstructured interview encounters with those being interviewed. Nevertheless, I would suggest that we can consider how her argument would apply to survey research too. For instance, the respondents/participants in Rabinowitz et al.'s research may well have been responding to what was discussed in previous chapters as social desirability pressures. (See in this regard Chapter 2, Section 2.3.1.2 and Chapter 3, Section "Possible Influence of 'Demand Characteristics'?" as discussed under Section 3.2.1.2.) In this case the "pressure" (in terms of the high school students' understanding of the mainstream cultural pluralist framework) would be to consider that there *are* a plurality of ethnic groups in some assumed ethno-racial set of groupings (which is taken as given – as Omi, 2001, notes) and that the pluralist goal is for people to be, in Rabinowitz et al.'s words, "willing to interact with members from different ethnic groups" (2005, p. 540). The students' responses could have been formed in relation to this (perceived) pressure.

Harris-Lacewell casts additional light on this point when she notes that according to Shipler (1997) when surveyors in the USA ask Whites about racial issues, the respondents may be offering "quickly formed responses." Shipler contends that such respondents should be understood to be "offering attitudes formed more

immediately" than those of Blacks who are likely to have thought about their positions more carefully beforehand (2003, p. 235). In other words, while Blacks may
have "well-developed beliefs" due to their need to have found a way of dealing
with racial issues, Whites may have less-developed views. This means, as Harris-
Lacewell puts it, that White respondents (or in the case of Rabinowitz et al.'s study
both Whites and Asians) would be "significantly more susceptible to measurement
error introduced through priming and questionnaire artifacts" (2003, p. 235). She
argues that with the focus on White (or high status group) attitudes in the study of
race politics (as noted in Chapter 2), surveyors need to give more attention to trying
to assess "the frequency and intensity with which different Whites normally think
about race in their daily lives" (2003, p. 235).

I would suggest here that Harris-Lacewell is pointing to an issue that has indeed
not been given sufficient consideration, namely, the way in which what she calls
"questionnaire artifacts" can be operating to *direct people to think about issues in
a particular way* (especially if their views are relatively unthought-through). My
proposal would thus be for researchers to take some responsibility for the way in
which their manner of setting questions itself implies a particular framing, and to
consider how to set up possibilities for reframing.

4.3.3 Accounting for Framing in Relation to Affirmative Action

Although Harris-Lacewell (2003, p. 235) contends that insufficient attention has
been paid to respondents' ways of forming responses in relation to racial issues during survey encounters, the notion that respondents in surveys may be responding in
terms of the frameworks provided by researchers has been explored by a number
of researchers in relation specifically to the framing of issues concerning affirmative action. In relation to attitudes on affirmative action, one can locate a body of
research material (springing from experimental and survey studies) suggesting that
the manner in which issues are framed by researchers through their questions, may
affect the opinions that respondents express toward affirmative action plans. Knight
and Hebl explain the argument that has been developed by some researchers in considering the importance of framing. In citing Cialdini and Rhodes (1997) in regard
to the "psychology of persuasion," they state:

> Generally speaking, a frame is "a psychological device that offers a perspective and
> manipulates salience in order to influence subsequent judgment" (Cialdini & Rhodes, 1997).
> Because people are influenced by changes in perspective, their perception of the desirability
> of options changes depending on the frame (Tversky & Kahneman, 1981, 1986). (Knight &
> Hebl, 2005, p. 550)

Knight and Hebl indicate how this argument has been applied in "the realm of
racial attitudes" in relation to affirmative action. Referring to work by Fletcher and
Chalmers (1991) on this, they note that

> the framing of a question used to assess opinions about affirmative action can dramatically
> influence people's answers, even though people typically have very strong opinions about
> racial issues (Fletcher & Chalmers, 1991). (Knight & Hebl, 2005, p. 550)

They thus suggest that even when people's opinions in relation to racial matters are "strong" (and would thus appear *not* to be malleable), different attitudes toward affirmative action can be drawn out by research framing. They illustrate their argument with examples:

> Whites [in the USA] support the idea of affirmative action when it is framed as providing equal opportunity and as helping minorities get ahead (Kluegel & Smith, 1983), yet they are opposed to affirmative action when framed as having negative consequences for Whites and men (Bell, Harrison, & McLaughlin, 2000). (Knight & Hebl, 2005, p. 551)

They also cite additional research in this direction (e.g., Fine, 1992; Taylor-Carter, Doverspike, & Alexander, 1995).

In describing further the background to their own research study aimed at considering different possible justifications for affirmative action, they indicate that as far as the diversity agenda is concerned:

> Although many researchers have speculated that framing affirmative action as enhancing diversity will increase nonbeneficiary support for its policies through eliciting self-interest [because diversity is seen as having positive effects for everyone and not only for the beneficiaries of affirmative action] few researchers have directly tested this theory. (2005, p. 552)

They indicate, though, that it is important when testing this theory, that research participants have some understanding of the "value of diversity" (2005, p. 552). They suggest that this understanding can be enhanced by "thoroughly explaining the benefits of affirmative action to nonbeneficiaries" so as to "make the message more concrete, personal, and meaningful." (They cite here the work of Petty and Cacioppo (1981), and of Pratkanis and Aaronson (2000).)

Their research study (with 216 White undergraduate students – 110 men and 106 women – at a small, private southern university) was directed at examining the responses to different messages provided to different groups of respondents. Three alternative kinds of justifications for an affirmative action plan were embodied in the messages: a *compensatory* justification, an *instrumental* one, and a *utilitarian* one – where the last one emphasized the value of diversity. They explain the import of their study:

> The current study sought to confirm and extend previous research by exploring how the justification given for different affirmative action programs affected nonbeneficiaries' acceptance of or resistance to the [affirmative action] plan. Across all different types of AAPs [affirmative action plans] and across all different types of participant characteristics, it seems that a utilitarianism justification that emphasized benefits to both minority and majority groups was the *most successful in inducing positive attitudes toward AAPs*. (2005, p. 563, my italics)

They point to the value of science (including their own contribution) as they see it:

> Through exploring how different justifications can influence self-interest and attitudes toward AAPs [affirmative action plans], perhaps science can help society realize the value of diversity initiatives and consequently develop an affirmative reaction to affirmative action. (2005, p. 563)

Whether or not we accept Knight and Hebl's way of presenting the frames to their (White) respondents, their research can be seen as supporting the idea that attitudes can be *(re)formulated* – and not simply "found" – via the research process itself. Or rather, "found" attitudes are recognized here to be in part a product of how the (research) framing is presented to respondents.

Niemann and Maruyama (2005) develop a related argument when they suggest that attitudes toward affirmative action are in the process of being formed in social life – and that researchers themselves can and do make inputs in this process. They indicate that on the one hand, affirmative action can be portrayed as "counter[ing] differential treatment and discrimination toward particular groups in society" (2005, p. 410). On the other hand, they point out that affirmative action can also be framed as "violating values of individualism and meritocracy." As they note, "to individuals supporting a meritocracy, almost any type of differential treatment is viewed as reverse discrimination" (2005, p. 410).

They point to the "diametrically opposed view [to this meritocratic argument] represented by critical race theory [CRT]." They indicate that CRT scholars emphasize that

> the color-blind perspective represses and renders irrelevant the important and impactful ways in which race shapes social relationships (Guinier & Torres, 2002; Roithmayr, 1999; Ross, 1995). (Niemann & Maruyama, 2005, p. 410)

Niemann and Maruyama suggest that in the light of the "battle" in society as to how to conceive affirmative action, researchers need to *take into account how their conceptualizations presented to respondents/participants (which in turn frame the results reported upon to wider audiences) may make a difference to people's outlooks*. Their own position on this is to side with the suggestions of CRT scholars who point to the ways in which race continues to affect social relationships. As they note, there is sufficient evidence that

> race matters: in media representations; ... in education; ... in immigration law; ... in social science research; ... and in the criminal justice system ... to name just a few of the seemingly countless contexts in which race matters. (2005, p. 411)

They clarify that their conclusion from their reading of the research to date is that "race matters," and that "at this stage of our human cognitive and social development, color blindness is impossible" (2005, p. 411). They indicate that this conception of theirs in turn informs their way of seeing, and evaluating, the way in which (if at all) researchers take cognizance of framing issues in relation to affirmative action.

Nevertheless, it must also be noted that Niemann and Maruyama still appear to be operating with some kind of *realist* research orientation, in the sense that their manner of outlining research studies (upon which they report in their article) is still couched in terms of the exploration of effects of variables on other variables identified in social reality. Hence, their understanding of the variable of *framing* as having an effect on *attitude formation* seems to be derived mainly from their account of research designs involving comparisons between different research respondents (exposed to different messages) to "find out" if and how the different framings are correlated with the attitudes that become generated. For example, when discussing Knight and Hebl's (2005) approach, they describe it using realist language. As they explain:

> Specifically, they [Knight and Hebl] examine whether or not appeals to broad benefits of diversity programs would be more effective than those that focused primarily on the benefits to the group receiving favorable treatment. Based upon responses of White college students, Knight and Hebl found that justifying programs using appeals to benefits for both minority and majority students were more effective than those that focused on benefits only to a single group. (2005, p. 421)

Thus it appears to me that although some researchers working with a "quantitative" research approach (focusing on variables and their relationship) have paved the way for alerting researchers to the possible impact on (primarily White) respondents of their manner of framing issues/questions (especially in relation to affirmative action[113]), they have not taken this sufficiently far. That is, they do not carry the argument to the point of making a case for regarding the status of any research "findings" in relation to affirmative action as being partly a product of the way the research itself is set up.

In the next section I discuss briefly a survey organized by Haley and Sidanius, which again points to the pliability of attitudes found/generated in research contexts, and which points also to the "race effect" on possible understandings of affirmative action. In discussing their argument, I make a number of additional points relevant to our ways of seeing the construction of race(d) groups. This provides a backdrop for my discussion in Section 4.6 of Dunn and Geeraert's (2003) constructivist argument and how it can be incorporated in survey research.

4.4   Haley and Sidanius's Survey Exploring the Positive and Negative Framing of Affirmative Action (Los Angeles, USA)

Haley and Sidanius organized a survey in Los Angeles County in which they explored both so-called nonbeneficiary and "beneficiary" groups' relationships to different possible framings of affirmative action. Their aim was to continue research work on the "positive and negative framing of affirmative action" – in this case in relation to "the public opinion of adult Whites, Blacks, and Latinos" (2006, p. 659). As part of their research, they developed six frames by creating informal focus groups, out of which these frames were generated (2006, p. 659). The frames were

---

[113] Other research of note here is that of Richardson (2005). Richardson explains that "by focusing on selected aspects of an issue, frames can *switch particular trains of thought to the forefront of audience members' consciousness, thereby affecting their political cognitions*" (2005, p. 504, my italics). Drawing on Dovidio et al.'s work on recategorization (see Chapter 3, Section 3.3), Richardson examines how people can be induced in research situations to "identify with a larger social category" – thereby affecting their attitudes to affirmative action (2005, p. 506).

- providing training to certain groups;
- engaging in outreach to recruit members of certain groups;
- considering group membership as "one factor among many";
- using group membership as a "tie-breaking" device;
- using quotas; and
- giving preferences to (relatively) underqualified applicants (2006, p. 665).

People's attitudes in relation to the frames were then explored via a telephone survey. The sample size was 328: 151 Whites, 129 Blacks, and 48 Latinos (2005, p. 660). Haley and Sidanius indicate that the aim was to establish "how often respondents tend to think about affirmative action in each of the six ways" (2006, p. 650). One of the substantive questions in which they were interested was "whether affirmative action attitudes depended on framing and/or on respondents' race/ethnicity" (2006, p. 661). They indicate that the results of their analysis of the data produced in the survey were that "opposition to affirmative action was significantly affected by frame" (2006, p. 661). They found that "there was very strong agreement across race/ethnicity concerning which forms of affirmative action were more or less objectionable" (2006, p. 662). That is, certain framings of affirmative action rendered it "objectionable" to respondents across race/ethnicity divides. Nevertheless, they indicate that consistent with STD, "Whites were more opposed to affirmative action than were minorities within each and every frame" (2006, p. 662). They elucidate that

> even when affirmative action was framed in the terms that people find most acceptable (i.e., "Giving training to certain groups so that they can compete equally"),Whites were still more opposed than minorities. (2006, p. 662)

They consider it noteworthy that

> both subordinate groups [Blacks and Latinos] had a tendency to think of affirmative action in the least objectionable ways (i.e., as training and outreach) rather than in the most objectionable ways (i.e., rather than as quotas or preferences for less qualified applicants). Whites, in contrast, showed a slight tendency to do the reverse – more often framing affirmative action in negative terms rather than positive terms. (2006, p. 663)

They state that it is very significant for them (in terms of STD) that SDO "made a statistically significant net contribution to the tendency to frame affirmative action in negative terms" (2006, p. 665). (See Section 4.2.2 for a definition of SDO.) In other words, the variable of SDO was correlated with the manner in which people tended to think about (or frame) affirmative action issues.

They remark that the results of the survey are in line with previous research (e.g., Bell et al., 2000; Bobo & Smith, 1994; Fine, 1992; Kinder & Sanders, 1990), which suggests that "opposition to affirmative action is an extraordinarily pliable attitude, significantly dependant on framing" (2006, p. 666). However, they add that (as they had anticipated), "Whites were consistently more opposed to affirmative action than were the other groups, regardless of framing" (2006, p. 666).

Considering the practical implications of the research, Haley and Sidanius suggest (following other researchers, such as Kinder and Sanders, 1990) that:

> Policy makers, employers, and others who desire to change people's (positive and negative) attitudes toward affirmative action should employ and encourage the use of certain frames as opposed to others. (2006, p. 666)

But they caution that "the link between affirmative action and dominance motives needs to be kept in mind and ... policy makers and employers will not be able to eliminate group differences in affirmative action attitudes so facilely" (2006, p. 667).

They indicate that although certain researchers have suggested that it may be possible to unearth people's different assumptions as a route to "help to build consensus among affirmative action supporters and detractors," their own research results (from their survey) "cast doubt on this idea." This is because "significant racial/ethnic differences in support for affirmative action persisted across each and every frame we examined" (2006, p. 667).

4.5 A Comment on Haley and Sidanius's Survey

The reason why I have included an account of Haley and Sidanius's survey in this chapter is to make three main points.

Firstly, in line with the other researchers whom I cited in Section 4.3.3, they agree that framing of issues relating to affirmative action can make a difference to the *production of attitudes* toward it – which appear to be somewhat "pliable" (2006, p. 666).

Secondly, they concentrate not only on the perspectives of "nonbeneficiaries" in relation to affirmative action (those identified as Whites in this case), but also on the views of others (those who were identified as Blacks and Latinos). Because they include these perspectives, they are able to show up for consideration to us that the manner in which debate between alternative ways of framing issues in (USA) society proceeds is likely to be influenced by *discrepancies between experiences and understandings of people along the dividing lines of racialized and ethnicized division in the USA.* Hence they suggest that attention needs to be given to the manner in which these experiences might enter into, and affect, the style of "debate" that takes place in the society. Instead of seeing debate as a matter of people engaging with one another in terms of their admission of the assumptions underlying the different frames, Haley and Sidanius suggest that this conception of social debate may be "facile." This would tie in with my argument in Section 4.3.1 with reference to the work of various authors who point out that people would need to cultivate the facility as well as interest to use language in a way that *enables human engagement across different frames of understanding/feeling.*

Thirdly, however, they seem themselves to accept that there *are* what they call "ethnic and racial groups" existing *in* the social system. While it could be argued that they wish to examine "the effects of race/ethnicity" (2006, p. 660) on the way in which frames are used and evaluated (and therefore that as researchers they need to employ these categories), the problem is that they do not at any point raise for discussion with respondents (during the telephone interview) or for consideration in their research write-up the question of *how we might envisage the categories.* They thus seem themselves to endorse the idea that there *are* these groups and that people are "members of the dominant ethnic group (i.e., Whites)" or "members of subordinate ethnic groups (i.e., Blacks or Latinos)" (2006, p. 660). Again, they might argue that the reason why they utilize these categories is in order to point to "socioeconomic gaps" that can be located in the society once we compare people in terms of the categories (2006, p. 660). But my concern is that once these categories are used without in any way problematizing their standing, it becomes very difficult for survey respondents and wider audiences of the research to *imagine how this "group" thinking can be reworked in a debate where the essentialism of race/ethnic categories themselves is put on the table for discussion.*[114]

As I indicated in Chapter 3, Morton et al. (2009) argue that "essentialism" can be considered as a variable that is differentially invoked in different contexts – in that appeals by (White) prejudiced people to essentialism can vary depending on whether someone is being excluded from a desired position for "being white." (See Chapter 3, Section 3.4.2.)[115] At this point, they note, many Whites (in the experimental situations that they set up) become more constructivist-oriented, challenging the meaningfulness of the race category and posing as color-blind. As Morton, Hornsey, and Postmes put it, "prejudice can be expressed in contradictory ways across contexts" (2009, p. 54). They cite as an illustration of incoherence in people's upholding of essentialism Federico and Sidanius's discussion (2002) of how White people may express an opposition to social policies that make use of race (such as affirmative action policies) as part of an apparent "principled objection."[116] They note, with Federico and Sidanius, that the principle seems to become activated strategically by prejudiced people depending on which group they believe is the "recipient of negative treatment" (2009, p. 46). They see Federico and Sidanius's work as pointing to the way in which "race categories" tend to be strategically deployed in different argumentative contexts.

Morton, Hornsey, and Postmes's interpretation of their own experiments and of Sidanius and colleagues' survey studies would seem to open the way for research around affirmative action to raise for consideration the contradictory ways in which social categories themselves are drawn upon in different social contexts. I would suggest, however, that the challenge is still to consider how indeed survey research,

---

[114] Harris-Lacewell (2003) points to a related concern of hers in relation to Sidanius and Pratto's (1999) work. (See also Footnote 110.)

[115] Their suggestions here can be seen to tie in with Bonilla-Silva's (2006) point that often one cannot find coherence (e.g., during interviews that he set up) in White people's storying around race. (See also Chapter 8.)

[116] One of the conclusions that Federico and Sidanius reached from this survey study among White adults in Los Angeles was that (apparent) "principled-objection" endorsement of opposition to affirmative action policies was "driven not merely by race-neutral values but also by dominance-related concerns like racism" (2002, p. 488).

through the manner in which questions are framed for participants, can contribute toward problematizing (rather than reinforcing) possible tendencies toward the essentialization of racialized categories.[117] Just as I have suggested that Rabinowitz et al.'s study can be revisited by considering whether their particular framing of questions might serve to reinforce apparently "given" social categories, so I would suggest that Haley and Sidanius's research likewise needs to be reviewed along similar lines, with a view to considering the social impact of research framings. In the next section, I consider the question of how survey research can possibly be mobilized in this direction, with reference to my discussion and extension of another example.

4.6 Dunn and Geeraert's Survey in Australia

Dunn and Geeraert indicate that the telephone survey that they commissioned in Australia was set in a context in which it has often been assumed that "support for anti-immigrant and anti-multicultural political groups was primarily rurally based" (rather than based also in urban areas) (2003, p. 1).[118] They contend that the geographies of racism are still "poorly understood" and that it is for this reason that they wished to organize a survey across different areas in the states of New South Wales and Queensland. A random sample of 5,056 residents from these states participated in the survey, which took place from October to December of 2001.

In order to offer an indication of the theoretical background of their study, they point to different "paradigms" of race studies, and they state that their work should be seen as invoking a paradigm which they call "new cultural geography" or "social constructivism" (2003, p. 1). They explain that over the last century, one can locate a move from what they call "environmental determinism" (as one paradigm), through what they call "old cultural geography" (as another paradigm) to "new cultural geography" – a third paradigm (2003, p. 1).

- In the first paradigm, they explain, the focus of researchers is on "identifying the environmental bases of 'races' and of culture more generally." This includes "measuring skin color and skull shapes, and linking those to environmental patterns and change" (2001, p. 2). (This conception relates to my discussion of the origins of the concept of "race" in Chapter 2, Section 2.2.2.)

---

[117] Harris-Lacewell also points out that one of her aims is not to "essentialize Blackness" by, for instance, claiming that Black people inherently have an "Afrocentric worldview which is more communal" (2003, p. 232).

[118] Johnson, Terry, and Louis set a wider context by noting that:

In Australia, renewed public awareness of racism and prejudice as pervasive social issues has been signaled by controversies concerning the rise and fall of the One Nation party, with a platform of cultural nationalism and opposition to Asian immigration; political and cultural policies toward Aboriginal Australians; and unfavorable attitudes toward asylum seekers. (2005, p. 56)

- In the second paradigm, the focus of researchers is on "measuring and mapping 'race' and ethnicity" in terms of culture. Here "culture" is seen as a container in which humans are born/raised – and it is conceptualized as static. In the context of Australia, they note, it includes "mapping the distribution of Indigenous peoples/tribes" (2003, p. 2). (This conception relates to my discussion of cultural racism in Chapter 2, Section 2.3.4.)
- In the third paradigm, the research focus is on seeing cultures and landscapes "as constructs of human action past and present." This in turn implies "deconstructing racial ideology" and "analyzing the politics of race." And, in relation to Australia, for instance, it implies an "analysis of the racialization of Indigenous people and their places" – as well as "analytic work on whiteness" (as a construction) (2003, p. 2).

They claim that although one can locate shifts in the emphasis adopted by scholars studying racism toward the third approach (an approach which they support), "the everyday belief that there are natural 'racial' categories of humankind is still widespread in everyday society" (2003, p. 1). Indeed from their survey, it appears that "about 78% of the respondents believed that humankind could be sorted by natural categories called 'races'" (2003, p. 1). They state that the reason why they have placed in quotation marks the term "race" throughout their article, is to highlight that in their own view "it is a constructed category rather than a natural grouping of humankind" (2003, p. 1).

They indicate that in terms of the new cultural geography or social constructivist perspectives, one can "identify different forms of racist beliefs and statements" (2003, p. 1). *Old racisms*, as they put it, "are based on supposed racial hierarchies and prohibitions on racial mixing." *New forms of racism*, they note (2003, p. 1), are "focused not through 'race' but upon cultural differences." (They cite Jayasuriya, 2002, in this regard.) New racism also involves exclusionary assumptions about what constitutes the nation – for example in the Australian context, this would include the "dominant perception that Australian national identity is Anglo-Celtic" (2003, p. 3). "New racism" can be expressed through people's "opposition to cultural difference" and in addition it includes the "failure to recognize the cultural disadvantages and privileges of racism" – that is, the failure to acknowledge the privileges that may accrue to people by virtue of their backgrounds (relative to others) (2003, p. 3). In considering "old" and "new" racisms, they suggest that these can be regarded as "distinct but related"; and they point out that "there is no . . . single definition of racism" (2003, p. 3).

They state that their questionnaire was designed to tap into the potential expression of both of these forms.[119] Questions were asked in the survey in relation to "the respondent's attitudes, their experiences of racism and cultural mixing, and [also their] gender, age, [and] cultural and educational background" (2003, p. 1).

---

[119] This tallies with Pillay and Collings's similar approach adopted in their survey (2004) in South Africa. (See Chapter 2, Section "Measuring Continuing Old-Fashioned as well as New Racism in South Africa" as discussed under Section 2.3.2.3.)

They point in particular to the wording that was used in respect of the *attitudinal questions* (as they call them – 2003, p. 1), as follows (2003, p. 2):

1. It is a good thing for society to be made up of people from different cultures.
2. You feel secure when you are with people from different ethnic backgrounds.
3. Australia is weakened by people of different ethnic origins sticking to their old ways.
4. There is racial prejudice in Australia.
5. Australians from a British background enjoy a privileged position in our society.
6. It is NOT a good idea for people of different races to marry one another.
7. All races of people ARE equal.
8. Humankind is made up of separate races.
9. You are prejudiced against other cultures.
10. Do you believe that there are any cultural or ethnic groups that do NOT fit into Australian society? (Response options here were YES or NO; and the respondent was asked which groups, if YES.)
11. In your opinion how would you feel if one of your relatives were to marry a person of . . .

> Asian background
> Aboriginal background
> Muslim faith
> Jewish faith
> Italian background
> British background
> Christian faith.

The response options for the first nine of these questions were: strongly disagree; disagree; neither disagree nor agree; agree; strongly agree. The response options for the final question (on marriage) were: not at all concerned; slightly concerned; somewhat concerned; very concerned; extremely concerned (2003, p. 2).

The questions taken as a whole were meant to provide for potential expressions of old as well as newer forms of racism. For instance, for Question 1, strongly disagree and disagree responses were seen as being an indicator of "opposition to cultural diversity" and in this sense an indication of (a form of) new racism; for Question 2, strongly disagree and disagree were seen as indicators of "concern about cultural difference" and again were seen as expressions of forms of new racism; for Question 3, strongly agree and agree responses were seen as thus indicative; for Question 4, strongly disagree and disagree were seen as indicators of denial of operative prejudice and thus as pointing to this dimension of new racism (namely, new racism as denial of racism); and for Question 5, strongly disagree and disagree were seen as indicating a denial that Anglo-Australians may enjoy privileges in Australia (and thus indicative again of new racism as denial of privileges accruing to some people by virtue of their background). Questions 6 and 7 in particular were seen as providing for the measurement of "older" forms of racist attitudes and were coded with this in mind – with strongly agree and agree on Question 6 being seen as an indicator of the "need to keep 'races' separate," and with strongly disagree and disagree on Question 7 being seen as an indicator of belief in "racial hierarchy" (2003, p. 2). Question 8 was included to tap into people's beliefs about "natural racial groups" (2003, p. 2). Question 9 was included to offer the option for respondents to self-identify as racist: strongly agree and agree responses to this question were taken as "an indicator of self-identified racism" (2003, p. 2). And Question 10 was aimed at seeing whether respondents felt that they had "the right to make judgments about cultural fit": Dunn and Geeraert also point out that naming particular groups here means that they were considered as "outgroups" (2003, p. 2). On the final question relating to possible concern with a marriage of a close relative to people from different backgrounds, Dunn and Geeraert remark that slightly concerned through to extremely concerned responses were taken as indicators of the "outgroup" status in Australian society of those from the respective backgrounds (2003, p. 2).

4.6.1 Dunn and Geeraert's Discussion of Results

Dunn and Geeraert begin their discussion of the results by noting that certain urban sociologists have suggested that city life seems to generate a more open approach to cultural diversity and to the experience of cultural difference than does rural living. They indicate that this kind of thinking around the rural–urban divide also penetrates the popular view of "red-necked ruralite" and "cosmopolitan urbanite" (2003, p. 3).[120] Yet they point out that the results of their research "provided little substantive evidence of a straightforward urban-rural difference of racist attitudes" (2003, p. 3). Although some regions appeared to have "very serious issues of racism," they suggest that these issues are linked to "histories of poor inter-communal relations" and that this points to *regional variation* rather than to rural–urban division. As they explain, "the regional level data fail to show a perceptible urban-rural dichotomy in attitudes" (2003, p. 4).

They present a table explicating the appearance of racist attitudes across different cities and rural areas, and they show that altogether the following results emerged:

> 7.34% of respondents expressed that "cultural diversity is not good";
> 10.7% felt "insecure in presence of cultural difference";
> 44.84% expressed that "ethnic diversity weakens nation";

---

[120] Dunn and Geeraert seem to be using the term "cosmopolitan" in a similar way to that used by Skrbis, Kendall, and Woodward (2004, p. 130) – as implying "the ability to draw upon and enact vocabularies and discourses from a variety of cultural repertoires." But Skrbis, Kendall, and Woodward also note that one can distinguish between indicators of "mundane or unreflexive forms of cosmopolitanism," which include "the types of food one consumes, consumption of heavily packaged or mediated cultural and tourist experiences," and more *genuine* forms of cosmopolitanism displayed in the ability to work across the symbols of alternative cultural repertoires (2004, p. 130).

8.5% expressed a "denial of racism in Australia";

42.6% expressed a "denial of Anglo-Australian cultural privilege";

13.3% expressed a "belief in racial sexual separation";

11.7% "do not believe in racial equality";

77.6% expressed a "belief in 'races'";

12% indicated a "self-identification as a racist";

44.9% could "identify groups that don't fit in Australia";

27.5% expressed Anti-Asian sentiment;

28.9% expressed Anti-Aboriginal sentiment;

52.8 % expressed Anti-Muslim sentiment; and

24.1% expressed Anti-Jewish sentiment.

Dunn and Geeraert also provide some graphs displaying the geographical distribution of incidences of respondents' self-identification as prejudiced and also of anti-Indigenous sentiment across certain areas; and they provide some maps showing, respectively, the distribution of racist attitudes, of Anti-Muslim sentiment, and of Anti-Asian sentiment across various Sydney Local Government Areas.

They state that it is possible to interpret the data from the survey in terms of their accord with the research expectation that racist attitudes are linked to levels of education and also to economic vulnerability. For instance, they indicate that across the Sydney Local Government Areas, "the generally most-racist opinion [as measured by Dunn and Geeraert's various indicators] was located within areas of lower socio-economic status and high recent migrant settlement" (2003, p. 4). In addition, they interpret the data as suggesting that:

> There is also a sense that those areas of much longer standing cultural diversity (Marrickville, Ashfield, Sydney and Leichhardt) are places where people have become more accustomed to, and perhaps appreciative of experiences of, cultural diversity. (2003, p. 4)

They caution that the geographies of racism are complex, for example:

> The highly affluent North shore LGA [Local Government Authority] of Pittwater had a much higher than average support for old racist attitudes of racial supremacy and racial separatism, and yet for the other indicators its responses were generally less racist (or about average). Respondents from the rural fringe LGA of Camden were third least supportive of old racisms, yet they were among the top groups of LGAs where concern about cultural difference was expressed. (2003, p. 5)

In terms of practical implications of their research, Dunn and Geeraert emphasize that those trying to fight against racism need to pay attention to regional variation when designing strategies such as "anti-racism campaigns, more inclusive statements of national and local citizenry, [and] tolerance building exercises" (2003, p. 5). And they state their hope that local governments and others should be able to utilize the data from their survey, coupled with their own understanding of "local inter-communal relations," to generate appropriate anti-racist initiatives which are "locally targeted and locally owned" (2003, p. 5).

4.7 Revisiting Dunn and Geeraert's Approach: Probing Their Proffered "Student Activities"

The final page (p. 6) of Dunn and Geeraert's article is labeled *Student Activities*. It consists of a whole page of statements and questions presumably for students (and others interested) to consider. I consider this page of the article crucial, as it raises a number of issues for us to think about. I believe that some of these questions could indeed have also been included in the questionnaire used for the telephonic survey itself and that if this was done, it would be some mechanism for helping respondents to reflect again on their understanding of racism and how their views can possibly be reconfigured. I refer in Section 4.7.1 to a few examples hereof. And in Section 4.7.2, I refer to possibilities for considering Dunn and Geeraert's style of write-up as novel in its presentation and as worth pursuing as a way of engaging with audiences.

4.7.1 "Activities" for Reviewing the Constructs of Culture and Race, and Possible Links to Racism

Under a heading called *Understanding the text* in their article (2003, p. 6), Dunn and Geeraert point to a number of ways in which students/audiences can reconsider the text that they have constructed. They facilitate our review of the text by asking us to consider a set of questions. In this section, I concentrate on showing how their questions can indeed facilitate our reviewing of the construct of "culture" and also our reconstruction of the category of "race," calling on us to consider implications hereof for addressing racism. I turn firstly to one of their questions on culture, that I regard as pertinent, as follows. (It appears as Question 5 under their heading of *Understanding the text* – where there are 22 questions to consider.)

5. A superorganic perspective of culture sees people as being born into a culture and they live their lives according to the dictates of that culture. How could such a notion reinforce racist thinking?

I suggest that this question, as well as serving us as audiences to reconsider their text, would also be valuable for respondents to consider. I suggest that it may be important to include such a question in the questionnaire itself, in order to prevent the essentialization of the categories that Dunn and Geeraert have taken pains to define as social constructions. To illustrate this point, let us consider again their first question on culture that they did pose in their questionnaire:

1. It is a good thing for society to be made up of people from different cultures (2003, p. 2).

I would propose that apart from posing this kind of question, it could well at some point in the questionnaire be asked as a further question, whether a superorganic perspective of culture is one which needs to be adhered to when thinking about culture.

(It could be explained to respondents on the telephone that such a conception of culture, as Dunn and Geeraert note, 2003, p. 6, sees people as "being born into a culture and they live their lives according to the dictates of that culture.") Such a question could be an open-ended one where response options are not restricted – and later the researchers could codify the responses, for audiences to reflect further upon. And it could be asked also at some point whether a "superorganic perspective" can be seen as reinforcing racist thinking (as Dunn and Geeraert have raised as a question for "Student Activities"). To aid the codification and analysis of questions such as these, some software designed for qualitative analysis could be drawn upon (cf. Richards & Richards, 1994). Also, in terms of possible financial and time constraints in dealing with the open-ended nature of the questions, a subset of the data could here be utilized instead of the whole set. In this way, at least all respondents/participants would have been asked to reflect upon the matters, and also as audiences we would have a glimpse of some of their reflections.

This would mean that the questionnaire could provide an opportunity for respondents (and audiences) to reflect upon, and possibly extend, their initial perspectives – also by recognizing that there is not only one way of seeing the term "culture" and indeed the term "racism."

While it may be argued that a survey method of research is not an appropriate mechanism for trying to expand people's horizons, it can be counter-argued that by *not* offering scope for reflection in the manner in which I have suggested, one still (as a researcher, via the questionnaire) cannot avoid complicity in the way in which social life develops. The choice to phrase questions in the way that Dunn and Geeraert have done (following a myriad of other survey researchers), without offering an alternative way of framing, cannot be assumed to be without consequences for people's thoughts and actions in social life.

The same reasoning can be used when considering the way in which they ask us as readers of their text to review the construct of race, and to think about implications of our usages for continued racism. For instance, under their heading *Understanding the text* (after Question 5 regarding the superorganic perspective on culture), they ask the following question (Number 6), which again I believe could well have been proffered for consideration to respondents:

6. Why do the instigators of the University of New South Wales Racism Project insert quotation marks around the word "race"?

They follow up this line of questioning under another heading called *Extension activities* (which consists of six questions) – where they ask a number of questions that I too believe could be included in the questionnaire for respondents. As one example, they ask (Number 1):

1. What evidence, if any, is there of racism in your local area/community? What are the most critical forms of racism within your local area? Speculate on other racisms that might be important (though not apparent) within your local area.

As another example of a question that I believe could be included, they ask (Number 4):

4. How is racism in your locality, or in others, influenced by national level issues, such as contemporary political debates over immigration, multiculturalism, and Indigenous affairs?

And as yet another example, they ask (Number 5):

5. How is racism influenced by dominant ideas about what constitutes national identity, e.g. the popular image of who is an Aussie, Briton, Kiwi, etc. How are such ideas circulated?

My view again is that these kinds of questions could be included in the questionnaire itself in order to act as a counterpoint to the questions that they did use in their questionnaire when asking people about "race issues." Let us consider the questions that appeared in the questionnaire, such as:

6. It is NOT a good idea for people of different races to marry one another.
7. All races of people ARE equal.
8. Humankind is made up of separate races.

I would suggest that because these questions can be argued to gear respondents in the direction of defining races as "existing," it is crucial to add at some point in the questionnaire *another way of seeing "race"* – as a contingent social construction, rather than an obviously given way of grouping (2003, p. 1). If, for instance, respondents were asked (via an open-ended question) why some scholars have chosen to place the term "race" in quotation marks, this could help to deconstruct the category. Again, some responses to this could be written up in the research report, thereby showing audiences too that this is an issue that requires reflection upon.

Considering the issue of quantification in the social sciences as a research approach, Young cautions us not to simply look for data in a form that supposedly can be counted – but rather to "actively seek ... presumptions and hidden assumptions" (2008, p. 223). She avers that "it is not quantification per se that is the problem, rather it is in failing to question such that we risk being unethical" (2008, p. 223). She suggests in this context that failing to hold up for attention hidden presumptions of, say, homogenized ethnicity can indeed be regarded as "unethical" – because the social consequences of retaining these presuppositions are not given due attention. Young makes these points as part of her calling on us to question the conceptual homogenization of "white Australia" too. She points in this regard to the "huge proportion of Australians [who] were not actually born here" and she suggests that "we are all migrants, whether newly arrived or 6th generation non-indigenous Australians" (2008, p. 222). She makes these points in the political context in which she observes how "each new significant wave of migrants [now] becomes the target of 'Australians'" (2008, p. 222). She puts the term "Australians" in inverted commas here as part of her suggestion that this category needs to be revisited.

It is worth noting in this regard that Ali makes similar proposals when considering the British and the USA social contexts. She comments that:

> The struggle to find appropriate names for collective identities whether forced or "voluntary", coupled with a desire to preserve "racial" or ethnic distinctions is a common feature of both British and USA literature. (2003, p. 6)

Ali points to "the ongoing singularity in hegemonic discourses of 'race,' and the binary structure that underpins most models of difference and discrimination" (2003, p. 6). She remarks that it is not surprising that some authors will choose rather to focus on "narratives of genealogical plurality" – as one way of under-cutting the "hegemonic discourse" (2003, p. 6). While Ali suggests that studies of interviewees' narratives of plurality offer a good route for this, I would suggest that it is also possible to try to introduce such an alternative discourse into questionnaire construction in survey research too. This could be by, say, introducing questions that allow for deliberations "in relation to mixedness" (as Ali expresses it, 2003, p. 30) – thus inviting a way of moving beyond "racialized constraints" by "beginning a process of deconstruction" (2003, p. 18).

I suggest therefore that questions in Dunn and Geeraert's survey calling to con-sciousness examples of what Young calls "fluid ethnic identity" (2008, p. 223) could conceivably open more space for people to envisage alternative ways of thinking and feeling around the various categories. In this way the survey questions can become used, to some extent, to unhinge "obvious" ways of seeing categories by providing alternative frames. As mentioned earlier, this way of approaching questionnaire-construction (as an opportunity for opening space for increased reflection on the part of respondents) also in turn would mean that audiences of the write-up are given more material to reconsider the standing of any categorizations that have been used during the research.

4.7.2 Inviting Audience Participation: A Novel Style of Write-Up?

Under a heading entitled *Skills* Dunn and Geeraert ask students/audiences to (re)consider some of the issues raised by their write-up of their article. They provide eight questions toward this end. I believe that such questions, along with the others they ask under their headings *Understanding the text* and *Extension activities*, pro-vide an aid for audience participation in reviewing the text. I feel that the questions should be seen (and expressed) as an important part of the text that they present, for all readers to consider as part of the article itself. For example, they point toward the concept of paradigms (Number 2 under *Skills*):

2a. T.S. Kuhn referred to paradigms in "The Structure of Scientific Revolutions" (1962). According to Kuhn, scientists work in communities, groups of researchers and teachers who share a common approach to their work. They are socialized into a research field from which they can problem solve from a mutually accepted framework. This is the paradigm through which they work.

To what extent are the authors Dunn and Geeraert justified in using the word "paradigm" to refer to the three phases of cultural geography?

2b. How do these three paradigms underpin shifts in thinking about ethnic and cultural studies in geography?

They also ask questions such as:

6. On the basis of the survey, comment on the expected racist attitudes experienced by an Indigenous person living in South Sydney, a Turkish-born person living in Auburn, a Vietnamese-born person living in Marrickville, a Shanghai-born person living in Ashfield, and a German-born person living in Pittwater.
7. On the basis of the survey, how comfortable would a practicing Muslim feel living and worshipping in: Warringah, Woollahra, Leichhardt, Council, and Kogarah LGAs [Local Government Authorities]?
8. On the basis of the survey, which LGAs appeared to express the least Anti-Asian sentiment?

Through all of these questions, Dunn and Geeraert offer what I consider to be an interesting and novel style of presentation of their research, especially insofar as we treat their section on *Student Activities* as material offered for all readers to think about (as very much part of the main text). For example, by asking us – under the heading of *Skills* in 2a – to consider the way in which Kuhn has used the word "paradigm" in his *The Structure of Scientific Revolutions*, they open up for consideration that science could indeed be conceptualized as a process wherein scientists "problem solve from a mutually accepted framework." Readers are invited to consider that the process of doing science might involve scientists working within frameworks that become "mutually acceptable" – which means that their collegial debate is not, as Popper (1994) implies, functioning to sidestep paradigmatic thinking. (See Chapter 3, Section 3.4.2.) They ask audiences to consider what may be involved in seeing "science" in this way.

In this manner (in 2a), the role of "science" in society in general, and in particular how work in relation to race/racism can be construed, is re-raised as a topic for consideration.

Furthermore, they ask us (in 2b) to reflect upon radical (paradigmatic) shifts in thinking about ethnicity and about culture. They therefore pave the way for unhinging thinking which assumes that "ethnicity" and "culture" are "things" that have always been treated and experienced in the same manner (within academic and other discourses).

In addition, I believe that the last three questions to which I pointed above (also under their heading of *Skills* – namely, Questions 6, 7, and 8) are helpful in that the categories that Dunn and Geeraert use to express people's background focus on where they are *born* – rather than assuming that somehow they "belong" unproblematically as "members" to some group. Nevertheless, I would suggest in this context that Dunn and Geeraert could also have raised further issues by asking us to consider not only the places of birth of, for instance, Turkish-born, Vietnamese-born, Shanghai-born and German-born people living in areas of Australia (see Question 6 under their heading of *Skills*), but also to what Young (2008) calls the *mixed ethnic heritage* of *white Australia* (2008, p. 221). According to Young, this has thus far been relatively hidden from view – and, as noted in Section 4.7.1, she pleads for researchers, as others, to reconsider the "unquestioning homogenizing of white Australia as predominantly British-Anglo origin" (2008, p. 221). Hence it can be suggested that the kind of questioning proposed by Young could likewise help to disrupt fixed notions of ethnicity here.

Dunn and Geeraert do, however, through the questions that they *have* raised in their *Skills* section, at least invite readers to develop a sense of empathy with how people may feel. This is by asking us to reflect on what it might mean (and feel) for Indigenous people as well as those born outside of Australia to experience attitudes of racism, and by asking us how comfortable people such as practicing Muslims might feel in geographical areas where respondents' answers to the survey questions have shown up forms of (overt or covert) racism. They also ask us to reflect on the finding that, say, anti-Asian sentiment appears to vary geographically (according to answers of respondents in the survey), and that this may be a function of the way in which inter-communal relations have been experienced within different regions. They thus open the space for people to rethink their ways of developing human relationships.

These examples to which I have pointed indicate to me that, via the write-up survey research, it is possible to point to issues for reconsideration at cognitive and emotional levels of understanding (where cognition and emotion are indeed recognized to be intertwined), while encouraging people to, as McIntyre-Mills puts it, "reconceptualize and reconstruct categories" (2008c, p. 237). I would propose that the *Student Activities* created by Dunn and Geeraert provide a possible mechanism for encouraging people to reconsider given constructions.

McIntyre-Mills further suggests that research can be used to acclimatize people to the idea that, in developing constructions/points of view "assumptions, beliefs and values and emotions play a key role as filters" (2008b, p. 201). On this point I feel that Dunn and Geeraert have not sufficiently exemplified this idea – although their constructivist position that they espouse should sensitize them to this. Dunn and Geeraert have in their write-up laid bare to readers that they are aware that a particular paradigmatic position (social constructivism) affected both the design of the survey (e.g., their identification of questions around both old and new racism) and their way of looking at the consequent "results." But I find that they do not make sufficiently transparent that they are aware that the results can also be considered to be *generated* partly in response to the way the questions were framed. Thus for instance, while they note that it appears that "about 78% of the respondents believed that humankind could be sorted by natural categories called 'races'" (2003, p. 1), they do not raise the issue of whether their way of using the term race within the questionnaire (without quotation marks) might have affected respondents' manner of expressing "beliefs."

Let us consider again their Questions 6, 7, and 8 in their *questionnaire* itself (2003, p. 2), namely:

6. It is NOT a good idea for people of different races to marry one another.
7. All races of people ARE equal.
9. Humankind is made up of separate races.

I would suggest that it is quite possible that by referring to "people of different races" in Question 6, the researchers incline respondents to see that there "are" different race groups, and that people are *of* some race. In Question 7, again, this style of language is present when speaking of "all races," as if there really are a variety of races (and linked to Question 6, this question implies that people are *of* one or other race). Thus when Question 8 is presented to the respondents, I would suggest that they have already been geared, via Questions 6 and 7, to seeing the world as composed of races. The nuanced thinking that Dunn and Geeraert express in their write-up, where they point out that "races" (in quotation marks) are socially constructed, is not presented as an option for the respondents to think about. And this could well have affected the way in which "results" became generated.

Dunn and Geeraert do not appear to me to be sufficiently reflexive about how their *own way of posing questions in the questionnaire might be responsible for orienting people in a particular direction* (which may indeed reinforce an essentialist conception of race). This also applies to their questions on culture in the questionnaire, which thus far seem to offer little scope for unhinging a view of culture as a "container" in which people are placed. For instance, considering their question "It is a good thing for society to be made up of people from different cultures" (2003, p. 2), the problem is that this way of posing the question can incline people toward a *particular conception of both culture and of diversity.* (See also my discussion in Section 4.3.1 above.) In my view, the question thus does not provide sufficient scope for people to call to consciousness as an option *an alternative conception of culture* to the one that the researchers themselves have associated with the "superorganicist paradigm," where culture is seen as a container into which humans are born (2003, p. 2). Thus it seems to me that they have not reflected sufficiently in their write-up on whether their question construction might have been unduly restricting options for thinking and acting in relation to the issues identified via the survey.

4.7.3 Some Final Points on Dunn and Geeraert's Scholarship

In a later article authored by Dunn, Forrest, Burnley, and McDonald (2004), the authors make the point that as they see it, "scholarship" on the treatment of diversity and of multiculturalism is thus far still "poorly developed." As they put it:

The scholarship on positive aspects of diversity, and more radical forms of multiculturalism, is by comparison more recent and still poorly developed. A social construction take on inter-communal relations can imagine a culturally inclusive, diverse and dynamic articulation of nation, which could theoretically challenge the apparent inevitability of out-groups. (2004, p. 426)

Considering the idea that "scholarship" can be directed toward imagining different ways of articulating culture (which challenges exclusionary thinking and practice), I would suggest that the survey commissioned in 2001 by Dunn and Geeraert (reported upon in 2003) falls short of evoking possibilities for what Dunn et al. (2004) call dynamic inter-communal relations – as explained in the quotation above. I have tried to show how they might have attempted this by, for instance, including some of their "activity" questions in their questionnaire itself and also how they might define anew their relationship with audiences engaging with their write-up text.

Meanwhile, in the text as it stands, I did not find any discussion of any variations in different respondents' responses from a variety of "cultural backgrounds" (as they call it, 2003, p. 1). Although they state (2003, p. 1) that they asked respondents about experiences of "racism and cultural mixing," they provide no indication of how people with different experiences around this, offered their accounts hereof. They do remark, though, that "there is a sense that areas of much longer standing cultural diversity (Marrickville, Ashfield, South Sydney, and Leichhardt) are places where people are accustomed to, and perhaps appreciative of, cultural diversity" (2003, p. 4). But I would suggest that far more detail on different people's perspectives on this would help us as audiences to gain a better appreciation of how the issue of "diversity" may be differently construed. And this again could help us to imaginatively extend our visions beyond the question of whether or not "it is a good thing for society to be made up of people from different cultures" (as in Question 1 of their attitudinal questions).

As far as efforts to explore people's experiences of "racism and cultural mixing" is concerned, it appears from Dunn and Geeraert's statement to the effect that they asked people about such experiences that this was an open-ended question; but this was not clear in their discussion of how their questionnaire was set up or how they dealt with responses to the question. A richer discussion on this could perhaps allow us to place in wider perspective the percentages that they report showing that, for instance, 8.5% of the respondents expressed a "denial of racism in Australia," and 42.6% of them did not feel that Anglo-Australians can be seen to enjoy a privileged cultural position. By juxtaposing certain people's account of "experiences of racism" (that presumably were recorded in the survey) with the answers to the attitudinal questions, we might be offered additional material for reviewing the statistical display of people's views. That is, the discussion around people's experiences of "racism and of cultural mixing" might provide some counterpoint to views expressing a denial of racism and might allow us as audiences to reconsider the meaning of racism itself (to include concerns with the possible ways in which, say, privileges may go unnoticed even by virtue of the language used to speak about issues). For instance, the language that defines "Australian national identity" and that forms the basis for judging that some groups (as defined) do not "fit" in Australia (according to Dunn and Geeraert's reporting 44.9% of respondents could identify groups that "do not fit") could be deconstructed as part of Dunn and Geeraert's write-up. They could ask us to reflect upon how this language itself (about supposed "national identity") might contribute to people's sense that they can judge which groups (as they define them) do not "fit." In short, I believe that more could be done with the write-up of results in order to activate what Omi (2001, p. 256) calls our "imagination" in imagining alternative ways of seeing the issues (and considering options for action to counteract both old and newer expressions of racism/social exclusion). (See also Chapter 3, Section 3.4.1.)

4.8 Conclusion

In this chapter, I examined a number of surveys where researchers have indicated that their research is relevant to the addressal of contemporary manifestations of racism. Through providing the detail, I argued that the surveys – like the experiments discussed in   Chapter 3 – can be seen as framing the research issues in a particular way, which itself is not without social consequence.

I suggested that Rabinowitz et al.'s research (2005) as well as that of Haley and Sidanius (2006) could operate to reinforce the notion that the social world is divided into blocs of racial/ethnic groups to which "members" belong. In the case of Rabinowitz et al.'s conclusions on possibilities for encouraging an egalitarian stance (springing from their survey results from "high status" high school students in Los Angeles), I suggested that their research framing seems to be linked to specific views of theirs on what this might involve in a so-called pluralist society. And such views, I argued, might run counter to *alternative definitions of egalitarianism* and *more radical forms of multiculturalism.* Considering Haley and Sidanius's survey (2006), I indicated that although they have pointed in their write-up of their research to experiments and surveys that offer an indication of the potential influence of research framings on people's (nonbeneficiaries' as well as beneficiaries') responses to *affirmative action*, they have not carried this understanding sufficiently forward. That is, they have not carried it to the point of reflecting back on the possible impact of their *own* research framing. I suggested that their approach also requires further extension in terms of raising for consideration the standing of social constructs (such as those of "groups") and the way in which these may be differentially drawn upon by people in specific argumentative contexts.

Turning to my discussion of Dunn and Geeraert's report on their survey in New South Wales and Queensland in Australia (2003), I pointed out that they espouse a social constructivist stance (and admit that their work is linked to this paradigm, as they call it). However, I proposed that in relation to the social constructions of "race" and "ethnicity," their questionnaire design – and their consequent write-up of results – could be enriched by including *as part of their questionnaire* some of the questions that they raised in their article in a final page called *Student Activities*. These questions, I argue, would allow respondents/participants to reflect again on the status of constructions such as race, culture, ethnicity, and so on, as part of their "responding" to the questions provided by the researchers. I suggested that if the opportunity is *not* created to enable respondents/participants to bring forward for consideration alternative understandings of these concepts, their givenness becomes hyper-accessible (and therefore all too easily reinforced).

As far as our understandings of multiculturalism is concerned, all the research examples discussed in the chapter encapsulate some vision of possible relationships that might be encouraged between (cultural) groupings. The research implicitly (through the question framing and through the interpretation of "results") can be seen as expressing these visions. But the researchers did not seem to show a reflexive orientation in relation to their starting visions and how these may be infusing their research (and influencing respondents as well as audiences). Dunn and Geeraert did lay bare their "paradigm" to us as audiences. But they did not in my view explore sufficiently the implications of this for the way in which we, as audiences, might consider their "results" generated via their survey. Nor did they show sufficient recognition that the way in which the questions were posed and framed for respondents may have restricted possibilities for accessing/expressing more radical forms of multiculturalism than normally imagined in diversity initiatives (as it seems that Dunn and Geeraert would wish to make provision for).

Nevertheless, I suggested that if we were to treat as material for their questionnaire some of the questions that they posed in their *Student Activities*, and if we were to consider as a novel form of textual write-up the inclusion of a variety of questions for readers to consider (such as offered in their *Student Activities*), their work can provide a style for constructively shifting the execution of survey research. This would be a style making provision for survey researchers to acknowledge their responsibilities in the discursive arena in terms of affecting via the research the manner in which issues become seen/discussed in the social fabric.

4.8.1   Revisiting Researcher Accountability in Survey Research

Considering the various write-ups of the surveys as discussed in this chapter, the researchers appear to put the focus on the way in which their surveys have offered information contributing to our understanding of the topics under consideration, which may be valuable for those wishing to make use of their findings. The focus in their write-ups thus appears to be on how findings produced via the surveys offer material of use to people in the wider society.

None of the survey researchers concentrated in their write-up on ways in which the research process itself – through the very decision to ask certain questions – might be rendering some modes of responding "hyper-accessible" for respondents. I would like to emphasize that the issue I am raising here goes beyond the question of whether "social desirability" pressures might have unduly influenced the respondents to respond in a particular manner. The researchers might argue that they have taken into account the so-called reactivity effect, where respondents respond (react) in terms of their understanding of researchers' and others' expectations. From a realist perspective, the researchers could argue that they have acknowledged this possibility and as far as possible designed their surveys accordingly.

My suggestion – from a constructivist-oriented perspective – is that in order to express a more accountable orientation, those setting up research need to take into consideration how research framings might impact on the way perspectives become generated in society – both by participants and by wider audiences of the research. As Ladson-Billings cautions us, the question as to "who has the power to shape the public perception … ?" (2003, p. 417) needs to be given serious consideration by taking into account researchers' complicity in the development of emergent social situations. (See Chapter 1, Section 1.5.3.)

I have suggested in this chapter that one way of designing surveys to take such considerations into account is by taking Dunn and Geeraert's approach and extending it along the lines that I proposed. In this way, I suggested, one could create a research process wherein juxtaposition of research frames (posing questions from a variety of frames) could be presented to participants so as to avoid a univocal way of framing. In this way, too, a dialogue between and around frames in the write-up of the research can more easily be set up as part of the writing style. And this then creates more scope for additional participation by original participants as well as audiences – in keeping with the ethical orientation proposed by Acquah (2007). I believe in this regard that Dunn and Geeraert's style of drawing out audiences' empathy in their questions posed at the end of their article (see Section 4.7 above) could also be one way in which an orientation to encouraging caring could be manifested via in this case survey research. That is, it is a way of taking on board Collins's (1990) plea for inquirers to work with an ethic of caring and of personal accountability – recognizing that they need to account for the possible impact of their research in generating options for human seeing, feeling, and living. Nonetheless, I suggest that more could be done with their survey in terms of displaying "imagination" (and evoking audience's imagination) in this regard (as, for instance, Omi, 2001, p. 256, also pleads for).

4.8.2 Extending Research Options

I have used a variety of examples of survey research showing how the researchers setting up the surveys deem the investigations as practically useful to people in society. The hope is that by identifying variables of relevance, and pointing to probable links between them (if applicable), the research can contribute to finding ways of addressing racism as it manifests in different (more or less covert) forms.

While I see that these researchers wish to present their work as contributing in this manner, I have suggested that there may be other ways of designing surveys, so that at the point of conducting the research, as well as at the point of write-up, hyper-accessible frameworks of understanding in society can become "unhinged." I have argued that if survey researchers could be more reflexive about how initial research framings may be contributing to the perspectives being developed in society – including through questions to which people are asked to respond – it may be possible to set up alternative ways of proceeding with this questioning. This in turn also means that any "information" collected, or rather, *generated* through the research process could create more scope for audiences also to be invited into reconsidering the issues at stake.

Another way of initiating a more in-depth exploration, and development, of perspectives would be to conduct a number of in-depth interviews with a set of respondents (as part of the survey), using a style of active interviewing that I explore in the next chapter. This too would enable any write-up of the research to include a richer dialogue (as, for example, I mention in Romm, 2007, p. 55). But it is also possible that those organizing the research might choose not to include this active interviewing option. And I would suggest that they would be justified in arguing that this is not a crucial component of accountable survey research as such.

Through the detail of my discussion around the surveys discussed in the chapter, I tried to show the points where one could, in my view, locate unnecessary restrictions in survey research. By locating these points, I hope to pave the way for survey researchers to

- create (more) efforts to increase their own theoretical literacy in relation to ways of framing "the issues," as well as find ways of engaging in a serious manner with the alternatives provided. As McIntyre-Mills suggests, this involves an orientation to working not primarily *within* frames of understanding, but *with*, and *around*, frames (2006a, p. 7);
- (re)consider their (consequent) way of designing questions so as to take into account different theoretical understandings (which may involve differently designed closed questions as well as open-ended ones, springing from alternative theoretical languaging);
- include options for asking questions to respondents in a manner that invites reflection on the part of participants (again, using closed- and/or open-ended questions);
- possibly (as another extension of the research, if viable) conduct some in-depth interviews with a number of respondents/participants, as a way of developing a dialogue around ways of seeing the issues (on which the researchers may have been concentrating);
- in the write-up of the research, include questions for readers to consider in the light of debates between radically diverse approaches to seeing and interpreting the "results" (which would involve drawing on, and finding ways of reconfiguring, different frameworks of understanding); and
- also include questions for readers aimed at activating their empathy. This would be in line with the suggestion expressed by a range of authors who question the duality between "thought" and "feeling" and who argue that human understanding can be seen to be already overlaid with emotional content. (See Chapter 1, Section 1.5.2.)

In response to possible claims that it may be unrealistic to expect that survey research(ers) can play the role of contributing in this way to activating thoughtful reflection and empathy in the social fabric, I have offered a glimpse in this chapter of how this may be attempted. And if we acknowledge that survey research (as with other forms of research) can be seen as exerting a powerful impact in society in helping to shape public opinion (including conceptions of possibilities for styles of human relationship), then we would do well to consider carefully our responsibilities (or what Collins, 1990, calls "personal accountability") in the way in which we choose to conduct such research.

However, as pointed out by Bonilla-Silva, "a significant amount of racial data cannot be retrieved through surveys"– especially because it is difficult (if not impossible) to "measure the effects of discrimination" in this way (1997, p. 471). Hence, while I propose that survey research can be (re)designed to aid the exploration of race-related issues in a (more) responsible way, I would suggest too that researchers conducting survey research need to point to possibilities for inquiry around the issues that could be provided by alternative research approaches – including experimental research (extended in the way I have suggested) and the approaches explored in the following chapters.

Chapter 5
Intensive Interviewing as Research: Generating In-Depth Talk to Explore Experiences/Cognitions of Racism

5.1 Introduction

In this chapter I consider intensive interviewing as a way of generating in-depth talk in relation to experiences/cognitions relevant to discussions around racism. As in earlier chapters, I structure the chapter by focusing on methodological and epistemological considerations, giving special attention to different interpretations of what is involved in this mode of inquiry.

Gray et al. offer an account of intensive interviewing as a research approach in the context of comparing it with survey research. They indicate that one of the qualities that can be used to distinguish it from survey research is that in survey research, the questions to be asked to respondents are determined (by researchers) "*before* data are actually collected," whereas in intensive interviewing "appropriate questions are often determined *as data are being collected* " (2007, p. 152). Gray et al. further indicate that in this approach, communication or conversation between "the researcher and those being studied" is regarded as being "a mutual effort" (2007, p. 152). The focus in the "methodology of intensive, or in-depth, or conversational interviewing" is on

> encouraging spontaneity in the respondent's comments, while minimizing the possibility that the interviewers will be so taken aback by a remark or turn of events that the momentum of the interview will be permanently disrupted. (2007, pp. 152–153)

They elucidate that:

> The manner and demeanor of the interviewer are governed not only by the study objectives and the cumulative information flow but also by a continuing assessment of what it will take to make or keep the interviewee most responsive. (2007, p. 153)

They indicate that intensive interviews are normally lengthy (about 2–3 h) and also that there may be multiple meetings with the same respondent (2007, p. 153).

As far as choices of methodological approach are concerned, Gray et al. suggest that intensive interviewing can be considered a suitable methodology "when other data-gathering methods would probably fail." For example, it can be used with people (such as "elites") who "may perceive themselves as too busy or too

N. Romm, *New Racism*, DOI 10.1007/978-90-481-8728-7_5,
© Springer Science+Business Media B.V. 2010

important to participate in a standardized survey research interview with a hired-hand interviewer" (2007, p. 153). And it may also be seriously considered

> for any category of respondent that is highly likely to be unwilling or unable to participate in other forms of research investigation, including convicted criminals, ... the elderly, ... and battered women, ... to name a few. (2007, p. 154)

They note that because of the characteristics of the intensive interview – namely, "being personal and encouraging respondents' introspection" – it can be used not only to explore "troubling and unfamiliar parts of life," but also to "make familiar experiences seem rich and fascinating" (2007, p. 154). They cite, for instance, McMahon's research toward her book on *Engendering Motherhood* (1995), where McMahon indicates that her book is "a story based on what participants told me about their lives" (1995, p. v). Gray et al. remark that:

> The notion of *engendering* is a process ideally captured through in-depth interviews because it is gradual and largely unconscious and thus requires the interviewer's encouraging respondents to be pensive and reflective. (2007, p. 154)

They give examples of respondents/interviewees in McMahon's study engaging in "self-examination and the development of insight that the women are able to share with us" (2007, p. 155).

In terms of a comparison between more quantitatively oriented research (oriented to seeking relationships of correlation/causality between quantified variables) and qualitative research (geared more to exploring the *dynamics of social relations* – cf. Ali, 2003, p. 28), intensive interviewing can be classed as *qualitative* in orientation. Gray et al. point out that further developments, and interpretations, of what is involved in qualitative research have arisen in response to the "postmodern critique of positivist science" (2007, p. 202). While in positivist-and post-positivist conceptions of science[121] it is assumed that the goal of scientific research is for researchers to "generate formal theories" on the basis of their understanding of the evidence to date, this goal is queried by many researchers engaging in more qualitative forms of inquiry (2007, p. 202). Gray et al. indicate that in these "creative approaches" to conceiving and practicing qualitative inquiry, informed by postmodernist arguments,

> there is much more genuine collaboration between researchers and the people they are studying. Even the term "research subject" is discouraged because it denotes a boundary that "objectifies" others and therefore impedes genuine empathy and understanding. (2007, p. 202)

---

[121]Certain theorists such as Hammersley define positivism narrowly as implying that scientific theories "can be confirmed, or at least falsified, with certainty" (1995, p. 5). Other theorists such as Keat and Urry (1975) define positivism (and post-positivism) as embracing also the Popperian argument, where it is recognized that science can neither verify nor falsify particular claims with certainty. (See Chapter 1, Section 1.5.1, and also Romm, 2001, pp. 20–25.) *Postmodernism* as an epistemology can be seen as taking issue with both the positivist and post-positivist *definition of truth* – and with the belief that we can specify (scientific) mechanisms for moving closer to truth, defined as an accurate representation of some posited extra-linguistic reality.

But despite Gray et al.'s suggestion that those practicing intensive interviewing may question the boundary between "researcher" and "researched" so as to enrich "empathy and understanding," their emphasis does not seem to be here on a concern with, say, the implications of the *potential power relationship* for the way in which "understanding" is developed. Douglas provides an example of such an alternative when she argues that it is important when engaging in research inquiries, to openly acknowledge any potential power in relation to research participants – because this means that the power invested in us as "researchers" is more likely to be used responsibly, with a sense of accountability and openness to challenge (1998, Chapter 5, p. 8). She points out how she tried to instantiate in the "here and now" of the research process, a concern with this in her study around Black women managers in Britain (which included herself as such a manager). As she puts it:

> In a study concerned with discrimination (i.e. the abuse or merely the irresponsible, and unconscious, use of power) I wanted to work in a mode that would see attending to power relations in the "here and now" of the [inquiry] process as a valid research issue. (1998, Chapter 5, p. 8)

Here Douglas emphasizes that attending to power relations was an important matter of principle in her approach, where questions of "knowing" were for her not divorced from processes of exploring new forms of human relating. She indicates in this vein that she herself entered the research with the assumption that "there may be many 'truths' about the means by which we [Black women managers] are excluded, and disadvantaged, and our development and growth suppressed." She wanted to work with "an epistemology of research that validated multiplicity of truths and realities" (1998, Chapter 5, p. 9). As I mentioned in Chapter 3, Parker and Lynn see certain connections between critical race theorizing and postmodernist thinking in their similar rejection of realist epistemologies, where "knowing" is conceptualized as a process of trying to get closer to "the truth" (2002, p. 11). Douglas shows how in her own research with, and concerning, Black women managers she chose to draw on an epistemology that provided for multiplicity of "truth" and (experienced) "reality." In the research examples that I discuss in this chapter I highlight to what extent, and how, this kind of epistemology can be catered for.

5.1.1 Backdrop to My Discussion of Examples

Before proceeding with the examples that I have chosen to discuss in this chapter, I would like to highlight as backdrop two further points to which Douglas has drawn attention.

Firstly, when Douglas invokes the category of "Black woman" as she describes her research involvement in Britain with other Black women, she clarifies that when she uses the term Black she means people who are perceived by others as being not White or who identify themselves as not White. She indicates that her use of the term is in line with Collins's view that we need to break with "our Cartesian framing of the world in which things must be either/or and cannot be both/and" (Douglas,

1998, Chapter 5, p. 9). As Collins emphasizes, in terms of an understanding of Black women's *both/and* conceptual orientation, "the act of being simultaneously a member of a group and yet standing apart from it [to reflect back on it], forms an integral part of Black women's consciousness" (Collins, 1990, as cited in Douglas, 1998, p. 9). The first example that I discuss in this chapter – the work of Essed – can be seen in terms of a conceptualization of categories that attempts to avoid binary thinking while enabling discussions reformulating the categories to proceed. (See also my Chapter 1, Section 1.3.)

Secondly, Douglas draws attention to the difficulties involved in this kind of research, namely, inquiries geared to facilitating the articulation of experiential and tacit knowledge. She remarks that:

> The emotions, which are often, attached to the experience of discriminatory incidents (frustration, irritation, shame, anger, boredom, despair, confusion, pain, sadness) means that they are often rationalized and treated as unimportant or suppressed. Returning to such incidents [via, for example, the interview process] is therefore not an easy process [for the participants]. (1998, Chapter 5, p. 8)

Besides the emotional content that Douglas sees as rendering it difficult to articulate felt experiences of discrimination, Douglas locates further difficulties:

> Uncovering and exploring discrimination as it takes place in everyday interactions is made more difficult by the fact that much of this knowledge is gained and held at a subjective, experiential, non-verbal level and hard to articulate. (1998, Chapter 5, p. 8)

Douglas argues that due to difficulties such as these, it is important to give credence to people's recounting of "subjective" stories, as a precursor to the development of a sense-making process in which patterns and themes become identified. (She avers that these themes become identified as people develop the facility to compare several of their own experiences as well as relate them to stories recounted by others.)

As I indicated in Chapter 3, critical race theorists have suggested, as does Douglas, that it is crucial to introduce the "recounting of experiences" via storying and restorying into the staple of research into new racism – because it is argued that this is a mechanism for injecting new discourses into the field of discussion of racism. The intensive interviewing processes that I discuss in this chapter can be seen as aimed in this direction. But I argue that the manner of justifying the methodological process and its epistemological underpinning still requires further exploration.

My discussion is set around different authors' styles of, and justifications for, conducting "intensive interviewing." Through my discussion of these various approaches, I show how one can go beyond Gray et al.'s account of it – where it is still ultimately seen as linked to "the interviewer seeking information from the interviewee" and establishing the requisite relationship to obtain this information (2007, p. 155). I review Gray et al.'s characterization of the "collaboration" involved in ways of practicing this form of qualitative research, by taking into account the epistemological arguments that I (further) develop through my discussion of the various examples.

5.1.2 Examples Discussed and Revisited

The first example that I discuss in the chapter is the work of Essed as she reports upon, and justifies her approach toward, the interviewing of Black women in the USA and the Netherlands. I revisit her discussion in the light of debates around active interviewing as a mode of encounter with participants and in the light of critical theoretical accounts of the status of research "results."

The second example that I discuss (briefly) is of a focus group that I facilitated in South Africa (around post-apartheid cross-racial friendships of school children). I use this example to offer suggestions for how focus group interviewing might be employed in acknowledgment of the interventive involvement of inquirers in the conduct as well as write-up of research.

5.2 Essed's Intensive Interviewing

5.2.1 Focusing on Experiences/Insights of Black Women

In her book *Understanding Everyday Racism* (1991), Essed reports on her study of the experiences of Black women in California (USA) and the Netherlands (1991, p. 54). She indicates that the empirical data of her study (gathered in the period of 1985–1986) consisted of "nondirective interviews with a group of 55 Black women, all but two of them aged 20–45, from a few large cities in California and the Netherlands" (1991, p. 4). She comments that it is possible that problems (of racism) in California are not necessarily the same as in other parts of the USA – and that the specific experiences of racism that she details in her book may therefore differ to some degree from other parts of the USA. She also states that for the sake of comparability with Black American women, she chose as interviewees in the Netherlands "immigrant women of African descent, from the ex-colony of Suriname" (1991, p. 4).

She points out that one of her aims in the study was to "make more explicit [than she saw as currently available] a Black female point of view in the general field of race and ethnic relations" (1991, p. 4). When she refers to "experiences" as expressed by interviewees, she does not mean only the "personal experiences Black women have with racism" (1991, p. 5). She indicates that, as she details in her book,

> a substantial part of their experiences are shaped vicariously, through friends, family members, and other Blacks, through the media, and cognitively, through their general knowledge of racism in the system. (1991, p. 5)

Like other authors who query the distinction between "experience" and "cognition," she points out that in her conception – in line with her interviewees – "*experience*" encapsulates processes of *developing insight/comprehension*. (In Section 5.2.2 I discuss Essed's view of the relationship between her own "understanding" as a researcher and the research participants' "comprehension" as she calls it.)

Essed makes the point that although her study concentrated on Black women, we need to bear in mind that "the experiences of Black women are structured by converging systems of race, class, and gender oppression" (1991, p. 5). Because Essed regards these systems of oppression as converging, her analysis can be seen as fitting into what she and Goldberg (2002, p. 9) call "theories of intersectionality," which they indicate "women of color" have been at the forefront of "developing, applying, and refining" (2002, p. 9). (See also my reference to this in Chapter 3, Section 3.5.2.2.) As far as the issue of class exploitation is concerned, Essed indicates that in her study in the USA and the Netherlands, she tried to

> minimize the role of class exploitation indirectly by selecting only women with higher education, namely, university students and professionals. They are a privileged group in terms of educational background and job opportunities, but the factor of class oppression plays an indirect role in their lives. Through family relations and life in segregated areas, Black women with higher education indirectly participate in the collective experience of class-based racism. (1991, p. 5)

In view of the link between the factors of race and gender in creating the experiences of discrimination as detailed by her interviewees, Essed indicates that it is often not feasible to separate these factors out analytically. She gives an example:

> Black women are systematically confronted in their aspirations with objections from Whites, who often attribute incompetence to them. One can place the problem of under-estimation in a gender context as well as in a racial context, but it is analytically difficult to determine in detail the specific impact of gender or race. (1991, p. 5)

Hence Essed introduces the concept of *gendered racism* to conceptualize the "experiences of racism in the lives of these Black women" (1991, p. 5).

When detailing her use of the term "everyday" in the phrase "everyday racism," Essed explains that the term allows us to attend to so-called micro processes of social interaction as well as "macro" structures of inequality. She believes that her study connects "structural forces of racism with routine situations in everyday life" (1991, p. 2). In elucidating her use of the phrase, she explains:

> Everyday racism is a complex of practices operative through heterogeneous (class and gender) relations, present in and producing race and ethnic relations. Such relations are activated and reproduced as practices. (1991, p. 50)

Micro and macro levels of analysis can become linked when making sense of everyday racism, as follows:

> From a micro point of view oppression can be implemented by creating structures of racial and ethnic inequality through situated practices . . . .. Racial inequality can only be maintained when other forces [seen from a macro point of view] operate to secure compliance and to prevent, manage, or break opposition. (1991, p. 51)

She argues that conceptualized in this way, it is possible to see how hard it is to escape the impact of racism on everyday life. She elucidates:

> Although individual Black women may work out strategies to break away from particular oppressive relations or situations, and frequently oppose racism, . . . they remain locked into the forces of the system, unless enough counterpressure develops to unlock these forces. (1991, p. 51)

Essed indicates that her account of the "interlocking forces of domination" parallels the theory of Omi and Winant on "racial formation" (1986), in which they explain how, in Essed's words,

> the situational activation of racial or ethnic dimensions in particular relations . . . reinforces racial or ethnic inequality and contributes to new forms of racial and ethnic inequality. (1991, p. 51)

In terms of this understanding, Essed notes:

> Everyday racism does not exist in the singular but only as a complex – as interrelated instantiations of racism. Each instantiation of everyday racism has meaning only in relation to the whole complex of relations and practices. (1991, p. 52)

She indicates that her conceptualization carries with it the suggestion that

> people are involved differently in the process of everyday racism according to gender, class, status, and other factors determining the content and structure of their everyday lives. (1991, p. 52)

For Essed it is thus important that researchers develop mechanisms to identify "how intertwining systems of domination are expressed and experienced in everyday life" (2001). Her proposed methodology (summarized in her 2001 article) is based on encouraging those affected by specific kinds of intersecting discriminations to identify (and make more visible to themselves and others, as a basis of discussion) their insights.[122] She notes that her approach "seeks to contribute, tentatively, to developing a method for intersectional analysis by incorporating the following possibilities":

- Modes to encourage women who are exposed to racism, as women, to take their own voices and insights seriously;
- Instruments for exposing covert forms of gendered racism [as the intersection of genderism and racism];
- Analytical tools to identify intertwined gender, race, ethnic, economic and educational factors in shaping specific expressions of everyday injustices;
- Tools to identify gendered racism within and beyond national boundaries and cross-culturally. A rational, systematic, and sensitive format to make inquiries about emotionally charged experiences such as everyday discrimination; and
- A mutually accessible conceptual language for lay persons and professionals to address everyday racism (in and outside of institutions) embedded in larger gender, economic, and historical structures.

---

[122]Crenshaw states in this regard that "the intersectional subordination of raced women is often underread" and that it is important to consider the various ways in which the lives of some women are "shaped, constrained, and sometimes lost by the nexus between gender, race, color, or ethnicity and other axes of subordination." She indicates that intersectional analysis specifically addresses "the manner in which racism, patriarchy, class oppression and other discriminatory systems create background inequalities that structure the relative positions of women, races, ethnicities, classes, and the like" (2000).

She suggests that such a methodology allows people (lay and professionals) to make inquiries about people's emotionally charged experiences (as explained also by Douglas in my introduction to this chapter) and to recognize that there are similarities as well as differences in the way in which systemic inequalities of all kinds manifest in everyday life.

With this methodological backdrop that Essed offers as the basis for her own research work, I now turn to a further set of methodological questions addressed by her.

5.2.2 The Link Between Lay People's and Professional's Understandings

As noted above, Essed (2001) proposes generating a mutually acceptable language that will provide for discussion between "lay persons" and "professionals" around experiences and understandings of everyday racism. In *Understanding Everyday Racism* (1991), she suggests that in the case of her interviewing of the American and Surinamese women of African descent she found that:

> These women are articulate, understand the issue of racism, have practical experience with the problem, are able to discuss different sides of the problem, and are able to give detailed descriptions of manifestations of racism. (1991, p. 55)

She goes on to state that:

> Real-life experiences are a rich source of information and provide insights into everyday racism that cannot be obtained in other ways. However, the reality constructions of Black women are checked for consistency with the structural properties of racism in the system. (1991, p. 55)

How, then, does Essed see the link between stories/accounts as told by participants and her theorizing around structural properties of "the system"? In order to consider this question, I need to draw attention to Essed's view of how her own understanding of everyday racism links up with the experiences that she locates through her nondirective interviewing process (with Black women who can be called "lay persons"). To provide some clarity to readers as to how she sees this connection, she suggests that:

> To prevent confusion, Black women's understanding of racism will be referred to as comprehension of racism . . . , while my analytic translation of Black women's comprehension will be referred to as *Understanding*. (1991, p. 55)

In explicating how she considers her theorizing as connected to the mode of comprehension of participants, she makes explicit how she envisages her own theorizing. She argues that her theorizing can be conceptualized as a "social scientific 'social representation' of generalized knowledge of racism," and it is this understanding/representation that helps to structure the "processing and interpretation of the empirical data" (1991, p. 56). She argues that similarly the participants can be considered as broadly speaking, operating in the same way in their "comprehension of racism." That is, "the meaning they attach to specific events can only have significance in terms of racism within a framework of their general knowledge of racism" (1991, p. 56). Thus to consider the link between her own understanding, and the women's comprehension, it is first necessary to consider how she envisages her own theorizing, as explained in Section 5.2.3.

5.2.3 Analytic Induction Combined with Structural Interpretation for Theorizing

In accounting for her own theorizing via-à-vis the interview material, Essed elucidates that it amounts to detailing the relevance of the concept of everyday racism as a tool of analysis. She admits that her way of approaching her interviewees "cannot be separated from my theoretical presuppositions about the concept of everyday racism" (1991, p. 54). She points out that her analysis of everyday racism draws on the logic of an analytic inductive approach (where understanding is induced from experiences as expressed by, e.g., interviewees[123]), as well as on the logic of "structural sociology" (1991, p. 55). In terms of the latter kind of logic, an understanding of social structure is developed by positing social structures that can be used to explain phenomenal events, including processes of social meaning making. (In Chapter 8, I provide detail on how structural theorizing can be seen as employing the logic of what is called "retroduction," and I show how this logic can be differently used within different structuralist positions.)

She indicates that her study can be considered as "dealing with subjective reality constructions as a base for theoretical analysis" (1991, p. 56). She places her discussion in the context of debates around the value of "interpretive sociology" (so labeled by Weber, 1949). She states that one of the problems that she sees in interpretive sociology, including the traditions of phenomenology, symbolic interactionism, and ethnomethodology, [124] is that "the definition of the situation" (as defined by

---

[123] As far as the logic of *analytic induction* is concerned, this is associated with the idea that social theorizing is *distinct from natural scientific theorizing* in that social scientists need to engage in the *interpretation of meanings* as the basis for their analyses (cf. Henwood & Pidgeon, 1993, p. 22). Analytic logic is used with the purpose of highlighting resonance between people's experiences in different social contexts – as drawn out through the analysis (Romm & Adman, 2000). This is seen as different from positivist-endorsed induction, which posits that scientists – whether natural or social ones – can induce theories about causal connections by using a similar logic whether natural or social phenomena are being explored. Essed is invoking here the *interpretive-oriented account* of induction. But this kind of induction, along with positivist-endorsed induction, has also been criticized by more structurally oriented sociology (cf. Layder, 1993, pp. 56–57). Essed proposes an approach that takes into account the criticisms leveled by structural sociology.

[124] Holstein and Gubrium provide an outline of how ethnomethodology (which focuses on the way in which actors "exercise interpretive discretion, mediated by complex layerings of interpretive influence") relates to phenomenology (which focuses on interpreting and explaining human action and thought) and other styles of interpretive inquiry (1994, pp. 262–268). They note that all of these approaches are concerned with "reality-constituting interpretive practice" (1994, p. 262).

people's meaning-making) is understood with reference to "a culturally homogeneous consensus model of society" (1991, p. 56). She sees an underlying consensus model operative in the work of, for example, Goffman (1963) and Garfinkel (1967). She argues that these approaches do not make sufficient provision for the "possibility that structural conflict (racism) is managed by the dominant group on a cultural or ideological level (overall denial and mitigation of racism)" (1991, p. 58).

She points out that it is for this reason that she redefines "experience" in her study not only to refer to "personal" experiences, but also to include "the impact of knowledge of general (structural) phenomena in one's definition of reality" (1991, p. 58). Experience *defined in this way* can then be seen as the "connecting element between the individual and social structure" (1991, p. 58). That is, once we recognize that experiences of racism in everyday life are not "merely individual experiences," we can see the experiences themselves as involving:

(a) Personal experiences (racism directed against oneself, usually witnessed, sometimes reported);
(b) Vicarious experiences (racism directed against other identified Blacks, which may be witnessed as well as reported);
(c) Mediated experiences (racist events directed against or affecting a larger [sub]group of Blacks, often communicated through the mass media);
(d) Cognitive experiences (the impact of knowledge of racism upon one's perception of reality). (1991, p. 58)

This definition of experiences allows us to appreciate that they can become extended as people come to develop a broader cognition in relation to the operation of racism across their own lives and in comparison with others' lives. Thus the array of information gleaned by, for example, researchers as they locate patterns in the data can in turn provide wider insights to people's comprehension of racism. Essed explains that in a context in which covert discrimination is hard to "prove" when taking into account as a criterion simply an actor's definition of the situation, it is necessary to develop a mode of theorizing that is not built solely on actors' own accounts. She explains the problem in relation also to the moral pressures put upon White people:

> The pressures of the moral rejection of racism and the encouragement of equality values have made an impact to the extent that individuals may have become blind to the racist implications of their comments and communications with Black people. Furthermore, Whites are generally motivated to present themselves to others as nonprejudiced. This has been illustrated with social psychological experiments … as well as through discourse analysis. (1991, p. 59)

Here Essed draws on the research of those conducting experiments and also discourse analysts who have provided examples through their work of what I discussed in Chapter 3 as racism "gone underground." (See Chapter 3, Section 3.7.1.)

Essed suggests that in such a socio-political context, it is reasonable to expect that Black women can "provide us with information about dominant group members that would probably not be obtained by using dominant group members themselves as informants" (1991, p. 59). She exhorts us to "take subjective experiences of racism seriously" in our effort to

> study how Black women in their daily lives strategically use beliefs, opinions, acquired knowledge about racism, and other heuristics of interpretation to account for their experiences. (1991, p. 59)

She explains that we need to develop "insights into these interpretation processes" if we are to "understand experiences of racism as an intrinsic part of everyday life" (1991, p. 59). But she argues that she also considers it important for her as an inquirer to "transcend individual perceptions" and look for "shared interpretations" (1991, p. 59). In this way, interviewees' perspectives are "placed in a broader framework of interpretive and evaluative processes" (1991, p. 60).

She indicates that she conceives her translation of "micro" events into "macro-level ('structural') concepts" as involving two steps:

- Analyzing how Black women apply general perceptions of race relations to the explanation of personal experiences and
- Comparing Black women's interpretations to my theoretical framework.

Now Essed proposes that to understand what she means by translating interpretations into her theoretical framework, she wishes to make a distinction between "interpretations of reality" and "evaluative conclusions that the experienced reality is indicative of racism" (1991, p. 60). This distinction allows us to see that in her schema:

> The interpretations that are used to reconstruct reality [during the interview process] are those of Black women. Whether or not we must evaluate specific events as racist is determined by assessing Black women's description of events against the working definition of racism [as proffered in the theory]. (1991, p. 60)

Essed introduces the idea that it is possible to come to what she calls an "objective" conclusion/evaluation concerning whether it is appropriate to classify certain recounted events (of unfair treatment) as "racist events" on the basis of information supplied to her by the interviewees. She indicates that this assessment can take place even in instances where the interviewees themselves may not have "see[n] the event in terms of racism" (including instances where they did not self-identify as Black or were ambivalent about defining themselves in these categorical terms) (1991, p. 78). She suggests that it is useful when considering the development of interpretations of events to make explicit the criteria that are being used to make assessments concerning their potential racism (1991, p. 79). To this end, she offers an outline of 6 steps that can be followed (as a "test sequence") in trying to arrive at defensible conclusions regarding the assessment of specific events. She entitles the sequence as "a procedure for the assessment of racist events" (1991, p. 79). The steps are as follows. (In Section 5.2.4.1, I show how she employs these steps with respect to actual examples.)

- Step 1 involves considering whether the interviewee regards the event as *acceptable* given the situational conditions. It is possible through considering this question to see that racism may become manifested in "seemingly acceptable practices" that, upon further examination (in view of the context), are *not* fully acceptable (1991, p. 80). She suggests that this is particularly important when considering covert racism in interaction situations – which Essed suggests involve cases of "racism expressed in seemingly acceptable practices that are, however, not (fully) acceptable within the particular context." Conversely, she notes that if an interpreter feels that an event is unacceptable (and can be classed as an instance of racism) while examination of the context suggests that it "has to be considered acceptable," then we may decide that the (subjective) judgment of the interpreter is "expressing insufficient situational knowledge" in this case (1991, p. 80).

- Step 2 involves considering whether *unacceptable behavior* (e.g., discrimination) can become "excused" with reference to certain reasoning. If it is deemed that the behavior was, for example, out of control of the actor, this may become considered as "acceptable reasons" (1991, p. 80). An examination of the excuses given for "unacceptable behavior" (and a consideration of whether they can be considered acceptable) thus needs to take place in coming to evaluations/conclusions regarding whether racism can be regarded as at play.

- Step 3 considers the behavior in the context of the question *Is it because I am Black?* Essed comments here that if there are no acceptable excuses, and it seems that the discrimination or prejudice has been directed against the Black individual because of her or his "racial-ethnic background," then this becomes relevant in the analysis (1991, p. 80). As she puts it, "when this is the case, and given that the actor is acting of his or her own free will, there are no reasonable excuses for discrimination" (1991, p. 80).

- Step 4 involves considering whether, in view of Steps 1–3, the specific event is excusable. Essed indicates that this question must be considered because sometimes other Blacks are blamed for causing discrimination (by being so vocal about their concerns). Such a judgment can be shown to lack "insight into racism" (1980, p. 80).

- Step 5 considers the question as to whether the event can be considered *socially significant*. She explains that for her, "not acknowledging the social relevance of racially discriminatory acts must be considered an example of insufficient comprehension of the implications of the event" (1991, p. 81). For example, sometimes people may believe that "feeling discriminated against is a personal problem." It is believed that "if you do not mention it, you will not have any problems with discrimination and you will not give people any reason to discriminate against you" (1991, p. 81). She suggests that, in the context of the Netherlands, it seemed to her a prevalent misunderstanding by the end of the 1970s that "if you were alert for discrimination, that meant that you were a failure in life" (1991, p., 81). She indicates that such kinds of misunderstanding need to be addressed in research analyses.

- Step 6 amounts to the *evaluation* as such. This involves placing "the specific event in an evaluative framework consisting of general racism knowledge, which can be supported by other argumentation such as comparisons with the experiences of specific other Blacks" (1991, p. 81).

Essed explains that in order to make the kind of evaluations that she proposes in *Step 6*, one needs to consider the social context in which racist events occur and one has to be equipped with "a social base of knowledge needed to understand these events" (1991, p. 88). She indicates that often people are not sufficiently equipped with the cognitive framework to "comprehend specific acts in terms of racism" (1991, p. 90).

She gives examples of how insufficiency of cognitive tools can lead to the failure to identify events in terms of the concept of "racism":

> Indications of this were found in the stories of Black women about the first time they recalled having experienced racism. First, personal experiences with hostility, discrimination, or, more generally, negatives attitudes or behavior from Whites add to the stock of knowledge about race relations, but these incidents do not mean that the women could already comprehend specific acts in terms of racism. (1991, p. 90)

Thus, even though the women could "recognize racial 'hostility' and 'unfairness' as children, none of them recalled being able to 'fully understand what was going on'" (1991, p. 90). She points out that these indications from these women are consistent with other research on political cognitions, which suggests that "insight into racism implies the ability to form abstract conceptions of the community" (1991, p. 90). Part of her interviewing process involved trying to locate how Black women in the USA as well as in the Netherlands "acquire knowledge of racism" (1991, p. 90).

As we have seen above, Essed also believes that in the current socio-political context, where the "dominance of Euro-American values" has become a hidden agenda resulting in more covert forms of racism, it is necessary for analysts to apply further evaluative criteria in deciding whether to label particular events (as recounted by interviewees) as involving racism (1991, p. 188). She argues that this is necessary because:

> Normative values inherent in Euro-American culture ensure that cultural difference is overemphasized and conceptualized in hierarchical ordering. . . . . Hidden under the surface of diversity, there is a strong tendency among Whites, in the United States as well as in the Netherlands, to assume the superiority of Euro-American values. (1991, p. 189)

She suggests that in this climate of "cultural racism," which she sees as specifically prevalent in Europe but also in the USA (1991, p. 218), "the concrete experiences of Black women [as recounted by them in the interviews] must be placed within [a] macro framework of culturalized racism" (1991, p. 189). In comparing the two countries on this score, she points to the relative lack of concern in the Netherlands with interracial dating, which she sees as "indicative of a more general difference in the systems of racism in both countries, namely, more racial racism in the USA and more cultural racism in the Netherlands" (1991, p. 218). As she sees it, "race" is not historically anchored in the Dutch class structure in the same way as in the United States. Indeed in the Netherlands (class-related) cultural traits are more important indications of status, whereas in the United States racial characteristics (White, blond) represent status symbols. (1991, p. 218)

But in both countries she argues that due to the management of "cultural difference" occurring in ways that can be argued to manifest racism, it is important for her, as analyst, to draw out the "hidden agendas" which may not (yet) be comprehended or theorized by (some of) her interviewees.

In the next section I provide more detail on some of the results of her research around Black women's experiences/cognitions.

5.2.4 Essed's Discussion of Research Results

Essed offers the results of her research by referring to examples that exemplify her way of analyzing interview fragments from her interviewees' stories. Through these examples, she provides us with details of the wordings as used by participants, so that we ourselves, as audiences, can consider her interpretations against our own, in relation to the interview fragments that she supplies. She also chooses to offer a detailed account of what she calls "an inventory of events in individual case story ([named as] Rosa N.)" (1991, p. 57) to provide an illustration of what she calls "the continuous and simultaneous battle over cultural meanings and structural resources" (in this case, the Netherlands) (1991, p. 185). She indicates that the story of Rosa N. is used by her as a case to highlight "intra-subjective comparison" – that is, comparison of events occurring in a single life in terms of consistent patterns of racism (1991, p. 57).

In outlining her manner of presenting results, I give an indication (Sections 5.2.4.1 and 5.2.4.2) of her approach in relation to two interviews – one from the Netherlands and one from the USA – from which she supplies interview fragments. I also show (Section "Details of Rosa N.'s Story" as discussed under Section 5.2.4.3) how in addition she utilizes the case of "the story of Rosa N." in the Netherlands in her analysis of "the hidden norms and values of dominant culture" (1991, p. 185). And I show (Section 5.2.4.4) how she constructs various tables, tabulating the distribution of manifestations of racism in various social contexts in the two countries as well as the frequency of occurrences of different forms of racism, as a pointer to the macro context in the two countries. In discussing her conception of the purpose of the cross-country comparison, she points out that her account is meant to be illustrative of "the general applicability of the concept of everyday racism as a means of qualifying processes of racism in different systems" (1991, p. 55). She states that her study was not designed to meet the requirements of "statistical representativeness" (1991, p. 55).

5.2.4.1 An Example from the Netherlands

One of the examples that Essed uses to explain how she analyses the interview material is from a women aged 30 in the Netherlands, who "has problems finding a job with Dutch temporary employment agencies" (1991, p. 82). Someone advises her to go to an agency "working explicitly (but not only) for Black clients." Through this agency she "finds the sort of job she wanted" (1991, p. 83). In response to the question of what she thought of the fact that it was only then that there appeared to be vacancies for her, the interviewee answers that:

> To be honest, I've never really given it much thought. . . .. I didn't worry about it . . .. But yes, if you listen a bit to all the studies that are done in that area, then you do have to wonder why it's like that, is it really just by chance? . . .. I can't tell you, look, this is how it is. I can say, look, this is what I've experienced, and you may interpret for yourself. But I think you will notice that often if things are difficult, or seem difficult, I try to find a solution, and that perhaps I don't even think that I'm being discriminated against . . .. I try to put myself in the place of the majority . . ..You know you are in a society where you are, first of all, eh, in the minority . . .. The majority, I assume, will more often get what he or she wants. (1991, p. 83)

Essed considers whether this interviewee finds the situation "acceptable" – and she interprets the interviewee's responses (where she indicates that she has not given it much thought) as implying a hesitant *No*. She also considers whether acceptable justifications for the (experienced) situation seem to be available. She interprets the interviewee as having both a *Yes* and *No* response to this question. The other agencies might have had good reasons for not finding her a job; but she is not sure whether it is "intentional or accidental that she did not get adequate job offers elsewhere." In response to the question of whether the interviewee attributes this to her *being Black*, Essed considers that the interviewee recognizes that this is relevant in the situation because she explains that the Dutch are the "majority" and she is a minority. But Essed notes that her approach here appears to be that "Yes, it is because I am Black, but I do not consider this discrimination. As a matter of fact you had better not start worrying about discrimination, because there is nothing you can do about it" (1991, p. 83). Essed suggests that here the interviewee seems to be working with the assumption that discrimination "is a fact of life because one cannot change the majority"; and she is thus not regarding discrimination as a condition that can be changed (1991, p. 84). Essed points out that some of the other interviewees who "problematized racism in society . . . do not view racial discrimination as a condition that cannot be changed" (1991, p. 84) – and thus differed from this interviewee's approach on this score. As to the issue of whether the specific event (the interviewee's not finding a job through the other agency) is excusable, Essed feels that the interviewee is implicitly finding that the other agencies *can be excused*. Essed sees this as implicit in her saying that "I try to put myself in their place" – implying that even she might act that way if in a similar position (1991, p. 84). The interviewee thus expresses that on this basis she "understands the other agencies."

Having analyzed the "interview fragment" from this interview (using steps outlined in Section 5.2.3 above), Essed notes that the interviewee's interpretation sequence "ends with Step 4" (1991, p. 84). Essed leaves it to the reader to continue the steps of analysis, to the point of making a judgment as to whether one might consider that racism could be said to be operating in a covert way – albeit difficult to detect (and indeed not even necessarily named by the interviewee as discrimination).

5.2.4.2 An Example from the USA

This interviewee, aged 21, has problems learning French. She is the only Black student in the class. Her difficulties in learning the language are "much increased when her French teaching assistant (TA) appears very impatient with her" (1991, p. 84). At one point "she becomes so nervous that she cannot quite understand a specific question addressed to her in French and subsequently responds quite out of line. The TA attacks her" (1991, p. 84). Essed analyzes the situation thus:

(1) *Acceptable? – No.*

Essed sees that the unacceptability in the interviewee's eyes can be gleaned from her account of the situation:

> One day she had me get up and do a little charade and I could not understand what she was asking me to do. I was taking certain words and thought this is what she meant and so I did that, but it wasn't it. She just stomps up to the front of the room, in front of the whole class. I was so embarrassed. She snatches the pencil out in front of me, pulls the card back, and parts it . . . .. The whole class was silent. (1991, p. 84)

(2) *Acceptable excuses? – No.*

Essed sees that because the interviewee indicates that she had "really wanted to learn," this implies that she does not believe that the TA was justified in her consequent actions, and was being unreasonably harsh with her.

(3) *Because you are Black? – Yes (hesitantly).*

Essed indicates that when this question was asked during the interview, the interviewee replied that:

> In this case I guess that would be the only thing . . . . That's what my [Black] roommate told me too. She says . . . are you the only Black in there? And I said yeah. She says is your TA White? I said well she's French. I don't know if they consider themselves White or not, and she says well then, there you go. . . . . But I don't know that, I can assume it, but I don't know. (1991, p. 85)

(4) *Specific event excusable? – No: as in (2) above.*

(5) *Specific event socially relevant? – No (hesitantly).*

Essed indicates that the interviewee is "very reluctant to see the experience as a case of racism" (1991, p. 85). She supplies further interview fragments to show how the interviewee expresses her account (which Essed indicates means that she is not comprehending the situation as a racist event and hence as socially significant):

> I thought of it [that it was because I am Black], but I try not to think that way. I try to make that my last resort, you know. I hate using my color as an excuse . . . . And I would hate

to think that she was. I mean, I just hate thinking that people are all trying to discriminate against me, and I am always trying to run away from that fact. (1991, p. 85)

Essed finds this example interesting "because it illustrates the fact that information about racism and even information about relevant questions to ask when assessing a situation for racism ... do not necessarily lead to comprehension of the racist event" (1991, p. 85). Through this example, where the interviewee expressed reluctance to conceptualize the experience as implying racism, Essed seems to be asking us, as audiences, to consider that – tied to similar experiences as expressed by her range of interviewees – there is a strong possibility that the TA's harsh response was indeed unduly harsh (and can be evaluated as an example of racism if taken to Step 6 of the "steps of analysis").

5.2.4.3 Comparing Various Examples

Essed indicates that by looking closely at these, and other, examples of "interview fragments" one can detect how "Black women expose cues and hidden messages enclosed in the situations." But she indicates that "overemphasis on situational evidence ... and insufficient inference from knowledge of the general processes of racism may depoliticize evidence of racism" (1991, p. 144). She finds it important, therefore, alongside the analysis of interview fragments, to provide a detailed account of the story of Rosa N. – a Black geriatrician in training in the Netherlands, being "the only Black in her group" (1991, p. 145). She believes that the experience of Rosa N. "forms a microcosm of everyday racism" (1991, p. 145). Each experience of Rosa N. "acquires meaning relative to the other experiences" and together provide instantiations of how "Black women in the Netherlands are subjected to strong pressure to assimilate culturally," while at the same time the dominant consensus operates to "suppress protest against racism" (1991, p. 145). Essed reiterates her definition of everyday racism before beginning her account of the story of Rosa N.:

> Everyday racism has been defined as a process in which socialized racist notions are integrated into everyday practices and thereby actualize and reinforce underlying racial and ethnic relations. (1991, p. 145)

It is against this definition of everyday racism that she asks us to "test" Rosa N.'s story.

Details of Rosa N.'s Story

Essed prefaces her portrayal of Rosa N.'s story by suggesting that it can be seen as providing an illustration of:

> Rosa N.'s extraordinary perseverance, despite multiple forms of oppression. Rejection, exclusion, problematization, underestimation and other inequities and impediments are regularly infused into "normal" life, so that they appear unquestionable. (1991, p. 146)

As far as the application of the label of *racism* is concerned, Essed argues that some of Rosa N.'s experiences are "obvious indications of racism." But many others are "concealed and subtle. Their understanding requires a certain degree of general knowledge of racism" (1991, p. 146). Essed clarifies that "everyday racism does not exist in the singular but only in the plural form, as a complex of mutually related, cumulative practices, and situations" (1991, p. 147). It is this "complex" to which Rosa N.'s story points (1991, p. 147). Essed also wishes to make the point that Rosa N., in recounting her story, "does not dismiss evidence of positive behavior by dominant group members as a means of [her] sustaining previous expectations of racism" – that is, she avoids what Pettigrew (1979) has called the "ultimate attribution error" (Essed, 1991, p. 147). As Pettigrew puts it, this error amounts to seeing *positive* behavior exhibited by those considered as "outgroup" as occurring in specified *situations*, but as not being *dispositionally caused*. That is, in terms of this error, positive behavior on the part of others defined as outgroup members is considered (unduly) as being a product of the situation, rather than being seen as linked to people's dispositions (1979, p. 465). Essed suggests (citing Pettigrew) that "prejudiced interpreters" tend to interpret *positive* behavior of those perceived as outgroup members as being caused by *the situation*, while in their own case, they see their own positive behavior as being dispositionally caused (i.e., as a function of their dispositions). Conversely, *negative* behaviors of perceived outgroup members tend to be attributed to *dispositional causes*, while negative behaviors on their own part are attributed to "the situation." Essed sees Rosa N.'s story as implying that she is not herself committing "attribution errors." Essed also points out that further research on attribution errors suggests that:

> Success is likely to be attributed to situational circumstances (e.g., as proof that there is no discrimination, rather than as a sign of the Black individual's exceptional ability to surmount problems of racism). Failure is likely to be attributed to dispositional factors (e.g., proof that Blacks are incompetent). (1991, p. 169)

Essed believes that this research (by Pettigrew and colleagues) is helpful in aiding us to appreciate some of the situations as described by Rosa N. in particular.[125]

Essed starts her portrayal of Rosa N.'s story by noting that she came to Holland in 1969 (from Suriname), and her main friends were Dutch medical students. Although she did not feel different from the Dutch, she was reminded that she was not Dutch:

> I can remember once making a phone call in a dorm when a Dutch boy said: "There's Rosa with that laugh of hers". And I thought: What does that mean? Strange! Because I was laughing very loud. But that doesn't happen any more, only when I'm with Rob. ... I had to get rid of a lot of the Suriname in me. Not consciously. (1991, pp. 148–149)

Essed indicates that later, Rosa N.'s vague feelings of "cultural deprivation" as expressed in this fragment appeared to develop into a more "focused understanding of racism" (1991, p. 149).

Essed cites a fragment of a story told by Rosa N. in her surgery class, where the teacher, a plastic surgeon, told a story about an industrial accident in a food

---

[125]It is worth noting here, in terms of my discussion of the reinforcement of bounded groupness in Chapters 3 and 4, that Pettigrew comments that "the more bounded the two groups [under consideration] the greater the ultimate attribution error is likely to be" (1979, p. 469). He cites research (such as that of McKillip, DiMiceli, and Luebke, (1977)) suggesting that the ultimate attribution error is linked to "high salience of group membership" (1979, p. 469).

processing plant, where a "Turk working on a cutting machine has sliced open his hand." Rosa N. comments:

> And he even started the story with: "the stupid Turk. His hand is not a can!" He said he didn't really have much confidence but still wanted to save the man's hand, because, he said, you know what it costs the Dutch government if that man loses his hand! He gets social security . . . . (1991, p. 149)

Rosa N. continues her story re the plastic surgeon's approach:

> Someone's heel is gone, that's another stupid foreigner in a factory, he says then. He talks about there being so many accidents. Only with foreigners. And he doesn't understand it, that's just how he tells the class the story. But he [doesn't add] . . . that it's foreigners who do this kind of work and that they are the highest risk group for having an accident. (1991, p. 149)

Rosa N. chose to deal with this situation as follows:

> I waited until the man was finished. . . . . I told him he shouldn't make remarks like that because they are offensive, and I chose that attitude because I thought: I must not become uncontrolled, agitated, aggressive. (1991, pp. 149–150)

Essed indicates here that Rosa N.'s (controlled) reaction suggests that

> taking an explicit stand against acts considered racist may incriminate not the agent of racism but the one who objects to the racism. Anticipating problems if she is not careful ("you are too emotional, too aggressive"), she speaks with utter self-control. (1991, p. 150)

Essed points out that because Rosa N. chose not to ignore situations such as this one, and others, she is becoming labeled as "oversensitive." Hence, as Rosa N. puts it, "now at my work, they find me oversensitive, probably because I just cannot let things pass. And I can absolutely not do that. I do not want to and I will not" (1991, p. 151).

Essed indicates how Rosa N. interprets her colleagues as not inclined to want to see parts of her daily realities that they may regard as "painful" experiences for her:

> They really don't want to see it; they don't know how to deal with painful things. I told them once what I had experienced in hotels. Now one of them reacted with: how strange, there must have been something behind it. The rest kept quiet. (1991, p. 151)

Essed offers more detail on the hotel situations as recounted by Rosa N., and she allows us as audiences to judge whether, as Rosa N. sees it, attitudes of the staff members are expressions of racism. But Essed makes the point that "she does not relate all these experiences to her colleagues, because she seemed to embarrass them with her stories about racism" (1991, p. 152). Meanwhile, Rosa N. has become afraid of being pigeonholed as, in her words, "Rosa is sensitive, you mustn't say anything discriminating. You know what I mean by them pigeonholing me. That I am the one who is oversensitive" (1991, pp. 152–153). Rosa N. also finds that her colleagues seem not to be interested in the "life that I've led" – but are more interested in "each other's stories, for that's something they know" (1991, p. 153).

Rosa N. also recounts a story of a patient considered mentally disturbed whose behavior had been recorded on video. She believed that some of the behavior was "typical of the Surinamese or Caribbean society" (1991, p. 153). But when she expressed her opinion, someone else (who had visited Suriname) was rather referred to for his opinion. She became upset and they regarded her as being too "emotionally involved." She explains: "they don't like that, you have to be detached when making a report. That is the general trend in Holland" (1991, p. 154).

Rosa N. furthermore recounts a situation where she is in a room with a patient, making notes, when a man comes in to clean the room and asks "When can I clean your room? Or you've got a new cleaner?" (1991, p. 155). She remarks that the shock when people realize that she is a doctor is for her "one more proof that the Dutch have a certain image of the Surinamese" (1991, p. 155). Meanwhile, she suggests that:

> You can see all too clearly that a Surinamese cleaner is treated differently here, by the . . . head custodian. I'm a doctor . . . .. Good day, good day, good day. Friendly nods. But to the others: "I told you to do that!" Or they're treated like an infant, but still uncivilly. (1991, p. 155)

But Rosa N. feels that she cannot bring up the subject of racism at the hospital because "they'll only trip me up" (1991, p. 155).

The interview with Rosa N. concludes by Rosa N. indicating that she reads a lot more about discrimination now because "now I would like to know much more about how I can deal with it" (1991. p. 156). Rosa N. indicates that this is because "you don't get any further if you [just] keep on thinking only about they do that and they do that and they do that" (1991, p. 156).

Essed for her part comments more generally that Black women in the Netherlands "seem to be at a turning point in which their orientation is changing from mere defense toward a search for the power to act and to build" (1991, p. 156). She also comments on Rosa N.'s experiences in terms of the issue of class exploitation. She states:

> If Rosa N. had become a cleaner rather than a doctor in the hospital, her story would have been one of racism structured by class exploitation and of class oppression permeated by racism. Indirectly she is confronted with the impact of class oppression in everyday racism. The head custodian bullies the Black cleaner, but he would never be anything but polite with Dr. N. Her own struggle, as it relates to the structural position of Black women within higher education, is directed more exclusively toward racial and ethnic marginalization. (1991, p. 170)

Essed notes that in considering the mechanisms of the exercise of structural power operative in the way in which Rosa N., and others, become marginalized, there seems to be no inherent connection with "'will', motivation, or desire" (1991, p. 171). The implications and consequences of the acts recounted by Rosa N. "and the realization [on the part of Whites] that one could have acted otherwise, are not inherently explicit for the actor(s) involved" (1991, p. 171). However, "the ideological climate fosters oppression of the elements that are seen as different and legitimizes practices that sustain hierarchical ordering of difference" (1991, pp. 171–172). And when Rosa N. tries to challenge the racism that she detects, her resistance is delegitimized. There is an implicit denial of any conflict. Therefore,

Essed notes, it is important to make explicit the implicit (in this case the implicit denial) "in trying to establish alternative definitions of reality" (1991, p. 172).

5.2.4.4 Some Pointers to the Macro Context in the Two Countries

In considering the "macro context of experiences of racism," Essed remarks that "like Rosa N. all other Black women experience racism in multiple situations" (1991, p. 175). In order to provide an idea of the *distribution of racism across different social contexts* in the USA as well as the Netherlands, Essed supplies two tables (1991, pp. 176–177) – one for the 27 interviewees in the USA and one for the 28 interviewees in the Netherlands. These tables summarize the different situations in which the interviewees had "direct, vicarious or mediated experiences of racism" (1991, p. 175). Her tables provide a summary of incidents in terms of the following coding categories: *Symbolic* (language, culture, science, religion); *Media*; *Politics*; *Education*; *Work*; *Housing*; *Neighborhoods*; *Family*; *Friends*; *Restaurants*; *Street*; *Hotel*; *Organizations*; *Services* (1991, p. 176).

Essed refers via these tables to the different ways in which racism may play itself out in the different countries. She comments that the "numbers" of incidents as presented in the tables require elucidation in the light of an interpretation of the social context. For example, she suggests that the marked presence of "neighborhood racism" as reported by interviewees in the Netherlands should be read in the context of the fact that in the Netherlands "Black women live in White-dominated neighborhoods" – while this is the case only for part of the US group (1991, p. 178). Also, the fact that Black women in the Netherlands more frequently report racism when riding a bus or street car should be interpreted in the light of the fact that most women in the Netherlands make use of public transport frequently, unlike those in California who tend to travel by car (1991, p. 178). Essed furthermore remarks on the numbers indicating that far fewer women brought up the issue of the media as a source of racism in the USA than in the Netherlands, where many criticized the media for perpetuating racism. She states that this also requires interpretation (1991, p. 178). It may suggest that:

> Black women in the Netherlands are more sensitive to ideological racism or that media representations of race issues are more problematic in the Netherlands than in the United States. (1991, p. 178)

She does not try to resolve the question of how the comparative information in this regard should be interpreted. She argues that the matter "requires further investigation" (1991, p. 178). But she points out that, given the need for interpretation of all the information supplied in the tables against the social context, it would be unwise to try to use the numbers reported in them for "generalization" (of the sort, e.g., attempted in survey research).

Essed also supplies a further table (pp. 180–181) tabulating the *frequencies of the forms of everyday racism* (as she calls them) across the two countries. She isolates in this table three main forms of everyday racism (with subcategories and subsubcategories). The three main headings are *Marginalization*,

Problematization, and *Containment*. The subcatgories under *Marginalization* are cognitive detachment; Eurocentrism/Whitecentrism; and obstacles impeding equal participation. The subcategories under *Problematization* are denigration of perspective/personality; cultural denigration; and biological/cultural denigration. The subcatgories under *Containment* are denial of racism; management of ethnic difference; pacification; denial of dignity; intimidation; retaliation; and other. (Each of the subcategories has further subcategories detailing specific indicators of the categories.)

Essed uses these tables to make a number of points. One of these that I wish to highlight is her comment that:

> Dutch racism problematizes Blacks more strongly through cultural determinism. . . . [T]his can be inferred from the overrepresentation of women who report the various forms of cultural and moral denigration of Blacks in the Netherlands. In the United States, more than in the Netherlands, racism operates through race. . . . . In everyday situations, many more Black women in the United States (70%) than in the Netherlands (14%) are more frequently confronted with the attribution of superiority on the basis of White skin color. (1991, p. 182)

Essed avers that apart from this variation in the strength of the operation of "culturalized or racialized" racism, "in both countries the mechanisms operate to impede Black mobility" (1991, p. 182). She remarks that it is noteworthy that in the Netherlands, the Dutch government "does not sanction employers who refuse to take Black workers."[126] She finds it "significant in this respect that 39% of women in the Netherlands and only 11% of the women in the United States report a chronic lack of initiative to facilitate the participation of Blacks in various institutions" (1991, p. 183).

Essed also indicates that 25% of women in the Netherlands report that "dominant group members get furious in situations where Blacks object to racism." But in the United States, only 7% "brought up the same problem" (1991, p. 182). She comments that this does not mean to her that "racism is sufficiently dealt with in the United States. " Rather, the figures suggest that "racism is not taken seriously [as an issue requiring serious attention] . . . in Dutch society" (1991, p. 182).

---

[126]This is consistent with the policy reported to me in an interview (2007) with a manager in the diversity and inclusiveness division at Shell (which has its headquarters in The Hague in the Netherlands). The interviewee indicated to me that while the operations of Shell in the USA and in South Africa are in line with legal provisions for affirmative action, in the Netherlands targets are set for employing more "ethnic minorities" – but these are not legally required to be met. She also indicated to me that different people in Shell see the targets differently – with some arguing the case for trying to meet targets on moral grounds, and others arguing that the "business benefit" needs to be shown in terms of the effectiveness for business of diversity in Shell. In this climate she tries in her work to collect stories that show "how diversity is good for business." She also makes use of Implicit Association Tests (IATs) (see Chapter 3, Section 3.7) to help people to acknowledge biases that they may be carrying in relation to those perceived as "different," and to open up discussions on possibly unacknowledged racism.

5.3 Revisiting Essed's Discussion

In my outline of Essed's research, I have indicated how she takes pains to elucidate her methodological approach that she chose to adopt. I also showed how she clarifies her conception of the link between her own theorizing and the comprehension that she sees as displayed by the interviewees in relation to their experiences as they recount (and in the process reflect upon) them. In this section I revisit her approach by commenting on the areas where I believe that it can be extended, drawing on, but developing, her account of her methodology and its justification. I focus on the following:

- The nondirective approach to interviewing;
- The status of her own theorizing in relation to the narrations (storying) of the interviewees; and
- Her account of intersectional analysis.

5.3.1 Essed's Nondirective Interviewing Approach

Essed characterizes her interviewing approach as having been nondirective (1991, p. 4). She allowed the interviewees to recount their experiences while encouraging them to be, in Gray et al.'s terms, "pensive and reflective" (2007, p. 154). She did not try to "direct" the conversation.

Essed describes the interview material as consisting of "verbal reconstructions of experiences" that became constructed during the interview process (1991, p. 3). She sees her interviewees as "narrators" recounting their "experiences in the context of their everyday lives" through the stories that they express and through their answers to questions asked during the interview (at appropriate points) as to whether they find the experiences "acceptable" and whether they believe that some of their experiences are linked to their being Black.

Seen in the light of Douglas's comments to which I referred in Section 5.1 on the difficulties in drawing out information "held at a subjective, experiential, non-verbal level and hard to articulate" (1998, Chapter 5, p. 8), it seems that Essed's approach in asking her narrators to reconstruct their experiences is one way of drawing out experiences and reflections thereon. Yet it is interesting to note that Douglas in her own one-to-one engagements with Black women managers (in Britain) takes what I see as a different role as "interviewer" to that portrayed by Essed. Rather than assuming a nondirective role, in asking "interviewees" primarily to *recount* their experiences and their reflections, Douglas consciously chose, during her encounters (that she chose to label as collaborative dialogue), to *open up conversation* in order, to "extend the participants' own sense-making processes" (including herself as one participant in the dialogue) (1998, Chapter 6, p. 7).[127]

---

[127]Douglas also initiated a collaborative inquiry group for Black women managers – as a "safe and secure" context where they could identify with the aim of transforming "habitual taken-for-granted responses." In establishing criteria for joining the group, she looked for women who, for

Douglas explains that she found that the "distance in roles" normally scripted between interviewer and interviewee frustrated her. Thus when one of her colleagues doing *her* research had asked her if she would participate in an interview (to which she agreed), Douglas already had begun to experience the restrictions that this can involve. After this colleague had "ended the session," she wanted to say to her "could we now drop the role and have a good conversation around these issues – woman to woman?" Nevertheless, she chose not to express these thoughts and feelings to the colleague, despite feeling that the interview process had been restrictive. Douglas remarks that upon reflecting more on this later,

> I realized our constructions of the interviewer's role inhibited the possibility of real dialogue. I had been constrained by our respective roles and I wondered whether she too had felt confined by the role. (1998, Chapter 6, p. 4)

Douglas began to consider the possibility of "breaking the rules" by asking "can the interview be reframed sufficiently for it to be mutually empowering and still remain an interview?" (1998, Chapter 6, p. 4).

In her own studies Douglas explored the possibility of indeed reframing "the interview" so as to incorporate her concerns with the restrictiveness of role definition. Hence, for instance, when entering into conversation with (other) Black women managers, she opened up with them questions such as "are we surviving?" and "are our survival strategies working in our interest"? She tried furthermore to extend their mutual sense-making by putting forward the idea that "thriving" is a radically different way of being.[128] She thus did not shy away from "directing" participants (including herself) toward asking the question "are we as Black women surviving or thriving?" as an entry point to hold a conversation on this, in which both parties' sense-making (and considerations of options for action) could become extended.[129] Douglas does not try to settle the issue of whether this "reframing" of the interview means that it "still remains an interview" (1998, Chapter 6, p. 4). But she

---

example, "were experienced in developing Black women" as she "hoped to tap a wider source of knowledge than just our personal experience." She also considered it important that they showed willingness to "collaborate as equals taking neither teacher, nor mentee roles." She indicates that the overall aim was to "create an ethos of critical reflectivity" rather than people "detaching the self and heavily [and defensively] protecting it" (2002, p. 253). Douglas's discussion of the importance of creating a context where people could feel "safe," tallies with Collins's expression of the need for this – see Chapter 1, Section 1.4.

[128] Douglas explains that her research concerns around this issue grew out of my work and life experiences as a Black woman in Britain working with organizations to implement their various equal opportunity policies. They also emerged from a more fundamental life question *"Is it possible for Black women to thrive in Britain?"* (2002, p. 250). She indicates that this life question became triggered for her "during a Maya Angelou poetry reading concert in Lewisham. Though inspired by the woman herself, I was most struck by the idea of 'surviving' and 'thriving' as distinctly different goals for the Black woman" (2002, p. 250).

[129] Ivey and Ivey argue in similar vein that in "intentional interviewing," participants can be facilitated to "restory" – that is, to generate new ways to talk about themselves in "new narratives" – as part of the process of reconsidering options for action. In this way, restorying becomes linked to possibilities for empowerment (2003, p. 27).

indicates that she decided to consider her one-to-one engagements as "collaborative dialogue."

An analogous style of engagement has been explored in some detail by Holstein and Gubrium in their book *The Active Interview* (1995). In the book they explain that active interviewing is not simply to be aimed at developing a deeper understanding of "the subject's [participant's] feelings" (1995, p. 9). Nor is it indeed a matter of trying to establish "mutual disclosure" so that both researchers and participants will have a better understanding of one another. It is about recognizing that so-called "mutuality of disclosure ... mediates, adds to, and shapes what is said in its own right" (1995, p. 13). As Holstein and Gubrium state (1995, p. 14), citing Pool (1957), "communicative contingencies and constructs of the interview literally activate opinion."[130] Holstein and Gubrium stress that interviews – no matter how they are conducted – cannot easily be argued to fulfill the task of excavating some underlying "true" opinion (as I similarly suggested in Chapter 4 could be said in relation to survey research as well). In view hereof, they suggest that active interviewing becomes consciously geared as follows:

> ... the active interviewer conscientiously, but cautiously, promotes multivocality .... . Asking the respondent to address a topic from one point of view, then another, is a way of activating the respondent's stock of knowledge .... . The contradictions and complexities that may emerge from positional shifts are rethought to signal alternative horizons and linkages. (1995, pp 77–78)

The interview is thus used as an occasion to elicit contradictions and complexities so that interviewees have a better sense of the variety of points of view that they themselves (through the interview encounter) can indeed appreciate (1995, p. 77). This is akin to Douglas's view that, with participants, complexities in ways of recounting and reflecting upon "experience" could become mutually explored. Douglas regards as important her (epistemological) orientation that she brought to the "interview" context, namely that "there may be many 'truths' about the means by which we are excluded, and disadvantaged, and our development and growth suppressed" (1998, Chapter 5, p. 9). The idea was to continue to explore with participants the related issues, and at the same time to re-envisage possible options for action. (As I indicated in Footnote 127, Douglas in addition set up a collaborative inquiry group with Black women managers – as a further space for rethinking their relation to Equal Opportunity practices in organizations. Furthermore, she became involved in various training and development programs – one of which I explore in detail in Chapter 7.)

In any case, Douglas's suggestions for using one-to-one engagements as an opportunity for co-exploring both parties' sense-making links up with Holstein and Gubrium's (1995) account of "active interviewing" – as a form of engagement in which interviewers acknowledge themselves as participants in the dialogue. Travers

---

[130]This ties in with my discussion in Chapter 4, Section 4.3.2, where I discussed Mann's (2006) account of interviewing perceived as an encounter where perspectives become (re)created, rather than "found."

(2006) considers that Holstein and Gubrium's approach – also elucidated in their book *Postmodern Interviewing* (2003) – has been influential in affecting our perceptions of both the conduct and the write up of interviewing processes. He summarizes their key argument in relation to interviews:

> They should be seen as interactional events, rather than, as in [traditional] survey research, or, for that matter, traditional symbolic interactionism, a window into people's minds. [The focus is on] how interview responses are produced in the interaction between the interviewer and interviewee. (2006, p. 270)

Travers comments that Gubrium and Holstein have managed to "reach a general audience" by not making qualitative research (such as their proposed style of interviewing) seem too "technically demanding or difficult," while emphasizing that we can consider the opinions and ideas formulated during interviews as constructions arising during the interview encounter (2006, p. 270). It is important to note that the postmodern bent of active interviewing as here defined is not merely a matter of, as Gray et al. seem to define it, developing "collaboration" between researchers and the people they are studying so that information can be better extracted. It is a matter of recognizing that the *results of the collaborative enterprise are to be seen as constructed through the specific relationship developed between the parties to the "interview" and the specific ways in which the interview unfolds*. Here it is explicitly recognized that the interview itself *brings forth* interpretations of the world through the way it proceeds. As Gubrium and Koro-Ljungberg put it:

> Viewing interviews as symbiotic events enables us to focus on sensitivity and flexibility and the way in which both interviewer and interviewee "feed off" each other as they coconstruct data. (2005, p. 711) [131]

In Douglas's terms, the interview can then be conceptualized and practiced consciously to engender styles of relating that enable people to extend their options for ways of seeing and for (continuing) action.

Because Essed does not indicate to us in her book how she believes her specific presence in the interviews (or way of asking questions, etc.) might have "made a difference" to the way the interviews unfolded, but merely indicates that the interviews were "nondirective," she does not in my view offer sufficient pointers to how she is conceptualizing her involvement in the process. It seems that as far as aiding participants to extend their "sense-making" (or way of visioning the issues) is concerned, she seems to have tried not to "direct" the interviewees in any way. She leaves this to another medium, namely, the medium of her write-up – where she offers her theorizing as a way of organizing the "translation of Black women's comprehension" into her own understanding (1991, p. 55). In Douglas's approach, however, and in other more active interviewing styles, the interview itself becomes an opportunity for interviewers to consciously enter input into the discussion, as a way of drawing

---

[131] This Gubrium is not the same person as the co-author of Holstein and Gubrium (1995, 2003), although Gubrium and Koro-Ljungberg cite favorably the work of Holstein and Gubrium (1995) for developing an understanding of interviewing that "enhances interactions and participants, and enriches analytic practices and data interpretations" (2005, p. 711).

out as well as generating different perspectives on the issues so that both parties can become mutually enriched in their "understandings." Furthermore, reflexivity is encouraged in relation to one's own role as "interviewer" – so that one is (more) aware of how one might be affecting the interview encounter and so that audiences in turn can judge the material in the light of commentary provided on one's own input/presence.

In short, I would suggest that one can extend further than does Essed the "traditional" approach to intensive interviewing to take more fully into account the considerations offered by, for instance, Douglas and by those supporting "active interviewing" as a style of approach (with the attendant more constructivist-oriented understanding of the interview process).

Before I close this section I wish to note that Douglas's as well as other active interviewers' understandings of active involvement in the research process differs from more realist-oriented accounts of practices of research interviewing. I illustrate this point with reference to Hammersley and Atkinson's realist-oriented account of interviewing processes, as discussed below.

5.3.1.1 Some Contention Around Hammersley and Atkinson's Approach to the Issue of "Reactivity"

Hammersley and Atkinson approach the issue of the presence of the researcher in the interview situation in terms of a discussion of "the problem of reactivity" (1995, p. 130). They define the reactivity effect as the effect(s) produced through the fact that "people respond to the presence of the researcher" in the research process (1995, p. 18). They suggest that as researchers, we can "minimize reactivity or we can try to monitor it." But we can also "exploit it" by seeing it as "informative," because "how people respond to the presence of the researcher may be as informative as how they react to other situations" (1995, p. 18). Hammersley and Atkinson consider that the issue of reactivity needs to be taken on board by researchers because "the effects of audience [in this case, the researcher] on what people say and do" are impossible to "eradicate" (1995, p. 130). Hence they suggest that, taking into account the problem of reactivity, "the goal must be to discover the correct way of interpreting what data we have" (1995, p. 131).

In other words, in Hammersley and Atkinson's understanding, researchers must aim at developing a "correct" interpretation of the data that become generated through the research process. They can strive to do this by considering what could have influenced the data to emerge in the way that they have – that is, by taking into account the presence of the researcher and the social context in generating the data that have come to the fore. Specifically considering processes of interviewing in the context of recognizing the possibility of the "reactivity effect," they suggest that:

> Interviewing can be an extremely important source of data: it may allow one to generate information that it would be very difficult, if not impossible to obtain otherwise – both about events described and about perspectives and discursive strategies. (1995, p. 131)

Having said this, Hammersley and Atkinson suggest that apart from read-ing/interpreting the data in the light of the "problem of reactivity," researchers may do well to combine interview material with other sources of data in order to work toward developing "correct" interpretations.

Many authors have criticized Hammersley for still operating with a model of interviews whereby they are seen as ideally (as far as possible) "locat[ing] valuable information inside the respondent and assign[ing] the interviewer the task of some-how extracting it" (as explained by Hoffman, 2007, p. 319). Hoffman indicates that a Foucauldian perspective (as in Foucault, 1973) suggests, on the contrary, that "there is no single 'Truth' for the interviewer to [try to] extract from the respondent" (2007, p. 324). In this approach, what becomes focused upon is the way in which the inter-view can (potentially) become mutually enriching for "both the researcher and the informant" as they develop their interaction (2007, p. 325). In Douglas's terms, this means that provision is made for mutually exploring multiple truths and multiple realities (Douglas, 1998, Chapter 5, p. 9).

McDonald similarly, in criticizing Hammersley and Atkinson's model of inter-viewing, poses the question of how we can disrupt the notion of the interview where the interviewer, "positioned as superior in relation to the interviewee, autho-rizes views about the interviewee and designates her own interpretations as true[r]" (2000). McDonald argues that what is missing in Hammersley and Atkinson's rec-ommendations for interviewing is "how emerging constructions of knowledge [can] privilege existing knowledge frameworks of the interviewer over those of the inter-viewee" (2000). She avers that Hammersley and Atkinson give insufficient attention to *this* problem. She indicates that the aim of her paper criticizing Hammersley and Atkinson's notion of interviewing practices is to try to

> convince the reader to [re]consider his/her assumptions about the role of the interviewer, the interviewee, and the ways in which knowledge is constructed through the interview process. (2000)

She suggests that ways of revisiting assumptions could include

> rigorous self-reflexivity on the part of the interviewer, shared exploration of dilemmas and power shifts involved in the research process, and acute listening to encourage a dialectic among knowledge of the interviewee and interviewer. (2000)

In considering Hammersley's own reference to the adoption of a "reflexive" approach, Speer and Hutchby make the point that "he does not provide any indica-tion of what such an orientation would look like in his own or others' work" (2003b, p. 353). They argue that his supposed "methodological commitment to reflexivity" thus means very little (2003b, p. 353). They present this criticism in the context of a debate with Hammersley over the issue of reactivity. (See also Chapter 2, Section 2.3.1.2; Chapter 3, Section 3.4.2; and Chapter 4, Section 4.3.2.) They note that con-cerns as expressed by Hammersley (and others) "about the problem of reactivity or researcher effect" are based on what Speer and Hutchby consider as an "unsustain-able distinction between 'natural' and 'non-natural' or 'researcher-affected' realms of social interaction" (2003a, p. 317). According to them, instead of maintaining the distinction between "natural" data supposedly unaffected by the research process and "researcher-affected" data, another approach is to admit the "subtlety of the ways in which our data collection practices [necessarily] ... constitute their objects" (2003a, p. 334).

In response to this position as expressed by Speer and Hutchby, Hammersley clarifies that a concern with reactivity as he sees it, "does not commit qualitative researchers to the idea that the task of research is to *eliminate* 'extraneous' factors with a view to 'uncovering "objective" reality' " (2003, p. 345). He argues that two separate issues here have become conflated that need to be distinguished from each other:

> First of all, there is the question of whether the aim of research is to provide knowledge of how the world operates *irrespective* of whether or not it is being researched. It seems to me that virtually all social research has this commitment. The second issue is whether, in order to produce such knowledge, we have to rely entirely or primarily on situations that are unaffected by the research process, or unaffected by variation in the researcher or in the research procedure. (Hammersley, 2003, p. 345)

Hammersley argues that his recommendation does *not* imply trying to find a way of studying the social world "as if it were not being studied" – an approach that he equates to a "naive form of naturalism" (2003, p. 345). His approach is rather to recognize that there are "methodological problems" that need to be addressed when seeking to gain knowledge of "how the [social] world operates." By making this statement, as I indicated in Chapter 1, Section 1.5.1, Hammersley indicates his allegiance to a realist epistemology – which propounds that researchers must strive to "provide knowledge," albeit that there is no firm foundation for establishing it.[132]

Speer and Hutchby, in rejoinder to Hammersley, indicate that they take a different starting point – which does not consider postulating a world unaffected by research input. They reiterate their position that "there is no such thing as a non-reactive piece of data in the sense that interactions can be stripped of their context" (2003b, p. 356). This means that so-called reactivity effects are a necessary part of all interactional events occurring between people, including in research contexts. In terms of their argument, these effects should be seen, and presented to audiences, as highlighting "ways in which research and research methods (like other persons and contexts) impact upon our data" (2003b, p. 358).

Although Hammersley believes that "virtually all social research" is aimed at establishing how the world operates independently of our knowing efforts, I have

---

[132]Hammersley calls his (realist) position *non-foundationalism* in order to distinguish it from "naïve" empiricist positions (1995, p. 72). In doing so, he follows Popper's suggestion that lessons can be learned from positivism, while rejecting the naïve empiricism (foundationalism) associated with positivism (1995, p. 19). As pointed out by Lincoln and Guba, "constructivists ... tend toward the *anti-foundational*" (2003, p. 273, my italics). *Anti-foundational,* they note, is the "term used to denote a refusal to adopt any permanent, unvarying ... standards by which truth can be universally known" (2003, p. 273).

tried to show in this book that *many researchers do not share this (realist) orienta-tion*. By stating that as he sees it "virtually all social research has this commitment" (2003, p. 345), he renders invisible all the efforts of those who have expressed, and practiced, alternative epistemologies in their inquiries, and who wish to put the focus on the way in which researchers can *take responsibility for their involvement in the co-construction of social realities*.

I have suggested in my discussion of Essed's approach that more attention could be given to accounting for her conception of the interview process itself in view of debates around its practice. In my view, Douglas's indication of her own attempt to make visible (to herself and others) her role, and to *acknowledge and take some responsibility for her intervention* in eliciting what she calls the "articulations" expressed by those with whom she converses, provides an illustration of a radi-cal shift in the traditional interview model – in keeping with the various criticisms that have been leveled against Hammersley and Atkinson's account. I believe this needs to be given serious consideration as an option for "intensive interviewing" as a way of generating inquiries around (new) racism.

In the next section I turn to my interpretation of Essed's conception of the status of her theorizing in relation to the storying of the interviewees.

5.3.2 Essed's Theorizing in Relation to the Narrations (Storying) of the Interviewees

Essed indicates that in addressing the "reality constructions" of Black women, as an analyst she checks these "for consistency with the structural properties of racism in the system" (1991, p. 55). She indicates that her theorizing around racism draws, inter alia, on structural sociology in order to explore the structural embed-dedness of racism in the system. She also indicates that her understanding of the "forces of the system" parallels the work of Omi and Winant (1986). (See also my Chapter 2, Sections 2.3.5 and 2.3.6 in regard to this position, as well as Chapter 3, Section 3.4.3, and Chapter 8.) As far as her theorizing is concerned, she indicates that she takes a theoretically pluralist stance, combining, for example, insights from structural sociology with insights from more interpretive-oriented traditions such as symbolic interactionism, phenomenology, and ethnomethodology when she focuses on the interpretation of interviewees' narrations. She points out that she does not pretend that she is "seeing/interpreting" without already bringing to bear a certain understanding – namely, her understanding of everyday racism.

She argues that on this score she sees a similarity with the narrations as recounted by the interviewees, in that their (level of) comprehension too amounts to drawing on some presuppositions in relation to the notion of racism (1991, p. 56). She sees her theorizing in relation to the actors' definitions/cognitions of their experiences as involving a process of placing these experiences (of all of the interviewees) "in a broader framework of interpretive and evaluative processes" – one which may not be available to the actors themselves, especially considering the covert ways in which racism currently manifests itself (1991, p. 60). She makes available (in her book) her own interpretations/evaluations as part of a process of "comparing Black women's interpretations to my theoretical framework" (1991, p. 60).

Interestingly, Douglas (1998), in referring to Essed's book (1991), indicates that she found it particularly helpful to her in aiding her to "recognize and name discrimination." She indicates that this recognition and naming is itself "a difficult process" (1998, Chapter 2, p. 13). She refers favorably to Essed's claim that, as Douglas puts it, "the identification of racism – particularly covert racism – is a complex process," which demands:

a) generalization about specific types of racist episodes and
b) abstract cognition about the processes and mechanisms of racism.

Douglas indicates that in her own situation, she had found that she could not "recognize and name the disjunctions" that she had been experiencing – as she had had no access until a certain stage in her life to some of the channels that might aid people to gain the necessary cognitive tools. That is, she had not had access to "media, books, or training that developed in me a conceptual framework for being able to make sense of these confusing experiences" (that she later came to name as racism) (1998, Chapter 2, p. 13). Douglas thus sees value in Essed's theoretical exposition in that in reading her book, amongst others, she became equipped with a conceptual framework that aided her own sense-making process.

Douglas's understanding of the import of Essed's theorizing (for her) is that it provided a way for her to make sense of what she otherwise regarded as "confusing" experiences that were painful to her, but that she had not been able to recognize or name. Nevertheless, it is still unclear (to me) whether Essed is posing her theoretical framework as a reality construction that should be seen as referring to some "real reality" existing independently of how different people might make sense of their experiences. When she states that the "reality constructions of Black women are checked for consistency with the structural properties of racism in the system," what status does she assign her own theoretical constructions in regard to these "properties"? It seems to me that on the one hand, she is suggesting that, at least, these constructions provide an "alternative definition of reality" to dominant discourses, which she sees as weighted in favor of denying the continued seriousness of racism (1991, p. 172). On the other hand, when she speaks of "properties of racism in the system" against which she "checks" people's interpretations, it gives the impression that she believes that someone (or set of people) operating as analyst(s) can access these properties.

Yet there is another way of interpreting her view of the status of her constructions – and that is to invoke the epistemological argument of a normatively directed critical theory. In a critical theoretical argument such as, say, proposed by Habermas (1974b, 1984, 1996), interpretations/evaluations are seen as consciously springing from some normative stance, which is rendered explicit so that audiences are aware of the value-laden character of the constructions, and so that discussion around constructions can proceed accordingly. (See also Chapter 3, Section 3.11; and Chapter 6, Section 6.3.2.)

In their Introduction to *Race Critical Theories* (2002), Essed and Goldberg note that:

> Critical theory necessarily requires a focus, among others, on race: and racial theory cannot help but be, *in a normative sense*, critical. Race, critique, and theory, we want to insist, are constitutive of the possibilities of thinking each other in any satisfactory way. (2002, p. 4, my italics)

Essed and Goldberg also make reference to the critical race theorists who developed their argument in the context of the discipline of law in the USA. They argue that "critical race theory" has been crucial in "reinvigorating the issues of race in a legal sense." But they are concerned that such theorizing has thus far been too caught up "in conditions and rationalities in the US context" (2002, p. 4). Furthermore, they express a desire that "critical race theory [should be] more generous in acknowledging its conceptual debt to the wider history of racial theorizing in the critical tradition" (2002, p. 5).

What I see as relevant from these remarks of Essed and Goldberg is that critical theorists and critical race theorists are recognized as embracing a normative orientation in their work, while at the same time inviting discussion around both the theorizing and the norms that are seen to guide it. (See Chapter 6, Sections 6.3.2.1 and 6.3.2.2 for more detail on this argument.) My suggestion is that a more explicitly expressed form of "race critical theorizing" as a way of envisaging the status of Essed's constructions would help us to shift/extend her account of the link between her own and others' "reality constructions" – by not expecting this to be adjudicated with reference to some supposed way of accessing "real reality."[133] (I return to this argument also in Chapter 8, when I discuss different accounts of how structurally oriented analyses can become developed and presented.)

5.3.3 Essed's Account of Converging Systems of Oppression

As part of her theoretical understanding that she presents, Essed indicates that "the experiences of Black women are structured by converging systems of race, class, and gender oppression" (1991, p. 5). She sees these systems as interlinked in the way in which they manifest in the particular experiences as recounted by her interviewees (which include experiences of indirectly participating in others' lives too).

In further explicating her views on how "intersectional analyses" of converging forms of oppression might be undertaken, she suggests a methodology that incorporates "concrete examples of convergent 'isms' [types of discrimination] operating in mutually reinforcing ways as they come together in the everyday lives of women of

---

[133]Some theorists naming themselves critical theorists still adhere to realist-oriented positions – see, for example, Morrow (1994) and Parks (2007). However, in Chapter 6, I indicate how critical theorizing is more often associated with questioning the fact/value distinction that underpins realist epistemologies.

color" (2001). Such a methodology, she believes, can be designed to point to ways in which categories and attendant images as employed in everyday life

> can be used ... to rationalize both the exploitation of women as workers, and the range of discriminatory practices that create glass ceilings and brick walls against women of color college students or professionals who aspire to social and economic mobility.

Here Essed points out how intersectional analyses provide a way for reviewing the social mechanisms that can operate to reinforce and at the same time justify the specific forms of discrimination as experienced by people in everyday life. Her approach involves using in her analysis existing categorical distinctions (such as man/woman, Black/White, worker/manager/owner) to highlight inequalities that manifest in people's everyday lives along these dimensions, while trying to reconfigure their meaning.

Collins indicates that she finds important Essed's understanding of institutionalized racism in the USA as providing an understanding of the social setting in which "efforts to preserve 'Blackness' become highly significant" (2000, p. 206). She considers Essed's understanding as helpful in pointing to everyday efforts on the part of those more powerful to "destroy not just actions that resist [racism], but the very ideas that might stimulate such resistance" (2000, p. 206). She sees the emphasis on "conserving African-derived ideas and practices as a form of resistance" – which takes the form of interrogating conditions that "have attempted to dehumanize and destroy the social and economic basis of Black society" (2000, p. 296). And she suggests that the category of *Black* in the way that Essed uses it needs to be understood with this in mind.

Nevertheless, the intersectional analyses proposed and practiced by Essed, Collins, and others have been criticized for tending to rely on a "list of social categories, as if they were all equally situated and interchangeable, without adequately addressing their structural differences" (cf. Thorvaldsdóttir, 2007, p. 4). In particular, it is argued that the category of "class" should not be reduced to the same ontological level (as a social construction) as the category, of, say, race or gender. Thorvaldsdóttir argues that the classic "race–class–gender" triad, which at first sight includes the "presence of the class term at all times," on deeper consideration can be seen to impede a sufficiently serious "critical theoretical engagement with the class concept" (2007, p. 3). In Chapter 8, I take up further the issue of how the concept of "class" might be envisaged in relation to other concepts, and I provide an indication of why those looking into (new forms of) racism have chosen to organize their analyses around the dynamics of racism in relation to, say, sexism and capitalism, without necessarily adjudicating on the ontological status of the different categories in the race–class–gender "triad." I would suggest that on this score, Essed's and others' proposals for intersectional analysis allow for continuing debate around the way in which various "isms" (such as sexism, racism, and capitalism) are to be conceptualized.

In my account of Essed's approach here I have concentrated on the way in which I believe her intensive interviewing process, as well as its write-up, can be extended.

I have used her work as a spur for suggesting that intensive interviewing encounters can be more explicitly justified in terms of a critical theoretical approach that acknowledges a normative intent, namely, to explore as well as undercut what can be regarded as different (intersecting) expressions of social domination. The theoretical use of the concept of racism then can be justified in terms of a pragmatically oriented critical theorizing. This means that what Essed calls Steps 5 and 6 in the analysis of social relationships (see Section 5.2.3 above), where decisions are made as to whether and how to apply the concept of racism, can be seen as including normative considerations; and these steps can be practiced (or taken) in a way that opens to discussion the purpose of the theorizing. In Chapter 8, I elucidate further how the use of the term racism can be conceived in this way, and how this tallies with Collins's suggestions for developing our inquiries so as to bring to the fore new ways of defining what is involved in the quest for "truth," while enhancing social discussion around issues of concern in view of the practical quest for "social justice" (2000, p. 38).

In the rest of the chapter, I turn to another way in which intensive interviewing might be practiced to open up discussion around issues that are otherwise scantly discussed – namely, via focus group research encounters (conceived in a particular way). I use as an illustration a focus group that I organized with a group of school children in South Africa.

5.4 Focus Group Discussion as Intensive Interviewing

Before I move on to an account of my organization of a particular focus group, I offer an indication of how focus groups can and have been conceptualized as a form of group interview. My reason for outlining focus group discussion in this chapter is to suggest, with Parker and Lynn, that it is a way of "narrowing the gap" between (professional) researchers and the people whose lives are being "researched" (2002, p. 17) – and can be seen as catering for the kind of ethical and epistemological orientation that I have discussed in previous chapters too. I explain my argument further in the course of my engagement with some alternative conceptions of what focus group interviewing might involve.

5.4.1 Some Conceptions of Focus Group Communication

Silverman suggests that when researchers study people's "communication in situ" (e.g., through focus groups in which people communicate around a topic), this can be very useful for those (such as policy makers) who later may be making decisions on the basis of an understanding of people's experiences and views. He suggests that studying people's way of communicating around the issues provides "far fuller evidence than provided by simple records of respondents' 'opinions' or 'attitudes'" (2000, p. 294). In my outline of focus groups, I concentrate not so much (as does Silverman) on their potential utility to the audiences of the research, but more on how researchers facilitating discussions can make contributions at the point of engagement with participants in the groups. I show in particular how they can enter the conversation with the aim of facilitating enrichment of the discussion. I thus follow up Parker and Lynn's comment that focus groups can be used as part of a methodological approach designed to narrow the distance between "researcher" and "researched" during the research process. I concentrate on the implications of this for researcher involvement in focus group discussions.

In my understanding of focus group research I differ from Hennink, who suggests the following role for moderators/facilitators of the discussion:

> A moderator needs to be flexible and spontaneous to be able to diverge from the prepared discussion guide and follow the natural flow of discussion while still covering the key issues of the research. .... A moderator also needs to be non-judgmental and 'neutral' by not contributing their own opinions and possibly biasing the discussion. (2007, pp. 30–31)

Hennink sees that moderators, in assuming a "neutral" role, are faced with the difficult task of "balancing the requirements of sensitivity and empathy on the one hand and objectivity and detachment on the other" (Stewart & Shamdasani, 1990, cited in Hennink, 2007, p. 31).

In contrast to this conception of moderators ideally trying to be "detached," Gregory and Romm (2001, 2004) offer a justification for seeing facilitators as participants in the group discussion, who, while paying attention to the process of the discussion, are *not required to shy away from adding content* thereto too. Just as I argued in Section 5.3.1 that one-to-one interviewing can become unnecessarily restricted by the traditional roles of "interviewer" and "interviewee" (as, for example, explained also by Douglas, 1998), so I suggest, in line with Gregory and Romm, that this applies to focus group interviewing too. Hence I suggest that in focus group interviewing, moderators/facilitators can justifiably add input into the discussion – as a way of furthering the conversation as well as helping to interrogate (starting) conceptualizations.[134] It can thus become a mechanism for generating what Bonilla-Silva calls more "straight talk" around issues that otherwise may not be brought to the fore (2006, p. 231).

In her discussion of the role of moderators, Hennink, following Stewart and Shamdasani (1990) offers two possible options for what she calls moderator involvement – namely, a *directive* and a *nondirective* role (or something in between – 2007, p. 178). Below I outline her suggestions and I indicate that focus group research can accommodate *another option* – namely, a consciously interventive approach.

Hennink defines a *directive* style of moderation as follows:

> *Directive moderation* is where the moderator plays an active role in facilitating contributions [of participants] and encouraging debate and discussion, through probing and follow-up

---

[134] Flick indicates that the notion that "individual views" are part of a dynamic social process is "an essential element of the social constructionist theoretical approach to reality [and] has been increasingly taken into account in the methodological literature" (2002, p. 119). My suggestion is that recognizing that views become "changed, asserted or suppressed" (as Flick, 2002, p. 119, puts it) in social exchange places a responsibility on facilitators to consider their involvement in this.

questions to the group. Directive moderation is used when the aim of the discussion is to elicit participants' opinions and experiences around quite specific, pre-determined issues. (2007, p. 177)

In directive interviewing, then, Hennink sees the moderator as setting out to "elicit" opinions and experiences – and adopting the required role to try to achieve this.

Hennink indicates that an alternative style of moderation is *nondirective*, which "allows the group discussion to flow more or less naturally" (2007, p. 177). She explains that:

This type of moderation ... allows greater opportunities for participants' views to emerge spontaneously and is heavily reliant on group interaction and independent discussion. (2007, p. 177)

She sees that in this type of moderation, researchers need not try to elicit views – as the group proceeds more through "independent discussion." She suggests that in practice, when adopting their roles, moderators will tend to be more or less directive or nondirective depending on the context. She indicates that experienced moderators "will be aware of the influence of different styles of moderation on the type and quality of the information obtained" (2007, p. 178). Clearly, for Hennink, the purpose of focus group interviewing – whatever style is adopted – is ultimately to "obtain information." However, in terms of Gregory and Romm's (2001) proposed interventive style of focus group interviewing, instead of treating the focus group session in this way, it is seen as an opportunity to *generate an intensive discussion in which new ways of seeing issues – including those proffered for consideration by facilitators – can be explored.* As I discuss the focus group that I facilitated, I illustrate how I tried to instantiate this conception of facilitator involvement (Sections 5.5 and 5.6).

In discussing the value of focus group interviewing as a research approach, Callaghan considers its theoretical value in, as she puts it, "relating structure and agency" (2005, Paragraph 1.1). She argues that it can make provision for us to appreciate human agency in social life, while still "recognizing the significance of existing relations and structures" that "mediate and develop individual and collective responses to them." That is, understandings that develop in a group can be recognized to be "not internal to the group but drawing on a wider repertoire of cultural knowledge from a community" (2005, Paragraph 6.11). She suggests that focus groups furthermore can

seek to render the taken-for-granted reflexive and, through the comparison of different styles [of living] and experiences, ... [can explore] both the ways in which people articulate things for themselves and ... [consider] those elements which are pre-conscious and tacit. (2005, Paragraph 7.2)

Thus, in her view, focus groups can aid people in social life to be more "reflexive about their social world" – by "subjecting their own experiences and motivations to examination" (2005, Paragraph 7.2). She states that it thus offers a way of exploring the manner in which socially sedimented patterns at the same time provide openings for people to develop novel responses (as human agents). I would propose that her account of the potential of focus groups to perform these functions is consistent with my understanding of interventive facilitation as a way of generating enhanced intersubjective examination of what Callaghan calls "experiences and motivations."

With this background account of my conception of focus groups and their potential, I now offer an outline of my experience with a focus group discussion that I organized in South Africa (2007) – around the topic of post-apartheid friendships. My exposition is brief (due to space limitations). I concentrate only on showing points at which I believe the "interventive" style that I used can be regarded as a fruitful way of facilitating both race-talk and post-race-talk in social contexts in which such talk is otherwise scantily engaged in.

5.5 Romm's Organization of a Focus Group Discussion Around Post-apartheid Friendships

The focus group session took place on 19 May 2007, with eight people (including myself). Six were school children of different ages (two aged 13 and four aged 18); one was the father (aged 43) of two of the White children. Half the children were Black and half were White.

The father of the White children had indicated to me (upon hearing I was writing a book on researching racism[135]) that he would try to see if he could arrange for me to meet and discuss with some children their experiences of their friendships. The focus group was thus organized. It lasted two-and-a-half hours.

Below I provide a truncated version – in narrative form – of some of the main issues raised and discussed. (The narrative draws on the extensive notes that I took during the discussion as well as on my verbal discussion with the father the following day around my and his memories of the meeting. The children themselves had indicated – at the end of our focus group discussion – that they did not wish to comment on my rendition that I would be entering into this book.)

I began the introductions by introducing myself as in the process of writing a book on researching racism, and I thanked them for taking part in the discussion. I indicated that, as they had heard, I was particularly interested in generating a discussion with them on the friendships that they had formed with one another. I indicated that therefore I would start the discussion by asking them questions around this and that I was expecting that they would all join the discussion by adding their experiences and reflections, and by engaging with one another's experiences and reflections. I also mentioned that if and when I added questions or points into the discussion, this was just another entry into it for them to engage with, as I regarded myself as a participant in the group as well as being the facilitator of the group discussion process.

---

[135]He heard about this through a participant in another set of (cross-racial) focus groups that I organized with adults to discuss racialized and postracialized social relationships (in Margate, South Africa, earlier in 2007).

I also asked the participants if they would like their names mentioned in the book and, particularly if they would like their names mentioned for making specific contributions to the discussion that they may wish to be attributed to them. They indicated that this was not their preference and that they preferred anonymity. In this narration, I assign anonymous names, with the father of the two White children being Graham; the three Black children being Ayanda, Bongiwe, and Thukiwe; and the three White children being Deborah, Henriette, and Rachel. Ayanda was 13 years old. Bongiwe and Thukiwe were 18 years old. Deborah was 13 years old. Henriette and Rachel were 18 years old. All were female.

I asked people to begin the discussion by speaking around how they chose their friendships – especially in the South African context (with its apartheid legacy). Deborah started off by commenting that she thought her parents had had a role to play in "bringing them up" in the way that they did – encouraging them to spend time with the various people whom they met at the school. Her father (Graham) stated that at the time when they began forming their friendships (around 1996), there had been a lot of interaction between Black and White children at the school to which they went.[136] I asked people to consider if the parents' views made a difference to their choosing of friends, and Henriette said that she herself was "educating" her parents in that "her friends are mainly Black" but that in any case her criteria for choosing people as friends are if they are "nice people." She indicated that her mom had grown up in the apartheid era and focused on the cultural side of Black people – namely, that they were less "educated" while she was more "educated." The history of educational resources thus might have impacted on her mom's attitudes. She indicated that she did not want to see it as a "thing" that she is hanging out with Black children (as well as with some White friends).

I asked whether, at school, the issue of seeming differences in "culture" was ever raised. Thukiwe suggested that sometimes, for example, on Sports days, Black people sit on one stand singing and cheering, while the rest of the school sits in another area. She suggested that they (at this stand) are the ones doing most of the "screaming and shouting." But "some White people will join the Black stand" if they wish to express themselves (by loudly cheering and shouting). Bongiwe remarked that this is not a "racial thing," but the "way you express yourself." Thus, when she herself has "had enough singing" she will go and sit at the quieter stand. I suggested then that we could define the "group" not in racialized terms, but as the "singing group." This means that if you are enjoying singing, you go and sit with that group at that point. I suggested that possibly in this way we can move toward deracializing our understanding of the different stands – rather than speaking of them as "Black" and "White," respectively.

---

[136]He later explained to me that this was a formerly White (government) school, where fees were relatively high and where many Black professionals chose to send their children post-apartheid (with increasing numbers of Black children entering the school each year). The school to which the other children went was likewise a fee-paying formerly White school (now called Model C schools).

But Ayanda indicated that she still experienced "pressure from Black people" and "even strain" because of her friendship with White girls. She indicated that she had become close friends with a White person. She began hanging out with her and because she had other White friends, she sat together with them – and was the only Black person in that group. When she herself spoke English, other (Black) people began to say to her that because she "sounded like White" she was "trying to be White." She still had her Black friends, but they did not understand why she was "wanting to be White." I suggested that they were using rigid color demarcations – and hence characterized her in this way.[137]

Bongiwe added to the discussion by mentioning that her main friends used to be her and another Black friend, with two White children (who were in the focus group). But her older brother does not like her playing with the White friends. I asked her why she thought he did not like it. And she indicated that the White boys at school used to bully her brother. Her brother was scared of them. I suggested that this context might explain why he seemed to be choosing color as a criterion for deciding the suitability of her friends. She said that she had not followed her brother's advice anyway. But she stated that as she got older, her other Black friends that she made asked her why she was "always hanging out with White girls instead of them." She told them that she felt comfortable with the White friends – because she found the Black girls were "fighting too much over boys." I asked her if she thought all of them tended to fight over this. And she said "not all – but it is a general attitude that comes from their social environment." She continued to reflect that possibly because they tend to react in a "loud" manner, this can appear as fighting. She stated that she liked to be quiet. I asked if she saw this as acting differently from the loudness that the other girls had suggested (during the discussion on the Sports stands) was seen as associated more with "Black" forms of cultural expression. And she said that sometimes she herself liked to be loud and sometimes quiet. She said that her mom and dad were both "quiet." But her extended family were "not quiet." She said that those "in White culture" do not understand this. I drew a picture and suggested that possibly the way we defined "groups" is that we think that all people in the group will have the same way of expressing themselves – and so we don't try to look past that at ways in which we can build up our manner of relating across cultural forms of expression.

---

[137]In making this statement I drew partly on Appiah's remarks (1994, 1996) that insofar as identities become constructed around being, say, black, this can lead to scripts associated with (in the case of the USA) being an "African American." As he notes, there will be "proper ways of being black . . ., there will be expectations to be met, demands will be made" (1994, p. 162). He criticizes this stance in that it does not provide for resisting "someone who demands that I organize my life around my 'race'" (1994, p. 163). He points out (1994, p. 164) that the downside of the application of a "recognition" stance that "demands respect for people as blacks" – which seems to be the concern of those criticizing Ayanda in this case for apparently not wanting to associate with "blackness" – is that it can lead to creating a set of expectations for people's behavior (and choices) that is "too tightly scripted" – as here experienced by Ayanda.

This led Bongiwe to raise the issue of being called a coconut – because she appears to adopt ways of speaking associated with being White.[138] I asked her if she regarded this as derogatory. She explained that being named this way was a way for the speaker to indicate that they saw her as "inside I'm White." I asked her how she responded to people calling her a coconut. And she said, "I ignore them." Graham stepped into the discussion and suggested to her that it was mainly the *boys* who told her that she is "acting White." Graham asked if she really could just ignore this. And she said that she "used to get cross" but, "now no more." I suggested to her that they do not appreciate that they are "pushing her into a group" when they name her as having to adopt what they consider to be Black ways of being. She said that when she is told she is trying to be White, she sometimes referred to her links with other Black friends. But because she also associates with White friends, she is still seen as that she is trying to be "better than Black." I said that this implies that "Whiteness" still has continuing status in the society (due to the way in which apartheid defined people's status) and that the response of the Black children could be seen as part of this context.

I asked Bongiwe what her parents thought of her association with White friends. And she said that her mom was worried that "some of the more White girls get too much freedom." Her mom thinks that Black parents are stricter. This generated a discussion in the group around whether one could regard White parents as being less strict with their children. Stories around parents' behavior ensued – with the Black children giving examples of their parents' strictness and with the White children offering examples of times when their parents were also strict. I asked how we can explain the perception of differences between White and Black parents' orientations, and Bongiwe said that normally Black parents consider that until one reaches age 21, one must still be a virgin and therefore at 16, say, they are not allowed to go on a date. This is different from "Western culture" where "at 16 you are allowed to date." The parents therefore tend to discourage friendships at this age with White children.

But Thukiwe stated that when her parents had met with Rachel, they welcomed her into the home. Rachel indicated that when she was first invited to supper, she did not know quite how to respond to the full plate of food put in front of her. She found the portion very large and indicated (in the focus group) that she was

---

[138]In a television talk show (*3 Talk*) hosted by Noeleen Maholwana-Sangqu on 20 October 2007 around the novel called *Coconut* by Kopano Matlwa (2007), Noeleen indicated that "I still don't understand it. What is it? Is it my accent? Is it the way I speak? Is it the way I live? Is it the way I dress? Is it that I hang out with White girls?" One of the (Black) panel members indicated that it is a serious label that one gives someone, and that "a 15 year old could feel hurt." She continued that "it is a label applied by Black people to other Black people implying 'you don't fit in,' and you are called upon to defend yourself." Phumla Nhlumayo – in offering me feedback on this chapter (May 2009) – pointed out to me that it is not only that one is called upon to defend oneself, but that one may be considered that one is "betraying other Blacks" by associating too much with Whites. She herself experiences this in her (good) relationship with her White manager, which leads to her "getting names from other Blacks saying she thinks she is White." She indicates that in this way the effects of apartheid still live on in the way she experiences the continued racialization of her social relationships.

used to "normal servings." She noticed that they had a "totally different way of doing" (in terms of traditions around eating). But besides the strain, she found it an interesting and intriguing experience. Thukiwe indicated that her dad also feels a strain when White friends come to visit. This is because her dad's English is not good – so he does not know what to talk about. When her friends come, he just greets them and then goes into his room. Her mom, however, whose English is good, can communicate better, and so can her sister.

Henriette said that she herself was concerned that "if you go to a house of another race, it is difficult conversation. One is scared to say anything offensive." So she finds the conversation difficult. She also indicated that she found that her [White] Afrikaans friends can be more racist than her English-speaking ones.[139] I asked her why she stated this. And she said it is mainly because she observes that "they don't have Black friends so they will never really learn." She was also shocked once when she went to one of her Afrikaans friends, and the family was moving house and had removal people there to help. One of the Black removal people was called a "Kaffir" by the friend's father.[140] I asked her whether she said anything thereafter to anyone. And she replied that "I did not say anything. It was not my place to say it."

I asked if her friend was aware that she was shocked by the use of the word Kaffir by her father. And she said "the friend sensed the mood" – even though she had stated nothing explicitly. At this point Graham asked people in the group to reflect on why it is so difficult for people to contest openly when someone uses the K-word (Kaffir). Why is it that peer pressure leads one to be afraid of the reactions of one's friends if one tries to confront the issue of racial insulting? He suggested that this shows that "racism is still there" (in the society) and therefore contesting it is seen as going against the grain – although there is now "more [social] equality."[141]

---

[139] Schutte notes that often English-speaking authors writing about South Africa attributed blame to Afrikaners and the Afrikaner-led (apartheid) government rather than to Whites in general for South Africa's "moral, political, and economic decline" (1995, p. 15).

[140] The term Kaffir – originally derived from an Arabic word (كافر) that is usually translated into English as "infidel" – was used by colonists during the Dutch and British colonial periods to describe Black people of the Southern African region (cf. http://en.wikipedia.org/wiki/Kaffir). During the twentieth century the term took on increasingly derisory meanings in South Africa, and as the nationmaster encyclopedia points out, it is used today in South Africa "only as a derogatory and offensive term of abuse" (http://www.nationmaster.com/encyclopedia/South-Africa-Kaffir-people). In 2000, the South African parliament enacted *Act No. 4 of 2000: Promotion of Equality and Prevention of Unfair Discrimination Act* that contains a clause relating to Hate Speech (speech that can be considered as hurtful, harmful, or promoting hatred). The clause is meant to prohibit the use of words such as Kaffir and other derogatory racial classifications (http://en.wikipedia.org/wiki/Kaffir).

[141] Phumla Nhlumayo's interpretation of this scenario (in offering feedback to me, May 2009) is that it shows that although we are supposedly living in a free world, the world is not free – in that Henriette did not feel free to contest the use of the language. But she indicates that especially for a child, it would have been difficult to raise this as an issue, also because she was a visitor in their home. She can thus see how, as visitor, Henriette did not feel that she could explicitly raise her concerns.

This led the discussion on to other instances of interactions where the children detected racism. Rachel indicated that with certain affirmative action policies, one of the White boys whom she knows has become "very racist" because "he can't get into medical school." There is a fixed quota for White people and due to this he was not able to get in (as the quota had been filled). She asked: "what do you say to him?" Thukiwe at this point said "I agree." Thukiwe stated that she expected them to be racist if they were excluded from medical school for this reason. She said "Black people ruling will not solve the problem." But I remarked that one also needs to take into account that thus far Black people have been disadvantaged educationally, and that one of the purposes of the policy of affirmative action is to try to rectify these imbalances.[142] Thukiwe asserted that the actual problem is the education system. Because of this, it is still the case that poor people will be mainly Black. At the moment, Black people are mostly attending "disadvantaged schools"[143] and, when it comes to accepting people for example, for jobs, then "as a Black person, they will look at the person as coming from a disadvantaged school." So the problem of Black people being disadvantaged will not be solved unless the schooling system is altered. That is, because the majority of poor people are Black, a race-based society will remain unless *this* issue in the education system is tackled. She indicated that she therefore does not agree with the affirmative action policy at this stage – as it is not likely to solve the problem. She stated that also, as regards appointments of teachers at her school, she does not believe that this should be done according to a policy of affirmative action.

Graham then stated that he would like to ask two questions, namely, "how many Black teachers are at the school?" and "what percentage of the children are Black?" Thukiwe answered that there were two teachers (out of about 15) and that the majority of the children were Black. She also indicated that the headmaster (responsible for appointments) was from Germany – and that he was "not likely to transform" (in the South African sense of setting out to introduce more Black teachers into the situation). Graham stated that it appeared then, that the Black children (the majority) were being taught according to a "Western educational system" and that surely one would need to hire more Black teachers to balance that. Thukiwe indicated that this would take place as a matter of course, as more Black people become qualified.

But I suggested that the concern of those propounding affirmative action is that it is quite possible that even with qualified people, the headmaster whom she had

---

[142] In Noeleen Maholwana-Sangqu's television show *3 Talk* on 10 May 2007 (advertised as exploring racism in South Africa), one White caller called in to indicate that he had wanted as a doctor to specialize in surgery in South Africa. But he had had no success in being accepted. He went for an interview abroad and was accepted. One of the White panel members stated that "at some stage you want to see where it [affirmative action] is going to stop" (in the country). The Chairman of the South African Human Rights Commission (also on the panel) – Jody Kollapen – responded that "in 1994 we did not inherit a country of equality" and that "mechanisms to address the inequalities of the past still have to be instituted." He suggested that "we need a proper application of affirmative action" – one that does not "forget the past" – to help "level the playing field" in South Africa.

[143] By this she meant formerly Black state schools (during apartheid) that are still monoracial and that continue to be under-resourced.

indicated is not inclined to "transform," could easily consider them as not being suitable for the job (in terms of his criteria of who, for instance, would fit in and who would make a good teacher). I stated that affirmative action policies were formulated to deal with this kind of scenario. Bongiwe pointed out that indeed many of the White teachers did not seem to know how to handle the children (for instance, when the children were "loud") and that it is possible that a Black teacher more acquainted with this way of expressing oneself would be more adept at relating to the children. She suggested the headmaster may not have considered this when selecting teachers, because as she saw it "Black people do not get teachers' posts." Thukiwe conceded that, yes, she had not thought of it this way and that this may be a problem. She also added that one of the (two) Black teachers was from Uganda, but she was considered as "weird" in her behavior. She continued that the children on the whole did not see her as Black or as White – but just as different because of her weirdness. I suggested that possibly it requires "work" in post-apartheid South Africa not to see people primarily as White or Black but, in this case, in terms of their qualities as teachers. And she said that the new Black teacher was initially seen (by most of the children) as Black, later she became described (in conversations around her) as simply "very nice" and now she is characterized as Mrs. M.

The conversation then moved on to affirmative action as far as rugby playing in South Africa (and choosing of teams at school) is concerned – but space does not permit me to delve into the debates that ensued around this.

5.6 Reviewing Romm's Focus Group Interviewing Approach

Due to space limitations in this book, I shall not enter into a detailed review of my way of proceeding as facilitator. In the light of my account in Section 5.4.1 of how I see the potential of intensive focus group interviewing, readers can engage with my narration of the gist of the discussion in the focus group. Readers can consider the ways in which I chose to involve myself in the content of the discussions – to introduce new points of view and new ways of approaching the issues (for further discussion and reflection). I have already indicated that I do not regard it as unduly interfering in the discussion if one chooses to add content (as well as attending to process issues) as one plays one's role as "facilitator." One could argue indeed that choosing *not* to "add content" itself cannot be seen as necessarily a more "neutral" stance – nor can it be considered as without consequences.

For instance, if I had chosen *not* to remark (in response to Thukiwe) that affirmative action policies are designed to deal with the scenarios with which the children seem to be faced in her school, then it is possible that no one (including Thukiwe), would have thought of making new points in this regard. As can be seen from my narration, Bongiwe used my remark to introduce some additional perspectives, as indeed did Thukiwe, as she considered the issue from another angle. Yet Thukiwe's earlier caution regarding the perpetuation of a racially based order due to the majority of poor people being Black and mainly attending "disadvantaged" schools, allowed people (including myself) to see this perspective too.[144] So multiple perspectives became introduced for consideration. (In later feedback to me, May 2009, Phumla Nhlumayo offered a yet wider perspective – which I now share with audiences of this book. She indicated that while the government introduced affirmative action to "put Black people into the picture," the problem is that it normally only helps people who have some "standard of education," while it "still leaves behind the others" – the majority. Furthermore, policies of affirmative action can detract attention from considering those who are relatively uneducated, who are not protected when, for example, factories close down or when people become retrenched. She indicated that in the light hereof she was not surprised to see that different views around the issue of affirmative action were coming to the fore in this focus group discussion.)

My suggestion overall is that facilitators need to take some responsibility for the choices that they make in regard to whether, when, and how to intervene in the discussion of issues, taking into account the possible consequences of both intervening and not intervening, in terms of considerations of how this might help the conversation to progress. They must of course be prepared to open to challenge during the discussion any of the statements that they might themselves express as part thereof – hence it is important that this kind of (dialogical) milieu is encouraged from the start.

I have tried here with reference to this brief account of my involvement in this focus group discussion to offer it as an example of my way of facilitating. I believe that it offers an illustration of how intensive focus group interviewing, thus facilitated, may advance participants', as well as audiences', ways of engaging with the issues being raised.

Apart from this focus group, I also undertook other focus group sessions with groups of adults – with the topic of focus being the development of post-apartheid relationships. Again, space does not permit a discussion of these, but I would like to make the point that if intensive focus group interviewing is to be used as a way of investigating while at the same time trying to work past (new) racism, this requires working with a range of participants over a range of topics. From this range, what Essed (1991) and Douglas (1998) call the further research work of generating

---

[144]It is worth noting in this regard that Zegeye comments that due to the way the government educational budget was spent during the apartheid era, "South Africa today has some of the best state schools in the world today [the formerly White ones], but also some of the worst" (due to the relative lack of money spent on Black schools) (2004, p. 872). He indicates that with the respondents whom he interviewed when exploring Black youth culture in Mamelodi, all of them "considered having a good education to be very important or important" (2004, p. 872). Nevertheless, "a significant proportion of the respondents were inclined to perceive a failure in efforts to provide them with an adequate education." As he states, "a large proportion of the respondents referred to the deficiencies in South Africa regarding black education in explaining their views that education for young black adults was not good enough to prepare them well for the future" (2004, p. 872). Thukiwe is likewise highlighting in the focus group here that the issue of the neglect of (still monoracial) Black schools needs to be focused upon.

themes and patterns, which can be drawn out of the (generated) data can ensue – ideally by checking understandings with some of the initial participants and at the same time using the analysis as a springboard for further discussion around the issues.

In the case of my own focus group sessions with adults, I undertook the process of "checking" my understanding of the initial meetings with groups of three participants at a time, while at the same time furthering the conversation again while offering my interpretation and analysis as open to discussion. In the case of the focus group interview with the children, I checked my interpretation with Graham, as we found it difficult to convene another meeting with the children (and they had earlier indicated that they were comfortable with my writing it up based on my notes). My understanding of "checking" interpretations with participants – that is sometimes construed as a way of ensuring validity of interpretations – is in line with Cho and Trent's remark that this process has been differently conceptualized by different authors within debates around the "validity" of qualitative research. They remark that techniques used in qualitative research such as "member checking" can operate within a range of epistemological outlooks, including one that "concedes that knowledge is a human construction" (2006, p. 327). That is, member checking (with participants) need not be coupled with an attempt to arrive at "valid" interpretations defined as appreciating and recording as accurately as possible the members' views (as might be expected within a realist epistemology). It can be seen as part of the process of developing enhanced intersubjective understanding as a dialogical process.

5.6.1 The Social Significance of Focus Group Inquiry to Deliberate on Nonracism

A question that may be asked – from readers – is whether the kind of intensive focus group interviewing that I argue can "make a difference" to participants at the moment inquiry (by extending their horizons for thinking through their experiences) can be regarded as socially meaningful. I answer this question by suggesting that while possibly a small number of focus group sessions, such as the ones I set up in 2007 (six in all), cannot easily be argued to make a difference in terms of people's understanding of, and acting out of, their human relationships, it is still possible to offer it as a research option toward this end.

In conversation with Carlis Douglas (August 2007), when I raised the point that I did not feel that the small number of sessions that I had had with the focus groups that I organized can be argued to have had much, if any, impact on people's way of living (even if they indicated in post-interview discussion that they felt that it led to enrichment of their understandings[145]), she remarked that there was another way of seeing this: If many, many more people choose to organize these group sessions,

---

[145] I asked people individually immediately after the discussion or 1 or 2 days later whether they had found the discussions boring or worthwhile. Most were very enthusiastic and indicated that

using the idea of inquiry with participants as a springboard for opening discussions that would probably not otherwise be entered into, then over time this could indeed make a "significant" impact.[146]

Meanwhile, in conversation with a young adult interviewee – with whom I held a 1-h telephone interview – who was referred to me by a participant from one of the adult focus groups that I had organized (also in 2007), she indicated to me that she herself found it very difficult in the course of her everyday life to raise topics around ways of relating cross racially. She indicated that this is not a "light subject" – also because for many Black people "there are too many painful past experiences." For this reason, she herself had decided to write a book around her own experiences as a Black person who was brought up in a White (and English speaking) home – and she wished to leave it to readers to slowly mull over her exposition, without forcing them to "form an opinion" on the spot. She hoped to open an interactive website so that readers, having thought through what she was saying in her book, could then enter into conversations with one another, as well as with herself around her experiences and reflections. Here again, another light is cast on the matter of attempts, via, say, focus group discussion "on the spot" to ask people to engage with these, after all, serious issues. My own view is that raising discussion involving "race-talk" and "post-race-talk" via focus groups can offer one medium, among other available media (such as, inter alia, novels, and autobiographies) for people to, indeed, set off the (needed) discussion around post-apartheid relationships, including options for working past seeing "diversity" in immutable terms (as Schutte, 1995, p. 198, puts it).

Writing in the context of the USA, Sue (2005) indicates that:

> During my 35 years of work on racism, diversity, and multiculturalism, I have come to realize that people and communities often do not wish to deal with such a potentially explosive topic because it pushes buttons in all of us and elicits strong emotions of defensiveness, guilt, anger, hopelessness and discomfort. (2005, p. 102)

Sue expresses concern that what he sees as people's reluctance to enter into race-talk, implies that people can be oblivious to the continuing impact of racism. Meanwhile, "cultural conditioning [has] taught us in many covert and overt ways that certain groups are lesser than others" (2005, p. 109). He suggests that ways need to be found to break past the "conspiracy of silence" that renders continued racism more or less invisible (2005, p. 109).

With the institutionalization of apartheid in South Africa until 1994, it is also not surprising that considerations around what it might mean to generate, and live,

---

they felt that these kinds of discussion are essential in post-apartheid South Africa. None indicated that they had been bored (although I gave them the option to state this) and they expressed amusement at my asking this.

[146] She suggested that this is especially insofar as group discussions are set up to create a forum that is both supportive of individual views as well as challenging – thus enabling people to extend their personal horizons. (This conversation that we had was in the UK, where we met, with Susan Weil, primarily to advance our co-authored book on the *Dynamics of Everyday Institutional Racism*.)

a nonracial society – that can work through the consequences of the apartheid system – are not everyday fare. As Noyoo explains:

> Racism has been a fundamental organizing principle in the relations between black and white in South Africa ever since the Dutch immigrants settled at the Cape of Good Hope. (2004, p. 364)

He goes on to suggest, citing Mbeki (2000), that:

> The transition to a nonracial democracy in 1994, and the subsequent creation of the constitutional and legal framework have not ended the inherited racist, discriminatory and inequitable divisions of the country and people. Despite collective intentions, racism continues to be the common bedfellow of South Africans. (Noyoo, 2004, p. 364)

Noyoo indicates that when he refers to racism, he is not implying the operation of only overt forms of racism, but is using "a definition of racism [that] has expanded beyond hurtful treatment" (2004, p. 364). Hence, while apartheid in its overtly hurtful form may be gone to some extent, "the unjust social relations it harnessed are still existing" (2004, p. 365). (See also my mention of this in Chapter 1, Section 1.1 and in Chapter 2, Section 2.3.5.1.)

In this social context, where "conflicts of interest" can take on "subtle dimensions," he proposes that:

> Social work should take the lead in identifying and rectifying the current oppressive patterns in South Africa, which are not easily identifiable because of the existing democratic dispensation. (2004, p. 365)

Noyoo thus makes the point that forms of racism in South Africa are less easily identifiable in the current "democratic dispensation."

Zegeye places such considerations in a broader perspective by pointing to the new theoretical discourse on racism that has emerged in various parts of the globe, where "the boundaries between gender, race, ethnicity, sexuality, and class are crossed, opening a new basis for discourse on racial politics" (2002, p. 267). He observes that:

> Applied to racial politics in South Africa, this means that the boundaries between black and white are no longer immutable, but flexibly, subjectively and historically defined. In its attempt to promote greater equality in South Africa, the state appears to recognize this significant aspect. (2002, p. 267)

But he argues that attempts to create greater equality in South Africa are strongly affected by "the conflicting demands made by global capital and the population of South Africa on a heavily-burdened government system" (2002, p. 270). Again I would suggest that in this social context identified by Zegeye, additional talk around the experience of inequality and the disproportionate poverty among "the black population of South Africa and especially black women" (2002, p. 269) needs to be instituted through increased public engagement in the way the issues at stake become defined. And, like Zegeye, I suggest that such discussion should proceed in a way that works through and past the seemingly "impregnable boundaries between black and white people" that are associated with racism (2002, p. 267).

However, as Hercules reminds us, based on his evaluation of one of the programs set up by the Department of Education (see Chapter 2, Section "Measuring Continuing Old-Fashioned as Well as New Racism in South Africa" as discussed under Section 2.3.2.3), the notion that "races" as bounded entities exist in South Africa still did not appear to have been worked through and past by the people whom he interviewed. In his understanding, the fundamental message even by those who wish to be progressive is to "promote 'peace between the races,' 'tolerance' and 'racial harmony'" (Hercules, 2006, p. 62).[147]

Upon receiving the report of Hercules, sent to me by the Director of Race and Values in the Department of Education (Granville Whittle) [148] following an interview that I had set up with him in September 2008, I e-mailed the latter with some comments. I remarked that Hercules had highlighted that, in his words, "the race concept is deeply entrenched and consolidated." I also highlighted Hercules's suggestion that in his opinion one would need therefore to develop "a learning process that problematizes the notion of race, seeks to debunk and deconstruct the race myth and attempts to deal with the serious question of building a nonracial classroom, school, society and community." And I pointed to the section in Hercules's report where he suggested that in order to activate the vision and meaning of the new Constitution, changes should be directed at the society at large to "socialize and educate the masses in new ways of self and social construction."

I mentioned to Whittle in my e-mail that I thought "the tenor of [t]his report matches what we were talking about in our conversation" around these issues. My discussion with him in our conversation (prior to his sending me Hercules's report) itself had indeed revolved around how the race concept has been thus far dealt with within the Department of Education. (I had raised this as the issue I was interested in conversing with him about.) He indicated to me in this conversation that it is very important via the "hidden curriculum" in schools – where students learn social values and ways of interacting – that people become more upfront about issues of race and racism. He indicated that many teachers (Black and White) still lacked

---

[147]One could argue that in my focus group interviewing approach I tried – at the point of interviewing – to participate with (other) participants in considering how deracialization could be set in motion. For example, we spoke about deracializing the different Sports stands on Sports days, thus making openings to review our understandings of the groupings at the different stands. Furthermore, by Thukiwe raising for consideration the class-based nature of being "Black and poor" and the fact that affirmative action is insufficiently equipped to deal with this, she helped us to redefine our understanding of the "race-based" social order in terms of concerns around poverty. This, I would suggest, points to potential in the social fabric for reviewing our relationships, not based on the essentialization of race categories. Of course, it is possible that the children in this focus group may have been somewhat atypical in their way of defying (as part of our discussion) apartheid-styled racial categorization. But my point is that this example can be used to point to, and at the same time draw out, a potential in the fabric to review socially entrenched categorizations – which thus far Hercules found to remain by and large entrenched.

[148]The expressed purpose of the Race and Values Directorate is "to promote equality, nonracialism and a culture of human rights in all education institutions" (cf. http://www.education.gov.za/functions/branchS_equity.asp).

training in ways of dealing with discrimination that might appear in the schools, and also many (White) teachers had come from a "brutal racist past" (socialized within an apartheid system) – and it is difficult to "change people's mindsets overnight." He indicated that in terms of research that has been undertaken in desegregated schools (i.e., schools that are not monoracial[149]), it appears that many Black children feel that they are marginalized. When he himself visits the desegregated (or otherwise called integrated) schools, the teachers report to him that "we don't see color; we deal with the learners." He stated to me that they "pretend to be color-blind." But "once you scratch the surface [by speaking further to them] you become aware of the stereotypes" that they are employing. He indicated that most of these schools have "White male principles" – and this also makes a difference to the symbols to which the children become exposed.

As far as dealing with overt racism in schools, he mentioned that there are some hotspot schools where incidents have been reported – for example, a Principal, teacher, or student might have made a racist remark. Then some intervention (organized by the relevant Province) occurs in the hotspot school. But when I asked him about mechanisms to address more covert forms of racism he pointed out that "in terms of subtle racism, thus far parents and teachers struggle to deal with diversity." It was at this point that he mentioned to me the training course that had been set up by the Department (of which Hercules, cited above, created the evaluation, 2006).

He further indicated that one of the problems in South Africa is that thus far "we have had only experience of reified cultures" – hence people are ill-equipped to consider what it might mean to generate a multicultural society. In a country like South Africa, he noted, there is a debate around whether to encourage a "bold nationhood" (so that people are urged to identify as South Africans) – but the issue still remains as to how they should relate to each other. (I made the point here that if people can learn to de-reify culture, then they can also learn that "nation" too is a social construction – and this can help to avoid/mitigate against xenophobia.)

He indicated that as far as helping to train teachers to focus on these issues, his sense is that the quality of teacher training is diverse across different institutions – while some institutions might be managing to facilitate discussion around "race," "culture" and "nation" in a way that is helpful to creating new human relationships, others are not.[150] He commented that it seemed to be the government policy after 1994 that "in the long term these issues would sort themselves out." Hence it was only post 2000 that it became evident that *some kind of intervention was needed* in order to generate a "nonracial political system." I mentioned at this point that it seems to me that the social meaning of race is still left largely undiscussed. I also mentioned that it is not helpful when people read categories presented to them on forms in schools, universities, banks, workplaces, and so on, as if they point to races

---

[149] He indicated that the majority of schools in South Africa are still monoracial.

[150] McKinney indicates in this regard that when she tried to open up discussions around "race" in a "historically 'White' and Afrikaans University" she found this difficult. She points to what she sees as various discourses in circulation and argues for the need to "deconstruct essentialist notions of both 'race' and 'culture'" (2007, p. 215).

as givens in the society. I mentioned it would be a good way for people to start problematizing the term race if on these forms there could be some indication that the categories are social constructs developed for specific purposes. This may help people to re-raise for consideration what it means to develop a nonracial society, where race categories are not essentialized.[151]

Nuttall indicates that at the current conjuncture in South Africa as she sees it, "multiple things are happening simultaneously" in terms of both debunking and reinforcing a race-based order (2006, p. 274). She states that "the very contest between these forces serves to create a paradoxically volatile stability" (2006, p. 274). She sees that in this (unfolding) context "radical new public spaces" are opening (e.g., through various cultural media) to "decry assaults on a democratic nonracist order" (2006, p. 274). In line with her appreciation of this emerging context, and in line with my interpretation of my conversation with Whittle, I suggest that focus groups – suitably facilitated – can provide an(other) avenue to keep alive the necessary reflective inquiry toward forwarding South Africa's constitutional commitments to nonracism.

5.7 Conclusion

In this chapter I examined "intensive interviewing" as a style of approach to exploring experiences around and discussions concerning (new) racism. I examined in detail Essed's interviewing approach (1991, 2001) – and argued that it could be extended to take on board Douglas's (1998) more *active interviewing* style at the moment of engagement with research participants. In terms of Douglas's account, the "interviewer" acknowledges her/his involvement as *person* in the research process and takes responsibility for the possible impact his/her presence might have on the way narratives becomes generated. I offered suggestions for how the interviewing style that I see as proffered by Essed can be further developed to cater for Douglas's concerns.

I also suggested that Essed's account of the way in which she translates (in her write-up) the comprehension as expressed by interviewees into her own theoretical understanding too can be extended. This could be by making more explicit how the theoretical assessments/evaluations can be seen to fit into an admittedly normatively

---

[151] In concluding the interview, I asked him if he had found our interview around the issues as meaningful for him – and he replied that he found it refreshing. I explained that my style of interviewing is that I do not want to leave the person feeling that I have been "extracting" information from them. And that is why I also tried to add contributions at the moment of the interview. He said that he is interviewed on a daily basis by people, and with lots of these interviewers he "feels that way" (as if it has been "extractive"). After I sent him (as I had said I would) the write-up of our conversation for him to extend/modify any of it, his response to this (via e-mail) was that "I think it captures our conversation very well. Thank you for the opportunity to respond to it. I am really looking forward to reading the book." He also indicated that he would be "very comfortable" with my identifying him as "Granville Whittle" (i.e., with my using his name rather than just his position in the Directorate).

oriented race critical theorizing. I indicated that in further chapters, and in particular Chapter 8, I continue discussion of race-conscious/race-aware "critical theory" as applied to considerations around (new) racism – giving specific attention to different stances that we may adopt toward proffered theoretical conceptualizations of, for example, race*d,* gender*ed,* and class*ed* social relationships.

I proceeded to discuss an illustrative example of how *focus group* interviewing as a form of active intensive interviewing might be undertaken. The example was from a focus group that I conducted in South Africa around post-apartheid friendships (2007). Using this example, I suggested that focus group interviewing – if it "takes off" in sufficient numbers – could become a mechanism for opening discussion around topics normally considered in everyday life as too sensitive to open – or perhaps not taken seriously enough by participants to open. By treating focus group sessions organized by researchers (that is, by those trying to initiate specific inquiry processes) as an opening to set up intensive discussion around people's experiences, space might be created for generating what Bonilla-Silva (2006, p. 231) defines as "straight talk" around issues that have been rendered largely undiscussable.

5.7.1 Revisiting Researcher Accountability in Intensive Interviewing

I noted in this chapter that a realist-oriented epistemology (such as, e.g., upheld by Hammersley, 1995) suggests that interviewers display their responsibility by using interview material, along with other material, to try to make "correct" interpretations about the operation of social reality. For Hammersley, interviewing, as all styles of research, needs to be seen as a tool to be used by researchers ultimately to "find out" about the social world. However, other authors have questioned this realist-oriented view and argued that the idea behind interviewing is not to try to uncover supposedly preexisting realities, but to collaborate in mutually extending horizons (e.g., Douglas, 1998).

Whether one is engaged in more directive (structured) or nondirective (relatively unstructured) conversation with interviewees, and whether one is engaging in individual or group interviews, I have suggested, in line with Mann (who follows Habermas on this score) that "*all* communication involves a range of 'unspoken presuppositions' that must be 'mutually understood' in order for a topic of discussion to be raised, and subsequently problematized" (2006, Paragraph 7.3). Considering Mann's deliberations, I would propose that as one relates (as professional inquirer or in "ordinary" talk) to people around topics of conversation, one should be alert to the ways in which, indeed, constructions can be problematized. For instance, Douglas (1998) notes that the language of "survival" as used by Black women managers (including herself), itself could be seen as restrictive, and that *problematizing this construction (by introducing the language of "thriving") could lead to new ways of seeing and acting.* To fail to encourage a process of problematizing in communicative encounters is thus not without social consequence. Hence I have suggested that we can consider interviewing as a process, where researchers *take some responsibility for aiding people (including themselves) to re-appraise ways of seeing or, in the language of critical race theory, to engage in "restorying" (creating new narratives).*[152]

5.7.2 Extending Research Options

Through my discussion of various ways of conceiving intensive interviewing as a research approach, I have focused on possibilities for those practicing it to reconsider the manner in which research, wittingly or unwittingly, might make a difference to the unfolding of social life. I propose that admitting responsibility for this implies that inquirers, inter alia:

- Recognize the interview encounter as being an interactive process (which is also conceded by Hammersley and Atkinson, 1995) and take this to the point of considering how the "interviewer's" presence may be impacting on the way people envisage their experiences (with experience itself being seen as also involving cognition, as explained by Essed, 1991 – see Section 5.2.1).
- Pay attention to power dynamics in the way in which the interview unfolds – so that, as Douglas indicates, at the moment of the interview, one is attending to the power relation as a research issue (1998, Chapter 5, p. 8).
- Pay attention to power relationships in the manner in which write-ups of the research are created and participants' statements theoretically "translated." As Ladson-Billings reminds us, this implies exploring ways of activating the principle of "the use of dialogue in the assessment of knowledge claims" (2003, p. 421).
- As part of the process of trying to activate social dialogue around the presentation of "results" include questions or entry points for readers to engage with diverse approaches to theorizing the issues seen to be at stake.
- Do not shy away from introducing a style of write-up that activates people's sense of empathy in relation to the narrations as recounted by participants in the interview situation. (Trying to activate audience empathy at the moment of write up can be seen as a way of following the spirit of the "ethic of caring" that Collins considers should be nurtured in our inquiries – Collins, 2000, p. 264.)

---

[152]Ali emphasizes that it is crucial to recognize the power of narrative, because knowledge is "carried by stories" in a way that differs from "that which has been promoted by Western scientific tradition" (2003, p. 30). She makes this argument in the context of considering how the dominant (hegemonic) discourse on racialized identity itself can become "subverted." Her book *Mixed-Race, Post-Race* detailing her (dialogical) interviews with children and their parents offers a narrative on mixedness. She believes that it is important as a way of intervening in the knowledge/power nexus around "race" to "start work on producing some kind of 'community of thought' in relation to mixedness, no matter how many differences may be contained within it" (2003, p. 30). See also Chapter 4, Section 4.7.1.

In short, I suggest that intensive interviewing, extended in the way I have suggested, offers a mechanism for attending to, drawing out, and finding ways of making sense of, differing experiences/cognitions relevant to discussions around (new) racism – with a view to expanding participants' and audiences' options for attentive engagement with issues brought to the fore.

Chapter 6
Ethnographic Research: Exploring the Quality of Social Life in Social Settings

6.1 Introduction

In this chapter I discuss ways of generating inquiries in relation to the quality of life in social settings via what is considered as another qualitatively oriented mode of inquiry, namely, ethnographic research. The chapter is set around my discussion of two examples of ethnographic research, namely, a study of a particular high school in the USA (undertaken with reference to Critical Race Theorizing – CRT) and an autoethnographic study of my own – in a university setting in the UK. But before I discuss these examples, I offer an indication of some definitions of ethnography and of some debates that have arisen around its practice. I give attention to the relevance of these debates for the investigation of racism. My exploration of the various arguments forms the backdrop to my discussion of my chosen examples.

Silverman defines ethnography as research that is "based on observational work in particular settings" (2000, p. 37). He states that the "initial thrust" of ethnography was the idea, generated by anthropologists, that "if one is really to understand a group of people, one must engage in an extended period of observation" (2000, p. 37). Anthropological fieldwork involves "immersion in a culture over a period of years, based on learning the language and participating in social events with the people of the culture" (2000, p. 37). He points out that following on from this way of conducting anthropological fieldwork, non-anthropologists can and do engage in ethnography – but they are "likely to study particular milieux in their own society" – for example, activities in classrooms, in hospitals, and other social locations can become "objects of research observation" (2000, p. 37).

Considering the problem that there may be aspects of the setting that cannot be "reached" through interviews (which can form part of ethnographic research) or through observation and analysis of people's interactions, Silverman suggests that this is not problematic – as long as it is recognized. He suggests that the problem of the partiality of the data that are obtained can be "easily resolved" by admitting that "all data are partial" (2000, p. 38). Thus he advises that researchers "make do with what you have and understand that there are multiple phenomena available in any research setting" (2000, p. 38). As the chapter proceeds, it will become clear that my concern with this account of ethnography is that it still carries the

N. Romm, *New Racism*, DOI 10.1007/978-90-481-8728-7_6,
© Springer Science+Business Media B.V. 2010

(unquestioned) assumption that ethnographers must strive to "reach" phenomena through their research observations.

Hammersley and Atkinson (1995) offer a similar definition of ethnography, which too encapsulates their view that the aim is to collect data that becomes presented (in relation to the issues being studied). As they put it:

> In the most characteristic form it [ethnography] involves the ethnographer participating, overtly or covertly [that is, known or not known to the other participants], in people's daily lives for an extended period of time, watching what happens, listening to what is said, asking questions – in fact collecting whatever data are available to throw light on the issues that are the focus of the research. (1995, p. 1)

They argue that what is important in ethnographic research is that (in keeping with the interpretive sociological tradition) it takes into account the distinctiveness of the social world – because the social phenomena to be studied are seen as "distinct in character from physical phenomena" (as studied by natural scientists). Ethnography thus falls within the scope of what they call "naturalism" – a position which avers that:

> As far as possible, the social world should be studied in its "natural" state, undisturbed by the researcher. Hence "natural" not "artificial" settings, like experiments or formal interviews, should be the primary source of data . . .. The primary aim should be to describe what happens in the setting, how the people involved see their own actions and those of others, and the context in which the action takes place. (1995, p. 6)

Hammersley (2003, p. 344) makes the point that in their book on ethnography, he and Atkinson explicitly criticized a "kind of naïve naturalism" to which some qualitative researchers can be taken as subscribing (see also Chapter 5, Section 5.3.1.1). In this naïve form of naturalism, it is believed that if (ethnographic) sociologists can somehow "blend into the situation" the social processes can proceed as if he or she is not there. He indicates that he and Atkinson do not subscribe to this "false naturalism" (2003, p. 344). Rather, their argument is that, along with trying to minimize reactivity effects (i.e., the effects of researcher presence on the processes operating in the social world), researchers should also try to *monitor* such effects. This then enables them to better consider "what conclusions can reasonably be drawn about those [social] processes on the basis of the data produced" (2003, p. 345). As Hammersley puts it, while researchers may indeed try to "minimize various sorts of reactivity," they should also recognize that "much can often be learned from how people actually respond to being researched" (2003, p. 345). He emphasizes, though, that the aim is ultimately – whatever methodology is being utilized – to "try to identify accurately the social processes operating in the situation so that we can understand them" (2003, p. 345).

Hammersley's insistence that researchers – including ethnographic ones – must be committed to what he calls the production of (accurate) knowledge is connected to his argument in his book *The Politics of Social Research* that researchers should, as a rule, have as their "overriding concern," a concern with "the truth of claims, not their political implications or practical consequences" (1995, p. 76). In other words, it is not a primary concern to researchers, as scientists, what the "political conse-quences" of their studies may be (as I pointed out in Chapter 1, Section 1.5.1). Their concern must be with "what happens" in the social world. Considering possible dis-agreements about the data and their theoretical interpretation that may arise in the research community, he suggests that those involved in this community should be

> willing to change their views if arguments from common ground suggest that those views are false; and equally important, they [should] assume (and behave as if) fellow researchers have the same attitude – at least until there is very strong evidence otherwise. (1995, p. 76)

In cases "where agreement does not result, all parties must [be prepared to] rec-ognize that there remains some reasonable doubt about the validity of their own positions" (1995, p. 76). He continues to state that:

The research community is open to anyone able and willing to operate on the basis of these rules; though their contribution will be judged wanting if they lack sufficient knowledge of the field and/or the relevant methodology (1995, p. 76).

He asserts that as long as the research community functions in this way, the chances are maximized of "discovering errors in empirical and theoretical claims and of discovering the truth about particular matters" (1995, pp. 76–77).

6.1.1 Controversies Around a Case Study as Reported by Hammersley

Hammersley offers his position on what it means to engage in the research com-munity in a chapter entitled "Research and 'Anti-Racism': A Critical Case" in his book (1995). Here he discusses a case study undertaken by Foster (1990) of a multi-ethnic, inner-city school in Britain, which was "formally committed to multi-cultural/anti-racist education" (1995, p. 66). Foster argued, on the basis of his study, that "there was little evidence of racism among teachers, or of school practices that indirectly disadvantaged black students" (1995, p. 66). Because Foster's conclu-sions "conflicted with general claims made on the basis of studies in other schools," Foster examined a number of these studies "that claimed to document racism on the part of teachers" (Hammersley, 1995, p. 66). Foster's argument in relation to these studies was that they:

- suffered from serious methodological flaws;
- involved vague and doubtful conceptions of racism;
- involved questionable assumptions about the motivations of the teachers involved in the incidents described and about the effects of those incidents. (Hammersley, 1995, p. 66)

Hammersley proceeds to use this case to consider ways in which people in turn criticized Foster's work, in which criticism he suggests mostly "seems to come from those committed to some version of 'anti-racism'" (1995, p. 67). He suggests that the criticisms of Foster's work can be classified under two broad categories:

1. First, there are factual criticisms – to the effect that various elements of Foster's arguments are false, including his theoretical and methodological assumptions.
2. Second, there are practical value criticisms: criticisms of Foster's motives, of his behavior as a researcher, and of the consequences of making public the arguments he presents. (Hammersley, 1995, p. 67)

As regards the factual claims, and the criticism of the theoretical and method-ological assumptions leading Foster to make these claims (point 1 above), Hammersley notes that some critics asked the question: "How can Foster as a White middle class male construct his own definition of racism to then use to judge the accuracy of Black working class students' definitions?" (1995, p. 70). Hammersley argues that this way of posing the question can lead to a *stalemate* – because it implies that Foster's arguments could be "valid" insofar as he expresses his defini-tion and proceeds to obtain information on this basis, explaining that *in terms of this definition of racism, this is what he found.* Hammersley suggests that this way of approaching Foster's study amounts to adopting a *relativist position*, which would indeed imply that some validity has to be accorded to Foster's study *on its own terms.*

Hammersley then explains another kind of argument offered by critics in rela-tion to point 1, namely, an argument springing from "standpoint theory" (see also Chapter 1, Section 1.3). He suggests that according to standpoint theory, "people's experience and knowledge is treated as valid or invalid by dint of their membership of some social category" (1995, p. 70). In terms of standpoint theory (as he sees it), it is argued that "Foster's arguments may be dismissed because they reflect his background and experience as a White, middle class, male teacher" (1995, p. 70). Hammersley notes that in comparison with a *relativist* stance, within *standpoint theory* it is suggested rather that "reality is obscured" to Foster – because of his background and experience. Hammersley comments that

> it is suggested [that] the oppressed (black, female and/or working-class people) have privi-leged insight into the nature of society. This argument produces a victory for one side, not the stalemate that seems to result from relativism. (1995, p. 70)

Hammersley questions standpoint theory by arguing that "we must ask on what grounds we can decide that one group has superior insight into reality" (1995, p. 71). He sees standpoint theory as having roots in the Marxist suggestion (as he inter-prets it) that some groups in society seem to be "blinded by ideology" and therefore are less able to appreciate the workings of social reality. But he considers it "an implausible claim that some category of people has privileged access to knowl-edge while others are blinded by ideology" (1995, p. 71). As I noted in Chapter 1 (Section 1.5.2), although Hammersley defines standpoint theory as according "privi-leged access to knowledge" to some members of society, there exist other non-realist understandings of standpoint theory, with which Hammersley does not engage (see also Romm, 1997). As the chapter proceeds, I shall show how these alternative epistemologies can be brought to bear in considering the practice of ethnography.

In further discussing the criticisms that have been leveled against Foster's research work, and specifically in relation to point 2 above (the "practical value" criticisms), Hammersley notes that an "instrumentalist" argument has been forwarded. He defines instrumentalism as embracing the view that "the validity of knowledge is defined solely according to whether action on the basis of it has desirable effects" (1995, p. 71). He states that forerunners of this instrumentalist argument are, for example, Dewey's pragmatist philosophy, as well as some aspects of Marxism, critical theory and some forms of feminism (1995, p. 71). Hammersley summarizes the import of instrumentalism as follows:

> The implication of this position is that research must be pursued in close association with practical activities and judged in terms of its contribution to these activities. If it facilitates their success it is true, if it does not it is false. Thus, the validity of Foster's work could be assessed in terms of whether or not it serves the fight against racism. (1995, p. 71)

But what Hammersley's summary account of instrumentalist/pragmatist epistemologies fails to highlight is the argument that *social inquiry is never without practical import*. In terms of *this* argument, "truth" seeking (insofar as the term truth is used at all), or rather social inquiry, should not be defined as ever being a socially neutral endeavor. As can be seen from my discussion of constructivist arguments starting in Chapter 1 and threaded through the other chapters, there is no need to conceptualize theorizing as itself being either "true" or "false." One can conceptualize it in terms of its facility to, say, aid the enrichment of social dialogue around issues of concern to people, as indeed I would suggest many of the arguments of critical theory imply (see also Chapters 7 and 8 for more detail on this conception of critical theorizing).

After considering what he sees as *relativist, standpoint* and *instrumentalist* approaches to the criticism of Foster's work, Hammersley believes that a "solution" to the disagreements that have arisen around the work can be found in the model of scientific research that he espouses. He summarizes his solution thus:

> I suggest that the assessment of substantive claims within a research community should be based on judgments about the plausibility and credibility of evidence. By "plausibility" here I mean ... consistency with existing knowledge whose validity is taken to be beyond reasonable doubt. By "credibility" I mean the likelihood that the process which produced the claim is free of serious error. (1995, p. 75)

Nonetheless, although Hammersley believes that he can thus provide a solution to the methodological and epistemological debates that arose around Foster's work – by putting forward the rules for participation in the research community that I outlined in Section 6.1 – others still criticize his understanding of methodology (relating to his understanding of theorizing) as well as his proposed epistemology. To provide an illustration of fundamental methodological criticism, I refer to the arguments of Layder (1993) – who explicitly takes issue with Hammersley on this score – as well as to the arguments of others espousing the need for more structurally oriented research. To offer alternative epistemological considerations in relation to ethnographic work, I refer to the argument of Alldred (1998) on what she calls discourse ethnography and to further considerations on reflexivity.

6.1.2 Criticism of Hammersley's Methodological and Theoretical Orientation: Moving Beyond Middle Range Theorizing

In considering Hammersley's approach to ethnography, Layder offers a critique of Hammersley's "model for theory-testing ethnography".[153] He avers that Hammersley's model is based on a theory-testing view that can be seen as represented in the work of Merton (who himself draws on a Popperian account of theory testing – cf. Merton, 1964, p. 559). Layder notes that "Merton's ideas have been very influential in social research (particularly of the theory-testing kind)" – especially his conception of what he names "middle range theory" (1993, p. 3). But middle range theory in Layder's view is based on a too narrow view of theorizing, where it is seen as possible and desirable to convert "larger theories" into forms that can be regarded as testable in (direct) relation to the empirical evidence. Layder provides an example of why he believes this approach is inadequate – especially when it is used to reject theorizing of the kind engaged in by, say, Marx "on the basis that it is too difficult to test" (1993, p. 27). He explains:

> Merton's idea that we should break up larger theories into narrower, more researchable, testable or observable portions may lead to an inadequate empirical application of the theory. For example, in trying to apply Marx's idea on class inequalities in society, it is of no use simply focusing on measurable indicators of inequality such as level of income, education and consumption, as if they in themselves could determine the validity or usefulness of the theory. (1993, p. 28)

Layder argues that Marx's framework of ideas and concepts such as that given in his understanding of the nature of capitalist exploitation cannot be sufficiently "registered" in the definition of theorizing supported by Merton and Hammersley. As Layder sees it, the Marxist focus on social structures and their historical development cannot be translated into observable portions in the way that Merton's conception of middle range theory implies.

He gives a further illustration of instances where a narrow theory-testing approach may be inadequate to do justice to theorizing around social relationships when he notes that "often power relations in factories and industrial organizations are hidden behind the scenes of the daily round of activity, and are seemingly unaccompanied by overt conflict" (1993, p. 29). Here he refers to the seemingly invisible but nevertheless constraining forces that can be argued to "lie behind the scenes" of what is immediately observable or that which people immediately experience. He suggests that a concentration on observation or experience as the basis for "testing" of theories (as proposed by a middle range approach to theorizing) would not be able to delve into these underlying features of the social structure.

---

[153]Layder labels his own preferred approach as a "realist" one in order to distinguish it from what he sees as the narrow theory-testing approach that he sees Hammersley as still espousing (1993, p. 7). However, the approach that Layder supports has been labeled as "scientific realism" by certain authors (e.g., Marsden, 1998; Joseph & Kennedy, 2000) – and it is this label that I use when referring to Layder's kind of approach. See also Footnote 10 in Chapter 1. In Romm (1991, 2001), I provide detailed accounts of the scientific realist position and its links to other forms of realism.

Layder argues that although Hammersley differs from Merton in assigning importance to qualitatively oriented ethnographic studies as a route to exploring social reality (while Merton's approach is inclined to favor quantitative measurement of variables), there are aspects of Hammersley's approach that are "strikingly similar to Merton's" (1993, p. 31). Layder believes that Hammersley is unduly influenced by the theory-testing idea that "a testable hypothesis or proposition [can be] logically deduced from an existing set of [theoretical] assumptions. The empirical data that is then collected either confirms or disconfirms the original hypothesis or proposition" (1993, p. 26).[154]

Layder's concern is that the (narrow) theory-testing approach supported by Hammersley (following Merton) can produce the effect that only those layers of reality that the analytic tools of this kind of theory-testing approach are equipped to handle will be shown up (1993, p. 52). Other layers that do not submit to being understood by being broken up in the way suggested by Merton will remain outside the domain of social theorizing.

Certain authors forwarding a specifically race-conscious approach to developing structurally oriented research have offered similar arguments concerning the appropriate manner of connecting theorizing with (observed) empirical reality. For example, Bell (1995) develops a racial realist approach to theorizing in order to make specific provision for looking into structural relations of racial inequality. And Zuberi and Bonilla-Silva likewise point to the importance of developing race-conscious understandings that are able to "engage the prevailing social structures" (2008, p. 334). They point out that such theorizing becomes a way of counteracting the influence of what can be called "small scale research" (akin to Merton's middle range theorizing) that as they see it is not equipped to create analyses at the level of social structure.[155]

In the light of these kinds of arguments, we can now consider again Hammersley's deliberations on the research undertaken by Foster, where he notes that Foster has been criticized by "anti-racists" on various grounds. Hammersley

---

[154]This is the Popperian idea of deduction as the logic of scientific discovery that I pointed to in Section 1.5.1, and discussed further in Section 3.1.1.1. Layder is aware of the argument advanced by those supporting this hypothetico-deductive position that the theoretical frameworks provided by larger theories *become untestable unless broken into smaller portions*. Layder counterargues that working with such theoretical frameworks need not amount to proceeding simply "to 'explain' all empirical evidence within the terms of the framework" (1993, p. 53). According to Layder, this way of using evidence to bolster theoretical frameworks reinforces the boundaries between different frameworks and is not conducive to "cross-fertilization of ideas from different frameworks" (1993, p. 53). But he believes that theoretical conceptualizations offering analyses at the level of social structure can and should be subjected to debate – and in this sense are *not untestable/unchallengable*. See also Chapter 8 in this regard.

[155]Zuberi and Bonilla-Silva make their point regarding the need for an alternative when they raise concerns, with Duberman (1999, whom they cite), about the current state of affairs where "too many scholars do 'small scale research backed by large-scale grants'" (2008, p. 334). They indicate in the light of this context that they concur with "feminist and Marxist scholarship" in this regard (2008, p. 334).

states that "'anti-racism' generally involves the core theoretical assumption that racism is institutionalized in British society" (1995, p. 74). Hence it is argued that the

> substantial inequalities in outcomes for members of ethnic minority groups – in terms of school achievement, jobs, freedom from harassment etc. – ... result from the fundamental structures of society, whether these are conceived in terms of capitalist social relations and or of national/cultural features (state racism, imperialist past, etc.). (1995, p. 74)

Hammersley states that the problem with Foster's argument according to this kind of anti-racist thinking is that "it seems to challenge a core assumption of their position" (1993, p. 74). This is because Foster's research suggests that "some of the evidence on which the position is based, establishing the ubiquity of racism, may be unsound" (1995, p. 74). In other words, Foster seems to have "discovered at least one place where racism is not endemic" (1993, p. 74). Hammersley argues that the best way to proceed here is to try to find a "reasonable basis on which social researchers ought to assess [empirical] claims" (1993, p. 75). That is, instead of clinging to particular theoretical assumptions about the structuring of social reality (leading to the belief that, say, racism is endemic), it would be best to find a way of assessing the evidence – or otherwise "suspend judgment for want of the necessary evidence" (1993, p. 75).

However, the argument of those forwarding an alternative view of the way in which theorizing relates to (observed) empirical reality is that it is not a matter of finding "the evidence" that (if agreed to be found) will supposedly help to confirm or disconfirm the theoretical position. The issue lies in the way in which theorizing itself is regarded as testable with respect to the realm of observation. Foster's "evidence" for what he believed to be a case disconfirming the ubiquity of racism can be (re)interpreted by considering, for instance, the power relations that might make it difficult for students to report instances of what may be understood as racism. Furthermore, covert ways in which racism may be played out might make it difficult for students to articulate and name the experiences as racism (as Essed, 1991, argues – see Chapter 5, Section 5.2.4). Thus even if it is "agreed" that the immediate evidence did not obviously point to "racism on the part of teachers," *this in itself may require theoretical explanation*. This, in any case, would be the argument springing from a view of research invoked by those questioning a narrowly oriented hypothetico-deductive approach.

In terms of a different conception of how theory relates to the realm of observation, the link between the two is often considered to be *logically indirect* – thus requiring theorists to engage in *more explanatory work* with respect to the possible operation of more or less invisible forces. As Keat and Urry state the argument, "for the [scientific] realist, a scientific theory is a description of *structures and mechanisms which causally generate the observable phenomena*, a description which *enables us to explain them*" (1975, p. 5, my italics).[156] (I return to a discussion of

---

[156]Although both Keat and Urry (1975) and Layder (1993, citing Keat and Urry) label this a realist epistemology, I call the approach "scientific realism" to specify its difference from (realist-oriented) positivist/hypothetico-deductive argumentation and to indicate the orientation to get to

this kind of logic in Chapter 8, where I delve into it with reference to a variety of examples.)

As will be seen in the discussion that follows, I take forward these various suggestions that we need to take on board an appreciation of theorizing that is broader in scope than so-called middle range theory. However, I question the realist orientation that is still expressed by certain authors – such as Layder (1993), Bell (1995), and Parks (2007) – espousing a scientific/critical realist argument. And I also question the attendant way in which "science" as a pursuit is seen as connecting in a relationship of authority to opinions/narratives generated in everyday life. In this regard I draw on Parker and Lynn's (2002) suggestions concerning how (professional) theorists' narratives, as well as those constructed by others, should be read – as envisaging, and calling forth, options for more humane modes of living (rather than as statements about humanly unmediated realities). I indicate implications hereof for considering the standing of the conceptualizations generated via critical race theorizing as expressing the perspectival character of human knowing.

Davidson and Layder, meanwhile, in outlining their realist-oriented position vis à vis the products of scientific activity (1994), indicate that they are in accord with Hammersley that although the scientific community can never guarantee the validity of findings that are generated within it, it still should be regarded as having some claim to authority in society. They state that they agree with Hammersley that

> to deny the "intellectual authority" of the researcher on the grounds that everyone's opinion is as important as everyone else's ignores the whole point of research, which is to generate opinions informed by evidence gathered in ways which are open to the scrutiny of (any) other researchers. (Davidson & Layder, 1994, p. 183)

Davidson and Layder believe that judgments about the quality of research can be made through a rational dialogue within the scientific community – which should function in terms of a healthy communication across different ways of theorizing and different ways of anchoring this in the empirical world. Participation by researchers in such a dialogue means that the research community as a whole is able to develop more integrated knowledge about reality. In this respect they agree with Hammersley that the research community, working in terms of rules for proper participation in it, is best equipped to develop processes for increasing our knowledge about social reality. However, they question Hammersley's criteria for how the contributions of those who may wish to participate in the research community might be "found wanting." Hammersley suggests that people's contribution will be "judged wanting if they lack sufficient knowledge of the field and/or the relevant methodology" (1995, p. 76). Clearly, Davidson and Layder would argue that Hammersley's suggested methodological approach itself can be "found wanting" because it is too middle-range oriented. Nevertheless, they concur with his belief in science as a process whereby inquirers can together *try to generate increasingly unbiased accounts of realities*. They do not consider that we should seriously entertain the idea that

---

grips with *structures and mechanisms* in reality (see also Romm, 2001, pp. 36–54). Some authors also refer to this kind of approach as critical realism (cf. Parks, 2007, who develops what he calls a critical race realist approach, as discussed in Section 6.3.1).

would-be scientists are engaged in making *value-full and emotionally-laden judgments* and that the challenge may be to try to bring together in discussion different assumptions, values, and felt concerns, including those of (professional) researchers and of others, as the basis for social knowing. It is this kind of alternative that I present below – with reference to Alldred's proposals for "discourse ethnography."

6.1.3 An Alternative Provided by Discourse Ethnography

Alldred begins her discussion of ways of conceiving ethnographic research by noting that she has "political and theoretical doubts about the representational claims [claims to portray the social world] that have conventionally warranted research" (1998, p. 146). She indicates that although claims of "objectivism and realism to guarantee my 'findings' do still provide the most powerful warrant for my research account," she has doubts about such claims (1998, p. 146). She avers that in particular when organizing research around groups that can be considered as marginalized, such as, for example, children (around which her discussion is set) or "any less powerful group that has little access to the practices of public knowledge production," representational issues cannot be ignored (1998, p. 147).

She argues that even when researchers claim to "present the voices" of participants, these metaphors of voice still do not solve the problem of what it might mean for researchers to provide a "re-presentation" (1998, p. 149). She indicates that representation or re-presentation may both imply that "an object exists and is then truthfully reflected in (portrayed by) its representation." But she indicates that another implication that can be associated with the image of representation or re-presentation is one that recognizes that "my research account is actively produced by me and embodies my perspective" (1998, p. 149). She states that what she calls "discourse ethnography" is an approach that works with this latter understanding, at the same time admitting the "power of the ethnographer's language" (1998, p. 153).

She proposes that it is important to take seriously in a discursive approach (to ethnography and to other styles of research) the "institutionalized power carried by researchers" (1998, p. 151). She suggests that this is especially in a context in which "conventional notions of language as reflective or representational (rather than constitutive)" are so taken for granted that the ethnographer's perspective is the "key warrant for the knowledge produced" (1998, p. 153). She explains:

> Claiming this representational status is so conventionalized in Western scientific discourse that the warrant [of claims to be able to better "portray" reality] need not be made explicit. Ethnographic techniques can embody a realist epistemology even when they have rejected (unitary) objectivism [and admitted that there may be different perspectives operative in the social world]. (1998, p. 153)

Thus even when ethnographers admit "the existence of different perspectives (hence studying the participants' [ones]), it is simply assumed that readers of the research will rest their faith in the researcher's own perspective as the basis for knowledge" (1998, p. 153).

Alldred's question now becomes how the centrality of researchers' "representations" can be challenged – so that cultural power is not seen to rest solely in their accounts (1998, p. 154). She believes that certain ways of practicing discourse analysis, which enable readers to consider indeed how the analysts' accounts have became produced, can be helpful in this regard (1998, p. 156). She gives an example of Marks's research with young people who were asked about their experiences of exclusion from school, noting that Marks (1996) wrote up the research in such a way that "she is not central in her warrant for research knowledge." She cites Marks as stating that "I cannot say how participants really experienced the exclusion. However, asking about the experience brings forth a number of productive ways of seeing the event" (Marks, 1996, p. 116, as cited in Alldred, 1998, p. 156).

Nevertheless, Alldred indicates that Marks also attends to the "broader social meanings within which research occurs". This leads her to examine the students' accounts by seeing them as part of the "powerful psychological discourses of self-regulating individuals". But meanwhile, Marks was aware that possibly her own involvement as researcher with the students "functioned to regulate some participants further by providing a space in which they drew themselves under disciplinary gaze to produce themselves as good children" (Alldred, 1998, p. 156). Hence even the account of discourses of self-regulating individuals could be partly a production of the specific relations created during the research process.

Commenting on the way that a number of discourse analysts proceed without a "realist warrant," Alldred argues that there is much from this that ethnographers can learn. For instance, she suggests that in a *discourse ethnography* (as a hybrid between ethnography and discourse analysis – 1998, p. 147), we can be more aware of "how power inheres in the processes of analysis 'back in the academy' as well as in the research encounter" (1998, p. 158). She proposes a "new ethnography" that attends to such matters (1998, p. 159).

In detailing her new ethnographic approach, Alldred addresses the question that she sees as raised by ethnographic research as to "how much to listen and how much to interpret" (1998, p. 162). She raises this question in the light of her understanding that:

> If we necessarily hear others through culturally dominant meanings, an unacknowledged perspective is most likely the hegemonic one. [Hence] the task of reflexivity ... is to make explicit the theoretical basis of interpretation. [This in turn] means taking greater caution over our representational claims and avoiding obscuring the perspectival nature of knowledge. (1998, p. 162)

As I have suggested in previous chapters, researchers can all too easily invoke an unacknowledged perspective when they pose their interpretations – especially insofar as these are presented as "found" results. One could argue that one of the problems with Foster's work (as cited by Hammersley, 1995) is in the way he presented his claims and the (realist) status that he accords them. In this regard, he could be argued to have not acted sufficiently accountably in the sense of showing sensitivity to *alternative ways of seeing* and *alternative concerns* that might be brought to bear in the (political) situation. His warrant as a "researcher" perhaps afforded his perspective too much social power – and it is this that the anti-racists (as Hammersley calls them) were clearly concerned about (particularly as they also did not agree with his theoretical interpretation in any case).

Alldred offers her deliberations on this issue as follows:

> We cannot ensure our preferred readings, but we must attempt to ward off ones we believe to be oppressive. These, as well as decisions about how to frame, how to write, how and where to publish, are more than mere "editorial control" over the accounts, and our politics are clearly highly significant. (1998, p. 163)

Alldred complains that because of the "taboo on speaking of politics in academic work (a legacy of objectivism)," she has had to find her own spaces for "discussing these concerns" (1998, p. 163). She suggests that more discussion needs to ensue between "researchers and activists" – but she states that because of the "presumption of realism" (where it is assumed that researchers must focus their efforts on the so-called production of knowledge) such discussion becomes blocked (1998, p. 163).

She suggests that reflexivity of researchers should include "making explicit the warrants we employ for the status of our accounts" and "attempting to dissemble them where we feel it is appropriate" (1998, p. 163). And she suggests also the use, in (narrative) writing up of the research, of *"active verbs such as 'producing'* (also avoiding the realist implication of pre-existing data)" (1998, p. 163, my italics). She indicates furthermore that we can pay attention to undoing the "metaphors of research which obscure the processes" through which material comes to the fore (1998, p. 163).

In short, Alldred suggests that a discourse ethnography sets out to address these "conventional silences" around the implicit "objective-realist warrants" that she sees as associated with the traditional practice of ethnography (1998, p. 164). She indicates that she hopes that the book of which her chapter is a part will contribute to "voice questions" around these issues, without the "pressure to find answers" (1998, p. 164).

Considering Alldred's indication that reflexivity of researchers in the new ethnography should include "making explicit the warrants we employ for the status of our accounts," this clearly offers an alternative to, say, Hammersley's understanding of reflexivity, where reflexivity – as the consideration of "bias" and attempts to "monitor" this – is still ultimately linked to strengthening the realist warrant (see Chapter 1, Section 1.5.1).[157] Walby indicates in this regard that although reflexivity and the social constructionist paradigm are not equivalent, the "fracturing of the positivist [and post-positivist] research paradigm and the proliferation of the social constructionist paradigm are linked with the reflexive turn" (2007, p. 1015). That is, while reflexivity can still be conceptualized within a view of science as striving

---

[157]Gergen and Gergen likewise indicate that sometimes those forwarding a commitment to reflexivity may put the focus on, as they put it, people pausing to "consider the biases". They indicate that alternatively reflexivity can take on a different meaning, where it implies recognition that "confronting the world from moment to moment is [at the same time] also confronting the self". The investigator hereby reveals his or her work as historically, culturally, and personally situated (2003, p. 579).

toward objectivity (as we have seen in, say, Hammersley's conception), Walby suggests that it is increasingly associated with an alternative practice – namely, one that "intervenes to diminish ... symbolically violent aspects of objectification." Here the concern is with the symbolic violence that is imposed by posing authoritative accounts of "the object" of study (2007, p. 1015). He continues that in *this* understanding of reflexivity:

> Reflexivity is helpful as a transgressive organizing metaphor for conceiving ways of reconfiguring social relations of research so as to question practices that retain the authority of "knowing" as a purely academic attribute. (2007, p. 1016)

Walby makes these remarks in the context of his discussion (and critique) of institutional ethnography, which he sees as research "designed to explicate ruling practices" within social institutions. He argues that the problem with the way of proceeding of certain self-named institutional ethnographers (such as Smith, 2005) is that it "takes the world as if it was to be *discovered* instead of interrogating the way ontology itself constitutes the world" (2007, p. 1017). He explains further:

> Making the everyday world and ruling relations problematic pardons institutional ethnography from thinking of itself as implicated in a social relations of research that takes the social world as an object of analysis. (2007, p. 1017)

Walby argues that in terms of what he calls "reflexive interventions," provision is specifically made for researchers to attend to the social relations of research (2007, p. 1017).[158] It is this notion of reflexivity that accords with definitions hereof that I outlined in Chapter 1, Sections 1.5.2 and 1.5.3. In this chapter I explore implications hereof for the practice of ethnography – with reference to some examples.

6.1.4 Examples Discussed and Revisited

The examples of ethnographic research that I discuss in this chapter involve explorations of the quality of life in the settings under examination, in terms of considerations around their racialization. I discuss these examples with a view to showing how styles of ethnographic research can be organized to take into account a notion of reflexivity including "reflexive intervention." With reference to a discussion of DeCuir and Dixson's (2004) account of the theoretical significance of storytelling of (Black) participants in a specific Academy in the USA, I show how "ethnographic validity" can be construed in other than realist terms – and can be considered as linked to the social relations set up between researchers instigating inquiries and others involved (participants and wider audiences). I suggest that

---

[158]This can be seen as similar to what Romm and Adman call "reflexive ethnography", which we distinguish from more traditional "qualitative ethnography". We indicate that the epistemology of reflexive ethnography is geared to highlighting "researcher honesty" and to nurturing the recognition that "there is no final answer" in the attempt to appreciate diverse interpretations of experienced worlds.

reflexive intervention involves reconsidering the research involvement in the development of social discourses. To this end I discuss ways in which the status of various stories becomes treated by those involved, and I consider this also in terms of the link between theorizing and quests for social justice.

I then turn to my own autoethnographic account of my involvement in a particular university setting in the UK. I here concentrate on how ethnographic research might open the space, as Cho and Trent put it, for aiding people (including the ethnographic narrator) "to differently perceive the world in which we live and to actively engage ... in changing this world" (2006, p. 332). I consider my reporting in terms of what it might mean to instantiate such a commitment. This again involves reconsidering the normative intent of social inquiry and implications hereof for the status of (narrative) constructions.

6.2 DeCuir and Dixson's Study of a High School in the USA

DeCuir and Dixson indicate that their study was set in an Academy "located in a major city in an affluent, predominantly White area in the southeastern United States" (2004, p. 26). They place the school setting in the wider social context, which they describe (following a number of researchers whom they cite, including Ladson-Billings and Tate, 1995) as follows:

> Because of the legacy of racism, schooling is problematic for African American students, particularly those students attending predominantly White schools .... For such students, feeling culturally alienated, being physically isolated, and remaining silenced are common experiences. (2004, p. 26)[159]

They propose that due to the

---

[159]Phumla Nhlumayo, upon reading this chapter and offering feedback to me (May 2009), pointed out that her son experienced a similar situation at a (predominantly White, and costly) school to which she had sent him in post-apartheid South Africa, hoping that he would thereby be exposed to the "White world". She indicated that he experienced that he became "judged according to color". Nevertheless, she still felt it important that he became exposed to a different style of teaching – as she found that the (Bantu) education of most of the teachers at Black schools (still springing from the apartheid era) was too focused on rote learning. She felt that most of the teaching at these schools (based on some of her other children's experiences) still tended to rely on this. She found that the "White schools" did offer a better education in this respect (and therefore if she could afford it, she would have sent all her children there). Furthermore, the advantage of these schools is that children become more fluent in speaking the kind of English that equips them in the Western-oriented "White world" and they learn cultural ways of behaving that are also necessary to operate in this world – such as, for instance, looking (White) people in the eye when speaking to them. She indicated that unless they learn this, they are not easily able to operate in this world. She lamented that it is unfortunate, though, that opportunities for cross-cultural learning seemed not to be encouraged at these schools (with still predominantly White teachers) – albeit that they are now supposed to be "integrated". This observation is supported by Granville Whittle, who mentioned in my interview with him (2008) that many Black children feel that they are marginalized – see Section 5.6.1.

insidious and often subtle way in which race and racism operate, it is imperative that educational researchers explore the role of race when examining the educational experiences of African American students. (2004, p. 26)

They propose that critical race theory (CRT) provides a useful perspective from which to examine the experiences of African American students, and they indicate that in their article they will be sharing with us some "counter-stories" of African American students at the high school – which they state were often "silenced" because "they were afforded very few opportunities to be heard" (2004, p. 26). They indicate that they define a counter-story, following Delgado and Stefancic (2001), as "casting doubts on the validity of accepted premises or myths, especially ones held by the majority" (2004, p. 27). They point out that the counter-stories that they will be narrating in their article – based on their involvement with participants – are part of their own counter-story that they present in relation to the high school.

In order to provide some indication of the setting where the study was located, they indicate that "during the 2002–2003 school year, 44 of the 559 students enrolled were African American" and that the "African American population was the largest population of students of color" (2004, p. 26). Of these students, two of their stories in particular are isolated for attention in their article – namely, 17-year-old Malcolm and 18-year-old Barbara (both pseudonyms). They were, respectively, from "middle-class" and "upper-class" families (2004, p. 26).

Before proceeding to offer their exposition of their stories, which DeCuir and Dixson set in the context of the "diversity" program to which the school was apparently committed, DeCuir and Dixson explain that they believe that the stories provide a route to expose and explore various elements of CRT. The elements that they isolate are CRT's view of the *permanence of racism*, of *Whiteness as property*, of *interest convergence*, and of the *need to criticize liberalism* (2004, p. 27). In discussing the results of their study, they refer to these concepts within the CRT literature.

6.2.1 Writing Up the Results in Relation to CRT Literature

6.2.1.1 Permanence of Racism

DeCuir and Dixson state that one of the basic premises of CRT is the notion of the permanence of racism. They indicate that according to Bell (1992, 1995), understanding of this permanence requires the adoption of a racial realist position that highlights "the dominant role that racism has played and continues to play in American society" (De Cuir & Dixson, 2004). They explain that the concept of the permanence of racism "suggests that racist hierarchical structures govern all political, economic, and social domains." It is these structures that are seen as "allocating the privileging of Whites and the subsequent Othering of people of color in all arenas, including education" (2004, p. 27).

As an illustration of how the stories of the African American students can be used to point to the continued applicability of the concept of the permanence of racism,

DeCuir and Dixson offer an account where Malcolm has spotted on an Internet site some hate speech (with threats of violence, including racist remarks) on the profile of one of the students in the school. Malcolm, as the only Black student on the disciplinary council, is party to the deliberations around how the student should be disciplined, and believes that he should be expelled. But the headmaster indicated that they couldn't expel him because of "legal liability." He was suspended for a month and made to watch *Eyes on the Prize* and *Black Like Me.*

DeCuir and Dixson indicate that a CRT analyses would concentrate on the "dismissal of the import and impact of the hate speech" – as well as how the Academy's governance practices "serve to support the permanence of racism" (2004, p. 28). Furthermore, it is important to explore the "culture of the school, one that allowed the student [with his profile] to feel comfortable in producing the threat" contained in the hate speech, as well as "the manner in which the threat encouraged racist and violent behavior and supported a hostile and alienating environment for African American students" (2004, p. 28). Also, from a CRT perspective the disciplinary process adopted at the school would need to be examined, including the meeting (where Malcolm's recommendation was not agreed to on the grounds of "legal liability") and where the headmaster decided the appropriate punishment.

6.2.1.2 Whiteness as Property

DeCuir and Dixson indicate that legal scholar Harris (1995, p. 280) argues that Whiteness can be considered as a "property interest" in the USA. Applied in the realm of education, they note that Ladson-Billings and Tate (1995) point to ways in which the "right to exclusion" associated with property rights can be argued to apply: "Tracking, honors, and/or gifted programs and advanced placement courses are but the myriad ways in which schools have been resegregated" (2004, p. 28). De Cuir and Dixson point to research examples from a variety of contexts where one can locate "policies and practices that restrict the access of students of color to high quality curricular, and to safe and well equipped schools" (2004, p. 28). They indicate that while some students of color may have been able to "penetrate these barriers to educational opportunity" this often implies indeed surmounting the barriers (2004, p. 28).

They also refer to an example from Barbara's story of the way in which she is faced with perceptions of the "ideal Black student," who is supposed to act in accordance with a view of "ideal" behavior that "is not receptive to African culture." They cite her saying that when you graduate "the girls have to wear all white"; and "it was this huge thing" when a friend of hers wanted to wear an African head-wrap but it wasn't white (2004, p. 28). In the end she had a headdress made that was white with African designs and symbols on it – but she had to "go through all of that just to be proud of where she came from" (2004, p. 28). DeCuir and Dixson explain that this story points to them to the fact that at the "shining moment" of graduation, they "are not allowed to express themselves culturally" (2004, p. 28). This example indicates to them how Whiteness as property operates in an exclusionary manner.

6.2.1.3 Interest Convergence

DeCuir and Dixon cite Bell (1980) as suggesting that the civil rights gains "should be interpreted with measured enthusiasm." This is because it is possible to interpret the gains of the civil rights movement as providing "rights" only insofar as these converged with the self-interest of Whites. That is, the granting of rights and the way in which they became instantiated could be argued to have not created a "major disruption to a 'normal' way of life to a majority of Whites" (2004, p. 28). Bell argues in particular that we must be cautious of suggesting that these gains amounted to "a substantive difference in the lives of people of color." DeCuir and Dixson (2004, p. 28) note that Bell points in this regard, for example, to:

- losses in human capital by way of dismissal of scores of African American teachers and administrators;
- school closures in Black neighborhoods;
- limited access to high-quality curricula in the form of tracking, inflated admissions criteria and other factors.

They see Malcolm's account of his first day at school as providing an illustration of how reification of Black/White categories impinges on Malcolm's experience, when he was asked – before people even said "hello" – about his football-playing abilities. He perceived that he was being treated in terms of what he calls a "horrible stereotype" regarding African Americans. He states that the White officials at the school were probably seeing him in terms of how the school could benefit from having African American students, that is, in terms of their interests and in terms of still rigid conceptions of what can be expected of Black students. This leads them to, in Malcolm's words, "expect us just to be Black athletes. That is what I think they see coming in" (2004, p. 29).

DeCuir and Dixson explain the applicability of the concept of "convergence of interests" here:

> Thus the school's interest in making its athletic program more competitive converged with some African American families' desires to provide a "rigorous education" for their children. (2004, p. 29)

They indicate that it is still questionable whether the children at the school actually experienced a high-quality education.

6.2.1.4 Critique of Liberalism

DeCuir and Dixson indicate that another tenet of CRT upon which they draw in their analysis relates to the critique of liberalism (2004, p. 29). They point to CRT scholars' being "critical of three basic notions that have been embraced by liberal legal ideology," namely:

- the notion of color-blindness;
- the neutrality of the law;
- incremental change.

They indicate while at "face value" these appear to be desirable goals, in practice,

> given the history of racism in the U.S. ... the idea that the law is indeed color-blind and neutral is insufficient (and some would say disingenuous) to redress its deleterious effects. (2004, p. 29)

They also indicate that considering the notion of incremental change, "gains for marginalized groups must come at a slow pace that is palatable for those in power" (2004, p. 29). They remark that within this incrementalist argument, the discourse favors equality rather than equity. But "in seeking equality rather than equity, the processes, structures and ideologies that justify inequity are not addressed and dismantled" (2004, p. 29). They consider it crucial to highlight the need for a discourse of equity, where it is recognized that "the playing field is unequal and [where] attempts are made to address the inequality" (2004, p. 29).

They believe that the Academy's "commitment" to diversity needs to be analyzed in relation to the CRT understanding of the critique of liberalism. They state that:

> In the 1999–2000 school year, the school created a diversity coordinator position .... In this position, the coordinator is responsible for teaching multicultural classes, organizing multicultural students activities, and providing diversity workshops for faculty. (2004, p. 29)

But DeCuir and Dixson locate a problem in this approach to addressing what were seen as "diversity" issues. They explain:

> A limitation of the liberal commitment to diversity was manifested in the Academy's hiring one person, an African American, to attend to the school's diversity initiative. This token commitment to diversity, which rested solely with one person, and encompassed a wide range of responsibilities, essentially ensured that change ... would not be sweeping or immediate. (2004, p. 29)

They comment that the people satisfied with incremental (and superficial) change of the kind introduced at the Academy "are those less likely to be directly affected by oppressive and marginalizing conditions" (2004, p. 29).

6.2.2 DeCuir and Dixson's Summary Discussion: Implications for Practice

In summarizing their way of proceeding in their analysis, DeCuir and Dixson comment that:

> Using a CRT framework to analyze Barbara's and Malcolm's counter-stories illustrates the ways in which the subtleties of race and racism can be illuminated. Furthermore, through uncovering covert racist practices and the policies that support them, educators, students, families and communities are able to devise strategies to counteract, resist, and/or forestall these practices' and policies' effects. (2004, p. 30)

They indicate that when applying CRT to the realm of education, *race* is made the "center of focus" and at the same time CRT "charges researchers to *critique* school practices and policies that are both overtly and covertly racist" (2004, p. 30). But they add that while CRT implies that race needs to be made the center of focus, a number of CRT scholars, such as Crenshaw (1991) and Williams (1997), have "included in their analysis the ways that social class and gender intersect with race." Hence they point out that it is possible to expand the "boundaries of CRT" – and that still new areas of scholarly inquiry are emerging (2004, p. 30).

Nevertheless, they emphasize that whatever kind of CRT analysis is undertaken, "researchers who seek to utilize CRT are cautioned to consider how their scholarship aids in the project of social justice and social change" (2004, p. 30). This "caution" relates back to the suggestion (introduced at the beginning of their article) that "CRT has an activist aspect, the end goal of which is to bring change that will implement social justice" (2004, p. 30).

6.3 Revisiting DeCuir and Dixson's Approach

In this section I revisit DeCuir and Dixson's approach by commenting on the areas where I believe that it can be extended, while relating the arguments back to the issues that I introduced in my introduction to this chapter. I focus on:

- the status of stories and counter-stories; and
- the link between theorizing and quests for social justice.

6.3.1 The Status of Stories and Counter-Stories

DeCuir and Dixson indicate that Malcolm's and Barbara's stories, as well as their own story that they construct in their article, should be read as offering counter-stories, which serve to "cast doubt on the validity of accepted premises or myths, especially ones held by the majority" (2004, p. 27). In considering the status of the various stories, they suggest that their highlighting (in their article) of these children's stories can be treated as a "means of giving voice to marginalized groups" (2004, p. 27). But it seems to me that what they do not concentrate on elucidating, or accounting for, is their own specific mode of interaction with the participants in the study, both in the process of "probing" their stories and in the process of writing them up. I suggest therefore that more explicit attention needs to be given to this.

In an endnote to their article (Endnote 1) they indicate that "the data presented in this article are part of a larger study. All the names used are pseudonyms" (2004, p. 30). I would propose here that it is important for us as audiences to have some sense of what this larger study involved and how, again, the researchers related to the various participants within the whole study. How did they express to participants their role as "researchers"? How did they see themselves as interacting with the participants in terms of their role? And how might the role they adopted and the way they presented the topic of the research have affected the way the interaction ensued? Would they be afforded some (institutionalized) authority already due to this role that they adopted? These kinds of considerations could well have been entered into their account of the study, so that we as audiences can better appreciate the context in which the stories of participants became recounted (remembered, reflected upon, and expressed).

Furthermore, in commenting on the status of their analysis, they point out that Malcolm and Barbara can be interpreted as having told counter-stories that can be used to expose and explore "the various elements of CRT" upon which they concentrate in their analysis. They also indicate that counter-stories generally can be conceived as those that "cast doubt on the validity of accepted premises and myths" that are prevalent in a society (2004, p. 27). But it would seem that they are presenting their own counter-story that they provide in their analysis as more than simply "casting doubt" on prevailing premises and myths. That is, they seem to be suggesting that by exposing certain "myths" (through, e.g., Malcolm's and Barbara's stories, and also through, for instance, their own understanding of the superficial nature of the "diversity" program at the school), they are at the same time displaying some "real reality" that they now present via their counter-story.

They indicate (2004, p. 27) that they agree with Bell that understanding the permanence of racism and the way in which it is built into "the American social structure" does involve adopting a "realist view" – or in Bell's terms a "racial realist" view (1995). In terms of the arguments that I presented in Section 6.1.2, this would mean that they also concur with, say, Layder (1993) that their vision does afford a "better" account of the dynamics at play in the Academy, because it invokes concepts of structure that allow us to recognize the conscious as well as unconscious forces at play in reproducing, in this case, racist practices.

They do not comment explicitly on what status we should give to their story in terms of its *merely disrupting* what they see as dominant (liberally oriented) conceptions (and helping us to cast doubt on these) or offering a *better portrayal of reality* "as it really is." However, it seems that they do not wish to question the epistemological understanding that as ethnographers their aim is to "tell it like it is." As I indicated in Chapter 1, Ladson-Billings (whom they cite) believes that these epistemological issues should *not be left unreflected upon* in the conduct of CRT. Thus, I would suggest that although it can be said that their invocation of concepts from CRT may be theoretically helpful in avoiding the pitfalls that authors such as Bell (1995) associate with liberal/narrow-range theorizing, more epistemological deliberation on their part is needed.

In reading various CRT writings, it is possible to locate a range of epistemological orientations – ranging from realist to non-realist (more constructivist-oriented) arguments. Bell explicitly adopts a *realist position*, using narratives as part of his theorizing to point to experiences of Black people in a context (the USA) where attempts to remove racism always seem to have only temporary effects. He expresses the historical context as follows:

> The [Civil Rights] Movement was the spiritual manifestation of the continuing faith of a people who had never truly gained their rights in a nation committed by its basic law to the freedom of all. (1999, p. 316)

To highlight what he sees as a "cyclical experience of blacks in this country" in terms of rights gained, lost, gained, and so on, he finds it useful to construct narratives that involve some "hypotheticals" (i.e., some degree of recognized fiction) as a way of "generating discussion in law school rooms" (1999, p. 316). The stories that he constructs for his students are meant to "reflect the contradictions and dilemmas faced by those attempting to apply legal rules to the many forms of racial discrimination" (1999, p. 316). The storytelling thus is meant to perform the function of inviting discussion around the many (real) forms of racial discrimination.

In excavating what is involved in adopting a realist position within CRT, Parks suggests that a Critical Race Realist (CRR) position requires some expansion to incorporate more "empirical modes of understanding race and racism" (2007, pp. 62–68). He indicates that CRT has been criticized for "struggling to define its substantive mission, methodological commitments, and connection to the world outside of academia" (2007, p. 70). He tries himself to provide a methodology that is based on an empirical social science operating to:

- expose racism where it may be found;
- identify its effects on individuals and institutions;
- put forth a concerted attack against it, in part, via public policy arguments. (2007, p. 70)

As part of this proposed methodology, he believes that the approach used by (many) lawyers to "marshal all possible evidence in support of her hypothesis and 'distract attention' from any possible contradictory information" needs to be combined with the social scientific orientation to "subject[ing] hypotheses to 'every conceivable test and data source', in an attempt to disconfirm the theory" (2007, p. 68). He believes that both of these ways of proceeding can have a place in a realist methodological approach, such as the one he proposes for what he calls CRR. In other words, theoretical hypotheses should not be too easily dismissed on the basis that some "observations"/evidence supposedly contradict the theory (as a Popperian approach implies). Nonetheless, this does not preclude using evidence to *help the development of empirically sound theorizing.*

Parks emphasizes that his suggestion to use an empirical social scientific methodology in this way does not imply supplanting CRT's narrative approach. Narratives can be used as part of the methodological repertoire as a "rich descriptive method" (2007, p. 63). He indicates that he agrees with Delgado that "the stories of outgroups aim to subvert the ingroup reality" (Delgado, 1989, as cited by Parks, 2007, p. 63). He sees this as consistent with the adoption of a CRR approach, where efforts are made to develop a theorizing of the continued racialized structuring of the social world. (He also sees that one of the advantages of narratives as part of CRR is that they can be used to help others, who are offered fresh insight via the narratives, to gain a sense of empathy – 2007, p. 63.)

However, as I noted in Chapter 3, Section 3.11.2, Parker and Lynn (2002) – drawing on a more constructivist-oriented epistemology – suggest that CRT "relies on the importance of perspective and context in assessing truth claims." In Parker and Lynn's epistemological and political conception of CRT, the "validation" of research is to be understood not in terms of its striving to offer accounts of a posited reality existing outside of the knowing process, but in terms of the way it can be argued to *forward the project of developing a more just society* – albeit that conceptions of justice may still be contestable. In the next section I consider in more detail some of these arguments.

6.3.2 The Link Between Theorizing and Quests for Social Justice

DeCuir and Dixson suggest that "implicit in CRT" is an understanding that the the-orizing should be helpful in serving "the project of social justice and social change" (2004, p. 30). They propose that CRT can play a role here, in that working through a CRT framework

> researchers are able to uncover and unmask the persistent and oppressive nature of the normativity of Whiteness, the co-option and distortion of oppositional discourses, and the ways in which policies that are offered as remedies to underachievement and educational disparity may not be in the best interest of marginalized groups. (2004, p. 30)

It seems that DeCuir and Dixson's suggestion (via the metaphor of "uncovering") is that because CRT is able to display with credibility to audiences ways in which the persistence of racism really functions in social institutions, it is likely to aid the project of social justice – because concerned people will then be able to take up the issues accordingly (based on what CRT has uncovered to date about the realities).

But critics such as Hammersley then maintain that the prior political commit-ment to fighting against racism is unduly guiding the theorizing – in that theorists then tend to look for empirical support for their theorizing framework (to which they have prior allegiance), rather than seeking possible disconfirming evidence. The scientific/critical realist response to Hammersley's kind of argument is that Hammersley's (hypothetico-deductivist) approach to supposedly "testing" theoriz-ing does not necessarily lead to better science, because the applicability of concepts such as that of racism rests not only on offering empirical support but also on being able to explain in terms of the theoretical concepts any events that (are observed to) occur (cf. Parks, 2007). Hence, for example, Malcolm's story regarding the way the hate speech of the fellow student was dealt with at the Academy can be seen as offering evidence of the institutional power stacked against Black people (through its insufficient mechanisms to deal with their being demeaned and threatened). The headmaster's reference to "legal liability" that prevents him from taking a stronger stance against the student also offers an indication of how the law can likewise be seen as stacked. Application of the CRT framework thus helps us to explain the inci-dent within the context of the institutional forces that serve to perpetuate racism at the level of the social structure. Likewise, the diversity initiatives that DeCuir and Dixson observe rest with one person taking responsibility for the entire program is explained in terms of the interests of those more powerful, who do not wish to implement a more radical approach to "diversity" that would lead to the alteration of basic structures. The theoretical framework of CRT again allows us to analyze this event at the level of social structure and thus to offer a better account of all levels of social reality than could be provided without the benefit of this framework. For this reason, it is argued, *CRT can offer a better appreciation of the realities under consideration* – which does not spring (just) from its being politically motivated (but indeed from its engaging in better theorizing).

As far as the ability to appreciate "disconfirming evidence" is concerned, as noted in Section 6.3.1, there is contention around how in any case pieces of "evidence" are to be seen as relevant to theorizing. Hammersley and others may consider that certain "evidence" – if found (in whatever case is under consideration) – should be recognized as implying that racism is *not* as "endemic" in society as those advancing CRT might wish to argue. However, scientific/critical interpretations of CRT suggest that there may be alternative ways of looking at the (apparent) evidence by placing it in a broader framework of understanding than allowed through the hypothetico-deductive approach. Thus again here, the argument is that it is not the political intention (to fight against racism) as such that may be guiding critical race theorists in their way of looking at evidence – but that what is "found" must always be *adequately theorized at the level of social structure* in order to generate a better appreciation of the realities.

Yet it is also possible to offer a more pragmatically defined epistemology as an approach to knowing processes in social life. This amounts to proposing that our theorizing can be judged as "better" not by virtue of claims to have found a way to better uncover "what really is," but by virtue of *serving to generate increased capacity in society for people to reconsider options for addressing issues judged to be of concern*. In this regard Ladson-Billings favorably cites Collins (1998, p. xxi) as consciously using her (theoretical) language as part of the political project of trying to re-humanize both our knowing and our being in society. Ladson-Billings notes that a technical-rational approach to knowing falls short of what is needed to "challenge the inequitable social, economic, and political positions that exist between the mainstream and the margins" (2003, p. 423). To work toward this end, she suggests, "the significant issues with which we grapple are paradigmatic and epistemological." In her view, working with technical-rational approaches to knowing such as those forwarded in epistemologies that strive for "objectivity" and that assume that knowledge can be divorced from political intention at the moment of knowing, cannot serve the project of trying to shift the relations between "the mainstream and the margins." Hence she emphasizes that alternative epistemologies are called for within CRT.

Ladson-Billings's understanding of the need to develop new paradigms and epistemologies as an intrinsic part of the CRT enterprise can be seen to tally with Habermas's focus on the use of "reconstructive theory" to aid the project of developing what he calls "democratic authority" as a basis for social organization. In Habermas's account of reconstructive theory, such theorizing is meant to serve the purpose of offering

a guide for reconstructing the network of discourses that, aimed at forming opinions
and preparing decisions, provides the matrix from which democratic authority emerges.
(1996, p. 5)

Habermas sees critical theorizing defined in this way as explicitly oriented to trying
to create the conditions for developing a "democratic authority," out of which new
goal directions for humanity can emerge.

In these accounts of the intended import of critical race theorizing and more
general critical theorizing, including what Essed and Goldberg (2002) call a race-
conscious critical theorizing (see Chapter 5, Section 5.3.2), the theory displays its
credentials by, inter alia, helping to *revitalize more genuinely democratic discursive
processes in the social fabric*. And it is in this way that the theorizing becomes
linked to the practical aim of trying to counteract dominative practices.

Furthermore, as I noted when discussing Walby's account of institutional ethnography above (Section 6.1.3), in setting out to explore "ruling practices" within
specific social institutions, again the epistemological emphasis is on shying away
from reproducing relations of authority in one's own approach to knowing. Hence
Walby (2007) calls for a reflexive orientation to reflect upon the relations with participants that might be set up during the research process and to consider the potential
power relations arising through the way the write-up is presented to wider audiences.
This is also in keeping with Douglas's (1998) remarks that processes of knowing in
projects intended to explore the abuse of power in social relations need to attend to
this in the knowing process itself (see Chapter 5).

I would suggest in the light hereof that DeCuir and Dixson's reference to "the
co-option and distortion of oppositional discourses" could be more fully explored
by (re)considering ways in which less distortive (and more democratic) discourses
might be facilitated in the social fabric. And I would suggest that Habermas's critical
theoretical approach to exploring the social basis of democratic authority provides
a useful entry point, along with CRT, to re-look at the quality of democratic versus
distortive discourses. For this reason, I now turn in more detail to a consideration of
some of Habermas's arguments (while also showing how they can be extended).

6.3.2.1 Considering and Extending Habermas's View of Social Discourse and Its Democratic Potential

Habermas's argument in relation to social discourse starts with his understanding
that "as historical and social beings, we find ourselves within a linguistically structured form of life" (2006, p. 122). It is within social discourse (as people are not able
to move outside of language to "access" the social world) that users "raise validity
claims with their speech acts" (2006, p. 123). It is here that they offer justifications
for any claims made. (As I indicated in Chapter 3, Section 3.11, Habermas believes
that all claims include empirical and normative components in some way, as the two
are inextricably linked.) Habermas suggests that in the "ideal speech" situation (as
he defines it), people feel bound only in terms of "the *binding power* of the reasons
that they offer to one another, and take from one another" (2006, p. 123) and it is

this that defines genuine communication. He also believes that it is through language that we

> know how to learn what we owe to one another; and each of us respectively, as members of a [communication] community, can self-critically appropriate our past histories, in light of such moral obligations. (2006, p. 123)

Considering the quality of discourse in the communication community, he posits the possibility of people gearing themselves toward a discursive process, where people can raise (and subject to challenge, via discursive reason) claims to truth, rightness, and sincerity. But validity claims to truth, as with claims to rightness, in Habermas's conception cannot be addressed by appealing to some (presumed) access to extra-linguistic reality. They can be approached only by people finding ways to communicate in relation to one another's assertions – ideally without the constraints of power relations impinging on their discussion (1996, pp. 52–53).

In his examination of "struggles for recognition in the democratic constitutional state," Habermas considers his own encouragement of a communicative community in the context of "the struggle of oppressed ethnic and cultural minorities for recognition within multicultural societies" (1994, p. 117). He points out that the idea of creating an "ethically neutral legal order" has been questioned by those who criticize the failure of de facto orders to make provision for cultural and social differences (1994, p. 111). He avers that claims for "cultural recognition" by certain groups need to be taken seriously, especially insofar as they point to "illegitimate divisions in society"; and he observes that failure of adequate cultural recognition is often connected with "gross social discrimination" (1994, p. 110). He remarks that thus far in prevailing conceptions of democracy across the globe, due to the "bankruptcy of state socialism" as an option for organizing society, the only remaining alternative seems to be that

> the status of a dependent wage earner is to be supplemented with rights to social and political participation, and the mass of the population is thereby given the opportunity to live in realistic expectation of security, social justice, and affluence. (1994, p. 108)

In other words, within this conception of rights, "a more equitable distribution of collective goods is [considered as needed] to compensate for the unequal conditions of life in capitalist societies" (1994, p. 109). He notes that many of those who have queried this way of conceiving rights have argued that systems of rights need to be formulated in *context-sensitive ways* with due recognition of possibly different social needs of people trying to defend themselves against "oppression, marginalization, and disrespect" (1994, p. 117). He gives as an example the way in which feminism has argued that "gender-specific differences in life circumstances and experiences do not receive adequate consideration, either legally or informally." This, he notes, is linked to the claim that "women's cultural self-understanding is not given due recognition." Thus the political struggle of women for "recognition" means that "the scale of values of the society as a whole [in question] is up for discussion" (1994, p. 117). Likewise Habermas argues that in other cases where specific collectivities of people call for recognition, coupled with a critique of "an illegitimate division of society," a public debate is called for around how people "want to deal with their history, with one another, with nature, and so on" (1994, p. 125).

While trying to offer a meaningful way of developing social discourses around alternative ways of life, Habermas reminds us of the "old question of whether it is even possible to transcend the context of our own language and culture or whether all standards of rationality remain bound up with specific worldviews or traditions" (1994, p. 121, see my related discussion in Chapter 4, Section 4.3.1). He comments:

> The overwhelming evidence of the fragmentation of multicultural societies and the Babylonian confusion of tongues in an overly complex global society seem to impel us toward … contextualist conceptions of worldviews that make us skeptical about universalistic claims, whether cognitive or normative. (1994, p. 121)

Habermas's argument regarding whether we should be oriented as humans in our communication to the principle of reaching for "consensus" in relation to "truth" (cognitive claims) and "rightness" (normative claims) is that we still should be thus oriented. That is, he still believes in the regulative ideal of consensus as guiding all human discourse. Nevertheless, he recognizes that the debate around this matter is still unsettled (1994, p. 121).

What he considers to be of particular concern, from his perspective, is when worldviews are displayed in dogmatic form that "lacks an awareness of the fallibility of their claims." He is thus concerned about fundamentalist worldviews that are "dogmatic in that they leave no room for reflection on their relationship with other worldviews with which they share the same universe of discourse." Furthermore, "they leave no room for 'reasonable disagreement'" (1994, p. 133). He proposes that multicultural societies (to be politically integrated) need to be organized around "sharpening sensitivity to the diversity and integrity of the different forms of life coexisting within a multicultural society" (1994, p. 134). Thus, while such societies need not be organized around a "substantive consensus on values," they need to be organized around some consensus on the legitimate enactment of laws and the legitimate exercise of power (1994, p. 135), where it is understood that:

> Unrestrained freedom of communication in the political sphere, a democratic process for settling conflicts, and the constitutional channeling of political power together provide a basis for checking illegitimate power and ensuring that administrative power is used in the equal interest of all. (1994, p. 135)

In considering the relationship between Habermas's encouragement of democratic deliberation and Derrida's approach to deconstruction (see Chapter 1, where I introduced the notion of deconstruction), Morris suggests that it is important to consider Derrida's argument that

> there is, at the very least, a need for a strong counter-cultural or counter-hegemonic presence in the mass media to offset the distortions and domination of existing social interests and the culture industries. (2006, p. 246)

Morris furthermore avers that:

To counter, for example, repetitions of racism, xenophobia, sexism and the numerous forms of colonization, Derrida calls us to start by recognizing that we ourselves come from "the other" in that difference is the very condition of identity. (2006, p. 247)

He continues to explain Derrida's position:

To recognize that a cultural identity is simultaneously a product of its own non-identity with itself as well as a product of relations with and to an other culture is to take a first step toward recalling the shared political space that all identities occupy in a communicative encounter. (2006, p. 247)

Morris sees Derrida's position here as bearing some similarity to that of Habermas – especially to the extent that we treat Habermas's conception of political communication as not necessarily oriented to producing *agreement* but as oriented to "*understanding* and an opening up to the other" (2006, 248, my italics). He indicates that Habermas's position could be seen as making provision for the notion that "the meaning of *understanding* far exceeds the moment of agreement ... since thought, like language, is always in motion, always moving under one heading or another" (2006, p. 248). He concedes (with Habermas) that in politics, a "moment of decision" is required for purposes of action. But he points out that "the call of profound understanding that arises from the irreplaceable place in which identities gather themselves is a call for an openness to the new, to the unique other" – and that this openness itself implies an openness to the "unforeseeable" and "unmasterable" (to use Derrida's terminology, 1992) (Morris, 2006, p. 248).

While Morris concentrates on pointing to the specific contributions that he feels Habermas and Derrida can both make to a "theory of democracy," Matuŝtĩk for his part concentrates on outlining the basis of what he calls the "new alliance" that emerged between Habermas and Derrida in their later writings (through the mutual understanding they developed in the late 1990 s until Derrida's death in 2004) (2006, p. 279). Matuŝtĩk notes in this regard that the notion of "communicative ideality" (as put forward by Habermas) "requires that we can overcome the structural violence issuing from material inequalities and distortions of power politics" (2006, pp. 282–283). He sees Habermas's position as pointing essentially "in the telos of speech oriented to an understanding of one another" to a form of communicative action that can have "no truck with violence" (2006, p. 282).[160] He suggests that in a social context that can be seen as becoming increasingly (symbolically and structurally) violent, Derrida joins Habermas on the "side of democracy" (2006,

---

[160]He also points out that on the international level, Habermas offers no kind words for the "self-centered course of a callous superpower" with its strategy of unilateral war. He points out too that the "language of crusades that accompanied the USA declaration of the war on terror (after 9/11) were snubbed by most commonsense Europeans" – but that these critical attitudes are "normative rather than anti-American" (2006, p. 283). He cites Derrida as indicating that in this political context he sides with "the camp that in principle, by right of law, leaves a perspective open to perfectibility in the name of the political, democracy, international law, international institutions and so on" (Derrida, 2003, as cited in Matuŝtĩk, 2006, p. 283). Habermas too calls for the need to strengthen world citizenry and its requisite institutions like the United Nations and the World Court (Habermas, 2003, as cited in Matuŝtĩk, 2006, p. 283).

p. 283). He considers that Habermas's critical theorizing and Derrida's deconstructive approach can be seen as sharing the belief/vision that although the "human race cannot heal all wounds of history, yet, freed from all pretension to heroism," there is scope for some hope (Matuštík, 2006, p. 293).

What I have tried to foreground via the above discussion is that critical theorizing around the quality of our social existence need not rest on theorists trying to offer an authoritative (expert) voice in the matrix of social discourse. Rather, it can rest on their intention to facilitate the review of issues identified as of concern to people, as part of a process of undercutting authoritative, undialogical, styles of human engagement within the broader project of fostering social justice. Such an orientation, as noted earlier, is also expressed by Collins (1990, 2000), who pleads for dialogue as a criterion for assessing knowing processes in society as an intrinsic part of the development of social justice projects aimed toward what she calls "lasting institutional transformation" (2000, p. 290).[161]

Nevertheless, more so than does Habermas or Derrida, Collins (in supporting a critical race theoretical emphasis) concentrates on highlighting for attention the encoded expressions of racism that she sees as encoded within the discourses of color-blind racism (see Chapter 2, Section 2.3.6.). She cites in this regard Davis's (1997) account of the way in which color-blindness can be seen (if appropriately deconstructed) to operate as a "form of camouflaged racism." In Davis's words:

> Because race is ostracized from some of the most impassioned political debates . . . , their racialized character becomes increasingly difficult to identify, especially by those who are unable – or do not want – to decipher the encoded language. (1997, p. 264)

Collins gives examples of the way in which Americans, for instance, can talk of "street crime" and "welfare mothers" in terms that imply that the discussions are race neutral – while supporting a "host of punitive policies that reinscribe social hierarchies of race and gender" (2000, pp. 279–280). Collins thus argues that critical theorizing needs to be explicitly race conscious in the sense of finding ways of decoding the racism encoded in color-blind rhetoric.

Collins also refers to Foucault's (1979) understanding of the way in which ruling practices in society can rely on "bureaucratic hierarchies and techniques of surveillance" to manage power relations (2000, p. 280). She suggests that in terms of Foucault's understanding we can appreciate that, in capitalist and socialist countries alike, bureaucratic styles of organization "become highly efficient in both reproducing intersecting oppressions and in masking their effects" (2000, p. 281). She gives some examples:

---

[161] Gergen and Gergen similarly attempt to "reframe validity" when they suggest that "if we abandon the traditional goal of research as the accumulation of products . . ., then a chief aim of research becomes that of establishing productive forms of [human] relationship" (2003, p. 598). This echoes Collins's understanding of the importance of tying the validation of social knowing to the project of fostering social justice – which she suggests should be understood in a "transnational context" (2000, p. 290).

Whether the inner-city public schools that many Black girls attend, the low-paid jobs in the rapidly growing service sector that young Black women are increasingly forced to take, the culture of the social welfare bureaucracy that makes Black mothers and children wait for hours, or the 'mammified' work assigned to Black women professionals, the goal is the same – creating quiet, orderly, docile, and disciplined populations of Black women. (2000, p. 281)

Collins suggests that critical theorizing can play a role in highlighting these, as other, "forms of disciplinary power" that can function to render docile these categories of Black women (2000, p. 282). But she argues that we must be careful meanwhile of creating a hierarchy between, for instance, Black feminist thought "in the academy," which becomes elevated "to the level of theory," and Black women's activism (and attendant theorizing in relation to issues of concern), which she argues can become devalued as "less theoretical" (2000, p. 282). She remarks that the issues that are of interest to "academics" seem to have become mismatched with issues of pressing concern outside of academia. She suggests that it is worth investigating how indeed the placement of Black feminist thought in the academy could serve, instead of fostering social justice, to "reinscribe social hierarchies" (2000, p. 282). In Chapter 8 I discuss further what may be involved in developing critical theorizing that is pragmatically directed to subverting social hierarchies, including through the way that "knowing" is practiced.

6.3.2.2 Returning to DeCuir and Dixson's Case: Further Commentary

Returning to DeCuir and Dixson's account of the case study at the Academy, I would now suggest – in the light of my exposition of the above arguments – that they could concentrate in their account on *highlighting issues of concern that were raised in the setting under consideration.* For example, they could highlight their understanding that despite its apparent commitment to diversity, the processes and policies supposedly set up at the Academy to attend to the school's diversity initiative, were experienced as, and could be theorized as, "superficial." They can present as part of their story that the employment of a single coordinator, who was deemed responsible for teaching multicultural classes and organizing multicultural students activities, implies for them a stance that is not sufficiently radical in orientation. This understanding they can present with the intention of opening for discussion what it might mean to create a program that is more radically oriented and that is more likely to generate meaningful institutional transformation.

The understanding becomes insightful (as far as a pragmatically oriented critical theory is concerned) to the extent that it helps to alert people to the possible need for an alternative way of approaching diversity issues at this, as at other, schools – in view of evidence/concerns brought to light that needs to be entered into processes of continuing discussion around goal directions to be pursued. I would suggest that such discussions could indeed be started at the school itself. DeCuir and Dixson could, say, try to introduce forums for speaking about (and challenging), inter alia, the justification for appointing only one person to handle the responsibility of the diversity program. And further to the ensuing discussions they could spur, through

298 6 Ethnographic Research

their write-up, further deliberations around this in more public discursive spaces – as part of the process of encouraging more discursive accounting for (and discursively accountable action in relation to) the treatment of issues raised as problematic via the case. Because DeCuir and Dixson do not indicate to us as audiences what their larger study to which they allude involved, we do not know whether, at any point, they tried to generate discussion around issues of concern raised by them (and others) at the Academy. But I would argue that a discursive orientation, both during the process of the research and in the style of presentation of "results," would be more in keeping with an extended critical theorizing – extended along the lines I have suggested above.

As far as any theoretical judgment as to whether the highlighted practices and policies (highlighted by DeCuir and Dixson in their write-up) really "are" racist – and must be seen as providing an instantiation of the "real" permanence of racism in the social structures of the USA – I would suggest the following. DeCuir and Dixson could indicate how they have chosen to theorize the case in terms of an understanding of the applicability of the concept of racism as a concept that draws attention to *issues of felt concern to various people and to a way of naming these concerns.* By offering their account in these terms, they need not pretend that they are offering a non-perspectival vision; rather, they are offering concepts to ignite further productive discourse around the issues that they, as others, may consider as important to address (see also my account in Chapter 8 – especially Section 8.5.1 – of the purpose of using concepts such as racism).

Relating this back to the debate to which Hammersley (1995) points in regard to Foster's work (1990), where Foster suggested that there was little evidence of racism on the part of teachers in the setting studied (in Britain), I would suggest that by others arguing that *continued issues of concern can be located* via the study, this already means that "the case" needs to be re-examined/reviewed. For example, the issue of whether students felt able to articulate their feelings/understandings is an issue that Foster would need to take seriously, to show that he is rendering himself *discursively accountable to the ways of seeing that might be brought to bear on the case in terms of other people's concerns.*

But my point is that by our trying to direct our inquiries toward some posited extra-linguistic reality hoping to make some "sound" conclusions about this (through, say, the scientific guidelines that Hammersley espouses), the problem of whose approach to "the situation" should be given more credibility is not resolved. Thus Hammersley tries to authorize *his* approach, while others can and do criticize this approach for not offering a sufficiently broad conception of social theorizing (and attendant methodology). The debate then only shifts to different researchers stating that their approach is the better route to properly "find out" about social reality. The alternative of a more constructivist epistemology that admits a pragmatic approach to knowing – where knowing is tied to the practical project of exploring new ways of both knowing and living – might provide a way out of this impasse. This implies accepting that, as Bonilla-Silva and Baiocchi put it, "all knowledge has a political foundation" (2008, p. 150), and operating in terms of this consciousness rather than striving for "neutrality" in our approach to social reality. In the following chapters I discuss further practical implications of adopting this conception of (critical) theorizing.

In the next section I offer an outline of another possible way of seeing and doing ethnographic research, which I believe can be valuable in inquiries around (new) racism – through what has been called "autoethnography." I offer an example of a case of my own involvement in a specific social setting and my writing it up.

6.4 Some Views on Autoethnography as Social Inquiry

Behar makes the point that when people write up autobiographical accounts of their involvements in social situations, no one objects to this "as a genre in its own right" (1996, p. 12). What bothers (scientific) critics, she suggests, is "the insertion of personal stories into what we have been taught to think of as the analysis of impersonal social facts." She continues:

> Throughout most of the twentieth century, in scholarly fields ranging from literary criticism to anthropology to law, the reigning paradigms have traditionally called for distance, objectivity, and abstraction. The worst sin was to be "too personal". (1996, p. 13)

She points out, though, that certain authors writing up their social involvements have begun experimenting with forms of writing where they "locate themselves in texts" – but she avers that this requires a "yet greater skill" than writing distantly (1996, p. 13). She explains that efforts at such writing require "a keen understanding of what aspects of the self are the most important filters through which one perceives the world and, more particularly, the topic being studied" (1996, p. 13). If the "personal" account is written with sufficient skill, drawing on "deep connections between one's personal experience and the subject under study," then the text is likely to "move" the reader (1996, p. 13). She suggests that:

> Efforts at self-revelation [at the point of write-up] flop not because the personal voice has been used, but because it has been poorly used, leaving unscrutinized the connection, intellectual and emotional, between the observer and the observed. (1996, pp. 13–14)

She emphasizes that writing in this way does not mean that "anything personal goes." Rather, the "exposure of the self" should be "essential to the argument" (1996, p. 14). She emphasizes that "a personal voice, if creatively used, can lead the reader not into miniature bubbles of navel-gazing, but into the enormous sea of serious social issues" (1996, p. 14).[162]

---

[162]Bell suggests that this idea of Behar's is similar to Clark's coining of the term "involved observer" to point to "observers" who are "in some way shaped by and connected to the individuals, groups and communities they are studying" and who do not try to become detached from the issues faced within these settings (2001, p. 52). Bell points out that in both Clark's (1973) understanding of the "involved observer" and Behar's (1996) understanding of the "vulnerable observer" reference is made in research write-ups to "the researchers' emotional relationship with and involvement in their work" (2001, p. 52).

In the example that I provide (in Section 6.5) of my own involvement in a particular (university) setting, I take forward the suggestion that ethnography can be approached in a way that is aimed at pointing to "serious social issues" through the prism of the self. I offer an account of my attempt to "make a difference" to the human relationships through taking seriously a complaint of racial discrimination on the part of some students leveled against the "home students" at the university. I write in a style that, as Behar endorses, is not meant to leave the reader "unmoved."[163]

In discussing autoethnography as a methodological approach, Walford points to a question surrounding its standing, namely, the question of "to what extent can such autobiographically-based stories reflect anything other than a constructed fiction?" (2004, p. 411). He notes that certain autoethnographers admit and even embrace the fact that "stories re-arrange, redescribe, invent, omit, and revise" (2004, p. 411). His response to this style of, and justification for, autoethnography is that "if people wish to write fiction, they have every right to do so, but not every right to call it research" (2004, p. 411). He is concerned that in some autoethnographical work (such as reported in, say, Ellis and Bochner, 1996) the boundaries between creative literature and social science research writing have become too blurred – doing justice to neither genre (2004, p. 411). He supplies his definition of creative literature, as follows:

> Good literature or good poetry should certainly try to encourage "connection, empathy and solidarity". Good literature is centrally a writerly text with multiple possible interpretations designed to engage the reader in a reflexive process of new understanding. (2004, p. 413)

He suggests that in contrast to such literature, the reports of social research

> need to be logically constructed and clear about what empirical claims (factual and explanatory) are being made and what empirical data have been generated that support those claims. The text is one where attempts are made to reduce ambiguity and to exhibit precision. (2004, p. 413)

Walford argues that there are "many forms of useful writing" in society – but in his view, "for that writing to be designated the report of 'research', it has to pass certain tests of validity and relevance" (2004, p. 413). He refers favorably to Hammersley's (1990) arguments in this regard.

Walford indicates that while he believes that "some forms of autoethnography are valuable," he rejects "the various forms of postmodern or postexperimental writing." He argues that these "newer forms of qualitative writing" cannot function "as a report of research" (2004, p. 414). He follows Hammersley in arguing that

---

[163]Lincoln and Denzin argue that it may be necessary to introduce a *political vulnerability* that goes beyond Behar's position. They call for an autoethnography that not only "breaks your heart" but that "challenges the reader to take action in the world [and] to reconsider the conditions under which the moral terms of the self and community are constituted" (2003, p. 623). They are concerned that Behar's position falls short of embracing a (moral) "call to action" (2003, p. 623). Nevertheless, I would suggest that Behar could be interpreted as calling for this – by trying to "move" readers so that they feel the need to address "serious social issues" (1996, p. 14).

ethnography, including autoethnography, cannot pass as "research" unless it meets the standards of research to which Hammersley points (see Sections 6.1 and 6.1.1).

As I have indicated, though, others have argued that the "stories" constructed by autoethnographers are indeed to be judged in terms of their being able to move readers so as to embrace a concern with "serious social issues" (to use Behar's 1996 terminology) – and that insofar as multiple interpretations of the text are made possible for readers, this is in keeping with the non-authoritative stance that, for instance, constructivism sees as important as a matter of principle. With this in mind, I proceed to tell my story.

6.5 Romm's Involvement in a Case of Felt Discrimination at a University in the United Kingdom

The case recounted here (and also in Romm, 2006b) was set in a university in the UK – in relation to a particular Masters class consisting of students from diverse backgrounds (whose meaning itself came to be defined in a particular way). In this narration I use pseudonyms for all participants excepting for Jin Yi, one of the students from China.[164]

The class consisted of students from many countries all over the world, including many from the Far East. The (two) home students – Christine and Gail – were conscious of the proportion in the cohort of "the Chinese," whom they later came to define (in writing) as "the numerous Chinese population." Meanwhile, during the course, many of the students – from a range of countries – and certain lecturers considered Christine and Gail as having a hostile attitude toward in particular "the Chinese" (as well as to the other "foreign" students).

At a certain point all of the students from the Far East signed a petition stating that their class representatives (one of them being Christine and the other being someone whom they regarded as led by her, namely, Raymond) had failed to keep harmony in the group (i.e., in the class as a whole). They asked on these grounds for new representatives to be elected. However, the re-election of representatives was held up for more than a month and in the meantime the experienced aggression increased. The students arranged for an appointment to see the Dean of the Business School to express their concerns with the attitude and behavior that they had experienced. Two of them were at the meeting (with the others on standby). I was also present in the meeting, as I was the course leader – on request of the students.

The students pointed out that Christine and Gail had in their view been insulting them and indeed had presumed to judge them as inferior on various counts: academically, ethically, and culturally. Below are some quotations from their conversation, which was tape-recorded. (The "[not clear]" inserted in the quotations below indicates points on the tape where the voices were unclear.):

---

[164]Mr. Jin Yi was happy to have his name revealed in my reporting of the saga – which he experienced as "horrible" throughout – so I have kept his real name in this recounting.

Jin Yi: [one of the students representing the concerns of "the Chinese" in the meeting]:

> ... And also in the Research module ... they think they have, you know, a high position they can judge academic and ethical and cultural things. So always when the students want to contribute they, they ... funnily enough we got a meeting with Dr. Smith [the Director of post-graduate programs] ... *[not clear]* they said we didn't want to contribute, but in every class ... *[not clear]*, just like what the English students do ....

Dean of School: mmmm

> Jin Yi: ... *[not clear]* they don't know if there are some standards to select the students, to give the offer to the students in the Business School, they don't know. So in the Research module they think they are better and they just ... *[not clear]*.

And further on during the conversation Jin Yi continues:
Jin Yi: [They say] we cannot stay here. We have no ...
Norma Romm: Capability.

> Jin Yi: Capability, capability to study here .... And then Dr. Smith [Director of post-graduate programs] goes to the class on the Friday ... *[not clear]* example ... *[not clear]* employer ... *[not clear]* employee ... *[not clear]* conflict ... *[not clear]* according to English law, these kind of things happen ... *[not clear]*. Quite Serious.

Dean of School: mmmm

> Jin Yi: And [Dr. Smith implied that] it is English culture, the students have the right to do these things ... *[not clear]*. So they have not stopped the trouble. And in the meeting they said the Chinese students do not contribute. During the leadership module, it is Ms. Probert who is our lecturer. I always give a contribution there ... *[not clear]* to discuss ... *[not clear]*. I am not finished my sentence and I am interrupted by Christine and Raymond .... I don't understand! The same things happened when we had the meeting with Dr. Smith. Some students used very rude words. ... *[not clear]* an English student [Gail] used "f...k" during the meeting when I was trying to ... *[not clear]*.

At the end of this meeting the Dean promised the students that the issues would be fully investigated. He admitted (earlier in the meeting) that he had understood that the issue at stake for the students was having to cope with feeling aggressed against; and he acknowledged that they had spoken with "passion" in recounting their experiences. I would like to add here that Jin Yi had spoken to me too with extreme upset (as had certain other of the students from Chinese background) at what they experienced as antagonistic treatment leveled against them due to their nationality (as they put it), as well as against some other students from other countries (such as India). It was not one incident but several that brought Jin Yi and fellow students to the edge to take the step of lodging with the Dean their account of their experiences – hoping that the matter could be looked into within the university. Unfortunately, the ensuing "investigation" never resulted in any written statements being taken from witnesses by the person supposedly investigating the issue (Dr. Smith) – thus it is not possible to establish what people might have said if questioned about the concerns complained about.[165]

Returning to (my narration of) the chronology, after a meeting that Dr. Smith arranged with Jin Yi and a fellow student (who had been present in the initial meeting with the Dean too), the students sent an e-mail to the Dean summarizing some points raised in their meeting with Dr. Smith and emphasizing that "we just want equal treatment." Yet when the Dean eventually (nearly a year late in terms of University Regulations) reported to Jin Yi about what he saw as the issues, and what witnesses had been used and what evidence collected, no mention was made of any references of the complainants to unequal treatment, to their concerns that they had experienced others as treating them as inferior (culturally, ethically, and academically), or to their expressed anxiety that their capabilities to study in the university had been called into question, and so on.

Interestingly, Jin Yi would (so he remarked to me much later) have preferred not to talk of Christine and Gail as "the English" and not to have to define as "the Chinese" himself and the other students on the course whose countries of origin was the Far East. Yet had he not used this terminology when addressing the Dean of the School and had he not made comparisons showing that "the Chinese" were feeling inferiorized, he would have been left (in all likelihood) in an even more vulnerable position. The university officers could have then stood more easily by their claim that issues of discrimination were never put on the table by the complainants. This claim was indeed made in a letter sent to Jin Yi by the Vice-Chancellor, after Jin Yi had asked for the handling of the "investigation" within the Business School to be looked into.[166] In one of his responses to Jin Yi, the

---

[165] Some witness statements were obtained by me more or less accidentally (but were never elicited by the University). One case in point is a statement from an exchange student from France who volunteered her views to the course leader (when matters were being investigated). She wrote that "Christine does not make enough effort to understand people from other countries who she thought were not as good as her," and that Christine created "an upsetting atmosphere in the class." She pointed out that she had "never seen such a case before." Another student (from Nigeria) also was keen to offer a statement expressing her "deep anger and bitterness" over the "matter which I [she] felt should have been dealt with properly and adequately during the MSc session." She continued that "Christine, Gail, and Raymond should have been disciplined and taught how to behave to foreigners." She indicated (to me) that she had never been questioned by anyone about the attitude of Christine and Gail to the other students. Meanwhile, an (external) lecturer who specifically stated (both verbally and in a written report sent to Dr. Smith) that a "small cohort of the Caucasians seemed to be openly hostile to the Chinese majority" was not on the list of witnesses (even as an anonymized name) that the Dean eventually offered to Jin Yi.

[166] Jin Yi had mentioned when he lodged his complaint to the Vice-Chancellor that although the Dean had promised in writing (subsequent to the "investigation") that action against those who had acted inappropriately and offensively would be taken, no one of whom he knew was informed of anything that had occurred; nor had a report (stating the substance of the issues and how they were examined by the investigator) been provided. To this the Vice Chancellor replied to Jin Yi that "the response of the Business School was not within the strict guidelines prescribed by University procedures [for dealing with student complaints in general]", while at the same time he stated that

Vice-Chancellor stated that had the issues been about (alleged) racial discrimination, the university policy on the prevention of harassment would have been activated (admitting that the university never did address the issue as involving such an allegation).

Taking into account the kinds of responses briefly mentioned above – we can repose the question whether by Jin Yi initially referring to "we" (the group of students whom he noted had felt affronted by those who seemingly posed as superior), he could be considered as essentializing the group classifications here. Was it necessary to have used the category for the purposes of drawing attention to its coercive application by Christine and Gail who saw "them" indeed as a group to which "the Chinese" belonged, and referred to "them" as "the Chinese population"? Furthermore, while drawing on a conception of an imaginery collective that had been imagined to exist as "the Chinese" on the course, could "the Chinese" try at the same time to subvert the status of the "collective" categorization? Had a dialogue opened between the parties (which unfortunately never did occur) they may well have been able to speak about, around and past the categories and they might have generated a different conception of what was involved in drawing on categories of collectivities. The collectivity constructions then might have become re-visioned as not referring to ontological givens, but indeed as potentially opening up a dialogue around central issues of concern to the concerned parties. As it stood, "the English" appeared to inferiorize "the silent Chinese" without acknowledging that one could interpret the cultural agenda of "the Chinese" as not predisposing people to speak in public unless specifically encouraged and unless the social atmosphere is made conducive to this. For "the Chinese" on the course (at least for those who still undertook to enter class discussions), being interrupted when trying to speak was prohibitive of meaningful involvement in the conversation. In this context, use of the collectivity construction "the Chinese" served to occlude their involvement rather than to point to potentially culturally distinct meanings and styles of interaction that could be drawn upon.

In my view, sadly, there were many missed opportunities for people in the Masters class referred to in my cited example to indeed meet one another – missed primarily because of the orientation on the part of Christine and Gail toward "the other" as something that could not hold anything new from which to learn. Instead of being curious about what "the other" might have held if they were prepared to enter a dialogue (which I would suggest certain students from the Far East did try to open, by for example, organizing a party to which they invited all students, and by making efforts to contribute input in the class), the dialogue was not pursued – and this had traumatic consequences for those involved (as reported to me and interpreted by me).

---

the matter was handled informally in the Business School "(Section 9 [of the Student Complaints Procedure] 'Informal Resolution')" – apparently unbeknownst to the complainants.

The dilemma for all those concerned about the coercive use of the overgeneralized collectivity construction used to identify "them" ("the Chinese") was how to work past this construction while not thereby enabling those tasked with investigating their complaint to pass off the matter as simply "tension [in the cohort] and lack of respect for individuals." (This is how Dr. Smith phrased matters in his report to the Dean, although he had said to myself and a colleague verbally 2 days before he submitted his report that from what he could ascertain "it is still very much a two-groups' culture. And one group is intolerant of the other. Perhaps Christine's group is far more intolerant.") In this political context as sensed by the (Chinese) students, they chose *to indeed utilize in their complaint the group construction (the construction of "the Chinese") considered to have been used to treat this (defined) group unequally.* But I believe from my discussions with Jin Yi that his invocation of the construction was not used as a device to imply the existence of a collectivity of people all with the same experience of the(ir) cultural framework (that facilitated their expressions).

From my reading of "the situation" (admittedly as read through my "personal" involvement) if all parties had been able to put in place this proviso regarding the status of the collectivity construction, space might be opened (in principle) for a genuine meeting from which all parties could learn.

But although I believe this was possible in principle, the potential for communication across the constructed "borders" within the setting became missed (see also Chapter 4, Section 4.3.1). This, I believe, was also due to the part played by personnel who failed to encourage a cultural climate for communicative exchange and who failed to take seriously the concerns of the Chinese students that the social relationships were being harmed, with "horrible" consequences for the Chinese students (as Jin Yi expressed it). In terms of the argument that I have developed in this chapter, as elsewhere, when people fail to take responsibility for the possible social impact of their way of seeing (e.g., the consequences of choosing not to recognize the Chinese students as complaining of racial discrimination), they become complicit in the furthering of a less-than-humane social fabric. I believe that the way in which the personnel proceeded in this case can be seen as an instance of how complicity in (new) racism becomes produced.

At the end of the academic year, after Jin Yi and others had obtained their results (as they were afraid to complain further during the year, for fear of repercussion), Jin Yi complained on behalf of the students first to a complaints officer, and later to the Vice-Chancellor, indicating that his original complaint had not been properly handled (according to Regulations) within the Business School. At this point, Christine and Gail put in their own complaint, arguing, inter alia, that I (and the course leader) had "masterminded" a process of "encouraging every action possible to make life unpleasant" for certain students (i.e., themselves). The university officers dealing with the complaints refused to connect up the two complaints, arguing that the Chinese students' one was "closed." After much (failed) effort on the part of the trade union to get the university to agree that the two complaints needed to be treated in an integrated fashion, so that documents related to the Chinese students' complaints could be at the disposal of the investigator,[167] I approached a (South African) lawyer, who agreed to take up my case (of victimization) on a no-win no-fee basis.[168] (I resigned at the same time.)

My victimization claim was based on the principle that I had done what is called a "Protected Act" in terms of the Race Relations law in supporting students who had complained of racial discrimination – by trying to find the channels in the university for this complaint to be addressed. This meant that I should have been protected from subsequent retaliation by, for example, Christine and Gail [who were called **X** and **Y** in the Tribunal hearing]. Although the university denied that a complaint of racial discrimination on the part of the Chinese students had ever been made (which would have afforded me protection), the Tribunal found otherwise.[169] Their judgment was that "The claimant's [my] support of Jin Yi in the pursuit of his complaint was conduct 'otherwise done under or by reference to' the 1976 Act and thereby constituted a protected act within the meaning of . . . that Act" (2005, p. 28).

The Tribunal did not however, find evidence of my having been victimized (i.e., the Tribunal did not find that I could be argued to have been treated unfavorably in relation to hypothetical and actual comparators[170]). At the review hearing (which I asked for so that the judgment could be reviewed), the chairman indicated to me that at the original hearing I had "won the point" re the racial discrimination complaint on the part of the Chinese students. I stated that *this had been crucial*, and that it was precisely because the university did not want to recognize this, that I was in a vulnerable position in relation to the home students [X and Y] asserting that I had "encouraged every action possible to make life unpleasant" for them in my support of the Chinese students. However, the Tribunal did not change their judgment. They did, nevertheless, refuse to award the university costs, for which the university had applied (in April of that year, after they heard that I had asked for, and been granted, a review). The university used as ground for their application for costs that in my

---

[167]The investigator of Christine and Gail's complaints was never given any of these documents (relating to the Chinese students' prior complaints) – as confirmed by the personnel officer who was one of the witnesses for the University testifying at the later Tribunal hearing (2004).

[168]My witnesses at the Tribunal were: Jin Yi (the Chinese student leading the complaint); the course leader of the Masters course; a trade union officer; and myself. The Tribunal hearing was in 2004 (May and September). The case number of the case was number 1806710/03. After the judgment (February 2005), I applied for a review, which was heard in June 2005. The Tribunal stood by its original decision – but the Tribunal chairman did indicate to me that I had "won" the point that there had indeed been a complaint of racial discrimination. It was also stated in their original report on their judgment that "any doubt about the matter" of whether a complaint of racial discrimination had been made was "answered" by various pieces of evidence (Tribunal Judgment, p. 28).

[169]The University's position as expressed to the Tribunal was that the complaint of the Chinese students had been "minor", and had not been a complaint of racial discrimination (Respondent's written submission, October 2004).

[170]I had argued that the Dean and the Director of post-graduate programs were actual comparators because they had been afforded the protection of the University – despite the University admitting (in writing to Jin Yi) that they had not acted in accordance with University Regulations in the handling the Chinese students' complaints.

taking up the matter in the first place at a Tribunal, or what they call "bringing the proceedings," I had acted "unreasonably and vexatiously" (University's application for costs, April 2005). In my objection to the university's costs application, which I was required to construct in 7 days, putting me under tremendous pressure, not to mention the worry that there was a chance of costs being awarded (as I did not know how the Tribunal felt), I stated:

> The University should be aware that the two-day hearing in May [2004] was extended at the request by the Chair of the Tribunal (during the course of the second day). He indicated that the case was clearly too complex to have been heard (unraveled) in the set limit. The fact that a further (4-day) hearing was set aside by the Chair implies that he (having heard my evidence under intense and extensive questioning by the respondent's barrister over nearly two days) did not consider my case baseless and frivolous (let alone unreasonable or vexatious). Otherwise, it surely would not have been extended by 200%. (April 2005)

I also tried to highlight the unfairness that had been introduced:

> By choosing to employ a barrister as well as their own solicitor the respondent can be seen as showing their intention to unbalance the fair representation of the parties concerned. The employment tribunals were set up as low cost courts (alternative to higher courts) to settle employment disputes inexpensively. The respondent surely had the obligation in terms of Tribunal guidelines to refrain from incurring (via an expensive legal team) costs disproportionate to the purpose of the court. (April 2005)

I asked the Tribunal to consider the broader implications of the unfairness introduced when public institutions are allowed to apply for costs against individuals when the individuals do not win their cases:

> How can a private individual be expected to risk taking up a case against a public institution in circumstances of such disparity [when public institutions have huge public funds at their disposal] – when it is indeed never possible (no matter what the judgment) for any particular staff member in the institution to lose any private funds? Was the University justified in introducing this disparity [by employing an expensive Barrister]? Is it normal practice? etc. (April 2005)

And I appealed to their sense of empathy, while raising questions for them to consider, as follows:

> Given that in my view the point of going to Tribunal was to allow my case to be heard by an independent body, I would like to ask (rhetorically): If I had not believed I had (and have) a good chance of "winning" (or proving my claims) would I have gone to all the time, trouble, and energy (besides finance) to organize to get to the UK twice from Cyprus, to now organize yet again to come this time from South Africa, to take leave from work (which does not get re-imbursed), etc? What motive could I possibly have for exhausting myself physically and emotionally, and spending so much effort (and cost) other than that I believe I have a very strong case for my claims? (April 2005)

Because the university had also argued that my original bringing of the proceedings had been misconceived (which apparently is some legal term that can be used in applying for costs), I stated:

> I do not know what the University is trying to suggest by saying that my bringing of the proceedings was "misconceived". My conception was that it was very important for the matter to be heard via an independent body . . .. The Tribunal indeed confirmed that I had supported

a group of students to get a complaint of discrimination heard – contrary to the vitriolic, unsubstantiated accusations that X and Y made about my behavior (and contrary to the barrister's denial, despite all the evidence, that the Chinese students had been complaining about the racist tendencies of X and Y). (April 2005)

All these points that I made in my objection to the Tribunal were meant to alert them to the problems that I now faced, placed in the broader context of the supposedly operative legal requirement to "protect" those trying to support others complaining of racial discrimination. Fortunately the Tribunal had agreed, on the basis of the original hearing (May and September 2004), that there *had* been a complaint of racial discrimination. And I believe this would have counted against the university when they made their application for costs. But it is interesting that a decision was still made in the university to apply – despite knowing that the Tribunal had disagreed with the university's denial that the Chinese students had ever complained of discrimination. Despite this, the university still could (without any repercussion for anyone therein) put in the claim that my bringing of the proceedings had been "misconceived" (thus putting me under huge pressure until the costs hearing indeed took place a few months later – namely, in June 2005).[171]

6.6 Review of Romm's Autoethnographic "Report"

As in my discussion of my focus group interviewing approach that I outlined in Chapter 5, I use my discussion of this autoethnographic example in this chapter to point to possibilities for styles of research around new racism that can proceed without "realist warrant" (as Alldred, 1998 calls it). Walford, following Hammersley (1990) in adopting a realist position, argues that any ethnographic report, if it is to be labeled as research, needs to be constructed so as to be "clear about what empirical claims (factual and explanatory) are being made and what empirical data have been generated that support those claims" (2004, p. 413). He sees this as a fundamentally different genre from poetry and literature, whose task is to "try to encourage "connection, empathy and solidarity" (2004, p. 413). I have attempted to show via this example, that through "reports" on one's involvements in unfolding social situations (as one experiences and acts in them as one sees them unfolding), one can point to one's perception of possibilities for generating (more) humane social relationships (and more human connection). One can admit that the data presented as one constructs the narrative are as seen through a perspective, namely, the

---

[171] In this case the University had indicated to my lawyer a few days before the original proceedings (in May 2004) that if I withdrew they would not "pursue me" for costs (and had suggested that if I continued, they might). I pointed out to the Tribunal (in my objection to the costs application received after I applied for a review of judgment – April 2005) that this way of threatening can easily become (ab)used as a mechanism to prevent private individuals from daring to access the Tribunal system of justice. As far as making decisions as to whether cases are misconceived, this depends on particular perceptions (in this case, a Tribunal's) of whether the applicant has been (un)reasonable in pursuing a case.

perspective of considering distortions of, as well as possibilities for, revitalizing humane social relationships. One can point to source material (as I have done in the text and in footnotes) while conceding to readers that all observed information is always in any case interpreted and is never "raw" (as indeed even Hammersley, in line with his critique of "naïve empiricism," admits – see again Chapter 5, Section 5.3.1.1, as well as Section 6.1 above).

In terms of my understanding of this illustrative example, I propose that when writing up "autoethnography," one can make statements without insisting on a real-ist warrant for one's claims. Hence, for instance, my claims that I made in relation to what I see as missed opportunities in the university setting are based on my reading of what "might have been" and what possibly "could have become" in the setting. And my claims regarding, say, the unfairnesses that can become (re)produced when taking up cases of victimization are based on my argument (involving empirical and normative components) that public institutions appear to be able to threaten people with costs (if they lose) on the grounds that their claims of victimization are "mis-conceived" (as was done in this case). This means that individuals have to take risks of possibly losing a case that might cost them personally (if they lose), while *no one in the institution is ever responsible for having to pay*. I presented this argument to the Tribunal (hoping to make a difference to their way of viewing the issue of costs, which might impinge not only on their judgment in my case, but possibly and hopefully also on others). And I present it in this book for additional audiences to take on board in their deliberations.

With the subtleties of "new racism" it is possible for institutions to decide that even when people complain of "wanting equal treatment," this is not to be construed as a complaint of racial discrimination and that it is in any event "minor" (as the university's barrister argued in her written submission, October 2004). I suggest that it required what CRT calls some "race-conscious" openness on the part of the Tribunal (and it may have been significant and helpful that there was one person who was not White thereon, of the three men[172]) to decide that the question as to whether a complaint of racial discrimination had been made was "answered" by the evidence.[173] I believe that some potential could be located (or rather, I tried to

---

[172]It was this person (of Indian descent) who asked the Dean how he thinks racism can be defined, thus bringing to the fore the definition and naming of racism within the Tribunal hearing.

[173]Sommers and Norton note in this respect that "denial of problem" kinds of behaviors "capture the subtle, ambiguous nature of modern racism" (2006, p. 131). They point out that many of the behaviors that psychologists consider indicative of racial bias (see Section 2.3.3) have not at this point entrenched themselves in "consensus lay conceptions of racism" (2006, p. 132). But they note that in a survey that they conducted "Non-White participants were significantly more likely than Whites to view subtle behaviors in the *discomfort/unfamiliarity* and *denial of problem* fac-tors as indicative of racism" (2006, p. 132). Sommers and Norton utilized closed and open-ended questions in their survey; and they also later invited vignettes in a subsequent study. They suggest that the vignettes also provided evidence for "between race differences in how people think about racism" (2006, p. 132).

activate this) in the Tribunal hearing(s) to "touch" the Tribunal (including in my objection to the university's costs application, as cited above). And if they were not hereby sensitized to my understanding of the issues, then hopefully audiences of this book (which may include Tribunal members too!) might take on board some of the concerns that I have expressed.

I do not see my reading of "the situation" (and my location of potential for less distorted forms of human relationship, to use Habermas's terminology) as authoritative. Because of the genre of narrative that I used, I see it as avoiding the problem of reinforcing relations of authority through the way in which authors try to authorize their accounts.

As far as possibilities go for reflexively reconsidering the orientation with which I have approached the narration, namely, one resting on a presumed potential for more discursively directed social relationships in the social fabric, I admit that readers may wish to read my narration with an alternative lens, not seeing (in the way I have) the possibilities for "fairer" human relationships as potentially workable into "the situation." My location of this potentiality in the way that I have done may thus be questioned. Furthermore, readers may wonder what "action options" can be pointed to through the narrative that I have presented – that is, how my account may open up possibilities for envisaging new forms of action and how, if at all, ethnographic research more generally can be developed toward this end. (In Chapter 7 I explore some research approaches directed toward designing action-oriented co-inquiry as a way of facilitating inquiry in action so as to strengthen the transformative potential of the inquiries.)

It is also possible that readers may wish to apply alternative angles on what it might mean to try, in Collins's words, to "reclaim spaces for thinking and doing" that might not be expected within "dominant culture" (2000, p. 285). Collins argues that in whatever manner people choose to operate in social settings, a useful way to consider our human being in society is to recognize that:

> Based on their personal histories, individuals experience and resist domination differently. Each individual has a unique and continually evolving personal biography made up of concrete experiences, values, motivations, and emotions. No two individuals occupy the same social space; thus no two biographies are identical. (2000, p. 285)

She also makes the point that:

> Individual biographies are situated within all domains of power [at macro- and micro-levels of social existence] .... Whereas the structural domain of power organizes the macro-level of social organization with the disciplinary domain managing its operations [see Section 6.3.2.1], the interpersonal domain functions through routinized, day-to-day practices of how people treat one another (e.g., micro-level of social organization). Such practices are systematic, recurrent, and so familiar that they often go unnoticed. (2000, p. 287)

Collins thus sees as valuable the enterprise of unpacking the details of people's biographies (as she does with reference to a range of examples in her book) as a way of showing that, on the level of the interpersonal domain, "resistance strategies ... can take as many forms as there are individuals" (2000, p. 288). She points out that through the process of reporting hereon, illustrations can be given of how "all sorts of ordinary people work to change the world around them" (2000, p. 288). She also points out that in terms of her understanding of Black feminist thought, it "views the world as a dynamic place where the goal is not merely to survive or to fit in or to cope" (as Douglas too illustrates – see Chapter 5, Section 5.3.1) (2000, p. 290). This means that (in terms of this thinking) "there is always choice, and power to act, no matter how bleak the situation may appear to be" (2000, p. 290). But likewise, in terms of this thinking, it is understood that "while individual empowerment is key, only collective action can effectively generate the lasting institutional transformation required for social justice" (2000, p. 290).

Collins's account hereof can be compared with Foucault's understanding of possibilities for human "resistance" at individual and collective levels, which both she and Foucault see as resting on different (what Collins calls "unexpected") processes than envisaged by, for example, Habermas. But Collins is concerned that a Foucauldian definition of "subjugated knowledge" (that runs counter to dominant culture) implies that it owes its (intellectual) force to the harshness with which it is opposed in mainstream thinking. She argues that such a definition of countercultural thinking fails to do justice to, for example, Black feminist thought, which owes its quality to "long-standing, independent, African-derived influences within Black women's thought" (2000, p. 291, Endnote 2).

In Chapter 8 I offer some further detail on Foucault's understanding of the connection of knowledge and power, and I indicate how its import for the theorizing of racism has been variously interpreted. For now, my point is that a variety of ways of seeing transformative potential as well as obstructions to "lasting institutional transformation" (as Collins, 2000, p. 290 puts it) can be brought to bear in considering "the case" as reported by me in my autoethnographic account of the specific racializing of the social relationships in the setting.

6.7 Conclusion

Bonilla-Silva and Baiocchi consider that one of the advantages of more qualitatively oriented research, as an alternative to surveys, is that it can take into account that "people do not express their positions and emotions about racial issues by answering 'yes' and 'no' and 'strongly agree' to questions." Instead, they "express their ideological positions in talk and text" (2008, p. 140). I have tried to show in this chapter how ethnographers and autoethographers can proceed to explore people's "talk and text" as generated in everyday life in the course of social interaction, and how they can account for their *own involvement in their interaction with (other) participants* (2008, p. 140). I have also tried to show via the examples discussed that they can *write up their narratives/accounts in a way that need not rely on realist warrants in order to pass as "research"* – as long as readers are prepared to award trust to them on other bases than judging the work in terms of claims to strive for "objective" understanding unmediated by human perspectives and concerns.

6.7.1 Revisiting Researcher Accountability in Ethnographic Research

My discussions in this chapter were directed at examining ethnographic (and autoethnographic) research in terms of my concern with social inquirers taking some responsibility for their involvements in the emerging situations being studied, while attending to power relations at the moment of doing research as well as write-up thereof. In the course of my discussion I showed how realist arguments in relation to the practice of ethnography, which account for the research endeavor in terms of its likelihood of getting closer to "correct" understanding of social realities, can be compared with more constructivist-oriented arguments.

I showed meanwhile how the particular realist argument supported by Hammersley (1990, 1995) and his attendant rules for participation in the scientific/research community are seen as restrictive by, for example, those who do not subscribe to this particular theory-testing approach to science. His approach to theorizing itself is not uncontested – even by those who concur with a realist-oriented view of scientific activity.

I made a case for an alternative approach to ethnography, which does not grant the same power to the ethnographer's language as is afforded within a realist approach. I suggested that critical race theorizing (with its focus on narrative construction as a methodology) can still move in the direction of trying to justify research with respect to a realist warrant (as in Parks's discussion, 2007). But it can also move in a more constructivist-oriented direction – as in Parker and Lynn (2002) and Ladson-Billings (2003). I suggested that certain arguments from a more general critical theoretical orientation such as that, say, expressed by Habermas in alliance with Derrida, coupled with Collins's understanding of Black feminist thought, can support non-realist interpretations of the doing, and justification, of ethnography. I proposed that because attention is given here to how our ways of *knowing* are linked to ways of *being* (and human relating) in social life, this style of ethnography reflexively examines the *social relations of research* as endorsed by, for example, Douglas (1998) and Walby (2007). I therefore suggested that more conventionally oriented ethnographic research, which swings in the dominant direction of treating its claims in terms of a realist warrant, needs to be revisited with this in mind.

6.7.2 Extending Research Options

My discussion in this chapter has revolved around my offering glimpses of how new forms of ethnography can proceed with the purpose of making a difference toward the quality of our human relationships (in terms of some vision of social justice, which itself becomes explored as part of the research process). I propose that in order to activate this potential of ethnographic research to thus "make a difference," ethnographers should orient themselves so that they:

- Recognize that at the moment of involvement in social settings, the language that one uses in interaction with others, as well as the examples that one sets in one's own mode of interaction, all can be seen as part of the situation, contributing to its unfolding.
- Pay attention to people's expressed concerns with inequalities and consider, with them, options for seeing and acting – as part of one's inquiry efforts.
- Write up reports/narratives without trying to authorize one's accounts as referring to facts and explanations independently of concerns that one is bringing to bear in seeing and understanding. This involves highlighting one's values/concerns and making explicit the way in which one is treating the status of one's account as serving to ignite social discourse and extended considerations for action around these, as other, concerns (as expressed and presented by others).
- Write up reports/narratives in a manner that tries to "touch" audiences, thus activating their empathy – as part of a recognition that authors carry some responsibility for the way in which their reports become received and possibly used within the wider social fabric.
- Try to facilitate forums for ethnographers to participate in wider social dialogue around the issues that they see as raised via their close involvement in the social settings into which they have been inquiring. This is consistent with Gergen and Gergen's proposal for inquirers to become "active participants in forging generative, communicative relationships, in building ongoing dialogues and expanding the domain of civic deliberation." (2003, p. 598)[174]

---

[174]Gergen and Gergen make this point in the context of their concern that although "much has been said about the value of global forums of exchange, national dialogues on prejudice, and the revitalization of communities (the 'civil society') ... efforts to achieve these ends have been scattered and have infrequently included social science researchers" (2003, pp. 598–599).

Chapter 7
Action Research: Exploring in Action the Meaning of Research as Change in Complex Living Systems

7.1 Introduction

In this chapter I discuss action research as an inquiry approach that can be harnessed toward exploring systemically concerns around racism and socially sedimented polarization as rendered problematic by actors in everyday situations. Before I look into its possibilities in this arena, I first show how action research has been conceived by different researchers as involving a conscious orientation of inquirers to concentrate on knowing as a form of action.

In outlining their view of the manner in which action research develops "extended" epistemologies that "go beyond orthodox empirical and rational Western views of knowing," Reason and Bradbury indicate that action research draws attention to, and encapsulates an understanding of, "knowing not just as an academic pursuit but also as the everyday practices of acting in relationship [with others] and creating meaning in our lives" (Reason & Bradbury, 2001, p. 9). In his presentation on participatory action research (2004), Reason likewise expresses that action research brings with it new understandings and definitions of "knowing" (new in terms of traditional Western epistemologies). As he states:

> If we want our research to be a truly living inquiry, we must go beyond the orthodox empirical and rational Western epistemology. We must consider ways of knowing that are rooted in everyday experience, and are expressed through story as well as through concepts, and which directly support our [people's] practice. (2004, p. 4)

Weil expresses a similar account of action research when she indicates that it involves

> inquiry that is borne out of the guts of problem situations that matter deeply to those who are living with them and within them ... who continually have that hollow feeling, that deep sense of unease that is seldom relieved by the processes, the procedures and outcomes of traditional forms of research and collaboration with universities. (1999, p. 2)

She elucidates that action research can be considered as inquiry

> undertaken with the intention of making a difference not through just a report, academic papers and dissertations, but in the real time of people's living and struggling with difficult and perplexing problems. (1999, p. 2)

N. Romm, *New Racism*, DOI 10.1007/978-90-481-8728-7_7,
© Springer Science+Business Media B.V. 2010

Action research thus entails working with, while at the same time making a difference within, what Weil calls "complex living systems" (1999, p. 2).

Action research can be said to embody the idea that, as Argyris and Schön put it, people "are in the situations they try to understand, and they help to form them by coming to see and act in them in new ways" (1996, p. 36). According to Argyris and Schön, action research contributes to the development of processes of "making things under [within] conditions of complexity and uncertainty" (1996, p. 37).[175]

Douglas (citing Romm in Flood, Romm, & Weil, 1997) summarizes her interpretation of the relevance of action research for her work addressing institutional discrimination:

> I began to understand my research as not simply an attempt to generate conceptual knowledge about change, institutional discrimination and equality of opportunities, but as a mechanism for impacting on the status quo. I wanted to experience research *as* change not just *for* change. (Romm, 1997; Douglas, 2002, p. 250)

Douglas emphasizes that in action research as she sees and practices it, knowing is not considered as an endeavor of forwarding conceptualizations that in turn might (later) "inform" people's quest for change. Knowing itself needs to become involved in what she (citing Schön, 1983) calls the "messiness of the 'swampy lowlands' . . . where individuals' perceptions, meanings and behaviors are entangled, and where what is being sought is often not clear" (2002, p. 250)

Douglas further clarifies (in Skype conversation with me around this issue, July 2008[176]) that as she understands it, those involved in inquiries "have the potential to consciously think about research as being a powerful intervention in any system – so as soon as I set out to inquire, the questions I ask will impact on the people." She continues:

> If research is simply to produce knowledge [as Hammersley suggests] then we do not have to worry about the questions and how we frame them. But if we believe that research is already an intervention and that questions are powerful and questions influence people in ways we do not understand always objectively – if we take that as a given – then we have a responsibility to think about the questions we ask and how we frame them. (Skype conversation, July 2008)

---

[175] Argyris and Schön label their proposed version of Action Research as *Action Science* (1974). They state that *Action Science* can be used to facilitate people's learning across alternative ways of asking and answering questions – from "single loop learning" to "double loop learning." They suggest that facilitators of action research processes may require some "detachment" in order to observe and locate people's possible defensiveness (1991, pp. 86–87). Whyte, who labels his own approach Participatory Action Research (PAR), avers that "Action Science calls for a [more] detached observer to document in detail the intervention process" (Whyte, 1991, p. 97). He indicates that he prefers to see (professional) researchers as *participants themselves involved in the action*, aiding the creation of new lines of action. For an overview of this debate, including accounts of different definitions of participatory action research, see Rahman (1991, pp. 14–18), Gaventa (1991, pp. 123–131), Flood and Romm (1996a, pp. 134–145), and Ellis and Kiely (2000).

[176] We held this conversation specifically in relation to her reading of my draft of this chapter – as part of a series of conversations toward the writing of the book being co-authored by Douglas, myself, and Weil exploring the *Dynamics of Everyday Institutional Racism*.

I added (as part of our conversation) that she seemed to be saying that "research *as* change" means that "you cannot separate out the research from the impact"; and it is for this reason that we have a responsibility to think about possible impacts. I mentioned that in my book I was attempting to put more flesh on the statement that research is not just *for* change, but is *already* change.

7.1.1 Action Research as an Inquiry Orientation in Relation to Alternatives

In trying to locate the origins of action research as an orientation to inquiry, Reason indicates that these

> are broad – they lie in the work of Lewin [for example, 1946] and other social science researchers around at the end of World War II; in the liberationist perspective that can be exemplified in Paulo Freire (1970); philosophically in liberal humanism, pragmatism, phenomenology and critical theory; and practically in the work of scholar-practitioners in many professions .... (2006a, pp. 187–188)

Considering the work of Freire in advancing a "liberationist perspective," Torres points out that "Freire's techniques [as an educationalist] for literacy teaching have all been adopted and adapted to fit a thousand projects where the learning situation forms part of a social conflict situation" (2002, p. 119). He indicates that Freire's ideas were able to take root especially in the 1960 s in Latin America, where "popular movements were able to organize political mass activities, sometimes confronting the capitalist state." He explains that "the 1960 s represents a period during which a political pedagogy like Freire's could arise in Latin America and have an impact on progressive educational settings worldwide" (2002, p. 121). He points out that in Freire's approach to (primarily) adult education, the process of "linking theory with practice in an indissoluble unity" becomes a "criticism of culture and the construction of knowledge" in a cultural revolution that implies the "conscious participation of the masses" (2002, p. 125). As Torres indicates, this approach to education evokes a co-inquiry process that is "anti-authoritarian" – "where 'teachers' and 'students' are teaching and learning together" (2002, p. 126).

McKay and Romm point out how Freire's approach to learning implies an inquiry process where people act as "co-investigators" in developing what he calls a "critical awareness of reality" (Freire, 1978, p. 78, as cited in McKay & Romm, 1992, p. 95). It is in this sense that Freire's approach to co-operative knowledge construction with a view to emancipatory social transformation becomes an action research endeavor (McKay & Romm, 1992, pp. 95–96).

Rahman meanwhile emphasizes that in order to "improve the possibility of liberation," the "gap between those who have social power over the process of knowledge generation, and those who have not" needs to be addressed as part of any liberation project (1991, p. 14). This means that attempts at "liberation" are not accomplished "by the masses being mobilized by a vanguard body with the latter's [apparently] advanced consciousness" (1991, p. 14) – as this reproduces the "control over the social power" that is invested in knowledge production (1991, p. 14).

Reason remarks that none of the origins of action research that can be located (whether in North America and Europe or in contexts such as Latin America and Africa) can be considered as "well linked to the mainstream of academic research in either North America or Europe" – where, as he understands it, "quantitative hypothetico-deductive research retains a dominance" (2006a, p. 188). He maintains that although this hypothetico-deductive tradition (see Chapters 3 and 4) has been "challenged by qualitative and interpretive approaches to research [see Chapters 5 and 6], the emphasis of the latter has been on *representation of the world* rather than action within it" (2006a, p. 188, my italics). This statement of Reason's is consistent with Hammersley's realist interpretation of, say, interviewing and of ethnographic research (see Chapter 5, Section 5.3.1.1; and Chapter 6, Sections 6.1 and 6.1.1), which Reason considers as indeed the leading manner of conceiving qualitative and interpretive approaches. Reason therefore states that the action research approach, where realism is challenged in favor of a more pragmatic approach to knowing, "inhabits the margins of academia" (2006a, p. 188).

In explicating his realist understanding of what is properly involved in the scientific enterprise, Hammersley makes the point (in opposition to pragmatic epistemological arguments) that social research as science should *not* be seen as an "intrinsically political enterprise" (1995, p. 80). He comments that:

> We find such views [of research as necessarily political] among feminists, critical ethnographers and many advocates of action research. .... This perspective suggests that rather than being primarily concerned with producing knowledge, research should be directed toward maximizing the success of particular practical or political projects. It seems that many "antiracists" adopt this view. .... On this basis research is required to serve the goal of bringing about social change of appropriate kinds and may even be judged primarily in terms of its success in this respect. (1995, p. 80)

Hammersley insists that this is *not* the basis on which good social science is to be judged. The basis for judgment should be an assessment of the efforts that have been made during the inquiry process to "produce knowledge" – where knowledge is defined in terms of a realist epistemology. To the extent that action research shies away from realism, Hammersley considers that it rightly inhabits a space in what Reason calls the "margins of academia" (2006a, p. 188). That is, he believes that academia should not embrace approaches that tie knowledge production to the pursuit of political goals.

Looking at, and reviewing, the contention around the "political" character of action research, Coghlan and Shani state that this is not in their view a preserve of action research – because, for them, *all* research can be considered as political. Their argument is that action research can be considered as "particularly political" in the sense that it explicitly

> emphasizes democratic participation, questioning, reflection, and is directed toward change, all of which may be threatening to existing organizational [and wider societal] norms. (2005, p. 544)

That is, action research is directed toward contributing to change toward more democratic, reflective and humane modes of human existence and is (pragmatically) inclined toward facilitating these developments. This inclination of action research can be seen as a style of research orientation that is what Zuberi and Bonilla-Silva call "unabashedly 'political' in the sense that it is deeply . . . rooted in the liberation movements of past, present and future" (2008, p. 334). Zuberi and Bonilla-Silva point out that as they see it, the epistemology of racial emancipation (which they espouse) is "political" not in the sense of "doing politicized, one-sided sloppy research," but in the sense of expressing "*solidarity* with the aspirations for social justice of oppressed people everywhere" (2008, p. 334). In line with the authors whom I have cited in earlier chapters who indicate the importance of tying episte-mological considerations (and definitions of "validity") to the (practical) forwarding of "social justice," many action researchers claim that action research is particularly suited to the task of instantiating research *as* change (as Douglas, 2002, p. 250, summarizes it).

7.1.2 Deliberations Around the Epistemological Underpinning of Action Research

Not all of those self-defining their research as action research adopt what can be called a pragmatic epistemology (of the kind criticized by Hammersley). For example, Lewin, whom O'Brien (2001, p. 1) notes coined the term "action research" as research oriented toward "leading to social action," can still be interpreted as adopting a realist epistemology. Lewin proposes an action research cycle composed of planning, action, and fact-finding about the results of action as a way to "organize research on the conditions and effects of various forms of action" (1946, p. 35). The connection between knowing and acting (or theory and practice) is thus conceptualized in terms of the idea that "good theorizing" about the results of action serves as a guide to generating effective action.[177] Seen in this way, as Greenwood and Levin remark, action research as a way of developing theory in action became synonymous with organizing

> a so-called natural experiment, meaning the researchers in a real-life context invited or forced participants to take part in an experimental activity. This research approach still fell very much within the bounds of conventional applied social science. (1998, p. 17)[178]

---

[177]Smith states that Lewin can hereby be seen as trying to "provide a rational basis for change through research" (2001, p. 3).

[178]In similar vein, Gustavsen argues that Lewin's conception of how hypotheses are formulated and tested in the action research process still relies too much on the input/control of the professional researcher and is not sufficiently dialogically oriented (1992, pp. 19–21). Romm and Adman (2000) point out that when action research is undertaken in terms of a *dialogical definition of knowledge*, the research process itself is assessed for validity in terms of its contribution to engendering more dialogical human relationships.

Viewing action research as a form of applied social science, the suggestion then is that by researchers working with people in practice to explore the effects of action, together they can develop utilizable knowledge (conventionally defined). The implication is that a realist approach, *oriented to developing knowledge* regarding "real life" social conditions and effects, provides the *necessary information that can in turn be utilized by actors as a basis for pursuing their goals.* This would be tantamount to what Douglas (2002, p. 250) calls research *for* change (rather than research *as* change).

Another way of interpreting action research in realist terms is espoused by McKernan who himself supports a realist epistemology as the basis for action research – albeit not the kind of realism associated with the philosophy of hypothetico-deductivism (implicit in, say, Lewin's approach). In responding to the pragmatic approach espoused by Reason, McKernan states that he himself feels that action inquiry is "quite better suited to the philosophy of realism" (2006, p. 204). McKernan locates an "absence of a supportive philosophical position in much action research" and argues that processes of action research are often

> wooden and mechanical, setting up a design for problem statement, hypotheses, experimentation, action monitoring, and conclusions in aid of solving some practical problem. (2006, p. 206)

He claims that the pragmatic orientation of action researchers geared to "solving some practical problem" means that action research can become "too baldy about utility" (2006, p. 204). He suggests that because of this practical bent, the knowing component of research may become lost under the pressure of "simple problem solving" (2006, p. 205). He believes that a better way of conceiving and practicing action research is by bearing in mind that:

> Because all practitioners are actors in social settings, then surely the aim of research is not merely to describe, interpret, or even collect knowledge about the world but to *develop a more profound situational understanding and knowledge* with which to reason about and guide us in choosing appropriate and improved behavior for action in social settings. (2006, p. 205, my italics)

McKernan's view is that if we envisage action inquiry with this in mind, then it is possible to criticize the "positivist hypothetico-deductive tradition of research," while not foregoing the quest to develop "a more profound situational understanding and knowledge" than might be supplied within a hypothetico-deductivist orientation (2006, p. 205).

McKernan draws on the epistemology of critical realism (akin to the realist epistemology that I elucidated in Chapter 6 with reference to the work of authors such as Layder, 1993, and Bell, 1995) to argue that "what we are after" is a "sophisticated set of values, embedded in practical, moral, and theoretical concerns" (2006, pp. 204–205). Critical realism, as he sees it, allows us to concede that there are values behind the quest for knowledge production, namely, "the deliberate attempt at securing justice, rationality and perhaps emancipation of actors" (2006, p. 206). But recognizing these value commitments *need not preclude positing a reality (albeit a changing one) toward which knowing processes are directed.* He explains:

> The conduct of action research becomes part of the reality situation and influences the outcomes that it describes. It is a critical aspect of the new reality. As such, research is a dialectic between a creative conceptualizor [inquiring and developing concepts] and the social setting it engages with. (2006, p. 206)

McKernan thus advocates action research as oriented toward exploring "reality situations" – underpinned by a critical realist stance. Within this stance, it is admitted that knowing is itself a force influencing the development of social reality, and is as such part of social reality, while research is oriented to developing "knowledge with which to reason about and guide us" (2006, p. 205).

In responding to McKernan's claims regarding realism as a better philosophical basis for action research than pragmatism, Reason indicates that his own pragmatism amounts to asserting the primacy of the practical ("I act") as a better starting point for human being than "I think" (2006b, p. 207). He indicates that as he reads the arguments of those supporting a critical realist position, "they are overconcerned with the problem of reality rather than the issue of practice" (2006b, p. 207). He suggests that he is not after a "theory of action" (that McKernan asserts that he is after), because this is what a *theorist* rather than a *reflective practitioner* would want (2006b, p. 208, my italics). He argues that theorizing (in his terms) "grows out of in-depth examination of [social] experience and new narratives" (2006b, p. 208). Here Reason's suggestion can be seen as aligned with a view of "restorying" as I explicated it in Chapter 5, Section 5.7.1 – where stories are seen as re-created as people develop their capacities to review their experiences and understandings.

This is also epistemologically consistent with McKay and Romm's (1992) interpretation of Freire's work through a non-realist position. We cite in particular Freire's conception of reality as dialogically defined. We argue that through his suggestion (1985) that people can come to see the world as "an object of critical reflection" (via a process of dialogue with others) he tries to encourage people to "recognize their capacity to participate in defining its character so that they do not blindly accept some given view of what 'reality' is" (1992, p. 10).[179] We suggest furthermore (1992, p. 117) that Freire encourages people to consider reality as a symbolic construction whose face should never be cast in concrete – thus leaving space for people to recognize the non-finality of any categorizations, which become seen as negotiable constructs to be revised through social interaction.

7.1.3 Strategies for Action Research as Living Inquiry

In his account of learning and change through action research, Reason outlines three broad strategies for action research practice that he believes have been illustrated

---

[179]McKay maintains that in calling for participation in processes of knowledge production Freire recognizes that not all social actors need enter the education situation with equal potential, creativity, or contributions. She suggests therefore that all social actors should participate to their *fullest ability* (1990, p. 98).

with examples (2001, p. 3). (These strategies are also detailed in Torbert, 1998, 2001; Reason & Torbert, 2001.)

- First-person action research/practice involves skills and methods to enhance the ability of people to foster an inquiring approach to his or her own life.
- Second-person action research/practice addresses our ability to inquire face-to-face with others into issues of mutual concern. The point of engaging in this inquiry (which often takes the form of small groups being set up to reflect upon participants' actions) is to "enhance our respective first-person inquiries" (2001, p. 5).
- Third-person action research/practice (which presupposes first- and second-person research/practice capacity) aims to create a wider community of inquiry – at a larger social scale – involving persons who may not necessarily be known to one another (Torbert, 2001, p. 256). Reason argues that although some work has been done in this arena (he cites in particular the work of Gustavsen), "one of the significant challenges in the field is how to develop third-person approaches to action research that engage large systems in democratic inquiry" (2001, p. 6).

Reason considers innovations in large-scale third-person action research as "in some ways the leading edge of action research practice" (2001, p. 7). He indicates that as he sees it, "first- and second-person inquiry will in many ways be fruitless unless at least in modest ways you are able to influence the wider third-person community to explore the issues that have engaged you" (2001, p. 7). He cites as an example of this attempt in Britain the work of Douglas (whose summary definition of action research I provided above).

Reason indicates that Douglas began her inquiries reflecting on the question of how "Black professional women like herself could thrive rather than simply survive in their organizational lives." (See also Chapter 5, Section 5.3.1.) Her *first-person* inquiry process included "reflective autobiography, careful recording and reflection on day-to-day activities, and experimentation with novel forms of behavior." Reason indicates that Douglas's *second-person* inquiry processes included "establishing a co-operative inquiry group of Black women" as well as "developing inquiring dialogue with Black and White members of the organizations with which she worked as a professional consultant." He suggests that her *third-person* inquiry processes were more tacit. These involved "increasing the amount of discussion and dialogue about issues of race and gender in the organizations she worked with, and influencing the development of policy and practice" (2001, p. 7).

And he indicates that, in a yet wider context, her write-up of her insights as developed via these inquiries

> provide us all with a better understanding of how institutional racism is built and maintained through very complex and subtle processes involving both Black and White people and their mutual inability to talk about questions of race. (2001, p. 8)

He states that her work suggests that we need to

address these issues at a level of third-person inquiry, while recognizing that this work cannot be undertaken except through processes which invite all those involved to engage [also] with ... first- and second-person inquiry. (2001, p. 8)

In Section 7.2.3, I point to Douglas's reflections on such co-inquiry processes in the context of her involvement in the *Through a Hundred Pairs of Eyes* anti-racist training and development program (Weil et al., 1985). (I base my account on her reflections as recorded in her thesis (1998) and as expressed in Skype conversation with Weil and me, June 2008.)

7.1.4 Dearth of Examples of "Race-Conscious" Action Research

Douglas's work (with others) in Britain can be considered as an example offering action inquiry options for addressing the complex and subtle processes that serve to maintain institutional racism. However, as Reason indicates, this is only one example, which needs to be carried further forward (as also encouraged by Douglas). Bell makes the point that in the USA, meanwhile, "race" is still not a common ingredient in the action research literature and has hardly entered the discourse (2001, p. 48). She indicates that when she was in graduate school, she herself was heavily influenced by the book *The Death of White Sociology* edited by Ladner (1973). It was this book that opened her eyes "to the idea that research could facilitate social justice and radical organizational change" (2001, p. 48). Throughout her graduate studies, she kept trying to integrate what she knew about Black sociology, with the arguments supporting action research that she found in certain writings (e.g., Lewin, 1951; Freire, 1970; Mitroff & Kilmann, 1978). But she found these efforts frustrating as she rarely found "references made to critical race theory or acknowledgement given to Black scientists for their contributions to the action research genre" (2001, p. 48). She suggests that perhaps this is not surprising because, following Nkomo (1992), she indicates that topics of "race, racism and institutional racism have been ignored in the managerial literature until very recently" (2001, p. 49). She laments that "an eerie silence [still] lurks when it comes to discussing action research techniques to dismantle racial oppression" (2001, p. 49).

In this context (in the USA), Bell considers it important to revitalize "the discourse between Black liberation research [such as developed as part of the civil rights movement] and participatory inquiry" (2001, p. 49). Her suggestion is to use racialized public occasions as action research opportunities to "deconstruct the forces of oppression" while identifying "allies, both within and across racial lines, who are also seeking ways to resolve the race question" (2001, p. 56).[180]

---

[180]Gazel reports on her own efforts to "walk the talk" in developing multiracial discourses. She points to efforts at applying a Freirian pedagogical approach – in which she has worked with over 3,000 students from "diverse racial, ethnic and class backgrounds" toward developing a "Multi-Racial Unity Living Experience [MRULE]" (2007, p. 533). She points out that the MRULE program is "sustained by a world-embracing vision for social justice, consistent challenges to the

Bell's concern with what she sees as a dearth of race-talk in (much) action research echoes Zuberi and Bonilla-Silva's more general concern with what they see as the relative absence of "race-affirming" approaches in social inquiry. In similar fashion to Bell, they advocate race-conscious styles of research, which they believe can "ultimately help to develop *real* communication across racial boundaries," and serve to "produce the knowledge and practices that can ... help abolish race as a category of exclusion" (2008, p. 333).

7.1.5 Examples Discussed and Revisited

In the two examples that I discuss in this chapter, I take forward Zuberi and Bonilla-Silva's suggestion regarding developing more possibilities for communication; and I indicate how the action research strategies proffered might serve as mechanisms for people to mutually explore ways of working in practice past "categories of exclusion" in their social relations. The first discussed example is that of Weil et al. (1985), as recounted in Douglas (1998) and Weil (1999) and as further reflected upon by both Douglas and Weil (in conversation with me through Skype communication, June 2008[181]). I see this example as providing an innovative way of setting up inquiry processes for people to engage with forms of new racism (in this case in organizational contexts in Britain). I indicate specifically how the "trigger method" proposed by Weil et al. (which makes use of video scenes with the purpose of triggering people's widening of horizons and attendant options for action) may be helpful for trying to trigger new patterns of response in the various organizational/social contexts in which people may be operating (in Britain as elsewhere). The idea behind the trigger method is to set up a forum for people to learn – through engagement in first-, second-, and third-person inquiry – how different patterns of influence may be interwoven in society, allowing them to develop "networked inquiry" (as Weil, 2008, in Skype conversation, summarizes it).[182] As I discuss the mode of inquiry, I point to its relevance to debates around knowing as social intervention.

The second example that I discuss involves a computer-aided manner of developing democratic dialogue through a structured design process (SDP) in face-to-face and virtual communication contexts with a view to developing understandings that support transformative actions. The computer software used to structure the dialogue is explicitly presented (by those explicating the processes) as aiding the

racial status quo from a macro and micro perspective, and the application of race, class, and gender intersectionality to theory and practice" (2007, p. 533).

[181]This Skype conversation was held between us around my write-up of their work in this chapter (along with other conversations around our co-authoring of our book exploring the *Dynamics of Everyday Institutional Racism* (Douglas, Romm, & Weil, in preparation).

[182]Earlier work in which Weil was engaged with adolescents and also with children led to her development of the trigger method as a way of opening up areas for collective engagement through preparatory co-inquiry in pairs and trios (personal communication by email, July 2008).

collective creation of inferences via a form of abductive logic (Christakis & Bausch, 2006). The example of this process that I detail in the chapter is set around concerns in Cyprus – with the focus being on a peace movement aimed at depolarizing the island (polarized along socially sedimented "Greek-Cypriot" and "Turkish-Cypriot" lines). I consider this as an(other) example taking up Reason's challenge to institute not only first- and second-person, but also third-person research practice as a way of generating research with "social influence." Again, with reference to this example, I revisit debates around the link between inquiry and action raised in earlier chapters.

7.2 Weil et al.'s Action Inquiry Around Institutional Racism in Organizational Contexts in Britain

7.2.1 Some Contextual Background

In order to provide some background to the anti-racist training package developed by Weil et al. (1985) to facilitate action inquiry around institutional racism, Douglas (1998) discusses the package in relation to other forms of racism awareness training that had been used to date (in the 1970 s) in Britain. She indicates to start with that:

> An objective exploration of Racism Awareness Training is difficult, as it became the site for enacting much of the confusion, challenge, dilemmas and contradictions of creating racial equality in organizations. (1998, Chapter 4, p. 24)

Having indicated the perspectival character of her understanding, she offers a number of points that she considers as weaknesses of the way in which racism awareness training had been hitherto undertaken. She outlines these as follows:

• Firstly, she indicates that:

> I perceived this solution [to issues of inequality] to be a "quick fix", arising from the establishment's anxiety to do something, rather than uncover and deal with more fundamental issues and processes of racial discrimination, disadvantage and oppression. (1998, Chapter 4, p. 25)

She remarks that she is not alone in this view, as many Black activists and racial equality specialists likewise considered that racism awareness training can divert attention away from "many of the other critical aspects of institutional discrimination": By placing attention on *individual action*, organizations could "avoid issues of structural and systemic change" (1998, Chapter 4, p. 25).

• Secondly, she states that

> in many instances Racism Awareness Training was contracted out of the organization, or consultants or specialists were brought in to do this work with very little intervention and/or support from the mainstream organization. (1998, Chapter 4, p. 25)

Organizations were thus able to "abdicate responsibility" for the process.

- Thirdly, she argues that the work of Racism Awareness Training "took place in a climate of rivalry and competition ... which bred a culture of defensiveness." She elucidates that:

> There was an *assumption* that critique equated to attack, that feedback must be negative and that evaluation was a process in which a detached observer told the practitioner what's wrong with their practice. The notion of collaborators critically reflecting on their practice was completely absent. (1998, Chapter 4, p. 25)

- Fourthly, she contends that unfair expectations were placed on the training – as it was

> often assumed that at the end of a two or three day training event participants would be able to radically change not only their own practices but those of their organization. (1998, Chapter 4, p. 26)

- Fifthly, she mentions that individuals in this approach were considered to be "powerful actors" – and were treated as "fully self-determining in making choices that impacted on others and on organizational systems" (1998, Chapter 4, p. 26). The implication was thus that one could operate at the level of "the individual" to change their attitudes and hence their practices. (See also my discussion in Chapter 8, where I consider further critiques of individual-level foci.)

- Sixthly, she indicates her concern that many models of racism awareness programs "worked from the premise that the individual should be jolted into consciousness." She indicates that notwithstanding her view that "awakening" of individuals is important,

> when we confront a huge and complex problem, and we see and feel our responsibility while having no ways in which we may constructively respond to the problem, we are often overcome by powerlessness, and helplessness. (1998, Chapter 4, p. 26)

Elaborating on this last point, Douglas argues that it is her observation that:

> Many programs left participants much more aware but no more able to act, and possibly even more paralyzed by the greater insights. This produced distress and anger that were then projected back on to the training and trainees. (1998, Chapter 4, p. 26)

Douglas now indicates that in contrast to these kinds of approaches to Racism Awareness Training, she participated (with Weil and others) in a training and development initiative that "took a very different approach" (1998, Chapter 4, p. 30). This was a program called *Through a Hundred Pairs of Eyes* (Weil et al., 1985). She explains that "Susan [Weil], a white woman colleague and friend," and she herself "were involved in both the development of the video package [that was used] and in the design and delivery of the training that followed" (1998, Chapter 4, p. 31).[183]

---

[183]Douglas indicates that in order to develop the video scenes, Susan Weil (then employed at the Center for Staff Development at London University) "brought together a team of Black academics, professionals and practitioners in the Race Equality field" to develop the training video (1998, Chapter 4, p. 31).

7.2.2 *The* Through a Hundred Pairs of Eyes *Program*

In their Preface to their training guide to be used by trainers on the action inquiry program, Weil et al. explain the title of the guide as inspired by Marcel Proust's statement that:

> The only real journey ... would not be to go to new places but to see with new eyes, to see the world with the eyes of another person, or a hundred others, to see the hundred different worlds that each of them sees, that each of them is. (Proust, as cited in Weil, *et al.*, 1985)

Through this quotation they elucidate that the program aims to invite people – with others – to extend their horizons via à vis their dealings with institutional discrimination.[184]

In their Orientation chapter of the guide, they make the point that a variety of people in Britain, as elsewhere, including managers and trainers, have expressed concerns about:

> The ways in which individuals, whist not deliberately discriminating or considering themselves racialist ... may be involved in the perpetuation of racism in institutionalized form. (1985, p. 1)

They refer to a series of surveys (carried out by the Policy Studies Institute in London, 1983) that point to "the significantly different reality experienced by people of Afro-Caribbean and Asian origin in all areas of their working life." They cite the Policy Studies Institute as reporting that:

> This survey gives us a depressing picture of their economic lives ... in Britain today. They are more likely than white people to be unemployed and those who are in work tend to have jobs with lower pay and lower status than those of white workers. (Policy Studies Institute, 1983, as cited in Weil et al., 1985, p. 2)

Weil et al. go on to explain that:

> Racism entails the attribution of negative and/or fixed characteristics to a particular [defined] group. This is strictly a sociopolitical process since "race" has no biological meaning. .... A racist ideology can become deeply embedded in a society and its institutions, offering both a covert and overt justification for the unequal treatment of specific groups for specific purposes. Although racism takes different forms in different societies at different times, its operations can always be linked to historical and structural factors relating to the distribution of power. (1985, p. 2)

They indicate that *Through a Hundred Pairs of Eyes* has been developed around a focus on

> promoting change on a variety of interrelated levels. These include [a focus on]: individual behavior and an organization's ethos and culture as well as its policies, structures and practices. (1985, p. 2)

---

[184]Weil et al. made this guide available to certain people in strategic positions in organizations as well as to the trainers who would be facilitating the training (Douglas and Weil, in Skype conversation with me, June 2008).

They urge that "we need to design effective methods for helping others redesign their relationships and build healthy and productive inter-racial relationships" (1985, p. 3). They indicate also that "to stand on the sidelines is to accept the current situation" – and is not a "neutral" stance (1985, p. 3).

They state that the program is based on what they call "the subjective trigger method." The "triggers" around which people are asked to develop their responses are video scenes that were constructed by a team of Black professionals (for the purpose of the program) out of their cumulative experiences of life and recurring patterns of interaction within organizations (including those presenting themselves as "equal opportunity ones").[185] Each of the scenes is meant to

> raise important issues about the covert and overt behaviors, work practices, and organizational policies and structures (or their absence) which perpetuate the disadvantage of black women and men. (1985, p. 3)

As far as the content of the scenes is concerned, seen as a whole they are intended to portray not only the operation of racism, but also "behaviors and practices which oppress in respect of gender, class and disability" (1985, p. 4).

Weil et al. point out that the "subjective trigger approach" has the following features:

- It is a short (30–45 s) video portrayal of a [constructed] situation or action directed at the viewer.
- It involves the viewer as an active or potential participant.
- It stimulates the viewer's experience relevant to the development of understanding and skills for effectively responding to such situations.
- It provokes a response which is the basis for at least 1–2 h learning activity both in small and large groups (1985, pp. 3–4).

They suggest that when trainers/facilitators are using the method for the first time with participants, "a brief introduction to the trigger method can be useful, particularly since there is little in people's everyday experience to prepare them for someone on a screen provoking them to respond actively" (1985, p. 43). They also suggest that "at the outset it is also helpful to clarify why the trigger is a particularly effective method for addressing institutional racism" (1985, p. 43). Further, they propose that when using the method, trainers/facilitators should start off by presenting not only one scene (out of the 54) but a cluster of them and also allow an

---

[185]Weil indicates that the trigger scenes were intended to present situations that were "all too familiar and therefore to which people in different organizational contexts could relate" (personal communication by email, July 2008). Furthermore, the idea was that participants should be chosen from organizations with one of the criteria being that Black and White colleagues should be involved together. McIntyre (personal communication by email, May 2009) asked me about potential risks associated with "triggering emotions in the work place" and wondered what protection the staff had here (after the training). Weil et al. clearly tried to make provision for this by considering the training as oriented to helping people to address their different emotions (through processes of co-learning).

opportunity for group discussion around these, while providing space for "raising and processing the diverse responses." They indicate that it is this diversity (of responses that participants hear) that "helps to challenge 'frozen' ideas and behaviors and establish the foundation for new learning and change." They point out that "this can be particularly constructive in groups with black and white people if a climate conducive to learning has been established prior to the session and during warm-up activities" (1985, p. 43).

They emphasize that "dealing with racism in groups is always emotive. Group leaders therefore need the will and skill to help group members to work through and learn from these emotions and behaviors" (1985, p. 19). They caution that there is

> always the danger that unless the … learning process is managed well, individuals may be overpowered by the size of the task. It is therefore essential that before leaving the training session, each group member has identified specific strategies for creating change at both individual and organizational levels. (1985, p. 19)

They also suggest the trainers/facilitators may find it useful to post up certain guidelines for the group members to consider as principles to underpin their participation during discussion processes (1985, pp. 22–24). The guidelines suggest that participants concentrate, for example, on:

- *Behavior of others rather than "personality"*: this means that reference is made in the process of discussion to what a person *does* rather than what is supposed he or she *is*.
- *"More or less" rather than "either/or"*: here they suggest that thinking in terms of "more or less" and the "use of continua" when characterizing behavior avoids "trapping ourselves into thinking in terms of categories."
- *Sharing of ideas and information rather than giving advice*: they suggest that with this focus we "leave people to decide for themselves, in the light of their own goals in a particular situation at a particular time, how to use the ideas and information."
- *Exploration of alternatives rather than "answers or solutions"*: they explain that if people look for a variety of means or procedures to attain a goal, the less likely they will be to "accept prematurely a particular answer or solution."
- *Value to the recipient not the needs of the provider of feedback*: they indicate that "help and feedback need to be given and heard as an offer, not an imposition."
- *Appropriate timing and location*: they explain that "because the … use of personal feedback involves many possible emotional reactions, it is important to be sensitive to when it is appropriate to provide feedback."
- *"What is said" rather than "why it is said"*: they point out that focusing on the "why" can involve making assumptions about the motives for why people are giving the feedback – and "can prevent us from hearing or cause us to distort what is said."

Weil et al. continue in the guide to outline guidelines for organizing the discussion around the "trigger scenes," such as working in pairs and trios at first, followed by large group discussion (pp. 48–50). They indicate that the work in the pairs and the trios should involve a rotation of roles, with one person facilitating each time and the other(s) taking notes in relation to people's responses, as a precursor to their together reflecting on the patterns and differences across their different understandings of the trigger. To guide this process, Weil et al. offer a number of questions that can be considered by the participants (in relation to the trigger scenes), such as:

- How did I feel?
- What was I thinking?
- What would I probably do at this moment?
- What would I really want to do? Why?
- Is there anything I would like to do later on?
- Has a similar thing ever happened to me and what did I do then?
- What might I consider to be an anti-racist response?
- What would I expect of the others if I were to make such a response?
- What in the organization or group would make this difficult or easy? (Weil et al., 1985, p. 45)

As people work in pairs and trios around their responses to these questions, it is intended that they will strengthen their reflexive co-inquiry capacities as they listen to, and engage with, the different reactions to the various questions. This prepares for the more conceptual discussion and debate in the large group discussion, where attention is moved "from individual responses to the wider implications of institutional racism" (1985, p. 52).

Weil et al. suggest that processes of large group discussion are to be directed at "analyzing the organizational challenge (the individual in context)." This involves people considering

> what ways of working, and what organizational policies and structures might need to
> be developed and implemented, if an organization is to support individuals effectively,
> including their efforts to challenge racism. (1985, p. 52)

The purpose of the analyses created "at this stage" is to "help individuals to identify the positive outcomes which might result from honest and open scrutiny of organizational work practices and policies" (1985, p. 53). They propose that to achieve an effective discussion, questions involving the *content* of the discussion – "the issues, the tasks and the concrete aims"– need to be given attention, as well as the discussion *process* involving "the maintenance of effective working relationships and of a climate conducive to learning" (1985, p. 5).

7.2.2.1 Some Scenes and Guideline Questions for Consideration

In keeping with their view that trainers/facilitators should play a part in facilitating the content (and not only the process) of the various discussions, Weil et al. designed lists of "discussion questions" in relation to all of the video trigger scenes, which they state can be used to help "support discussion" around the issues arising from the scenes (1985, p. 54). Below I provide three examples of such scenes and attendant discussion questions as detailed in the guide.

Scene 24 (1985, p. 128)

Transcript

A black woman and a white man and camera meeting around table. The door opens and another white man enters the meeting room.

Man who has entered looks at white man and camera, excluding black woman. "What time are you finishing tonight? I need to prepare this room for tomorrow ..."

Black woman "About 6.15 (continues with work in a pre-occupied way) Yes?" (half look at colleagues).

1st white man (continues to ignore black woman, and looking at white man and camera) "So what time is it going to be then?"

Black woman (assertively) "At 6.15!" (looks at men, and around table). 1st white man continues to ignore her. 2nd white man looks away self-consciously, averting 1st man's and camera's eye contact. 1st white man looks at 2nd white man, shrugs, turns to camera expectantly, continuing to exclude black woman. Black woman looks at camera, and 2nd white man.

Weil et al. indicate that this trigger can be used to illustrate ways in which White people's verbal and non-verbal behavior can render Black people "invisible" – thus excluding and isolating them (1985, p. 128). They point to the way in which the response of the man seated at the table (which can be regarded as a "common response" in groups) can "heighten feelings [on the part of black people] of enforced solitude, betrayal (especially when espoused values and practices are in contradiction), anger and frustration" (1985, p. 128).

They suggest that this trigger can be used to show that "organizations need to consider the cumulative influence of such incidents on its workers and upon the overall effectiveness of the organization" (1985, p. 128).

To stimulate discussion around these issues, they offer certain discussion questions, as follows (1985, pp. 128–129):

- In such situations what strategies could be used to indicate support for the woman without undermining her authority?
- What opportunities do such situations offer for the following:

    (i) Reducing the likelihood of them recurring (i.e., strengthening an anti-racist ethos which is intolerant of such behavior)?

    (ii) Learning more about the day-to-day pressures on and experiences of black colleagues (i.e., strengthening a work climate conducive to learning)?

(iii) Strengthening team relationships (i.e., the capacity for mutual support in dealing with racism, and initiating change within the organization)?

- In what ways might the group's experience of this situation [i.e., the participants' understanding of the trigger] – and anti-racist responses to it – be used as a "case study" (to highlight organizational needs, and to draw attention to the need for anti-racist action at all levels)?
- In your organization, what might be the reactions to a formal or informal complaint by a black person regarding racism in the organization? Would attention be focused on the black person (i.e., "hypersensitive"); the white person (i.e., "racialist"); the organization (i.e., "racist")?
- If a black colleague were to tell you that such incidents occur covertly or overtly between 10 and 15 times a day for herself or himself or other black people in the organization, in which ways might you react or respond to such information? To what extent would your organization's espoused policies and practices influence your response?
- In what ways does your organization make it easy or difficult for people to raise issues of racism?

Scene 32 (1985, p. 141)

Transcript

White man to camera: "Now don't get me wrong ... I don't care if he's blue, green or yellow .... I just don't think he is the right sort of person for this job ... and I don't have to justify it (pauses). Frankly, I'm thinking that there are just too many people around here who are going overboard on this "race thing"... and it's causing too many waves ... It never used to be like this (Long challenging look to camera). "Don't you think it's gone too far ... really?"

Weil et al. indicate that "this trigger raises issues about the kind of resistance anti-racism and equal opportunities policies can meet when there are serious attempts to implement them." Furthermore, the trigger "illustrates the kind of defensive attempts to undermine progress in which viewers are likely to be invited to collude 'on the side of racism'" (1985, p. 141).

Their suggested discussion questions for group discussion around this trigger scene are, for example:

- What messages are being communicated by the phrase "I don't care if he's blue, green or yellow"?
- What is likely to make this person feel that it is legitimate to say these things? Why might you be expected to collude?

- What added skills do managers, interviewers, and other decision-makers require in dealing effectively with white workers who are resisting equal opportunities initiatives?
- In what ways can clear policies, procedures, and guidelines assist in situations such as these?
- How might you react if you were to hear a black person say to you or another that "white racism has gone too far … really" assuming it was spoken in the same reasonable tone as in the scene?

Scene 35 (1985, p. 144)

Transcript

Two black men (Afro-Caribbean and Asian), white man and camera seated around table, with a report in front of each person.

White man (referring to report): "Now in your report, the two of you stated the black view quite clearly but I'm surprised you didn't state the Asian view" (the two black men exchange looks; white man seeks support from camera).

Black man: "I think you've misunderstood how we've used the term "black'. Do the two of you not see Asians as black?"

The two black men await a reply from camera. White man looks self-consciously to camera

---

Weil et al. indicate that issues arising from this scene relate to the implicit support of the "hierarchy of color ideology," which "seeks to

> pit those who are lighter skinned (e.g., Asians) against those who are darker skinned (e.g., Afro-Caribbeans) through the granting of certain limited or economic privileges and status to those who are lighter skinned. In the past 20 years, a key issue in black consciousness has been recognition of how all people of color are targets of racism. (1985, p. 144)

They point out that this issue is related to the way in which the term "black" is increasingly being used in a political way, albeit that "there are many Asian and Afro-Caribbean people – particularly older ones – who choose not to refer to themselves as black." They comment that

> how ever they define themselves, their experiences in Britain include experiences of racism. It is just that the positive use of the term "black" to acknowledge this collective experience is a relatively new [political] phenomenon. (1985, p. 144)

Weil et al. also remark that meanwhile,

> white people who think of Asian and Afro-Caribbean people as two completely distinct categories are often unaware of how such divisiveness helps to perpetuate white control. (1985, p. 145)

They summarize that "work based on this scene enables viewers to deepen their understanding of these issues" (1985, p. 145). And they offer an indication of guideline questions for participants in group discussion to consider, such as:

- Why is it important that the "Asian view" has not been expressed [as such]? What might he [the white person] be expecting or hoping from this being accepted as a valid criticism [of the report]?
- How much confidence would you have in this man's commitment to working with black people as equals?
- What are the issues around the use of the term "black"? What does it mean to you? In what ways do these issues reflect white and black interpretations of history and black experiences in Britain today?
- What may inhibit some groups who are treated as "nonwhite" from wanting to be associated with this term? What pressures do white people put on black people to deny their association with terminology which reflects a political consciousness?

As indicated earlier, Weil et al. believe that the discussions that ensue in the pairs, trios, and the large group communications in relation to the set of video scenes (of which I have provided three examples above) should be of value to participants in acting differently within their organizations, so as to interrupt patterns of racism.

7.2.2.2 Model of Facilitation

Although Weil et al. (1985) do not explicitly spell out in the training guide a model of facilitation as involving the facilitation of discussion *processes* as well as the development of new *conceptions*, this model of facilitation can be seen as implicit. This is because the guide concentrates not only on proposing how facilitators might encourage (dialogical) *processes* for discussion around the "trigger scenes," but also provides the trainers with *content* ideas in relation to ways of conceiving institutional racism (which move beyond seeing racism as rooted primarily in individual prejudice).

Weil suggests (June 2008, in Skype conversation with Douglas and me) that given the then current dominant model of facilitators as expected to operate as "empty vessels" (see Chapter 5, Section 5.4.1, where I discuss this approach in the context of focus group interviewing) it was necessary to enable trainers to not feel "trapped" by this model. They needed to recognize that they could legitimately be "present" as persons as they participated in the discussions taking place. Douglas and Weil, who themselves facilitated training sessions with trainers as well as worked directly with (other) participants (as direct trainers), tried to embody this alternative view of facilitation by bringing themselves as persons into the sessions.

Douglas indicates (June 2008, in the same Skype conversation) that her way of "living" this view of facilitation was "right from the start bringing things about myself into it" so that participants came to expect her to be "present" as a person (and not therefore, in Weil's terms, as an "empty vessel"). She recalls that sometimes people would invite her views by asking her "what are your perceptions" – thus recognizing her as "not just a facilitator but also a person who might have a view." And Weil recalls further that "we certainly brought ourselves to it because of comments about the fact that how rare it was to hear a white woman and black woman in dialogue about racism." Douglas adds that "sometimes people would say I am learning from what you are doing and also watching you and Susan [Weil] relate." She indicates that the way in which people experienced her and Susan struggling with issues of racism was very "impactful" for people (as they commented on it at the time and indeed many years later too, when she "ran into them").

Weil remarks that although she agrees that they implicitly encouraged a model of facilitator presence, where "authenticity includes our own presence," she believes that they were "not as present as we may be now." In later work she came to work more fully with this understanding of facilitation. Douglas points out, though, that even at that time, because they themselves brought content to the sessions, they did expect other trainers (whom they worked with while using this facilitation style) to "add content too." She indicates that in any case, the guide made the assumption that one "needed the content and not just the process" and that trainers/facilitators "would be expected" to make such contributions.[186]

7.2.2.3   Evaluation and Monitoring of Learning

Weil et al. mention that the evaluation and monitoring of training and organizational change in the organizations where "trigger sessions are being used as one anti-racist strategy" is an issue that is beyond the scope of their guide to deal with. They do suggest, though, the importance of setting up a group (in each organization) focused around generating plans and policies that will enable the outcomes of training to be evaluated and monitored. They also refer those reading the guide to further reading on the subject of evaluation in their reading list; and they urge that "both quantitative and qualitative methods for assessing perceived and actual changes in the organization's actual work practices, policies and structures be used" (1985, p. 70). In processes of evaluation of the training package, they suggest that:

> Interviews, open-ended anonymous questionnaires, participant observation and case studies are [all] needed to complement statistics and official records (such as from monitoring activities) to ensure that more than one perspective is considered in evaluating the impact of anti-racist action on all levels of the organization. (1985, p. 70)

Meanwhile, they suggest that as far as feedback from participants on the course (the anti-racist training package) is concerned, "feedback and course evaluation

---

[186]This view as expressed by Douglas is in keeping with her views on active involvement of "interviewers" as persons in conversation – see Chapter 5, Section 5.3.1. As I point out in that chapter, this understanding of facilitation is also expressed by Gregory and Romm (2001), who offer a detailed exploration of how one might account for facilitators making content interventions in group processes – as an alternative to process models of group facilitation. We explain this with reference to our involvement in an action research project involving quality initiatives in a region of the National Health Service in the UK.

should focus on both the process and the content of learning" and should include feedback on:

  i) how leadership functions were exercised;
 ii) how the learning climate was developed and maintained;
iii) the design, content and process of the session and its relevance to identified aims and expectations. (1985, p. 72)

In their own facilitated sessions, the evaluation sheets that they designed for participants to fill in were complemented with "ongoing commentary" as sources of feedback (Weil, 2008, in Skype conversation with Douglas and me, June 2008). But Weil notes that there is no further documentation that could give us an indication of how people might have been influenced by the program because Weil et al., as the program designers, did/do not have an "ongoing relationship" with the people in the organizations who bought the material. She adds that, even if this documentation had been sought, trying to "say neatly this is what came out" may not be an appropriate way of speaking in this kind of complex systemic context.

In the next two sections I provide some indication of Douglas's (1998) and Weil's (1999) sharing with wider audiences their interpretations of what fairly could be said to have "come out" of the program. Then in Section 7.2.5, I refer to Douglas's and Weil's continuing (summary) reflections on how they regard the significance of the "trigger method."

7.2.3 Douglas's Reflections on the Program

Douglas reports on the program as part of her thesis on *Black Women Managers in Britain* (1998) by explaining that through her own participation in the program she learned "the challenge of establishing relationships across differences, but I also learnt that it was possible to do this." She indicates that as she sees it, the *Through a Hundred Pairs of Eyes* anti-racist program aided people to "cross one of the most difficult chasms that must be somehow crossed in the forming of such relationships" – namely, the chasm created by "the intense anger and rage of the oppressed person." She states that in many programs (in which she had been involved) "members of the oppressor groups (men or White people) experienced the anger as a personal attack (and sometimes it was!) and retreated. Their retreat triggered further anger" (1998, Chapter 4, p. 30). However, in this program – compared with others – she experienced "greatest success in establishing cross-race and cross-gender relationships that were not based on denial or avoidance of issues of racism and sexism" (1998, Chapter 4, p. 30). She indicates that she is "still not sure" that she has "been able to identify the various contributors" to making this possible, but she believes the following to have been important in supporting this shift:

• Based around video scenes;
• Shared analysis of Institutional Discrimination;

- Attention to building a climate conducive to learning about challenging issues;
- "Doing with" not "to."

7.2.3.1 Based Around Video Scenes

Douglas suggests (from her experience with the program) that it seemed important to start the discussions with reference to the constructed video scenes that were presented. This meant that people could "experience themselves being confronted with the dilemmas [that may arise] in context, and yet there is distance from the experience as 'it is only a response to a video scene'" (albeit that it presented situations that would be familiar to them) (1998, Chapter 4, p. 31). As participants took turns in listening to each other's responses (in pairs and trios) to the scenes, "they were able to hear the very different ways in which the same situation could be perceived and experienced by another." This, she believes, laid the groundwork for "important learning" (1998, Chapter 4, p. 31). She also believes that the variety of video scenes (triggers) that were supplied in the guide as a *totality* meant that people could see that they are not "ONE incident" but are expressions of "patterns of everyday incidents that sustain dynamics of institutional racism in multiple forms" (Skype conversation with Weil and me, June 2008). That is, the trigger method could "shine a light on complexity" and help people to understand that "something that seems small is more embedded [in recurring patterns] than you might think."

7.2.3.2 Shared Analysis of Institutional Discrimination

Douglas points to the way in which the training guide presented/conceived institutional discrimination as "a complex and seamless weave of interactions between individuals, institutional structures, culture and the taken-for-granted unobserved context of society" (1998, Chapter 4, pp. 32–33). She believes that it is important that institutional discrimination was presented as an "ideology that influenced the perceptions of individuals and informed their decisions and behaviors, rather than as inherent characteristics of the individual." She states that she observed that this manner of working with the concept of "institutional discrimination" meant that

> as participants engaged with the significance of this analysis, they were able to move from the labeling of individuals as "racist" or "sexist", and to seeing racism and sexism as learnt behavior internalized by **all** of us to a greater or lesser degree. With this came greater possibilities for empathy, dialogue and connection. It also allowed us to find ways of holding the paradox of justifiable rage and non-attributable blame (1998, Chapter 4, p. 32).

The theoretical understanding that was adopted to conceive institutional discrimination thus was helpful in "allow[ing] us to be better able to untangle personal responsibility from that of the collective" (1998, Chapter 4, p. 32). She recalls that this theoretical conceptualization became "liberating" and opened up more scope for people to engage openly with one another around the complexities of their responses.

7.2.3.3 A Climate Conducive to Learning About Challenging Issues

Douglas states that she regards it important that before the training events started "priority places were allocated to Black and White pairs – preferably from the same organization – and not to individuals"; and furthermore, "participants were asked to establish a learning contract that would continue beyond the training event." She suggests that these processes helped participants to "focus on some of the challenges that joint learning would present." She regards it as also important that in trying to establish a climate conducive to learning "we asked participants to consciously work with us in establishing a context . . . [embracing] the paradox of mutual support and acceptance *and* challenge" (1998, Chapter 4, p. 32). She sees all these processes as helpful in creating a climate conducive to learning about challenging issues.

7.2.3.4 "Doing with" Not "to"

Douglas attributes as a contributory factor to what she experienced as "success" of the program, the way in which she and Susan were themselves entering the process as co-learners rather than as "experts." She points out that learning around the racism that may have been at play in their relationships meant that she and Susan (as Black and White partners)

> sometimes very much struggled to find ways of tackling the dynamics of racism, while continuing to value the other, *and* the relationship. We did not mask the complexity of our relationship and tried to use it as opportunities for furthering our own and others' learning. (1998, Chapter 4, p. 32)

She regards it as

> interesting to observe that although we never stated this commitment explicitly to participants, on most courses participants commented on how much they had learnt from watching our own relationship. We modeled dealing with racism as a continual learning and unlearning process encompassing reflexive challenge and support. (1998, Chapter 4, p. 32)

Considered as a whole, Douglas concludes that she experienced the program – based on her involvement therein and her discussion with participants around it – as helpful in creating a new basis for relationships between Black and White colleagues. She indicates that she believes that one of the strengths of the program is the way in which it worked against the potentially "hostile climate breeding defenses rather than reflexivity" that she saw as associated with many other training programs. She indicates that in these programs – that fed the culture of defensiveness – "there was an *assumption* that critique equated attack, [and] that feedback must be negative" (1998, Chapter 4, p. 25). The *Through a Hundred Pairs of Eyes* program was able to generate what she calls "deep learning" – partly, she thinks, because of its not locating "racism" as a label to be applied to individuals (thus rendering them defensive) – but allowing for people to participate in genuine co-inquiry around their own and others' responses within their organizational contexts.

But she also learned subsequently as she reflected further "on the lessons learned" and as she further actively worked on equality issues in organizations, that "the legislative and organizational systems were not the only locations in which these struggles were fought." She points, for instance, to the importance of "Black self-help and/or political organizations" as also crucial locations for developing new ways of seeing and acting in relation to experiences of racism (1998, Chapter 4, p. 33).

7.2.4 Weil's Reflections on the Program

In her inaugural lecture reflections (1999), Weil offers commentary, inter alia, on the *Through a Hundred Pairs of Eyes* program. As part of her commentary on this, she indicates that she sees "complex human activity systems and interactions" as constituted by our "authoring different stories as we interact with and participate in and re-author our way through the complex interweaving of power, culture, context and everyday choice and action" (1999, p. 6). She remarks that the team of those involved in the development of the videos and the training guide for the *Through a Hundred Pairs of Eyes* program

> began with a shared frustration. We all knew there was more to challenging racism than having good paper-based equal opps policies or sheep dipping everybody in one or two day racism awareness training events. (1999, p. 6)

She points out that the purpose of the *Through a Hundred Pairs of Eyes* program was to enable "new forms of social and organizational learning as a process of inquiry" in relation to the perpetuation of institutionalized racism (1999, p. 6). She now invites her audience (at the inaugural) to imagine (based on one of the trigger scenes) that:

> You are meeting with a first rate colleague. He has asked for some time alone with you. You have no idea what it is about. In your view, and others, he has been doing a smashing job, and he agrees, "the work is going well". But that's not the problem. "It's the racism that I am finding impossible to deal with, and not the type you're thinking about. That would be easier. It's all the hot air about how nonracist you all are that gets me. But no one wants to look at what they are doing every day, much less listen to what my experience of working here is. I've tried everything I can so what do you think we should do?". (1999, p. 7)

She elucidates to the audience that the Black person in this trigger scene

> has given you feedback that until now has been invisible, unknown to you, about the nature of his everyday experience. Or, to put it another way, he has expressed the unspoken known that now demands a different kind of response. (1999, p. 7)

She indicates that this is the kind of scenario expressed via the video triggers – and in the light of the triggers people were invited to reflect, first individually and then in pairs and trios, on particular questions (such as those that I outlined in Section 7.2.2.1).

She states that through the processes of reflection where people considered the questions individually, in pairs, and in trios:

> Even very "clued up", reflective, insightful people were always shocked at what emerged. The range of interpretations, choices, assumptions, so diverse, often so unexpected. And

the many things that surfaced that were often unspoken, taboo subjects in the organization itself. (1999, p. 7)

She indicates further that as she experienced it,

the relief at being able to have these kinds of dialogues, to explore, to learn and surprisingly, to be challenged but also to support in such social learning, to engage in new forms of sense making without being beaten up . . ., was often so palpable. (1999, p. 7)

She points out that these processes were

only the beginning of a number of cycles of inquiry. We would ask people then to work with their notes from the reflective rotation of roles [as had been organized in the pairs and trios]. We would consider contradictions, tensions, and possibilities. We would begin to explore possibilities for action, often using drama to re-enact and re-play and expand repertoires of choice. (1999, pp. 7–8)

As can be seen here, Weil concentrates on the processes that she believes were helpful in aiding people to move toward expanding what she calls their "repertoires of choice" – so as to interrupt previously entrenched patterns of response that precluded this kind of learning.

She indicates that she considers that the training guide was itself helpful in its detailed content provision of "in depth historical and social analysis of the themes embedded in each scene, along with powerful questions to trigger inquiry beyond the individual level" (1999, p. 8).

And she refers to the way in which:

We would enact possibilities that might make a difference. We would explore where spaces for change could be created. What would that entail? What could people do individually and what did they need to do with others? What openings might fruitfully be created (in terms, e.g., if there were general concerns about client service quality)? What were the opportunities for building in ethnically diverse considerations early on, rather than as add-ons later? (1999, p. 8)

According to Weil, few of the participants

had ever experienced what it might mean to actively learn constructively from within this tension zone [working together in "mixed groups" to discuss these issues], in ways that both did not deny complex issues nor end up in polarization and anger. (1999, p. 8)[187]

She expresses that they experienced a "very different form of co-inquiry that enabled curiosity and genuine questioning of yourself and others rather than 'getting it right' as a group norm" – and that this experience was itself often transformative for people as they developed new ways of reflexive and challenging learning.

In Weil's account of this work, she indicates that she is aiming to provide audiences with what she calls "a taste of work that takes us into borderlands" (1999, p. 8). She argues that although social theorists "such as Habermas, Giddens, Layder,

---

[187]She elucidates that the work that she and Douglas facilitated involved working with Black and White groups (primarily in trainer training) and that people through this process experienced ways of engaging in critically reflexive and challenging learning that "did not lead to paralysis by guilt" (Skype conversation, June 2008).

and Foucault" have offered socially relevant social theorizing in relation to working "the borderlands," the implications of the theorizing "remain so under explored in terms of research into what it may mean to live, learn and make choices within these challenging and ever-shifting contexts for action" (1999, p. 8).

Using the *Hundred Pairs of Eyes* as an illustrative example of a critically reflexive way of doing action research, she indicates (in similar fashion to Reason in his rejoinder to McKernan, 2006) that action research should not be seen as directed toward "technical problem solving." Rather, it is about

> theorizing that was [in this case] grounded in everyday reality, but also guided by other influences, social, critical, and historical. All this was obviously not pain or struggle free. This is complex social learning at the edges of uncertainty. (1999, p. 8)

She argues that it is this kind of theorizing (grounded in "the everyday" while making provision for "learning at the edges of uncertainty") that she believes is properly associated with "action research." She summarizes that what she envisages here is "learning that is at once tense, scary, unsettling and simultaneously potentially exhilarating, renewing, re-humanizing without denying the contested contradictory living test" (1999, p. 8).

Weil thus uses the "story of the triggers" (as she puts it) to point to these kinds of possibilities for learning – which she believes became enabled via, and were embedded in, the *Hundred Pairs of Eyes* program (as well as other projects in which she has been involved). She remarks that this story is "part of the living history of SOLAR's shore" (1999, p. 8).[188]

She indicates that the program opened up for her new horizons at the time in relation to how organizational learning could be understood; and the program contributed to showing how action research can indeed work on multiple levels – involving first-, second-, and third-person inquiries (Skype conversation with Douglas and me, June 2008). (See also Section 7.1.3, where I proffered Reason's outline of these three levels of inquiry.)

7.2.5 Summary Reflections on the Significance of the "Trigger Method"

In continuing to reflect on the significance of the "trigger method" as an innovative mode of co-inquiry, Douglas and Weil offer their summary deliberations (in continued Skype conversation with me, June 2008). Weil proposes that the point of the trigger method was to introduce an approach that was neither just an "historical account" of racism" nor a "racism awareness" package, but a fresh way of developing inquiry in action. And she provides a metaphor to express the relief that she considers that people felt from "going into the core of the onion [institutional

---

[188]SOLAR stands for the Center for Social and Organizational Learning and Action Research founded by Weil at the University College Northampton.

racism] and all its mutually interacting layers." The trigger method allowed people to come to terms with "the cumulative impact of those incidents [drawn out by the video scenes] on the individuals." People came to understand that what seemed to be "one incident" can "spawn so many other things" and can be "spawned by so much that is unknown, such as historical events and patternings."[189] Douglas likewise indicates that through the development of the themes as raised by the triggers, something that "seems so small" is recognized to be "an expression of a very old and more complex process and that ONE incident can form so many other things."

Considering the importance of the trigger method for working at the "systemic" level to intervene in systems of power that sustain institutional racism, Douglas and Weil indicate that although they were trying to provide an opening to thinking about mutual influences on multiple levels, they cannot be sure of the "impact" on, for instance, policy levels. Douglas states that she "personally does not know" to what extent policy might have been impacted upon in different organizations and whether the triggers are "well suited" for strategic interventions. But she indicates that because people occupying strategic positions in organizations had been brought together in the training, it is possible that they did become more attuned to the unattended consequences of seemingly "micro" moments, and therefore became actively involved in progressing policies that could be supportive for challenging racism. What seemed crucial for both Douglas and Weil, however, was also the development of a human/humane social fabric constituted by people's capacities to recognize how that which may appear to be small incidents "carry so much more" – so that people faced with these kinds of incidents would be willing to expand their repertoires of possible responses. Any "implementing" of new policies in any case would require this (social) basis.

7.3 Revisiting the *Through a Hundred Pairs of Eyes* Program

In this section I revisit Weil et al.'s initiative by commenting primarily on three issues that I believe require further consideration, namely, the question of the "pragmatic" intent of this, as other, action research endeavors; the question of how practical "worth" might be evaluated; and the question of the development of "theorizing" as part of action research inquiry. As will be seen from the text below, these issues are very much interrelated within discussions on action research.

7.3.1 The Pragmatic Intent of the Inquiry Process

Douglas (1998) and Weil (1999) both comment on the importance to them of facilitating learning processes in the organizations with the intent to "make a difference" at and through the moment of inquiry. As Douglas puts it, it was

---

[189]She points out that she elucidated this in her notion of CRAR as outlined in Weil (1998).

important to her to find a way of enabling people to "constructively respond" to the problems raised, rather than their feeling "overcome by powerlessness, and helplessness" (1998, Chapter 4, p. 26). And as Weil notes, she considered it crucial that the program was geared to help people to "enact possibilities that might make a difference" (1999, p. 8).

Douglas makes the point (Skype conversation, June 2008) that as she sees it, the idea was for the "facilitators" of the inquiries/learning processes to enter the sessions as themselves learners, co-learning with others through the inquiries. She remarks that the "doing with" principle of action research was instantiated in this case as she and Weil (according to comments that she received) were able to exemplify a form of human relationship where people could indeed grapple with the tensions that may arise from racialized relationships, while finding ways of working through them (1998, Chapter 4, p. 32). She finds it important that people still commented on this aspect of the experience, as other aspects, many years later.

In their training guide, Weil et al. (1985) give much attention to the ways in which they urge trainers/facilitators to encourage human relationships between participants based on ways of relating that (as far as possible) do not reinforce and yet also do not deny power relationships. (See Section 7.2.2.) Their suggestions for organizing the inquiring process were thus directed toward developing enhanced systemic understandings coupled with an ongoing (more) reflexive quality of democratic relationship. In this sense, it was hoped that the inquiries would enact what Douglas calls research *as* change and not just "for" change (2002, p. 250).

Yet the question can still be raised as to whether the intent to "make a difference" by helping to set up the human relational conditions for people to constructively respond to their lived situations may be at the expense of developing sufficiently incisive theoretical understandings. This question relates to what Mehta calls the "wider debate regarding whether action research necessarily means privileging local action at the expense of analytic rigor" (2008, p. 242). Weil (1999, p. 8) herself alludes to this in her comment on the solution-oriented focus of some action research. While McKernan advises a realist epistemology as the grounding for action research so as to revive the idea of action research as geared to insightful *understanding* (2006, p. 205), Weil offers the suggestion that understanding in action is about "complex social learning at the edges of uncertainty" (1999, p. 8). She suggests that there is no need to consider that action research is geared to understanding social realities independently of people engaging in (critically reflexive) styles of interaction with others who are themselves trying to inquire around particular social issues and (located) problems. As she puts it:

> CRAR [Critically Reflexive Action Research] does not aim to create one representation of reality, but, rather, the unraveling (and documentation) of multiple realities and rhetorics that are in mutual and simultaneous interaction. (1998, p. 58)

Her argument is that CRAR as a form of action research is intended to *evoke new possibilities for experiencing our relationship with the world*, allowing us to live more comfortably with uncertainty in facing complex problems (understood as constructed collectively). (See also Weil, 1997.) By enabling people to gain a better appreciation – via the reflexive inquiries – of the complex dynamic of mutually interactive influences at the level of individuals, groups, organizational policies, culture, and wider-socio-political influences, she believes that the critical edge of action inquiry is not lost under the pressure of "action."

However, Johansson and Lindhult note that a concern that has been leveled by some "critical researchers" (as they name them) is that a practice-oriented action research process can all too easily run the risk of being "co-opted by dominant interests, and unable to recognize subjugating powers" (2008, p. 108). They admit that an answer by those more pragmatically inclined could be that this kind of criticism "seriously underestimates the practical knowledge of people, the intelligence inherent in praxis and the creative aspects of action in response to situations" (2008, p. 108). But they still feel that it is necessary to bear in mind the caution that it *is* important to find ways of exploring "asymmetrical power relations, [and] invisible structures that are restricting people" (2008, p. 110).

Johansson and Lindhult refer to the tension that they identify between those inquirers with a more "pragmatic" bent (directed by perceptions of lived problems) and those "critical researchers" wishing to gear inquiry toward gaining an increased appreciation of "invisible structures." They suggest that action researchers should at least consider carefully the kind of emphasis that they may be encouraging through the way the inquiries become organized (2008, p. 111). They also suggest that action researchers may wish to consider the kinds of dialogical approaches that might be being implicated in the manner of inquiring. For instance, they argue that the Habermasian style of dialogue can be seen as associated more with a pragmatic orientation due to its focus on speech oriented toward consensus, whereas, as they put it, "the type of dialogue we associate with the critical orientation is ... more in line with the thinking of Freire and Foucault than Habermas" (2008, p. 101).

In the following chapter, I give more attention to some of these critical theoretical positions – and I relate the discussion hereof to arguments of Zuberi and Bonilla-Silva, who argue that "critical social scientists on race matters can provide ... all sorts of intellectual ammunition against dominant representations about racial groups and racial inequality" (2008, p. 338). For the moment, it is worth noting Weil's argument that one of the tasks of action researchers, which she does not see as separable from the "pragmatic" intent of action research, may be to explore the significance of various critical theorists' theorizing for "people's living, learning, and making choices" within "challenging and ever shifting contexts for action" (1999, p. 8).

Regarding the claim that might be made by "critical researchers" (as understood by Johansson and Lindhult) that action inquires may become directed toward solving narrowly defined problems rather than impacting on large-scale power systems, Douglas and Weil both admit that whether the inquiries that they initiated in the *Through a Hundred Pairs of Eyes Program* could be interpreted as "affecting the power systems" remains an open question (Skype conversation, June 2008). Douglas thus prefers to label the intervention that occurred as "the development of people in strategic roles" (rather than, say, "strategic intervention"). This being the case, Johansson and Lindhult might suggest that it is still not clear when and how action research (including the "trigger method" as elucidated by Douglas and Weil) can become directed toward getting to grips with and finding ways of addressing, in their terms, "invisible structures."

However, Douglas and Weil could comment on this point that the *Through a Hundred Pairs of Eyes Program* could indeed bring into view (for participants and wider audiences) the more or less invisible manner in which institutional racism becomes reproduced at various intertwined levels such as:

- individuals with their restricted repertoires of response;
- groups (insofar as these become a basis for restrictive human interaction);
- organizational policies (that were experienced as further restricting people's sense of possibilities for action);
- culture (including what Douglas calls climates of hostility and/or defensiveness which are not conducive to learning);
- wider sociopolitical and historical forces toward which the triggers also point (by, say, drawing attention to the historically-produced meanings of "black" as a social category).

The program could be argued to have opened up possibilities for people to engage in collective learning around these multiple restrictions – thus subverting the notion that racism is a label that can simply be attached to "individuals." And this, it could be suggested, did lay the groundwork for enabling people to indeed find ways of challenging what Weil et al. call the "structural factors relating to the distribution of power" (1985, p. 2).

7.3.2 Evaluation of the Worth of the Program

Weil et al. indicate that evaluation of the outcomes of the project was to be left largely in the hands of the actors in the different organizations (for which the training had been organized). They do suggest, though, that the training based on *Through a Hundred Pairs of Eyes* could

> become a ... perhaps futile exercise if organizations are not committed to action on the outcomes of learning which this program is designed to stimulate. This [action] will inevitably entail the need for a range of organizational strategies conducive to overcoming institutional racism (Weil et al., 1985, p. 12).

Although Weil et al. felt that the formal evaluation of the program in terms of its contribution to addressing institutional racism was not part of their remit as trainers/facilitators of the learning program, they make suggestions in their training guide as to how the capacity for this might be furthered. For instance, they recommend that not only quantitative but also qualitative "methods for assessing perceived and actual changes in the organization's actual work practices, policies and structures be used" (1985, p. 70).

Weil comments in this regard that those involved in designing the program did not have an ongoing relationship with the organizational actors that would allow them access to any documentation that might have been collected on this. But she also states the view that it is always difficult to decide in any particular case what "neatly" the outcomes of interventions in the unfolding of emergent social realities might be (Skype conversation, June 2008). In this respect, she concurs with Greenwood and Levin's more nuanced view of the transformative possibilities of action research – where trajectories of change cannot be clearly determined as part of the action research remit. As Greenwood and Levin put it, "for us the change process has an open starting point and often no absolute final goal" (1998, p. 18). Weil indicates that she regards this stance as indeed central to a complexity approach.

McKay and Romm propose that in "active research" – as a form of action research that does not necessarily follow the format of "diagnosing, planning action, taking action, and evaluating action" (as Coghlan & Shani, 2005, p. 534, put it) – the intent is more to "contribute toward activating across an array of spheres of action (more) diffuse processes of critical awareness and action" (2008a, p. 165). We argue that in cases where transformative action is seen as needing to occur at a variety of interlinked levels or spheres of activity, active research acknowledges its concern with "the struggle over cultural meanings in relation to multiple social locations over an unknown period of time" (2008a, p. 153).[190] This broad "goal" of action would also seem to be implied by Weil et al., as, for instance, manifested in Douglas's (1998) and Weil's (1999) account of the multiple and mutually interactive levels that they were trying to render (more) visible and on which they were trying to work.

Although Douglas and Weil do not feel that they can easily document the "results" of the inquiries, this does not preclude them from creating their own deliberations, as for instance, they do when they offer an indication of why they regard the program as having been worthwhile based on their sense of achievements generated by it. As an example, Douglas comments on the success of the program in aiding people to "cross the chasms" created by "the intense anger and rage of the oppressed person." She compares this program with others in which, as she understood it, the chasms became deeper as many men and White people retreated, thus "triggering further anger on the part of the Black people" (1998, Chapter 4, p. 30). She believes that it is fair to state on the basis of the evaluation sheet feedback and other commentary of participants that the *Through a Hundred Pairs of Eyes* program helped to build up "cross-race and cross-gender relationships that were not based on denial or avoidance of issues of racism and sexism" (1998, Chapter 4, p. 30).

Weil supports this view of Douglas when she refers to people's relief at being able to "have these kinds of dialogues." She considers that this relief was noticeable in its "palpability" (1999, p. 7). And she also highlights what she considers to be

---

[190]McKay and Romm suggest that in processes of "active research" (as we call it), it is understood that the exploration of the issues at stake "gives, and will give, rise to a range of both intended and unintended impacts – in the short, medium, and long term" (2008a, p. 164).

people's achievements in "explor[ing] possibilities for action, often using drama to re-enact and re-play and expand repertoires of choice" (1999, pp. 7–8). She adds that by working in ways that prevented any of the issues from becoming polarized within the co-inquiry groups, an "inherently systemic approach" was being activated in the work (as she now articulates it).

Mehta offers a way of defending this manner of communicating "results" as forwarded by Douglas (1998) and by Weil (1999) when she makes the point that "the researcher is never a *tabula rasa*. Consequently, the final research product is a 'situated' account given by a particular researcher at a particular point in time" (2008, p. 237). She remarks that in the light of the situated character of all practices, including the ones that those involved in action research endeavors choose to create, "the final output can only be a reconstructed account of facts, events, observations and theory as interpreted by the researcher" (organizing the write-up) (2008, p. 237).

Broad and Reyes adopt a similar position when they indicate that the tendency in traditional research has been to valorize the understandings of those individuals who "publish about the phenomena." Individuals who have published, become "elevated to the level of experts" (2008, p. 141). Their position, which they pose as a more ethical one, is that:

> As individuals we can claim a certain perception that is our own knowledge, but always we must be vigilant of ourselves, that we do not usurp the rights of the collective ownership of much of that knowledge. (2008, p. 141)

Broad and Reyes suggest, as with Mehta (and others), that due to the "powerful nature of knowledge ownership and control," those organizing write-ups need to consider when they may be "entitled to make a paper or presentation" as well as to consider the question of "what is to be considered a research 'result'" (2008, p. 141).

As I indicated in Chapter 1, I believe that those rendering "public" their view of research enterprises in which they have been involved can earn trust of others (such as other participants involved and wider audiences) by offering their interpretations while admitting their presence in their constructions, and by pointing to an engagement with issues that they see of social concern. In considering write-ups of action research endeavors, Stringer et al. call this a process of "shar[ing] knowledge gain [or interpretations developed] in one context with people in other contexts in which they work" (2008, p. 124).

Stringer et al. propose that the case of their own sharing around the action research inquiries in which they have been involved, "the spirit of the work in which people have been engaged and the collaborative relationships that characterize our operation enrich the emerging international action research community" (as a community of anyone interested in this kind of research orientation) (2008, p. 124). They suggest that it is important in working toward this "sharing" of "the spirit of the work" that new discourses be developed (over and above traditional "academic" ones) that are "more readily relevant and accessible to people's everyday worlds." It could be argued that Douglas and Weil's accounts/evaluations of quests to develop enhanced cross-racial relationships through the "trigger method" do offer an accessible vision of how the "spirit" of work around this method as supported by the guide and program as a whole might become instantiated. This invites us to engage with their reflections on its worth and to consider possibilities for ways of using/developing it in other geographical contexts too.

7.3.3 Theorizing Around Institutional Racism as Part of the Program

Weil remarks that theorizing should, in her view, properly relate to "living, learning, and making choices" within "challenging and ever-shifting contexts for action" (1999, p. 8). Thus even the conceptualization of institutional racism as elucidated in the training guide (Weil et al., 1985) as a starting point for discussion should be seen as just this – a starting point for continued discussion around meaning(s) in living "complex systems." Clearly for Weil et al., theorizing in action inquiry is linked to what Burns calls sense-making "around the complex, interdependent overlapping 'messes' which characterize human lives" (2007, p. 1).[191] Burns's reference to this manner of sense-making invokes many systemic thinkers' arguments criticizing models of linear causation that assume that "outcomes" in social life can be traced in some way (by research specialists) back to specific "causes" which can serve to explain them (Burns, 2007, p. 1).[192] As indicated in Section 7.2.5, Douglas and Weil see "live" theorizing around institutional racism as involving a process of "unpacking" the incidents (expressed via the trigger videos) with respect to the reproduction of recurring patterns and possibilities for interrupting these. They believe that the trigger method is helpful in enabling people to gain some appreciation of the complexity of the entanglement of "perceptions, meanings and behaviors," as Douglas puts it (2002, p. 205).

When discussing the training guide's definition of institutional discrimination, Douglas remarks (1998) on why she considered this conceptualization as helpful. She notes that it seemed important that institutional discrimination was presented as an "ideology that influenced the perceptions of individuals and informed their decisions and behaviors, rather than as inherent characteristics of the individual." She states that she observed that this manner of conceptualizing "institutional discrimination" meant that it was possible to develop (practical) scope for "empathy, dialogue and connection." It also "allowed us [those involved] to find ways of holding the paradox of justifiable rage and non-attributable blame" (1998, Chapter 4, p. 32). That is, by theorizing "racism" as not an act of individuals, but as "behavior and practices" internalized by all people to some extent (insofar as they live in

---

[191] In his acknowledgments to his book *Systemic Action Research* (2007) Burns indicates Weil's influence on him through her creation of SOLAR (see Note 188) and through some of their joint work.

[192] Similar points have been made by, inter alia: Ozbekhan (1968, 1970), Churchman (1971, 1979), Mitroff (1994), McKay (1997), Checkland and Holwell (1998), Midgley et al. (1998), Midgley (2000, 2001), Flood (2001), Fuenmayor (2001a, 2001b), Nelson (2001), McIntyre-Mills (2003, 2006a, 2006b), Vargas (2005), Weil et al. (2005), and Christakis and Bausch (2006).

a racialized society), people were better able to reach toward defining options for building their social relationships.

The question of the status of the theorizing that may be drawn upon, as well as developed, within action research inquiry is thus linked to the issue of the helpfulness of the concepts in inviting people to develop their styles of sense-making and living together. Johansson and Lindhult argue that the drawing upon, as well as the continued emergence of, relevant theorizing during action research processes can be seen as utilizing a logic that is neither inductive nor deductive, but abductive. They note that according to this logic of inquiry, single cases (i.e., people's understanding of cases/settings) are interpreted "from a hypothetical general pattern. From that, new empirical evidence is sought" (2008, p. 113). They indicate that it is in this way that action inquirers can use the "evidence" of people's social experience in addressing experienced situations, while at the same time drawing upon analytic conceptualizations of "patterning" in social life, in a "back and forth" movement between "the empirical" and "the theory."[193] Douglas remarks that she sees the method used in the trigger scenes as one of "using small incidents and taking them apart in order to understand the [broader] dynamics in them" (Skype conversation with Weil and me, 2008). This too would fit in with a definition of abduction as a way of generating an appreciation of interweaving patterns (in this case, that can be seen to constitute institutional racism). (I discuss abductive logic further in Section 7.4.2.2, where explicit reference is made to the operation of this mode of inference as guiding the inquiry process.)

Reflecting on the question of how "soundness" of theorizing may become assessed by others, Douglas indicates that she takes on board Collins's suggestion (1990) that our manner of evaluating the quality of inferences made can justifiably be tied to an assessment of the *kinds of people* that we consider those involved in the inquiry to be. She refers to Collins's suggested criteria for "quality assurance" as invoking criteria such as inquirers' dialogical orientation, their capacity for empathy, and their commitment to learning (1998, Chapter 6, p. 13).

Referring to these kinds of criteria by which (co-)inquirers can try to earn trust in their manner of proffering ideas as "insightful," Douglas provides for readers of her thesis an outline of the kinds of struggles that she reports in her journal in relation to her own learning about institutional discrimination. She indicates (1998, Chapter 10, p. 2) that:

> I filled many pages of a journal as I struggled with the insight that my understanding of Institutional Discrimination had been changed and tried to identify the precise nature of the learning I had gained. I asked questions such as:
>
> - What was the difference that I perceived in myself?
> - How did this change come about?
> - What do I now know that I did not know then?

---

[193] Huxham makes the point that in cases where action researchers claim that research data toward the "development of theory" is being generated, "while data from long-term interventions may be used in isolation to generate theory, data from short-term ones must necessarily be used in combination with other data as a contribution to theory" (2003, p. 242).

She indicates that as she considered these "very puzzling questions," she could find no easy answers. She realized that over the period of the various stages of her inquiries around institutional discrimination (of which her involvement in the *Through a Hundred Pairs of Eyes* program had been one stage) "there had been many 'Aha!' moments" when she felt that "new insights had been gained." Yet she remarks that "as I 'stood' at the 'closing chapter' of the study I had great difficulty in specifically isolating the discrete units of 'new' learning" (1998, Chapter 10, p. 2).

She explains that she came to appreciate that:

> Learning which empowers the individual to become subject rather than object is not simply about the acquisition of new knowledge and skills. It demands new ways of being in the world and a different level of consciousness. It is not possible to move from surviving to thriving simply by adding new competencies. It is a shift that demands new ways of perceiving and relating to oneself, others and the world. (1998, Chapter 10, p. 2)

Douglas thus displays to us the kind of person that she believes she became as part of her involvement in the various co-inquiries. By offering her personal account, she indicates to us as audiences that we can judge any of the insights that she presents partly on the basis of our understanding of her (presentation of) journey of development. This tallies with Collins's remark that when engaging with the written work of certain theses presented by "scholars," the students in her class rightfully "refused to evaluate the rationality of [the] written work without some indication of [the person's] personal credibility as an ethical human being" (2000, p. 265). Collins emphasizes that:

> The entire exchange [between her and her students in this class] could only have occurred as a dialogue among members of a group that had established a solid enough community to employ an alternative epistemology in assessing knowledge claims. (2000, pp. 265–266)

Thus, returning to my point about the status of theoretical accounts, Douglas believes (following Collins) that the assessment of any presented "insights" rightfully should bring to bear criteria developed through an "alternative epistemology."

7.4 Action Inquiry Toward a Peace Movement in Relation to Cyprus

7.4.1 Some Contextual Background

In this section I use an example of inquiry directed around forwarding a peace movement in Cyprus, toward trying to re-unite the island currently divided along Turkish Cypriot and Greek Cypriot lines. I consider this example as an illustration of what Reason calls endeavoring to develop "a rationale for mutual viability" in situations where "discourses of identity boundaries are not adequate to the challenge of crossing boundaries" (2004, pp. 11–12). Reason urges action research to rise to the challenge of confronting the problem of "conflicting traditions of meaning" in situations where these conflicts generate the potential for "alienation and hostility" (2004, p. 11). This he notes, citing Gergen (2003), is a challenge facing many "second order" democracies (See also my discussion in relation to struggles for recognition in Chapter 6, Section 6.3.2.1.)

In the Cyprus political context, Philippou suggests that "identity and the politics of recognition are the cornerstones of the Cyprus problem." She points to the historically generated "nationalism of each community" – fuelled also by Greece and Turkey (2007, p. 71). She notes that a "coup organized by the dictatorial government of Greece against the government of Cyprus led to a Turkish military intervention in 1974, which divided Cyprus into two parts."[194] Subsequent to this, she indicates, the "UN [United Nations] General Assembly has co-ordinated a number of unsuccessful negotiation talks" – the most recent one being the Annan Plan, which was rejected by 75% of Greek Cypriots in a referendum in 2004 (2007, p. 71). She points to (qualitative) studies of Greek-Cypriot children, which suggest that these children tend to construct the Turks as "Others=Enemies," drawing on discourses of identity that "essentialize identity ... and erect a firm boundary which keeps 'us' (the Greeks) separate from 'them' (the Turks)." She cites, for instance, the research of Spyrou (2002). She indicates also how in current discourses, "Europe" has become used "as a discursive tool to justify Cyprus's place in the EU [European Union] and ... its Greekness has been put forward to justify its Europeanness" (2007, p. 74).

Philippou suggests that the EU as an actor in the conflict has had an "ambiguous impact" on it – although it has the potential to act as a constructive catalyst for a "lasting transformation of the Cyprus conflict" (2007, p. 75). She proposes, though, that in order for the evocation of "Europe" to be used positively, we need to explore how the concept of Europe can be used as a tool to revisit constructions of identity. She suggests that "ethnocultural definitions of Europe" are likely to have the consequence of encouraging divisions within Europe in general and Cyprus in particular (2007, p. 76). She contends that Europe could be defined in other terms – for example, as "incorporating both 'western' and 'eastern' cultural foundations, thereby moving away from exclusive definitions/constructions of Europe" (2007, p. 76).

Remarking on social/political contexts where "identity issues" are linked to people's conceptions of "survival, and fears of the other," Chigas indicates that where conflicts seem intractable, these can still become addressed through "a process that works directly to change the underlying human relationship, promoting mutual understanding and acknowledgement of people's concerns" (2003, p. 2). She suggests that in the case of Cyprus, the conflict can be interpreted as "ethno-national," and as "pervading all aspects of the community's life" (2003, p. 2). In this case, she points out, "traditional mediation and negotiation by themselves are not adequate to address this kind of conflict" because "a transformation in the conflictual

---

[194]Yilmaz indicates that on 13 February 1975 a "Turkish Federal State of Cyprus [TFSC]" was proclaimed in the Northern part of the island. Greece protested this move, while Turkey recognized it. On 15 November 1983 the TFSC declared its independence as the Turkish Republic of Northern Cyprus. Again, it was recognized only by Turkey. He refers also to the failed negotiations around the Annan Plan (2004) proposed with the help of the United Nations, and to the current "stalemate" (2006, p. 9).

relationship of the parties is required" (2003, p. 2). She notes that a proposed way of dealing with seemingly intractable conflicts characterized by "distrust and dehumanization" (2003, p. 2) is to introduce "unofficial interventions with unofficial actors" – called "Track II diplomacy" (cf. Montville, 1991).[195]

Yilmaz similarly indicates that the idea behind instituting Track II diplomacy (defined by Montville as separate from Track 1 official government actions to try to resolve conflicts) is to help participants to "examine the root causes of their conflict" and "identify obstacles to better relationships." At the same time it is aimed at helping participants to "arrest dehumanization processes and ... focus on relationship building" (Yilmaz, 2006, p. 11). (See also Hadjipavlou-Trigeorgis, 1993; Broome, 1998; Lassila, 2006.) Yilmaz makes the point that while it is advisable to avoid "over-optimism" in considering the value of Track II diplomacy, it can become workable – especially insofar as it helps to "reduce the salience of group boundaries" (2006, p. 11). (This relates to my discussion of perceived salience of boundaries in Chapter 3, Section 3.4; and Chapter 4, Section 4.3.1.)

Track II diplomatic efforts can be seen as creating wider political impact in society through what Christakis calls a process of "osmosis" – where ways of working are intended to work their way through into more formal political processes (personal communication via e-mail, April 2008[196]). The actors in the civil society dialogues in the meantime try to develop options for action to deal with issues identified as of concern. By gaining media coverage, they publicize their efforts, thus also gaining increased contacts for further participation in future activities and discussion forums, thus spreading their influence.[197]

---

[195]Chigas is named as one of the people acknowledged for her contribution to Laouris et al. (2007) as reported in Section 7.4.3. The idea that the peace movement in Cyprus can be conceptualized in terms of the notion of Track II diplomacy was first suggested to me in personal communication by email (April 2008) with one of the facilitators of some of the SDP sessions – namely, Marios Michaelides.

[196]This statement of Christakis was made in answer to a question that I asked him by email (April 2008) about how the issue of political "impact" might be considered. Lassila meanwhile points out that there are various ways in which Track 1 and Track II actions can become linked. While some authors consider them as "distinct branches" that have no interaction (because they are distinct activities), others point to instances of "direct relations" of the Track II to the Track I (2006, p. 12). Lassila also emphasizes (as would Christakis) that it is important not to "put Track I at the top of the hierarchy, with all the 'unofficial' tracks [such as Track II] poised to change the direction of Track I" (2006, p. 4). He supports the idea and practice of "multi-track diplomacy" that "no one track is more important than the other, and no track is independent from the others" (2006, p. 4).

[197]For example, from 12 to 17 April 2007, three radio programs and one TV program were hosted around this work; and from 6 to 14 July 2007, there were two radio programs, one newspaper interview and two TV programs. The media involved were: Radio CyBC; Radio Mayis; Radio Astra; Rik2 TV; KIBRIS newspaper; BRT TV and KIBRIS TV (see http://blogora.net/page/Interviews). Christakis and Damdelen also presented the *Civil Society Dialogue* project during the live radio broadcasting of the LIFE EARTH CONCERT (2007).

7.4.2 The Structured Design Process (SDP) Methodology

Christakis and Bausch explain that SDP – which has been used in a variety of "co-laboratories" across the globe, including in the civil society dialogue project in Cyprus – is a "specialized process aimed at problem solving and design through collaborative teamwork and the participation of stakeholders" (2006, p. 47).[198] Its strength as they describe it lies in its capacity to "enable participants to offer observations and explanations, make distinctions and decisions, and generate alternative action scenarios" (2006, p. 47). They emphasize that the SDP is intended to provide a specific way of facilitating dialogue; and in other writings they indeed add an additional "D" to capture their understanding of the importance of dialogue – referring to the approach as *SDDP* (cf. Schreibman & Christakis, 2006; Laouris & Christakis, 2007; Laouris et al., 2007, 2009).

Christakis and Bausch indicate that they believe the SDP helps to instantiate Foucault's argument that "power is an emergent characteristic in the complex behavioral relationships between people" (2006, p. 60). They refer to Foucault's (1980) suggestion (as they interpret it) that "power is manifested in the distinctions made by individuals and accepted by groups" (2006, p. 60). Christakis considers it crucial therefore that "monopolies on distinction making" (whereby observations are constructed) need to be "prohibited" (2004, p. 481). Christakis and Bausch also indicate that the dialogic design process can be considered as a process of engaging in what Habermas calls "communicative action," where, ideally, "participants express themselves freely, forthrightly and truthfully" (in Habermas's sense of these terms) – without "external power relations" impinging on the discussion (2006, p. 129).[199]

---

[198] In the USA Christakis has worked, inter alia, with the Americans for Indian Opportunity (AIO) since 1987, using this methodology for generating dialogue around action options for Native American communities within the USA and for Indigenous people globally. He explained to me (via email, August 2008) that he "started working with AIO in 1987, since I was invited to work with them following a conference presentation that he had given at the time (at an international conference). LaDonna Harris (founder of the AIO), who was at the conference, had been "looking for a conflict resolution approach to help the tribes. She had tried everything and was not satisfied because it was alien to the Native American style of dialogue and consensus building. She tried SDD, fell in love with it, and has been an advocate and a promoter ever since." Christakis became an elected member of the AIO Board in 2006 in appreciation of his contributions (cf. http://www.aio.org/21228%20Ambassador%20Newsletter.pdf). Christakis pointed out to me (email communication, August 2008) that he has since "started calling myself Greek Native American instead of Greek American." (As I commented in Chapter 1, Section 1.4, this to me as an indication of how a sense of belonging to a community can be developed through joining with others in terms of some purpose.) In 2008–2009, Christakis facilitated some sessions of virtual encounters between a set of international stakeholders whom he considered as experienced in Structured Design Process (SDP) as a methodology for generating e-democracy, in order to consider factors that might be potential roadblocks to Obama's vision of bottom-up democracy. See http://obamavision.wikispaces.com for the full account of how the SDP sessions were set up and outcomes generated (which were communicated to Obama's team at http://change.gov/open for questions).

[199] Christakis and Bausch note that SDP draws on a variety of "consensus methods" to help to structure the dialogical process (2006, p. 25). Their reference to these methods, and to the development

Christakis and Bausch contend that via the SDP, as people develop "high quality observations" and explanations through a process of discourse (2006, p. 141), "equitable power relations" are generated at the same time.[200] They suggest that trying to generate such relationships "cannot be induced by posting 'rules of equitable power relations' on the wall of a meeting facility" – rather, participants must *experience* this through the "social fabric of the dialogue process" (2006, p. 60). They believe that the SDP is equipped to achieve this.

They see the SDP as supporting what they call a "people science" (2006, p. 143). As they put it:

> The people science is developed on the following premise: *externalizing the knowledge and wisdom of people affected by a complex issue is necessary for the definition and resolution of the issue.* (2006, p. 143)

They suggest that people science goes hand in hand with a commitment to a new model for participative democracy – where "people must discover their wisdom in order to exercise their collective power" (2006, p. 145). But they argue that "because of the complexity of the Information Age [with vast amounts of information to process], we need a structured ... approach to deal with differences in values, disciplines, languages, and priorities" (2006, p. 145).

In order to be able to address the complexity to which they point, they indicate that SDP dialogues are aided by a computer software package (called the *Cogniscope*):

> The software records observations and meanings, produces, iteratively, representations resulting from the design dialogue, and enables stakeholders to review the representations and amend them through additional discourse. It keeps track of the logic expressed in stakeholder pair-wise decisions, produces the graphic language patterns of relationships among observations, and displays them on a large screen, with the flexibility to amend these observations and the patterns continuously. (2006, p. 50)

They point out that "one of the principle advantages of using the software is the efficiency gained in the exploration of relationships among a large number of ideas" (2006, p. 50). The reference to "pair-wise decisions" in the previous quotation is a reference to stakeholders/designers being asked to decide amongst a set of factors that have been isolated as potentially helping to achieve goals/visions "whether the accomplishment of proposal *A* would help significantly in accomplishing *B*" – and so on (2006, p. 26). The computer package is able to track everybody's paired relational judgments (in relation to the potential influence of the factors on each other). In this way it produces a "tree of meaning" of the "most influential agents/factors" –

---

of a consensual linguistic domain, should be read in the context of their reference to Habermas and his suggestions for consensual understanding being the regulatory ideal toward which discourse is directed. See also Chapter 6, Section 6.3.2.1; and see Romm (2006c).

[200] This view of theirs ties in with Churchman's proposal that we need to make provision in the inquiry process for the necessary social discourse that can sweep in alternative values, ways of life, ways of seeing, and ways of understanding that form the basis of intersubjectively-generated thinking and being (Churchman, 1979, p. 9).

which encompasses the cumulative results of the various people's judgments. The graphic representation of the tree is a way of highlighting the "root causes" (at the roots of the tree) that need to be tackled as priority, because these are seen to "exert strong leverage" in "ameliorating the situation" (2006, p. 27).

Christakis and Bausch explain further what is involved in SDP, by pointing to various stages of the structured dialogue process (2006, pp. 66–67). But firstly they note that all of these stages are set off by what they call a *triggering question* set by the "design team" in collaboration with representatives of stakeholders. They indicate that the development of the triggering question may be aided by references to literature around the situation deemed problematic, and by interviewing people (2006, pp. 65). The stages of the SDP then proceed as follows (though this need not be interpreted as completely linear, as movement between stages can also occur):

1. A *definition stage* of inquiry where participants in the co-laboratory participate in: stating their observations; inductively creating "affinity clusters" where similar observations are grouped in clusters; and "abductively discerning the most influential observations by producing and interpreting an influence tree pattern among important observations" (2006, p. 66). (A voting process is used to decide what factors among the clusters are sufficiently important to enter the process of creating the influence tree; this is followed by pair-wise judgments on the relative influence of different factors – see Section 7.4.3.)
2. A *design stage* of inquiry where participants become involved in "proposing and clarifying action options for addressing the roots of the influence tree pattern." Participants again construct "affinity clusters" – this time by exploring similarity among action options and proceeding to select action options that are most salient for decision-making.
3. A *decision stage* of inquiry, focusing on the design of alternative scenarios that focus on the question "Which are the preferred options and why?"(2006, p. 66). Participants can work in small teams at this stage, presenting their action scenarios and rationales in a plenary. Ideally the participants try to converge on a "consensus action scenario" (2006, p. 66).
4. An *action planning* stage of inquiry, where participants are engaged in answering the question "When will we do what we can do and who will do it?"

The idea behind the SDP methodology is that participants begin by "proposing distinctions" (observations) based upon contemplated action options, and these distinctions in turn "spark new ideas for action," and so on – in an "iterative pattern" (2006, p. 58).

7.4.2.1 Facilitation of the Co-laboratories: Process Facilitation

Christakis and Bausch emphasize that within the SDP methodology for inquiry, the facilitator(s) should concentrate only on facilitation of the SDP *process* and should leave the content to the "experts" in content – namely, the stakeholders. They explain their position in this regard:

The stakeholders are identified as the content experts. They engage in the generation of observations, the distinctions and descriptions of observations, and the selection of design pathways to action. (2006, p. 61)

Christakis and Bausch are adamant that those assuming the role of facilitators in a co-laboratory should *not* intervene in content discussions. As facilitators their responsibility, and their only involvement, should be to "maintain an equitable group process" (2006, p., 61). As they state:

As process experts [knowledgeable on how to manage the SDP approach], they do not provide any opinions on the validity of any content observations whatsoever. They offer no contributions or observations related to content. (2006, p. 61)

They indicate that their rationale for adopting this (process) model of facilitation is that it "excludes the facilitation team entirely from assuming a dominant role in the dialogue around content" (2006, p. 61). This argument of theirs is in line with their calling of the approach a "people's science." They indicate that this does not preclude stakeholders from soliciting the views of "technical [professional] experts" – who may be considered as having certain expertise to which the stakeholders in a particular co-laboratory do not have access. But the stakeholders then would "evaluate the implications of their statements" and finally they have "complete control over the content of the design" (that they produce during the SDP for aiding action) (2006, p. 61). Christakis also indicates that those considered as "professional experts" could of course be invited – as stakeholders – to co-laboratories, in which case their observations and explanations would be put forward and discussed along with those of others on equal footing during the SDP/SDDP (personal communication by e-mail, August 2008).

In further work developing/expanding the SDDP, it has been suggested that a "knowledge management team" (which includes the "lead facilitator" and some stakeholders) can operate alongside the "facilitation team" in helping the group to develop the trigger question as well as to structure their observations/explanations into clusters. Such a team may be particularly useful as an aid when a *virtual* communication component is introduced into the co-laboratories – as they can perform a co-ordinating function in "virtual" space (cf. Laouris & Christakis, 2007; Laouris & Michaelides, 2007; Laouris et al., 2007). Laouris et al. indicate that the expansion of the SDDP to accommodate "hybrid" modes of use that include face-to-face and virtual communication components capitalizes on the use of modern technology so that the methodology can:

(a) make possible the participation of remote participants located at different places;
(b) break the process in smaller asynchronous chunks of time, thus making it more manageable and accessible to the diversity of stakeholders required for disciplined dialogue on complex issues;
(c) significantly shorten the time and lower the cost required for achieving reasonable results in terms of diagnosis and agreement on a collaborative action plan.

Laouris et al. indicate that in the hybrid mode of use of the SDDP, which includes some virtual communication,

> the participants can respond/interact at their own convenience in a way that can be synchronous or sequential, but does not require each one listening to every other one at all times. The Knowledge Management Team can take the information, distill it and use it to move the process to the next step. (2007, p. 18)

In this mode, then, it seems that there is some scope for the knowledge management team to play a role (albeit a limited one) in "content" – by helping to "distill ideas," as Laouris et al. put it.

7.4.2.2 Use of Abductive Logic in the Co-laboratories

Christakis and Bausch explain that when participants "explore influence relationships among the observations" and construct hereby a "tree of influence," they are invoking abductive logic. They indicate that the exploration of abductive reasoning as a mode of reasoning has been credited to Peirce (see also Baldwin, 1901; Eisele, 1985; Chiasson, 2001; Burch, 2006). While for Peirce *induction* proceeds by making inferences from "samples" to conclusions about "general populations" (i.e., from the particular to the more general), and *deduction* proceeds by making inferences from general populations to samples (i.e., from the general to the more particular), Burch points out that *abduction* for Peirce "has the air of educated guess about it" (2006, p. 3). That is, Peirce sees abductive (or otherwise called *retroductive*) logic as using experience as its basis for making inferences (in conjectural form) that in turn help to render the experience comprehensible.[201]

Christakis and Bausch draw on Peirce's (1958) argument that abductive reasoning is "useful for the construction of hypotheses" (2006, p. 72). The hypotheses in the structured dialogic design process are generated as people "relate their observations in paired judgments" to construct a "tree of meaning." Christakis and Bausch indicate that after participants have constructed an initial tree of meaning – aided by the *Cogniscope* software – they continue, as a group, to

> analyze the cross-impacts existing among the observations they have made. If there is a need to amend the preliminary pattern of influences after the interpretation, they can do this efficiently again with computer assistance, and produce a new version of the tree pattern. (2006, p. 72)

They state that in many cases in which they have used the SDP methodology, participants share their experiences, via, for instance, "storytelling," thus contributing to the "richness of the dialogue" (2006, pp. 72–73). In this way, step-by-step, the SDP dialogue "progressively clarifies the situation [for participants] and opens the way to greatly enhanced decision-making and action planning" (2006, p. 72).

---

[201]Chiasson (2001, p. 1) remarks that Peirce's use of the different words *abduction* and *retroduction* seems to point to different foci; but Paavola (2004, p. 4) suggests that we can consider that Peirce used these terms interchangeably (to point to a form of logical inference distinct from induction and deduction).

7.4.2.3 The Status of Meanings Produced: (Pragmatic) Creation of Narratives?

As indicated above, Christakis and Bausch's make reference to Peirce to explain the (abductive) logic being used to construct the "tree of meaning" which "clarifies the situation." It is worth noting here that Peirce explicitly ties his conception of this logic to a pragmatist epistemology[202] (see Section 7.1.2) in which, as Reason notes, the concern is with "practice" and not with adjudicating on (extra-linguistic) "reality." Although an implicit pragmatist epistemology is evoked by Christakis and Bausch – through the reference to Peirce and to the idea that trees of meaning are to be viewed as "sparking ideas for action" (2006, p. 62) – they do not as such spell out this epistemology in their write-ups of the various uses of the methodology. That is, they do not make reference to the extent to which this (pragmatic) way of conceptualizing "knowing" is given expression during their facilitated co-laboratories.

Flanagan, who has used the SDDP in various design contexts in the USA, indicates that reference can be made by those managing/facilitating the process to the notion that what is being produced through the engagement between the participants are indeed *narratives for collaborative action* (2008, p. 80). He offers certain cases of articulating the narrative nature of that which emerges through SDDP – for example, the case of attempts to expand a particular city's "creative economy" (the City of Bedford in the USA). He indicates that it was helpful for participants/stakeholders (who were convened to discuss this with a view to action) to work with the notion that they were engaged in constructing in narrative form a systems view of relations among a "prioritized set of requirements" for addressing (seen) challenges (2008, p. 83).

Flanagan also points out that seeing the results of discussions as "scripts" is a way of reminding participants that any narrative that emerges should be interpreted as an evolving one – because "living stories are more compelling than static stories" (2008, p. 83). He argues that keeping the story "open" is important because new information can become available and/or prior information can become irrelevant. The *Cogniscope* software is supportive of evolving narrative construction because it "provides the capacity to weave the new information into and around the more familiar information" (2008, p. 83). Like Christakis and Bausch, he indicates that an initial "tree of meaning" can be revised in the light of people's additional experiences/stories that they may wish to add. But he makes it clearer than they do that the maps (expressing influence patterns) are indeed themselves "read (interpreted) by participants in the design group in the form of a story" (2008, p. 85). In the City of Bedford case, as he reports it, the influence map that was generated became "the script for a story of the system of requirements that the group most strongly feels must be addressed to achieve success in the design project" (2008, p. 85). He points out that stories are in turn linked to visions, and that when striving

---

[202]Burch indicates that in some of his writings Peirce characterized his approach as "pragmaticism" to point to his proposed form of pragmatism (2006, p. 5).

for "transformational design," this frequently requires approaches that "distribute ownership of complex design requirements among many voices" – such as he sees provided by the SDDP (2008, p. 86).

I now turn to a summary example of work with the SDDP in the context of Cyprus – in this case using the SDDP in a hybrid mode, which included a combination of virtual and face-to-face interactions as well as synchronous and asynchronous communication between participants.

7.4.3 Cyprus Peace Revival Inquiries: August–December 2006 (as Reported by Laouris et al., 2007)

Laouris et al. indicate in their report that the participants of the SDDP co-laboratory that occurred from August to December 2006 were "Cypriots based both on the island and abroad . . . who had relevant experience and have contributed significantly to the Cyprus peace process" (2007, p. 5). The authors of the report (Laouris et al.) include some members of the "facilitation team," some of the "knowledge management team" and some of the participants in the co-laboratory.[203] The report begins by offering an introduction elucidating various attempts to resolve "the Cyprus problem," including peace-building initiatives to date in which some of the participants have been involved. It then explains how the SDDP was used to structure the reported-upon co-laboratory. The idea was to make use of virtual technologies (along with the *Cogniscope*) to enable remote participation of certain participants – toward identifying leverage points around which further actions of peace builders could be focused (Laouris et al., 2007, p. 3). They indicate that their hope was that the products documented in the report

> may prove extremely useful to any organized effort to re-launch the peace process in Cyprus. The search for a sustainable solution to the Cyprus problem can only be based on the knowledge and wisdom produced collectively by the community of stakeholders, and consideration of the problems and obstacles as perceived by those concerned. (2007, p. 17)

As far as the composition of the group of participants in the co-laboratory is concerned, Laouris et al. note that because the dialogue was spread over a period of 3 months and engaged remote participants by means of web technologies, there was some variation in the composition of the group from session to session (2007, p. 8). They remark that at the onset of the process 25 individuals contributed their ideas – but only 11 remained active throughout the dialogue (eight physically present and three remote participants) (2007, p. 8). They note that the 25 participants contributed

---

[203] This composition of the authorship is not spelled out explicitly in the report – but can be gleaned by comparing the author list with an indication at the end of the report of the composition of the knowledge management team and those involved in the SDDP. Also, in their "credits", the authors thank the participants of the co-laboratory for their "valuable comments and contributions" (2007, p. 22).

together 120 factors in response to the triggering question *"What factors contribute to the increasing gap between the two communities in Cyprus?"* (2007, p. 17). These factors emerged as participants offered ideas, clarified and further discussed them (2007, p. 11). The authors note that the "number is relatively high, compared to analogous exercises" (2007, p. 18). They suggest that "the increased number of factors in the context of this 'peace process revival' could be an indication of an increased effort to understand the situation and explore ways to get out of the impasse" (2007, p. 18). It could also be an indication that participants were "quite knowledgeable of the situation" (2007, p. 19).

In order to help people to collaboratively develop their further understanding of the impasse, with a view to moving toward a different future, the co-laboratory provided a forum for them to help identify points for priority action in the design situation. (Christakis and Bausch label "the situation" understood through the "triggering question" as a "design situation" in order to highlight that the situation is being understood with a view to designing options for action – 2006, p. 160.)

In the map that ensued, 20 factors (that had been clustered from out of the factors that had been voted as important and that therefore "made it" into the stage of constructing the "influence tree") were structured. This structuring was done through pair-wise voting. (see Section 7.4.2.) Through this process, seven Levels emerged in the "tree" – also called a "root cause map" (see Fig. 7.1).

7.4.3.1 Reading the Map: Some Commentary from the Authors

In interpreting the map, Laouris et al. indicate that the dominating root causes (influences) in the "deepest Layer 7" appear to be:

> Factor 72: MEDIA AS PUPPETS OF POLITICAL PARTIES; and
> Factor 47: THE PERSONAL AND FINANCIAL INTERESTS OF POLITICIANS AND ORDINARY PEOPLE ON BOTH SIDES

They remark that when seen in connection with the Layer 6 factors, namely,

> Factor 18: LEADERS ON EACH SIDE DO NOT WANT TO SHARE POWER; and
> Factor 58: DISEMPOWERMENT OF THE NGOs IN NORTH CYPRUS & WEAK NGOs IN THE SOUTH WHO ARE SUPPRESSED,

"one is justified to conclude that the greatest obstacles lie within the political leaders and the media" – as indeed also was expressed in previous co-laboratories (2007, p. 19). They indicate that whether the problems of political leadership and the (mis)use of the media "can be attributed to them sharing [assuming] a different political ideology/line" (from those seen as opponents), or is "simply the result of putting personal interests over the common good and/or political corruption" is an issue that requires "further analysis and discussion" (2007, p. 19). In any case, with reference to a number of examples, they suggest that there may be justification for the understanding of the participants of the current co-laboratory that

> political leaders (as well as ordinary people) may put more value to their personal and financial interests than to the common good and to the resolution of the Cyprus problem. (2007, p. 20)

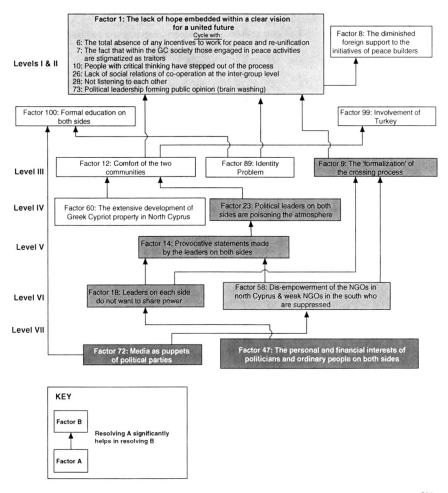

Fig. 7.1 Construction of root cause map (Source: Laouris et al., 2007, p. 16 – with added KEY[204])

The authors continue to offer their interpretation of the way in which the influence tree became constructed. For instance, regarding Factor 6 (one of the connected set of factors at the top of the influence tree), they suggest that:

The fact that factor 6, "The total absence of any incentives to work for peace and reunification", climbed at the top layer of the influence map can be viewed as "good news." The obvious advantage is that it encourages peace builders to move forward without waiting for any support from any side. It also serves as a human quality filter. Those who choose to be active and remain engaged without anticipating some later advantage, recognition or

---

[204] A slightly modified version of this picture can be found in Laouris et al. (2009).

reward, are the kind of people who have clear minds and hearts.[205] It is in fact to the honor of the participants of this workshop that they did not vote factor 6 as a root-cause. (2007, p. 21)

Commenting on what they see as the broader significance of trying to find a resolution to the "Cyprus problem," they suggest that:

> If Cyprus had managed to resolve its problem through a process combining political peace negotiations and citizens' contributions and participation, the UN would have been significantly empowered to take analogous action [trying to encourage involvement of civil society] in other regions of the world. (2007, p. 21)[206]

They believe that the issues of polarization in Cyprus (and efforts in civil society to try to generate a way out of the impasse) is significant for many other social contexts too.

Speaking generally, they suggest that when political leaders (and they cite the Cypriot leaders as a case in point) focus on feasibility and viability of proposed solutions, they may lose sight of the need for "idealization" of new futures (2007, p. 22). This relates back to Christakis and Bausch's definition of the term "future," which they see as "the state of a social system that is more than a mere extrapolation of the past and present" (2006, p. 160). Laouris et al. refer to systems thinkers' arguments made in the 1970 s to the effect that transforming systems involves people "letting go of the need to know how and trusting that the creative how will be discovered along the way" (2007, p. 22). They offer a word of hope by citing Ozbekhan's (1970) reference to the "Will to act" – which as they see it transcends concerns regarding "the need to know how" and instead trusts that this "will be discovered along the way" (2007, p. 22). But they argue that this implies that "there is a political leadership in place" capable of "transformative leadership" (2007, p. 22) – which again would relate back to Factor 47 in the influence tree constructed by the participants.

---

[205]Laouris et al. suggest that clarity of mind and hearts "is very important when actors engage in a group dialogue committed to put together their unbiased ideas and thoughts trying to design a process based on their collective wisdom" (2007, p. 21). When they propose that *hearts* should be engaged, this implies (as I read it) that they do not define "bias" in terms of trying to become detached from one's own and others' concerns. Rather, their use of the word "bias" means here the *incapacity to examine carefully alternative perspectives around concerns* that may be brought to bear.

[206]Yilmaz makes a similar point when he argues that the new Cypriot state (if established) "would be a model to which many other nations and peoples will look to guide the resolution of their own conflicts and ethnic tensions" (2006, p. 1). He argues that it is indeed for this reason that that the UN, "acting on behalf of the International Community ... has always given a special importance to the Cyprus problem" (2006, p. 1).

7.5 Revisiting the Inquiries

In this section, I comment on some of the points emerging for me from Laouris et al.'s account of the inquiries. To avoid repetition with points I have made earlier (in regard to other examples of research in the book) the discussion is brief.

7.5.1 Reconsidering the Role of Facilitators as "Outside" the Discussion Process

Christakis and Bausch suggest that their assigning a role to facilitators as being "outside" the content discussions/structuring of ideas is in order to sidestep any undue power of the facilitator (whose ways of seeing may be given undue attention if they were to "intervene"). I have suggested elsewhere in the book that issues of power relations can be differently handled (as, e.g., expressed by Douglas – see Chapter 5, Section 5.3.1). As far as the processes involved in the SDDP are concerned, I suggest that there is no reason why in principle the facilitators, as concerned citizens, cannot add their observations during the co-laboratories, as well as be afforded (equal) voting power within the situation. Incorporating the notion of facilitators being able to add ideas as part of the discussion would of course require some extension of the SDDP methodology, but it is in keeping with the fact that facilitators do appear to play a role in adding content *at the point at which report writing takes place.*

For example, Laouris et al. (2007) include some of the facilitators (as well as some of the knowledge management team and participants) in offering their interpretations and further analyses in their "reporting" on the process. These interpretations are not without import for the participants as well as for wider audiences who are able to read the report/interpretations of the relationships between factors in the influence maps that have been constructed. Indeed insofar as participants are also contributing to the report, a discussion over "content" issues would surely be occurring. This means, as I see it, that facilitators do not remain outside of content intervention in the arena of discussion and analysis. Whether this occurs "within" the co-laboratory setting or "afterward" (in report write-ups), their understandings are being put forward. I would suggest therefore that facilitators should be prepared to acknowledge their involvement in the construction of conceptions of "the situation."

Laouris's position in this regard (proffered as part of an e-mail discussion originally instigated by Vera Vratuša, in which I played a part, 2008) is to suggest that the first reporting on any co-laboratory consists [merely] of "logistical data" such as WHERE the discussion took place, WHO participated, WHAT the triggering question was, and HOW LONG the co-laboratory endured, plus the "outputs of the [Cogniscope] software: tables and graphs." He suggests that:

> If we then decide to write a longer report, we use [as basis] the discussion that took place after the MAPPING [of the influence tree]. Those interpretations and ideas go into such a report. If a later publication will be produced, then optimally it must be co-authored by participants and KMT. (Yiannis Laouris, by e-mail, July 2008)

In response, I suggest here (as I did by e-mail) that there are always decisions involved in what those reporting decide to highlight from the discussion that occurred in the co-laboratories. Hence I consider it important that as part of their involvement in report writing, facilitators and KMT authors should be specifically attuned to consider (in conversation with others) the possible consequences of what is being chosen to highlight for attention.

Vratuša's commentary on the SDDP team of facilitators/KMT meanwhile is from the perspective of what she calls a "critical sociology of knowledge." From this perspective, she considers a still unaccounted-for direction taken by SDDP facilitators insofar as they do not reflect sufficiently on their own social position (e.g., how they are being formed by "her/his social habitus") and how this may be affecting the choices that they make. She points out that she raises what she calls these "self-reflecting concerns" so as to urge facilitators/knowledge management team to consider more carefully the issue of who becomes defined and invited as stakeholders to join the co-laboratories (in view of the "power relations" in the social setting in question). Furthermore, she points out that the setting of the triggering question (by the "design team" with certain stakeholders) becomes a way of formulating the context. She remarks that:

> As sociologists we all know well that a very important form of social power is to control the formulation of what will be the issue for research or decision-making. (Vratuša, by email to certain SDDP facilitators, July 2008)

Vratuša's invitation to set up a forum for encouraging self-reflection on the part of facilitators/knowledge management teams set off a series of electronic communications – with Laouris's contribution (mentioned above) being one.[207] The discussion involved a number of different facilitators and management team members of SDDP processes, as well as others interested (including myself). The discussion was informal (although it had been proposed that possibly it could later become formally managed by means of an SDDP process). In any case, via the informal exchanges, different arguments were expressed and exchanged with no attempt made to arrive at a shared view with which all could be said to "agree.". (Re)definitions of the meaning(s) of "impartiality" were offered as part of the exchanges.

My input was to suggest that decisions around whom to invite as stakeholders in any "co-laboratory" are not without social consequence and also that definitions of the triggering question (by KMT members plus chosen stakeholders) may shape the way discussion ensues during co-laboratories. Furthermore, that which becomes highlighted in report writing (in which facilitators/KMT members are involved) may well affect continuing discourse in society. For these reasons, I supported

---

[207] Having seen the queries raised by Vratuša in an email forwarded to me by Christakis, I suggested that these should be taken seriously, because, as I remarked, self-reflection provides a route to "admitting and accounting for, one's way of being involved" (July, 2008). Some of the interchanges around her invitation can be seen at: http://www.blogora.net/page/On+Reflective+Practice (entitled "Practicing Self-reflection"). Other exchanges took place directly over the email (as some people experienced difficulty at times accessing the site).

Vratuša's plea for enhanced self-reflection to account for such involvements. Vigdor Schreibman thanked me for this "excellent review and my conclusions" and agreed that "further self-reflection on these issues will be helpful," especially "to help orient Vera [Vratuša] with regard to the dynamics of SDDP and whether this process can help to transform the existing situation toward the values of democratic sustainability" (July 2008). He thus emphasized the overall (pragmatic) purpose – namely, enhancing "democratic sustainability." At the same time he indicated that Vratuša's experiences in Belgrade offers a reminder to us of "our planetary failing to transform the dysfunctional existing situation" (on the planet) – and he pointed out that her training in Belgrade offers her "vital experiences" to contribute to an understanding of "the social dynamics that require transformation."

As part of the exchanges, Vratuša sent a paper (to the group) that she was planning to present at the International Sociological Association (ISA) conference in September 2008, in which she pointed to her concerns that thus far there seems to be insufficient attention across the globe to researching ways of realizing "political, social and economic democracy" through a serious consideration of the "social source of private property and environmentally unsustainable production for profit instead of for the satisfaction of human needs.".

Vratuša mentions in her paper her primary concern that serious exploration of possibilities for transforming social relations can be argued to constitute a "blindspot" among (many) researchers, insofar as research is not directed toward

> finding solutions for the problems of transformation of dominant social relations to the benefit of the increase in satisfaction of needs and democratic participation of the majority of citizens, instead of the increase in profit and power of the few. (2008)

She argues that because of this blind spot, a "complex re-colonization disaster" is becoming reproduced. She calls for self-reflection as a way for researchers to take seriously their potential complicity – through their research foci – in this "disaster."

Another response in the set of exchanges (this time by Kevin Dye) was to ask, as part of the dialogue around self-reflective practice, whether the advised separation between facilitators/KMT members and stakeholders may possibly "obscure the fact that facilitators/KMT are stakeholders as well" (in any set of issues being discussed). This would tally with my view that the rigid separation need not be maintained, especially once we admit that facilitators/KMT are in some ways contributing to the direction of the social discourse. Dye also makes the further point (in response to one of Vratuša's e-mails) that it should indeed be recognized that at times there may be different agendas between sponsors of co-laboratories and (other) stakeholders, and that this too needs to be taken into account.

In any case, the variety of responses indicates to me that within the group of those interested in discussing this issue (of facilitator/KMT involvement), the matter of whether facilitators/KMT *must* see themselves as striving not to become involved in definitions of the context and in futures creation is not to be regarded as settled.

Burns in his book *Systemic Action Research* (2007) makes what I regard as a pertinent point in regard to facilitators' uneasy roles. He suggests that a facilitator's choosing *not* to try to stand "outside" the joint discourse (among participants/stakeholders) may require *more intricate processes of trust building* with the different participants than a facilitator who adopts the guise of not being involved (2007, p. 103). In terms of his argument, facilitators' admitted involvement (coupled with what Vratuša would call their recognition of their commitment toward developing more workable relationships) is a more constructive approach. In the case of research involving attempts to explore as well as invent new forms of human relationship, I would suggest that facilitators' attempts to activate processes for people's knowing and living together cannot be settled by any recipes – and that whatever route is taken by facilitators is at least recognized to be a choice that needs to be accounted for.

7.5.2 Conceptualizing the Status of the Influence Tree Developed

Laouris et al. organize their write-up of the construction of the influence tree by noting that it graphically represents the participants' perception – as a collectivity – of "the current [design] situation." They remark that whenever SDDP processes are used,

> depending on the number and type of participants in the structured dialogue, the influence structure of the factors may incorporate a *variety of perspectives* into an overall understanding of the current situation. It is only natural that individual participants perceive the situation from a limited point of view. The application of SDDP to facilitate structured dialogue enables stakeholders to integrate a variety of perspectives on a particular problem situation. Thus, a much more complete and spherical perspective emerges. (2007, p. 17)

Here they point out that the status of the influence tree – with its location of root causes – is that it incorporates a "more complete perspective" than would be arrived at without the application of the structured dialogical process. This is not to say that it is seen as representing some "truth" existing outside of people's (collective) inquiry efforts. Rather, it graphically represents participants' collective understanding. They argue that ideally, to gain increasing comprehensiveness of perspective, it is to be advised that organizers of co-laboratories should "ensure the participation of actors who can offer a [suitably wide] variety of perspectives" (2007, p. 17). They indicate that

> in the case of the present co-laboratory, practically all participants were peace pioneers. Therefore, the resulting map cannot be read as a universal map that incorporates the viewpoints and perspectives of the whole Cyprus. (2007, p. 17)

Laouris et al. argue that to gain a yet wider "spherical" perspective, further efforts can be made to include different viewpoints and perspectives to re-construct the influence trees. Meanwhile, the influence tree constructed with the specific participants points to their understanding of which kinds of actions may need to be prioritized to provide "leverage" in the "design situation." Christakis and Bausch state that their way of seeing the consensus-building process (toward developing consensus on leverage points for transformative action) is in line with a Habermasian view of communicative action (2006, p. 129). As I noted in Chapter 6,

Habermas addresses the issue of how communication oriented toward "consensus" may be envisaged in situations where communicators bring different traditions of reasoning as well as meaning systems to bear on the discussion. Debate between Habermas and other authors on the character of "communication" across different languages/paradigms is still ongoing and I refer to some of these debates in the next chapter.

For the moment, I wish to point out that I see the main strength of the SDDP approach as lying in its initiating processes of "knowing" through stakeholders co-constructing – through abductive logic – what Christakis calls a "collective relational tree" locating relationships of influence among a set of factors deemed relevant by them (personal communication by e-mail, May 2008). Insofar as all those involved (and wider audiences) recognize that the location of "root causes" in this way may be helpful in deciding what issues are to be considered as requiring priority attention, this manner of considering networks of causality concurs with Reason's suggestion that action inquirers are not "overconcerned with the problem of reality" – and rather concentrate their attention on "the issue of practice" (2006b, p. 207).

The SDDP approach is based on the notion that it is preferable to work with people in exploring the emergence of their social situations, with the aim of developing insightful ways of considering the arena of possible action. The aim is to develop ways of appreciating "what *could be*, rather than what [supposedly] *is*" – hence Christakis and Bausch (2006) as well as Laouris et al. (2007) point to the importance of future visioning. This future-oriented approach ties in with a point made by Lassila in relation to the concept of "conflict *transformation*." Lassila states that "conflict transformation" (rather than the more commonly used term "conflict *resolution*") points to a deliberate focus on *systemic change*. As he expresses it, "transforming deep-rooted conflicts is only partly about 'resolving' the issues of the conflict – the central issue is systemic change or transformation" (2006, p. 4).

It seems, then, that the purpose of the co-laboratories is indeed to try to engender the social infrastructure for trying to, as Lassila puts it, "establish new patterns" (of human relationship) (2006, p. 4). However, I would suggest that both within the SDDP co-laboratories and as the participants/facilitators/knowledge management team share their understandings of possibilities for transformative action with wider audiences, their intention of *forward-looking "knowing"* rather than supposedly "accurate" understanding of "the situation" could be rendered more transparent.

Gustavsen argues that in order to avoid people seeing the process of theorizing around issues as "trying to establish the one and only true and right way," theorizing in practice can rather be seen as a process of "testing ideas, generating new associations [between ideas] and generally enriching our thoughts and actions" (2001, p. 19). He notes that in order to avoid buttressing the (still dominant) view of theorizing in a mode that tries to offer authoritative commentary on the operation of "reality," the reports that are generated through the dialogical search conferences that he has organized/supported shy away from offering undue "analyses." He suggests that besides reporting on the processes of the dialogue, and the statements developed during the conference, only "modest interpretations" are sometimes added in the report, to the extent that it is believed that the interpretations "will help the process forwards." Beyond this, "the report contains no analysis" (2001, p. 21). In this way, he argues that both during the conference (where the focus is on moving action forward) and during report writing, the pragmatic underpinning of the methodology becomes evident (2001, p. 19).

Gustavsen maintains that Habermas's theorizing itself can be interpreted as privileging theoretical discourse (of "professional" researchers) over and above other discourses. He avers that Habermas is wary that "participation in action will lock the researcher into the practical side of the equation in such a way that the ability to participate in theoretical discourse will become lost" (2001, p. 18). However, as I noted in Section 7.2.4, there are other ways of interpreting Habermas's position. I follow up the question of the development of social theorizing, including Habermas's reconstructive theorizing, in Chapter 8.

7.6 Conclusion

7.6.1 Taking into Account Researcher Accountability in Action Research

In this chapter I offered two examples of setting up opportunities for "action inquiry" with the focus on co-research as a way for people to reconsider their way of working and living, with particular reference to moving past socially sedimented polarizations. I used these examples to illustrate innovative possibilities for systemic inquiry – aimed at working on multiple levels to transform the conflicts and tensions created through the historical sedimentation of racialized/ethnicized constructions.

Considering the first example (the *Through a Hundred Pairs of Eyes Program* aimed at addressing institutional racism), I showed in relation to the three transcripts of scenes that I chose (Section 7.2.2.1), how issues that I located earlier in the book can become the focus of "live" discussion and critically reflexive co-inquiry with a view to opening up possibilities for individual and collective action. The way in which new racism can be seen to operate more or less invisibly, unless drawn attention to (Chapter 2, Section 2.2), the way in which quests to implement equal opportunities become disparaged by "symbolic racists" (Chapter 2, Section 2.3.1), and the political character of the category of Black as a social category (Chapter 2, Section 2.3.5.1; and Chapter 3, Section 3.4.2) form the basis for the scenes that I have chosen to present. I argued that the understandings developed through the inquiries as initiated via this anti-racist training and development package (whose import for participants is linked to their expansion of repertoires for action) can be said to emerge via a logical process of *abduction*. That is, I argued that this "logic" could be used to account for, and defend, the manner of theorizing around institutional racism as embodied in the program – albeit that the write-ups/reporting thereof (by Douglas and Weil) do not explicitly refer to any specific logic for developing theorizing.

I used the second example to offer an illustration of the more explicit use of abductive logic to enable people – through computer-aided dialogue – to consider possible ways of prioritizing their action options. In this case, the example was set in the context of a peace movement aimed at generating new ways of living together in Cyprus (across the divisions between Greek and Turkish Cypriot communities). I indicated that the view of facilitation subscribed to by those propounding the importance of SDDP to aid participants to construct a tree of "influence patterns" is a *process model* of facilitation. However, I suggested that it could (and should) be extended. I proposed that especially in cases of attempting to build trust between people, facilitators can *enter the trust-building process by showing the propensity to work with others in setting up increasingly dialogical relationships in the social fabric* (including between themselves and other participants), supported by ongoing self-reflection on their own complicity in the unfolding of the defined context. I suggested that in this way their discursive accountability may become better expressed.

7.6.2 Extending Research Options

I have concentrated in the chapter on locating what I consider to be the strengths of action inquiry directed around expanding people's horizons for seeing and acting in "lived time" in social life practice. However, a concern that has been leveled by some critics of the "pragmatic" bent of action inquiry is that the concentration on practice may be at the expense of *incisive theorizing*. Moreover, certain authors have argued that, whether in action research or other research enterprises, the concept of race (and in particular its featuring in manifestations of new racism) is still *under-theorized* and that more "race consciousness" needs to be injected into our social inquiries.

Marks, for instance, argues that "tools of analysis" when used by people (during whatever kind of inquiry process) "need a theoretical base" (2008, p. 49). She argues that especially in the case of research around new racism, it is difficult to "produce meaningful explanations for simultaneous progress" (in addressing some forms of racism) *and* "stagnation" (in that new forms of racism have taken hold) (2008, p. 48). She notes that certain writers have tried to confront this "difficulty" by pointing to the increasing significance of "class" as a tool of analysis, while recognizing that this did not imply a decline in racism (2008, p. 58). Other authors have insisted on retaining race as a concept that does not reduce it to "an epiphenomenon of some other category" (such as class). She argues further that even accounts of "multiple oppression" (and the attendant use of the word "intersectionality") have "done little to explain how race conflict emerges and expresses itself over time" and how "ruling ideas" exert pressure on people – even as they may try to resist these ideas.

Marks suggests that we still need to work toward producing a "convincing theory" that can explain, as Winant (2000, p. 81) mentions, how "Jim Crow was defeated, apartheid abolished, and colonialism discredited … yet racial classification and subordination persist" (2008, p. 60). Following on from the work of Du Bois (1903), she argues that we need to move toward creating "a convincing racial theory that addresses the persistence of racial classification [albeit in new forms] and stratification" (2008, p. 62).

The question thus remains whether action inquiry as I detailed it in this chapter may need to move in the direction suggested by Marks (in terms of theorizing "race" and its continued meanings in current discourses), and what this might involve. For instance, to further contextualize and develop the peace movement inquiries in Cyprus, it might be necessary to include, say, the additional line of inquiry proposed by Philippou when she suggests that we need to consider how the concept of Europe has become constructed in terms of "ethnocultural definitions." According to her, these definitions already incorporate an exclusivist orientation – one that restricts genuine engagement between (more) "western-oriented" and "eastern-oriented" traditions (2007, p. 76). (See Section 7.4.1.) In terms of her argument, it would seem that further investigation of "Europeanness" and the structural embeddedness of racism in the way in which normative standards become defined, may need to be undertaken. (See also Chapter 2, Section 2.3.4.1.)

Kundnani also can be said to be calling (albeit from a different perspective) for more incisive understanding of the way in which social exclusionary patterns become reproduced, by noting that across the globe apparently "enlightened" secular states can be seen to embody forms of exclusion precisely to the extent that they exclude "from the public sphere groups that define themselves by religion" (2007, p. 187). He states that the clearest example of the danger of such a form of exclusion is France, where the "ban on oversized religious symbols" in the public sphere "was aimed at preventing Muslim girls from wearing the hijab" (2007, p. 187).

Kundnani reminds us that the struggle against these new (coded) forms of racism "is not a fight for a particular religion or culture but a fight for universal human rights and against the vast economic and political inequalities of our world" (2007, p. 187). He suggests that this "fight" involves a "battle of ideas"; and at the same time it should involve

> building up community-based organizations that are capable of . . . raising issues and creating a movement for justice based on real solidarity, rather than imposed and divisive identities. (2007, p. 188)

Meanwhile, as Vratuša (2008) points out, there is cause for concern that across the globe forums for the majority of people to genuinely participate in defining a "desirable form of (re)construction of the basic social relations" are yet to be established (on an international level). She believes that the international discourse is tilted toward the value patterns of "the elites" – with their agenda of trying to "diminish the costs of control of the disinherited majority of the population" – rather than engaging a genuine democratic discussion around possibilities for radical transformation of (capitalist-oriented) social relations. She believes that those involved in "research" need to be aware of this "social and historical context of power relations" so that they can take this into account as part of their self-reflecting on how research "makes a difference" through the way it is conducted.

In terms of concerns such as those brought forward by, say, Kundnani (2007), Philippou (2007), Marks (2008), and Vratuša (2008), it might be suggested that our theorizing in relation to the historical development of exclusivist practices – as part of the process of imagining possibilities for increased inclusiveness on various scores – may require further attention than has thus far been given via the examples of action inquiry as I interpreted them in this chapter. In Chapter 8, I pursue this question by considering the arguments of those proposing the need for "structurally oriented" theorizing around (new) racism. I discuss these arguments by further considering the value of abductive/retroductive inference as a way of developing theoretical insight. My argument overall is that inquirers need not shy away from what Marks calls developing "theoretical bases" to make sense of new racism – but that the status of the theorizing should be understood as rooted in the co-inquiry processes on which I have indeed concentrated in this chapter.

In this chapter I focused on ways in which action inquiry can be seen to present "sound" social theorizing as a process of *learning with others* through the development of *critical reflexive capacity* and as a mode of *being-in-the-world*. I illustrated possibilities for co-inquirers to orient themselves to listening, caring, and learning as part of their knowing and being (and as a basis for trust earning). I suggested that in this way co-inquirers can instantiate approaches to knowing such that, as Douglas explains, research is seen *as* (already) change (2002, p. 250).

I propose that the practice and write-up of action inquiry can work toward exemplifying such an "alternative" epistemology (which ties knowing to the quality of human living) insofar as those participating:

- Excavate the *meaning of critical reflexivity as a way of being and learning with others* (and as a criterion through which people can assess others' personal accountability – to use Collins's terminology, 2000, p. 265).
- Make explicit to themselves and others the way in which the epistemology *ties "knowing" to concerns with undercutting different forms of domination*, including those forms potentially embedded in knowing processes.
- Make explicit to themselves and others *the way in which inferences are being generated* about the dynamics of (new) racism through drawing on people's collective wisdom (including their emotionally laden concerns).

On this last point, I proceed to Chapter 8 for a more detailed discussion.

Figure Credit

Figure 7.1 printed with permission; from Laouris, Y., Michaelides, M., Damdelen, M., Laouri R., Beyatli D. & Christakis, A. a systemic evaluation of the state of affairs following the negative outcome of the referendum in Cyprus using the structured dialogic design process. *Systemic Practice and Action Research*, 22(1), 45–75 @ 2009 Springer SBM. AND Figure 7.1 printed with permission:

from Laouris, Y., Michaelides, M., Damdelen,, M., Laouri, R., Beyatli, D., & Christakis, A. A systemic evaluation of the state of affairs following the negative outcome of the referendum in Cyprus using a structured dialogic design process. Retrieved at: http://www.futureworldscenter.org/Research/Full%20Papers/ RevivingPeaceArticle2007_04_13.pdf @ 2007 Future Worlds Center.

Chapter 8
Research Conducted in Terms of Retroductive Processes: Rethinking the Theorization of Racism

8.1 Introduction

In this chapter I examine possibilities for investigating the structuring of modes of social organization with the help of retroductive processes of inquiry. I suggest that an appeal to (some version of) retroductive logic – as a form of logical inference – can provide a justification for proffering social-structural analyses of the kinds outlined in Chapter 2, Sections 2.3.5 and 2.3.6, and as pointed to through my discussions in other chapters too. (See in particular, Chapter 5, Section 5.2.3; Chapter 6, Section 6.1.2; and Chapter 7, Sections 7.3.3 and 7.6.2.) I point to various opportunities for forwarding what Marks calls "convincing theorizing" (2008, p. 49) in which analyses of, inter alia, racism are developed at the level of social structure. Before I address the question of how such research can be justified (or in my terms, accounted for), I start off by showing how retroductive logic has been conceived by Peirce (whose suggested definition hereof I cited briefly in Chapter 7, Section 7.4.2.2).

As I indicated in Chapter 7, Peirce proposes that the form of logical inference that he calls abductive or retroductive reasoning can and must operate over and above induction and deduction to "open up new ground" in processes of theorizing (1911, p. 2).[208] Indeed he notes that he considers "retroduction ... to be the most important kind of reasoning, notwithstanding its very unreliable nature, because it is the only kind of reasoning that opens up new ground" (1911, p. 2). He defines retroduction as a logical inference that allows us to proceed from

> finding ourselves confronted by a state of things that, taken by itself seems almost or quite incomprehensible ... to supposing that perhaps there is ... another definite state of things ... which would shed a light of reason upon that state of facts with which we are confronted, rendering it comprehensible. (1911, p. 2)

---

[208]Like Chiassis (2001), Paavola comments that Peirce (1958) seemed to use the terms abduction and retroduction interchangeably – using "various names for this third mode of inference [over and above induction and deduction] throughout his long career" (2004, p. 16). While Chiassis argues that a different emphasis may be implied by the different use of the terms, Paavola sees the two terms as indeed interchangeable.

He remarks that the "characteristic formula" of reasoning that he calls retroduction is that it involves reasoning from a *consequent* (any observed/experienced phenomena that confront us) to an *antecedent* (i.e., a posited state of things that helps us to render comprehensible the observed phenomena). Or, as he otherwise puts it, it can be considered as "regressing from a consequent to a hypothetical antecedent" (1911, p. 4). He believes that this form of "probable reasoning" is, as he apprehends it, "what Aristotle meant by {apagögé}" in his "train of thought." But he suggests that apagögé "should be translated not by the word abduction, as the custom of translators is, but rather by reduction or retroduction." He indicates in his lectures on *Reasoning and the Logic of Things* that he "shall generally call this type of reasoning retroduction" (1898).[209]

Hanson (1958), following Peirce, and drawing on his argument, also wishes to give due attention to abduction/retroduction as a form of inference separate from inductive and deductive inference. Marsden points to Hanson's summary account of the form taken by this mode of inference:

(1) Some surprising phenomena, $P_{1,2,3}$ are observed.[210]
(2) $P_{1,2,3}$ would be explicable if H [a hypothesis about an unobservable state of affairs] were true.
(3) Hence, there is reason to think that H is true.

Marsden indicates that in this formulation, although there is no logical necessity between P and H, retroduction is still seen by Hanson (1958, 1961) as a form of logical inference – one that, however, expresses its "conclusions ... only problematically or conjecturally" (1998, p. 299). Marsden elaborates on this logic as part of his suggestion that Marx adhered to this manner of practicing science, and that his work should be read and understood in the light hereof (1998, p. 299). In this regard Marsden follows Sayer (1983), who likewise refers to the importance of recognizing this form of logic in order to appreciate "the procedures of what Marx practiced as science" in his exploration of capitalism as a social formation (1983, p. 141). Sayer argues that there is a connection between the view of explanation that he sees Marx as invoking in *Capital* (1965) and the retroductive account of theory development. That is, he argues that we can reconstruct the logic of Marx's *Capital* by reading it in terms of the retroductive mode of developing theoretical explanations.[211]

---

[209]Chiassis suggests that this is because *abduction* implies "moving away" from observables (toward generating a hypothesis) whereas *retroduction* incorporates the notion of "going backwards" to provide an explanation (Chiassis, 2001, p. 2).

[210]Paavola states that in Peirce's argument, the event(s) do not necessarily have to be "surprising" – although a good strategy is to work from "anomalous or surprising phenomena." As he explains, "although it is possible to start abductive [retroductive] inference from non-anomalous phenomena, it is often a good strategical point to concentrate on anomalous phenomena" (2004, p. 13).

[211]Sayer postulates the methodological unity of the natural and social sciences, arguing that the logic of retroduction properly guides the study of both natural and social reality.

Sayer elucidates that the use of retroductive logic implies that one is oriented to postulating (albeit conjecturally) the existence of *underlying mechanisms* or *structures* in reality as part of the process of explaining discernible phenomena. This is because retroductive logic proceeds by "postulat[ing] mechanisms which should they exist would explain how the phenomena under investigation come to assume the forms in which they are experienced" (Sayer, 1979, p. 40). In terms of retroductive logic, the logical link between "H" (causal mechanism) and "P" (observable phenomena) consists in the fact that "H" posits a mechanism which, "*if it existed*, would offer an explanation for P$_1$, P$_2$, P$_3$, and so on" (Sayer, 1983, p. 116, my italics). In other words, the logic is used to postulate mechanisms whose posited existence helps us to make sense of the events (phenomena or appearances) as we experience them in their observable form.

Sayer's reference to retroductive logic is used by him to suggest that Marx proceeded, via retroduction, to generate theoretical accounts of, for instance, the causal power of capitalist social structures and mechanisms that, once theorized, help to explain experienced phenomena. Sayer insists that it is important to maintain the distinction between social *mechanisms* and the *phenomenal forms* that we experience in order to be able to provide adequate explanations for the latter's appearance. Unless efforts are made to get to grips with *underlying causal mechanisms*, "causes" may come to be understood in terms of constant conjunctions between observed phenomena (as they are in the positivist and hypothetico-deductivist traditions) – leading people to leave unexplored the *causal power of capitalist relations of production in generating outcomes*. The focus on retroductive logic thus involves a critique of various forms of positivist/hypothetico-deductivist empiricism.[212]

This ties in with Layder's argument (1993) to which I referred in Chapter 6 (Section 6.1.2) in relation to his critique of "middle range theorizing" as an approach to scientific inquiry. In similar vein to Sayer, Layder argues that what is properly involved in the process of such inquiry (whether applied in the natural or social sciences) is different from what is supposed within a positivist/hypothetico-deductive-oriented understanding of science. He points out that

> a key aspect of the [scientific] realist project is a concern with causality and the identification of causal mechanisms . . . in a manner quite unlike the traditional positivist search for causal generalizations [stating a relationship of causality between variables]. (1993, p. 16)

Layder's suggestion is that besides testing specific hypotheses about relationships between variables (as, for instance, seems to be the primary focus of the researchers'

---

[212] Keat and Urry put forward a similar argument when explaining their realist position as an alternative to positivism (1975, p. 54). They indicate that they do not wish to identify themselves with the positivist suggestion (including the Popperian argument) "that there is any specifiable set of logical relationships between theories and perceptual [observation] statements" (1975, p. 233). For a discussion of the debate between scientific realists endorsing Marx's approach and Popperian-oriented authors who question the positing of unobservable entities as a way of explaining causality, see Romm (1991, pp. 64–66 and 92–93). And for more detail on the scientific realist argument in relation to various other approaches, see Romm, 2001, pp. 37–54.

work I discussed in Chapters 3 and 4), space should be made for theory-constructing approaches that go beyond looking for such relationships (1993, p. 31). Theorizing should also not, however, be confined to the emergent theorizing suggested by certain more qualitatively oriented researchers – because, he argues, the attendant view of structure still does not allow us to assign analytic weight to structures beyond the "immediate environment of actors" (1993, p. 56).[213]

Joseph and Kennedy for their part argue that a crucial consequence of Marx's use of retroductive reasoning toward an understanding of social structures is that it points to the *historization* of these structures (2000, p. 514). That is, the "causal connections" that may be observed between any phenomena (or variables in positivist/hypothetico-deductive terms) are seen to be linked in turn to *structures that are historically variable*. This means that "causal regularities" can become recognized to be *transformable if the underlying structures that are postulated to generate them, themselves become changed*. In contrast, theories that are unable to theorize the socialization and historization of specific modes of social organization become "trapped in the realm of fetishized relations" – unable to imagine their transformation.

While authors such as Sayer (1983), Layder (1993), Marsden (1998), and Joseph and Kennedy (2000) adopt a (scientific) realist argument in posing the utility of retroductive logic to explore structures and their causal mechanisms and possibilities for transformation, this is not the only manner in which the use of retroductive logic can be seen. Indeed, as Burch notes, even when Peirce calls himself a "realist" or is called by others a "realist," it must be kept in mind that his realism is more an "internal realism" – in the sense that "the world" as it is comprehended is considered by Peirce as interpreted through mental concepts as well as evolving (Burch, 2006, pp. 8–9). Burch thus considers that the labels of "anti-foundationalist" and "fallibilist" aptly apply to his position (2006, p. 9).[214]

I point to this interpretation of Peirce's argument in order to show that retroductive logic need not always be associated with a scientific realist position.[215]

---

[213]Layder refers in particular to those following Strauss's grounded theorizing approach, which shies away from making claims about the way in which structural conditions necessarily become relevant to the "interactional/processual phenomena under study" (Strauss, 1987, p. 80, as cited in Layder, 1993, p. 56). As I explained in Chapter 5 (Section 5.2.3), Essed develops an approach that incorporates analytic induction with structural deliberation; and as I showed in Chapter 6 via my chosen examples, ethnography can also move beyond what Layder would criticize as "middle range."

[214]Lincoln and Guba point to the affinity between constructivism and anti-foundationalism when they note that "constructivists ... tend toward the anti-foundational" (2003, p. 273). (See also Footnote 132.)

[215]Paavola argues that Peirce's understanding of the status of retroduction – more so than the views of Hanson – has scope to broaden our conception of human rationality so as to encompass a "distributed cognition" approach, which emphasizes that:

Human cognition is not confined to individuals and within individuals' minds but is distributed in essential ways to surrounding physical, social, and cultural environments and to long-term temporal processes. (2006, p. 5)

What can be called a non-realist interpretation of retroductive logic is also made by McIntyre-Mills when she defines it as a mode of inference that allows people to

> trace the connections across institutions in society and demonstrate how society shapes life chances . . . . It also involves understanding what the terms mean and why, in terms of the different stakeholders' assumptions and values. (2006b, p. 391)

In McIntyre-Mills's account, retroductive logic need not go hand in hand with striving to develop a more or less value-free understanding of the workings of social systems (as "objects" to be disclosed). Value-full understanding (and discussion around different values that may be brought to bear) is catered for in her approach. She links retroductive logic to Churchman's argument (1979) concerning the need to sweep in a range of felt concerns and values as part of the process of defining systemically issues at stake to be addressed. As she explains in the context of her book exploring Indigenous ways of life in Alice Springs (Australia):

> This book is about "unfolding" and "sweeping in" . . . the issues that can be explained retroductively as historical, economic, intergenerational violence associated with marginalization, alcohol and poverty. An economy that supports the class/culture system is [considered as] written in the socio-demographic patterns of disadvantage (educational outcomes, unemployment and incarceration), morbidity and mortality and life chances. That is why the intervention to break the interlinked cycles has to be at the level of regional governance [promoting citizenship rights and responsibilities]. (2003, p. 11)

She indicates that the challenge for retroductive thinking in this case was linked to the policy goal of "addressing power, empowerment and governance needs of people marginalized in terms of conceptual, geographical and cyberspace/time" (2003, p. 12). The results of a history of colonization and marginalization – spelt out in alcoholism, cultural despair, and a sense of real powerlessness – needed to be addressed by "breaking the cycle," through Indigenous people "refocusing the direction of development" (2003, p. 14). She points out that refocusing this direction involved moving away from "the market rules" philosophy, toward exploring the liberative potential of other frameworks for living (2003, p. 14). In this way, she offers an account of how the historical contextualization via a form of retroductive reasoning offered a route for enabling people to become more equipped to "co-create the designs of their . . . futures" (2003, p. 16).

In the course of the chapter, I discuss various interpretations of what is involved in the "logic" of retroduction, and I show how an understanding hereof can aid us to re-examine as well as refresh the theorizing of race issues. My suggestion on the whole is that while it is possible to invoke retroductive processes of inference within both realist and more constructivist-oriented approaches, the latter approaches offer more scope for linking our ways of developing theorizing to practical processes of forwarding social justice projects.

According to Paavola a distributed cognition approach allows us to undercut the view that making inferences is a matter of "processes within one's mind" in which one tries to make a connection with "nature" (or some posited external extra-linguistic world); and it opens up possibilities for instead developing "new kinds of conceptualizations concerning human activity" (2006, p. 12).

I structure this chapter by delving – as my prime example – into the theorizing that Bonilla-Silva advances (which I argue can be understood in terms of the logic of retroductive inference). I show that there are various ways in which Bonilla-Silva's self-understanding of his work can be interpreted. And I suggest that insofar as we are able to interpret the texts as veering in a constructivist/pragmatic direction (see Table 8.1 in Section 8.3.3), they can more readily be used to support the orientation as pleaded for, by example, Douglas (1998, Chapter 6, p. 13), Collins (2000, p. 289), and Ladson-Billings (2003, p. 399), who call for inquirers to exemplify via the inquiry process the practicing of non-dominative social relations.

Before I look into these arguments around what it may mean to employ retroductive processes of inference in constructivist/pragmatic-oriented fashion, and what the social implications hereof might be, I first (Section 8.2) offer a summary elucidation of Sayer's account of Marx's retroductive mode of explanation as a way of theorizing around *capitalism* and I show how similarly certain theorizations of *racism* can likewise be argued to invoke this mode of inference. With this backdrop to elucidating retroduction as a mode of inference, I then (Section 8.3) consider in some detail Bonilla-Silva's systemic approach to exploring racism while providing an indication of how he sees the relationship of his work to Marxism. I indicate how an understanding of retroductive logic can provide an account of how he justifies his conceptualization of racialized social systems.

In Section 8.4 I delve further into how we might consider his deliberations around the status of his theorizing. I suggest that he seems to be appealing to critical theoretical arguments that in some way offer a critique of realist epistemologies. I revisit his approach to theorizing by drawing out further the implications of some of his statements about his inquiry endeavors. I suggest that these need indeed to be further drawn out and extended so as to incorporate more fully the concerns raised by authors such as Collins (1990, 2000), Douglas (1998), and Ladson-Billings (2003) in relation to the dominance of styles of knowing that separate "epistemology" from "ethics." Finally, in Sections 8.5 and 8.6, in discussing the various arguments, including a re-look at Bonilla-Silva's deliberations on the USA and on Brazilian social relations, I remark on how his work can be seen to cast light on the issues raised by the debate between Bourdieu and Wacquant that I introduced in Chapter 2 (Section 2.4) in relation to the apparent global dominance of the US discourse on "race relations."

8.2 Retroductive Logic: The Potential for Theorizing Around Structures

In Sayer's account, the use of retroductive logic implies an endeavor to advance our understanding of (natural or social) mechanisms or structures that are posited to have causal efficacy, albeit that they are themselves rarely observable. Sayer argues that Marx implicitly draws on this mode of inference in his theorizing of capitalism as a social formation. For instance, Marx suggests that any consideration of the "laws of the market" regulating the supply and demand of commodities and determining the wage level of workers in capitalism needs to be related back to an understanding of the *essential relation between "capital" and "labor" that characterizes the capitalist mode of production (although this is itself not observable).* It is only with reference to an understanding of the constitution of the entity called "capitalism" that we can properly explain the way that outcomes become generated in the society (1983, p. 141). This implies a particular view of causality, namely, the causality that arises because the essential structure of certain entities – in this case, capitalism – produces certain outcomes. According to Sayer, it is *this* kind of causality that retroductive logic is properly geared to come to grips with.

Just as Sayer recovers Marx's retroductive approach as a way of examining capitalism, we can apply a similar inspection of the style of inference used by certain authors theorizing racism in terms of social-structural mechanisms. As an example, we can consider the argument of Stewart, who creates a model to explain the continued racial outcome disparities that we find "in the Western world," where, as he puts it, "race is perhaps the most salient representation of inequality" (2008, p. 111). He points to "persistent, significant racial disparities in education, earnings, wealth, health, mortality and other indicators of social well being" (2008, p. 111). In developing his model, he uses an allegory of "swimming upstream" – where different swimmers swim in different directions to start with in the rivers (social institutions), disadvantaging the upstream swimmers. Via this allegory, he suggests that inequality becomes produced through "countless social interactions taking place in various locations and levels in society" (2008, p. 118). He presents his allegory by comparing the swimming scenario with social situations embodying:

(1) Competition for Social Status and Resources;
(2) Institutions;
(3) Racial Classification/Structure;
(4) Confronting Racial Discrimination;
(5) Receiving Racial Privilege;
(6) Social Outcomes;
(7) Racial Disparities in Outcomes;
(8) Reactions to Racial Treatment;
(9) Relationship between Racial Disparities across Institutional Contexts.

In explicating his account of the "mechanisms of racial privilege" (2008, p. 111), he criticizes the inadequacy of certain quantitative methodologies. For instance, he criticizes "variable analytic research" which examines disparities between people's wages by suggesting that if we control for certain "background factors," the Black-White wage disparity becomes "reduced to insignificance" (2008, p. 120). The background factors (considered as variables) that have been drawn upon in studies of the US labor market are factors such as "years of education," "work experience," [and] "skills" (2008, p. 120). Stewart points out that this way of proceeding is not equipped to assess "the complex social interactions that create wage inequality."

Thus although the studies are often cited as "evidence of race neutrality in the labor market" (because it appears that factors other than race are determining the outcomes), a *deeper examination of the "results"* indicates that they are *not equipped to offer any conclusions* as to whether "racism exists or does not exist in the American labor market" (2008, p. 120). Nor are "comparative analyses" – which try to determine "what distinguishes successful minority actors from the unsuccessful mass" by locating variables such as "family structure, culture and motivation" – equipped to explore the *underlying mechanisms producing racialized inequality.* One of the reasons why comparative analysis (using identified variables) is inadequate to this task is because it "often overlooks the dependence of current characteristics on *prior treatment and reactions"* (2008, p. 121, my italics). Due to the deficiency of these "variable-based models of difference" (variable analysis and comparative analysis), Stewart calls for a "theoretical shift" in approach (2008, p. 121).

In providing his account of how to examine racial privilege and disadvantage, I would suggest that Stewart invokes a retroductive style of inference not unlike the one that authors such as Sayer attribute to Marx. That is, Stewart cautions against stopping the analysis at the level of (what are taken to be) observed correlations (as observed via, say, the mathematical regressions). Instead of taking at face value what appears to be observed, he moves beyond these and provides an allegory detailing the mechanisms that he sees as functioning as a totality to effect the reproduction of structured inequality. He thus moves toward developing a systemic approach to the theorizing of race, by viewing outcome disparities in terms of different, broader theoretical lenses than he sees as supplied through the "variable analysis."

What is important to note here too is that Stewart indicates that observations as made by people (including by scientists) need not be regarded as themselves theory- or value-neutral. For example, the "observations" produced by the variable-oriented research to which he refers can be regarded as indeed generated through the specific way of organizing the research. (This is related to my argument in previous chapters concerning the way in which the research process itself can lead to certain "data" becoming presented via the way the research is designed.) It is in this sense Stewart argues that the mathematical regressions of quantitative variable analysis are only *seemingly* objective: they already carry with them a specific way of looking at "the data" in the first place, that is, in a way that in this case renders invisible to our vision the prior (racialized) treatment of people and their reactions to this.

Stewart finds it important to trace (observed) disparities in education, earnings, wealth, health, mortality and other indicators of social well being, and so on, back to the complex interaction of events across various social institutions – through his allegory of racial privileges and disadvantages built into the "swimming against the stream" scenario. This can be seen as bearing some similarity to Essed's (1991) emphasis on examining events as reported in this case through her interviewees, by assessing them in relation not only to other events in their lives but also in relation to events as experienced across their different lives in order to show how an understanding of racism can serve to explain many of the incidents as reported upon. (See Chapter 5, Section 5.2.3.)

Stewart indicates that he regards his allegory as a way of showing how researchers can shift focus (from narrow variable-based analyses) toward "aim[ing] to [better] locate the sources of racial inequality" (2008, p. 122). While he offers some examples of research that can be seen as oriented in this direction, he suggests that future research should be aimed at

> revealing the connectedness of social interactions – racial treatment [including racial discrimination and racial privilege], perceptions, and coping responses – across time and space. More specifically, future research should examine how the tenor of social interactions in one institution (e.g., education) at a particular time are either reinforced or weakened by the tone of social interactions in another institution (e.g., labor force) – or the same institution at a later time. (2008, p. 123)

He adds that "future research . . . should expand beyond the labor force and immigrants to include a broad array of populations and a variety of institutions (e.g. familial, health care, and residential)" (2008, p. 124).

Stewart indicates that while he uses the "allegory of the swim meet" to point to the importance of institutionally directed research, the allegory "does not capture the historical dynamics of race." He points out that literary techniques such as allegories can "involve limitations" (2008, p. 124, Endnote 1). But he clearly wishes to take a historical perspective in explaining the development of racialized social formations. He regards this as important in "our goal [both] of understanding and eradicating racial inequality" (2008, p. 124). Hence I suggest that his proposed approach spurring structurally oriented research in terms of an historical lens is consistent with the account of retroduction that I have outlined above. However, he does not concentrate on spelling out how the attendant understanding might become put forward as indeed offering "understanding." As the chapter proceeds, I show with reference to a detailed exposition of the work of Bonilla-Silva that there may be various ways of viewing the arguments/insights of those forwarding structural-oriented theorizing. As mentioned earlier, I use the work of Bonilla-Silva as a springboard to discuss these. But first it is necessary to show how Bonilla-Silva himself presents his case for offering a structural interpretation of racism that goes beyond "idealist" definitions of racism and incorporates a concern with (material) structures – in particular, the materiality (as he puts it) of racism.

8.3   Bonilla-Silva's Approach to Rethinking Racism via a Structural Interpretation

Bonilla-Silva begins his presentation of a structural interpretation of racism by claiming that "the area of race and ethnic studies lacks a sound theoretical apparatus." He suggests that many analysts of racial matters have "abandoned the serious theorization and reconceptualization of their central topic: racism" (1997, p. 465). He argues that one of the problems with these analyses is that they tend to define racism in "idealist" terms – thus neglecting its material basis. The narrow idealist focus, in which racism is defined as a set of *beliefs or ideas* (such as in the definition of it by Schaefer, 1990, p. 16, as cited in Bonilla-Silva, 1997, p. 465), implies that:

> First, racism is defined as a set of ideas or beliefs. Second, those beliefs are regarded as having the potential to lead individuals to develop prejudice, defined as "negative attitudes toward an entire group of people" (Schaefer, 1990, p. 53). Finally, these prejudicial attitudes may induce individuals to real actions of discrimination against minorities. (1997, p. 466)

As can be gleaned from my discussion of the exemplars of social psychological experiments and surveys in Chapters 3 and 4, I believe that Bonilla-Silva's commentary on how racism is envisaged by those focusing on "prejudicial attitudes" can be considered as still currently pertinent insofar as the research focus appears to be on people's *cognitions and categorical representations*. It is for this reason that I suggest that these approaches need to be shifted/extended through, inter alia, developing an increased "theoretical literacy" – as argued for by, for example, Douglas (1998, Chapter 4, p. 16), Harris-Lacewell (2003, p. 246), McIntyre-Mills (2003, pp. 33–34), and Morton, Hornsey, and Postmes (2009, p. 36) (See, e.g., Chapter 3, Section 3.4.2; and Chapter 4, Section 4.3.2).

And I also argued in Chapters 5, 6, and 7 that certain theorizations of racism proffered as part of interviewing, ethnographic, and action research approaches too can become extended with a view to reflexively (re)considering the manner in which theoretical constructions are being developed. (See, e.g., Chapter 5, Section 5.3.2; Chapter 6, Section 6.3.1; and Chapter 7, Section 7.5.2.)

I now turn to considering Bonilla-Silva's relationship to the way in which racism has been studied within what he calls the "orthodox Marxist" or "neo-Marxist" positions – which he sees as strtucturally oriented, but not sufficiently oriented to exploring the specific structuration of a *racialized* social order.[216] To be able better to appreciate Bonilla-Silva's critique of these positions, I commence (Section 8.3.1) by providing a brief outline of certain self-labeled Marxist accounts of the primacy of the concept of "class" as a central analytic tool.

8.3.1 The Marxist Focus on Class Analysis

Stating an argument that Bonilla-Silva labels as neo-Marxist in orientation (1997, p. 466), Miles points out that the purpose of a Marxist-oriented theory is to focus on the concept of class as "anchored in production relations, a structural feature of social formations" (1996, p. 5). Miles contends that it is only by proceeding through the first analytic step of mapping out *class* positions in the social formation, that we can begin to recognize the structural underpinnings of the production of race differentiation and the way in which this has been utilized within the development

---

[216]Bonilla-Silva considers as "orthodox Marxists" those who "regard class and class struggle as the central explanatory variables of social life [and] reduce racism to a legitimating ideology used by the bourgeoisie to divide the working class." He argues that neo-Marxists "share to various degrees the limitations of the orthodox Marxist view: the primacy of class, racism viewed as an ideology, and class dynamics as the real engine of racial dynamics" (1997, p. 466).

of capitalism (1996, p. 5). As he explains, this way of proceeding in our analyses allows us to better understand the "processes by which 'race difference' is socially constructed and the processes by which resources and rewards are . . . produced" (1996, p. 6).

Miles avers that putting forward *class* rather than race as the central analytic tool enables us to consider the ways in which issues of race are handled in various (capitalist) societies – by referring back to the constraints that are set by the needs of capital and the nature of capitalist production. For example, he believes that immigration policies in Britain can be explained (albeit not necessarily predicted) by making reference to these needs (1996, p. 7). Miles here follows authors such as Keat and Urry (1975), Keat (1981), and Sayer (1983), who argue that it is not necessary for researchers to put their focus on generating predictions in order that their theorizing is regarded as credible; more important is that they can provide *plausible explanations* by referring back to structures that render the events explicable.

McLaren follows a similar line of argument (while being interviewed by Rikowski) when he suggests that "we need to understand not only the theoretical concepts that Marx offers us but also the way in which Marx thinks" (2005, p. 478). He emphasizes that the importance of Marx's works is that they "constitute a critique of relations [of production] historically specific to capitalism" (2005, p. 478). When Rikowski questions McLaren about whether his own Marxism "swamps concerns with 'race', gender [and] with social movements in general" (2005, p. 496), he agrees that it is "important to continue this discussion" (2005, p. 497). He answers as follows:

> But let me shift here to your comment about privileging class oppression over other forms of oppression. I hold that in general class struggle modifies the particularities of other struggles, that there is a strategic centrality to class struggle in that capitalism is the most powerful and far-reaching process of commodification imaginable. (2005, p. 497)

He adds that there is no need to believe that the "stress on class detracts from antiracist efforts in [say] education or efforts to de-claw patriarchy" (2005, p. 497). He argues that such a position would be an "insult to feminists and activists of color who have historically played an important role in the struggle against capitalist exploitation" (2005, p. 497).

McLaren states that the main point he wants to make is that "capitalism will find ways to survive the challenge of multiculturalism and feminism by co-opting these struggles" (2005, p. 497). He points out that he supports projects that bring into view "the relation between capitalism and racism, and capitalism and sexism and capitalism and heteronormativity" (2005, p. 497). But he emphasizes that there is

> a strategic centrality to my work that I won't deny, or apologize for, that seeks to unite new social movements with the old social movements, so that anti-capitalist struggle becomes a unifying priority. (2005, p. 497)

McLaren and Farahmandpur further argue that, as they see it, Marx's analysis of capitalism is today even more "desperately needed" than it was in Marx's time (2005, p. 4). They point to the "dangerous politics that we face today," where "limitless concessions" are granted to transnational corporations and

> private interests [are permitted to] control social life in the pursuit of profits for the few (i.e. through lowering taxes on the wealthy, scrapping environmental regulations, and dismantling public education and social welfare programs). (2005, p. 5)

In the light of the global "intensification of class polarization and the upward redistribution of wealth" (2005, p. 4), they urge us to recognize the relevance of Marx's work – which enables us to expose "the historically specific limits of the capitalist mode of production" (2005, p. 4). They summarize their position:

> That Marxism appears to have lost its epochal footing and does not yet enjoy a new refunctional status as the official opponent of neoliberalism and the downsizing of democracy does not mean that educators [and others] should remain inactive until history is suddenly served by a wake up call that will make Marxism relevant again. (2005, p. 5)

Mocombe likewise points to the continued relevance of Marxism in terms of a theoretical framework offered "at the global institutional or world system" (2006, p. 399). He elucidates that:

> The upper class of owners and high-level executives, based in the corporate community of developed countries like the United States, represent today's dominant bourgeois capitalist class whose various distributive powers lead to a situation where their policies . . . determine the "life chances" of not only local social actors, within the globalizing developed nation, but global ones as well. (2006, p. 399)

He argues that considering the desires of the corporate community to "continue to grow and make profits," the corporate-driven agenda of the developed world (in line with the structure of their social relations) in turn creates conditions such that the

> developing countries must establish open markets as the basis for development and social relations, but these markets when established are unable to compete with those of competitors in the West, and therefore get usurped by the capitalists of the West who take advantage of the labor force – which is cheapened in order to compete globally with other, cheaper, prospective markets – and other resources of the developing country. (2006, p. 399)

Mocombe thus calls for an increased theoretical focus on the locus of causality of what he calls "class-based structural differentiation" across the globe (2006, p. 398).

Harvey sets the Marxist argument in the context of the 2008 world financial crisis and its aftermath – which, he argues, can be seen as evidence (as Marx and Engels' *Communist Manifesto*, 1848, foresaw) of a "violent, brutalizing, and perpetually revolutionizing capitalism" (2008, p. 7). Using some of the wordings of the *Communist Manifesto*, he points to wages of workers being "ever more fluctuating" and livelihoods being "more and more precarious" while insecurities over jobs, social provision, and pensions generate collective anxieties where "all that is solid" seems to be "perpetually melting into air" (2008, p. 6). He points out that while some "corporate heads" that "innovated us into this mess" have lost their jobs, they

> have had to pay nothing back of the many millions they earned in the halcyon years and some received incredibly generous golden handshakes when they stepped down – $161 million in the case of Stan O'Neal of Merrill Lynch and $40 million for Charles Prince of Citicorp . . . . And just to add insult to class injury, those companies and lawyers employed

in the "foreclosure mill", as it is now called [in relation to house foreclosures] are reaping the handsomest of profits. Who said class differences (neatly intertwined, as is all too often the case, with race and gender) are irrelevant to the sociality of our postmodern times? (2008, p. 5)

Meanwhile he argues that over the last 30 years a no-holds-barred corporate capitalism has emerged across the globe. He notes that:

> In China, Bangladesh, Indonesia, Guatemala and Vietnam, contemporary descriptions of the catastrophic conditions of laboring could be inserted into Marx's chapter on "the Working Day" in *Capital* without anyone being able to tell the difference. And the most rabid forms of exploitation rest, as is so often the case, on the backs of women and people of color. (2008, p. 12)

He contends that with a capitalist class that "many now regard as being by definition transnational," we need to try to gauge the economic situation as well as "the political possibilities of our time." But he comments that, unfortunately, many workers, "desperate for jobs, are corralled into supporting local alliances to promote development packages and projects that offer sweet subsidies to highly mobile multinational capital to come to or stay in town" – thus rendering any prospective "unity of the working classes" far more difficult (2008, pp. 14–15).

He re-iterates that the issue concerns the "predatory practices" of "the capitalist classes" in all their manifestations – including the practices that led to workers in the USA and Europe "losing not only their homes but also their hard-won pension and health-care rights" (2008, p. 16). He indicates that this is what he calls the "accumulation of dispossession" in the current situation (2008, p. 17). And, he points to the continued necessity for "both progressive and permanent revolutions of the sort that capitalism so successfully and vigorously prosecutes" – through an "organizational form of class struggle" that is able to "jump geographical scales" and "move smoothly from the local to the global and back again" (2008, p. 19). He argues that there is good reason why "Marx and Engels return to the proletariat again and again as the central agent of radical and transformative change" (2008, p. 16).

8.3.2 Bonilla-Silva's Reconsideration of Marxist Analyses: Lacunae in Theorizing Racialized Social Systems

Faced with these kinds of Marxist-oriented arguments, Bonilla-Silva concedes the value of such thinking in attuning us to the (historically specific) structures of capitalism as a social formation. Nevertheless, he is concerned that in Marxist and neo-Marxist modes of analysis, racialized differentiation is seen as somehow a *by-product of class dynamics,* and as such, it becomes difficult to conceptualize the structuring of what he calls *racialized social* systems (1997, p. 468, 2006, p. 9). His contention is that Marxist-oriented authors stressing the primacy of class may not be analytically equipped to delve into the full significance of the materiality and structuring of racism in the social fabric (1997, p. 468). He explains that by *structure* he means (following Whitmeyer, 1994, p. 154) "the networks of (interactional) relationships among actors as well as the distributions of socially meaningful characteristics of actors and aggregates of actors" (1997, p. 469). And by *materiality* he means "the economic, social, political, or ideological rewards or penalties received by social actors for their participation ... in social structural arrangements" (1997, p. 469).

In order to offer a "structural interpretation" of racism that enables it to be viewed as involving a specific "materalty or structure," Bonilla-Silva considers it crucial that the concept of *racialized social system* is accorded theoretical importance (1997, p. 469). He elucidates his use of the term:

> This term refers to societies in which economic, political, social, and ideological levels are partially structured by the placement of actors in racial categories or races. Races typically are identified by their phenotype, but ... the selection of certain human traits to designate a racial group is always socially rather than biologically based. (1997, p. 469)

Bonilla-Silva indicates that the reason why he suggests that racialized social systems are only *partially structured* by race is because modern social systems also articulate "two or more forms of hierarchical patterns." It is in view hereof, he notes, that certain researchers have focused on intersections of different forms of oppression.[217] (See also my discussion on intersectionality in Chapter 3, Section 3.5.2.2; and Chapter 5, Section 5.2.1.)

He points out that because "historically ... racialization occurred in social formations also structured by class and gender," one of the consequences is that the racial structuration of subjects becomes "fragmented along class and gender lines" (1997, p. 470). Hence

> not all members of the subordinate race receive the same level of rewards and (conversely) not all members of the subordinate race or races are at the bottom of the social order. (1997, p. 470)

But he suggests that this does not "negate the fact that races, as social groups, are in either a superordinate or a subordinate position in the social order" (1997, p. 470).

As regards the important question concerning the bases on which actors are moved to struggle, he emphasizes that this "is historically contingent and cannot be ascertained a priori." (He cites, for instance, Anthias and Yuval-Davis, 1992 on this.) He provides as empirical examples class interests taking precedence over racial ones in the countries of Brazil, Cuba, and Puerto Rico; while he suggests that in other situations, "racial interest may take precedence over class interests as in the case of Blacks throughout the U.S. history" (1997, p. 471).

In any case, to say that a society can be characterized as a racialized social system is to draw attention to the way in which "the placement of people in racial categories involves some form of hierarchy that produces definite social relations between the races" (1997, p. 469). Furthermore, it is to point out that (contrary to the Marxist

---

[217]He refers for example to Segura's (1990) work on race, class, and gender as the primary axes of social hierarchy in modern societies, and Essed's (1991) work on "gendered racism" (1997, p. 469).

insistence on the primacy of class) racialized forms of social relationship need to be given specific consideration as such.

He defines a racialized system (which may be more or less empirically manifested) as one where life chances are differentiated along racialized lines. He explains that

> ultimately a racialized social order is distinguished by this difference in life chances. Generally, the more dissimilar the races' life chances, the more racialized the social system, and vice versa. (1997, p. 470)

He also elucidates that the specific ways in which racialized hierarchies are formed is variable. He cites Omi and Winant's indication (1994) that

> domination of Blacks in the United States was achieved through dictatorial means during slavery, but in the post-civil rights period this domination has been hegemonic [resting on different forms of social control]. Similarly [he notes] the racial practices and mechanisms that have kept Blacks subordinate changed from overt and eminently racist to covert and indirectly racist. (1997, p. 470)

Although he remarks (1997, p. 466) that Omi and Winant's perspective provides an important theoretical approach in that they conceptualize race as "an organizing principle of social relationships that shapes the identity of individual actors at the micro level and shapes all spheres of life at the macro level," he does not concur with them on certain points. He believes that their perspective

> still gives undue attention to ideological/cultural processes, does not regard races as truly social collectivities, and overemphasizes the racial projects ... of certain actors (neoconservatives, members of the far right, liberals), thus obscuring the social and general character of racialized societies. (1997, p. 466)

It is worth noting in this regard that Omi and Winant comment that "academic and political controversies about the nature of racism have centered on whether it is primarily an ideological or structural phenomenon" (2002a, p. 138). They indicate that those putting the emphasis on racism as *ideology* consider racism as "first and foremost a matter of beliefs and attitudes, doctrines and discourse" (2002a, p. 138). Those emphasizing the *structural embeddedness of racism* "see racism as primarily a matter of economic stratification, residential segregation and other institutional forms of inequality which then give rise to ideologies of privilege" (2002a, p. 138). Their own view is that

> it is crucial to disrupt the fixity of these positions by simultaneously arguing that ideological beliefs have structural consequences and that social structures give rise to beliefs. (2002a, p. 138)

They aver that "today, racial hegemony is 'messy'" in that it cannot be understood via any *either/or* position. As they put it: "The complexity of the present situation is the product of a vast historical legacy of [*both*] structural inequality *and* invidious racial representation" (2002a, p. 139, my italics). They thus believe that our theorizing should be attuned to recognize that both structure and ideology can interact and mutually determine each other.

I would suggest that Omi and Winant's argument in this respect can be seen to concur in large part with that of Bonilla-Silva, who too wishes to emphasize the adaptable character of racism, which continues to be infused in the social formation aided by the development of new ideologies (such as color-blind racism). The question on which I wish to concentrate now is how we should regard the standing of the concept of *racialized social system* that Bonilla-Silva defines as so important in his theorizing. I discuss this by offering an account in the next section of how Bonilla-Silva draws on the concept in his study (and interpretation) of racial structures.

8.3.3 The Standing of Bonilla-Silva's Theoretical Conceptualizations: Excavating Mechanisms Reproducing Racial Privilege

From Bonilla-Silva's discussion of the concept of *racialized social system*, it seems that he is arguing that the employment of this concept allows us theoretical scope to appreciate the ways in which raced relations as hierarchical relationships develop in different social formations. Relating this to my account of retroductive logic as presented in the introduction to this chapter, it could be suggested that Bonilla-Silva is considering the concept of racialized social system as helpful in locating more or less invisible mechanisms reproducing racial privilege. As he notes:

> Accordingly the task of analysts interested in studying racial structures is to uncover the particular social, economic, political, social control, and ideological mechanisms responsible for the reproduction of racial privilege in a society. (2006, p. 9)

By employing the concept of racialized social system, Bonilla-Silva contends that we become equipped to delve into the structures leading to the development of observed (and experienced) racial privileges and racial disadvantages across different societies. And we become equipped to better recognize the ways in which racism can transmute over time in any specific social formation (while still reproducing racially structured hierarchy).

With reference to the concept of racialized social system, Bonilla-Silva explains how the structures that give rise to racial privilege become reproduced:

> Since actors racialized as "white" – or as members of the dominant race – receive material benefits from the racial order, they struggle (or passively receive the manifold wages of whiteness) to maintain their privileges. In contrast, those defined as belonging to the subordinate race or races struggle to change the status quo (or become resigned to their position). Therein lies the secret of racial structures and racial inequality the world over. They exist because they benefit members of the dominant race. (2006, p. 9)

With the concept of racialized social system at our theoretical disposal, then, we are able to understand that the dominant racial group would try to justify and account for its manifold privileges received from the racial order. He draws explicitly on Marx and Engels' concept of ideology in *The German Ideology* (1970) to make reference to what he calls "racial ideology."

> It should surprise no one that this group [a constructed dominant race] develops rationaliza-
> tions to account for the status of the various races. And here I introduce ... [another] key
> term, the notion of *racial ideology.* (2006, p. 9)

Drawing on a Marxist understanding of ideology, Bonilla-Silva suggests that we can
appreciate how the ruling *material* force of society (in this case, the materiality of
racial privilege) can operate at the same time as a ruling *intellectual* force – with
the dominant party in social relationships being able to exert a "master framework,"
which serves as the dominant framework for thinking in the society.[218] He points
out that this does not imply that the master framework is all-powerful and that subordinate groups are unable to develop oppositional views. But he suggests that "it
would be foolish to believe that those who rule a society do not have the power to at
least color (pun intended) the views of the ruled" (2006, p. 10).

All in all, in relation to the concept of ideology (with specific reference to racial
ideology), he suggests that

> because the group life of the various racially defined groups is based on hierarchy and
> domination, the ruling ideology expresses as "common sense" the interests of the dominant
> race, while oppositional ideologies attempt to challenge that common sense by providing
> alternative frames, ideas, and stories based on the experiences of subordinate races. (2006,
> p. 10)

He sees his own project as part of an oppositional movement to explore possibilities
for moving beyond the "common sense" which glues together the racialized social
fabric and its attendant relations of racial domination.

In line with his view that one cannot make predictions about "the bases on which
actors are moved to struggle" (1997, p. 471), he points out that it is not possible to
predict how people occupying a privileged position in the racial order (i.e., Whites)
might perceive their interests, especially because contradictory interests may be at
play. For example, he asks us to consider the question: "Do white workers have
more in common with white capitalists or with black workers?" (2006, p. 10). He
suggests that despite his not being able to make definite predictions in relation to
this question, it makes sense that:

> Because all actors awarded the dominant racial position, regardless of their multiple struc-
> tural locations (men or women, gay or straight, working class or bourgeois) benefit from ...
> the "racial contract", *most* have historically endorsed the ideas that justify the racial status
> quo. (2006, p. 10)

---

[218] After reading a draft of my Chapter 8 (May 2009), Susan Weil suggested to me that – besides
what she saw as the need to make my storyline clearer throughout (which I believe I have better
accomplished now) – she found that she could find no bases for engagement with the kinds of
statements that I was making here (in citing Bonilla-Silva). She found that my way of expressing
Bonilla-Silva's argument did not seem to tally with the terms of engagement that I set out in
previous chapters. She indicated that in the way in which I was setting out his argument thus far,
he had not "become a human being for her" – and she found this problematic. Readers may wish to
consider her commentary here. Perhaps indeed I have not managed to show up the person "behind"
the statements, as I am engaging too academically with the question of how we can reconstruct the
logic of his approach to theorizing hierarchy and domination (which is my focus in this section).

As I indicated in Chapter 2, Bonilla-Silva believes that the current ideology that is mainly used to sustain the racial order is color-blind racism. He argues that while experiments and surveys may have some uses as research approaches in investigating new forms of racism such as color-blind racism, it is difficult – if not impossible – via these methods to examine "how people explain, justify, rationalize, and articulate racial viewpoints" (2006, p. 11). For this reason, he relies mostly on interview material (and a critical exploration of views expressed during interviews) in order to study the operation of color-blind racism as an ideology (2006, p. 11). He indicates that the interview material on which he relies in explicating his understanding of color-blind ideology was generated from interviews undertaken with college students and other respondents in the USA – 1997 and 1998 (2006, p. 12).

Considering the study of racial ideology, his view is that it can be conceived for analytic purposes as comprising what he calls "frames, style, and racial stories" (2006, p. 10). He suggests that in the case of color-blind racism, it is a curious ideology in the sense that it is "slippery" – functioning in a "now you see it, now you don't" style. But its slipperiness is precisely what renders it a powerful ideology operating to defend the "contemporary racial order" (2006, p. 25). As he explains:

> ... the language of color-blindness is slippery, apparently contradictory, and often subtle. Thus, analysts must excavate the rhetorical maze of confusing, ambivalent answers to straight questions; of answers speckled with disclaimers such as "I don't know, but ..." or "Yes and no"; of answers almost unintelligible because of their higher than usual level of incoherence. (2006, p. 53)

Meanwhile, when engaging with interviewees, analysts also need to be attuned to the "storylines" that become drawn upon in "the 'matter-of-fact' world" where people create "social representations" as they converse with others (2006, p. 75). For example, storytelling might include the "past is past storyline" or the storyline that "I didn't own any slaves," or stories that include accounts of "someone close who is racist" (thus excluding oneself from this attribution) (2006, pp. 75–95). He argues that in processes of storytelling, people are "least aware that they are using a particular framework" (2006, p. 75). Most importantly, he explains that "the central component of any dominant racial ideology is its frames or *set paths for interpretation*" (2006, p. 26). It is these that underlie people's style of presentation of arguments and their storytelling processes.

In discussing the frames underpinning the ideology of color-blind racism, Bonilla-Silva indicates that he has gleaned (and isolated) four frames from the interview material. (See Section 8.3.4 for more detail.) These frames, he contends, can be considered as penetrating the arguments of "an overwhelming majority of the white respondents" (2006, p. 26). Although they themselves may not have used the language used by Bonilla-Silva in his analysis of their arguments, Bonilla-Silva has isolated these frames, along with styles of argumentation and stories told. He points out in this regard that although he believes that "people's accounts count," it is also important for those studying social meaning making not to relinquish their responsibilities to place people's accounts in wider theoretical context, which may involve "outstripping the conceptual resources of those being studied" (2006, p. 24, Endnotes 77, 79, and 80). He cites in particular the philosopher of science Fay in this regard (1996, p. 34) – who has advanced arguments in keeping with the critical theoretical tradition such as that developed by, inter alia, Habermas (1974b).

Before turning to a discussion of Bonilla-Silva's way of detailing the frames of color-blind (new) racism, I offer as further backdrop to this discussion an outline of his account of the standing of his own "conceptual resources" (or conceptualizations that he forwards). In order to help readers to "follow" my ensuing discussion, I now present Table 8.1 that provides a rendition of how we might understand differently what is involved in generating structurally oriented conceptualizations – depending on the epistemological orientation that we adopt. This table should act as a support for readers to make sense particularly of the material in Section 8.3.3.1, where I discuss Bonilla-Silva's self-understanding, and where I show that it can be interpreted as veering in either realist- or constructivist-oriented directions. The table should also be consulted to help make sense of my discussion in Sections 8.4 and 8.5, where I continue to "unpack" his proffered approach. Furthermore, the conclusion of the chapter (Section 8.7) can also be read in relation to the table.

Table 8.1 Comparing some alternative understandings of retroductive inference

	Retroductive logic understood in terms of a realist view of science	Retroductive logic understood in terms of a more constructivist- and pragmatic-oriented approach
Understanding the status of concepts in relation to observed phenomena	The theoretical concepts proffered by analysts postulate mechanisms in (natural and social) reality whose existence helps explain phenomena that appear	In social life in particular, we can try to trace connections across social institutions with a view to considering how societies can be said to differentially shape life chances as experienced (observed) and discussed by people
Defining the main research goal	Researchers should direct themselves toward developing accounts of structures that are likely to be causing phenomenal (empirical) appearances. They should embrace the ideal of objectivity in attempting to develop sound theorizing (that takes on board empirical information, while not being unduly narrow in analytic focus)	Inquirers engaged in social inquiry should sweep in – in a value-full manner – a range of considerations to be discussed as part of thinking systemically about issues seen to be at stake (with the help of retroductive inquiry processes). This is inextricably linked to the purpose of reconsidering the directions of our historical development

Table 8.1 (continued)

	Retroductive logic understood in terms of a realist view of science	Retroductive logic understood in terms of a more constructivist- and pragmatic-oriented approach
Using retroductive logic as a route to "knowing"	Although retroductive reasoning is necessarily conjectural, it may be regarded as a form of logical inference that should be used to advance our understanding of reality	Use of retroductive logic needs to include an admission that logic and emotion are not separable (as binaries) and that our ways of thinking and visioning in social life are filtered through our emotions/concerns
Deciding on the strengths of class-based analysis in relation to, say, race-based (or other category-based) analyses when examining (retroductively) social patterns	Concepts should be judged on the basis of their explanatory power in aiding our comprehension of real structural constraints that primarily determine outcomes	There is no need to make judgments in regard to the theoretical primacy (or not) of certain forms of analysis (such as, say, class- or race-based analysis) and there is no need to label any one form of oppression as more important than others. This is crucial for the practical project of developing coalitions
Considering the helpfulness of structurally oriented theorizing in relation to political practice	Sound and incisive theorizing should be helpful to actors in that their actions become better theoretically informed in relation to realities that need to be confronted	To the extent that theorizing opens conceptual spaces toward generating social justice projects that involve workable (political) coalitions, it is valuable
Acknowledging the importance of theorizing that points to the historization of social formations	A historical lens (such as that implicit in retroductive logic) is important in that it allows us to understand that structures posited to exist are capable of historical transformation	A historical lens in theorizing/storying enables people to respond to challenges that are seen to be of concern, as part of together considering values that can become embodied in historical reconstruction. In order to develop new forms of human relationship, our inquiry processes and the manner in which "knowing" is assessed must be practiced in such a way that potential relations of domination here are attended to as research issues themselves

8.3.3.1 Bonilla-Silva's Self-understanding of His Analytic Work

To start with, I suggest that Bonilla-Silva's citing of Fay (1996) is important in terms of the question of what standing we should assign to his own theoretical conceptualizations. In support of the critical theoretical tradition in the social sciences, Fay has put forward the view that critical theorizing does not pose as rooted in striving for value-freedom as an ideal for scientific inquiry. Critical theoretical accounts are instead presented as being *admittedly based on particular concerns that theorists may bring to bear in developing their theorizing.* Fay argues that critical theorists can and should operate in terms of a concern with enabling actors to reconsider their own "needs, wants and purposes" in the light of identified "structural conflicts in the social order" (1975, p. 165). The function of critical theorizing is to aid people to explore new ways of interpreting the social world of which they are part, so that they can develop their actions accordingly. Fay does not believe that theorizing can or should be divorced from the practical (political) intention to aid people toward rethinking and regenerating their ways of life. In this sense he sides with a pragmatically inclined inquiry approach. (See also Chapter 6, Section 6.3.2.)

In considering more realist-oriented views of theorizing, Fay warns that we should not regard theorizing as an instrument to guide and direct people in terms of a so-called (more) "objective" understanding of the situation (1975, p. 102). He is concerned that such a view of theory eventuates in a form of social manipulation whereby people can become manipulated by theorists proposing to have superior, more "objective," understandings of the interests of people. It is for this reason that critical theorists, he suggests, do not endow those posing as scientists with what he calls "expert authority" (1975, p. 107).

I would like to point out at this juncture that when offering me feedback on her reading of this (draft) section of the chapter (May 2009), Susan Weil raised as an issue for consideration how the writing practices of authors such as Fay and Bonilla-Silva can be seen (if at all) to support this "valid and valuable intention" – that is, the intention of forwarding less "objectivist" approaches. She was finding the style (as she read my renditions of the arguments) as not sufficiently supportive of their expressed intentions. She suggested that some "postmodern irony" could perhaps be injected here – namely, to point to the irony of writing about social possibilities while not writing in a manner that displays new options for engaging with audiences. She also indicated that I myself "seemed to be disappearing" in my write-up of these arguments – and she suggested that I make a clearer appearance! I have tried in response to her commentary to offer pointers throughout the chapter as to where I am heading in the chapter – namely, by displaying my preference for constructivist and pragmatic approaches that support the development of more humane styles of knowing and living. But it is worth noting at this point Weil's commentary that she is not (yet) seeing the "human being" of these authors (through my write-up in this chapter). This could be because I am concentrating on showing how they are spelling out their epistemological arguments, rather than on whether (if at all) their way of expressing these supports their intention. Nevertheless, as I have indicated earlier, I believe that we can indeed point to a tension in the arguments of

Bonilla-Silva and others whom he favorably cites, between veering in more realist or constructivist/pragmatic directions. And this tension could be manifested also in the irony that Weil is identifying – namely, that the writing style may belie an "objectivist" orientation, despite trying to offer alternatives (such as those that I elucidate via the right-hand column of Table 8.1). Bearing this in mind, I continue to discuss their arguments below.

Bonilla-Silva and Zuberi make the point that "today, few philosophers of science would agree in *toto* with [an] objectivist and realist stand" – that is, one that posits the possibility of accessing reality independently of observers (2008, p. 26).[219] They cite Fay's argument (1996, p. 204) that in both the natural and social sciences

> nature is never encountered in an unvarnished way; experience, sensations, and other perceptions require a priori conceptual resources in order to occur; and the language in which we articulate our thoughts are inherently permeated by our conceptual commitments. (2008, p. 26, Endnote 26)

However, Bonilla-Silva and Zuberi argue that admitting this does not imply the adoption of a relativist position that accords equal value to all ways of seeing and cognizing. Rather, they indicate that their position is that the value of theorizing can be judged in terms of the notion that "science and scientists (social or otherwise) can be responsible, responsive to community needs, and, hopefully, multicultural" (2008, p. 26). They indicate that their position in regard to the "color" of scholarship in terms of whether it is able to incorporate "the knowledge/experience of nonwhites" (2008, p. 18) is similar to that of Ladson-Billings (whose argument I introduced in Chapter 1, Section 1.5.3 – as pivotal to the epistemological discussions in this book). They point out that the central issue for her is not just to "color the scholarship" but to

> challenge the hegemonic structures (and symbols) that keep injustice and inequity in place. The work is not about dismissing the work of European-American scholars. Rather, it is about defining the limits of such scholarship [especially insofar as it fails to incorporate epistemologies that admit the political character of research]. (Ladson-Billings, 2003, p. 421, as cited in Bonilla-Silva & Zuberi, 2008, p. 27, Endnote 28)

Bonilla-Silva considers it important to explicitly admit as influencing his scholarship the political commitments toward forwarding justice and equity. Hence in the context of discussing his attempt to "describe the main components of color-blind racism and explain their functions," he points out that another goal is also operative. This is the important political goal to "uncover the basic profile of the main ideology reinforcing contemporary racial inequality" (2006, p. 13). This means that by definition his work

> is a challenge to post-Civil Rights white common sense; to the view that race no longer matters; and to anyone who believes that the problems afflicting people of color are fundamentally rooted in their pathological cultures. (2006, pp. 13–14)

---

[219]Bonilla-Silva makes a similar point when he suggests that the understanding of social science as a social product (rooted in political contexts) is becoming increasingly acceptable as a position (2006, p. 13).

He argues that accepting the political nature of his work does not mean that he can resort to "sloppiness" or "one-sidedness" in his work (2006, p. 14). This is why he takes pains to

> support my arguments with systematic interview data and reference where my data analysis differs from that of mainstream analysts so that readers can find alternative interpretations to mine. (2006, p. 14)

He also deals with the issue of what "authority" should be accorded to his work. Considering the question as to whether he has been "conferred a special gaze," he contends that:

> In truth, given the situational and partial character of all knowledge, neither I, nor my potential critics hold the monopoly over the right way of interpreting data. All of us try our best to construct robust explanations of events and hope that in the tilted market of ideas (tilted toward the interpretations of the powerful) the most plausible ones achieve legitimacy. (2006, p. 14)

Having pointed out that as he sees it, no one has the monopoly over interpreting data and developing explanations that account for them, he asks the following question:

> But if research is political by nature and my interpretation of the data is guided by my theoretical and political orientation, how can readers ascertain if my interpretation is better than those of other analysts? (2006, p. 15)

His answer to this question is that his explanations, as well as those provided by other analysts, "ought to be judged like maps" – with reference to their

> *usefulness* (Does it help to better understand whites' views?), *accuracy* (Does it accurately depict whites' arguments about racial matters?), *details* (Does it highlight elements of whites' collective representations not discussed by others?) and *clarity*. (Does it ultimately help you move from here to there?) (2006, p. 15, my italics)

Of course, all of the terms used by Bonilla-Silva in this passage themselves can be viewed differently depending on the understanding of science that we wish to apply here (as more or less realist- or constructivist-oriented – see Table 8.1). For example, according to a critical theoretical position of the kind proposed by Fay – where it is acknowledged that all interpretation is value-full – when researchers "depict" other's views, they are already *offering a specific interpretation* (cf. Romm, 1991, 1998c, 2001). Hence when Bonilla-Silva asks us to judge whether his depictions of Whites' arguments are *accurate*, this could be understood as implying that he has *created constructions for us to consider as a plausible way of interpreting* their arguments. In this way he would acknowledge that we do not have the means of checking in an unmediated manner what people being studied "really" are arguing independently of us assigning an interpretation. As indicated earlier, Bonilla-Silva and Zuberi make the point that "today, few philosophers of science would agree in *toto* with [an] objectivist and realist stand" (2008, p. 26, Endnote 26). This accounts for Bonilla-Silva's remarks in the context of proffering his particular interpretations of "whites' arguments," that other analysts may well offer alternative interpretations.

It seems that Bonilla-Silva is in any event cautioning us as readers to be aware that interpretations may be tilted toward those of "the powerful" in the market of ideas. So when considering the plausibility of his interpretations of "the data" and of his explanations for the appearance of the data, our awareness hereof can be factored into our assessment of the interpretations that he presents as part of his research. Weil, in her continuing commentary on this draft chapter (May 2009), mentioned here that it is worth highlighting that in terms of my intentions for the whole book, I am making the point that "truth making" is all too easily controlled by dominant credentializing processes in society – as, for instance, has been spelled out in detail by Collins (1990, 2000). In earlier chapters, I referred to Collins's concerns with finding ways of countering prevailing "truths" that function to obscure the "forms that new racism take in the post-civil rights era" (2005, p. 5). Like Bonilla-Silva she expresses concern with the way in which these apparent truths have taken hold in the "market of ideas" – and her focus has been on credentializing alternative ways of knowing as part of the process of exploring new avenues for generating "quality" explorations of new racism that can revitalize social justice projects. She puts the focus on finding ways of knowing that can serve the project of, in her terms, "foster[ing] our humanity" (2000, p. 289). I return to her argument in Section 8.4.

Interestingly, when offering the criterion of "clarity" as a way of judging his interpretations, Bonilla-Silva defines this as "Does it ultimately help you move from here to there?" (2006, p. 15). Here he proposes a pragmatic criterion as a possible way of judging the value of the interpretations.[220] If audiences find that the analysis is helpful in activating ways of moving forward (to address highlighted social injustices), this in itself becomes a criterion for judging the worth of the analysis (see again Table 8.1). This, then, would tally with arguments that I introduced in Chapter 7 too in regard to the practical edge of "action inquiry" as a way of proceeding: People's ways of drawing on, as well as developing, social theorizing to enable them (through co-inquiry) to revisit their ways of framing issues and their considerations of options for action become criteria for considering the value of the theorizing. (See especially Chapter 7, Section 7.3.1.)

Nonetheless, unless the map analogy proffered by Bonilla-Silva is indeed tied to an epistemology that breaks with "objectivism" and with a concern with "finding out," use of the analogy could give the impression that he believes that his analysis can be seen as "mapping" in some way an independently existing social world – and that it is by virtue hereof that the map becomes useful. But the map analogy can also be interpreted in a more constructivist fashion (in terms of arguments that I developed in Chapter 7, Section 7.1.1). In this case, it would be treated as a construction that *helps us to form a social world in-the-making, according to values that are regarded as important.*

---

[220]Weil notes, though, in her response to this draft chapter (May 2009) that "we don't always know what 'there' is, or what else it might mean to try to forward some vision of 'there'". This is why, in her view, the principles of critically reflexive action inquiry (cf. Weil, 1997, 1998) need to be made more central.

Bonilla-Silva here in any case opens the space for readers to consider that his interpretations are at the same time admittedly offering action options and clarifying these for us. He also at the end of his book offers a range of suggestions for "moving from here to there" – which I discuss in Section 8.3.6.

Before I proceed to discuss some of the detail of his analysis of color-blind ideology, I would also like to point out that Bonilla-Silva shows recognition that his theoretical ensemble that he brings to bear in his analysis has "etched in it" certain assumptions. As he puts it:

> Although this is not a theory book, my analysis of color-blind racism has etched in it the indelible ink of a "regime of truth" about how the world is organized. Thus, rather than hiding my theoretical assumptions, I state them openly for the benefit of readers and potential critics. (2006, p. 8)[221]

When utilizing the phrase "regime of truth," Bonilla-Silva refers (2006, p. 21, Endnote 50) to Foucault's *The Order of Things* (1973). By referring to the Foucauldian phrase "regime of truth," Bonilla-Silva suggests that any claims that he makes are to be understood as containing certain assumptions about "the world." That is, he does not present his claims as statements about the world free of the influence of specific (paradigmatic) assumptions. He tries to state these openly so that readers can appreciate how his analyses may be influenced hereby and also readers (who may also be critical of the assumptions) can enter into a dialogue with the work in an understanding of his view of these assumptions. I offer a fuller discussion of Bonilla-Silva's drawing on Foucault's argument, and implications hereof in terms of reflecting back on starting assumptions, in Section 8.4.

8.3.4 Frames of Color-Blind Racism

Having indicated to us as readers that his discussion of color-blind racism is set in the theoretical context of an exploration of *ideology* in a sense akin to Marx and Engels' use of the term (2006, p. 9), Bonilla-Silva proceeds to identify four frames of color-blind racism. He starts by first explaining how he is defining the notion of a frame. He explains that frames provide a "path" that people follow when interpreting racial phenomena (as they see them) or indeed in helping them not to "see" in some cases – for example, to avoid seeing "facts hidden by color-blind racism" (2006, p. 26). He explains further that:

---

[221] Weil in her feedback to me (May 2009) found this point made by Bonilla-Silva to be "immensely important" and suggested that it may be more important than "retroductive theory." This fits in with her focus on rendering assumptions open via critically reflexive co-inquiry. McIntyre-Mills, however, found that my exposition of retroductive inference in the chapter (May 2009) was "splendid"; and she suggested in her feedback that she considers it very important that I was able via the chapter to highlight its relevance in social life.

Dominant racial frames ... provide the intellectual road map used by rulers to navigate the always-rocky road to domination and ... derail the ruled from their track to freedom and equality. (2006, p. 26)

He elucidates the way in which interviews conducted with college students and other respondents – via qualitative interviewing of 66 White and 17 Black interviewees (2006, pp. 152–154) – pointed to the use of these frames. (He specifies that the interviews were conducted in the respondents' homes using a "structured interview protocol," and lasted about an hour each – 2006, p. 13. He admits that his sample size for the study, especially as regards the 17 Black interviewees, may be seen as small – thus limiting the possibility of generalization. But he points to its significance "given the limited number of systematic qualitative studies of Blacks' views"; and he also points out that the interviewing was part of a larger survey study – 2006, p. 152. That is, the cases for in-depth interviewing were randomly selected from a larger (random) sample of White and Black people who had been surveyed.)

He indicates that his analysis of the data herefrom revealed four central frames of color-blind racism. These frames are *abstract liberalism, naturalization, cultural racism*, and *minimization of racism*. He avers that "all these frames are essential to whites' explanations of racial matters" (2006, p. 152). He points out that while *White* respondents/interviewees can be seen to draw directly on these frames, content analysis of the interviews suggests that "blacks are significantly less likely than whites to use the frames of color-blindness directly" (2006, p. 152). Nevertheless, three of the frames (*abstract liberalism, naturalization*, and *cultural racism)* have "impacted blacks' consciousness" (2006, p. 152). The ideology of color-blind racism can thus be said to "dominate the space of what people [including black people] think is feasible and thinkable" (2006, p. 152).

8.3.4.1 Abstract Liberalism

The frame of *abstract liberalism* involves using in abstract manner ideas such as "equal opportunity," "not using force to achieve social policy," "choice," and "individualism." For example, these ideas can be used in an abstract way to oppose affirmative action policies on the grounds that they involve "preferential treatment" of certain groups.[222] But Bonilla-Silva notes that this frame involves

---

[222]See my discussion in Chapter 4, Section 4.5, where I showed also how Morton, Hornsey, and Postmes (2009) interpret experiments suggesting that prejudiced people can invoke abstract principles of fairness and equality (and at the same time contest the meaningfulness of racial categories) especially when it is believed that White people may become excluded from a desired position for "being white." They note, also citing the research of Lowery et al. (2006), that "people are likely to be particularly concerned about fair treatment when their ingroup may be the recipient of negative treatment, but are less concerned when an outgroup is similarly disadvantaged" (2009, p. 46). This can be seen as tying in with Bonilla-Silva's argument that color-blind racism is slippery. (See also Chapter 3, Section 3.4.2.)

ignoring the fact that people of color are *severely* underrepresented in most good jobs, schools and universities and, hence, it is an abstract utilization of the idea of "equal opportunity". (2006, p. 28)

Meanwhile, the idea of treating people as "individuals" with "choices" enables Whites to justify "the right of choosing to live in segregated neighborhoods or send their children to segregated schools" (2006, p. 28). But this requires "ignoring the multiple institutional and state-sponsored practices behind segregation and being unconcerned about these practices' negative consequences for minorities" (2006, p. 28).

In considering the frame of abstract liberalism in relation to the views of *Black* respondents, Bonilla-Silva notes that when questions about *affirmative action* were asked, Blacks "overwhelmingly expressed support" for such policies (2006, p. 153). Typical responses when asked during the interviews whether it was "unfair to whites" were to answer: "What do you call fair?" and to suggest that Blacks have had, and still have, a "hard time" (2006, p. 153). Thus concrete experiences became appealed to in order to express support for the policies. However, when it came to interpretations of *segregation*, the views expressed by these interviewees were not as "monolithic." Some of them suggested that school residential segregation was "natural"; some felt that "blacks have something to do with residential segregation" or that it was "no-one's fault"; and some felt that racial segregation was "not a problem." And, "significantly, some used the abstract liberalism frame directly to account for school or residential segregation" (2006, p. 155). That is, segregation was seen as a product of people's choices – and it was suggested that there is no scope for intervention to help change the situation" (2006, pp. 156–157).

8.3.4.2 Naturalization

The frame of *naturalization,* Bonilla-Silva notes, is a frame that "allows whites to explain away racial phenomena by suggesting that they are natural occurrences" (2006, p. 28). For example, in terms of this frame, "whites can claim 'segregation' is natural because people from all backgrounds 'gravitate toward likeness'" (2006, p. 28). Bonilla-Silva explains that here "preferences for primary associations with members of one's race are rationalized as nonracial because *they* (racial minorities) do it too" (2006, p. 28).

The naturalization frame functions to legitimize a racialized social order as "the way things are" (and therefore as natural). Bonilla-Silva comments that with being socialized in a "white habitus" and influenced by Eurocentric culture, it is not surprising that "whites interpret their racialized choices . . . as 'natural'" (2006, p. 39). But he offers his perspective – namely, that "they are the 'natural' consequence of a white socialization process" (2006, p. 39).

As indicated above, Bonilla-Silva detects that this naturalization frame was present in some of the responses of Black respondents too – for example, when they "relied on the naturalization frame mixed with abstract liberalism to explain segregation" (2006, p. 159). He gives an example of a Black interviewee attributing neighborhood segregation to "natural tendencies in people," as follows (2006, p. 159):

> I mean whites tend to stay with whites because they're comfortable. But given, you know – I'd say if we tried to mix a little more, we might tend to get together more and all, integrate more and all, but as it stands now and all, we tend to be comfortable [with] our race and that's the way it generally goes. (2006, p. 159)

Bonilla-Silva thus indicates how the naturalization frame – where race is regarded as referring to some "thing" in social reality of which people are naturally "members" (and with which people feel "comfortable") – can be seen as penetrating the discourse of many of the White, and some of the Black interviewees. But despite the operation of this frame in this way, Bonilla-Silva indicates that "most blacks point out that whites have something to do with segregation or that whites do not want to live or share resources with blacks" (2006, p. 159).

8.3.4.3 Cultural Racism

Bonilla-Silva refers to Taguieff's understanding that in this form of racism, the presumed cultural practices of "minorities" are seen as deficient. Bonilla-Silva argues that the cultural racism frame as defined by Taguieff in the context of Europe is "very well established in the United States" (2006, p. 40), where cultural characteristics supposedly "in" the group are used to account for their being worse off in the society (2006, pp. 39–40). He indicates that the frame of *cultural racism* here relies on "culturally based arguments such as 'Mexicans do not put much emphasis on education' or 'blacks have too many babies' to explain the standing of minorities in society" (2006, p. 28).[223] He remarks that this frame has been given attention by "many commentators" and does not require much (further) discussion by him. (See Chapter 2, Section 2.3.4.) But he makes the point that the invocation of cultural criteria (that in cultural racism can be seen to replace biological ones) are "as effective in defending the racial status quo" (2006, p. 29).

As regards cultural racism and the views of the Black respondents, he notes that "few blacks bought completely the cultural explanation." Yet this can be argued to have "bounded the way many blacks discuss issues such as discrimination or the specific charge that they are lazy" (as a cultural characteristic) (2006, p. 157). He indicates that the influence of this cultural frame did not come as a surprise to him, because in an earlier survey (from which some Black interviewees were chosen to be interviewed in depth) about a third of the Black respondents had agreed that blacks are "violent," about a third with the idea that they are "lazy," and about a

---

[223]Commenting on the way in which such arguments have also been used in Africa, Abimbola Olateju (originally from Nigeria) indicated to me in personal conversation (December 2008) that the problem is that when White people make blanket statements such as these, they fail to grant credibility to other reasons that can account for poverty – and they thus close off considerations around these possible explanations. It is in this failure that she sees their arguments as flawed. She made this point in the context of our discussing the substance of this book.

third with the notion that "blacks are welfare dependent" (2006, pp. 157–158).[224] The cultural stereotypes have thus arguably taken some hold in the views of many of these respondents (2006, p. 158).

8.3.4.4 Minimization of Racism

The minimization of racism frame is one that suggests that "discrimination is no longer a central factor affecting minorities' life chances" (2006, p. 29). Bonilla-Silva sees this frame as operative when it allows Whites to accept

> the neglect and slow response of government officials toward a mostly black population during Hurricane Katrina, and many other cases ... [while still] accusing minorities of being "hypersensitive," or using race as an "excuse," or of "playing the infamous race card." (2006, p. 29)

He explains that a significant feature of this frame is that it

> involves regarding discrimination exclusively as all-out [overt] racist behavior, which, given the way "new racism" practices operate in post-Civil Rights America ... eliminates the bulk of racially motivated actions by individual whites and institutions by fiat. (2006, pp. 29–30)

Because subtle and institutional forms of racism are not given attention in the minimization of racism frame, it becomes possible hereby to ignore the continued persistence of racism.

In considering the views of Blacks on this score, Bonilla-Silva points out that:

> Notwithstanding how color-blind racism affects blacks' understandings of various racial issues, the reality of discrimination is such that few blacks believe discrimination is no longer significant. (2006, p. 160)

With reference to their answers on the question of the significance of discrimination, he indicates that the Blacks interviewees "believe discrimination is salient, that it affects them personally, and that it operates in crude and subtle ways" (2006, p. 162).

8.3.5 A View of Things to Come

Bonilla-Silva indicates that one self-criticism that he has with the interviews conducted and his analysis thereof is that "the respondents are black and white only" (2006, p. 13). He indicates that although he still posits "color-blind ideology [as being] the general ideology of the post-Civil Rights era," it is also important to show "how other people of color fit into the notion of color-blind racism" (2006, p. 13). For increased comprehensiveness, he finds it necessary to also provide a sketch of "the future of racial stratification in the United States" – based also on "data from other sources" (2006, p. 13).

---

[224]In the same survey, 50, 20, and 53% of Whites had agreed with these respective stereotypes (2006, p. 158).

In offering his "view of things to come" based on a range of "data sources," Bonilla-Silva begins what he calls his "sketch" by pointing out that "Latinos are now officially the largest minority group in the nation." He suggests that the "Latino population explosion, generated by immigration, has already created a number of visible fractures in the United States that seem to be shifting the racial terrain" (2006, p. 177). He suggests furthermore that

> in addition to the Latino population explosion, other trends have emerged that challenge our traditional biracial divide (white vs nonwhite) and, more specifically, our black-white understanding of racial politics in the United States. (2006, p. 177)

He points in this respect to the visibility of Asian Americans in racial discussions, which he attributes to their demographic gains (their being now 5% of the population) and to the perception that they are "doing very well economically" (2006, p. 178). Another illustration of the changing racial terrain is "our recent national discussion on the status of 'multiracial' and 'biracial' people" (2006, p. 178). He indicates that the

> struggles by people in the multiracial movement to force changes in the way the Census bureau gathered racial data – specifically to include a multiracial category – ... ended with the addition of the "More than one race" item in the 2000 Census Schedule. (2006, p. 178)

And finally he points out that the rate of interracial dating and marriage between Latinos and Whites and Asians and Whites has skyrocketed (2006, p. 178). He remarks that many demographers and some public intellectuals have "heralded this development as signifying the erosion of racial boundaries" (2006, p. 178).

He comments that as he is writing his revised edition of his book, "we all ponder about what will be the future of race in America" (2006, p. 178). In this context, he himself postulates an "emerging triracial system" (see Fig. 8.1) that he anticipates will be comprised of

> "whites" at the top, an intermediary group of "honorary whites" – similar to the coloreds in South Africa during apartheid – and a nonwhite group or the "collective black" at the bottom. (2006, p. 179)

He hypothesizes that:

> The white group will include "traditional whites", new "white" immigrants and, in the near future, totally assimilated white Latinos, ... lighter skinned multiracials, and other subgroups; the intermediate racial group or honorary whites will comprise most light-skinned Latinos ..., Japanese Americans, Korean Americans, Asian Indians, Chinese Americans, and most middle Eastern Americans; and finally, the collective black group will include blacks, dark-skinned Latinos, Vietnamese, Cambodians, Filipinos, and Laotians. (2006, p. 179)

He contends that within this triracial system that he envisages (which he sees as a Latin- or Caribbean-like racial order) "race conflict will be buffered by the intermediate group, much like class conflict is when the class structure includes a large middle class" (2006, p. 179). And in this scenario,

Americans, like people in complex racial stratification orders, will begin making nationalist appeals ("We are all Americans"[225]), decry their racial past, and claim they are "beyond race". (2006, p. 179)

Bonilla-Silva puts forward this scenario in the context of his understanding of how race-talk has become eclipsed in "the Americas," where, as he puts it:

Despite claims of nonracialism ("We don't have racism here. That is an American problem"), racial minorities in Latin American countries tend to be worse off, comparatively speaking, than racial minorities in Western nations. (2006, p. 181)

He emphasizes that in making his claims about how he anticipates the emergence of a triracial system in the USA similar to Latin-Americanization, it is of course possible that some groups may end up in different strata to the ones he envisages – for example, it is possible that Filipinos could "become 'honorary whites' rather than another group in the 'collective black' strata" (2006, p. 180). He also points out that his thesis does not exclude "categorical porosity as well as 'pigmentocracy'" (2006, p. 180). That is, the categories could be somewhat porous, also depending on, for example, individual people's "skin tone, phenotype, hair texture, eye color, culture and education, and class" (2006, p. 182). Thus his "map" cannot be used to make individual-level predictions. But it could well be useful for group-level ones. As he explains:

The former [the individual-level] refers to individual members of a racial strata moving up (or down) that stratification system (e.g. a light-skin middle-class black person marrying a white woman and moving to the "honorary white" strata) and the latter [group level] refers to the rank ordering of groups and members of groups according to phenotype and cultural characteristics (e.g. Filipinos being at the top of the "collective black" given their high level of education and income as well as high rate of interracial marriage with whites). (2006, pp. 180–181).

Nevertheless, in setting out his "sketch of things to come" Bonilla-Silva adds an important stipulation: "Lastly, since I am predicting the future, I truly hope that we can prevent the crystallization of this racial order altogether or at least derail it partially" (2006, p. 181).[226] He offers various possibilities for action to try to

---

[225] In this regard, Obama indicates that when he made his speech at the 2004 Democratic National Convention, in which he stated that "there is not a black America and white America and Latino America and Asian America – there's the United States of America," he did not mean to imply that such a situation was already in place (2007, p. 231). He indicates that when he hears commentators interpreting his speech to mean that "we have arrived at a 'postracial politics' or that we already live in a color-blind society, I have to offer a word of caution" (2007, p. 232). He cautions that "to say that we are one people is not [and should not be] to say that race no longer matters – that the fight for equality has been won, or that the problems minorities face in this country today are self-inflicted" (2007, p. 232).

[226] Commenting on Bonilla-Silva's, as others', considerations around the "changing color/culture-line" in the USA and the social operation of the various distinctions, Kretsedemas suggests that:

It is not a matter of predicting which tendency will dominate but understanding how they will interact with each other, creating rationales for assigning differences and justifying exclusions that can vary by place and time. (2008, p. 827)

Fig. 8.1: Preliminary map of triracial order in the USA as anticipated by Bonilla-Silva (Source: Bonilla-Silva, 2006, p. 180)

"Whites"
Whites
New whites (Russians, Albanians, etc.)
Assimilated white Latinos
Some multiracials
Assimilated (urban) Native Americans
A few Asian-origin people

"Honorary Whites"[227]
Light-skinned Latinos[228]
Korean Americans
Asian Indians
Chinese Americans
Middle Eastern Americans
Most multiracials

"Collective Black"
Vietnamese Americans
Filipino Americans
Hmong Americans
Laotian Americans
Dark-skinned Latinos
Blacks
New West Indian and African immigrants
Reservation-bound Native Americans

"derail" the (sketch of the) racial order as depicted in Fig. 8.1 – possibilities that I discuss in the next section.

Before considering his sketch, it is worth noting that Collins likewise theorizes the tenacity of the "racial triangle" – which she describes as a triangle of "White, native and Black" – in terms of the "continuity it provides to American national identity" (2006, p. 35). She suggests that the triangle (as she describes it) "constitutes benchmarks against which individuals and groups measure racial

He states that in this conceptualization, he follows Omi and Winant's (1986) treatment of racial-ethnic identities as "fluid and unstable complexes of meaning constantly contested and transformed through political struggle" (Omi & Winant, 1986, p. 55, as cited by Kretsedemas, 2008, p. 828).

[227]Collins makes similar observations when she notes that "unlike prior waves of European immigrants who could in fact become White, recent racial/ethnic immigrant groups can at best become 'honorary Whites'" (2006, p. 47). She makes this point as part of her noting that "only White Americans can shed their racial and ethnic identities to stand for the generalized national citizen" (2006, p. 47).

[228]Collins has also commented that "the Latino population constitutes varying mixtures of all three 'racial' categories" (with the three being "White, native, and Black" in her description of the triangle) and therefore constitutes a challenge to the "racial triangle." She points out that "actual population groups have never fit smoothly" into given categories, and that the "triangle" should be seen as constituting "benchmarks against which individuals and groups measure racial categorization" – rather than offering a way of predicting how particular individuals or groups might indeed become placed (2006, p. 35).

categorization and the political power it engenders" (2006, p. 35). She considers that the "tenacity of the triangle" points to ways in which

> American society can undergo massive reorganization of its basic social institutions and ethnic populations in response to phases of capitalist development, yet somehow manage to replicate a seemingly permanent racial hierarchy. Whites were on the top at the founding of the nation-state reliant on agrarian capitalism; they remain so today. Native Americans and African Americans were on the bottom, and these groups remain so today. Despite massive reorganization of social institutions in the United States during transitions from industrial capitalism to a global capitalism reliant on the service industry, the basic contours of the triangle persist. (2006, p. 35)

These remarks of Collins are in line with her view of new racism as "past-in-present forms of racial oppression" (2005, p. 201) and her concern with trying to develop new visions and attendant social movements to counter it. (See Chapter 2, Section 2.3.6.)

8.3.6 Some Possibilities for Action

Bonilla-Silva indicates that in his first edition of his book *Racism Without Racists* (2003) he chose not to concentrate on taking a position on "what is to be done" (2006, p 239). However, a few years after finishing the book, he questioned that choice, and decided that he had a responsibility to his readers to try to answer the "burning question of what is to be done?" (2006, p. 229). Part of his reasoning for his (new) choice was his knowledge that behind the "norms of science" which require scientists to try to assume a "detached" position as scientists "lurks a pro-status quo position" (2006, p. 229). On his understanding that science can all too easily operate in support of the racialized order (and attendant hierarchical patterns), he chose now to take a strong position in forwarding his own suggestions as to how one might address the issues as highlighted via his analysis. To this end, in his second edition of the book (2006), he proposes both individual-level and collective strategies for consideration.

8.3.6.1 Individual-Level Strategies

On the level of individual strategies, he suggests that as far as Whites are concerned, he agrees with others who have proposed that they could become what are called "race traitors" by doing "undercover work in whites-only spaces" with a view to "tell[ing] the world when whites do or say things that disadvantage minority groups" (2006, p. 230).[229] In offering this as an option for action, he asks us to "imagine

---

[229]McWhorter points out that those asking Whites to commit race treason are not pleading for them to commit treason in a legal sense. They are calling on them to commit "the much more personal and intimate treason that consists of all those subtle and not-so subtle acts of betrayal that imply a refusal to bow to the authority of the white power structure" (2005, p. 549). McWhorter comments that due to the way in which racism is built into the structures of society, "white power structures require so few gestures of fealty these days to keep themselves intact that one hardly

what would happen if whites never know for sure if what they say or do in private, whites-only spaces could be potentially leaked to the public" (2006, p. 231). He here indicates that what Whites say in "private" should enter the public domain – so that there can be more "straight talk" around racism. (See also Chapter 5.)

He also suggests that Whites can engage in actions such as:

> Why not tell your neighbors that you are concerned about the neighborhood being perceived as racist because it is all white and America is a wonderfully diverse country? .... Why not tell your white co-workers that their comments about the new black worker are problematic and will not help her become a full member of the organization? (2006, p. 231)

His concerns here can be seen to tie in with Weil et al.'s (1985) understanding of how everyday racism can become reinforced by a myriad of choices on the part of people – that can be reviewed and accordingly altered. (See Chapter 7.)

Also on the level of individual strategy, he suggests that young people can

> create teams – one white and one black, two whites and two blacks, etc. – to test whether race affects a host of social transactions such as trying to rent an apartment, purchase things at the mall, apply for jobs, hail a cab, and the like. The teams could try to assess the "race effect" in these affairs by sending teammates alone to the various settings and then comparing notes afterward with their teammates. (2006, p. 231)

Bonilla-Silva believes that this strategy "could bring to the fore clear and convincing evidence of how discrimination occurs in the streets of the United States" (2006, p. 231).[230] He suggests that if this strategy were to "catch on," it could "uncover the many faces that racism takes on in the real world" (as experienced by the teammates) (2006, p. 232). And this, he believes, could provide "legal ammunition for lawsuits and serve as an embarrassment factor for those cases where there is no legal recourse" (2006, p. 232).

Bonilla-Silva thus indicates how people's way of involving themselves in the social world can operate to create the relevant experiences (such as experiences of discrimination), which serve as a springboard for further action (on the part of themselves and others).

---

ever gets a good opportunity to betray them" (2005, p. 549). She believes that the focus of those calling for race treason has been primarily on "negative acts of refusal on the parts of whites." She stresses that in her view the "positive [act] of fighting injustice is more important" (pp. 550–551). Like Bonilla-Silva, she believes that a collective movement toward "justice or transformation" is crucial. (See Section 8.3.6.2.)

[230]Collins also provides an example of how two students in one of her classes, one African American and the other White, "told of how they switched names on their respective papers when they suspected that the Black student's lower grades reflected the professor's prejudice." She notes that when the papers were returned to them "the Black student got her same old 'C' whereas the White student received her 'A', even though they had submitted each other's work!". She indicates that "coalition strategies such as these become especially important in integrated settings where differential treatment is hard to detect" (2000, p. 288).

8.3.6.2 Collective-Level Strategies

In relation to collective-level strategies, Bonilla-Silva states that, as he had suggested in the first edition to the book, "we need a new civil rights movement if we want to attack frontally the system responsible for the production and reproduction of racial inequality" (2006, p. 232). He indicates that he did not say much about this in the first edition, but in his second edition he ventures to do so.

In the first place, he suggests that a civil rights leadership (for a new movement) needs to avoid become trapped in the "battles and issues of the past." He reminds us that "new racism style discrimination . . . does not involve the overt, nasty practices of the past." Hence the "new civil rights movement will require new leaders who understand the nature of contemporary racial dynamics" (2006, p. 232). He also points out that when considering leadership positions, gender issues will have to be dealt with in a "more systematic way" than has been done in the past. He comments that the "old rampant sexism of the civil rights movement," in which women were given "little space in leadership positions, having their issues excluded because they were supposedly 'divisive' . . ., has to go" (2006, p. 233). He suggests that even if there is no other reason for taking this position (i.e., even if one does not try to argue for it on other grounds),

> given that women of color are central to the new working class, particularly the organized segment of the class, the new movement will have to be inclusive in its agenda and leadership. (2006, pp. 233–234)

He argues that in his view the new movement needs to be a "racially pluralist, gender/class/race conscious movement" (2006, p. 234).

Considering the way in which race and class issues have been dealt with in previous "movements," he argues that, "this new civil rights movement . . . will have to deal with issues of class and racial diversity in a more straightforward manner" (2006, p. 232). He explains that:

> It is no longer possible for the black middle class, who led the struggle of the past, to present *their* issues as *the* issues of all blacks and it is no longer possible for blacks to continue believing they are *the* most important minority group in this country. (2006, p. 232)

As far as addressing the question of *racial plurality* within the "new civil rights movement" is concerned, he indicates that if Black leaders wish to represent minority community viewpoints, they will have to exhibit a "pluralist" style of leadership"; and likewise, "blacks must [also] begin to understand that a Latino or an Asian can represent them, too" (2006, p. 233). As far as *class* issues are concerned, he indicates that

> the issues before us are, more than ever, the issues of the black, Latino, and Asian working class, i.e., the need for adequate and decent schools, jobs, social services, medical care, housing, and transportation. (2006, p. 232)

He claims that for this segment of the minority community, one needs a movement "that deals in a straight manner with their class/race issues." He elaborates further that what is here required is "not 'equality of opportunity' [which in any case is thus far only abstract – as explained in Section 8.3.4.1] but 'equality of results'"

(2006, pp. 232–233). Faced with what he sees as a possible hopelessness of those who might have become pessimistic about such prospects, he comments that, in participating in the new social movement,

> We all need to regain the energy we seem to have lost, drop the pessimism that has filled our souls, and get over the individualism and materialism that has eaten so many of us from within. (2006, p. 236)

In clarifying this statement of his, he refers to the work of bell hooks (2006, p. 241, Endnote 22). As I indicated in Chapter 3, Section 3.4.2, hooks is concerned that while the civil rights movement under the leadership of Martin Luther King had emphasized what she calls a "love ethic," the "Black Power movement" put the emphasis "more on power" (1994, p. 291). She considers it crucial that "we must collectively return to a radical political vision of social change rooted in a love ethic and seek once again to convert masses of people, black and nonblack" (1994, p. 292). She suggests that

> without an ethic of love shaping the direction of our political vision and our radical aspirations, we are often seduced, in one way or another, into continued allegiance to systems of domination – imperialism, sexism, racism, classism. (1994, p. 289)

Bonilla-Silva appreciates hooks's advice that a way of people being with one another that is non-exploitative needs to be practiced in "lived practices of interaction" (hooks, 1994, p. 287).

8.4 Revisiting Bonilla-Silva's Approach to Theorizing

I suggested in Section 8.3.3 that Bonilla-Silva's way of developing his theorizing can be accounted for by appealing to some notion of retroductive inference. In operating according to such logic, theorists/scientists are not required to concentrate on trying to generate *predictions* in relation to observable events and their connections. They are required to direct their focus more at the level of systemic theorizing so as to be able to provide *explanations* for whatever observable occurrences (and connections between them) become manifested – explanations which make sense of the totality of manifestations.

   In a *scientific realist* approach to the utility of retroductive logic, it is assumed that if theorists are repeatedly able to provide plausible explanations for observable events in terms of their concepts (which posit the existence of structural generative mechanisms), this lends support to the idea that the causal mechanisms do exist. It is possible to read Bonilla-Silva's work as implying that his conceptualizations, if considered plausible by other analysts as well as by others in society, should be treated as probably referring to *real structural characteristics* of the social world. When he states that "all of us try our best to construct robust explanations of events and hope that . . . the most plausible ones achieve legitimacy" (2006, p. 14), this statement of his could imply that plausible explanations are indeed plausible *because they refer ultimately to some independently existing realities* (existing independently of our knowing processes).

Yet Bonilla-Silva cites favorably critics of the Enlightenment dream of "pure objectivity," and in this context he remarks that when scientists pose problems, develop theories, use methods, and perform analyses, they are bringing to bear their "selves" as researchers (2006, p. 13). Thus (as with many others before him) he criticizes Weber's (1949) "call for a separation between researcher, method, and data" (2006, p. 13). And this goes hand in hand with an admission that *his theorizing should be understood as springing from his "presence" therein* – including his specific concerns, values, and so on.

Moreover, Bonilla-Silva (2006, p. 24) and Bonilla-Silva and Zuberi (2008, p. 26) cite favorably Fay's work – albeit in endnotes – on the philosophy of social science. Fay (following the critical theoretical tradition) considers that theoretical statements can be judged as true/worthwhile in terms of their posing insights that help people to rethink their mode of social being and living. Here the search for "truth" is not seen as separable from a concern with social justice.

For example, as I noted in Chapter 6, Section 6.3.2, Habermas indicates that what he calls his reconstructive social theory is meant to serve the function of offering

> a guide for reconstructing the network of discourses that, aimed at forming opinions and preparing decisions, provides the matrix from which democratic authority emerges. (1996, p. 5)

Habermas's critical theorizing can thus be read as directed toward highlighting the potential for developing an enhanced communicative fabric in society, out of which new goal directions for humanity can emerge. (See also Delanty, 1997, p. 87.) Bonilla-Silva's reference to the criterion of worthwhile theorizing to be judged in terms of the (practical) question "Does it ultimately help you move from here to there?" (2006, p. 15) can be seen as calling forth this kind of critical theoretical argument – albeit that as Weil points out in her feedback to me (May 2009) "we do not always know where 'there' is" or indeed "what (else) it may mean to move to 'there'." (Weil would thus appreciate it if more critically reflexive co-inquiry practices were to be explicitly called for within "critical theorizing" – see also Chapter 7, Section 7.3.1.)

In reviewing Bonilla-Silva's orientation, it is also important to bear in mind his favorable citing of Foucault's conception that statements made by theorists (and others) can be understood as embodiments of a "regime of truth" – that is, as infused with assumptions about how the world is organized (2006, p. 8). By speaking of his own examination of color-blind racism as having etched in it a "regime of truth," Bonilla-Silva implies that he recognizes that his way of speaking about "the world" is indeed a way of speaking (a narrative), which can be counterposed against other ways of constructing interpretations. It is worth highlighting here that when Foucault points to "regimes of truth" – which, as *regimes*, would seem *not* to provide scope for reflection on paradigmatic assumptions – he simultaneously can be seen as making space for a different form of theorizing (i.e., one which *is* able to reflect back on starting assumptions). Thus Rajchman interprets Foucault's location of regimes of truth as pointing to an alternative, namely, to a "style of critical investigation based ... in the supposition of critical moments in which we start to depart from those conditions or 'regimes' and invent new ways of talking and seeing" (2007, p. 21).

Rajchman indicates that Foucault follows Habermas's concern with creating "public spaces" for "actively critically thinking together" (2007, p. 15) – although Foucault does not agree with Habermas's postulate of a regulative ideal of consensus governing discursive reason.[231] According to Foucault (as interpreted by Rajchman), people have to "constantly invent or re-invent the means, the techniques, the strategies and the spaces" for revisiting their relationship to "historically determined forms of power" – as part of the effort to say "we don't want to be governed like this anymore" (2007, p. 14). Rajchman argues that Foucault tried to isolate a different style of critical thinking (than that proposed by Habermas), which is

> more closely tied to material conditions – uncertain and questioning, "dissensual" or "problematizing," associated as well with fiction and aesthetics rather than with sociological expertise or academic positions. (2007, p. 10)

Thus Rajchman sees Foucault as indeed opening more space for dialogue (and different forms of dialogue) than that provided for in Habermas's account of reconstructive theorizing. Nevertheless, it should be remembered that Foucault appreciates Habermas's critique of ideologies, including an ideology of science that presents itself as forwarding information (more or less) free of presuppositions and antecedents. Foucault agrees that exposing these is "precisely the advantage of critique" (cf. Foucault's conversation with Mouloud, as reported in Foucault, 2007).

Foucault makes the point in relation to the purpose of philosophical reflection in the present period to which we belong that "here it is a matter of showing specifically and in what ways the one who speaks as a thinker, a scientist, and a philosopher is himself [or herself] a part of this process" (cf. 2007, p. 84). He points to the importance of reflecting upon one's own complicity (as thinker, scientist, philosopher) in the unfolding of the social world of which one is both an element (of the emergent relations) and an actor (cf. 2007, p. 85). This relates to Bonilla-Silva's suggestion that one needs to be aware that *already by thinking/theorizing (about racism in his case) one is making some kind of political intervention* and cannot avoid taking some responsibility for this (2006, p. 229).

As far as the content of Foucault's ideas on *racism* are concerned, Bonilla-Silva takes on board Foucault's suggestion that constructions of racial identities are *historically created* through specific discourses. Bonilla-Silva and Zuberi (2008, p. 26, Endnote 27) refer to McWhorter's discussion of Foucault's account of the origin of "race" as a socially meaningful category. In her presentation of the Foucauldian exploration of the question "where do white people come from," McWhorter (2005) indicates that according to Foucault, the "thematics of blood" seems to have

---

[231] See also Flood and Romm (1996a, pp. 48–50) for a consideration of the relationship between Habermas's and Foucault's arguments.

gained historical importance in the second half of the nineteenth century. She cites Foucault's statement that it was then that

> a whole politics of settlement (*peuplement*), family, marriage, education, social hierarchiza-
> tion, and property, accompanied by a long series of permanent interventions at the level of
> the body, conduct, health, and everyday life, received their color and their justification from
> the mythical concern with protecting the purity of the blood and ensuring the triumph of the
> race. (Foucault, 1978, p. 149)

McWhorter indicates that Foucault traces race discourses as far back as the early seventeenth century, but argues that "those early discourses did not mobilize a concept of race like the one that has been operative in the 20th century" (Foucault, 2003, as cited in McWhorter, 2005, p. 540). Foucault suggests that "the earliest concepts of race were neither biological nor even morphological; race was a matter of lineage, language, and tradition, correlated perhaps with religion and character." However, she points to a "gradual mutation of the idea of race as it was adapted for use in a variety of political contexts in Europe" (McWhorter, 2005, p. 540). (See also Chapter 2, Section 2.2.2.)

Most importantly, Foucault emphasizes that in order to understand the construction and deployment of racialized identities in specific social formations, they must be "studied in relation to the networks of power that generated them" (McWhorter, 2005, p. 540). That is, the power relations that serve to sustain the established racial hierarchies have to be explored. And Foucault hopes that by attempting to expose the way in which the notion of race has become historically constructed, the political space is created for reconfiguring, inter alia, the networks of power sustaining racism. Hence McWhorter states that "Foucault meant for his work to have political effects, to disrupt power formations and make new configurations possible" (2005, p. 544).

Bonilla-Silva for his part proposes that his theorizing (specifically around racism) might function to have "political effects" by, for instance, serving to "tilt the balance" in the already tilted market of ideas (tilted toward the interpretations of the powerful) (2006, p. 14). Bonilla-Silva and Zuberi note (2008, p. 26, Endnote 26) that they do not hereby wish to conceptualize knowledge production as "the mere expression of power relations" as in certain postmodernist arguments – such as those offered by, say, Baudrillard (e.g., 1983) and Lyotard (e.g., 1984). They believe that Ladson-Billings (2003) helps to cast light on the question of how knowledge production should be conceived when she suggests certain criteria for assessment – such as an assessment of its contribution to challenging "injustice and inequity" (2008, p. 27). By their citing Ladson-Billings in this regard, they also can be interpreted as invoking her concern with developing an epistemology that problematizes the manner in which power relations can infuse our forms of "knowing" in society (as I explained this in Chapter 1, Section 1.5.3.)

Regarding the issue of how the new social movement that Bonilla-Silva envisages can work toward generating visions of a more just social order, he does not try to adjudicate on the debate around how "capitalism" is to be transformed in this process. It is noteworthy though, that like Obama (whose arguments I cited in Chapter 2,

Section 2.2.1), he indicates that the issues before us are, more so than ever, "the need for adequate and decent schools, jobs, social services, medical care, housing, and transportation" (2006, p. 232). Obama (2007) likewise expresses concern that thus far in the USA and indeed the global economy, policy-making has been skewed in favor of the "corporate sponsors and wealthy donors" (2007, p. 35) – at the expense of the needs of the working class. He expresses concern that in the USA "we ran up the national credit card so that the biggest beneficiaries of the global economy could keep an even bigger share of the take" (2007, p. 188). Obama refers to Warren Buffet's statement (stated in conversation with Obama) that: "If there is class war in America, then my class is winning" (2007, p. 189). He points to his own, as well as Buffet's, concerns about this. He remarks that he was surprised to hear Buffet – the world's foremost capitalist – reflect an understanding that:

> How well we respond to globalization won't be just a matter of identifying the right policies. It will also have to do with a change of spirit, a willingness to put our common interests and the interests of future generations ahead of short-term expediency. (Obama, 2007, p. 191)

On the issue of how capitalist patterns of existence can be modified, Obama takes the line that the wealth that it produces needs to be "distributed fairly and wisely" – so that wealth can be ploughed into education, infrastructure, and providing safety nets for those who "lose out in a market economy" (2007, p. 190). He also cites as problematic that "between 1971 and 2001, while the median wage and salary income of the average worker [in the USA] showed literally no gain, the income of the top hundredth of a percent went up almost 500 percent" (2007, p. 192). He expresses dismay at the "levels of inequality [that] are now higher than at any time since the golden age" (2007, p. 192).

Interestingly, with the global financial crisis to which I referred earlier in the chapter, when discussing Harvey's (2008) Marxist-oriented view hereof, the *New York Times* (11 April 2009) makes the point that

> all the conservative shouting about how Obama is a socialist has had the unexpected effect of educating a sizable portion of the public to think of socialism as synonymous with "European socialism" (i.e., democracy plus private industry plus nice, soft, 400-thread safety nets) instead of Soviet-style "socialism" (i.e., totalitarianism plus gigantism plus poverty).[232]

Of course, the "socialism" advanced by Obama would not be of the kind recommended by Harvey, who sees the problem as lying in the way in which capitalist *production*, rather than *distribution*, processes are organized in the social system. Nevertheless, Obama can be seen as trying to inject new codes for people to consider as meaningful options for re-organizing economic and social life.

As Lakoff (2009) points out:

> The word "code" [when speaking about the Obama Code] can refer to a system of either communication or morality. President Obama has integrated the two. The Obama Code is

---

[232]The question of the kind of "socialism" now gaining more legitimacy in the USA is discussed further at: http://greenpagan.newsvine.com/_news/2009/04/11/2669333-morning-skim-capitalism-vs-socialism.

both moral and linguistic at once. The President is using his enormous skills as a communicator to express a moral system. . . . . His economic program is tied to his moral system. (2009, p. 1)[233]

Lakoff argues that Obama's Code introduces a different language of causality than the language of "direct causation" in terms of which "conservatives tend to think." He believes that Obama's systemic thinking (with its attendant break with linear causality) is more equipped to come to grips with global economics (as well as global ecology) as "examples of systemic causation." He avers that Obama has understood that:

> The global economic collapse is . . . systemic in nature. That is at the heart of the death of the conservative principle of the laissez faire market, where individual short-term self-interest was supposed to be natural, moral, and the best for everybody. (2009, p. 7)

He argues that the old "rational actor model," can be shown to be "fallacious" in the light of the "twin disasters of global warming and global economic breakdown. Both must be dealt with on a systematic, global, long-term basis" (2009, p. 7). He states that "President Obama understands this, though must of the country does not" (2009, p. 7). He postulates that as Obama proceeds, he seems to be trying to find a way of situating the meaning of concepts such as "freedom, equality, prosperity, unity," and so on, within his view of values such as "empathy, [and] social as well as personal responsibility," while also redefining American patriotism and developing new visions of democracy (2009, p. 8).[234]

This would be consistent with Bonilla-Silva's favorable citing of hooks, who calls for a "love ethic" to shape the direction of people's political visions as well

---

[233]This seems to be similar to the stance adopted by Nelson Mandela in South Africa, when he stated in his opening address at the 50th National ANC conference held in Mafikeng (December 1997) that:

> According to this thesis to which we must subscribe, success must also be measured with reference to a system of social accountability for capital, which reflects its impact both on human existence and the quality of that existence. (http://www.anc.org.za/ancdocs/history/mandela/1997/sp971216.html)

[234]Commenting on Obama's election campaign, Shane indicates that Obama was calling for the creation of a "transparent and connected democracy" and that in terms of his innovative objectives, "Americans have within their grasp a host of communication tools that could sustain a robust democratic culture of sharing, creativity and participation. . . . . Senator Obama . . . is promising to lead a transformation in our political life" (2008). In December 2008 and January 2009, Christakis facilitated some SDDP dialogues (following the methodology that I discussed in Chapter 7) designed to consider the challenges that might be faced in employing technology to create a "connected democracy." Some of the most influential inhibiting factors that emerged as needing to be addressed were, for instance, the insufficient attention given by the Obama administration toward capacitating facilitators of e-democracy; the problem of corporate control of the means of democracy, and the problem of the digital divide. (See http://obamavision.wikispaces.com for an account of how the partipants were chosen for this SDDP and how influence maps were generated and interpreted. An account is also offered here by Christakis and co-organizer Gayle Underwood of the SDDP logic and its use in this application.)

as radical aspirations – in order to create moves away from "imperialism, sexism, racism, classism" (1994, p. 289). The theorizing that offers conceptions as to how best to move away from these forms of domination, however, cannot present itself as authoritative, because this goes against the grain of practicing non-dominative human relationships.

It is for this reason that Collins emphasizes that in developing a "politics of engagement" we become empowered when we reject "the dimensions of knowledge that perpetuate objectification, commodification, and exploitation" (2000, p. 289). Considering this in relation to her discussion of Black feminism (see Chapter 1, Section 1.3; and Chapter 6, Sections 6.3.2.1 and 6.6), she suggests that "African-American women and others like us become empowered when we understand and use those dimensions of our individual, group, and formal educational ways of knowing that foster our humanity" (2000, p. 289). She considers it important to invoke Black feminist epistemologies as counterpoints to dominative ways of knowing that may be argued to stifle possibilities for "fostering our humanity." She argues that within such a (epistemological and ethical) stance, conceptual spaces also become created for identifying "new linkages" between different forms of activism toward fostering social justice projects. She points out that this is important because "just as oppression is complex, so must resistance aimed at fostering empowerment demonstrate a similar complexity" (2000, p. 289). And she argues that in order to create practical linkages, we need to develop an inclusive perspective that refrains from "labeling one form of oppression [such as based on, say, race, gender, class, sexuality, and nation] as more important than others, or one expression of activism as more radical than another" (2000, p. 289). In this way, she argues, we can avoid having to adjudicate between the explanatory power of analyses based on categories such as, say, race, gender, or class as having any particular (analytic) primacy; and instead we can focus on developing conceptual spaces for creating coalitions in practice.

8.4.1 A Note on Interpreting Texts

The issue of what is involved in interpreting *texts,* which would include my interpretation of all the authors discussed in this and previous chapters (such as Bonilla-Silva, Foucault, Ladson-Billings, hooks, Collins, etc.), is itself a subject of heated debate. In line with the constructivist position that I have espoused (and detailed with reference to various examples in the book), I do not believe that one can posit a "correct" reading of any text or set of texts.[235] In this regard, I concur with Kaufmann's account (which she explains in the context of exploring Foucault's contribution). As she expresses it:

> I have come to recognize that ... every text I read is interpreted and rewritten through my own biography, and my autobiography is rewritten as I read it through alternate texts .... According to this understanding, not only is there no "real" Foucault for me to use as

---

[235] See Romm (1998c) for my exposition of realist-oriented and constructivist-oriented understandings of processes of interpreting texts.

the underpinning theoretical framework for my work but also each use of theory is constructed through the autobiography of the researcher and interpreted and rewritten through
the autobiography of the reader. (2004, p. 578)

Kaufmann suggests that as one reads and interprets texts, the texts themselves
become rewritten through their being (re)constructed by readers, while at the
same time readers interact with (and thus learn from) their engagement with
texts. The rewriting of the text by readers opens up a suggested way of seeing
it (for other audiences also to consider), so that in this sense it becomes a living
document.

In terms of Kaufmann's language, then, I see my interaction with, inter alia,
Bonilla-Silva's work in this chapter, as both a *reading* and *(re)writing* of the texts.
With this reminder to readers of my constructivist-oriented engagements with the
texts, I proceed in the next section to cast (what I regard as) further light on some
of Bonilla-Silva's statements that he has provided in sketching his account of Latin
American racism.

As noted above, Bonilla-Silva compares the racism that he understands as
operative in Latin America with his anticipated crystallization of a triracial stratification system in the USA – which he considers as crystallizing unless it becomes
"derailed" (2006, p. 181). To cast additional light on Bonilla-Silva's sketch, I offer
some detail on an argument developed by Dos Santos and Da Silva (2006), who
have concentrated on examining the patterning of the Brazilian social fabric. By
comparing their argument with his (Section 8.5), I show how one can lend support to his statements on the operation of color-blind racism in this context. I also
show how this can be interpreted through a constructivist/pragmatic-oriented lens
(Section 8.5.1). Finally (Section 8.6), I show how one could interpret both his and
Dos Santos and Da Silva's theoretical claims (and attendant practical proposals) in
view of the debate between Bourdieu and Wacquant (1999) and Hanchard (2003)
that I introduced in Chapter 2, Section 2.4.

8.5 A Way of Considering Racism in Latin America
with Special Reference to Brazil

In providing his understanding of the racialization of social relations in Latin
America, Bonilla-Silva emphasizes that despite claims made by some that issues
of racism are "past" and are irrelevant here, the issues can be seen as ever-present.
As noted in Chapter 2, Section 2.2.1, Bonilla-Silva expresses concern that, despite
the operation of discrimination in practice in Latin America, "any one trying to
address racial divisions is likely to be chided" (2006, p. 184).

Bonilla-Silva's account of the way in which "collective blacks" have tended
toward the bottom of a racialized (but not officially recognized) system in Latin
America (2006, p. 179) is lent support by Dos Santos and Da Silva in their discussion of racism in Brazil. I now provide some detail on their argument and I show
how it compares with that of Bonilla-Silva (although they have not cited him in their
text).

Dos Santos and Da Silva state that in the late 1970s,

> when there was a resurgence of social movements of Afro-Brazilians protesting the racial discrimination that they suffer every day, the myth of Brazilian racial democracy was still generally accepted and proclaimed. (2006, p. 13)[236]

They indicate that up until 1978, Brazil had "gone almost 20 years without any statistical information on the color or race of its population" (2006, p. 13). However,

> with the inclusion of a question on color/race in the censuses of 1980 and 1991 and some components of the National Survey of Sample Households, it became possible to obtain more accurate statistical information on the reality of racial inequalities in Brazil. (2006, p. 14)

They remark that they are using the term "race"

> not as a biological concept denoting physically and mentally distinct varieties of human being but as ... a concept denoting only a form of social classification .... Race, as a [social] reality, is therefore limited to the social world. (2006, p. 27)

They support the inclusion of a concept of race in the censuses and in the survey of sample households, because it allows "statistics on racial inequality" to come to the fore (2006, p. 14). However, they are concerned that despite the statistical information that has been available, there is an "inertia in seeking solutions to our pattern of racial inequality." To account for what they see as the "lack of moral indignation at Brazilian racism," they suggest that "we are socialized not to regard Afro-Brazilians as ordinary citizens, our equals in law, because the Brazilian mass media have made them either invisible or stigmatized" (2006, p. 14). Their argument in this regard concurs with Bonilla-Silva's view that in Brazil (as in other Latin American countries) racism is largely ignored and not spoken about.

To try to render more visible the continued discrimination in particular against Afro-Brazilians, they emphasize that:

> The statistics, both the official ones supplied by the state and the unofficial ones from private institutions, have shown that Afro-Brazilians ... suffer the most prejudice in the labor market. They suffer the highest unemployment rates and are paid the least, even for the self-same jobs. (2006, p. 15)

Dos Santos and Da Silva thus show that in terms of labor-market statistics, "the labor market became much more affected by racism in the 1990s" (relative to earlier) (2006, p. 17). This would lend support to Bonilla-Silva's view of a trend toward crystallization, rather than a dismantling, of a racialized social order in contemporary Brazil. Furthermore, in line with Bonilla-Silva's conception of the intersection of gender and race issues – with reference to which he cites, for example, Essed's notion of "gendered racism" (1997, p. 469) – they point out that:

---

[236]Nascimento concurs with this account when she argues that in Brazil, as in other Latin American societies, a covert "whitening policy" has been at play, where "a Latin or Iberian identity is routinely applied to indigenous, black, or mestizo populations with pride, as if they were European" (2004, p. 871). However, "the racial democracy ideology created a taboo identifying the unmasking of its anti-racist pretense" (2004, p. 870).

Suffering double discrimination for being both Afro-Brazilian and women, they [Afro-Brazilian women] have the highest rates of unemployment in all six metropolitan regions surveyed in 1998, and in 1999 they had the highest unemployment rate nationally. (2006, p. 17)

They situate these statistics in the context of Brazil's lack of economic growth, which has meant that

most workers have had no wage increase and a considerable number have lost their jobs, temporarily or for good, but the problems of white workers have been nothing like the penury to which Afro-Brazilians have been reduced, nor has the gender discrimination against white women in the labor market been anything like that suffered there by Afro-Brazilian women. It is racism that lies at the root of this inequality. (2006, p. 20)

They argue that despite the existence of the data that they present here, there still persists "a failure to see the data ... in government, trade unions, and social movements" – even though certain "activists in the Afro-Brazilian movement and some intellectuals have been effectively challenging the myth of Brazil as a 'racial democracy' ever since the 1970s" (2006, p. 20).

Like Bonilla-Silva, they locate a taboo in Brazilian society around "talking about racism." And like Bonilla-Silva, they suggest that the taboo in speaking about race issues does *not* mean that Brazilians are color blind. On the contrary, they suggest that:

It seems that we are *blind to racism* and its malignant consequences because neither causes us any moral difficulty either as human beings or as citizens. We practice discrimination against nonwhites but are loathe to admit it. (2006, pp. 20–21, my italics)

They try to account for people's ability to deny continued racism, despite the available data, which should tell us that "something is going on" (2006, p. 21). They suggest the following:

Moral indifference with regard to the social fate of individual nonwhites is so widespread that we remain unaffected when we are faced with Brazilian racial inequality. They do not touch us or bother us, not even as citizens who expect and insist on a full and total application of the Brazilian constitution. (2006, p. 21)

They suggest that this in turn can be explained in terms of the fact that "we have been (and still are being) socialized against seeing nonwhites as ordinary citizens" (2006, p. 21). They argue that through the messages that people receive on a daily basis,

Brazilians assimilate the invisibility of nonwhites in the media, with their underlying prejudices and consequent discrimination against them, and feel no guilt about this situation. .... Because we have been (and are still being) socialized to live with racial discrimination and inequality, we believe them to be normal. (2006, p. 24)

They see a continuity as well as a rupture between present-day racism and racism in colonial times. As they state:

While we have no wish to adopt the simplistic position that present-day racism is a mere reflection of colonial slavery, the interdependence between today's images and those of the past cannot be denied. (2006, p. 24)

They consider the continuity as consisting in "the questionable use of images that focus on the otherness of nonwhites." They point out that these images "crystallized by different means . . . have, over time, caused racism to seem quite natural" (2006, p. 24). And it is because of its naturalness that it becomes unnoticed. Part of the racism can be seen as manifested in the seemingly natural "ideal of the Brazilian, created to satisfy the needs of the dominant culture and those alone" (2006, p. 24). An unnoticed exclusionary orientation means that in practice "few opportunities [are available] to the socially excluded" (2006, p. 24).

In similar vein to Bonilla-Silva, they try to unpack the dominant mode of thinking, which they see as "aimed at neutralizing the tensions produced by diversity." They themselves see a diversity in Brazilian society along "cultural, social, economic, and political differences." But they argue that the dominant attitude – which rules the labor market – is that "we are all 'the products of racial mixing', even though our ethical and aesthetic aspirations are directed toward an ideal of whiteness" (2006, p. 25). They explain the operation of this normative ideal of Whiteness in practice:

> Whenever we come across the notorious "good appearance" phrase in a classified job advertisement, we know that the selection of candidates will have whiteness as a basic prerequisite, regardless of their skills and abilities. Overcoming such prejudices in a society as conservative as that of Brazil will require superhuman effort. (2006, p. 25)

In order to begin to institute a social fabric that "will have done with racism," they suggest that:

> It is essential that we substantially increase the quantity and improve the quality of the images that refer to negritude, and this means establishing a new order in the mass media that will depend on placing legal limits on the actions of corporate executives in the communications field. (2006, p. 25)

They thus recommend that legal restraints be put on those who perpetuate the normative ideal of Whiteness in the society. They suggest that insofar as it is postulated that this entails a limit of people's "freedom of expression," it can be counter-argued that at the moment such a concept of freedom can be seen to generate the opposite of freedom. The abstract concept in practice in this social context is "based on a way of thinking that in reality imprisons every one of us because it reduces 'others' (non-Caucasians) to less-than-human status" (2006, p. 25). As Zuberi and Bonilla-Silva similarly argue, "the modern Cartesian subject is not truly universal, but an idealized White, bourgeois, male, atomistic, heterosexual construct" (2008, p. 333).

Just as Bonilla-Silva (2006) tries to portray the way in which abstract liberalism functions as a frame in color-blind ideology, so Dos Santos and Da Silva likewise show how the abstract ideal of freedom of expression serves to exclude and dehumanize those deemed as "others" (with special reference to the Brazilian context).

In order to begin to address problems of racism in the society, they suggest that it is necessary to think of alternative models of producing and distributing images that will increase the visibility of Afro-Brazilians in the communications media and no longer represent them in a negative way. (2006, p. 26)

They are aware that in making this proposal, they may be criticized by the "advocates of so-called abstract universalist thought … for considering human beings only in terms of groupings of cultural significance such as race and gender" (2006, p. 26). But they argue that although they recognize that this way of creating groupings (in terms of these classifications) can be criticized, the problem is that unless we use these terms, we become unable to "analyze the concrete (in)equality of Brazilians" (2006, p. 26). They are aware that others can criticize them for

> defending skin color as an aspect of identity more important than other identifiers such as being Latin American, Brazilian, or coming from Brazil's Northeast, South, São Paulo, Rio de Janeiro, Minas Gerais, Bahia, or being working-class, or having a particular religion, and, above all, as something more important than just being a member of the human race. (2006, p. 26)

They indicate that "universalist thinkers" have argued that by continuing to use the categories referring to groupings along "race" lines, they "condemn themselves to perpetual imprisonment by race because they will be making an ideal of racial identity" (2006, p. 26). But again they re-iterate that "defenders of abstract equality need to develop some mechanism for seeing and understanding that we do not yet have equality among all human beings" (2006, p. 27). Or, as Zuberi and Bonilla-Silva put it, to be race conscious in orientation as an alternative to the rhetoric of abstract equality "is to be aware of the system of racial stratification, and to recognize the acts of survival and creativity of those marginalized by the racial hierarchy" (2008, p. 333). For Dos Santos and Da Silva, as for Zuberi and Bonilla-Silva, engaging in race-talk does not imply "essentializing" race, but rather, as the latter put it – citing also Collins and Ladson-Billings on this score – to acknowledge "the 'racialized identity' and the common history of oppression shared by people of color" (2008, p. 333).

Finally, Dos Santos and Da Silva state their proposal for the development of a dialogue around the issues that seem to be at stake:

> In sum, we believe that, in order to understand racial inequality in Brazil and our indifference to it, scientists of all types, together with other individuals, social movements, and institutions, need to discuss the subject freely rather than accuse each other. (2006, p. 27)

They thus appeal on these grounds for a lifting of the taboo around race-talk. Dos Santos and Da Silva offer their word of caution when they express concern that unless people have an orientation toward "seeing" racism, they can well be indifferent to it. Although they have stated that "racial discrimination has … become something that has been expressed objectively through statistical data," they are cognizant that the "data" can be *rendered invisible in various ways* (2006, p. 14). As Bonilla-Silva also has noted, it is always possible to explain the data in terms that allow people to deny continued racism (2006, p. 208). (See Chapter 3, Section 3.11.)

How, then, might we treat any (theoretical) statements made in relation to racism in a way that can be conducive to creating some kind of social dialogue? My argument is that it is important to treat as open to continuing discursive encounter any statements made by people – whether so-called professional researchers or others – when they (retroductively) provide explanations of perceived "facts." I suggest that it is in this way that the basis for trust earning through inquirers showing an orientation to discursive accountability, as I have outlined it in previous chapters, can become built. This, however, implies that retroductive logic is not defined as a process whereby it is hoped to arrive at "correct" accounts – as if these can be arrived at by somehow matching statements with "real reality." Rather, it becomes understood as a *process that aids co-inquirers to find ways of seeing and acting that can build what is taken to be (and discussed to be) more just and equitable ways of being together.* This would tally with the definition of retroductive logic as proffered by McIntyre-Mills (mentioned in my introduction to this chapter) as well as with the implicit and explicit definitions of abductive/retroductive logic embedded in the examples of action research that I detailed in Chapter 7.

8.5.1 Possibilities for Creating a Dialogue Around Issues of Racism

As I indicated in the introduction to this chapter, retroductive logic can be used in a "scientific realist" manner, which implies that by referring back from our observations to posited structures that explain them, we can try to develop our knowledge regarding independently existing structures (existing outside of the knowing process). But I have indicated throughout the book that it is also possible to suggest that when researchers create theoretical conceptualizations to account for what is "observed," these conceptualizations do not have to be assessed in terms of their supposed reference to "what really is the case" independently of a dialogue involving those concerned. Nor are those involved in the dialogue required to distance their emotions/concerns/values from their engagement with the issues that they see to be at stake.

In terms of a more constructivist-oriented approach to processes of retroductive inference, I suggest that we can now re-look at Dos Santos and Da Silva's understanding of an operative racism in Brazil as follows:

Dos Santos and Da Silva examine the patterns of employment and income levels in Brazil, and so on, which point to the disparities that can be observed between, say, Afro-Brazilians and other social groupings. From their account of these patterns of inequality, and their understanding of an indifference hereto within the overall society, they infer that:

> It is as if Afro-Brazilians did not exist, as if they were not part of Brazilian society and played no role in it. Denying their existence, dehumanizing them in this way, is in fact the essence of racism. (2006, p. 21)

They thus posit the existence of racism through *excavating the patterns of inequality* and through noting how an *ideology of dehumanization* serves to buttress the system. But they also are aware that not everybody would agree with their account of "the facts" (which they may not see in the same way as they do) and not everybody would even agree that it is worthwhile to continue to analyze society using the racial categories that they have used.

They have also pointed to their concern that "few opportunities [are provided] to the socially excluded" (2006, p. 24). And they have noted that in their view it is important that:

> Even when we talk about inclusion, it is important to know whom we are including, with what aim, and for what purposes, because, as a rule, the differences we see in the other tend to acquire a negative value. (2006, p. 24)

They argue that the normative ideal of Whiteness still tends to pervade (albeit in an unnoticed way) the social conversation, including conversations around possibilities for "inclusion." Hence they call for a dialogue around the meaning of the term "difference" (which in turn relates to conversations around issues of diversity). (See in this regard my discussion of this in Chapter 4, Sections 4.3.1 and 4.3.2.)

But how might the dialogue be conducted in a way that does not amount, in Dos Santos and Da Silva's terms, to people "accusing each other" – either of unnecessarily using race categories or of insensitively trying to avoid "race-talk" (2006, p. 27)? McIntyre-Mills considers that retroductive logic can be used by people to gain an appreciation of patterns of exclusion through *engendering a dialogue around what the terms used by various people to explain differences in life chances mean and why* (2006b, p. 391). Considering Dos Santos and Da Silva's account of the patterning of life chances in Brazil, I would suggest that retroductive logic can help analysts (professional and otherwise) to "trace" ways in which society can be argued to differentially shape life chances. The "tracing" process could involve not only a statistical analysis of survey data (on which Dos Santos and Da Silva seem to concentrate), but also other research procedures – as, for instance, I have detailed in Chapters 3–7. Furthermore, as part of the inquiry process, as McIntyre-Mills emphasizes, *a variety of stakeholders' usage of terms needs to be explored, taking into account the assumptions underpinning their use and also the values infusing their* use.

Drawing on and extending a critical systemic humanist approach, McIntyre-Mills proposes that:

> We need to address and redress the Cartesian split between body and mind, and the rational and reductionist approach to do research on slices of reality and worse to split the researcher from the researched (as the expert). .... In the new millennium the challenge is to ensure that ... the powerful do not silence those currently with limited access to communicate their knowledge narratives. This is not an argument for universalizing language or knowledge narratives, because the cognitive meaning maps associated with specific language, specific place, specific time and specific discourses could be a vital use for future planning. (2006b, p. 367)

McIntyre-Mills does not see that it is necessary for inquirers to try to bracket their values and emotions in processes of developing fruitful dialogue. She concurs with Collins (2000, pp. 70–71) that the (traditional Western) dualities informed by the Cartesian split between mind and body need to be revised to accommodate people as whole beings entering the (co)-inquiry process. And she echoes Collins's view that "dialogues associated with ethical, principled coalition building create possibilities for new versions of truth" (2000, p. 38).

If we reconsider Dos Santos and Da Silva's account in this light, they too could be argued not to be divesting their values from their own "analysis." Thus it can be said that *when they discuss problems of exclusion, they introduce their value of, for instance, admitting diversity in a way that does not impose the normative ideal of Whiteness.* Also, they appeal emotionally to our sense of humanity (and empathy) when they discuss the *dehumanization involved* in creating "otherness" in the context of, inter alia, Brazilian social relations. Although they have not tried to clarify for readers the way in which they have brought to bear certain values (and attendant emotions) in their analysis, and the way in which they might see these as becoming part of a social dialogue, I would suggest that their approach can be extended to make this more explicit. This would allow us to open up a discussion on the standing of their (theoretical) statements and on how they believe that these can be entered into a dialogue with others around their claims and their concerns.

Furthermore, in relation to their statement that "overcoming such [racial] prejudices in a society as conservative as that of Brazil will require superhuman effort" (2006, p. 25), it is crucial to remember both Collins's (1990, 2000) and hooks's (1994, 2001) advice on envisioning (as well as trying to activate) forms of human relationship that manifest human caring. As indicated above, Bonilla-Silva refers to hooks's plea to (re)activate a "spiritual and moral compass." This is also in line with Collins's plea to regenerate an ethic of caring, including through the way in which "knowing" is practiced.

8.6 Revisiting Bourdieu and Wacquant's Concerns with Reference to the Brazilian Case

Before closing the chapter, I would like to comment on how the discussion above can be seen to relate back to the concerns expressed by Bourdieu and Wacquant when they lament the spread across the globe of the US way of treating race issues. (See Chapter 2, Section 2.4.) They have expressed concern, for instance, that the "endless media repetition progressively transforms [ways of seeing issues] . . . into universal commonsense" (1999, p. 42). They give an example of the discourse of multiculturalism, which in the USA

> refers – if in distorted and veiled forms – to the enduring sequelae of the exclusion of blacks and to the crisis of the national myth of the "American dream" correlative to the generalized increase in inequalities over the past two decades. (1999, p. 42)

They argue that the discourse of multiculturalism – with its promise of equal opportunities – can readily become employed to set the terms of (and limit) the social conversation on race issues across the globe. (See also Chapter 4, Section 4.3.1.) They continue their argument by stating that "among the cultural products now being diffused on a planetary scale," the most "insidious" ones are *not* those which are "easy to spot" (1999, p. 42). They emphasize that:

> Rather, they are those isolated and apparently technical terms such as "flexibility" (or its British equivalent, "employability") which, because they encapsulate and communicate a whole philosophy of the individual and of social organization, are well-suited to functioning as veritable political codewords and mottoes (in this case: the downsizing and denigration of the state, the reduction of social protection and the acceptance of the generalization of casual and precarious labor as a fate, nay a boon). (1999, p. 42)

Markedly, Bourdieu and Wacquant's argument here bears some similarity to Dos Santos and Da Silva's account of how racism becomes more or less invisible in Brazil (under code words that mask its operation) while at the same time those viewed as "other" in the labor market are subject to a precarious existence. Nonetheless, Bourdieu and Wacquant (1999) and Dos Santos and Da Silva (2006) can be seen as offering different readings of the structuring of Brazilian society. In regard to the debate around social relations in Brazil, Bourdieu and Wacquant argue that the American tradition has tended to superimpose a model of a dichotomy between "black and white" even in countries such as Brazil, where, according to them, "the operative principles of vision and division of ethnic differences, codified or practical, are *quite different*" (1999, p. 44, my italics). As noted in Chapter 2, they criticize Hanchard (1994) in particular for "applying North American racial categories to the Brazilian situation" (1999, p. 44). They propose that instead of this, it is preferable to proceed by dissecting "the constitution of the Brazilian ethnoracial order" according to its own logic (1999, p. 44).

Referring to anthropologist Wagley (1965), they state that he

> showed that the conception of "race" in the Americas admits of several definitions according to the weight granted to descent, physical appearance (itself not confined to skin color), and to sociocultural status (occupation, income, education, region of origin, etc.), depending on the history of intergroup relations and conflicts in the different geographic zones. (1999, p. 45)

They argue that Wagley's understanding of varied operative definitions of race in particular social contexts implies that the meaning of "race" (insofar as the term is used) needs to be understood in its complexity. They cite the example of Brazil, where they argue that

> racial identity is defined by reference to a continuum of "color", that is, by use of a flexible or fuzzy principle which, taking account of physical traits such as skin color, the texture of hair, and the shape of lips and nose, and of class position (notably income and education), generates a large number of intermediate and partly overlapping categories (over a hundred of them were recorded by the 1980 Census) and does not entail radical ostracization or a stigmatization without recourse or remedy. (1999, p. 45)

They consider it notable that the "segregation indices" in Brazilian cities are "strikingly lower" than in the USA metropolitan areas, and it is also notable for them that in Brazil there is "no social and legal category" for people of "mixed race" (1999, p. 45). Here they suggest that mixed race is not regarded as a meaningful category because the category itself would imply that distinct races exist in the first place to later be "mixed."[237]

Bourdieu and Wacquant's contention is that race is not reified in Brazil in the same way in which it is in North America – and they argue that insofar as "stigmatization" (of those regarded as "other") is operative, it functions differently, because "race" has a more fuzzy meaning. But as we have seen from Dos Santos and Da Silva's account – written more recently than Bourdieu and Wacquant's one – they find that the analytic tool of "racism" indeed still aids us in rendering visible the *racialized patterns of inequality* in Brazilian society – a society arguably divided along racialized lines. The debate between Bourdieu and Wacquant and their critics thus would seem to revolve to some extent around their interpretations of the complexity of the social relations in different contexts, as well as their interpretations of the way in which theoretical tools are used/applied in different contexts.[238]

Following Bonilla-Silva, I would argue that even if we recognize more complex forms of racism emerging in Latin America, this does not imply that the analytic tool of "racism" is irrelevant. The analytic tool is still relevant precisely in order to keep open discussions around issues of "race" – in whatever way these may be conceptualized.

8.7 Conclusion

In this chapter I detailed a view of retroductive reasoning as a mode of inference that enables us to develop analyses at the level of social structure – that is, to move beyond "middle range theorizing." (See Chapter 6, Section 6.1.2.) Considering the structuralist argument of Bonilla-Silva, in which he engages critically with Marxist-oriented structuralist accounts, I pointed out that we do not need to try to settle the debate around the efficacy of "class analysis" as the basic way of approaching issues of (new) racism – as would be implied in a Marxist approach. Nor do we need to define retroductive logic as aimed at grasping "real" causal mechanisms

---

[237]This is similar to Ali's remarks on the terminology of mixed race that I mentioned in Chapter 4, Section 4.7.1, where she criticizes the implication of "mixing previously singular 'racial' identities." The terminology of "mixed race" itself can serve to "re-inscribe and reify 'race'" (2003, p. 6). That is, it can be seen as introducing a language that still "constructs and maintains" the idea of "race" (2003, p. 6).

[238]Bonilla-Silva and Zuberi indicate their concern that Wacquant (2002) made no reference in his argument to the work of authors contributing to the volume "The Death of White Sociology" (edited by Ladner, 1973). They find it "difficult to understand" why Wacquant chose not to make connections between his own work criticizing certain sociological practice in the USA and these authors' exposition of the way in which "White Sociology" poses as science (2008, p. 16).

independently of inquirers engaged in co-inquiry processes to explore what they perceive to be the issues at stake. What *is* important is to set up the relevant inquiries so that any attendant theoretical insights can be seen as serving to create, rather than delimit, possibilities for coalition between those engaged in social justice projects as advised by Collins (2000, p. 289) – as I have tried to summarize in the right-hand column of Table 8.1.

In developing/drawing out constructivist/pragmatic-oriented understandings of the value of retroductive inquiry processes, I also pointed to McIntyre-Mills's understanding of retroductive thinking as being a way of "redressing," as she calls it, the traditional (Western) Cartesian-based dualities between, say, mind and body, reason and emotion, opinion and fact, and so on (2006b, p. 367). Retroductive logic then can be seen as making provision for people as "whole" people – together with others – revisiting their assumptions/concerns/values in the light of a consideration of alternatives and in the light of an orientation to co-creating different futures.

The future-oriented outlook of retroductive inference as understood by McIntyre-Mills bears out the accounts (and examples) of abductive inference that I detailed in Chapter 7. McIntyre-Mills explains how retroductive logic can be linked to efforts at systemic intervention to "address power, empowerment, and governance needs of people marginalized in terms of conceptual, geographic and cyberspace time" (2003, p. 12). She sees retroductive inference as part of a process of "unpacking the complexity layer by narrative layer using interactive dialogue for [future] design" (2003, p. 6). This concurs with Douglas's suggestions that I cited in Chapter 7, Section 7.2.3, namely, that it is possible to (co-)explore "patterns of everyday incidents that sustain dynamics of institutional racism in multiple forms" as part of the process of imagining and practicing alternative forms of human being together.

Abductive/retroductive inference here is not seen as aimed at observing in a neutral (supposedly theory- and value-free) way what appears as incidents/events in social reality in order to generate apolitical theoretical understandings. Rather it is seen as a process of, as Essed notes (1991, p. 56), making sense of the "events" by considering their broader significance in relation to manifold incidences as experienced in individual lives and across lives. An admitted race-conscious starting point for theorizing as part of critical theorizing need not pose as free of concerns that are being brought to bear. But it forms, indeed, a starting point for further dialogue around both how to interpret "events" and how to consider their broader social implications. And it can be argued that without such a race-conscious starting point, due to the weightiness of color-blind rhetoric in the social fabric, concerns about racism can easily be disappeared/rendered taboo in our discourses. Hence Dos Santos and Da Silva point out that people can choose to orient themselves to not "seeing" racism and/or to be indifferent to it (2006, p. 14). Race-aware stances thus serve, at this juncture (as understood within race critical theorizing), as a counterweight to dominant discourses that serve in various ways to render "race" and its impact on people's lives more or less invisible. However, I suggested that theorizing at the level of social structure to look into the systemic reproduction of, inter alia, racial hierarchies needs to be combined more consciously and purposively with epistemological discourses that call for inquirers to practice problematizing potential authority relations in what Douglas calls the "here and now" of the research process itself (1998, Chapter 5, p. 8).

Ladson-Billings indicates that the "epistemological limbo – between the old epistemological discourse and the new – is a place where many scholars of color find themselves" (2003, p. 415). As I indicated in Chapter 1, and illustrated with examples throughout the book, she follows Collins in forwarding a notion of personal accountability, combined with an empathetic expression of caring for others and an orientation to dialogue as part of the development of ethical inquiry processes. In her account, as in Collins's (1990, 2000), these ethical issues cannot be separated from epistemological ones, because knowing is to be judged in terms of ethical considerations. Of course, "ethics" in social research here is clearly not seen as a matter of following some "codes of conduct" – the following of which renders the research "ethical." Rather, ethics is linked to the person's expressing an ethics of caring, connectedness, and accountability. (See also Romm, 2001, pp. 96–97; McIntyre-Mills, 2003, p. 43, 2008a, pp. 147—149.)

I consider that linking epistemology inextricably with ethics as pleaded for expressly by authors such as Collins and Ladson-Billings needs to be explicitly taken on board in any social theorizing around new racism – in order that it can be seen to embrace exemplary (accountable) styles of both knowing and living. To activate the potential of structurally oriented theorizing to express orientations to what I call discursive accountability, I suggest that we need to focus upon the following points (which as a whole can be seen as embodying the suggestions encapsulated in the right-hand column of Table 8.1, while still appreciating the merits of retroductive logic). I suggest that inquirers become oriented so as to:

- Recognize that at the moment of creating inferences with respect to the persistent patterning of social inequality, the inferences, and the attendant statements/analyses produced, need to be accounted for through a serious engagement with alternatives. This means that when posing analyses at the level of social structure, possibilities for rethinking the building up of the analyses need to be seriously entertained – as a matter of developing our human engagements with others as (co-)inquirers. In this way provision is made for Collins's plea for developing an orientation where we shy away from "labeling one form of oppression as more important than others, or one expression of activism as more radical than another" – as part of the process of "creat[ing] conceptual spaces to identify some new [practical] linkages" (2000, p. 289). This is important for her because coalition building as part of the project of "fostering social justice" requires engagement with others' understandings (2000, p. 290).
- Exemplify a commitment to attend to (and to shift) potential relations of domination during the inquiry process – recognizing (with Douglas, 1998, Chapter 5, p. 5) that this is a "valid research issue" in itself.
- Explore the manner in which any proffered analyses offer theoretical resources that, however, can be revisited/extended/utilized in a novel way by different audiences as they (re)consider their relevance in helping them to work toward more human/humane ways of living.

- Write up analyses/theoretical accounts without trying to authorize one's accounts as referring to "realities" independently of the concerns that one is admittedly bringing to bear. This implies presenting analyses in a manner that encourages further discussion and reconsideration as part of the social process of working with alternative values and concerns toward creating viable futures. This links up with Collins's tenet that "dialogue remains central to assessing knowledge claims" (2000, p. 276) as well as her caution that dialogue is not akin to "adversarial debate" but is more akin to a "call and response discourse" between speakers and listeners – where specific expressions of concerns are provided for without aiming to create a univocal story (2000, p. 261).

Chapter 9
General Conclusion: Reviewing Research Approaches, Conceptualizing Mixed-Research Designs, and Writing into One Another's Stories

9.1 Introduction

In this concluding chapter I first summarize the way in which this book has been structured to re-examine various research options for organizing inquiries around new racism. I then offer some reflections on the justification for what Bonilla-Silva and Baiocchi call "mixed-research designs" (2008, p. 140). The argument that I forward is that mixed-research designs are feasible to the extent that it is recognized that any methodological options (including those employed in mixed-research designs) always need to be adapted for use in particular contexts. Instead of considering methods for collecting/generating data and methodologies (as designs for inquiry that make use of methods) as entities to be taken "off the shelf" (as Midgley, 1997, p. 261, puts it) and then used in combination with others, I suggest, following Midgley, that mixing methods/methodologies requires their *creative use* in situ. This means that the research approaches that are "mixed" become (re)moulded through the way in which they are used within the research project overall. Before proceeding to elucidate this argument, I offer a summary below of the course of the book thus far.

9.2 Summary Overview of the Book

In Chapter 1, after indicating that the book is aimed at revisiting approaches to investigating new racism, I presented a narrative account of myself as a background for readers to better understand my concerns in writing the book. This led on to my outlining of my preference for adopting a more constructivist- than realist-oriented epistemological orientation in the debate concerning the understanding of research as an enterprise in society. I suggested that such an orientation provides more scope for researchers (professional or otherwise) to acknowledge a responsibility for the manner in which processes of "knowing" may be impactful on the unfolding of social outcomes – albeit that the social impact of research can itself never be understood outside of human discourse.

N. Romm, *New Racism*, DOI 10.1007/978-90-481-8728-7_9,

In Chapter 2, I offered an exposition of a number of conceptions of, and ways of theorizing, new racism – showing that different arguments can be brought to bear in explaining the persistence of racism across the globe. In Chapters 3–8, I discussed in detail a number of methodological approaches that have been used to explore issues relating to (new) forms of racism. I pointed to the accounts of authors explaining their use of them, while also showing that at times these approaches can be restrictive.

As I proceeded, I offered constructively oriented criticisms of realist-oriented arguments that insist that researchers be committed to producing accurate under-standings of the social world as it operates *irrespective* of whether it is being researched or not (to use Hammersley's terminology, 2003, p. 345). Hammersley states that it seems to him that "virtually all social research has this commitment" (2003, p. 345). However, I showed that from a constructivist alternative, the quest is *not* to try to seek knowledge of a social world as it operates without it being "reac-tive" to our research efforts. Such a quest can be seen as a wild goose chase with no goose, because we cannot ever establish whether we have "found" such a world – as we have no mechanisms for matching our statements with a posited social world operating outside of our discourses. Threaded throughout the book (and building up my arguments with reference to examples), I pointed to options for redefining both human knowing and human living. I indicated why many of those concerned with the exploration of new racism have forwarded ways of defining "validity" in social research in terms that are not based on commitments to a form of realist epistemology – where research gains its validity through researchers' striving to attain accurate/unbiased representation of a posited external world. For example, I have shown how the criteria offered by Collins (1990) – such as the commit-ment to care, dialogue, and personal accountability – can be invoked in defining research validity. I elucidated the importance of these criteria within what I call a trusting constructivist epistemological argument, where the focus is on people being awarded trust in their research endeavors on the basis of their (display of) serious engagement and involvement with views and concerns as expressed and discussed by others.

In the light of the link between epistemology and ethics that I showed is impor-tant within the constructivist-oriented approach forwarded in the book, I examined various available methodologies that I chose to consider as research options. In view of this link, I offered suggestions for *organizing the research process to allow for increased participation of research participants in framing/reframing issues* in terms of different understandings and concerns that can be brought forward. And I showed how research reporting could be styled to *express the status of research products as admittedly having been generated through the research*, while also expressing an orientation on the part of authors to recognize and account for their own and others' (value-laden) concerns as part of their presentation of theoretical accounts.

My discussion of experimentation in Chapter 3 became an opening for me to provide a variety of theoretical perspectives that can be used to reframe the issues raised by the experimenters whose arguments I chose to discuss. I concentrated on exploring different angles on themes that recur through the book. When discussing Nier et al.'s (2001) experimentation with White participants in the USA, I considered in detail their views on recategorization as a way of possibly generating more inclusive social categorizations. However, I showed that their views on categories and on groups (including their views on race relations) might serve to reproduce an essentialization of the categories under discussion. I argued that this aspect of their research (and related research that they have conducted with minority groups too in the USA as elsewhere) has not been adequately (reflexively) reflected upon. I showed how one might review their theoretical conclusions, as well as the methodological approach leading to these, in the light of alternative ways of posing the starting questions that they have raised. I showed, for example, that so-called debriefing sessions in experiments could become an opportunity to open a space for reconsideration – including through cross-racial discussion across race(d) groupings – of starting conceptions. Such an engagement with alternatives could then be better expressed in (theoretical) write-up of "results." Moreover, through encouragement of audience feedback (Nyamnjoh, 2007) additional participation of research participants (those initially involved) and of wider audiences can be provided for.

Meanwhile, in presenting my argument for shifting processes of experimental research, I expanded upon the experiment reported by Monteith et al. (2001) in which they set out to explore the reactions of their White American participants to measurements of "implicit racial bias" (obtained by using the Racial Implicit Association Test – IAT). Through the research they tried to establish whether enabling people with biased IAT scores to themselves detect their own implicitly held prejudices could become a route to intervening positively in the social world. I suggested a number of ways in which this interventive component of experimental research can be further capitalized upon. I also offered an indication of how an alternative relationship with participants in their experiment with White participants as well as in a subsequent experiment with African American participants could be set up, and indeed how cross-racial discussions could be encouraged through such research. I suggested furthermore that once the image (and self-image) of experimenters as geared to uncover the workings of a posited external "factual reality" becomes shifted, this provides space for us to explore the *generative potential* of experiments as an aid for increased reflection by both participants and wider audiences on what Douglas calls their "organizing frames for engaging with the world" (1998, Chapter 10, p. 17)

In Chapter 4, I used the research of Rabinowitz et al. (2005) to make the point that survey research investigating attitudes (in this case of "high status group" people in the USA) around racialized issues can all too easily reproduce taken-for-granted social categorizations. I then showed how certain researchers conducting survey research (such as Haley and Sidanius, 2006) have acknowledged the way in which the framing of research questions can influence the kinds of responses that are given by respondents/participants (in this case, from what they call dominant as well as subordinate groups). But I suggested that this acknowledgment has normally not been carried to the point of reviewing "reactivity" in the context of considering how research itself can be seen as part of a process of *forming attitudes/opinions* in relation to race(d) issues. I pointed to ways in which survey research could more fully incorporate this understanding and could be shifted so as to enable those setting up such research to be more accountable for their involvements in social life. To this end, I examined specifically and further developed Geeraert and Dunn's constructivist argument (2003) that they proffered when exploring racialized attitudes in Australia via their survey. I compared it with arguments developed earlier in the book, showing implications of this for discursively accountable survey research. I made suggestions for how survey researchers could set up their questions in such a way as to invite participants to reflect on the language that is being used. I showed too how they could invite both participants and wider audiences to reconsider what may have become taken-for-granted conceptualizations (including, say, conceptions of multiculturalism) through the way in which questions become posed to people both during the administration of the survey and during write-up thereof.

In Chapter 5, I went on to discuss the engagement in intensive interviewing as a research approach for exploring new racism. I compared more traditional understandings of interviewing with alternatives. I showed, for instance, how Douglas, in her research with (other) Black woman managers in Britain, questions the traditional understanding of the relationship between "interviewer" and "interviewee" and calls for a revision of the role separation (1998, Chapter 6, p. 4). Douglas indicates in addition that when engaging in any processes of inquiry, she does not assume the power to "know" but rather operates by keeping in consciousness "a tentativeness about stating 'reality'" (1998, Chapter 7, p. 7). Yet she points out that (paradoxically) her decision to operate in terms of a tentativeness in making claims about "reality" *does not prohibit her from finding a way of operating in relation to others and their concerns.* In Chapter 5, I elaborated on the implications of Douglas's epistemological and ethical orientation for intensive interviewing – comparing it with positions such as the one offered by Hammersley (1995, 2003). I showed how her considerations can be brought to bear in reconsidering the example of intensive interviewing provided by Essed (1991) in relation to Black women in the Netherlands and the USA (that I discussed in detail in the chapter). I also offered an outline of focus group interviewing as an intensive interviewing approach – and I illustrated with reference to an example of a focus group facilitated by me in South Africa (2007) how some responsibility can be taken for researcher involvement in such inquiries. I suggested that intensive interviewing can be seen (and practiced) in terms of the intent to create openings that otherwise may not be created in society for what Bonilla-Silva (2006) calls straight talk around more or less "taboo" subjects (such as, for instance, "race-talk") by setting up forums for live mutual exchange as part of the inquiry process.

In Chapter 6, in considering ethnography and autoethnography as research options, I presented as an example of ethnography a case of research in the USA (DeCuir & Dixson, 2004) undertaken in terms of critical race theorizing (CRT). According to Ladson-Billings, one of the important contributions of CRT is that it offers researchers "an opportunity to stand in a different relationship to the research (and researched)" than that provided for within what she calls "Euro-American cultural logic" – insofar as the latter involves an "aggressive seizure of intellectual space" (2003, p. 417). For her, the point of focusing on storytelling in (qualitative) research is "that it [this focus] can be used to demonstrate how the same phenomena can be told in different and multiple ways depending on the storytellers" (2003, p. 417). The issue of the power to define "reality" is thus a central issue of concern for her (and according to her, for CRT).

My discussion in Chapter 6 was organized around considering a variety of interpretations of CRT as an entry into revisiting DeCuir and Dixson's approach. For example, I pointed to Bell's (1992, 1995) self-named realist position ("racial realism") – which I argued differs from the hypothetico-deductive-oriented realism supported by Hammersley (1990) and bears more similarity to the realist stance adopted by Layder (1993). Layder classes Hammersley's style of ethnography as oriented to middle range theorizing (1993, p. 31) – an approach to theorizing that he believes needs to be supplemented with more structurally oriented thinking (such as that promoted by Marx). However, Layder does not raise as an issue of concern the unequal power relationships that may be introduced by authorizing certain interpretations and analyses of institutions/structures and their "real" operation. I elaborated upon Alldred's understanding of discourse ethnography (1998) and Walby's account of "reflexive intervention" (2007) to point to options more in keeping with the interpretation of CRT that I see Ladson-Billings as supporting. I indicated how these options can be seen to link up with the critical theoretical arguments developed by, for instance, Habermas (1984, 1993, 1994) in his critical theorizing – especially as extended with reference to Collins's (1990, 2000) suggestions – and how all these approaches can be used to revisit the study reported by DeCuir and Dixon (2004). Finally, with reference to debates around the value of autoethnography as a research approach, I offered a brief example of a case of my own autoethnographic research (in a setting in the UK) – considering it in terms of criteria of assessment that can be invoked within constructivist arguments.

In Chapter 7, I discussed in detail further arguments for considering research as a "political" enterprise – in the sense that it cannot be regarded as neutral in its social impact. I concentrated on exploring the views of proponents of action research who argue that such research includes an orientation to develop more humane forms of social organization as part of the research remit. As Weil summarizes, the value of action inquiry lies in its enabling people to "work with learning and change" through setting up processes whereby people can consider, in practice, "the appropriateness of assumptions deriving from different paradigms of thought, and their influence on our choices of action and inquiry, our languages and our metaphors" (Weil, 1998, p. 43). I showed that this conception of action research tallies with the constructivist arguments that I have forwarded in the course of the book. I also highlighted how this interpretation of action research differs from realist-oriented interpretations that may be espoused.

I wished through this chapter to point to the details of the contribution that action research can make, through a pragmatic use of the logic of abduction, toward exploring while transforming forms of new racism. I chose what I regard to be two innovative action research approaches (with research examples from Britain and from Cyprus) to make this point. I suggested that these should be added to the repertoire of approaches to be used in the field. Mehta indicates that many supporters of action research as a mode of inquiry suggest that any methodology/method[239] that can be harnessed to aid the facilitation of inquiry in action can be appropriately incorporated, depending on "how [it is] used and to what end" (2008, p. 246). This is in line with Selener's comments that action research is "methodologically eclectic and innovative" (1997, p. 111). The two approaches that I discussed can be seen as possible options among others that can be (suitably) employed by those forwarding action inquiries.

In Chapter 8, I undertook an exploration of the way in which abductive/retroductive logic can be used to aid theorizing around the structuring of specific modes of social organization, which become, in Marx's terms, "fetishized" insofar as people cannot imagine their transformation. I suggested that the strength of retroductive inference in the analysis of new racism is that it enables us to move from experienced "consequents" to explanatory "antecedents" theorized at the level of social structures – without insisting on direct logical links being made between the two. I offered examples – concentrating on the one provided by Bonilla-Silva (2006) – of how racism can be theorized at the level of structure (thus theorizing beyond the "middle range") in terms of the invocation of retroductive logic to create analyses of racism. I also suggested that in terms of this logic, there is no need to consider cognition as separable from emotion – and thus no need to uphold the dualisms of, say, mind/body, fact/opinion, thought/feeling, and so on, associated with the adoption of realist understandings of the knowing process. This is particularly so when we extend criteria for assessing the theorizing by taking into account Collins's epistemological arguments (1990, 2000) and other arguments proposed by various other critical theorists.

Taking on board the structurally oriented theorizing of Bonilla-Silva, who propounds that we need to move beyond seeing racism as primarily rooted in "prejudice," I suggested that we can review the exemplars of social psychological experiments and surveys in Chapters 3 and 4. That is, we can undercut the theoretical starting position that seems to link racism primarily to negative feelings and attitudes. We can make the point that this theoretical starting point leads to attendant solutions being proposed by the researchers to try to address such feelings and attitudes, through, for instance, creating "recategorizations" of "the other"

---

[239]Mehta here uses the terminology of *method* when she suggests that "much depends on how methods are used" (2008, p. 246). However, she seems to be using the term in a similar way to my use of the term *procedure* – where, for example, different methods/techniques of data collection might be harnessed (such as questionnaires, observation of behavior, structured or unstructured interviews, etc.) as part of the research. For example, Nier et al.'s experimentation (as a procedure) involved a number of techniques of data collection (2001); and as De Vaus (1996) notes, survey research too is not necessarily limited only to questionnaires as a source of data. Also, while "intensive interviewing" as a way of proceeding does seem to imply a concentration on one way of conversing with participants (i.e., intensively), even it can involve variation (as I showed in Chapter 5). And ethnography too can involve a number of techniques (as mentioned by Hammersley and Atkinson (1995)), as can action research – which can draw on the use of any "tool" that helps to facilitate inquiry in action.

(as proposed by, say, Nier et al., 2001) or through trying to foster "egalitarian attitudes" (Rabinowitz et al., 2005). These approaches to racism (with the focus on studies of "prejudice") can be argued to be unnecessarily restrictive. As Omi and Winant note, though, it may not be necessary to uphold an either/or position in this regard, where racism is seen as *either* rooted in people's prejudicial responses *or* in social structures (1994, p. 138). Douglas concurs with this when she points to the "unending debates about behavior or attitude change; change of individuals or change of culture" that often governs "analysis of the problem" of racism. She too prefers to distance herself from this "either-or, dichotomized way of thinking" (1998, Chapter 4, p. 15). More important for her is to "gain insight into the variety of assumptions that underpin different perspectives on the 'problem' and also the solutions offered" (1998, Chapter 4, p. 16).

My discussion in Chapter 8 was directed toward considering how one can account for modes of inference that provide for structurally oriented inquiry (of the kind undertaken by, say, Collins, 2005, Bonilla-Silva, 2006, Stewart, 2008, etc.), and how we might consider the status of the proffered theorizing. As far as research procedures to be used in supporting systemic theorizing of this kind are concerned, Bonilla-Silva (2006) indicates that he used interviewing along with reference to other research material (including analyses of historical records) to build up his theorizing around color-blind racism. He and Baiocchi comment that although survey research can be useful to "gather *general* information on actors' views," they believe that it is "time to rely more on data gathered from in-depth interviews and mixed-research designs" (2008, p. 140). (They suggest in this regard that they are following Du Bois's (1899) model – 2008, p. 150, Endnote 11.) They thus show a preference, alongside some usages of quantitatively oriented research, for in-depth interviewing and mixed-research designs. This preference of theirs should also be read in the light of the problem that Collins (2000) identifies, namely, that methodologies modeled on the natural sciences (such as, say, experiments and surveys) propose an emotional detachment of researchers when dealing with their "object of study" – which becomes, indeed, treated as an object (2000, p. 255). From Collins's ethical perspective, she finds untenable this relationship of researchers with what is being "researched."

I have suggested in Chapters 3 and 4 that it is possible to (re)design quantitatively oriented methodological options so that they can incorporate some of the concerns as have been expressed by Collins, by using them in a way that may differ from their more "normal" use. This is by, for instance, admitting the possible ways in which the research framing can *generate* rather than simply "discover" results, and by establishing more space for researchers to interact with respondents/participants outside the frames initially provided. In addition, I have suggested in Chapters 5, 6 and 7 that the use of qualitatively oriented approaches too needs to go hand in hand with researchers' careful consideration of the manner of justifying the approach by accounting for what Collins calls the "criteria for methodological adequacy" that are being drawn upon (2000, p. 256). My argument overall that I have put forward is that no matter what methodological approaches are being utilized (whether on their own or in mixed designs), researchers should not avoid *considering the way in which, and purposes for which, the approaches are being employed* in terms of the research being *implicated in the unfolding of the social fabric*. In the next section I explore further arguments for ways of treating the different methodological options that may be incorporated in mixed-research designs.

9.3 Mixed-Research Designs

As McKay and Romm note, debates around possibilities for developing coherent mixed-research designs center around the question of what it might mean to mix different approaches, given that they each seem to invoke *different paradigmatic assumptions* about the nature of the "reality" being investigated, the meaning of "knowing," and the relationship between "researchers" and "those being researched" (2008b, pp. 391–392). When inquirers develop mixed-research designs, can they work with these differing underlying assumptions, or do they need to override some of the assumptions in the process of drawing on a variety of research procedures? For example, if, say, experimental research has been developed as an approach geared to *locating causal relationships between variables* that are seen to inhere in the social world, can this be properly "combined" with alternative approaches that entail a *questioning of this view of social reality, of how it can be inquired into, and of how (professional) researchers should properly relate to participants*?

In order to create a mixed-research design, it would seem that it is necessary to *alter* some of the "original" philosophical understandings of the (separate) methodologies, given the differing paradigmatic assumptions that each otherwise carries. Vogt comments that while "different kinds of coding, measurement and analysis are frequently employed in the same study," the issue remains as to whether one can "mix [underlying] philosophical paradigms" (2008, p. 10).[240] He answers this question tentatively by pointing out that "perhaps pragmatism allows this. But does it allow mixing purposes, problems or constructs?" (2008, p. 10). Some authors have argued that when combining methodologies, each different one should be used largely "as is" in order to try to retain the rationale of the approach as developed by original creators thereof (cf. Flood & Jackson, 1991). The idea here would be to try to show respect for the range of alternative standards that can be invoked to judge the quality of research – and to afford credibility to each one. That is, a diversity of criteria for developing sound research would then be activated by those organizing the "mixing" of the separate approaches.

---

[240]If, as Kuhn (1962) suggests, paradigms are *incommensurable* it would seem that one cannot mix the approaches in any coherent fashion. For this reason, Flood and Romm propose that we rather speak of (in)commensurability to show that some translatability (or rather, bases for comparison between approaches) can be constructed (2006a, pp. 7–8). We point out that the apparently incomparable options can be *made comparable by* setting out relevant terms for discussion around them.

Midgley (2000, pp. 225–228) looks at the question of mixed-research designs from another angle, similar to the one I wish to forward in this book. He argues that instead of trying to take "off the shelf" the separate approaches, it is often a more suitable (and dynamic) approach to *adapt* them in a *creative way*, in terms of an overall research design. He argues that inquirers have a pivotal role in deciding how to use/adapt various "available" (or if necessary newly developed) options; and they are in this sense in a "unique position of responsibility" (2000, p. 229). Boyd et al. further explain:

> It is not usually a matter of "stitching" methods together in an additive fashion (although this can be done): a whole *system* (interrelated set) of purposes can be pursued through the *synergy* of different methods. (Boyd et al., 2007, p. 1309)

Here Boyd et al. – following Midgley (2000, p. 226) – emphasize that if inquirers consider carefully the purposes for which the inquiries are being undertaken, they are able to create a "synergy" between the different methods (or methodologies) that become drawn upon.

McKay and Romm interpret the approach that we used in exploring HIV/AIDS in the informal economy in Zambia (following a similar design developed by McKay (2003), in a previous four-country study), as offering an illustration of Midgley's (2000) and Boyd et al.'s (2007) account of the effort to creatively develop a synergy between methods/methodologies. We add to Boyd et al.'s account that when (re)working various research approaches that become utilized, these can become adapted through infusing each one with a *consciously considered intervention component*.[241] In stating our stance in relation to methodological pluralism we suggest that:

> This injection [of an intervention component] into the methods/methodologies used (as well as into their interconnection) implies infusing a reflected-upon intention into the employment of the methods/methodologies – an intention that is considered anew with each use of the method/methodology (and which can be accounted for in the social context in which the method/methodology is to be employed). (2008b, p. 392)

---

[241] In the case of the Zambian research, the inquiry processes employed were a survey; rapid rural assessment workshops; a peer education training process; and a national workshop. When administering our survey, the idea of using the survey was to employ it with the (intervention) intention of *rendering more discussable* issues that would normally have been considered undiscussable, but which nevertheless were regarded as questions that needed to be addressed. In rapid assessment workshops, the intervention intention was not only to raise issues for discussion at local level, but to create space for developing social capacity, including possibilities for *intervention at national as well as sectoral level*. In the peer education process, the intention was that capacitated peer educators could *continue with learning/discussion processes* after the formal research process had "ended," and could encourage the development of options for action (at various levels of action) to *address informal sector workers' discussed needs*. In the national workshop, the intention was to strengthen the debate around ways of dealing with HIV/AIDS in the light of concerns brought forth from (more or less vulnerable) participants as well as from research assistants and research consultants (McKay & Romm, 2008b, p. 392). In the overall design, each methodological stage set up opportunities for further stages. The mixed research design was thus sequential in this case rather than concurrent – to use the terminology of Creswell and Plano-Clark (2007).

Mehta makes a similar point when she suggests that in considering the use of methods, it is important to bear in mind "the political opportunities that exist in a given context and the spaces that are available or that can be opened up to influence." She states that:

> While surveys can be highly extractive [using people's responses to extract information], they can generate data that can speak to powerful people. They can also complement qualitative and participatory research. Similarly, qualitative research can be extractive and ridden with power politics. Thus a lot hinges on the intention of the researcher, her approach to research and her research participants, rather than the methods per se. (2008, p. 246)

Mehta's observation that "much depends on the researcher" again puts the focus on the need for responsibility to be taken for the way in which methodologies and methods are used and the way in which they may be "mixed" (if they are mixed). In the light of the focus on responsibility (or what can also be called discursive accountability), McKay and Romm aver that

> the debate around methodological pluralism can be revisited by highlighting (as Midgley, 2000, suggests) the responsibility of inquirers, and in addition by considering how inquirers can *try to cater – in each context of use of a method/methodology/overall research design – for their involvement in the unfolding of social outcomes.* (2008b, p. 393)

McKay and Romm propose that the use of particular methods/methodologies – whether or not "mixed" in an overall design – requires us to consider (with others, through a discursive process) their interventive possibilities. As I have suggested throughout this book, instead of regarding methods/methodologies as a means (primarily) to "produce knowledge" (as Hammersley, 1995, 2003, puts it), researchers need to concern themselves with their impactful involvements in the social world via their research efforts. Research designs created for exploring racism should thus be consciously harnessed toward the political project of working toward more humane, genuinely democratic, social alternatives. I have concentrated in this book on offering suggestions for how the different research approaches that I explored in Chapters 3–8 can – if suitably shifted/expanded – be harnessed toward this end. Likewise, I suggest that our ways of combining approaches in mixed research designs too need to be developed in terms of similar considerations (in discursive engagement with others) of the complicity of research in the organization of our social being. That is, we need to *acknowledge responsibility for our involvement in the social world through our use of the research processes and through our way of presenting any products/results generated thereby.*

I would now like to make the further point that even when inquirers choose not to "mix" approaches in any particular project, they still can operate in terms of a consciousness that recognizes that there is *value in what other inquirers* may be doing – toward building up a variegated "story" around new racism and ways of addressing it. Collins suggests in this regard that there is much to be gained by allowing for a story to become built up "from a multitude of different perspectives" – accepting that different authors of stories (including ones developed by those defining themselves as professional researchers and by others) each can contribute "missing parts to the other writer's story" (2000, p. 38). It is important here also, as Collins notes, not to concentrate only on accounts written up in books and journals, but to include as credible those accounts that may be expressed in any communications shared with others – including accounts that may be reported in sources such as masters and doctoral theses, lectures, and so on. This is especially because, as she remarks (citing Kuhn, 1962; Mulkay, 1979), "in general, scholars, publishers, and other experts represent specific interests and credentializing processes" (2000, p. 253).[242]

To sum up, I have argued in relation to the use of methodological approaches to explore new racism that a responsible approach implies that we:

- Actively rework/shift "traditional" uses of methodological approaches, and decide in different research contexts how and whether to combine different ones – in such a way as to make provision for considering with others the possible impacts in society of both *processes* of inquiry and their *generated products*. This at the same time requires acknowledging that, as Collins points out, issues of control in social life can be seen as manifesting also in ways in which criteria for methodological adequacy or inadequacy become defined (2000, p. 39) – with certain approaches often dubbed inadequate in terms of invoked "scientific" paradigms of research. (It is for this reason that I have concentrated on spelling out alternative criteria as the book proceeded.)
- Operate styles of reasoning/logic that enable "understanding" (or insight generation) to be inextricably linked with "caring"– thus reworking the reason/feeling binary and instantiating forms of empathetic knowing and living.
- Accept that there will be diverse ways of approaching our inquiries around new racism as well as diverse theoretical perspectives on "the problem" that become proffered – and that different writers can contribute what Collins calls "missing parts to the other writer's story" (2000, p. 38).

Considering this last bullet point, for me this does not imply trying to generate a unity of perspective, but rather an *enrichment* hereof, with a view to *enriching the consideration of possible options for action too*. My discussions of theoretical fluency that I introduced in the various chapters imply engaging with others' stories and considering how these evoke alternative possibilities for addressing "the problem." Gaertner et al. make the point that research that they cite "across time, populations, and paradigms ... illustrate[s] how aversive racism – racism among people who are good and well-intentioned – can produce disparate outcomes between Blacks and Whites" (2005, p. 384). I have argued in this book (mainly in Chapter 3, Section 3.4.2) that Gaertner et al. still can be seen to be relying on particular research approaches and more specifically on a "scientific" paradigm of research in order to generate their story (which they would probably not call a story) around aversive racism. I have tried to show that there are alternative ways of proceeding

---

[242]It is worth noting here that Carlis Douglas and Susan Weil, in commenting (during August 2008) on my exploration in Chapter 7 of their action research inquiries, found important that I managed to acknowledge, and render credible, various normally scantly used ways of referencing their recounting, such as in a PhD thesis, in an inaugural lecture, and in personal communications.

that question the starting framework (along with their implied view of science) and that the different stories generated can together create a more evocative account, evoking different action options. I have also suggested that in reading each other's stories and helping to write "missing parts," all participants can at the same time begin to unfold "their" stories differently, producing new understandings on their part that they otherwise may not have appreciated (if they are unduly restricted methodologically and theoretically).

This means too that we accept that people (and their stories) *can develop along new lines*, and that they (like methods/methodologies/theories) can be treated as being in-the-making. Kalungu-Banda, in offering lessons that he believes he has learned from Nelson Mandela's life, indicates that when we regard "others," and believe that we can trace a pattern in their behavior, this "does not entitle us to think we know the lot" about them. He continues:

> The pattern we may have noticed is not hard information: it can be negated at any time by the choices of that person we think we know inside out. That is what makes any human being a mystery. (2006, p. 22)

Taking up this lesson from Kalungu-Banda, my suggestion therefore is to treat theorists/writers and the theories/stories they tell as unfolding, emergent phenomena – that for this reason cannot be understood/appreciated via stable categories. As we engage with "their" stories, we can appreciate that these stories at the same time are [can be] in the process of shifting.

9.4 Some Concluding Notes

9.4.1 A Note on the Terminology of "Mixing" in "Mixed-Research Designs"

The terminology of mixing used by some authors referring to mixed-research designs could create the impression that the research approaches that become mixed each have their "own" identities, which they then bring into the "combination." White and Taket refer to this model of mixing as implying that there exists a "set of unitary distinct categories" each with a stable identity. They argue that this in turn invokes an underlying "homogenizing and sterilizing" perspective on diversity (1997, p. 391). As I noted in Chapter 4, Section 4.7.1, Ali expresses similar concerns with the category of mixed races – which she indicates brings with it the assumption that singular "races" exist in the first place to be "mixed." She points to "the ongoing singularity in hegemonic discourses of 'race', and the binary structure that underpins most models of difference and discrimination" (2003, p. 6).

In keeping with my attempt to deconstruct the idea of unitary, homogeneous entities "existing" in social reality – including entities such as "methods" and "methodologies" – I suggest that it is preferable to recognize that what becomes mixed in mixed-research designs should be treated as already differentiated and also as potentially evolving. This makes more provision for being able to appreciate, with Kalungu-Banda, that what we seem to be presented with (e.g., a person, method, or methodology) "is not hard information: it can be negated at any time by the choices of that person we think we know inside out" (2006, p. 22). Applied to the issue of utilization of methodologies, we can be surprised by the innovative ways in which people can use methodologies in a fashion that we had not foreseen, and which show us that "information" about the methodologies' potential usage need not be treated as "known."

9.4.2 A Note on Plurality of Cultural Expressions and of Methodological Approaches: Pluralism as an Opportunity for Learning

Vogt refers to the "intensity of debates" about methodological options and notes that in order to understand these debates it may be necessary to "apply concepts from social psychology and cultural anthropology" (2008, p. 18). He suggests that methodological groups often develop with loyalties to "favored research approaches" and with "ethnocentric ideas" concerning what are seen as other research group cultures. He indicates that in this context "allegiance can replace choice, which in turn chokes off innovation" (2008, p. 18). He admits that his ideas about how researchers often proceed in terms of some favored approach are not new, and that already Kuhn (1962) indicated that often researchers stick to what they see as the "tried and true" approach (2008, p. 10). Taking on board the arguments around making provision for diversity of cultural expressions that I developed in Chapter 4 (Section 4.3.1), these arguments can be applied to consider the relationship between methodological options treated as "cultural alternatives." My suggestion is that researchers can, and should, develop the facility to learn from what "the other" can offer, and use this as a basis for extending their initial understandings of particular approaches to which they might have been committed.

When discussing different models of pluralism in terms of which people can operate, Kundnani points out that one model is to try to preserve the initial identity of the various cultures – in a kind of static multiculturalism. But another approach makes provision for more dynamic forms of multiculturalism, where participants are open to engage in *discussion around social values as part of a process of mutual learning* (2007, pp. 6–7). Invoking (and encouraging) this latter interpretation of pluralism, I argue that it is important for researchers/inquirers to consider the various methodological options as *starting points to renew their considerations, with others, around the value of social research/inquiry.* And I suggest – in terms of all of the illustrations that I have forwarded in this book – that what we cannot leave out of the discussion are concerns around the possible social impact of all social inquiry.

9.4.3 A Note on the Discursive Intent of My Use of Categories

In the course of the book, I have made use of categorical distinctions – between, say, old-fashioned and new(er) forms of racism, between realist-oriented and more constructivist-oriented epistemologies, between different kinds of methodological approaches, between multiculturalism and more radical multiculturalism, and so on. However, my intention, via the use of the categories, was to *create openings for continued discussion around issues* that I have raised for attention in the book – by inviting people to (re)consider my way of seeing differences between the alternatives as defined by the categories.

For example, in the case of describing different methodologies, using categories such as experimentation, surveys, intensive interviewing, and so on, I am not assuming that the categories refer to entities with specific "identities." Rather I am assuming that as I talk, and invoke categories, so this raises for discussion issues around how social research can be (responsibly) engaged in. I have tried to show, for instance, that the doing of "experimentation" need not be confined to a particular definition thereof, and that increased provision can be made by those conducting experiments (and naming their research as such) for, for instance, qualitative input on the part of participants and wider audiences. In this way, the boundaries between "experiments" and "other" forms of research can be treated as porous and indeed by treating the boundaries as porous we can *encourage a relationship between research approaches where researchers are able to take on board arguments/suggestions developed by those forwarding "other" research options (and attendant purposes).*

As far as the categories of "realist-oriented" and "more constructivist-oriented" to describe epistemological positions is concerned, these categories as used in the book were a way of my highlighting that as I see it, there is no need to conceptualize research processes in terms of their contribution to producing knowledge of realities posited to exist outside of the knowing process (as in what can be called realist-oriented understandings of science). The pervasive belief – that authors such as Collins (2000), Ladson-Billings (2003), and Reason (2006a) consider as still dominant, rendering alternative epistemologies marginalized – is that the scientific community can manage to "get closer to the truth" through the mechanisms of science. But this self-understanding of science, I have argued, needs to be understood in relation to constructivist alternatives.

The longstanding dispute about whether or not science should be seen as advancing our knowledge of realities existing independently of discourse cannot be resolved with reference to "the evidence" about what science "really" can achieve. But my argument is that just because we can never know whether so-called scientific investigation is leading to advancements of knowledge defined as reflection of external realities, researchers do need to be particularly wary of presenting it as a process of developing such knowledge. Hence, working with a conception of knowing as a process of developing constructions might be considered preferable not because it can be proved that theorizing constitutes, rather than reflects, "realities," but because – as I have argued via my illustrations in the book – it can be seen to *provide more scope for inquirers to relate to others in a discursively accountable way.*

My proposal in this regard goes hand in hand with my suggestion that one can award trust in people's capacities to make judgments about ways of seeing and acting, without expecting them to have to justify themselves with reference to the soundness of their vision in relation to "the realities" (Romm, 2001, p. 284). Requirements on inquirers to "keep trust" could be requirements on them to be *discursively oriented to defending choices of vision and action in serious engagement with alternatives.* I have presented this value (which is admittedly a value) as an option, or way of life, to be given consideration – in contexts of "professional" social inquiry as well as in everyday discourse. And I present it as an option that, at this point, can be seen to differ from realist-oriented approaches to ways of knowing and living.

Of course it is possible that those whose arguments I have called realist in orientation and also those who self-categorize their position as realist oriented might claim that I have misrepresented their statements concerning what is involved in the scientific enterprise and have in effect caricatured their position. Speaking (admittedly) from a constructivist perspective, I would contend that there is no manner in which we can finally ground a complaint that another person has "really" been *caricaturing* as opposed to *categorizing* an argument. The charge of caricature implies that there is an experience that the other has not respected, or tried to come to grips with, the rationale of a position taken. We can never know whether this experience is justified or not – but what we can do is try to set up an alternative style of relating, so that our relationship can become experienced as more constructive (for furthering the discussion). (See also Romm, 1998c.)

This therefore brings me back to the point that at the end of the day, our ways of categorizing and dealing with possible complaints of caricaturing, are inextricably connected to the quality of human relationship that we wish to establish between those engaged in discussion. In processes of debate, people may decide that their reasons for wanting to identify themselves with some aspect of a category (as advanced by themselves at some point in time or by others) can be modified/extended. They may reconsider the way in which they wish (or whether they wish) to be thus identified. By arguing around the relevance of some suggested category to (aspects of) their work/behavior, they can at the same time refine/develop their approach. This makes provision for Kalungu-Banda's point (2006, p. 22) that we can treat the patterns that we discern in people's positions/ways of behaving as capable of *unfolding* in different directions as we interact with them. And as people and their "positions" unfold (to us) so the categories we may be employing can shift their meaning, as they become qualified/modified. It is in this way that I would argue that categories can meaningfully become defined through the course of social interaction. And whether the categories continue to have relevance as categories depends on whether the different parties still afford them relevance (and whether they can convincingly use them in a way that does not generate distrust).

In short, treating categories as openings for human discourse is a way of treating the categories as well as an attendant way of treating our social relationships. It is for this reason that I have concentrated as an important theme in this book on the status that we assign to any categorizations.

9.5   Some Unexplored Areas for Further Inquiry

I conclude this book by pointing to various unexplored areas herein to which I wish to alert readers and which other inquirers may choose to try to "fill" in some way as part of the ongoing debate around (experiences of) forms of new racism. Three areas around which I have *not* tried to offer advice for exploring (in terms of my methodological discussions in Chapters 3–8) are the following:

1. Options for exploring the complicity by Africans in Africa perpetuating conceptions of White superiority;
2. Options for exploring hierarchies not based on only Whiteness as supreme;
3. Options for exploring the meaning of racism in regard to possible conceptualizing of Black racism.

9.5.1   Complicity by Africans in Africa Perpetuating Conceptions of White Superiority

When conducting my research toward the writing of this book, I did not find examples of research specifically exploring the way in which within Africa certain Africans may themselves be perpetuating what are called new forms of racism through their (more or less) covert perpetuation of norms of White superiority. My extensive investigation of research around new racism showed up articles writing about new racism in various geographical arenas, but not about Africans in Africa perpetuating what is called normative Whiteness. References that I found to this were linked more to South Africa, where for example the Human Rights Commission report in South Africa referred to the "veritable history of dominance by the European culture and world view in South Africa to the extent that such a unipolar world view has come to be taken for granted" (2000, p. 57). (See Chapter 2, Section 2.3.4.) I also showed in Chapter 5 in relation to my research example set in South Africa how one could consider the use of the term "coconut" as pointing to the conceptions of users of the term that those "coconuts" presumably trying to act as "White" were trying to claim some kind of superiority. However, in wider Africa I did not find articles referring to arguments around this concern and therefore did not include these in this book.

Upon getting feedback from Carlis Douglas on my Chapter 2, she pointed out this unexplored area to me. At first I did not understand what she meant when she suggested that I have not attended to new racism in Africa. But she offered an illustration of this to me springing from experiences that she and her (Nigerian) husband had had when they visited Nigeria (from the UK where they live) trying to set up work opportunities.

I offer below the gist of our Skype conversation in this regard (August 2008) – with Carlis Douglas being abbreviated as CD and Norma Romm as NR:

CD: My husband had some interviews with different companies in Nigeria with respect to work. On a number of occasions we were told that they were excited about what he is doing, but if he wanted to be taken seriously he needed a White man to offer the presentation [at the time when he made his formal presentation].

NR: Were the people who told him he needs a White person presenting Black?

CD: Yes, and they were supportive and were friends and were wanting to see success – they were being helpful [in telling him to bring along a White person].

NR: For whom were the presentations?

CD: The presentations were to Black people. [He was told that] he would get more credibility if done by a White man. They said, "look, he does not have to know very much – as long as he is White. If you walk into the room with him immediately your credibility is established".

CD: This conversation came from so many different people.

NR: Were these different people on different occasions?

CD: Yes, and on one occasion I had a conversation about the fact that this had happened – the response was "Well you know you just have to be real, this is how things are".

NR: You lose the work if you resist this.

CD: It is not named as racism.

NR: How do they see it?

CD: Pragmatism – it is pragmatic to have a White person with you to increase credibility.

CD: My sense was that the issue of racism – having a discussion of racism in Africa – is not something they feel is an issue. They don't see it as an issue. So if you say to them it is a perpetuation of racism, they will not agree.

NR: Even if you try to sensitize them to this?

CD: They see it as normal that if you want to increase your credibility, you need a White person.

CD: The internalization of racism is less visible [than reactions to colonization]. We don't know enough about this.

NR: Yes, we don't know about racism in Africa that is unspoken about.

CD: When responding to the old fashioned kind – colonialism – they resist that, but they do not seem to recognize new racism as a conception of hierarchy; this is less explicit. They seem not to be recognizing other ways in which the hierarchies become perpetuated.

CD: *I wonder if discussions taking place around racism have happened in one part of the world and not in others – therefore there is a dearth of information around this. We have had more of a discussion historically in the USA and parts of Europe (my italics).*

NR: So there is probably more awareness of this there. And in other places, we get only glimpses, for example, via this anecdote.

CD: These conversations are anecdotal pieces of experience.

The conversation then led to our discussing what it might mean to engender further reflection and how reflections driven by "action" purposes might differ from reflections driven by "theory" (thus linking up with issues around action research that I discussed in Chapter 7).

The point I wish to make here is that Douglas brings to attention that in this book I have not examined the implicit perpetuations of hierarchical thinking (with Whiteness affording credibility) that, she believes, need to be opened up to exploration in Africa. My sense, with Douglas, is that there is a dearth of information on this and that discussions on new racism have tended to take place in other parts of the world.[243]

I would suggest that this is a gap in this book – and ways of organizing research around unrecognized perpetuation of more or less invisible hierarchies in Africa need to be explored (through further research). I would suggest that this would be a way of people writing into my story parts that I have not been able to write.

9.5.2 Not Only Black and White

As I mentioned in Chapter 1, when offering me feedback on my draft Chapter 1 (January 2009) Sisinyane Makoena suggested to me that I should point out in this book that new racism may not just be a matter of social relations around Whiteness and Blackness.

She suggested (in personal communication) that one of the strengths of this book as she sees it is that I am proposing that "everybody should come together and come with their views and unpack them and make them more open and more visible." But she pointed out that I seemed to be concentrating only on hierarchical thinking in relation to Whites and Blacks and had made no mention of hierarchies among Black people. She gave the example of her marriage to a Zulu man that was opposed by his family – who still do not regard her as on the same level as a Zulu woman. (See Chapter 1, Section 1.7.) She indicated that it is difficult to raise this

---

[243] Since Carlis Douglas alerted me to this, I asked in conversation around this book (in December 2008) Abimbola Olateju (from Nigeria) whether she had any experiences of this kind of thinking. She mentioned that Nigerians in both South Africa and Nigeria sometimes use skin-whitening chemicals (even on their children) and that perhaps this points to a similar kind of mentality of Whiteness as "better." When I asked her why she thought that this skin whitening was proceeding, she indicated that she had not considered this further and had never asked the people doing it. In relation to this anecdote of hers, I would suggest that further more in-depth exploration might be advisable to offer another glimpse of African complicity in perpetuating these hierarchies.

subject with the relatives, but her husband urges them to try to accept that in the new South Africa there is no place for this kind of thinking. Her husband feels that after apartheid there should be more social space for reviewing the rigidities of ethnically based judgments; but she feels that thus far in her case the social space for opening discussion is limited.

Furthermore, in reading parts of my Chapter 2, Veronica McKay too pointed out to me (by e-mail, September 2008) that "we also have ethnic discrimination among ethnic groups in South Africa – also since these groups and differences were focused on during apartheid."[244] She further noted a link between this and my brief mention in Chapter 2 of some understandings in regard to Black "foreigners" in South Africa.

I have not ventured in this book to discuss in any detail these different kinds of hierarchical thinking (in South Africa or elsewhere). But I would suggest that further exploration of (defined) Black people's anecdotes/examples of experienced discrimination by other Blacks in relation to their ethnic/national backgrounds is an area that could become linked to the discussion of manifestations of new racism and its various social manifestations across the globe.[245]

9.5.3 Black People's Racial Labeling – Connections with Racism

Another area to which I have not given attention in this book relates to the issue of what is sometimes called Black racism vis-à-vis Whites and others.[246] In considering this issue, Bonilla-Silva contends that it is important to define racism as a "sociopolitical concept that refers . . . to racial ideology that glues a particular social order" – rather than to define it in terms of individual attitudes that may be held by

---

[244]Jubber indicates in this regard that "ethnicity and ethnic identity, rather than being less salient [after apartheid], have become more salient post-1994" (2007, p. 536). He notes that in particular South African coloreds – particularly sensitive to "issues of identity" – have tried to bring such issues to the fore for social discussion (2007, p. 536).

[245]This would take into account Baber's argument that we can also apply the concept of racism to the racialization of identities in India. He notes that normally "'racism' is thought of as something that white people do to us. What Indians do to one another is variously described as 'communalism', 'regionalism' and 'casteism' but never 'racism'" (2004, p. 701). He argues that once we recognize that racial constructs are constructs of "power, ideologies and differential resource allocations," we can begin to better appreciate the social relations in India in terms of an understanding of "how racism works overtly and covertly even though race as such does not exist" (2004, p. 712). He contends that the so-called clash of cultures between Muslims and Hindus in India too can be understood as a "specific form of 'cultural racism' at work" (2004, p. 713). And even among Muslims in India, he notes divisions between Shias and Sunnis emerging as status distinctions – again racializing the religious distinctions (2004, p. 714).

[246]Often when I mentioned to White people in South Africa that I was writing a book on researching new racism, they asked whether I was including emerging forms of Black racism in relation to Whites in South Africa – to which I replied that this was not my focus, with my concentration being rather on ways of exploring (persistent) forms of racism advantaging White people across the globe.

people. He considers it crucial that people understand that "individual-level expla-nations are, for the most part, deficient and incomplete at explaining big national and international issues" (such as racism) (2006, p. 220). As he puts it, we need to move to a different level to understand the "centrality of larger social forces" (2006, p. 220). This, he suggests, also helps to recast the issue that has been posed by some authors concerning the (so-called) racism of Black people who use deroga-tory racial labels. Considering in particular the context of the USA, he argues that once we treat (White) racism as enmeshed in a system of power, if we wish to con-sider Black racism on the same terms we need to ask: Are blacks likely to develop a racialized social system in the United States with blacks as the dominant race?" (2006, p. 173). He avers that the most likely scenario for the future of the USA is that:

> Race relations will become Latin American-like, that is, . . . a new triracial order will emerge with a pigmentocratic component to it [where "epidermic capital" – such as light skin color, eye color, etc., will continue to function as a form of capital[247]]. As in Latin American-like society, any form of race-based contestation will become increasingly more difficult, which, as in Latin America, will allow white supremacy to reign supreme, hidden from public debate. (2006, p. 173)

Because Bonilla-Silva offers a structural definition of racism as linked to disadvan-tages in life chances for people in groups defined as not-White, he does not believe that it is helpful to speak of Black racism in the same way as one can speak of White racial ideology that glues the social order. To the extent that Black people may use racial language to label Whites and others in derogatory ways, this is not the same as developing an ideology entrenching a material social hierarchy. And according to him, this social context has not changed sufficiently for us to be able to apply the term "racism" to the views of Black people.

Bonacich, Alimahomed, and Wilson offer a (more Marxist-oriented) structural understanding of racism on a global scale when they suggest that the entire global system of racialized exploitation of labor "depends upon racial understandings – that the lives of some people, and some workers, are less important than those of the dominant group (typically White and Western)" (2008, p. 352). They argue that "under colonialism, this domination was overt and clear. Now it is obscured by corporate rather than state domination" (2008, p. 351) – where corporations are able to "search the world for the most rightless and disempowered workers" (2008, p. 351). They consider that subordinate racialized workers are thus in a position of "being forced to accept bargains of desperation" – often characterized by low wages and unsafe working conditions (2008, p. 351). They see the attendant racism as rooted in the structural position of those globally subordinated along racialized lines – and, in somewhat similar fashion to Bonilla-Silva, they thus reserve the term "racism" for an understanding of racism at a structural level.

---

[247]Bonilla-Silva points out that "the incorporation of groups into the USA white category has shown, so far, to have some epidermic boundaries, that is, groups and individuals added to the category have been European looking" (2006, p. 196).

Debates about the definition of racism and whether Black people might be termed "racist" continue in "popular" discourse. For example, one blogspot (2009) discusses the definition advanced by Martha Barry – racial justice programmer at the YMCA of Greater Milwaukee – who defines racism as "prejudice plus privilege plus power to oppress" (cf. http://freeracine.blogspot.com/2009/03/redefining-racism.html). She thus invokes the institutional/collective account of racism that I introduced in Chapter 2, Sections 2.3.5 and 2.3.6, where racism is defined in terms of what Bonilla-Silva calls the "perpetuation of [racial] inequality in the social order." Some responses to this as given on the blogspot argue that this "lets off the hook" non-White people from being able to be considered as "racist." In terms of this definition, they seemingly cannot be racist as they lack the requisite institutional power. However, other commentators argue that the purpose of linking (collective) power to the definition of racism

> is not to let minorities off the hook [but to] also acknowledge that racism does not just exist on an individual basis. It is very collective. So, while not all individual whites have "power" they are part of a collective power structure.

The same commentator later suggests that we refrain from trying to compare White racism (which he sees as linked to a system of power) with the individual orientations of certain Black people who may not "like White people." He notes that *White racism* and *Black people's derogatory labeling* of others are "two different problems with two different solutions." He indicates that it is for this reason that he supports Martha Barry's insistence on including the dimension of collective power in the definition of racism – so as to highlight that we cannot approach these different issues in the same way. However, many commentators in the blog (who appear to me to be White) do not support this view and instead consider racism as a matter of (racial) prejudice – no matter who is harboring it.

It may be noted in this regard that, as African American activist and writer Victor Lewis, on a tour to Australia pointed out (1996), it can be considered as in the interests of White people not to view racism as a system of power – because "if it's viewed as a system of individual attitudes then we can conceive of it as something that a person either has or doesn't have." This in turn means that White people do not need to concern themselves with trying to "interfere with, to disrupt and afflict those institutions which persist in squashing the life possibilities of people of color." As he notes, "if we look at racism as a system of [collective] power instead, then not being part of the problem is not an option [for people – including for Whites] because racism is woven into the very fabric of our social order." A definition of racism that is linked solely to individual prejudice thus for him lets off the hook Whites in terms of (collectively) organizing to try to address their collective White privilege and power.

I have not in this book tried to deal with the issue of whether and in what conditions we might consider Black people's uses of derogatory labels for Whites and others as "racist" – as my focus has been on the continuity between past and present forms of racism privileging those defined as White. Other writers may wish to explore further the contestation and implications for definitions of racism in regard to Blacks' racial labeling of Whites and others – also considering at the same time what it might mean to shy away from using such labeling in order to try to construct what Bonacich, Alimahomed, and Wilson call "a better world" (2008, p. 352).

Meanwhile, my focus in this book has been on offering proposals/options for inquiry around new forms of racism in a manner that can be regarded as consistent with the quest to co-construct experiences of more humane forms of knowing and living.

References

Achterberg, P. (2006). Voting in the new political culture: Economic, cultural and environmental voting in 20 Western countries. *International Sociology, 21*(2), 237–261.

Acquah, B. K. (2007). Community involvement in social research in Botswana. In A. Rwomire & F. B. Nyamnjoh (Eds.), *Challenges and responsibilities of social research in Africa: Ethical issues* (pp. 127–132). Addis Ababa: The Organization for Social Research in Eastern and Southern Africa (OSSREA).

Adindu, A., & Romm, N. R. A. (2001). Cultural incongruity in changing Africa. In A. Rwomire (Ed.), *Africa's development crisis* (pp. 53–69). Westport, CT: Praeger.

Alant, C. J., & Romm, N. R. A. (1990). A brief exploration of some assumptions of a humanist conception of society. In C. J. Alant (Ed.), *Sociology and society: A humanist profile* (pp. 43–50). Johannesburg: Southern Book Publishers.

Ali, S. (2003). *Mixed-race, post-race: Gender, new ethnicities and cultural practices.* Oxford: Berg.

Alibhai-Brown, Y. (2000). *After multiculturalism.* London: The Foreign Policy Center.

Alldred, P. (1998). Ethnography and discourse analysis. In J. Ribbens & R. Edwards (Eds.), *Feminist dilemmas in qualitative research: Public knowledge and private lives.* London: Sage.

Alleyne, B. W. (2002). *Radicals against race.* Oxford: Berg.

Alvarez, S. E. (2003). *Reflections and refractions on Brazilian and U.S. racial formations and transnational antiracist politics.* Comments prepared for workshop on Hemispheric Perspectives on Race and Ethnicity, Chicano/Latino Research Center, University of California at Santa Cruz. Retrieved December 2003, from http://lals.ucsc.edu/hemispheric_dialogues/papers/7_S_Alvarez.doc

Alvesson, M., & Sköldberg, K. (2000). *Reflexive methodology.* London: Sage.

Amin, A. (2004). Multi-ethnicity and the idea of Europe. *Theory, Culture and Society, 21*(2), 1–24.

Amirauz, V., & Simon, P. (2006). There are no minorities here: Cultures of scholarship and public debate on immigrants and integration in France. *International Journal of Comparative Sociology, 47*(3–4), 191–215.

Anderson, M. (2003). Immigrant youth and the dynamics of marginalization. *Young, 11*(1), 74–89.

Anthias, F. (1999). Institutional racism, power and accountability. *Sociological Research Online, 4*(1), http://www.socresonline.org.uk/socresonline/4/lawrence//anthias.html

Anthias, F., & Yuval-Davis, N. (1983). Contextualizing feminism: Ethnic, gender and class divisions. *Feminist Review, 15*, 62–75.

Anthias, F., & Yuval-Davis, N. (1992). *Racialized boundaries.* London: Routledge.

Anthias, F., & Yuval-Davis, N. (1996). *Racialized Boundaries* (2nd ed.). London: Routledge.

Appiah, K. A. (1994). Identity, authenticity, survival: Multicultural societies and social reproduction. In A. Gutmann (Ed.), *Multiculturalism: Examining the politics of recognition* (pp. 107–148). Princeton, NJ: Princeton University Press.

Appiah, K. A. (1996). Race, culture, identity: Misunderstood connections. In K. A. Appiah & A. Gutmann (Eds.), *Color conscious: The political morality of race* (pp. 30–105). Princeton, NJ: Princeton University Press.

Arber, R. E. (2000). Defining positioning within politics of difference: Negotiating spaces "in between". *Race, Ethnicity and Education, 3*(1), 45–63.

Arber, R. E. (2003). The presence of another: The Prescience of racism in post-modern times. *Journal of Educational Change, 4*, 249–268.

Argyris, C., & Schön, D. A. (1974). *Theory in practice*. San Francisco: Jossey Bass.

Argyris, C., & Schön, D. A. (1991). Participatory action research and action science compared. In W. F. Whyte (Ed.), *Participatory action research* (pp. 85–96). Newbury Park, CA: Sage.

Argyris, C., & Schön, D. A. (1996). *Organizational learning II: Theory, method, and practice*. Reading, MA: Addison-Wesley Publishing.

Asante, M. K. (2007). Barack Obama and the dilemma of power: An Africological observation. *Journal of Black Studies, 38*(1), 105–115.

Ashburn-Nardo, L., Monteith, M., Authur, S. A., & Bain, A. (2007). Race and the psychological health of African–Americans. *Group Processes and Intergroup Relations, 10*(4), 471–491.

Augoustinos, M., Walker, I., & Donaghue, N. (2006). *Social cognition: An integrated introduction*. London: Sage.

Baber, Z. (2004). "Race", religion and riots: The "racialization" of communal identity and conflict in India. *Sociology, 38*(4), 701–718.

Bakan, D. (1974). Psychology can now kick the science habit. (Keynote address, American Psychological Association annual conference.) *Psychology Today, 11*, 26–28.

Baldwin, J. M. (1901). *Dictionary of philosophy and psychology* (Vol. 1). London: Macmillan.

Banaji, M. (2008). *The implicit association test: A talk with Mahzarin Banaji and Anthony Greenwald*. Retrieved December 2, 2008, from http://www/edge.org/3rd_culture/banaji_greenwald08/banaji_greenwald08_index.htm

Banathy, B. A. (1999). The difference that makes a difference. (Incoming presidential address delivered at the 42nd annual meeting of the International Society for the Systems Sciences, Atlanta, USA, 1998.) *General Systems Bulletin, 28*, 5–8.

Barry, D., & Michael Elmes, M. (1997). Strategy retold: Toward a narrative view of strategic discourse. *Academy of Management Review, 22*, 429–452.

Baudrillard, J. (1983). *Simulations*. New York: Semiotext(e).

Behar, R. (1996). *The vulnerable observer: Anthropology that breaks your heart*. Boston: Beacon Press.

Bell, D. A. (1980). Brown v. Board of Education and the interest convergence dilemma. *Harvard Law Review, 93*, 518–533.

Bell, D. A. (1992). *Faces at the bottom of the well: The permanence of racism*. New York: Basic Books.

Bell, D. A. (1995). Racial realism. In K. Crenshaw, N. Gotanda, G. Peller, & K. Thomas (Eds.), *Critical race theory: The key writings that formed the movement* (pp. 302–312). New York: The Free Press.

Bell, D. A. (1999). The power of narrative. *Legal Studies Forum, 23*(3), 315–351.

Bell, E. E. (2001). Infusing race into the U.S. discourse on action research. In P. Reason & H. Bradbury (Eds.), *Handbook of action research: Participative inquiry and practice* (pp. 48–58). London: Sage.

Bell, M. P., Harrison, D. A., & McLaughlin, M. E. (2000). Forming, changing, and acting on attitudes toward affirmative action programs in employment: A theory-driven approach. *Journal of Applied Psychology, 85*, 784–798.

Berbrier, M. (2004). Assimilation and pluralism as cultural tools. *Sociological Forum, 19*(1), 29–61.

Berry, J. W. (1984). Cultural relations in plural societies. In N. Miller & M. B. Brewer (Eds.), *Groups in contact: The psychology of desegregation* (pp. 11–27). Orlando: Academic.

Berry, J. W., Trimble, J. E., & Olmedo, E. L. (1986). Assessment of mutual acculturation. In W. Lonner & J. W. Berry (Eds.), *Field methods in cross-cultural research* (pp. 219–342). Thousand Oaks, CA: Sage.

Bhavnani, R. (2001). *Rethinking interventions in racism.* Staffordshire: Commission for Racial Equality with Trentham Books.

Bhavnani, R., Mirza, H. S., & Meetoo, V. (2005). *Tackling the roots of racism: Lessons for success.* Bristol: The Policy Press.

Bigler, R. S. (1999). The use of multicultural curricula and materials to counter racism in children. *Journal of Social Issues, 55,* 687–705.

Biko, S. (2002). *I write what I like.* Chicago: University of Chicago Press.

Blinder, S. B. (2007). Dissonance persists: Reproduction of racial attitudes among post-civil rights cohorts of White Americans. *American Politics Research, 35*(3), 299–335.

Bobo, L. D. (1999). Prejudice as group position: Microfoundations of a sociological approach to racism and race relations. *Journal of Social Issues, 55,* 445–472.

Bobo, L. D. (2001). Racial attitudes and relations at the close of the twentieth century. In N. Smelser, W. J. Wilson, & F. Mitchell (Eds.), *America becoming: Racial trends and their consequences* (pp. 263–297). Washington, DC: National Academy Press.

Bobo, L. D. (2003). *Affirmative Action and Higher Education Before and After the Supreme Court Rulings on the Michigan Cases: Inclusion's Last Hour?: Affirmative Action Before the Bush Court.* Presentation given at Stanford University, January 17, 2003.

Bobo, L. D., Kluegel, J. R., & Smith, R. A. (1996). *Laissez-faire racism: The Crystallization of a kindler, gentler anti-black ideology.* Retrieved from the Russell Sage Foundation (29 pages) http://epn.org/sage/rsbobo1.html

Bobo, L., & Smith, R. A. (1994). Antipoverty policies, affirmative action, and racial attitudes. In S. H. Danziger, G. D. Sandefur, & D. H. Weinberg (Eds.), *Confronting poverty: Prescriptions for change* (pp. 365–395). Cambridge, MA: Harvard University Press.

Bobo, L. D., & Thompson, V. (2006). Unfair by design: The war on drugs, race, and the legitimacy of the criminal justice system. *Social Research, 73*(2), 445–472.

Bonacich, E., Alimahomed, S., & Wilson, J. B. (2008). The racialization of global labor. *American Behavioral Scientist, 52*(3), 342–355.

Bond, H. M. (1933). Educational research and statistics: The cash value of a Negro child. *School and Society, 37,* 627–630.

Bond, H. M. (1958). Cat on a hot tin roof. *Journal of Negro Education, 27,* 519–525.

Bonilla-Silva, E. (1997). Rethinking racism: Toward a structural interpretation. *American Sociological Review, 3,* 465–480.

Bonilla-Silva, E. (2001). *White supremacy and racism in the post-civil rights era.* London: Lynne Rienner Publishers.

Bonilla-Silva, E. (2003). *Racism without racists.* Lanham: Rowman & Littlefield.

Bonilla-Silva, E. (2006). *Racism without racists* (2nd ed.). Lanham: Rowman & Littlefield.

Bonilla-Silva, E., & Baiocchi, G. (2008). Anything but racism. In T. Zuberi & E. Bonilla-Silva (Eds.), *White logic, White methods: Racism and methodology* (pp. 137–151). Lanham: Rowman & Littlefield.

Bonilla-Silva, E., & Zuberi, T. (2008). Toward a definition of White logic and White methods. In T. Zuberi & E. Bonilla-Silva (Eds.), *White logic, White methods: Racism and methodology* (pp. 3–27). Lanham: Rowman & Littlefield.

Bouchard, M. (2004). *Panel presentation on "cultural copy".* Presented at the fourth international conference on Diversity in Organizations, Communities and Nations, UCLA, Los Angeles, July 2004.

Bourdieu, P., & Wacquant, L. (1999).On the cunning of imperialist reason. *Theory, Culture & Society, 16*(1), 41–58.

Boyd, A., Geerling, T., Gregory, W. J., Kagan, C., Midgley, G., Murray, P., & Walsh, M. (2007). Systemic evaluation: A participatory multi-method approach. *Journal of the Operational Research Society, 58*(10), 1306–1320.

Branscombe, N. R., Wann, D. L., Noel, J. G., & Coleman, J. (1993). Ingroup or outgroup extremity: Importance of the threatened social identity. *Personality and Social Psychology Bulletin, 19,* 381–388.

Brendl, M. C., Markman, A. B., & Messner, C. (2001). How do indirect measures of evaluation work? Evaluating the inference of prejudice in the Implicit Association Test. *Journal of Personality and Social Psychology, 81*(5), 760–773.

Brewer, M. B., & Miller, N. (1984). Beyond the contact hypothesis: Theoretical perspectives on desegregation. In N. Miller & M. B. Brewer (Eds.), *Groups in contact: The psychology of desegregation* (pp. 281–302). Orlando, FL: Academic Press.

Brewer, M. B., & Miller, N. (1996). *Intergroup relations.* Pacific Grove, CA: Brooks/Cole.

Broad, G., & Reyes, J. A. (2008). Speaking for ourselves: A Columbia–Canada research collaboration. *Action Research, 6*(2), 129–147.

Bromgard, G., & Stephan, W. G. (2006). Responses to the stigmatized: Disjunctions in affect, cognitions, and behavior. *Journal of Applied Social Psychology, 36*(10), 2436–2448.

Broome, B. J. (1998). Overview of conflict resolution activities in Cyprus: Their contribution to the peace process. *The Cyprus Review, 10*(1), 47–66.

Brubaker, R. (2004). *Ethnicity without groups.* Cambridge: Cambridge University Press.

Brubaker, R., & Cooper, F. (2000). Beyond "identity". *Theory and Society, 29,* 1–47.

Brubaker, R., Loveman, M., & Stamotov, P. (2004). Ethnicity as cognition. *Theory and Society, 33,* 31–64.

Brug, P., & Verkuyten, M. (2007). Dealing with cultural diversity: The endorsement of societal models among ethnic minority and majority youth in the Netherlands. *Youth & Society, 39*(1), 112–131.

Bruner, J. S. (1951). *Cognition and the limits of scientific inquiry.* Unpublished paper read at the Institute for the Unity of Science at the American Academy of Arts and Sciences. Jerome S. Bruner Papers: Harvard University Archives, HUG 4242.28.

Bruner, J. S., & Postman, L. J. (1949). On the perception of incongruity: A paradigm. *Journal of Personality, 18,* 206–223.

Bruner, J. S., Goodnow, J. J., & Austin, G. A. (1956). *A study of thinking.* London: John Wiley & Sons.

Bryman, A. (1992). *Quantity and quality in social research.* London: Routledge.

Burch, R. (2006). *Charles Saunders Peirce.* Stanford Encyclopedia of Philosophy. Retrieved from http://plato.stanford.edu/entries/peirce/

Burns, D. (2007). *Systemic action research: A strategy for whole systems change.* Bristol: Policy Press.

Butler, J. (1994). Contingent foundations: Feminism and the question of "postmodernism". In S. Seidman (Ed.), *The postmodern turn* (pp. 153–170). Cambridge: Cambridge University Press.

Byng, M. D. (2008). Complex inequalities: The case of Muslim Americans after 9/11. *American Behavioral Scientist, 51*(5), 659–674.

Callaghan, G. (2005). Accessing habitus: Relating structure and agency through focus group research. *Sociological Research Online, 10*(3), http://www.socresonline.org.uk/10/3/Callaghan.html

Carmichael, S., & Hamilton, C. (1967). *Black power: The politics of Black liberation in America.* New York: Vintage.

Checkland, P. B., & Holwell, S. (1998). Action research: Its nature and validity. *Systemic Practice and Action Research, 11,* 9–21.

Chesler, M. (1976). Contemporary sociological theories of racism. In P. A. Katz (Ed.), *Toward the elimination of racism* (pp. 21–71). New York: Pergamon Press.

Chiasson, P. (2001). *Abduction as an aspect of retroduction.* Retrieved from http://www.digital-peirce.fee.unicamp.br/abachi.htm

Chigas, D. (2003). *Track II (citizen) diplomacy.* Conflict Research Consortium, University of Colorado, Boulder. Retrieved from http://www.beyondintractability.org/essay/track2_diplomacy/

Cho, J., & Trent, A. (2006). Validity in qualitative research revisited. *Qualitative Research, 6*(3), 319–340.

Christakis, A. N. (2004). Wisdom of the people. *Systems Research and Behavioral Science, 21*(5), 479–488.

Christakis, A. N., & Bausch, K. C. (2006). *Co-laboratories of democracy: How people harness their collective wisdom and power to construct the future.* Greenwich, Connecticut: Information Age Publishing.

Churchman, C. W. (1971). *The design of inquiring systems: Basic concepts of systems and organizations.* New York: Basic Books.

Churchman, C. W. (1979). *The systems approach and its enemies.* New York: Basic Books.

Cialdini, R., & Rhodes, K. (1997). *Influence at work: The psychology of persuasion.* Retrieved from http://www.workingpsychology.com/whatfram.html

Clark, K. B. (1973). Introduction to an epilogue. In J. A. Ladner (Ed.), *The death of White sociology* (pp. 399–413). New York: Random House.

Clayton, D. (2007). The audacity of hope. *Journal of Black Studies, 38*(1), 51–63.

Cobley, P. (2003). *Narrative: A new critical idiom.* London: Routledge.

Coghlan, D., & Shani, A. B. (2005). Roles, politics and ethics in action research design. *Action Research, 18*(6), 533–545.

Cohen-Cole, J. (2005). The reflexivity of cognitive science: The scientist as model of human nature. *History of the Human Sciences, 18*(4), 107–139.

Collins, P. H. (1990). *Black feminist thought: Knowledge, consciousness and the politics of empowerment.* London: Harper Collins.

Collins, P. H. (1998). *Fighting words: Black women and the search for justice.* Minneapolis, MN: University of Minnesota Press.

Collins, P. H. (1999). Producing the mothers of the nation: Race, class and contemporary U.S. population policies. In N. Yuval-Davis (Ed.), *Women, citizenship and difference* (pp. 118–129). London: Zed Books.

Collins, P. H. (2000). *Black feminist thought: Knowledge, consciousness and the politics of empowerment* (2nd ed.). London: Harper Collins.

Collins, P. H. (2005). *Black sexual politics: African Americans, gender, and the new racism.* New York: Routledge.

Collins, P. H. (2006). *From Black power to hip hop: Racism, nationalism and feminism.* Philadelphia: Temple University Press.

Crenshaw, K. (1991). Mapping the margins: Intersectionality, identity politics, and violence against women of color. *Stanford Law Review, 43*(6), 1241–1299.

Crenshaw, K. W. (1997). Color blindedness, history, and the law. In W. Libiano (Ed.), *The house that race built* (pp. 280–288). New York: Pantheon.

Crenshaw, K. (2000). *Background paper for the expert meeting on the gender-related aspects of race discrimination.* WCAR, Zagreb, Croatia. Retrieved November 21–24, http://www.wicej.addr.com/wcar_docs/crenshaw.html

Creswell, J. W., & Plano-Clark, V. L. (2007). *Designing and conducting mixed methods research.* Thousand Oaks, CA: Sage.

Crisp, R. J., & Hewstone, M. (1999). Differential evaluation of crossed category groups: Patterns, processes, and reducing intergroup bias. *Group Processes & Intergroup Relations, 2,* 307–333.

Crisp, R. J., Hewstone, M., & Cairns, E. (2001). Multiple identities in Northern Ireland: Hierarchical ordering in the representation of group membership. *British Journal of Social Psychology, 40,* 501–514.

Crisp, R., Ensari, N., Hewstone, M., & Miller, N. (2002). A dual-route model of crossed categorization effects. *European Review of Social Psychology, 13,* 35–73.

Crisp, R., Walsh, J., & Hewstone, M. (2006). Crossed categorization in common ingroup contexts. *Personality and Social Psychology Bulletin, 32*(9), 1204–1218.

Dasgupta, N., & Greenwald, A. G. (2001). On the malleability of automatic attitudes: Combating automatic prejudice with images of admired and disliked individuals. *Journal of Personality and Social Psychology, 81,* 800–814.

Dasgupta N., McGhee D. E., Greenwald A. G., & Banaji M. R. (2000). Automatic preference for White Americans: Eliminating the familiarity explanation. *Journal of Experimental Social Psychology, 36*, 316–328.

Davidson, J. O. C., & Layder, D. (1994). *Methods, sex and madness*. London: Routledge.

Davis, A. (1997). Race and criminalization: Black Americans and the punishment industry. In W. Libiano (Ed.), *The house that race built* (pp. 264–279). New York: Pantheon.

Davis, J. (1997). *Alternate realities: How science shapes our vision of the world*. New York: Plenum.

Deal, M. (2007). Aversive disablism: Subtle prejudice toward disabled people. *Disability and Society, 22*(1), 93–107.

DeCuir, J. T., & Dixson, A. D. (2004, June/July). "So when it comes out, they aren't that surprised that it is there": Using critical race theory as a tool of analysis of race and racism in education. *Educational Researcher, 33*(5), 26–31.

De Houwer, J. (2001). A structural and process analysis of the Implicit Association Test. *Journal of Experimental Social Psychology, 37*, 443–451.

De Houwer, J. (2003). A structural analysis of indirect measures of attitudes. In J. Musch & K. C. Klauer (Eds.), *The psychology of evaluation: Affective processes in cognition and emotion* (pp. 219–244). Mahwah, NJ: Lawrence Erlbaum.

De Houwer, J. (2006). Using the Implicit Association Test does not rule out an impact of conscious propositional knowledge on evaluative conditioning. *Learning and Motivation, 37*, 176–187.

De Houwer, J., Geldof, T., & De Bruycker, E. (2005). The Implicit Association Test as a general measure of similarity. *Canadian Journal of Experimental Psychology, 59*(4), 228–239.

Delanty, G. (1997). *Social science: Beyond constructivism and realism*. Buckingham: Open University Press.

De la Rúa, A-F. (2007). Networks and identifications: A relational approach to social identities. *International Sociology, 22*(6), 683–699.

Delgado, R. (1989). Storytelling for oppositionists and others: A plea for narrative. *Michigan Law Review, 87*(8), 2411–2441.

Delgado, R. (Ed.). (1995). *Critical race theory: The cutting edge*. Philadelphia: Temple University Press.

Delgado, R., & Stefancic, J. (2001). *Critical race theory: An introduction*. New York: New York University Press.

Denzin, N. K. (2001). The reflexive interview and a performative social science. *Qualitative Research, 1*, 23–46.

Department of Education, South Africa (2008). *A guide for schools: Into higher education*. National Information Service for Higher Education: A Project for Higher Education South Africa (HESA).

Derrida, J. (1992). *The other heading: Reflections on today's Europe* (P.-A. Brault & M. B. Naas, Trans.). Bloomington, IN: Indiana University Press.

Derrida, J. (2003). Autoimmunity: Real and symbolic suicides. In G. Borradori, J. Derrida, & J. Habermas (Eds.), *Philosophy in a time of terror* (pp. 85–136). Chicago: University of Chicago Press.

De Souza, R. (2002). *Hearing different voices: Methodological pluralism in nursing education and research*. Paper presented at the conference on research: Contributing to the Future of Nursing, Hamilton, New Zealand, NZNO.

De Souza, R. (2004). Motherhood, migration and methodology: Giving voice to the "other". *The Qualitative Report, 9*(3), 463–482. Retrieved from http://www.nova.edu/ssss/QR/QR9-3/desouza.pdf

De Vaus, D. A. (1996). *Surveys in social research*. London: UCL Press.

Dewey, J. (1929). *The quest for certainty: A study of the relation of knowledge and action*. New York: Minton Balch and Company.

Dobbs, M., & Crano, W. D. (2001). Outgroup accountability in the minimal group paradigm: Implications for aversive discrimination and social identity theory. *Personality and Social Psychology Bulletin, 27*(3), 355–364.

Dos Santos, S. A., & Da Silva, N. O. I. (2006). Brazilian indifference to racial inequality in the labor market. *Latin American Perspectives, 33*(4), 13–29.

Douglas, C. (1998). *From surviving to thriving: Black women managers in Britain.* Unpublished thesis, University of Bath. Retrieved from http://www.bath.ac.uk/carpp/publications/doc_theses_links/c_douglas.html

Douglas, C. (2002). Using co-operative inquiry with Black women managers: Exploring possibilities for moving from surviving to thriving. *Systemic Practice and Action Research, 15*(3), 249–262.

Dovidio, J. F. (1993). The subtlety of racism. *Training and Development, 47*(4), 50–57.

Dovidio, J. F. (2001). On the nature of contemporary prejudice: The third wave. *Journal of Social Issues, 4*, 829–849.

Dovidio, J. F., & Gaertner, S. L. (1986). Prejudice, discrimination, and racism: Historical trends and contemporary approaches. In J. F. Dovidio & S. L. Gaertner (Eds.), *Prejudice, discrimination, and racism* (pp. 1–34). Orlando, FL: Academic Press.

Dovidio, J. F., & Gaertner, S. L. (1993). Stereotypes and evaluative intergroup bias. In D. Mackie & D. L. Hamilton (Eds.), *Affect, cognition, and stereotyping: Interactive processes in group perception* (pp. 167–194). San Diego, CA: Academic Press.

Dovidio, J. F., & Gaertner, S. L. (1999). Reducing prejudice: Combating intergroup biases. *Current Directions in Psychological Science, 8*(4), 101–105.

Dovidio, J. F., & Gaertner, S. L. (2000). Aversive racism and selection decisions 1989 and 1999. *Pyschological Science, 11*(4), 315–319.

Dovidio, J. F., Gaertner, S. L., Niemann, Y. F., & Snider, L. (2001). Racial, ethnic, and cultural differences in responding to distinctiveness and discrimination on campus: Stigma and common group identity. *Journal of Social Issues, 57*(1), 167–188.

Dovidio, J. F., Gaertner, S. L., Validzic, A., Matoka, K., Johnson, B., & Frazier, S. (1997). Extending the benefits of recategorization: Evaluations, self-disclosure, and helping. *Journal of Experimental Social Psychology, 33*, 401–420.

Dovidio, J. F., Kawakami, K., & Gaertner, S. L. (2000). Reducing contemporary prejudice: Combating explicit and implicit bias at the individual and intergroup level. In S. Oskamp (Ed.), *Reducing prejudice and discrimination* (pp. 137–163). Hillsdale, NJ: Erlbaum.

Duberman, M. (1999). *Left out: The politics of exclusion/essays/1964–1999.* New York: Basic Books.

Du Bois, W. E. B. (1899). *The Philadelphia Negro: A social study.* Philadelphia: Philadelphia University of Pennsylvania Press.

Du Bois, W. E. B. (1903). *The souls of Black folk.* New York: Knopf.

Dunn, K., & Geeraert, P. (2003). The geography of "race" and racisms. *Geodate, 16*(3), 1–6.

Dunn, K. M., Forrest, J., Burnley, I., & McDonald, A. (2004). Constructing racism in Australia. *Australian Journal of Social Issues, 39*(4), 409–430.

Echebarria-Echabe, A., & Guede, E. F. (2007). A new measure of anti-Arab prejudice: Reliability and validity evidence. *Journal of Applied Social Psychology, 37*(5), 1077–1091.

Eisele, C. (1985). *Historical perspectives on Peirce's logic of science* (Vol. 1). Berlin: Mouton Publishers.

Ellis, C., & Bochner, A. P. (Eds.). (1996). *Composing ethnography: Alternative forms of qualitative writing.* Walnut Creek, CA: Alta Mira Press.

Ellis, J. H. M., & Kiely, J. A. (2000). The promise of action inquiry in tackling organizational problems in real time. *Action Research International* (online journal), Paper 5. Retrieved from http://www.scu.edu.au/schools/gcm/ar/ari/p-jellis00.html

Entzinger, H., & Biezeveld, R. (2003). *Benchmarking in immigrant integration.* Report written for the European Commission under contract No. DG JAI-A-2/2002/006. Retrieved from http://publishing.eur.nl/ir/repub/asset/1180/SOC-2003-011.pdf

Essed, Ph. (1991). *Understanding everyday racism: An interdisciplinary theory*, London: Sage.

Essed, Ph. (2001). *Toward a methodology to identify continuing forms of everyday discrimination*. Retrieved from www.un.org/womenwatch/daw/csw/essed45.htm

Essed, Ph. (2002). Reflections on "everyday racism". In Ph. Essed & D. T. Goldberg (Eds.), *Race critical theories* (pp. 460–468). Oxford: Blackwell.

Essed, Ph., & Goldberg, D. T. (2002). Introduction: From racial demarcations to multiple identifications. In Ph. Essed & D. T. Goldberg (Eds.), *Race critical theories* (pp. 1–11). Oxford: Blackwell.

Esses, V. M., Dovidio, J. F., Jackson, L. M., & Armstrong, T. L. (2001). The immigration dilemma: The role of perceived group competition, ethnic prejudice, and national identity. *Journal of Social Issues, 57*(3), 389–412.

European-American Collaborative Challenging Whiteness (2005a). Reflections on Erica Foldy's first-person inquiry. *Action Research, 3*(1), 55–61.

European-American Collaborative Challenging Whiteness (2005b). When first-person inquiry is not enough: Challenging whiteness through first- and second-person action inquiry. *Action Research, 3*(3), 245–261.

Fals-Borda, O. (1985). *Knowledge and people's power: Lessons with peasants in Nicaragua, Mexico, and Columbia*. New Delhi: Indian Social Institute.

Fay, B. (1975). *Social theory and political practice*. London: George Allen and Unwin.

Fay, B. (1996). *Contemporary philosophy of social science*. Oxford: Blackwell.

Fazio, R. H., Jackson, J. R., Dunton, B. C. W., & Carol, J. (1995). Variability in automatic activation as an unobtrusive measure of racial attitudes: A bona fide pipeline? *Journal of Experimental Social Psychology, 33*, 451–470.

Fazio, R. H., & Olson, M. A. (2003). Implicit measures in social cognition research: Their meaning and use. *Annual Review of Psychology, 54*, 297–327.

Feagin, J. R., & Sikes, M. P. (1994). *Living with racism: The Black middle class experience*. Boston: Beacon Press.

Federico, C. M., & Sidanius, J. (2002). Racism, ideology, and affirmative action, revisited: The antecedents and consequences of "principled objections" to affirmative action. *Journal of Personality and Social Psychology, 82*, 488–502.

Fekete, L. (2004). Anti-Muslim racism and the European security state. *Race & Class, 46*(1), 3–29.

Fine, T. S. (1992). The impact of issue framing on public opinion: Toward affirmative action programs. *Social Science Journal, 29*, 323–334.

Finlay, L. (2002). Negotiating the swamp: The opportunity and challenge of reflexivity in research practice. *Qualitative Research, 2*(2), 209–230.

Flanagan, T. (2008). Scripting a collaborative narrative: An approach for spanning boundaries. *Design Management Review, 19*(3), 80–86.

Fletcher, J. F., & Chalmers, M. C. (1991). Attitudes of Canadians toward affirmative action: Opposition, value pluralism, and nonattitudes. *Political Behavior, 13*, 67–95.

Flick, U. (2002). *An introduction to qualitative research* (2nd ed.). London: Sage.

Flood, R. L. (2001). The relationship of "systems thinking" to action research. In P. Reason & H. Bradbury (Eds.), *Handbook of action research: Participative inquiry and practice* (pp. 133–144). London: Sage.

Flood, R. L., & Jackson, M. C. (1991). *Creative problem solving: Total systems intervention*. Chichester: Wiley.

Flood, R. L., & Romm, N. R. A. (1996a). *Diversity management: Triple loop learning*. Chichester: Wiley.

Flood, R. L., & Romm, N. R. A. (Eds.). (1996b). *Critical systems thinking: Current research and practice*. New York: Kluwer.

Flood, R. L., & Romm, N. R. A. (1997). From metatheory to multimethodology. In T. Gill & J. Mingers (Ed.), *Multimethodology* (pp. 291–322). Chichester: Wiley.

Flood, R. L., Romm, N. R. A., & Weil, S. (1997, June). *Critical reflexivity: A multi-dimensional conversation*. Conference paper presented at the Fourth World Congress on Action Research, Cartegena, Columbia.

Foster, P. (1990). *Policy and practice in multicultural and anti-racist education*. London: Routledge.

Foucault, M. (1973). *The order of things: An archaeology of the human sciences*. New York: Random House.

Foucault, M. (1978). *The history of sexuality* (Vol. 1) (R. Hurley, Trans.). New York: Vintage Books.

Foucault, M. (1979). *Discipline and punish: The birth of the prison* (A. Sheridan, Trans.). New York: Vintage Books.

Foucault, M. (1980). *Power/knowledge: Selected interviews and other writings, 1972–1977*. New York: Pantheon.

Foucault, M. (2000). Interview with Michel Foucault. In James D. Fabion (Ed.), *Power: The essential works of Foucault, 1954–1984* (Vol. 3, pp. 239–297). New York: Free Press.

Foucault, M. (2003). *Society must be defended: Lectures at the Collège de France, 1975–1976* (D. Macey, Trans.). New York: Picador.

Foucault, M. (2007). *The politics of truth* (S. Lotringer, Ed. with an introduction by J. Rajchman). Los Angeles: Semiotext(e).

Fraser, N., & Nicholson, L. (1994). An encounter between feminism and postmodernism. In S. Seidman (Ed.), *The postmodern turn: New perspectives on social theory* (pp. 242–261). Cambridge: Cambridge University Press.

Freire, P. (1970). *Pedagogy of the oppressed*. New York: Herder & Herder.

Freire, P. (1978). *Pedagogy in process: The letters to Guinea-Bissau*. London: Writers and Readers Publishing Cooperative.

Freire, P. (1985). *The politics of education: Culture, power, and liberation*. South Hadley, MA: Bergin and Garvey Publishers.

French, J. D. (2003). Translation, diasporic dialogue, and the errors of Pierre Bourdieu and Loïc Wacquant. *Nepantia: Views from the South, 4*(2), 375–389.

Fuenmayor, R. (2001a). The oblivion of Churchman's plea for a systems approach to world problems (I): The inseparability of systems thinking and world issues in the modern epoch. *Systems Practice and Action Research, 14*(1), 11–28.

Fuenmayor, R. (2001b). The oblivion of Churchman's plea for a systems approach to world problems (II): The rise of the modern constellation. *Systems Practice and Action Research, 14*(1), 29–45.

Fuss, D. (1989). *Essentially speaking: Feminism, nature, and difference*. New York: Routledge.

Gaertner, S. L. (1973). Helping behavior and racial discrimination among liberals and conservatives. *Journal of Personality and Social Psychology, 25*, 335–341.

Gaertner, S. L., & Dovidio, J. F. (1981). Racism among the well intentioned. In E. Clausen & J. Bermingham (Eds.), *Pluralism, racism, and public policy: The search for equality* (pp. 208–222). Boston: G.K. Hall.

Gaertner, S. L., & Dovidio, J. F. (1986a). The aversive form of racism. In J. F. Dovidio & S. L. Gaertner (Eds.), *Prejudice, discrimination, and racism* (pp. 61–89). Orlando, FL: Academic Press.

Gaertner, S. L., & Dovidio, J. F. (1986b). Prejudice, discrimination, and racism: Problems, progress and promise. In J. F. Dovidio & S. L. Gaertner (Eds.), *Prejudice, discrimination, and racism* (pp. 315–332). Orlando, FL: Academic Press.

Gaertner, S. L., & Dovidio, J. F. (2000). *Reducing intergroup bias: The common ingroup identity model*. Philadelphia: Psychology Press.

Gaertner, S. L., & Dovidio, J. F. (2005). Understanding and addressing contemporary racism: From aversive racism to the common ingroup identity model. *Journal of Social Issues, 61*(3), 615–639.

Gaertner, S. L., Dovidio, J. F., Nier, J. A., Hodson, G., Houlette, M. A. (2005). Aversive racism: Bias without intention. In L. B. Nielson & R. L. Nelson (Eds.), *Handbook of employment discrimination research: Rights and realities* (pp. 377–395). Dordrecht: Springer.

Gaertner, S. L., Mann, J. A., Dovidio, J. F., Murrell, A. J., & Pomare, M. (1990). How does cooperation reduce intergroup bias? *Journal of Personality and Social Psychology, 59*, 692–704.

Gaertner, S. L., Mann, J. A., Murrell, A. J., & Dovidio, J. F. (1989). Reducing intergroup bias: The benefits of recategorization. *Journal of Personality and Social Psychology, 57*, 239–249.

Gaertner, S. L., Rust, M. C., Dovidio, J. F., Anastasio, P. A, Bachman, B. A., & Rust, M. (1993). The common ingroup identity model: Recategorization and the reduction of intergroup bias. In W. Stroeber & M. Hewstone (Eds.), *European review of social psychology 2:* (pp. 247–278). Chichester: Wiley.

Gaertner, S. L., Rust, M. C., Dovidio, J. F., Bachman, B. A., & Anastasio, P. A. (1996). The contact hypothesis: The role of a common ingroup identity in reducing intergroup bias among majority and minority group members. In J. L. Nye & A. M. Brower (Eds.), *What's social about social cognition?* (pp. 230–360). Newbury Park, CA: Sage.

Gallagher, C. A. (2008). "The end of racism" as the new doxa: New strategies for researching race. In T. Zuberi & E. Bonilla-Silva (Eds.), *White logic, White methods: Racism and methodology* (pp. 163–178). Lanham: Rowman & Littlefield.

Garfinkel, H (1967). *Studies in ethnomethodology.* Englewood Cliffs, NJ: Prentice Hall.

Gaventa, J. (1991). Toward a knowledge democracy: Viewpoints on participatory research in North America. In O. Fals-Borda & M. A. Rahman (Eds.), *Action and knowledge: Breaking the monopoly with participatory action research* (pp. 121–131). New York: The Apex Press.

Gazel, J. (2007). Walking the talk: Multiracial discourses, realities, and pedagogy. *American Behavioral Scientist, 51*(4), 532–550.

Geci, K-S., Hemson, D., & Carter, J. (2009). Putting people first versus embedding autonomy: Responsiveness of the democratic development state to effective demand-side governance in South Africa's service delivery. *Systemic Practice and Action Research* (in press).

Gergen, K. J. (2003). Relational practice and orders of democracy. *Action Research, 1*(1), 39–56.

Gergen, M. M, & Gergen, K. J. (2003). Qualitative inquiry: Tensions and transformations. In N. K. Denzin & Y. S. Lincoln (Eds.), *The landscape of qualitative research: Theories and issues* (2nd ed., pp. 575–610). London: Sage.

Giddens, A. (1984). *The constitution of society: Outline of the theory of structuration.* Berkeley, CA: UCLA Press.

Gill, P. (2001). Narrative inquiry: Designing the processes, pathways and patterns of change. *Systems Research and Behavioral Science, 18*, 335–343.

Goffman, I. (1963). *Stigma: Notes on the management of spoiled identity.* Englewood Cliffs, NJ: Prentice Hall.

Goldberg, D. T. (2002). Modernity, race, and morality. In Ph. Essed & D. T. Goldberg (Eds.), *Race critical theories* (pp. 283–306). Oxford: Blackwell.

Gomez, A., & Huici, C. (1999). Orientación política y racismo sutil y manifiesto: Relaciones con la discriminación [Political orientation and subtle and blatant prejudice: Relations with discrimination]. *Revista de Psicología Social y Aplicada, 14*, 159–180.

Gordijn, E. H., Koomen, W., & Stapel, D. A. (2001). Level of prejudice in relation to knowledge of cultural stereotypes. *Journal of Experimental Social Psychology, 37*, 150–157.

Govan, C. L., & Williams, K. D. (2004). Changing the affective valence of the stimulus items influences the IAT by re-defining the category labels. *Journal of Experimental Social Psychology, 40*, 357–365.

Gray, P. S., Williamson, J. B., Karp, D. A., & Dalphin, J. R. (2007). *The research imagination: An introduction to quantitative and qualitative methods.* Cambridge: Cambridge University Press.

Green, E. (2008). Barack Obama's U.S. Presidential Bid Bridges Racial Divisions. Report written on 18 January 2008 in *America.gov – Telling America's story.* Retrieved from http://www.america.gov/st/elections08-english/2008/January/200801181212531xeneerg0.8178675.html

Green, E. G. T., Staerklé, C., & Sears, D. O. (2006). Symbolic racism and whites' attitudes toward punitive and preventative crime policies. *Law and Human Behavior, 30*, 435–454.

Greenwald, A. (2008). *The Implicit Association Test: A talk with Mahzarin Banaji and Anthony Greenwald.* Retrieved December 2, 2008, from http://www/edge.org/3rd_culture/banaji_greenwald08/banaji_greenwald08_index.htm

Greenwald, A. G., McGhee D. E., & Schwartz, J. L. K. (1998). Measuring individual differences in implicit cognition: The Implicit Association Test. *Journal of Personality and Social Psychology, 74*, 1464–1480.

Greenwood, D. J., & Levin, M. (1998). *Introduction to action research*. London: Sage.

Gregory, W. J., & Romm, N. R. A. (2001). Critical facilitation: Learning through intervention in group processes. *Management Learning, 32*(4), 453–467.

Gregory, W. J., & Romm, N. R. A. (2004). Facilitation as fair intervention. In A. Ochoa-Arias & G. Midgley (Eds.), *Community operational research* (pp. 157–174). New York: Kluwer Academic/Plenum Publishers.

Gubrium, E., & Koro-Ljungberg, M. (2005). Contending with border making in the social constructionist interview. *Qualitative Inquiry, 11*(5), 689–715.

Guinier, L., & Torres, G. (2002). *The Miners' Canary: Enlisting race, resisting power, transforming democracy*. Cambridge, MA: Harvard University Press.

Gumede, W. (2008). Mbeki must face up to South Africa's xenophobia. *The Independent*. Retrieved May 21, 2008, from http://www.independent.co.uk/opinion/commentators/william-gumede-mbeki-must-face-up-to-south-africas-xenophobia-831476.html

Gustavsen, B. (1992). *Dialogue and development: Social science for social action*. (Vol. 1). Assen, The Netherlands: Van Gorcum.

Gustavsen, B. (2001). Theory and practice: The mediating discourse. In P. Reason & H. Bradbury (Eds.), *Handbook of action research: Participative inquiry and practice* (pp. 17–26). London: Sage.

Habermas, J. (1974a). Rationalism divided in two: A reply to Albert. In A. Giddens (Ed.), *Positivism and sociology* (pp. 195–223). London: Heinemann.

Habermas, J. (1974b). *Theory and practice* (J. Viertel, Trans.). Boston: Beacon Press.

Habermas, J. (1984). *The theory of communicative action* (Vol. 1): *Reason and the rationalization of society* (T. McCarthy, Trans.). Boston: Beacon Press.

Habermas, J. (1993). *Justification and application: Remarks on discourse ethics*. Cambridge: Polity Press.

Habermas, J. (1994). Struggles for recognition in the democratic constitutional state (S. W. Nicholsen, Trans.). In A. Gutmann (Ed.), *Multiculturalism: Examining the politics of recognition* (pp. 107–148). Princeton, NJ: Princeton University Press.

Habermas, J. (1996). *Between facts and norms* (W. Rehg, Trans.). Cambridge: Polity Press.

Habermas, J. (2003). Fundamentalism and terror. In G. Borradori, J. Derrida, & J. Habermas (Eds.), *Philosophy in a time of terror* (pp. 25–43). Chicago: University of Chicago Press.

Habermas, J. (2006). How to respond to the ethical question. In L. Thomassen (Ed.), *The Derrida-Habermas reader* (pp. 115–127). Chicago: University of Chicago Press.

Hacking, I. (1995). The looping effects of human kinds. In D. Sperber, D. Premack, & A. J. Premack (Eds.), *Causal cognition: A multidisciplinary debate* (pp. 351–383). Oxford: Clarendon Press.

Hacking, I. (1999). *The social construction of what?* Cambridge, MA: Harvard University Press.

Hadjipavlou-Trigeorgis, M. (1993). Unofficial inter-communal contacts and their contribution to peace-building in conflict societies: The case of Cyprus. *Cyprus Review, 5*(2), 68–87.

Haley, H., & Sidanius, J. (2006). The positive and negative framing of affirmative action: A group dominance perspective. *Personality and Social Psychology Bulletin, 32*(5), 656–668.

Hall, J. R. (1999). *Cultures of inquiry: From epistemology to discourse in sociohistorical research*. Cambridge: Cambridge University Press.

Hammersley, M. (1990). *Reading ethnographic research*. London: Longman.

Hammersley, M. (1995). *The politics of social research*. London: Sage.

Hammersley, M. (2003). "Analytics" are no substitute for methodology: A response to Speer and Hutchby. *Sociology, 37*(2), 339–351.

Hammersley, M., & Atkinson, P. (1995). *Ethnography* (2nd ed.). London: Routledge.

Hammersley, M., & Gomm, R. (1997a). Bias in social research. *Sociological Research Online, 2*, http://www.socresonline.org.uk/socresonline/2/1/2.html

Hammersley, M., & Gomm, R. (1997b). A response to Romm. *Sociological Research Online, 2*, http://www.socresonline.org.uk/socresonline/2/4/7.html

Hampden-Turner, C., & Trompenaars, F. (2000). *Building cross-cultural competence*. New Haven, CT: Yale University Press.

Hanchard, M. (1994). *Orpheus and power: The Movimento Negro of Rio de Janeiro and São Paulo, Brazil, 1945–1988*. Princeton, NJ: Princeton University Press.

Hanchard, M. (2003). Acts of misrecognition: Transnational Black politics, anti-imperialism and the ethnocentricism of Pierre Bourdieu and Loïc Wacqant. *Theory, Culture & Society, 20*(4), 5–29.

Hanson, N. R. (1958). *Patterns of discovery: An inquiry into the conceptual foundations of science*. Cambridge: Cambridge University Press.

Hanson, N. R. (1961). Is there a logic of scientific discovery? In H. Feigl & G. Maxwell (Eds.), *Current issues in the philosophy of science* (pp. 20–35). New York: Holt, Rinehart and Winston.

Haraway, D. (1991). *Simians, cyborgs and women: The reinvention of women*. London: Free Association Press.

Harris, B. (2003). Xenophobia: A new pathology for a new South Africa? In D. Hook & G. Eagle (Eds.), *Psychopathology and social prejudice* (pp. 169–184). Cape Town: UCT Press.

Harris, C. I. (1995). Whiteness as property. In K. Crenshaw, N. Gotanda, G. Peller, & K. Thomas (Eds.), *Critical race theory: The key writings that formed the movement* (pp. 276–291). New York: The Free Press.

Harris-Lacewell, M. (2003). The heart of the politics of race: Centering Black people in the study of White racial attitudes. *Journal of Black Studies, 34*(2), 222–249.

Harvey, D. (2008). *Introduction to Marx and Engels' Communist Manifesto*. London: Pluto Press.

Hayman, R. L. (1995). The color of tradition: Critical race theory and postmodern constitutional traditionalism. *Harvard Civil Rights-Civil Liberties Law Review, 30*, 57–108.

Henkel, K. E., Dovidio, J. F., & Gaertner, S. L. (2006). Institutional discrimination, individual racism, and hurricane Katrina. *Analyses of Social Issues and Public Policy, 6*(1), 99–124.

Hennink, M. M. (2007). *International focus group research: A handbook for the health and social sciences*. Cambridge: Cambridge University Press.

Henry, F., & Tator, C. (2002). *Discourses of domination: Racial bias in the Canadian English-language press*. Toronto: University of Toronto Press.

Henry, P. J., & Sears, D. O. (2002). The symbolic racism 2000 scale. *Political Psychology, 23*, 253–283.

Henwood, K. L., & Pidgeon, N. F. (1993). Qualitative research and psychological theorizing. In M. Hammersley (Ed.), *Social research: Philosophy, politics and practice* (pp. 14–32). London: Sage.

Hercules, A. (2006). *Program evaluation report (by Sonke consulting) on the advanced certificate in education (ACE) – Values and human rights in education, 2003–2005*. Johannesburg.

Hewstone, M. (1996). Contact and categorization: Social psychological interventions to change intergroup relations. In C. N. Macrae, C. Stangor, & M. Hewstone (Eds.), *Stereotypes and stereotyping* (pp. 323–368). New York: Guilford.

Hodson, G., Hooper, H., Dovidio, J. F., & Gaertner, S. L. (2005). Aversive racism in Britain: The use of inadmissible evidence in legal decisions. *European Journal of Social Psychology, 35*, 437–448.

Hoffman, E. A. (2007). Open-ended interviews, power, and emotional labor. *Journal of Contemporary Ethnography, 36*(3), 318–346.

Hollinger, D. (1995). *Postethnic America: Beyond multiculturalism*. New York: Basic Books.

Holstein, J. A., & Gubrium, J. F. (1994). Phenomenology, ethnomethodology and interpretive practice. In N. K. Denzin & Y. S. Lincoln (Eds.), *Handbook of qualitative research* (pp. 262–272). London: Sage.

Holstein, J. A., & Gubrium, J. F. (1995). *The active interview*. London: Sage.

Holstein, J. A., & Gubrium, J. F. (2003). *Postmodern interviewing*. Thousand Oaks, CA: Sage.

hooks, b. (1994). *Outlaw culture*. New York: Routledge.

hooks, b. (2001). *All about love: New visions*. New York: Perennial.

Hornsey, M. J., & Hogg, M. A. (2000). Subgroup relations: A comparison of mutual intergroup differentiation and common ingroup identity models of prejudice reduction. *Personality and Social Psychology Bulletin, 26*, 242–256.

Hursthouse, R. (2007). *Virtue ethics*. Stanford Encyclopedia of Philosophy. Retrieved from http://plato.stanford.edu/entries/ethics-virtue/

Huxham, C. (2003). Action research as a methodology for theory development. *Policy and Politics, 31*(2), 239–248.

Ivey, A. E., & Ivey, E. *Intentional interviewing and counseling*. Pacific Grove, CA: Thomson.

Jackson, J. W. (2002). The relationship between group identity and intergroup prejudice is moderated by sociocultural variation. *Journal of Applied Social Psychology, 32*, 908–933.

Jacobsen, C. M. (2008). Theory and politics in research on Muslim immigrants in Norway. *Tidsskrift for Islamforskning (Research on Islam Repositioned), 2*(3), 27–52.

James, A. (2008). Making sense of race and racial classification. In T. Zuberi & E. Bonilla-Silva (Eds.), *White logic, White methods: Racism and methodology* (pp. 31–45). Lanham, MD: Rowman & Littlefield.

Jayasuriya, L. (2002). Understanding Australian racism. *Australian Universities Review, 45*(1), 40–44.

Jayasuriya, L. (2003). Australia: Immigration and identity. Interview in *The World Today*. Retrieved October 30, from http://www.abc.net.au/worldtoday/content/2003/s978819.htm

Jervis, R. (1997). *System effects: Complexity in political and social life*. Princeton, NJ: Princeton University Press.

Johansson, A. W., & Lindhult, E. (2008). Emancipation or workability? Critical versus pragmatic scientific orientation in action research. *Research, 6*(1), 95–115.

Johnson, D. W., & Johnson, F. P. (1975). *Joining together: Group theory and group skills*. Englewood Cliffs, NJ: Prentice Hall.

Johnson, D., Terry, D. J., & Louis, W. R. (2005). Perceptions of the intergroup structure and anti-Asian prejudice among White Australians. *Group Processes and Intergroup Relations, 8*(1), 53–71.

Johnston, L., & Hewstone, M. (1990). Intergroup contact: Social identity and social cognition. In D. Abrams & M. A. Hogg (Eds.), *Social identity theory: Constructive and critical advances* (pp. 185–210). New York: Harvester Wheatsheaf.

Jones, J. M. (1983). The concept of race in social psychology: From color to culture. In L. Wheeler & P. Shaver (Eds.), *Review of personality and social psychology* (Vol. 4, pp. 127–149). Beverley Hills, CA: Sage.

Jones, J. M. (1986). Racism: A cultural analysis of the problem. In J. F. Dovidio & S. L. Gaertner (Eds.), *Prejudice, discrimination, and racism* (pp. 279–314). Orlando: Academic Press.

Joseph, J., & Kennedy, S. (2000). The structure of the social. *Philosophy of the Social Sciences, 30*, 508–527.

Jubber, K. (2007). Sociology in South Africa: A brief historical review of research and publishing. *International Sociology, 22*(5), 527–546.

Kalungu-Banda, M. (2006). *Leading like Madiba: Leadership lessons from Nelson Mandela*. Cape Town: Double Storey Books.

Kaufmann, J. (2005). Autotheory: An autoethnographic reading of Foucault. *Qualitative Inquiry, 11*(4). 576–587.

Keat, R. (1981). *The politics of social theory: Habermas, Freud and the critique of positivism*. Oxford: Basil Blackwell.

Keat, R., & Urry, J. (1975). *Social theory as science*. London: Routledge & Kegan Paul.

Kiguwa, P. (2006). Social constructionist accounts of intergroup relations and identity. In K. Ratele (Ed.), *Inter-group relations: South African perspectives* (pp. 111–136). Cape Town: Juta.

Kinder, D. R., & Sanders, L. M. (1990). Mimicking political debate with survey questions: The case of White opinion on affirmative action for Blacks. *Social Cognition, 8*(1), 73–103.

Kinder, D., & Sanders, L. (1996). *Divided by color: Racial politics and democratic ideals.* Chicago: University of Chicago Press.

Kinder, D. R., & Sears, D. O. (1981). Prejudice and politics: Symbolic racism threats to the good life. *Journal of Personality and Social Psychology, 40*(3),: 414–431.

Kluegel, J. R., & Smith, E. R. (1983). Affirmative action attitudes: Effects of self-interest, racial affect, and stratification beliefs on Whites' views. *Social Forces, 61*, 797–824.

Knight, J. L., & Hebl, M. R. (2005). Affirmative reaction: The influence of type of justification on nonbeneficiary attitudes toward affirmative action plans in higher education. *Journal of Social Issues, 61*(3), 547–568.

Koppelman, A. (1996). *Antidiscrimination law and social equality.* New Haven, CT: Yale University Press.

Kovel, J. (1970). *White racism: A psychohistory.* New York: Pantheon.

Kretsedemas, P. (2008). Redefining "race" in North America. *Current Sociology, 56*(6), 826–844.

Kuhn, D. P. (2008). Dem's prejudice may cost Obama votes. *Politico.* Retrieved September 20, 2008, from http://www.politico.com/news/stories/09/08/13669.html

Kuhn, T. (1962). *The structure of scientific revolutions.* Chicago: University of Chicago Press.

Kuhn, T. (1970). *The structure of scientific revolutions* (2nd ed. enlarged). Chicago: University of Chicago Press.

Kundnani, A. (2007). *The end of tolerance: Racism in 21st century Britain.* London: Pluto Press.

Ladner, J. A. (Ed.). *The death of White sociology.* New York: Random House.

Ladson-Billings, G. (2003). Racialized discourses and ethnic epistemologies. In N. K. Denzin & Y. S. Lincoln (Eds.), *The landscape of qualitative research: Theories and issues* (2nd ed., pp. 398–432). London: Sage.

Ladson-Billings, G. (2004). New directions in multicultural education: Complexities, boundaries, and critical race theory. In J. A. Banks & C. A. M. Banks (Eds.), *Handbook of Research on Multicultural Education* (pp. 50–65). San Francisco: Jossey-Bass.

Ladson-Billings, G., & Tate, W. (1995). Toward a critical race theory of education. *Teachers College Record, 97*(1), 47–68.

LaFromboise, T., Coleman, H. L. K., & Gerton, J. (1993). Psychological impact of biculturalism: Evidence and theory. *Psychological Bulletin, 114*, 395–412.

Laitin, D. D. (1988). Political culture and political preferences. *The American Political Science Review, 82*(2), 589–593.

Lakoff, G. (2009). The Obama Code. *Truthout.* Retrieved February 24, 2009, from http://www.truthout.org/022409R

Laouris, Y., & Christakis, A. N. (2007). Harnessing collective wisdom at a fraction of the time using structured design process in a virtual communication context. *International Journal of Applied Systemic Studies, 1*(2), 131–153.

Laouris, Y., & Michaelides, M. (2007). *What are the obstacles that prevent the wide public from benefiting and participating in the broadband society?* Conference proceedings, Cost 298 Conference, Moscow. Retrieved from http://www.cost298.org

Laouris, Y., Michaelides, M., Damdelen, M., Laouri, R., Beyatli, D., & Christakis, A. (2007). *A systemic evaluation of the state of affairs following the negative outcome of the referendum in Cyprus using a structured dialogic design process.* Retrieved from http://www.futureworldscenter.org/Research/Full%20Papers/RevivingPeaceArticle2007_04_13.pdf

Laouris, Y., Michaelides, M., Damdelen, M., Laouri, R., Beyatli, D., & Christakis, A. (2009). A systemic evaluation of the state of affairs following the negative outcome of the referendum in Cyprus using a structured dialogic design process. *Systemic Practice and Action Research, 22*(1), 45–75.

Lassila, J. (2006). *Multi-track, track two and track 1,5 diplomacy?* Crisis management initiative (CMI) background paper 2. Retrieved June 2006, from http://www.cmi.fi/?content=news&id=401

Layder, D. (1993). *New strategies in social research.* Cambridge: Polity Press.

Lemert, C. (1994). Post-structuralism and sociology. In S. Seidman (Ed.), *The postmodern turn: New perspectives on social theory* (pp. 265–281). Cambridge: Cambridge University Press.

Leontidou, L. (2001). *Shifting configurations of "the other" in European border towns.* Paper presented at the Dialogue Workshop on Racism and Xenophobia, Brussels, April 5–6, 2001.

Lewin, K. (1946). Action research and minority problems. *Journal of Social Issues, 2,* 34–46.

Lewin, K. (1951). *Field theory in social science.* New York: Harper and Row.

Lewis, V. (1996, Autumn). Men, sex, politics. *XY Magazine, 6* (1). Retrieved from http://www.xyonline.net/ColourP.shtml

Leyens, J.-P., Cortes, B., Demoulin, S., Dovidio, J. F., Fiske, S. T., Gaunt, R., Paladino, M-P., Rodriguez-Perez, A., Rodriguez-Torres, R., & Vaes, J. (2003). Emotional prejudice, essentialism and nationalism: The 2002 Tajfel lecture. *European Journal of Social Psychology, 33,* 703–719.

Lincoln, Y. S., & Denzin, N. K. (2003). The seventh moment: Out of the past. In N. K. Denzin & Y. S. Lincoln (Eds.), *The landscape of qualitative research: Theories and issues* (2nd ed., pp. 611–640). London: Sage.

Lincoln, Y. S., & Guba, E. G. (2003). Paradigmatic controversies, contradictions, and emerging confluences. In N. K. Denzin & Y. S. Lincoln (Eds.), *The landscape of qualitative research: Theories and issues* (2nd ed., pp. 253–291). London: Sage.

López, G. R. (2001, January–February). Revisiting white racism in educational research: Critical race theory and the problem of method. *Educational Researcher, 30*(1), 29–33.

Lorde, A. (1984). *Sister outsider: Essays and speeches.* Freedom, CA: Crossing Press.

Louis, B. (2005). The difference sameness makes: Racial recognition and the narcissism of minor differences. *Ethnicities, 5*(3), 343–364.

Lowery, B. S., Hardin, C. D., & Sinclair, S. (2001). Social influence effects on automatic racial prejudice. *Journal of Personality and Social Psychology, 81,* 842–855.

Lowery, B. S., Knowles, E. D., & Unzueta, M. M. (2007). Framing inequity safely: Motivated perceptions of racial privilege. *Personality and Social Psychology Bulletin, 33*(9), 1237–1250.

Lowery, B. S., Unzueta, M. M., Knowles, E. D., & Goff, P. A. (2006). Concern for the ingroup and opposition to affirmative action. *Journal of Personality and Social Psychology, 90,* 961–974.

Lyotard, J-F. (1984). *The postmodern condition: A report on knowledge* (G. Bennington & B. Massumi, Trans.). Minneapolis, MN: Minnesota University Press.

MacIntyre, A. (1981). *Whose justice? Which rationality?* South Bend, IN: University of Notre Dame Press.

MacPherson, W. (1999). *The Stephen Lawrence inquiry: Report of an inquest.* London: HMSO.

Mandela, N. (1997): *Report by the President of the ANC, Nelson Mandela, to the 50th National Conference of the African National Congress.* (Opening address, delivered on December 16, 1997, Mafikeng.) Retrieved from http://www.anc.org.za/ancdocs/history/mandela/1997/sp971216.html

Mann, R. (2006). Reflexivity and researching national identity. *Sociological Research Online, 11* (4), http://www.socresonline.org.uk/11/4/mann.html

Marks, C. (2008). Methodologically eliminating race and racism. In T. Zuberi & E. Bonilla-Silva (Eds.), *White logic, White methods: Racism and methodology* (pp. 47–62). Lanham, MD: Rowman & Littlefield.

Marks, D. (1996). Constructing a narrative: Moral discourse and young people's experience of exclusion. In E. Burman, G. Aitken, P. Alldred, T. Billington, B. Goldgerb, A. J. Gordo-Lopez, C. Heenan, D. Marks, & S. Warner (Eds.), *Psychology, discourse, practice: From regulation to resistance* (pp. 114–130). London: Taylor and Francis.

Marsden, R. (1998). The unknown masterpiece: Marx's model of capital. *Cambridge Journal of Economics, 22,* 297–324.

Marshall, H. (1992). Talking about good maternity care in a multi-cultural context. In P. Nicholson & J. Ussher (Eds.), *The psychology of women's health and healthcare* (pp. 200–224). Basingstoke: Macmillan.

Marx, K. (1965). *Capital.* London: Lawrence and Wishart.

Marx, K., & Engels, F. (1970). *The German ideology.* London: Lawrence and Wishart.

Marx, K., & Engels, F. (1988). *Manifesto of the Communist Party* (S. Moore, Trans. in cooperation with F. Engels). London: Pluto Press.

Massey, D. S., & Denton, N. A (1993). *American apartheid: Segregation and the making of the underclass*. Cambridge: Harvard University Press.

Matlwa, P. (2007). *Coconut*. Aukland Park: Jacana Media.

Matuštík, M. B. (2006). Between hope and terror: Habermas and Derrida plead for the impossible. In L. Thomassen (Ed.), *The Derrida-Habermas reader* (pp. 278–296). Chicago: University of Chicago Press.

Mayr, E. (1952). Concepts of classification and nomenclature in higher organisms and microorganisms. *Annals of the New York Academy of Science, 56*, 391–397.

Mbeki, T. (2000). *Keynote speech*. Opening session of the National Conference on Racism. Johannesburg, August 30, 2000.

McConahay, J. B. (1983). Modern racism and modern discrimination: The effects of race, racial attitudes, and context on simulated hiring decisions. *Personality and Social Psychology Bulletin, 9*(4), 551–558.

McConahay, J. B. (1986). Modern racism, ambivalence, and the modern racism scale. In J. F. Dovidio & S. L. Gaertner (Eds.), *Prejudice, discrimination, and racism* (pp. 91–125). Orlando, FL: Academic Press.

McConahay, J. B., & Hough, J. C. (1976). Symbolic racism. *Journal of Social Issues, 32*, 23–45.

McDonald, K. J. (2000). Authorization of knowledge in the interview process. *Educational Insights, 6*(1), http://www.ccfi.educ.ubc.ca/publication/insights/archives/v06n01/mcdonald.html

McIntyre-Mills, J. J (2003). *Critical systemic praxis for social and environmental justice: Participatory policy design and governance for a global age*. New York: Kluwer Academic/Plenum Publishers.

McIntyre-Mills, J. J. (2004). Facilitating critical systems praxis (CSP) by means of experiential learning and conceptual tools. *Systems Research and Behavioral Science, 21*, 37–61.

McIntyre-Mills, J. J. (2006a). Introduction to volume 1: The contribution of West Churchman to sustainable governance and international relations. In J. J McIntyre-Mills (Ed.), *Rescuing the enlightenment from itself* (pp. 1–19). New York: Springer.

McIntyre-Mills, J. J. (2006b). *Systemic governance and accountability: Working and re-working the conceptual and spatial boundaries*. New York: Springer.

McIntyre-Mills, J. J. (2008a). Systemic ethics: Expanding the boundaries of rights and responsibilities. *Systems Research and Behavioral Science, 25*(2), 147–150.

McIntyre-Mills, J. J. (2008b). Reconsidering relationships across self, others, the environment and technology. *Systems Research and Behavioral Science, 25*(2), 193–213.

McIntyre-Mills, J. J. (2008c). Systemic ethics: Social, economic and environmental implications of eating our yellow cake in South Australia. *Systems Research and Behavioral Science, 25*(2), 225–248.

McKay, V. I. (1990). Critical education: A contradiction in terms? In C. J. Alant (Ed.), *Sociology and society: A humanist profile* (pp. 96–105). Johannesburg: Southern Book Publishers.

McKay, V. I. (1997). The importance of reflection and action research in the training of community educators: A sociological contribution. *Educare, 26*, 4–14.

McKay, V. I. (2003). *Consolidated report on HIV/AIDS interventions in the informal sector: A four-country study*. Geneva: International Labor Organization.

McKay, V. I., & Romm, N. R. A. (1992). *People's education in theoretical perspective: Toward the development of a critical humanist approach*. Cape Town: Longman.

McKay, V. I., & Romm, N. R. A. (2006a). *Capacity building for educators of adults in three Southern African countries: South Africa, Botswana, and Namibia* (with contribution also by H. Kotze). Report for an ADEA-commissioned study (Association for the Development of Education in Africa). Retrieved from http://www.adeanet.org/biennial-2006/en_papers_A-2006.html

McKay, V. I., & Romm. N. R. A. (2006b). *The NQF (national qualifications framework) and its implementation in non-formal education – With special reference to South Africa,*

Namibia, Botswana and Kenya (with contributions also by J. Kebathi & H. Kotze). Report for an ADEA-commissioned study (Association for the Development of Education in Africa). Retrieved from http://www.adeanet.org/biennial-2006/en_papers_A-2006.html

McKay, V. I., & Romm, N. R. A. (2006c): *Assessment of the impact of HIV and AIDS in the informal economy in Zambia.* Lusaka: International Labor Organization.

McKay, V. I., & Romm, N. R. A. (2008a). Active research toward the addressal of HIV/AIDS in the informal economy in Zambia: Recognition of complicity in unfolding situations. *Action Research, 6*(2), 149–170.

McKay, V. I., & Romm, N. R. A. (2008b). A systemic approach to addressing HIV/AIDS in the informal economy in Zambia: Methodological pluralism revisited. *International Journal of Applied Systemic Studies, 1*(4), 375–397.

McKernan, J. A. (2006). Choice and quality in action research: A response to Peter Reason. *Journal of Management Inquiry, 15*(2), 204–206.

McKillip, J., DiMiceli, A. J., & Luebke, J. (1977). Group salience and stereotyping. *Social Behavior and Personality, 5*, 81–85.

McKinney, C. (2007). Caught between the "old" and the "new"? Talking about "race" in a post-apartheid university classroom. *Race, Ethnicity and Education, 10*(2), 215–231.

McLaren, P., & Farahmandpur, R. (2005). Marx after post-Marxism. In P. McLaren & C. Y. Companeros (Eds.), *Red seminars: Radical excursions into educational theory, cultural politics and pedagogy* (pp. 3–24). Cresskill, NJ: Hampton Press.

McLaren, P., & Rikowski, G. (2005). Pedagogy for revolution against education for capital: An e-dialogue on education in capitalism today. In P. McLaren & C. Y. Companeros (Eds.), *Red seminars: Radical excursions into educational theory, cultural politics and pedagogy* (pp. 455–507). Cresskill, NJ: Hampton Press.

McMahon, M. (1995). *Engendering motherhood: Identity and self-transformation in women's lives.* New York: Guilford Press.

McWhorter, L. (2005). Where do white people come from? A Foucauldian critique of whiteness studies. *Philosophy and Social Criticism, 31*(5–6), 533–556.

Mehta, L. (2008). The politics of researching citizenship and marginality. *Action Research, 6*(2), 233–253.

Mellor, D. (2003). Contemporary racism in Australia: The experiences of Aborigines. *Personality and Social Psychology Bulletin, 29*, 474–486.

Merton, R. K. (1964). *Social theory and social structure.* London: The Free Press.

Midgley, G. (1997). Mixing methods: Developing systemic intervention. In J. Mingers & A. Gill (Eds.), *Multimethodology* (pp. 249–290). Chichester: Wiley.

Midgley, G. (2000). *Systemic intervention: Philosophy, methodology and practice.* New York: Kluwer Academic/Plenum Publishers.

Midgley, G. (2001). Systems thinking for the 21st century. In G. Ragsdell & J. Wilby (Eds.), *Systems thinking for the 21st century: Understanding complexity* (pp. 249–256). New York: Kluwer Academic/Plenum Publishers.

Midgley, G., Munlo, I., & Brown, M. (1998). The theory and practice of boundary critique. *Journal of the Operational Research Society, 49*, 467–478.

Miles, R. (1996). Racism and class structure. In J. Hood-Williams, G. Mundy, & D. Stuart (Eds.), *Skills and reasoning for the social sciences* (pp. 3–18). Greenwich: Greenwich University Press.

Miller, G. A. (1963). Thinking, cognition, and learning. In B. Berelson (Ed.), *The behavioral sciences today* (pp. 139–150). New York: Basic Books.

Miller, N. (2002). Personalization and the promise of contact theory. *Journal of Social Issues, 58*(2), 387–410.

Miller, N., & Brewer, M. B. (1986). Categorization effects on ingroup and outgroup perception. In J. F. Dovidio & S. L. Gaertner (Eds.), *Prejudice, discrimination, and racism* (pp. 209–230). Orlando, FL: Academic Press.

Milner IV, H. R. (2007). Race, culture and researcher positionality: Working through dangers seen, unseen, and unforeseen. *Educational Researcher, 36*(7), 388–400.

Mitroff, I. I. (1994). The cruel science of world mismanagement: An essay in honor of C. West Churchman. *Interfaces, 24*, 94–98.

Mitroff, I. I., & Kilmann, R. H. (1978). *Methodological approaches to social science: Integrating divergent concepts and theories*. San Francisco: Jossey-Bass.

Mocombe, P. C. (2006). The sociolinguistic nature of black academic failure in capitalist education: A reevaluation of "language in the inner city" and its social function, "acting white". *Race, Ethnicity and Education, 9*(4), 395–407.

Monteith, M. J., Voils, I. C., & Ashburn-Nardo, L. (2001). Taking a look underground: Detecting, interpreting, and reacting to implicit racial biases. *Social Cognition, 19*(4), 395–417.

Monteith, M. J., & Winters, J. (2002). Why we hate. *Psychology Today, 35*(3), 44–50 & 87.

Montville, J. V. (1991). The arrow and the olive branch: A case for track two diplomacy. In V. D. Volkan, J. V. Montville, & O. Julius (Eds.), *The psychodynamics of international relationships* (Vol. 2, pp. 161–175). Lexington, MA: Lexington Books.

Morawski, J. G. (2005). Reflexivity and the psychologist. *History of the Human Sciences, 18*(4), 77–105.

Morris, M. (2006). Between deliberation and deconstruction: The condition of post-national democracy. In L. Thomassen (Ed.), *The Derrida-Habermas reader* (pp. 231–253). Chicago, IL: University of Chicago Press.

Morrow, R. A. (1994). *Critical theory and methodology*. London: Sage.

Morton, T. A., Hornsey, M. J., & Postmes, J. (2009). Shifting ground: The variable use of essentialism in contexts of inclusion and exclusion. *British Journal of Social Psychology, 48*, 35–59.

Mulkay, M. (1979). *Science and the sociology of knowledge*. Boston: Unwin Hyman.

Murji, K. (2007). Sociological engagements: Institutional racism and beyond. *Sociology, 4*(5), 843–855.

Myrdal, G. (1944). *An American dilemma*. New York: Harper & Row.

Nascimento, E. L. (2004). Kilombismo, virtual whiteness, and the sorcery of color. *Journal of Black Studies, 34*(6), 861–880.

Navas, M. S. (1998). Nuevos instrumentos de medida para el nuevo racismo [New instrument to measure the new forms of racism]. *Revista de Psicología Social Aplicada, 13*, 223–239.

Nelson, H. (2001). Continuing the traditions of ISSS: Systems science in the service of humanity. In G. Ragsdell & J. Wilby (Eds.), *Understanding complexity* (pp. 283–287). New York: Kluwer Academic/Plenum Publishers.

Ng, R. (1995). Teaching against the grain. In R. Ng, P. Staton, & J. Scane (Eds.), *Antiracism, feminism, and critical approaches to education* (pp. 129–153). Westport, CT: Bergin & Garvey.

Niemann, Y. F., & Maruyama, G. (2005). Inequities in higher education: Issues and promising practices in a world ambivalent about affirmative action. *Journal of Social Issues, 61*(3), 407–426.

Nier, J. A. (2006). Does the Implicit Association Test (IAT) measure racial prejudice? Introductory paragraph to issue 15 in J. A. Nier (Ed.), *Taking sides: Clashing views in social psychology* (2nd ed.). Berkshire: McGraw-Hill Education.

Nier, J. A., Gaertner, S. L., Dovidio, J. F., Banker, B. S., Ward, C. M., & Rust, M. C. (2001). Changing interracial evaluations and behavior: The effects of a common group identity. *Group Processes and Intergroup Relations, 4*(4), 299–316.

Nkomo, S. M. (1992). The emperor has no clothes: Rewriting race in the study of organizations. *Academy of Management Review, 17*, 487–513.

Noyoo, N. (2004). Human rights and social work in a transforming society: South Africa. *International Social Work, 47*(3), 359–369.

Nuttall, S. (2006). A politics of the emergent: Cultural studies in South Africa. *Theory, Culture and Society, 23*(7–8), 263–278.

Nyamnjoh, F. (2007). Toward a predicament-oriented approach to social research ethics. In A. Rwomire & F. Nyamnjoh (Eds.), *Challenges and responsibilities of social research in*

Africa: Ethical issues (pp. 1–10). Addis Ababa: The Organization for Social Science Research in Eastern and Southern Africa (OSSREA).

Obama, B. (2007). *The audacity of hope: Thoughts on reclaiming the American dream.* Edinburgh: Canongate.

Obama, B. (2008). Speech delivered on 18 March 2008 at the Constitution Center in Philadelphia. Retrieved from http://www.huffingtonpost.com/2008/03/18/obama-race-speech-read-th_n_92077.html

O'Brien, R. (2001). *An overview of the methodological approach of action research.* Retrieved from http://www.web.ca/~robrien/papers/arfinal.html

Olson, M. A., & Fazio, R. H. (2004). Reducing the influence of extrapersonal associations on the Implicit Association Test: Personalizing the IAT. *Journal of Personality and Social Psychology, 86,* 653–667.

Omi, M. (2001). The changing meaning of race. In N. Smelser, W. J. Wilson, & F. Mitchell (Eds.), *America becoming* (pp. 243–262). Washington, DC: National Academy Press.

Omi, M., & Winant, H. (1986). *Racial formation in the United States.* New York: Routledge.

Omi, M., & Winant, H. (1994). *Racial formation in the United States* (2nd ed.). New York: Routledge.

Omi, M., & Winant, H. (2002a). Racial formation. In Ph. Essed & D. T. Goldberg (Eds.), *Race critical theories* (pp. 123–145). Oxford: Blackwell.

Omi, M., & Winant, H. (2002b). Reflections on "racial formation". In Ph. Essed & D. T. Goldberg (Eds.), *Race critical theories* (pp. 455–459). Oxford: Blackwell.

Ospina, S. (2008). Celebrating the legacy of Orlando Fals-Borda. *Action Research, 6*(4), 440–441.

Outlaw, L. (1990). Toward a critical theory of race. In T. Goldberg (Ed.), *The anatomy of racism* (pp. 58–82). Minneapolis, MN: University of Minnesota Press.

Ozbekhan, H. (1968). *Toward a general theory of planning.* Paper presented at the Symposium on Long-range Forecasting and Planning, Bellagio (Lake of Como). Retrieved from http:www.panarchy.org/ozbekhan/planning.1968.html

Ozbekhan, H. (1970). On some of the fundamental problems in planning. *Technological Forecasting, 1*(3), 235–240.

Paavola, S. (2004). Abduction through grammar, critic, and methodeutic. *Transactions of the Charles S. Peirce Society: A Quarterly Journal in American Philosophy, 40* (2), 245–270. Retrieved from http://www.helsinki.fi/science/commens/papers/abductionthrough.html

Paavola, S. (2006). *Abductive logic of discovery with distributed means.* Presented at a Conference on Abduction and the Process of Scientific Discovery, Lisbon. Retrieved May 4–6, 2006, from http://www.helsinki.fi/science/networkedlearning/texts/paavola-2006-abduction-distributed.pdf

Pampallis. J. (2008). Introductory essay. In *Submissions on apartheid in education* (pp. 4–11). Johannesburg: STE Publishers (on behalf of the Department of Education).

Parekh, B. (1997). Dilemmas of a multicultural theory of citizenship. *Constellations, 4*(1), 54–62.

Parker, P. (1990). For the white person who wants to know how to be my friend. In G. Anzaldua (Ed.), *Making face, making soul/Haciendo caras: Creative and critical perspectives by women of color* (p. 297). San Francisco: Aunt Lute Foundation Books.

Parker, L., & Lynn, M. (2002). What's race got to do with it? Critical race theory's conflicts with and connections to qualitative research methodology and epistemology. *Qualitative Inquiry, 8*(1), 7–22.

Parks, G. S. (2007). *Critical race realism: Toward an integrative model of critical race theory, empirical social science, and public policy.* Cornell Law School working paper series, paper 23: Cornell University. Retrieved from http://lsr.nellco.org/cornell/clsops/papers/23

Patterson, O. (1997). *The ordeal of integration: Progress and resentment in America's "racial" crisis.* Washington, DC: Civitas/Counterpoint.

Peirce, C. S. (1911). *The Peirce manuscripts.* Commens Peirce Dictionary (Retroduction). Retrieved from http://www.helsinki.fi/science/commens/terms/retroduction.html

Peirce, C. S. (1931–1958). *Collected papers* (8 vols., C. Hartshorne. P. Weiss, & A. Burks, Eds.). Cambridge, MA: Harvard University Press.

Peirce, C. S. (1989). *Cambridge lectures on reasoning and the logic of things.* Commens Peirce Dictionary (Retroduction). Retrieved from http://www.helsinki.fi/science/commens/terms/retroduction.html

Pettigrew, T. F. (1979). The ultimate attribution error: Extending Allport's cognitive analysis of prejudice. *Personality and Social Psychology Bulletin, 5*(4), 461–476.

Pettigrew, T. F., & Meertens, R. W. (1995). Subtle and blatant prejudice in Western Europe. *European Journal of Social Psychology, 25,* 57–75.

Petty, R. E., & Cacioppo, J. T. (1981). *Attitudes and persuasion: Classic and contemporary approaches.* Dubuque, IA: Brown.

Petty, R. E., & Cacioppo, J. T. (1986). *Communication and persuasion: Central and peripheral routes to attitude change.* New York: Spring-Verlag.

Pfeifer, J. E., & Bernstein, D. J. (2003). Expressions of modern racism in judgments of others: The role of task and target specificity on attributions of guilt. *Social Behavior and Personality, 31,* 749–766.

Pfeifer, J. E., & Ogloff, J. R. P. (2003). Mock juror ratings of guilt in Canada: Modern racism and ethnic heritage. *Social Behavior and Personality, 31,* 301–312.

Philippou, S. (2007). On the borders of Europe: Citizenship education and identity in Cyprus. *Journal of Social Science Education, 6*(1), 68–79.

Pillay, N. S., & Collings, S. J. (2004). Racism on a South African campus: A survey of students' experiences and attitudes. *Social Behavior and Personality, 32*(7), 607–618.

Pool, I. de S. (1957). A critique of the twentieth century anniversary issue. *Public Opinion Quarterly, 21,* 190–198.

Popper, K. R. (1959). *The logic of scientific discovery.* London: Hutchinson.

Popper, K. R. (1969). *Conjectures and refutations.* London: Routledge & Kegan Paul.

Popper, K. R. (1978). *Unended quest: An intellectual autobiography.* London: Fontana/Collins.

Popper, K. R. (1994). *The myth of the framework: In defence of science and rationality.* London: Routledge.

Pratkanis, A. R., & Aaronson, E. (2000). *Age of propaganda: The everyday use and abuse of persuasion.* New York: W.H. Freeman and Company.

Pratto, F. (2002). Integrating experimental and social constructivist social psychology: Some of us are already doing it anyway. *Personality and Social Psychology Review, 6*(3), 194–198.

Pratto, F., Sidanius, J., Stallworth, L. M., & Malle, B. F. (1994). Social dominance orientation: A personality variable predicting social and political attitudes. *Journal of Personality and Social Psychology, 67,* 741–763.

Rabinowitz, J. L. (1999). Go with the flow or fight the power? The interactive effects of social dominance orientation and perceived injustice on support for the status quo. *Political Psychology, 20,* 1–24.

Rabinowitz, J. L., Wittig, M. A., von Braun, M., Franke, R., & Zander-Music, L. (2005). Understanding the relationship between egalitarianism and affective bias: Avenues to reducing prejudice among adolescents. *Journal of Social Issues, 61*(3), 525–545.

Rahman, M. A. (1991). The theoretical standpoint of participatory action research. In O. Fals-Borda & M. A. Rahman (Eds.), *Action and knowledge: Breaking the monopoly with participatory action research* (pp. 13–24). New York: The Apex Press.

Rajchman, J. (2007). *Introduction to Foucault's the politics of truth* (S. Lotringer, Ed.). Los Angeles: Semiotext(e).

Reason, P. (2001). Learning and change through action research. In J. Henry (Ed.), *Creative management.* London: Sage. Retrieved from http://people.bath.ac.uk/mnspwr/Papers/LearningChangeThroughActionResearch.htm

Reason, P. (2004). *Action research: Forming communicative space for many ways of knowing.* Presented at the international workshop on Participatory Action Research, Dhaka. Retrieved March 2004, from http://www.bath.ac.uk/~mnspwr/Papers/DhakaFormingCommunicativeSpace.htm

Reason, P. (2006a). Choice and quality in action research practice. *Journal of Management Inquiry, 15*(2), 187–203.

Reason, P. (2006b) A Response to J. A. McKernan. *Journal of Management Inquiry, 15*(2), 207–208.

Reason, P., & Bradbury, H. (2001). Introduction: Inquiry and participation in search of a world worthy of human aspiration. In P. Reason & H. Bradbury (Eds.), *Handbook of action research: Participative inquiry and practice* (pp. 1–14). London: Sage.

Reason, P., & Torbert, W. R. (2001). Toward a transformational science: A further look at the scientific merits of action research. *Concepts and Transformations, 6*(1), 1–37.

Reay, D. (2004). "Mostly roughs and toughs": Social class, race and representation in inner city schooling. *Sociology, 38*(5), 1005–1023.

Reay, D., Hollingworth, S., Williams, K. Crozier, G., Jamieson, F., James, D., & Beedell, P. (2007). A darker shade of pale? Whiteness, the middle classes and multi-ethnic inner city schooling. *Sociology, 41*(6), 1041–1060.

Richards, D. (1980). European mythology: The ideology of progress. In M. K. Asante & A. S. Vandi (Eds.), *Contemporary Black thought* (pp. 59–79). Beverley-Hills, CA: Sage.

Richards, T. J., & Richards, L. (1994). Using computers in qualitative research. In N. K. Denzin & Y. S. Lincoln (Eds.), *Handbook of qualitative research* (pp. 445–462). London: Sage.

Richardson, J. D. (2005). The influence of editorial framing on reader attitudes toward affirmative action and African Americans. *Communication Research, 32,* 503–528.

Richardson, S., & McMullen, M. (2006). Research ethics in the UK: What can sociology learn from health? *Sociology, 41,* 1115–1132.

Rist, R. C. (1974). Race, policy and schooling. *Society, 12*(1), 59–63.

Roithmayr, D. (1999). Introduction to critical race theory in educational research and praxis. In L. Parker, D. Deyhle, & S. Villenas (Eds.), *Race is ... race isn't: Critical race theory and qualitative studies in education* (pp. 1–6). Boulder, CO: Westview Press.

Romm, N. R. A. (1990a). Gouldner's reflexive methodological approach. In C. J. Alant (Ed.), *Sociology and society: A humanist profile* (pp. 13–22). Johannesburg: Southern Book Publishers.

Romm, N. R. A. (1990b). A critical evaluation of South African political theory. In C. J. Alant (Ed.), *Sociology and society: A humanist profile* (pp. 34–40). Johannesburg: Southern Book Publishers.

Romm, N. R. A. (1991). *The methodologies of positivism and Marxism: A sociological debate.* London: Macmillan.

Romm, N. R. A. (1994). Symbolic theory. In N. R. A. Romm & M. Sarakinsky (Eds.), *Social theory* (pp. 322–326). Johannesburg: Heinemann.

Romm, N. R. A. (1995a). Participation in defining Tanzanian realities. In P. Forster & S. Maghimbi (Eds.), *The Tanzanian peasantry: Further studies* (pp. 3–22). Aldershot: Gower.

Romm, N. R. A. (1995b). Knowing as intervention. *Systems Practice, 8,* 137–167.

Romm, N. R. A. (1996). Inquiry-and-intervention in systems planning: Probing methodological rationalities. *World Futures, 47,* 25–36.

Romm, N. R. A. (1997). Becoming more accountable: A comment on Hammersley and Gomm. *Sociological Research Online, 2,* http://www.socresonline.org.uk/socresonline/2/3/2.html

Romm, N. R. A. (1998a). Nurturing sustainability through triple loop learning: Discursive accountability as responsible action. *Systemist, 20*(1), 40–52.

Romm, N. R. A. (1998b). Interdisciplinary practice as reflexivity. *Systemic Practice and Action Research, 11*(1), 63–77.

Romm, N. R. A. (1998c). Caricaturing and categorizing in processes of argument. *Sociological Research Online, 3,* http://www.socresonline.org.uk/socresonline/3/2/10.html

Romm, N. R. A. (2001). *Accountability in social research: Issues and debates.* New York: Kluwer Academic/Plenum.

Romm, N. R. A. (2002a). A trusting constructivist approach to systemic inquiry: Exploring accountability. *Systems Research and Behavioral Science, 19*(5), 455–467.

Romm, N. R. A. (2002b). A trusting constructivist view of systems thinking in the knowledge age. In G. Ragsdell, D. West, & J. Wilby (Eds.), *Systems thinking and practice in the knowledge era* (pp. 247–253). New York: Kluwer Academic/Plenum Publishers.

Romm, N. R. A. (2002c). Responsible knowing: A better basis for management science. *Reason in Practice, 2*(1), 59–77.

Romm, N. R. A. (2006a). The social significance of Churchman's epistemological position. In J. J. McIntyre-Mills (Ed.), *Rescuing the enlightenment from itself* (pp. 68–92). New York: Springer.

Romm, N. R. A. (2006b). An exploration and extension of Churchman's insights toward the tackling of racial discrimination as a world problem. In J. J. McIntyre-Mills (Ed.), *Rescuing the enlightenment from itself* (pp. 289–331). New York: Springer.

Romm, N. R. A. (2006c). Review of Christakis and Bausch's book entitled co-laboratories of democracy. *Systemic Practice and Action Research, 19*(4), 399–401.

Romm, N. R. A. (2007). Issues of accountability in survey, ethnographic, and action research. In A. Rwomire & F. Nyamnjoh (Eds.), *Challenges and responsibilities of social research in Africa: Ethical issues* (pp. 51–76). Addis Ababa: The Organization for Social Science Research in Eastern and Southern Africa (OSSREA).

Romm, N. R. A., & Adman, P. (2000). *Table: A theoretical elucidation of research designs.* Retrieved from http://www.thesolutionorganisation.com/ontology%20Table.pdf

Romm, N. R. A., & Adman, P. (2004). Exploring the complexity of human dynamics within 360-degree feedback processes: The development of (active) qualitative inquiry. *Journal of Business and Society, 17*(1&2), 170–189.

Romm, N. R. A., & Hsu, C-Y. (2002). Reconsidering the exploration of power distance: An active case study approach. *Omega, 30*(6), 403–414.

Romm, N. R. A., & Rwomire, A. (2001). Some sociological reflections on child abuse: Implications for action. In A. Rwomire (Ed.), *African women and children* (pp. 49–66). Westport, CT: Praeger.

Romm, N. R. A., & Sarakinsky, M. (Eds.). (1994). *Social Theory.* Johannesburg: Heinemann.

Ross, T. (1995). Innocence and affirmative action. In R. Delgado (Ed.), *Critical race theory: The cutting edge* (pp. 551–563). Philadelphia: Temple University Press.

Rydgren, J. (2003). Meso-level reasons for racism and xenophobia: Some converging and diverging effects of radical right populism in France and Sweden. *European Journal of Social Theory, 6*(1), 45–68.

Sayed, Y., Soudien, C., & Carrim, N. (2003). Discourses of exclusion and inclusion in the South: Limits and possibilities. *Journal of Educational Change, 4*, 231–248.

Sayer, D. (1979). Science as critique: Marx versus Althusser. In J. Mepham & D.-H. Ruben (Eds.), *Issues in Marxist philosophy* (Vol. 3, pp. 27–54). Brighton: Harvester Press.

Sayer, D. (1983). *Marx's method: Ideology, science and critique in "capital".* Brighton: Harvester Press.

Scarman, L. (1981). *The Brixton disorders.* CMND 8427. London: HMSO.

Schaefer, R. (1990). *Racial and ethnic groups* (4th ed.). Glenview, IL: Little Brown Higher Education.

Schmidt, G. (2008). From granting the right (?!) answers to posing odd questions: Perspectives on studying and presenting Muslim minorities in a politicized, Western context. *Tidsskrift for Islamforskning (Research on Islam Repositioned), 2*(3), 11–26.

Schoennauer, A. W. (1967, January–February). Behavior patterns of executives in business acquisitions. *Personal Administration, 30*, 22–32.

Schofield, J. W. (1986). Causes and consequences of the colorblind perspective. In J. F. Dovidio & S. L. Gaertner (Eds.), *Prejudice, discrimination, and racism* (pp. 231–253). Orlando: Academic Press.

Schön, D. A. (1983). *The reflective practitioner: How professionals think in action.* London: Temple Smith.

Schreibman, V., & Christakis, A. N. (2006). *New technology of democracy: The structured design dialogue process.* Retrieved from http://www.harnessingcollectivewisdom. com/pdf/newagora.pdf

Schutte, G. (1995). *What racists believe.* London: Sage.

Sciolino, E. (2007). Far right Swiss party divides nation on immigrant issue. *International Herald Tribune.* Retrieved October 7, 2007, from http://www.iht.com/articles/2007/10/07/ news/swiss.php

Seale, C., & Filmer, P. (1998). Doing social surveys. In C. Seale (Ed.), *Researching society and culture* (pp. 125–145). London: Sage.

Sears, D. O. (1988). Symbolic racism. In P. A. Katz & D. A. Taylor (Eds.), *Eliminating racism: Profiles in controversy* (pp. 53–84). New York: Plenum.

Sears, D. O. (2005). Inner conflict in the political psychology of racism. In J. F Dovidio, P. Glick, & L. A. Rudman (Eds.), *On the nature of prejudice: Fifty years after Allport* (pp. 343–358). Malden, MA: Blackwell.

Segura, D. (1990). Chicanas and the triple oppression in the labor force. In National Association for Chicano Studies (Ed.), *Chicana voices: Intersection of class, race and gender* (pp. 47–65). Albuquerque, NM: University of New Mexico Press.

Selener, D. (1997). *Participatory action research and social change.* New York: The Cornell Participatory Action Research Network.

Sellers, R. M., Smith, M. A., Shelton, J. N., Rowley, S. A., & Chavous, T. M. (1998). Multidimensional model of racial identity: A reconceptualization of African American racial identity. *Personality and Social Psychology Review, 2,* 18–39.

Shane, P. M. (2008). Voting for democracy: The Obama vision of open government and public engagement. *The Huffington Post.* Retrieved October 30, 2008, from http://www.huffingtonpost.com/peter-m-shane/voting-for-democracy-the_b_139262.html

Sharma, A. (1997). Professional as agent: Knowledge asymmetry in agency exchange. *Academy of Management Review, 22,* 758–798.

Sheppard, N. (2008). AP's racist poll: If Obama loses it's because he's black. *Newsbusters.* Retrieved September 20, 2008, from http://newsbusters.org/blogs/noel-sheppard/2008/09/20/aps-racist-poll-if-obama-loses-its-because-hes-black

Shipler, D. (1997). *A country of strangers: Blacks and Whites in America.* New York: Alfred A. Knopf.

Shipman, M. D. (1982). *The limitations of social research.* London: Longman.

Sidanius, J., & Pratto, F. (1999). *Social dominance: An intergroup theory of social hierarchy and oppression.* New York: Cambridge University Press.

Silverman, D. (2000). *Doing qualitative research: A practical handbook.* London: Sage.

Simpson, L. (2000). Communication and the politics of difference. *Constellations, 7*(3), 430–442.

Singh, G. (2000). The concept and context of institutional racism. In A. Marlow & B. Loveday (Eds.), *After MacPherson: Policing after the Stephen Lawrence inquiry* (pp. 29–40). Dorset: Russell House Publishing.

Sitas, A. (2004). Thirty years since the Durban strikes: Black working-class leadership and the South African transition. *Current Sociology, 52*(5), 830–849.

Sivanandan, A. (2007). Foreword to A. Kundnani's book. *The end of tolerance* (pp. vii–viii). London: Pluto Press.

Skrbis, Z., Kendall, G., & Woodward, I. (2004). Locating cosmopolitanism: Between humanist ideal and grounded social category. *Theory, Culture & Society, 21*(6), 115–136.

Skrentny, J. D. (1996). *The ironies of affirmative action.* Chicago: The University of Chicago Press.

Smith, D. E. (2005). *Institutional ethnography: A sociology for people.* Walnut Creek, CA: Alta Mira Press.

Smith, M. K. (2001). Action research. *The Encyclopedia of Informal Education.* Retrieved from http://www.infed.org/research/b-actres.htm

Sniderman, P. M., & Tetlock, P. E. (1986). Symbolic racism: Problems of motive attribution in political debate. *Journal of Social Issues, 42,* 129–150.

Sommers, S. R., & Norton, M. I. (2006). Lay theories about white racists: What constitutes racism (and what does not). *Group Processes and Intergroup Relations, 9*(1), 117–139.

Sonn, C., Bishop, B., & Humphries, R. (2000). Encounters with the dominant culture: Voices of indigenous students in mainstream higher education. *American Psychologist, 35*, 128–135.

South African Human Rights Commission (2000). *Faultlines: Inquiry into racism in the media.* Johannesburg: SAHRC.

Speer, S. A., & Hutchby, I. (2003a). From ethics to analytics: Aspects of participants' orientations to the presence and relevance of recording devices. *Sociology, 37*(2), 315–337.

Speer, S. A., & Hutchby, I. (2003b). Methodology needs analytics: A rejoinder to Martyn Hammersley. *Sociology, 37*(2), 353–359.

Spyrou, S. (2002). Images of "the other": "The Turk" in Greek-Cypriot children's imaginations. *Race, Ethnicity and Education, 5*, 255–271.

Squires, J., & Weldes, J. (2007). Beyond being marginal: Gender and international relations in Britain. *British Journal of Politics and International Relations, 9*(2), 185–203.

Stangor, C., Lynch, L., Duan, C., & Glass, B. (1992). Categorization of individuals on the basis of multiple social features. *Journal of Personality and Social Psychology, 62*, 207–218.

Stathi, S., & Crisp, R. J. (2008). Imagining intergroup contact promotes projection to outgroups. *Journal of Experimental Social Psychology, 44*, 943–957.

Stewart, D., & Shamdasani, R. (1990). *Focus groups: Theory and practice.* Newbury Park, CA: Sage.

Stewart, Q. T. (2008). Swimming upstream: Theory and methodology in race research. In T. Zuberi & E. Bonilla-Silva (Eds.), *White logic, White methods: Racism and methodology* (pp. 111–126). Lanham, MD: Rowman & Littlefield.

Strauss, A. (1987). *Qualitative analysis for social scientists.* Cambridge: Cambridge University Press.

Strickland, B. (2004). Things fall apart: Black struggle in imperial America and the need for an adequate theory of emancipation for the 21st Century. *The Black Scholar, 34*(3), 2–8.

Stringer, E., Guhathakurta, M., Masaigana, M., & Waddell, S. (2008). Guest editors' commentary. *Action Research, 6*(2), 123–127.

Sue, D. W. (2005). Racism and the conspiracy of silence. *The Counseling Psychologist, 33*(1), 100–114.

Sydell, E. J., & Nelson, E. S. (2000). Modern racism on campus: A survey of attitudes and perceptions. *The Social Science Journal, 37*(4), 627–635.

Taguieff, P-A. (1999). The new cultural racism in France. In M. Bulmer & J. Solomos (Eds.), *Racism* (pp. 206–213). Oxford: Oxford University Press.

Tarman, C., & Sears, D. O. (2005). The conceptualization and measurement of symbolic racism. *The Journal of Politics, 67*(3), 731–761.

Tatum, B. D. (2003). *Why are all the Black kids sitting together in the cafeteria?* New York: Basic Books.

Taylor-Carter, M. A., Doverspike, D., & Alexander, R. (1995). Message effects on the perceptions of the fairness of gender-based affirmative action: A cognitive response theory-based analysis. *Social Justice Research, 8*, 285–303.

Teasley, M., & Tyson, E. (2007). Cultural wars and the attack on multiculturalism: An Afrocentric critique. *Journal of Black Studies, 37*(3), 390–409.

Thorvaldsdóttir, T. (2007). *"Equal opportunities for all" – Intersectionality as a theoretical tool to move equality policies forward.* Retrieved from http://www.umu.se/kvf/aktuellt/ppf/tthorvaldsdottir.pdf

Torbert, W. R. (1998). Developing wisdom and courage in organizing and sciencing. In S. Srivastva & D. Cooperrider (Eds.), *Organizational wisdom and executive courage* (pp. 222–253). San Francisco: New Lexington Press.

Torbert, W. R. (2001). The practice of action inquiry. In P. Reason, & H. Bradbury (Eds.), *Handbook of action research: Participative inquiry and practice* (pp. 250–260). London: Sage.

Torres, C. A. (2002). From the pedagogy of the oppressed to a luta continua: The political pedagogy of Paulo Freire. In P. McLaren & P. Leonard (Eds.), *Paulo Freire: A critical encounter* (pp. 119–145). London: Routledge.

Travers, M. (2006). Postmodernism and qualitative research. *Qualitative Research 6*(2), 267–273.

Tsing, A. L. (1993). *In the realm of the diamond queen*. Princeton, NJ: Princeton University Press.

Tversky, A., & Kahneman, D. (1981). The framing of decisions and the psychology of choice. *Science, 211*, 453–458.

Tversky, A., & Kahneman, D. (1986). Rational choice and the framing of decisions. *Journal of Business, 59*, 251–278.

Van Dijk, T. (2000). New(s) racism: A discourse analytic approach. In S. Cottle (Ed.), *Ethnic minorities and the media: Changing cultural boundaries*. Buckingham: Open University Press.

Van Dijk, T. (2002). Reflections on "denying racism". In P. Essed & D. T. Goldberg (Eds.), *Race critical theories* (pp. 481–485). Oxford: Blackwell.

Van Oudenhoven, J. P., Prins, K. S., & Buunk, B. (1998). Attitudes of minority and majority members toward adaptation of immigrants. *European Journal of Social Psychology, 28*, 995–1013.

Vargas, J. H. C. (2005). Genocide in the African diaspora. *Cultural Dynamics, 17*(3), 267–290.

Vogt, W. P. (2008). The dictatorship of the problem: Choosing research methods. *Methodological Innovations Online, 3*(1), 1–18.

Vratuša, V. (2008). *Problems of privatization and participation research from the sociology of knowledge perspective*. Paper prepared for RC10 of the International Sociological Association Conference, Barcelona. Retrieved September 5–8, 2008, from http://www.wikispaces.com/file/view/V_Vratusa_ISA_2008_RC10_Privatisation_and_participation_research_problems_in_Sociology__of__knowledge_perspective3.pdf

Wacquant, L. (2002). Scrutinizing the street: Poverty, morality and the pitfalls of urban ethnography. *American Journal of Sociology, 107*(6), 1468–1532.

Wagley, C. (1965). On the concept of social race in the Americas. In D. B. Heath & R. N. Adams (Eds.), *Contemporary cultures and societies in Latin America* (pp. 531–545). New York: Random House.

Walby, K. (2007). On the social relations of research: A critical assessment of institutional ethnography. *Qualitative Inquiry, 13*(7), 1008–1030.

Walford, G. (2004). Finding the limits: Autoethnography and being an Oxford University Proctor. *Qualitative Research, 4*(3), 403–417.

Walters, R. (2007). Barack Obama and the politics of blackness. *Journal of Black Studies 38*(1), 7–29.

Washington, J. (2008). Obama's candidacy sparks race dialogue. *The Associated Press*. Retrieved September 23, 2008, from http://www.sltrib.com/ci_10538614

Weber, M. (1949). *The methodology of the social sciences* (E. A. Shils & H. A. Finch, Trans. & Eds.). New York: The Free Press.

Weil, S. (1996). From the other side of silence: New possibilities for dialogue in academic writing. *Changes, 14*, 223–231.

Weil, S. (1997). Social and organizational learning and unlearning in a different key: An introduction to the principles of critical learning theatre (CLT) and dialectical inquiry (DI). In F. A. Stowell, R. L. Ison, R. Armson, J. Holloway, S. Jackson, & S. McRobb (Eds.), *Systems for sustainability: People, organizations and environments* (pp. 373–381). New York: Plenum.

Weil, S. (1998). Rhetorics and realities in public service organizations: Systemic practice and organizational learning as critically reflexive action research (CRAR). *Systemic Practice and Action Research, 11*, 37–62.

Weil, S. (1999). *An inaugural in 7 waves: Strangers on the shore? Living and learning new cultures of inquiry*. Inaugural professorial lecture given at University College Northampton, May 1999.

Weil, S., Annamonthodo, P., Brandt, G., Cheung, D., Douglas, C., Gunning, M., & Phoenix, A. (1985). *Through a hundred pairs of eyes* (Organizational development materials including 210 page guide and trigger video with 54 incidents). London: Institute of Education/CSDHE/Local Government Training Board.

Weil, S., Wildemeersch, D., & Jansen, T. (2005). *Unemployed youth and social exclusion in Europe: Learning for inclusion?* Aldershot: Ashgate.

White, L., & Taket, A. (1997). Critiquing multimethodology as metamethodology. In J. Mingers & A. Gill (Eds.), *Multimethodology* (pp. 379–405). Chichester: Wiley.

Whitehead, K., Wittig, M. A., & Ainsworth, A. (2005). *Implications of ethnic identity exploration and ethnic identity affirmation for intergroup attitudes among adolescents.* Manuscript under review at the time as cited by Rabinowitz et al., 2005.

Whitmeyer, J. (1994). Why actors are integral to structural analysis. *Sociological Theory, 2,* 153–165.

Whyte, W. F. (1991). Comparing PAR and action science. In W. F. Whyte (Ed.), *Participatory action research* (pp. 97–108), Newbury Park, CA: Sage.

Wieviorka, M. (1993). Racism and modernity in present-day Europe. *Thesis Eleven, 35,* 51–61.

Wieviorka, M. (2004). The making of differences. *International Sociology, 19*(3), 281–297.

Williams, P. J. (1997). *The rooster's egg.* Cambridge, MA: Harvard University Press.

Wimmar, A. (1997). Explaining xenophobia and racism. *Ethnic and Racial Studies, 20*(1), 1096–1114.

Winant, H. (2000). Race and race theory. *Annual Review of Sociology, 26,* 169–185.

Yilmaz, M. (2006). The Cyprus conflict and the question of identity. *Turkish Weekly.* Retrieved March 14, 2006, from http://www.turkishweekly.net/articles.php?id=108

Young, I. M. (1990). The ideal of community and the politics of difference. In L. J. Nicholson (Ed.), *Feminism/postmodernism* (pp. 300–323). New York: Routledge.

Young, J. (2008). Ethics, categories and identity: Counting on quantification. Ethnicity in Australian history. *Systems Research and Behavioral Science, 25*(2), 215–224.

Yuval-Davis, N. (2004). *Human/women's rights and feminist transversal politics.* Lecture 2 in the Bristol Lecture Series on the Politics of Belonging. Retrieved June 2004, from http://www.bristol.ac.uk/sociology/ethnicitycitizenship/nyd2.pdf

Yuval-Davis, N. (2006). Intersectionality and feminist politics. *European Journal of Women's Studies, 13*(3), 193–209.

Yzerbyt, V. Y., Estrada, C. Corneille, O., Seron, E., & Demoulin, S. (2004). Subjective essentialism in action: Self-anchoring and social control as consequences of fundamental social divides. In V. Y. Yzerbyt, C. M. Judd, & O. Corneille (Eds.), *The psychology of group perception: Perceived variability, entitativity, and essentialism* (pp. 101–126). London: Psychology Press.

Yzerbyt, V., Rocher, S., & Schadron, G. (1997). Stereotypes as explanations: A subjective essentialist view of group perception. In R. Spears, P. J. Oakes, N. Ellemers, & A. Haslam (Eds.), *The social psychology of stereotyping and group life* (pp. 20–50). Oxford: Blackwell.

Zegeye, A. (2002). Introduction: Globalization and post-apartheid South Africa. *Journal of Asian and African Studies, 37*(3–5), 265–270.

Zegeye, A. (2004). Of struggles and whistles: Mamelodi's Black youth culture. *Current Sociology, 52*(5), 850–878.

Zuberi, T., & Bonilla-Silva, E. (2008). Telling the real tale of the hunt: Toward a race conscious sociology of racial stratification. In T. Zuberi & E. Bonilla-Silva (Eds.), *White logic, White methods: Racism and methodology* (pp. 329–341). Lanham, MD: Rowman & Littlefield.

20th Century History. (2000). *Austrian far-right party in power.* Retrieved from http://history1900s.about.com/library/holocaust/aa020600a.htm

Author Index

Subject Index

LaVergne, TN USA
27 July 2010
191005LV00004B/19/P

9 789048 187270